Where print meets digital and engaging content meets academic rigor

THE
JUSTICE SERIES

across the CJ curriculum...

Transportation first became an official aspect of England's punishment system in the seventeenth century but not a major component until the eighteenth century.

The Transportation Act of 1718 allowed transportation as a substitute to execution and also made it a punishment in its own right.

CJ2012
Fagin

Corrections
Alarid & Reichel

American colonies

Prisoners became indentured servants and the British gave up all responsibility for them.

Transportation sentences were typically seven years for noncapital offences or for life for those who had had their death penalties commuted.

Policing
Worrall & Schmalleger

Criminal Investigation
Lyman

Criminal Procedure
Worrall

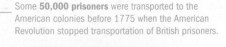

718 — 1775

Some **50,000 prisoners** were transported to the American colonies before 1775 when the American Revolution stopped transportation of British prisoners.

Australia

Rather than becoming indentured servants in Australia, prisoners remained the responsibility of the British government, which continued to have control over them.

Juvenile Delinquency
Bartollas & Schmalleger

Coming in 2013:

1788 — 1868

From 1788 to 1868, more than **160,000 convicts** were transported from England and Ireland to Australia. Transportation ends throughout Australia in 1868.

Norfolk Island, about 1,000 miles east of Sydney, became the most notable penal colony because of the unbearable discipline.

Norfolk Island jail

CJ2013
Fagin

Criminology
Schmalleger

CORRECTIONS

CORRECTIONS

Leanne F. Alarid
University of Texas, San Antonio

Philip L. Reichel
University of Northern Colorado

PEARSON

Boston   Columbus   Indianapolis   New York   San Francisco   Upper Saddle River
Amsterdam   Cape Town   Dubai   London   Madrid   Milan   Munich   Paris   Montréal   Toronto
Delhi   Mexico City   São Paulo   Sydney   Hong Kong   Seoul   Singapore   Taipei   Tokyo

Editorial Director: Vernon R. Anthony
Senior Acquisitions Editor: Eric Krassow
Assistant Editor: Megan Moffo
Editorial Assistant: Lynda Cramer
Director of Marketing: David Gesell
Marketing Manager: Cyndi Eller
Senior Marketing Coordinator: Alicia Wozniak
Marketing Assistant: Les Roberts
Senior Managing Editor: JoEllen Gohr
Senior Project Manager: Steve Robb
Senior Operations Supervisor: Pat Tonneman
Creative Director: Design Development Services,
  John Christiana
Text and Cover Designer: Mary Siener
Media Project Manager: Karen Bretz
Full-Service Project Management:
  GEX Publishing Services
Composition: GEX Publishing Services
Printer/Binder: R. R. Donnelley & Sons, Inc.
Cover Printer: Lehigh/Phoenix Color Hagerstown
Text Font: MinionPro-Regular 10/12

Charles Manson is one of the most well known prisoners in the United States. He has lived for the past three decades in a California prison. Manson was convicted as a serial killer on March 29, 1971. He was found guilty of first degree murder and conspiracy to commit murder for the brutal killing of Sharon Tate, her unborn child, and four other people who were visiting the Tate house that night.

Cover Image: © Mary Evans
Picture Library / Alamy

Credits and acknowledgments borrowed from other sources and reproduced, with permission, in this textbook appear on the appropriate page within the text.

Library of Congress Cataloging in Publication Data
Alarid, Leanne Fiftal
  Corrections / Leanne F. Alarid, Philip L. Reichel. -- 1st ed.
    p. cm.
  Includes bibliographical references and index.
  ISBN 978-0-13-257104-3 (pbk.)
  1. Corrections--Study and teaching. 2. Punishment. 3. Criminal justice, Administration of--Study and teaching. I. Reichel, Philip L.
II. Title.
  HV8754.A43 2013
  365--dc23
                    2011045414

10 9 8 7 6 5 4 3 2

ISBN-10: 0-13-257104-8
ISBN-13: 978-0-13-257104-3

Dedicated to Crazyhorse,
my mentor and best friend.
L.F.A.

Dedicated to my parents,
Joe and Virginia Reichel.
P.L.R.

Brief Contents

Contents

Each chapter opener includes a quote and lists the chapter objectives to pique interest and focus students' attention on the topics to be discussed.

The book exhibits a balance between text, photos, and figures to present the information in both a text format and a visual format.

Each chapter Introduction presents a current event or story related to chapter content followed by a discussion question. This sparks interest and promotes critical thinking about chapter concepts.

PART 2 Sentencing and Sanctions 54

Each objective has an associated icon that also appears in the related chapter section and in the end-of-chapter material. The icon is a navigational tool, making it easy to locate explanations of or find review material for a particular topic, and is also a visual key to aid memory and retention of information related to the topic.

Key statistics are set in large blue type for easy identification.

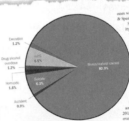

Think About It features pose questions related to chapter content, promoting critical thinking, discussion, and application.

Important quotes pulled from the text reflect the central ideas in the chapter.

PART 4   Correctional Issues and Challenges   182

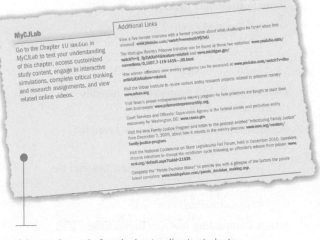

A box at the end of each chapter directs students
to chapter-specific resources and additional links
to extend learning and investigation.

At the end of each chapter, a real-life case example poses analytical discussion questions related to chapter content, promoting critical thinking and application of chapter concepts.

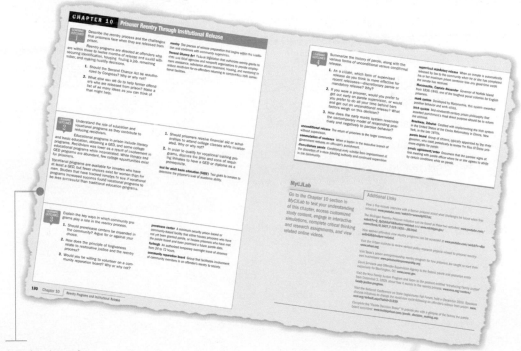

The chapter summary displays the chapter's key information as a chart with images and critical-thinking review questions embedded throughout. This visual format is designed to be a helpful study and review tool.

Preface

Introducing the Justice Series

When best-selling authors and instructional designers come together, focused on one goal—improve student performance across the CJ curriculum—you come away with a groundbreaking new series of print and digital content: the *Justice Series*.

Several years ago we embarked on a journey to create affordable texts that engage students without sacrificing academic rigor. We tested this new format with Fagin's *CJ 2010* and Schmalleger's *Criminology* and received overwhelming support from students and instructors.

The Justice Series expands this format and philosophy to more core CJ and criminology courses, providing affordable, engaging instructor and student resources across the curriculum. As you flip through the pages, you'll notice this book doesn't rely on distracting, overly used photos to add visual appeal. Every piece of art serves a purpose—to help students learn. Our authors and instructional designers worked tirelessly to build engaging infographics, flow charts, pull-out statistics, and other visuals that flow with the body of the text, provide context and engagement, and promote recall and understanding.

We organized our content around key learning objectives for each chapter, and tied everything together in a new objective-driven end-of-chapter layout. Not only is the content engaging to the student, it's easy to follow and focuses the student on the key learning objectives.

Although brief, affordable, and visually engaging, the Justice Series is no quick, cheap way to appeal to the lowest common denominator. It's a series of texts and support tools that are instructionally sound and student approved.

Additional Highlights to the Authors' Approach

- Evidence-Based Practices in all areas of corrections are given close attention and become a key aspect of the book's content.

- Theories of punishment are introduced early and connected to correctional policies and best practices.

- The historical foundation for critical thinking of contemporary correctional policy initiatives is provided, along with issues such as reducing risk, decreasing prison violence, improving prisoner reentry, prisoner rights, and narrowing death penalty discretion.

- Information about women offenders and female correctional staff is incorporated throughout the book rather than in one specific chapter. This integration of gender emphasizes the similarities and differences of the correctional supervision of men and women.

- Student learning is enhanced through a very clear writing style with interesting contemporary examples and remarkably up-to-date information.

Groundbreaking Instructor and Student Support

Just as the format of the Justice Series breaks new ground in publishing, so does the instructor support that accompanies the series.

Interactive Lecture PowerPoint Presentations

The *Interactive Lecture PowerPoints* will enhance lectures like never before. Award-winning presentation designers worked with our authors to develop PowerPoints that truly engage the student. Much like the text, the PowerPoints are full of instructionally sound graphics, tables, charts, and photos that do what presentation software is meant to do—support and enhance your lecture. Data and difficult concepts are presented in a truly interactive way, helping students connect the dots and stay focused on the lecture. The *Interactive Lecture PowerPoints* also include in-depth lecture notes and teaching tips so you have all your lecture material in one place.

A New Standard in Testing Material

Whether you use a basic test bank document or generate questions electronically through *MyTest*, every question is linked to a learning objective, page number, and level of difficulty. This allows for quick reference in the text and offers an easy way to check the difficulty level and variety of your questions. *MyTest* can be accessed at **www.PearsonMyTest.com**

MyCJLab

MyCJLab is a dynamic program designed to support the way students learn and instructors teach. We've integrated our groundbreaking interactive simulations and media into a new, robust course management and assessment program. With *MyCJLab*, instructors can either manage their entire course online or simply allow students to study at their own pace using personalized assessment tools.

> *When best-selling authors and instructional designers come together, focused on one goal—improve student performance across the CJ curriculum—you come away with a groundbreaking new series of print and digital content: the Justice Series.*

From practical game-like simulations to media enhanced critical thinking exercises, instructors can tailor the course to the needs of their students. In addition, our new media search tool organizes current criminal justice–related videos, news articles, and other media from the Internet for quick and easy access in and out of the classroom.

Whether you're an expert in digital learning or new to online enhancements, *MyCJLab* provides student engagement and instructor support for all levels of learning and teaching. *Note:* An access code is needed for this supplement. Students can purchase an access code at **www.MyPearsonStore.com** or from the *MyCJLab* site at **www.MyCJLab.com**.

To access supplementary materials online, instructors need to request an instructor access code. Go to **www.pearsonhighered.com/irc**, where you can register for an instructor access code. Within 48 hours after registering, you will receive a confirming e-mail, including an instructor access code. Once you have received your code, go to the site and log on for full instructions on downloading the materials you wish to use.

▶ Acknowledgments

This book is the result of an opportunity provided to us by Eric Krassow to be part of a cutting-edge series. We greatly appreciate Eric's support and enthusiasm for this book. We would also like to thank Megan Moffo, our assistant editor, for keeping us on task and providing practical suggestions for improving the book. Thanks goes out to Mary Siener, text and cover designer at Pearson; Steve Robb, project manager at Pearson; Kelly Morrison, project manager at GEX Publishing Services; Mike Lackey, image lead/manager at Pearson Image Asset Services; and Lily Ferguson, photo researcher at Bill Smith Group. Finally, we thank the numerous reviewers for their innovative and important suggestions that we incorporated into this series.

▶ About the Authors

Leanne F. Alarid is associate professor in the Department of Criminal Justice at the University of Texas–San Antonio. Dr. Alarid is the author of *Community-Based Corrections* (9e, 2012), and over 40 journal articles and book chapters. She is co-editor of four books including *Behind a Convict's Eyes: Doing Time in a Modern Day Prison* (2004) and *In Her Own Words: Women Offenders' Views on Crime and Victimization* (2006). She received the Founder's Award by the Academy of Criminal Justice Sciences in 2011 for her contribution to education and service. She was recognized as one of the top 20 female scholars in the country out of female Ph.D. graduates in criminal justice between 1996 and 2006. Dr. Alarid has worked as a counselor for a girls' group home and as a correctional case manager at an adult halfway house in Denver, Colorado.

Philip Reichel is a tenured full professor in the Department of Criminal Justice at the University of Northern Colorado. During more than 30 years in academia, Dr. Reichel received awards for his teaching, advising, service, and scholarship. Especially notable awards were his university's Distinguished Scholar award in 2003 and Advisor of the Year in 2005. He is the author of *Comparative Criminal Justice Systems: A Topical Approach* (2008), editor of the *Handbook of Transnational Crime and Justice* (2005), and has authored more than 30 articles and book chapters. His areas of expertise include corrections, comparative justice systems, and transnational crime. He is active in the American Society of Criminology and the Academy of Criminal Justice Sciences.

CORRECTIONS

An Evidence-Based Approach to Corrections

"I will restore the basic principle that government decisions should be based on the best available, scientifically valid evidence and not on ideological predispositions of agency officials or political appointees."

—President Barack Obama, campaign speech during the Science Debate, 2008

1 Describe how corrections is part of the larger criminal justice system and how decisions made along the way contribute to case dismissals, convictions, and potential disparity.

2 Compare and contrast both diversion and postsentencing options, and institutional- and community-based corrections.

3 Explain the key reasons for the rise in incarceration rates since the 1980s and the overall effect that it has had on individuals, communities, and the crime rate.

4 Analyze the relationships among mass media, public opinion, and the making of correctional policy.

5 Characterize the meaning of evidence-based practices and why it is significant to improving the correctional system.

1

HOW DO MEDIA SOURCES INFLUENCE PUBLIC PERCEPTIONS OF CRIME?

In January 2011, Representative Gabrielle Giffords welcomed members of the public at a constituent event held at a local shopping plaza in Tucson, Arizona. That morning, 22-year-old Jared Lee Loughner entered and opened fire using a 9mm handgun. By the time Loughner was apprehended, he had killed 6 people and wounded 13 others. Representative Giffords suffered brain trauma and was severely wounded in the attack. Among those who died were federal judge John Roll, one of Giffords's staff members, and a 9-year-old community visitor. Investigators said that the incident was a deliberate, planned attempt to murder Giffords. There was also evidence to indicate that Loughner obtained a gun in advance; that he visited Internet websites that encouraged hate, violence, and anti-government extremism; and that he had a mental illness.

The horrific shooting tragedy in Arizona reopened the debate not only about gun control laws, but also about the influence of media exposure in certain violent crimes.

DISCUSS Do the media cause or contribute to violence? Are the media neutral in the reporting of violent incidents, or do they affect people in other ways? How? What impact do the media have on public perceptions about crime in general?

▶ Corrections: An Integral Part of the CJ System

In the context of the criminal justice system, **corrections** is an important component that follows the court process after a defendant has been found guilty or that aids the court during the process prior to the sentence. We begin first by briefly introducing how criminal cases get to court through the police.

Police

When a crime is committed, a victim or witness reports the situation to the **police**. In serious cases, the police take the report in person and may collect evidence or testimony. In less serious cases, the victim reports by phone or the Internet. Other than traffic enforcement, it is clear that the police rely on *citizens* to bring most crimes to their attention. Then, based on the quality of this information, police can investigate further and then decide whether there is enough evidence to act. In less serious cases, such as exceeding the speed limit, police can decide to issue a warning or a **citation**. In more serious cases, such as domestic violence, an officer must arrest one or both defendants if there are visible injuries. When an arrest is made, the police drive the suspect to a city or county jail to be **booked**. In the most serious felony cases, the reporting officer relies on detectives to spend the time collecting evidence.

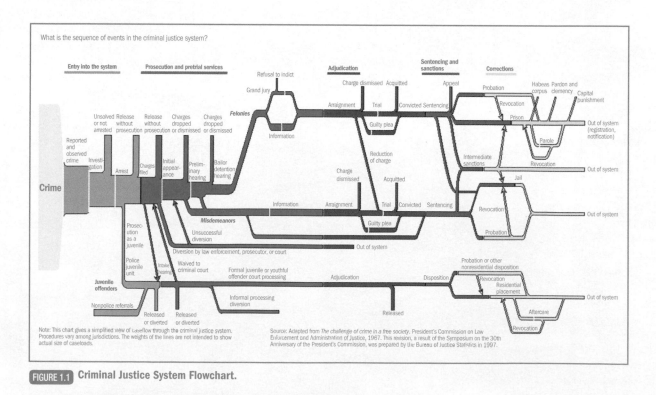

FIGURE 1.1 Criminal Justice System Flowchart.

GLOSSARY

corrections The network of government and private agencies responsible for the pre- and post-conviction custody, supervision, and treatment of persons accused or convicted of crimes.

police Law enforcement officials who are sworn to uphold the law, keep social order, and preserve public safety.

citation A police-issued ticket ordering a citizen to pay a fine for a minor law violation.

booked When a suspect is identified and fingerprinted in jail after being arrested for an alleged crime.

jurisdiction A predefined geographic area.

dismissed When a case is dropped for lack of evidence and does not proceed any further.

pretrial supervision The community supervision of a defendant who has not yet been convicted but is waiting for his or her next court hearing date.

The police enforce the law, keep social order, and preserve public safety for their particular **jurisdiction**. For example, local police have boundaries within a city or county, while state police focus on highways and interstates within the state. A federal law enforcement agency enforces laws in places that are considered federal areas (such as national parks and post offices) or enforces violations of federal law (such as counterfeiting or terrorism) anywhere in the United States. In using their discretion, the police truly are the gatekeepers of the criminal justice system. Following an arrest or a citation, the case moves to the courts, which is the next social control agency.

Pretrial/Courts

The courts depend on the police's ability to identify the right suspect and to collect enough quality evidence, if needed, to corroborate the case. There are four main decision points that prosecutors have: initial case screening, charging, plea offers, and case disposition. At the initial case screening, prosecutors will likely **dismiss** cases if the evidence is weak or inadequately linked to that defendant for a particular offense. Depending on the jurisdiction and the severity of the offense, between one-third and one-half of all cases are dismissed.

Prosecutors will go forward with charging cases in which they believe there is enough evidence to hold the defendant accountable for the crime. A small percent of defendants (between 1 percent and 5 percent) request a criminal trial and enter a plea of "not guilty," in which case, the decision lies in the hands of a judge or jury. While the average criminal trial lasts only one to three days, the court's dockets are typically filled 12 to 18 months out, so a trial may not be decided until 18 months after the initial arrest. During this time, defendants with pending

There are four main decision points that prosecutors have: initial case screening, charging, plea offers, and case disposition.

court appearances are out in the community on a bond that secures their reappearance, or they are on some form of **pretrial supervision** in the community.

The pretrial release decision is made following arrest so that defendants who qualify can be effectively released and supervised in the community prior to their next court date. This allows defendants to return to work or school and to prepare for their defense, and it keeps local jails from becoming too crowded while a criminal case is pending. A risk assessment instrument has been developed for the federal system to predict who would likely pose a threat to the public safety or likely not return for a later court appearance (Lowenkamp & Whetzel 2009).

▶ Corrections as Community-Based or Institutional

Misdemeanor or first-time felony offenders may be offered **diversion**. Upon successful completion of diversionary supervision, the offender's charge is dropped and the individual does not have a formal record of conviction. If the offender on diversion supervision does not comply with the conditions, a formal execution of the sentence ensues and a record of the conviction remains.

The last two decision points for prosecutors are plea offers that lead to a recommendation to the judge for case disposition. Most defendants plead guilty, after which they are formally sentenced by the court. A wide variety of sentencing options are available within the correctional system continuum of sanctions. The **continuum of sanctions** means that correctional supervision typically involves combining one or more options within the community or an institutional setting to achieve more than one goal. In cases of petty offenses and misdemeanors, a citation may be issued for the payment of a fine. For nonviolent felony offenses, community-based supervision may be an option, while for predatory felony cases, the focus may be achieving public safety.

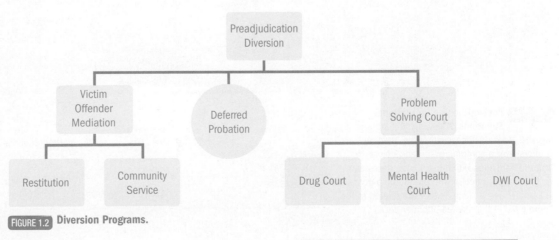

FIGURE 1.2 Diversion Programs.

Compare and contrast both diversion and postsentencing options, and institutional- and community-based corrections.

GLOSSARY

diversion A form of community supervision for individuals who have not been formally sentenced but who agree to complete stipulations such as treatment or community service in exchange for having their charges dropped.

continuum of sanctions One or more sentencing options within the community or an institution that can be combined with one another to achieve a range of sentencing goals.

community corrections Court-ordered supervision and treatment while the offender remains at liberty in the community.

net widening When offenders receive a level of correctional control or punishment that is greater than what they really require, resulting in bringing more people into the system.

institutional corrections Incarceration of offenders in a jail or prison, apart from the community.

Community Corrections

Community corrections programs depend on correctional resources available in the community to assist the offender in seeking help and abiding by certain conditions. The philosophy behind community corrections assumes that most offenders have made poor decisions along the way, but their need to retain responsibility and/or change overrides their threat to public safety and therefore they do not require incarceration. Community correctional programs are more likely than jails and prisons to offer rehabilitation programs that meet the offender's court-ordered conditions. In addition, the offender can enlist the help of his or her family for support. Forms of community corrections include probation, restitution, electronic monitoring, and day-reporting centers. At times, all of these add-on alternatives may be used to excess and thus offenders on probation are required to do too much or to do more than they need for adequate punishment. Had these programs not been available, judges would have used straight probation anyway, but sometimes they have a tendency to use a sanction just because it's there—not because it truly benefits an offender. This principle is called **net widening**.

95% about 95 percent of incarcerated prisoners will be released someday, so we must consider their reentry back into the community.

Institutional Corrections

Institutional corrections house offenders in an institutional environment, apart from their community, friends, and family. Visits are restricted to weekends if at all. Institutional corrections operate under the philosophy that some people need to be separated from the elements of daily life to protect others' safety or to pay for their crimes by having their freedom taken away. Jails are primarily for pretrial detainees who have not been convicted of a crime. Jails also detain people convicted of misdemeanors who are serving less than one year of time. Prisons are long-term institutions designed to house convicted felons who are serving more than one year of time. Furthermore, about 95 percent of incarcerated prisoners will be released someday, so we must consider their reentry back into the community. Only a very small number of offenders are locked up permanently. Some of the programs pictured in the orange boxes in Figure 1.3 can be used during stays of incarceration, on a case-by-case basis.

FIGURE 1.3 **Postsentencing Correctional Sanctions.** Following sentencing, the judge decides whether the offender is eligible for a community sentence. Note that the sanctions within the orange boxes can be used in conjunction with probation, parole, jail, and prison as long as they are related to the crime itself or the risk the offender poses.

▶ Incarceration Rates

Despite recent declines in the use of prison, the U.S. **incarceration rate** per 100,000 men and women remains the highest in the world, surpassing all other countries. While other countries have been relatively steady, U.S. rates were similar to other European countries until the 1970s, but beginning in the 1980s, the United States began to increase incarceration for drug offenders and lengthen sentences for repeat and violent offenders. The war on drugs had a pronounced negative effect on increasing the percent of incarcerated women—who now comprise nearly 7 percent of the overall prisoner population in the United States. Tonry (2004) provided evidence that severe punishment has had little effect on decreases in crime. Over the last 40 years, the United States reached a high of over 700 people per 100,000. This number is more pronounced and deeply affects Latino and African-American communities.

Using arrest and incarceration as a control mechanism dates back to the end of the Civil War. Although slavery ended, many people of color were incarcerated for minor offenses and treated differently than Caucasians. Historians contend that dehumanization and differential treatment was simply transferred from slavery on plantation farms to prisons. Then it took a different form with regard to the southern states' use of the convict leasing system. By the 1950s, African-Americans constituted about one-third of inmates admitted to prison (Mauer 1999). People of Hispanic descent have also experienced hardships with the criminal justice system on account of their heritage.

One perspective on why this is the case is that police may target people of a certain race/ethnic group more often than Caucasians and that increased police contact results in a greater likelihood of an arrest for some people because of their race or ethnicity. Studies investigating the "driving while black" (or "driving while brown") phenomenon and various points in the criminal justice system, such as the charging decision or

Despite recent declines in the use of prison, the U.S. incarceration rate per 100,000 men and women remains the highest in the world, surpassing all other countries.

7% women now comprise nearly 7 percent of the overall prisoner population in the United States.

sentencing, support a view of racial bias in some jurisdictions. Another view suggests that while young males across all racial groups engage in criminal offenses in their teens and early 20s (as suggested by self-report data), African-American males engage in more violent felony offenses and continue offending behavior for a longer duration than males of other racial groups (Walker, Spohn, & Delone 2012). A third observation suggests that the war on drugs has worsened racial disparities in that it has affected both men and women from low-income, urban communities. These views by themselves clearly do not explain all cases, nor are they limited to African-Americans. History shows that arrest and incarceration has long been a tool to control and limit the lives of Native Americans, Latinos, and, most recently, undocumented immigrants (Walker, Spohn, & Delone 2012).

Racial disparities in corrections continue to widen and affect entire communities, many of which are poor communities that lack political influence. The corrections system, especially incarceration, hinders **economic mobility** of individuals and their children and thus hinders their ability to move up the economic ladder (The Pew Charitable Trusts 2010). These disparities, in turn, reinforce stereotypes that some people hold about dangerousness and who is perceived to be a criminal. It is precisely for these reasons that in this book, one common underlying theme that runs throughout is drawing attention to the history and contemporary situation of racial disparity and socioeconomic differences in the correctional system, where applicable.

> **LEARNING OUTCOMES 3** Explain the key reasons for the rise in incarceration rates since the 1980s and the overall effect that it has had on individuals, communities, and the crime rate.
>
> **GLOSSARY**
>
> **incarceration rate** The proportion of people in jail and prison per 100,000 residents in a given area.
>
> **economic mobility** The likelihood that individuals can rise and maintain a higher socioeconomic status than they were born into, through employment and earnings.

Think About It...

About 7.3 million people are *currently* under some form of correctional supervision in the United States. Of this number, 2.3 million are serving time in local, state, and federal institutions, like the women pictured here. These numbers don't even count the estimated 20 million people with felony records and the millions of people who have misdemeanors criminal records but are not currently in the system. The grand total could be as many as 100 million people nationwide with a criminal record of some kind (Cassidy 2010). Does knowing this change your perception of offenders?

Source: Rob Schoenbaum/ZUMA Press/ Newscom

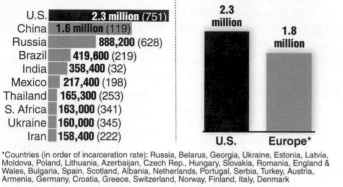

A dubious distinction

In 2007, the U.S. had about 723,000 inmates in jails and 1.6 million in prisons, more prisoners than any other country.

U.S. vs. all other nations
Nations with the largest prison populations, latest available data (rate per 100,000 residents)

U.S.	2.3 million (751)
China	1.6 million (119)
Russia	888,200 (628)
Brazil	419,600 (219)
India	358,400 (32)
Mexico	217,400 (198)
Thailand	165,300 (253)
S. Africa	163,000 (341)
Ukraine	160,000 (345)
Iran	158,400 (222)

U.S. vs. Europe
Total U.S. inmate population compared to the 36 largest European inmate populations

U.S. 2.3 million   Europe* 1.8 million

*Countries (in order of incarceration rate): Russia, Belarus, Georgia, Ukraine, Estonia, Latvia, Moldova, Poland, Lithuania, Azerbaijan, Czech Rep., Hungary, Slovakia, Romania, England & Wales, Bulgaria, Spain, Scotland, Albania, Netherlands, Portugal, Serbia, Turkey, Austria, Armenia, Germany, Croatia, Greece, Switzerland, Norway, Finland, Italy, Denmark

Source: Pew Center on the States, World Prison Brief: King's College London
Graphic: Pat Carr
© 2008 MCT

FIGURE 1.4 Incarceration Rates between the United States and Europe.
Source: Carr/MCT/Newscom

▶ Media Influence on Public Opinion and Correctional Policy

The **mass media** provide us with global news, entertainment, and education and has perhaps the greatest influence on how most people learn and develop opinions about various social issues. The media also play a significant role in influencing public opinion and encouraging political involvement in the punishment of offenders. Public opinion on crime and punishment issues remain deeply rooted in television programs depicting crime scene investigations, courtroom dramas, and scenes of the agitated, difficult prisoner. News programs and newspapers remain wedded to headlining only the most horrific crimes that have occurred that particular day, while at the same time ignoring more common crimes (Dowler, Fleming, & Muzzatti 2006). This creates a public perception that violence is random and frequent, while ignoring the true likelihood of victimization of violence and its contributing factors.

Despite concerns about the economy, employment, education, health care, and dwindling social security, violent crime in the urban core dominates local news stations' aims to increase ratings for a specific target audience (Yanich 2004). When it comes to discussing punishments for particular crimes, the media are not privy to attorney conversations about the lack of evidence that lead to possible dismissals, charge reductions, and plea bargaining, so only the maximum possible penalty is reported. When the actual sentence is later publicized, it is not surprising that citizens feel angered or disconnected with what they perceive as injustice. Being that crimes are rarely followed through the entire justice process, people rely on what they see on the latest episode of *Law and Order* or read on the latest blog and personal website page as

viewers think that they are getting information about public issues when, more often than not, they are simply gathering factoids that have no useful purpose in public debate

representative of the "real" judicial process. Few people actually understand the realities of sentencing options and the correctional process. Yanich warns that

viewers think that they are getting information about public issues when, more often than not, they are simply gathering factoids that have no useful purpose in public debate.... But, the news system communicates them to make us think that they do. Who among us can take the time to deconstruct a news story about a violent crime when we are bombarded by images of victims, suspects, and yellow crime scene tape? To understand that the reality that we are being shown is designed to hold us as consumers until the next commercial break and not to inform us as citizens? The danger is that we think that we are being informed, when in fact, we are only being sold. (2004, 560)

Research on media influence and crime indicates support for **cultivation theory**, otherwise known as the "mean world syndrome." Cultivation theory suggests that violence in the media, by itself, does not cause individuals to become violent. Rather, repeated and cumulative exposure to violence eventually creates a sense of insecurity and irrational fear of violent victimization and anxiety about certain types of people (Gorham 2006). This leads to a potential for widespread "moral panic" about child abductions, child molestations, and homicide (Zgoba 2007).

The relationship between media and crime has other uses as well, such as criminals who directly contact the media themselves to use writers and reporters to convey a specific message. Another way criminals may use mass media is to create or visit websites to network with like-minded people. It is no wonder why repeated exposure to extreme crimes leads the average person to become confused and fearful about crime in general. When it comes to public opinion on punishments and treatment for people who break the law, the public seems to recognize that

violence in the media, by itself, does not cause individuals to become violent. Rather, repeated and cumulative exposure to violence eventually creates a sense of insecurity and irrational fear of violent victimization

Analyze the relationships among mass media, public opinion, and the making of correctional policy.

certain types of offenders need community-based treatment or shorter sentences (Applegate & Davis 2006; Applegate, Davis, & Cullen 2009) than other types of offenders (Cullen, Fisher, & Applegate 2000). Public opinion on more extreme forms of punishment, such as support for the death penalty, is more strongly related to resentment and the inability to connect with racial minorities than to views on the moral decline of society or fear of uncontrolled violence (Unnever & Cullen 2010).

Crime Control Policy

Media influences and public opinion are also related, in part, to the formation of **crime control policy**. Throughout the book, you will consider philosophies, practices, and procedures that are being used to implement crime control policy. Many of these policies were developed in piecemeal fashion by state and federal legislatures for responses to an immediate problem or in reaction to something other states are doing. Crime policies in the United States appear to be distinctly different—more punitive—than crime policies in other Western countries in the world.

More punitive crime policies have led to responses that have relied substantially on incarceration. This has caused correctional spending to increase faster than most other government budget items. Correctional spending is now the fourth largest line item in most states' budgets after education, health care, and transportation (Vera Institute of Justice 2010). Annual corrections' costs accounts for over *$173 billion* at state and local levels. These expensive approaches, coupled with our recent economic troubles, have led to budget shortfalls and underfunded community supervision programs left to supervise a high number of clients. Despite increasing corrections expenditures, recidivism rates remain high with about half of all persons released from prison returning within three years. To complicate the problem, offenders cycle in and out of the justice system from the same communities that are also underserved and impoverished.

▶ Evidence-Based Practices

The Bureau of Justice Assistance (BJA) started the **Justice Reinvestment Initiative** in 2006 to address these budgetary concerns. In 2010 a National Summit was held and BJA was joined by nonprofit organizations such as the Pew Center on the States, the Council of State Governments Justice Center, and the Public Welfare Foundation. In February 2011 the report from the National Summit was released. The report concluded that incarceration is a very high cost response with very low positive returns on investment. Included in its recommendations were that correctional programs become more cost effective by using objective assessments to separate the offenders that pose the greatest risk to public safety from offenders who should be in community corrections programs that work. Technical assistance and financial grants were provided to states that used collected data to identify strategies to reduce costs and support the data analysis, policy recommendations, implementation, and measurement phases of the project.

The four-step Justice Reinvestment Initiative process is as follows:

1. Analyze trends to understand factors driving jail and prison population growth.

2. Develop and implement policy options to generate savings—examples include respond to offender risks and needs based on sustainable, evidence-based approaches; develop new approaches to promote successful offender reintegration.

TABLE 1.1	Making Crime Policy: Why the United States Is Different.	
	United States	**Other Westernized Countries**
Judges and Prosecutors	Elected at state and local levels—influenced by politics and short-term terms	Career civil servants—receive special training and remain there as a career
Legislative Organization	Vulnerable to voting according to party lines or according to what other states are doing	Various parties are present
Funding	Reliance on federal funding; vulnerable to loss of federal funding; 50 state systems	Centralized single system
Sentencing and Release Decisions	Micromanaged by legislators	Managed by the courts and corrections system
Legislative Style of Decision Making	Political action committees; lobbyists; appeal to human emotions	Rational decision making

Source: Derived from THINKING ABOUT CRIME: Sense and Sensibility in American Penal Culture by M. Tony (2004) Oxford University Press.

An outcome is a way to measure whether a program or practice works. Outcomes will differ for each program, and there may be separate outcomes for various segments of a single program. Goals are typically focused on the offender and may include the following:

- Reduced number of new crimes committed while on supervision
- Reduced number of new crimes after supervision
- Reduction in the number of people who stay out of jail and/or prison
- Offender change in thinking patterns

- Increased number of drug-free days
- Increased number of days offender is working or employed while on supervision
- More effective assessments—matching risk and need with supervision levels

3. Reinvest money saved back into selected high-risk communities and other prevention-oriented strategies.

4. Measure the impact of policy changes and reinvestment resources.

At about the same time as the Justice Reinvestment Initiative began, the term **evidence-based practices** (EBP) also surfaced on the criminal justice scene. EBP is used in fields such as medicine, education, social work, and mental health. EBP allows academics and practitioners to come together with programs that work and make a difference on intended outcomes. In corrections, the chief concerns (and thus the intended outcomes) are achieving public safety through no new crimes while on supervision and reducing offender recidivism after supervision.

Before EBP, academic research may have been passed over as not necessary because practitioners may have felt that they could tell what works based on years of experience and anecdotal evidence. Some agencies had been reluctant to try anything new or better because "this is what we've always done." EBP challenges anecdotal evidence by requiring programs to prove with statistical evidence that what they do works. If it doesn't work, agencies are required to change to a curriculum or technique that has been shown in

EBP challenges anecdotal evidence by requiring programs to prove with statistical evidence that what they do works.

another jurisdiction to work with the offender population or risk funds going elsewhere to agencies that are adhering to performance-based outcomes.

How to Determine What Works

Evidence-based practice encourages academics to engage in policy-relevant research, while at the same time, requires agency practitioners to use programs that have been empirically shown through methodologically sound academic research to meet the intended outcome. So, only studies conducted with a strong methodology and those that have found a true difference are counted. This is harder to find than it sounds as only a small percent of published studies meet all the criteria for a quality study.

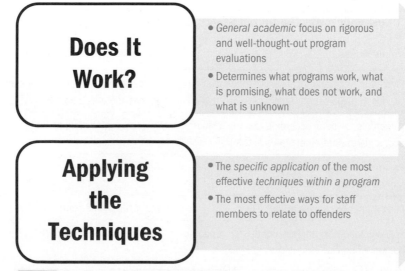

Does It Work?

- *General academic* focus on rigorous and well-thought-out program evaluations
- Determines what programs work, what is promising, what does not work, and what is unknown

Applying the Techniques

- The *specific application* of the most effective *techniques within a program*
- The most effective ways for staff members to relate to offenders

FIGURE 1.5 Two Parts to Evidence-Based Practices.

Once a published study has been judged to be of high quality, or "rigorous," it is considered to be part of the overall score card kept on the results of each correctional program or intervention. From there, a program needs a certain number of valid studies to be placed into one of four categories: what works, what's promising, what doesn't work, and what we need to know more about.

EBP Techniques

The "what works" literature is more general in terms of correctional philosophies achieved (such as deterrence, rehabilitation, and incapacitation), but it can also be targeted toward a specific outcome (such as recidivism reduction). Using EBP techniques, however, is more specific to *how* treatment interventions are implemented by practitioners when time and resources are

Using EBP techniques, however, is more specific to how treatment interventions are implemented by practitioners when time and resources are limited.

limited. Agencies are increasingly required to continue to add to the body of knowledge by measuring what they do and having an evaluator statistically examine their data.

The basis of applying EBP techniques in corrections (pretrial or postconviction) begins with a valid assessment instrument to measure the level of risk the offender poses and

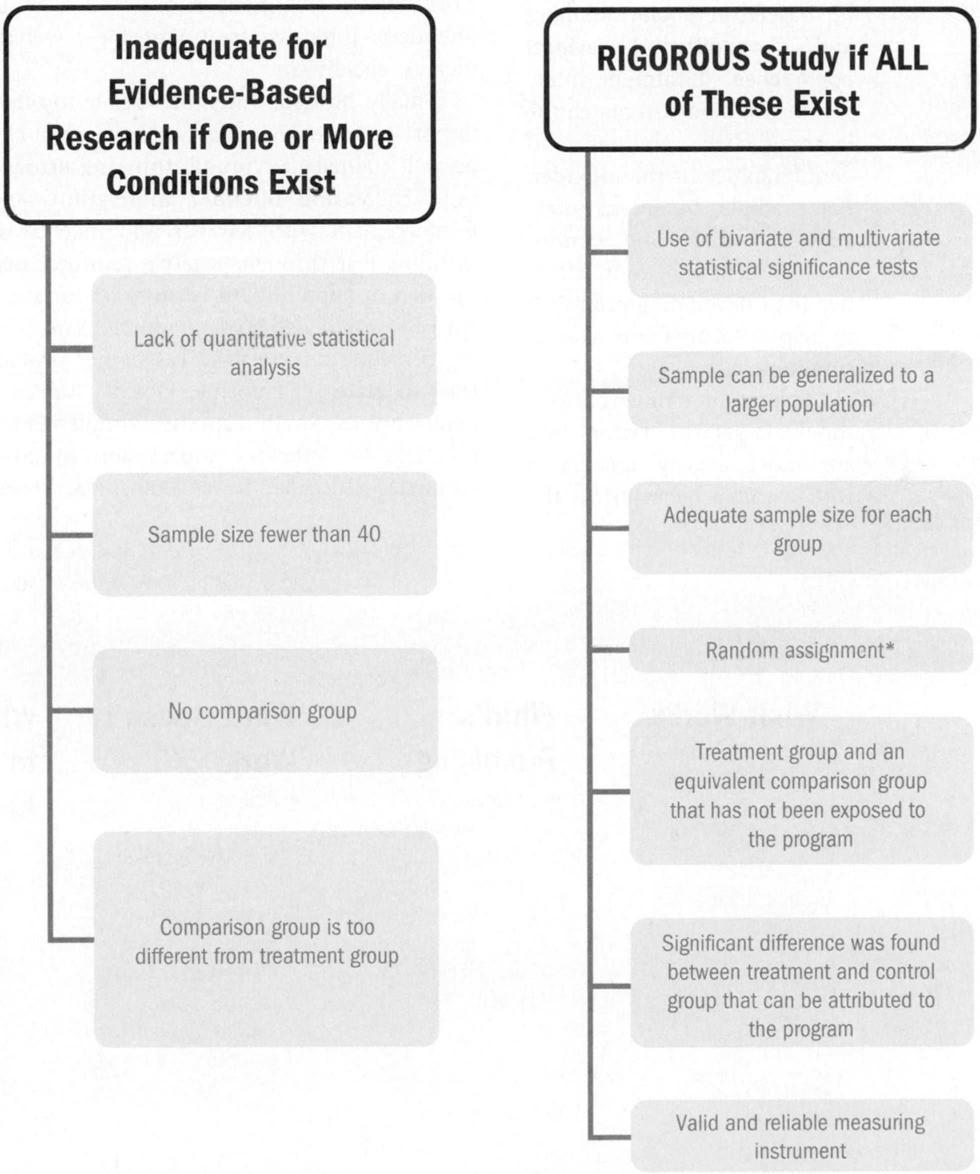

Inadequate for Evidence-Based Research if One or More Conditions Exist

- Lack of quantitative statistical analysis
- Sample size fewer than 40
- No comparison group
- Comparison group is too different from treatment group

RIGOROUS Study if ALL of These Exist

- Use of bivariate and multivariate statistical significance tests
- Sample can be generalized to a larger population
- Adequate sample size for each group
- Random assignment*
- Treatment group and an equivalent comparison group that has not been exposed to the program
- Significant difference was found between treatment and control group that can be attributed to the program
- Valid and reliable measuring instrument

* True random assignment is rare in the social sciences, so there are plenty of quasi-experimental and matched group designs that are still considered rigorous.

FIGURE 1.6 **How to Identify RIGOROUS Studies Used in EBP.**

GLOSSARY

Justice Reinvestment Initiative
A data-driven approach to encourage states to reduce correctional spending and reinvest savings in strategies designed to prevent crime. States and localities collect and analyze data on factors related to prison population growth and costs, implement changes to increase efficiencies, and measure both the fiscal and public safety impacts of those changes.

evidence-based practices
Correctional interventions for which there is consistent and solid scientific evidence showing that they work to meet the intended outcomes, such as recidivism reduction.

social learning Changing old behavior through modeling new skills and desirable behavior.

cognitive behavioral approaches Changing thinking patterns and habits that lead to criminal behavior, such as self-control, anger management, social perspective taking, moral reasoning, problem solving, and attitudinal change.

the problem areas (needs) that should be emphasized with the offender during his or her sentence. One of the most effective assessment instruments at the current time is the Level of Service Inventory-Revised (LSI-R). Once the risk and needs are accurately measured, correctional supervision and treatment can commence. Risk and needs assessments are also used to make decisions about prison custody level, housing, and institutional release.

Another technique of EBP is that intervention should be based on **social learning** and/or **cognitive behavioral approaches**. Treatment interventions should also match the learning styles, abilities, and demographics of the offender. For example, treatment interventions that are gender focused seem to be more effective than developing programs to help both men and women simultaneously.

Treatment interventions should target risk factors that are most closely associated with criminal behavior for the

greatest gains in recidivism reduction. These factors include the following:

- Antisocial attitudes, values, beliefs, and emotional states (criminal thinking)
- Pro-criminal associates and isolation from pro-social associates
- Egocentrism, weak problem-solving and self-regulation skills
- Criminal history
- Familial factors (low levels of affection and cohesiveness, poor parental supervision and discipline practices, neglect and abuse)
- Low levels of personal, vocational, and educational achievement
- Substance abuse

Correctional treatment should actually target higher-risk offenders. Intensive treatment for lower-risk offenders can increase recidivism.

Finally, how staff members relate to offenders is extremely important to achieving lasting behavioral change. Staff should be well trained in criminal thinking errors, establishing rapport, increasing offender motivation, and using positive reinforcement with rewards and incentives over the use of instilling fear through negative reinforcement. The quality of the visit or appointment is more important than the quantity. An EBP would also favor graduated sanctions over incarcerating someone for violating his or her probation or parole. At least six states—California, Florida, Kansas, New Hampshire, Pennsylvania, South Carolina—implemented evidence-based practices for offender supervision in 2010. An additional six states—Indiana, Iowa, Louisiana, Nevada, Oregon, and

What Works
- Must have two or more RIGOROUS evaluations showing *significant difference* on the outcome between the group exposed to the program and the group not exposed

What's Promising
- At least one rigorous study showing effectiveness or a significant difference between two groups

What Doesn't Work
- At least two rigorous studies that have reported *no significant* difference on the outcome between the group exposed to the program and the group not exposed

What We Need to Know More About
- Not enough research conducted to draw any conclusions

FIGURE 1.7 **Uniform Criteria for Classifying Correctional Practices.**
Source: "Uniform Criteria for Classifying Correctional Practices" in PREVENTING CRIME: What Works, What Doesn't, What's Promising by L. W. Sherman, D. Gottfredson, D. MacKenzie, J. Eck, P. Reuter, & S. Bushway. Washington, DC: National Institute of Justice, 1997.

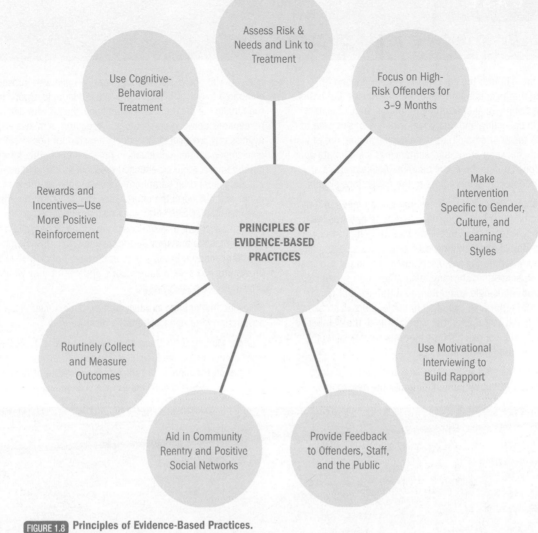

Circles around center:
- Assess Risk & Needs and Link to Treatment
- Focus on High-Risk Offenders for 3–9 Months
- Make Intervention Specific to Gender, Culture, and Learning Styles
- Use Motivational Interviewing to Build Rapport
- Provide Feedback to Offenders, Staff, and the Public
- Aid in Community Reentry and Positive Social Networks
- Routinely Collect and Measure Outcomes
- Rewards and Incentives—Use More Positive Reinforcement
- Use Cognitive-Behavioral Treatment

Center: **PRINCIPLES OF EVIDENCE-BASED PRACTICES**

FIGURE 1.8 **Principles of Evidence-Based Practices.**
Adapted from: Crime and Justice Institute (2004)

applying EBP techniques in corrections begins with a valid assessment instrument to measure the risk the offender poses and the problem areas (needs) that should be emphasized with the offender during his or her sentence.

Virginia—are considering the use of evidence-based or best practices in the future.

In conclusion, the complexity of public opinion, the interests of the media, and the factors that influence passing or not passing crime control legislation is indeed an important consideration as you read this book. Further, understanding the importance of using programs and strategies that work are a part of the evidence-based approach. We will refer to the two parts to EBP in this book as "does it work?" and "applying EBP techniques." A final goal of this book is to provide a base for that knowledge so you can intelligently engage in a discussion of both philosophies of punishment as well as effective and salient correctional strategies.

Using EBP to Address Racial Disparities

Cases that are brought into the corrections system depend on decision making that occurs beforehand. No one knows that better than Milwaukee County district attorney John Chisholm. Chisholm was interested in collecting and analyzing evidence-based data to identify possible racial or ethnic bias in cases originating out of his Wisconsin county between arrest and sentencing. The ultimate goal was to build public confidence in the criminal justice process and to explain case outcomes from the courts to the corrections system.

This was quite challenging because most case information in his office was maintained as hard copy files, and none of it was kept at any one agency. A team of experts listed key data that were necessary to assemble for each individual defendant to determine how a system operated during key discretion points in the process: arrest, initial case screening, charging, plea offers, and sentencing. Data were entered in a single computerized database, not only by individual defendant, but also including multiple charges, some of which were dismissed and others that were charged. The database also accounted for the various charges that may lead to different plea agreements and different sentences.

The data revealed a disparity in misdemeanor possession of drug paraphernalia cases. About 73 percent of non-white defendants charged with possession of drug paraphernalia were prosecuted, compared to only 59 percent of white defendants. Upon closer examination of the data, the disparity originated with differences in perceptions between prosecutors. Prosecutors with less experience aggressively prosecuted individuals arrested for possession of crack pipes but not individuals in possession of other forms of paraphernalia. More experienced prosecutors decided against pursuing most drug paraphernalia cases, seeing them as too minor and not worth the effort. Once the source of the disparity was identified, District Attorney Chisholm encouraged his junior prosecutors to view possession of paraphernalia as a treatment issue that qualified for dismissal or diversion rather than prosecution. He also implemented a policy that required prosecutors to seek a supervisor's approval if they wanted to prosecute such charges.

Following that change in policy and practice, racial disparities in possession of drug paraphernalia disappeared.

Source: McKenzie, W., Stemen, D., and Coursen, D. (2009). Prosecution and racial justice: Using data to advance fairness in criminal prosecution. New York, NY Vera Institute of Justice. Retrieved online from **www.vera.org/centers/prosecution-and-racial-justice**.

The case in Milwaukee County raises several interesting questions:

1. Given that district attorneys like Chisholm are elected to their position, what are the potential ramifications for one's political career of doing a study such as this? Is Chisholm a change agent or is he destined to end his D.A. career prematurely?

2. Decisions made by prosecutors are considered to be one of the most influential in the system, yet these decisions are rarely scrutinized. Should the scrutiny held to Milwaukee County prosecutors be expanded to other counties and even other states?

3. When it comes to issues of racial/ethnic disparity, how important is it that the public has confidence in our criminal justice system?

Source: © Visions of America, LLC /Alamy

Describe how corrections is part of the larger criminal justice system and how decisions made along the way contribute to case dismissals, convictions, and potential disparity.

The three main social control agencies of the criminal justice system are the police, the courts, and the corrections system.

The police are the gatekeepers of the system.

The courts depend on the efficiency and professionalism of the police to determine whether the suspected law-breaker is the right suspect and whether this suspect broke the law in the manner that he or she is being accused.

Corrections serve to carry out the sentence of the court.

1. What role do local police play, if any, in racial and economic disparity in jails and prisons?

2. How can prosecutors and/or judges correct racial and economic disparities that exist in their jurisdiction?

3. Do gender disparities exist in the corrections system? If so, where and how can these disparities be corrected?

4. If a case is dismissed, can the same case be brought up for prosecution at a later time? If so, how? If not, why not?

5. What circumstances about an offender's past might make him or her a good candidate for pre-trial community supervision?

corrections The network of government and private agencies responsible for the pre- and postconviction custody, supervision, and treatment of persons accused or convicted of crimes.

police Law enforcement officials who are sworn to uphold the law, keep social order, and preserve public safety.

citation A police-issued ticket ordering a citizen to pay a fine for a minor law violation.

booked When a suspect is identified and fingerprinted in jail after being arrested for an alleged crime.

jurisdiction A predefined geographic area.

dismissed When a case is dropped for lack of evidence and does not proceed any further.

pretrial supervision The community supervision of a defendant who has not yet been convicted but is waiting for his or her next court hearing date.

Compare and contrast both diversion and postsentencing options, and institutional- and community-based corrections.

Corrections programs involve not only individuals who have not yet been sentenced, but also misdemeanants and felons who have been formally convicted or have pled guilty.

Offenders who are in jail or prison are separated from the elements of daily life to protect the safety of others or to pay for their crimes by having their freedom taken away.

1. What factors determine if a case or an offender is qualified for diversion and who makes the decision?

2. Which crimes and/or offender situations would be best suited for community supervision, and why?

3. What crimes and/or offender situations would best qualify for institutional corrections, and why?

diversion A form of community supervision for individuals who have not been formally sentenced, but who agree to complete stipulations such as treatment or community service in exchange for having their charges dropped.

continuum of sanctions One or more sentencing options within the community or an institution that can be combined with one another to achieve a range of sentencing goals.

community corrections Court-ordered supervision and treatment while the offender remains at liberty in the community.

net widening When offenders receive a level of correctional control or punishment that is greater than what they really require, resulting in bringing more people into the system.

institutional corrections Incarceration of offenders in a jail or prison, apart from the community.

LEARNING OUTCOMES 3

Explain the key reasons for the rise in incarceration rates since the 1980s and the overall effect that it has had on individuals, communities, and the crime rate.

The U.S. incarceration rate per 100,000 men and women remains the highest in the world, yet incarceration is the most expensive option and yields only a small impact on the crime rate.

Incarceration negatively affects the emotional mobility of individuals and can impact entire communities, especially those areas that are underserved and are composed primarily of families of Latino and African-American heritage.

Increases in the prison population since 1980 are related to politicization of criminal behavior based on emotions, changes in sentencing laws for drugs and violent offenses, decreased rates of release on discretionary parole, and decisions made about responding to parole and probation violators.

1. How much of the correctional system is a response to earlier decisions made by legislators, police, and courts?

2. If the United States has the highest incarceration rates in the world, is it because Americans are just more violent or criminal than the rest of the world, or are there other reasons? If so, what?

3. Why do incarceration rates have such a small impact on crime rates?

4. Can we build our way out of the crime problem enough to make a significant decrease in the crime rate? If so, how many people would need to be incarcerated to make this difference and at what cost? If not, what are other options?

incarceration rate The proportion of people in jail and prison per 100,000 residents in a given area.

economic mobility The likelihood at which individuals can rise and maintain a higher socioeconomic status than they were born into, through employment and earnings.

LEARNING OUTCOMES 4

Analyze the relationships among mass media, public opinion, and the making of correctional policy.

Media sources inform public opinion of crime and responses to it more often than learning experiences at school, home, or other settings.

Citizens are generally in favor of rehabilitation and prevention programs and support alternatives to incarceration when available.

U.S. crime policy making is unique compared to other Westernized countries, due to its system of electing or appointing state/local judges and prosecutors, legislative micromanagement of sentencing/parole, and state reliance on federal funding.

Correctional policy trends may not be representative of public opinion in the long-term, but they have affected the overall expansion of the corrections system, the growth of women under correctional supervision, the incarceration rate, and the burgeoning cost.

1. What other ways do the media inform public opinion on social issues?

2. How have legislators been major definers of the "crime problem"?

3. If citizens are in support of alternatives to prison, why haven't we developed more programs and options in this direction?

4. What other ways exist to develop rational crime policies?

5. If we continue down the same path of prison expansion, how might other societal institutions be affected?

mass media Broadcast and print forms of expression for consumer news, education, and entertainment, such as television, movies, internet, DVDs, video games, radio, books, newspapers, and magazines.

cultivation theory Repeated viewing and cumulative exposure to violence in the media eventually creates a sense of insecurity and irrational fear of violent victimization and about people in the world in general.

crime control policy A course of action to respond to criminal behavior in the best interest of the public.

Characterize the meaning of evidence-based practices and why it is significant to improving the correctional system.

EBP requires agencies to use programs that have been empirically shown through methodologically sound academic research to work, thus becoming more effective over time at reducing recidivism.

Specific EBP techniques for lasting behavior change include assessing risk/needs, using cognitive behavioral approaches, having a program duration between three and nine months, targeting high-risk offenders, being responsive to demographics of the population, using motivational interviewing, and using rewards/incentives.

It is important that EBPs are continually measured through data collection, evaluation, and dissemination of that EBP practice or intervention so that minor adjustments may be made.

1. How does EBP help achieve public safety?

2. How is EBP different from correctional supervision used two decades ago?

3. Is EBP applicable to correctional officers in prison who are tasked with supervision of inmates but not treatment? If so, how? If not, why not?

4. Is EBP seen as more demanding for offenders overall or as an intervention that is less punitive?

5. How is EBP different from the Justice Reinvestment Initiative?

Justice Reinvestment Initiative A data-driven approach to encourage states to reduce correctional spending and reinvest savings in strategies designed to prevent crime. States and localities collect and analyze data on factors related to prison population growth and costs, implement changes to increase efficiencies, and measure both the fiscal and public safety impacts of those changes.

evidence-based practices Correctional interventions for which there is consistent and solid scientific evidence showing that they work to meet the intended outcomes, such as recidivism reduction.

social learning Changing old behavior through modeling new skills and desirable behavior.

cognitive behavioral approaches Changing thinking patterns and habits that lead to criminal behavior, such as self-control, anger management, social perspective taking, moral reasoning, problem solving, and attitudinal change.

MyCJLab

Go to the Chapter 1 section in *MyCJLab* to test your understanding of this chapter, access customized study content, engage in interactive simulations, complete critical thinking and research assignments, and view related online videos.

Additional Links

Visit the National Conference of State Legislature website and click on the "bookstore" tab to learn what criminal justice books legislative staff members are reading: **www.ncsl.org**.

Check to see what correctional policies were a part of the 2010 legislative session in your state: **www.ncsl.org/default.aspx?tabid=20763**.

Visit the VERA Institute of Justice, Center on Sentencing and Corrections to review recent legislative trends in reducing prison populations: **www.vera.org/content/continuing-fiscal-crisis-in-corrections**.

View *The Mean World Syndrome*—a video by George Gerbner and Michael Morgan, about the effect of media violence on perceptions of the world using cultivation theory: **www.youtube.com/watch?v=ylhqasb1chl&feature=related**. A shortened explanation of this video is entitled *Media as Storytellers: Nothing to Tell, but a Lot to Sell.*

Watch a short video explaining evidence-based practices from George Keiser, the division chief of the National Institute of Corrections: **http:// nicic.gov/EvidenceBasedPractices**.

Listen to how EBP can be applied in community corrections and to treatment programs by scrolling down to the list of previous podcasts from July 6, 2009: **www.corrections.com/podcasts**.

Why Do We Punish?

1 Name and describe the five primary punishment philosophies.

2 List and summarize the three key elements for effective deterrence.

3 Compare and contrast selective and general incapacitation.

4 Summarize rehabilitation's development from a reclamation focus to a reentry emphasis.

5 Explain the keys ways in which retribution differs from revenge.

6 Describe how restorative justice principles are used in sentencing, during community supervision, and in prison.

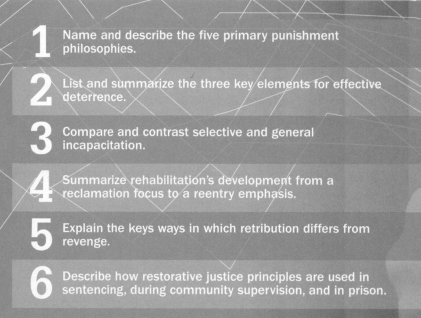

Source: James Steidl/Shutterstock.com

2

WHAT DOES SOCIETY HOPE TO ACCOMPLISH WHEN PUNISHING CRIMINAL OFFENDERS?

In 2010, in three different U.S. jurisdictions, the following sentences were imposed:

- As part of a probation agreement for causing an accident that killed Army Sgt. Thomas E. Towers, Jr., Andrew Gaudioso was ordered to send the soldier's family a postcard, via the probation department, every week for 15 years. If he fails to send the postcards he could be sent to prison for the remainder of the 15 years. Towers's father agreed to the unusual stipulation because he thought it would force Gaudioso to think about what he did at least once a week (Hudak 2010).

- In October, a federal judge ordered Grammy-winning rap artist, T.I. (Clifford Harris, Jr.) back to prison for 11 months. He violated the terms of his supervised release on federal weapons charges when he was arrested on suspicion of drug possession. T.I. said that he had now learned his lesson ("T.I. says new prison sentence is his final lesson" 2010).

- A Michigan teenager, as part of his sentence to a juvenile detention center, was ordered to read three books per month. He was directed to begin with one of his victim's favorite books, *The Catcher in the Rye*, which the judge said might teach the boy about responsibility (Reynolds 2010). That sentence add-on is consistent with a belief by some organizations—such as Changing Lives Through Literature (http://cltl.umassd.edu/home-flash.cfm)—that literature can transform lives and that reading should be used as a probation condition in lieu of prison sentences.

Source: Ayessemedia/ Dreamstime.com

DISCUSS Do we punish in order to force an offender to remember the wrong, to learn a lesson, to change, or for some other reason?

▶ Why Punish?

Important questions result from asking why we are punishing someone. The answers we come up with, independently or collectively, help us determine whether justice has been done. Equally important is how our view of punishment's goals affects the correctional process and helps us evaluate the success of correctional programs. This chapter directs our attention to those issues by describing key reasons for punishment.

In our representative democracy, the people's will is expressed through elected legislators. That means we should be able to identify punishment philosophies in each state and at the federal level by finding the relevant statutes or other legislative documents. Unfortunately, not all legislators have put into writing their understanding of their constituencies' reasons for applying criminal punishment. A few states that have done so provide interesting variation:

Alabama: The Alabama Sentencing Commission is directed to consider sentencing laws and practices that, in part (a) promote respect for the law, (b) provide just and adequate punishment for the offense, (c) protect the public, (d) deter criminal conduct, and (e) promote the rehabilitation of offenders (Alabama Sentencing Commission 2000).

California: The court rules for California identify the general objectives of sentencing as (a) protecting society, (b) punishing the defendant, (c) encouraging the defendant to lead a law-abiding life in the future and deterring him or her from future offenses, (d) deterring others from criminal conduct by demonstrating crime's consequences, (e) preventing the defendant from committing new crimes by isolating him or her for the period of incarceration,

(f) securing restitution for the victims of crime, and (g) achieving uniformity in sentencing (Judicial Council of California 2010).

Colorado: The Colorado Revised Statutes explains that the purposes of sentencing are (a) to punish a convicted offender, (b) to assure the fair and consistent treatment of all convicted offenders, (c) to prevent crime and promote respect for the law, and (d) to promote rehabilitation (State of Colorado 2010).

Texas: The Texas penal code's provisions are intended to ensure public safety through (a) the deterrent influence of the penalties provided in the code, (b) the rehabilitation of those convicted of violations of the code, and (c) such punishment as may be necessary to prevent likely recurrence of criminal behavior (State of Texas 2009).

Vermont: State policy requires that principles of restorative justice be included in shaping how the criminal justice system responds to persons charged with or convicted of criminal offenses. Policy objectives are to (a) resolve conflicts and disputes by means of a nonadversarial community process, (b) repair damage caused by criminal acts to communities in which they occur and to address wrongs inflicted on individual victims, and (c) reduce the risk of an offender committing a more serious crime in the future that would require a more intensive and more costly sanction, such as incarceration (State of Vermont 2002).

There is an interesting connection among these five states' reasons for punishing offenders. Especially similar are references

LEARNING
OUTCOMES
1
Name and describe the five primary punishment philosophies.

GLOSSARY

deterrence Discouraging future criminal acts by both the offender and others in the population.

incapacitation Restricting an offender's freedom of movement through isolation from the general population.

rehabilitation Providing the offender with skills, attitudes, and norms that enable him or her to be law-abiding.

retribution Just and adequate punishment.

restoration Restoring the victim, community, and offender through accountability, respect for the law and the legal process, and attention to victim needs.

to deterring the offender from future criminal acts (including people who have not yet offended, California adds), protecting the public (specifically for California, through incarceration), rehabilitating the offender, and punishing the offender (justly and adequately, Alabama notes). Also mentioned are goals of promoting respect for the law (Alabama and Colorado), uniformity in sentencing (California and Colorado), securing restitution for the victim (California), and repairing the damage caused by criminal acts (Vermont).

Those objectives provide the broad base from which a discussion of punishment rationales builds. Specifically, this chapter discusses the reasons for punishment as primarily focused on **deterrence** (discouraging future criminal acts by both the offender and others in the population), **incapacitation** (isolation of the offender from the general population), **rehabilitation** (providing the offender with skills, attitudes, and norms that enable him or her to be law-abiding), **retribution** (just and adequate punishment), and **restoration** (restoring the victim, community, and offender through accountability, respect for the law and the legal process, and attention to victim needs).

The concepts of deterrence, incapacitation, rehabilitation, retribution, and restoration provide the structure for society's system of penal sanctions and for this book. Their importance in understanding the theory and practice of corrections is emphasized by how they relate to the main ideas in several chapters of this book. In Chapter 3, for example, the philosophies help explain the development of correctional practices over time. Throughout the textbook, the philosophies provide an important perspective when discussing what, if anything, works in corrections.

▶ Deterrence

The deterrence philosophy of punishment assumes that actions serving a useful function (that is, they are utilitarian) are desirable when they benefit the general welfare of society. Reducing crime, the argument goes, certainly benefits the general welfare, so punishment that serves to reduce crime is utilitarian and desirable.

The aim of punishment is to prevent future offenses by example to both the offender and to others. When applied to the offender, punishment is said to be acting as a **specific deterrent** by showing the criminal that his or her action brought more pain than pleasure. When others hear about a criminal being punished, that punishment serves as a **general deterrent** by showing people who might be considering a criminal act the consequences they will suffer. Both specific and general deterrence are important when understanding the deterrence philosophy.

Specific Deterrence

When punishment is applied to someone who has already misbehaved, it is acting as a specific deterrent with the goal of discouraging that person from offending again. It is assumed that punishment will have that effect because proponents of the deterrence philosophy believe everyone is a rational, pleasure-seeking, and pain-avoiding person with free will.

DISCUSS *Do you think humans mostly have free will and behave in a rational manner after weighing the consequences of their actions? How should the answer to that question affect punishment decisions?*

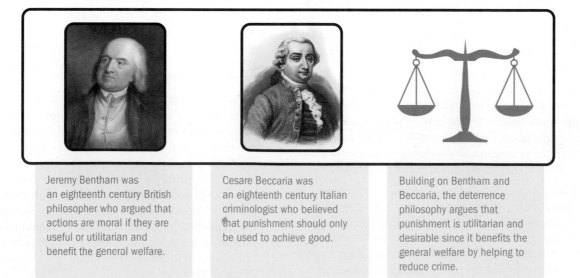

Jeremy Bentham was an eighteenth century British philosopher who argued that actions are moral if they are useful or utilitarian and benefit the general welfare.

Cesare Beccaria was an eighteenth century Italian criminologist who believed that punishment should only be used to achieve good.

Building on Bentham and Beccaria, the deterrence philosophy argues that punishment is utilitarian and desirable since it benefits the general welfare by helping to reduce crime.

FIGURE 2.1 **How Utilitarianism Influenced the Deterrence Philosophy.**
Sources: © Classic Image/Alamy and © MARKA/Alamy

FIGURE 2.2 How Deterrence Theorists View Humans.

This doctrine that punishing persons for their misdeeds will make them less likely to commit the misdeeds again is a guiding principle for many (maybe most) Western criminal justice systems. The proposition seems intuitively correct, but contemporary research has failed to find consistent evidence of the deterrent effects of punishment (Fagan & Meares 2008, 182). It seems that formal punishment alone has a very limited ability to deter crime. The lack of a specific deterrent effect might be due to problems society has in achieving three key requirements of an effective deterrence system:

- **Certainty**

  Problematic because certainty is reasonably achieved only if citizens are willing to be constantly monitored so that all criminal acts are known to the authorities and can thereby be punished

- **Severity**

  May be possible, but there is the problem that "severe" for one person may be "mild" to another

- **Swiftness**

  Will likely be achieved only by restricting the due process currently provided defendants and the rights to appeal now granted to convicted offenders

contemporary research has failed to find consistent evidence of the deterrent effects of punishment

Even if specific deterrence is not as effective in reducing reoffending as we might hope, deterrence theory may still be a desirable punishment rationale if it has a general deterrent effect.

General Deterrence

When the aim of punishment is to discourage other people from committing a crime in the first place, it is said to have a general deterrence function. As the holiday season approaches, local department stores may seek to deter

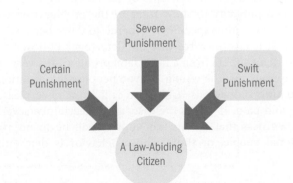

FIGURE 2.3 **Key Requirements for an Effective Deterrence System.**
Punishment acts as a deterrent only when it is accomplished with certainty, severity, and swiftness. For purposes of specific deterrence, this means that having caught offender Jones—and wanting to deter him from future acts—society's punishment must be unavoidable. It must be severe enough (but not disproportionately severe) that Jones considers it more painful than any pleasure he got from the act, and it must be applied to Jones soon after the crime occurred. When all these conditions are met, Jones is likely—deterrence theory argues—to be a law-abiding citizen.

Maybe people are not rational, calculating individuals using free will to achieve pleasure and avoid pain.

shoplifting by increasing their willingness to press charges against shoplifters. The store manager believes that the publicity resulting from shoplifters being prosecuted and punished will discourage other people from shoplifting.

In order for punishment of one offender to have a deterrent effect on others, the others must believe that they will be punished, that the punishment will be more painful than any pleasure they get from the act, and that the punishment will be administered soon after their wrongful act. In addition to those conditions, Newman (1985) adds the requirement of publicity because that condition is necessary for the others to know about the punishment someone else received.

Just as certainty, severity, and swiftness are difficult to achieve for purposes of specific deterrence, they are also problematic for general deterrence. Publicity, however, is more attainable today with our advanced media technology. But if the public is informed less about criminals being punished and more about the problems of making arrests and getting convictions (a lack of certainty), the increased use of what are seen as lenient penalties (a lack of severity) and the excessive time it takes for punishment to actually be applied (a lack of swiftness), publicity may be more harmful than helpful in having punishment be a general deterrent.

We have used the concepts of certainty, severity, swiftness, and publicity to show some of the problems of using punishment, either specific or general, to deter behavior. Of course, it is also possible that the deterrence philosophy of punishment suffers from a more fatal problem—its very core assumptions may be wrong. Maybe people are not rational, calculating individuals using free will to achieve pleasure and avoid pain. If this is the case, all the certainty, severity, and swiftness that society can muster will be to no avail. Irrational people, or those whose behavior is determined by biological, psychological, or social factors rather than through free will, are not going to be deterred by punishment (Katz 1988).

▶ Incapacitation

When incapacitation is used as a punishment, a person's ability to move about freely is impaired or restricted. Historically, the incapacitation of criminals has been achieved through imprisonment. The idea is that by removing a criminal from free society, that person is prevented from continuing to cause harm to people or property.

Most people agree that prison is necessary for some criminals. Where we disagree is about the size of that "some" category. One group would reserve imprisonment for those very few offenders who must truly be locked away for society's protection. Imprisonment, in other words, is acceptable on a limited scale. "Confine only specific offenders or offender types," say these folks. Others see imprisonment as acceptable and desirable on an extensive scale for a wide range of offenders. This "lock 'em all up" approach views imprisonment as protecting society from criminals whether or not any rehabilitation or specific deterrence occurs. Zimring and Hawkins (1995) refer to the limited approach as **selective incapacitation** and the expansionist approach as **general incapacitation**.

Both selective incapacitation and general incapacitation are based on the premise that a particular group of offenders is responsible for a large percentage of crime. If that group (whether rather small or rather large) can be removed from society—that is, incapacitated—the crime rate will decline while they are imprisoned. Even if the assumption is correct, distinguishing those criminals who fall into the overly active population from the more occasional offenders is not an easy task. Selective incapacitation has often relied on an ability to distinguish the two groups on the basis of individual characteristics, whereas general incapacitation more often relies on characteristics of the crime itself.

Both sentencing philosophies have appealing aspects, but each also has the potential to be unfair. In selective incapacitation, when trying to define the criteria for identifying individual dangerousness, bias and discrimination play a role. For argument's sake, assume that persons most likely to continue their criminal behavior will be those who come from a low-socioeconomic area of the inner city, are high school dropouts, and are unemployed. If these characteristics are included among those used to identify persons likely to continue committing crime, there is a potential for discrimination by race and ethnicity. Unfortunately, in contemporary U.S. society, there is a disproportionate number of African-Americans and Latinos who are unemployed high school dropouts living in low-income areas of the inner city. Not all of them, however, commit crimes. Even those who are criminal may not be any more likely to continue their criminal involvement than would be a

Think About It...

If people refrain from committing a crime because they fear the punishment they might receive, that punishment is serving a deterrent function. Do you think signs such as this one can deter someone from distributing drugs near a school? Is anything really accomplished if drugs are distributed instead to persons under age 18 when they are more than 1,000 feet from a school?

Source: KPA/Hackenberg/KPA/ Hackenberg/Newscom

European American offender with a high school diploma who is living in suburbia.

Redding (2009, fn. 14) reminds us that there is considerable research identifying the risk factors associated with criminal behavior (for example, criminal history, early age of criminal offending onset, substance abuse, association with deviant peers), but it remains difficult to accurately identify those people most likely to continue their criminal ways—some of them may commit serious crimes over a prolonged period, but many may not. However, as discussed in Chapter 4, increased reliance on evidence-based practices when sentencing may be changing this problem.

General incapacitation may avoid the problem of racially and ethnically biased sentencing by imposing prison sentences based on what offenders did rather than who they are. For example, if members of a community decide that drug offenders present a serious and continued threat to the public safety, they can develop a policy of longer prison terms for anyone convicted of a drug offense. In this manner, Anglo drug dealer Patterson and Hispanic drug dealer Jaramillo both receive long prison sentences. Presumably, Patterson's and Jaramillo's educational level, employment status, and neighborhood will not influence the length of imprisonment. In this manner, Patterson and Jaramillo are punished because the community believes drug offenders are dangerous—not because it thinks either Patterson or Jaramillo is necessarily a dangerous individual.

Zimring and Hawkins (1995) agree that the policy of general incapacitation may resist stereotypes of dangerousness, but they are not so sure that it can avoid the problem of false positives wherein an offender is incorrectly included among the likely-to-repeat group. This overpredicting will mean some people will be imprisoned for an unnecessarily long time. Even ignoring the ethical aspects of that situation, the mere cost involved in constructing prisons to house these offenders presents a problem to proponents of general incapacitation.

The value of selective and general incapacitation as punishment rationales continues to be debated. As with all the rationales, a key to deciding if incapacitation is a desirable basis for making punishment decisions will ride on how effectively it achieves its goal. The answer may depend on what is meant by "effective." Consider, for example, the problem of replacement. If Patterson completes 100 drug deals a year in his community, the effect of his imprisonment would be 100 fewer drug deals in that community. But what if drug dealer Tanaka begins to service Patterson's former clients and essentially makes 100 more drug sales than he does when Patterson is around? The community has lessened Patterson's criminal behavior but has not lowered the amount of crime occurring because Tanaka has replaced Patterson. Has imprisonment achieved the goal of incapacitation? The answer seems to be yes regarding Patterson, but no regarding the community's crime rate.

However, even Patterson's punishment may cause other problems because incapacitation may provide him with opportunities to learn techniques for committing other offenses. To the extent that prisons might be "schools for crime," offenders may complete their prison sentences with greater knowledge about ways to commit an even wider variety of crimes. Although incapacitation may have temporarily

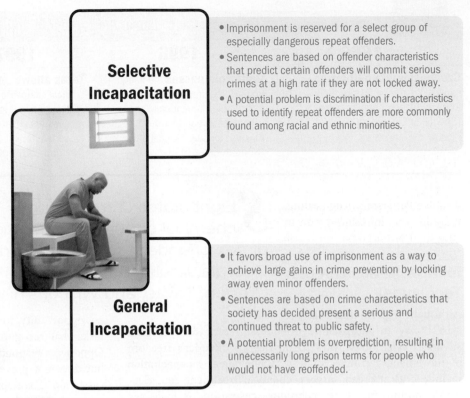

Selective Incapacitation

- Imprisonment is reserved for a select group of especially dangerous repeat offenders.
- Sentences are based on offender characteristics that predict certain offenders will commit serious crimes at a high rate if they are not locked away.
- A potential problem is discrimination if characteristics used to identify repeat offenders are more commonly found among racial and ethnic minorities.

General Incapacitation

- It favors broad use of imprisonment as a way to achieve large gains in crime prevention by locking away even minor offenders.
- Sentences are based on crime characteristics that society has decided present a serious and continued threat to public safety.
- A potential problem is overprediction, resulting in unnecessarily long prison terms for people who would not have reoffended.

FIGURE 2.4 Key Features of Selective and General Incapacitation.
Source: Comstock/Thinkstock

GLOSSARY

selective incapacitation
Imprisonment is reserved for those very few offenders who must truly be locked away for society's protection.

general incapacitation
Imprisonment is acceptable and desirable on an extensive scale for a wide range of offenders as a means of crime prevention.

technological incapacitation
Using technologies such as critical organ surgery, chemical treatment, and electronic monitoring to restrict an offender's freedom of movement.

General incapacitation may avoid the problem of racially and ethnically biased sentencing by imposing prison sentences based on what offenders did rather than who they are.

Use of Surgical and Chemical Castration in the Twentieth and Twenty-First Centuries

1966	1996	1997	1999
Czechoslovakia authorizes surgical castration for sex offenders who volunteer for the procedure (Council of Europe 2009).	**California passes** the nation's first law requiring chemical castration of repeat child sex offenders on parole. Offenders may opt for surgical castration (Norman-Eady 2006).	**Texas allows** voluntary surgical castration of incarcerated sex offenders and Florida requires chemical castration for certain repeat offenders (Norman-Eady 2006).	**Oregon requires** chemical castration for certain sex offenders (Wong 2001).

disabled Patterson's drug dealing, it could have introduced him to auto theft or burglary.

Incapacitation through Technology

Although imprisonment is the classic way to incapacitate offenders, recent technological advances offer other ways to restrict an offender's freedom of movement. Examples of this **technological incapacitation** include critical organ surgery, chemical treatment, and electronic monitoring. One technique, castration of male sex offenders, continues to receive considerable attention and can involve either surgery or chemical treatment. Although females also commit sex offenses, treatment responses for them rely on psychological (Gannon & Cortoni 2010) rather than technological measures. As such, this particular example of technological incapacitation is relevant only to male sex offenders.

Eight states currently allow chemical or surgical castration of sex offenders: California, Florida, Georgia, Louisiana, Montana, Oregon, Texas, and Wisconsin (Norman-Eady 2006). The chemical treatment is mandatory in some states but is a condition for release from custody in all eight. Voluntary surgical castration is an option in California, Florida, and Texas for offenders who must undergo treatment.

Chemical Treatment

- This includes chemical intervention such as antabuse for alcoholics and methadone for heroin addicts in an attempt to force abstinence or to reduce sexual drive or interest (that is, chemical castration).

Critical Organ Surgery

- This includes operating on specific regions of the brain in an attempt to lessen a propensity toward violence (that is psychosurgery) or surgical removal of both testicles in order to reduce sexual drive or interest (that is, surgical castration).

Electronic Monitoring

- Freedom to move about is restricted through the use of monitoring devices that inform authorities of the offender's location and/or movements.

FIGURE 2.5 Common Types of Technological Incapacitation.

> Eight states currently allow chemical or surgical castration of sex offenders: California, Florida, Georgia, Louisiana, Montana, Oregon, Texas, and Wisconsin

Proponents of chemical castration argue that it is a humane and effective treatment for some sex offenders when used in conjunction with counseling therapy. The medication decreases offenders' sexual drive and provides an opportunity for them to engage in cognitive-behavioral tasks that recognize and control unacceptable sexual urges. Opponents respond by noting that the medication decreases—but does not prevent—erections and ejaculation so chemical castration is not appropriate for all sex offenders. In addition, some sex offenders are motivated by anger, hatred, or power rather than by sex. Those people will not be affected by chemical castration because their crimes do not rely on sexual urges or fantasies.

It is difficult to determine whether castration effectively reduces recidivism. Studies of both surgical and chemical castrations have shown lower reoffense rates by offenders undergoing the treatment in comparison with either control groups or with the reported pretreatment behavior of the offenders themselves (Meyer & Cole 1997). However, such studies are few in number and often rely on self-report data. A more rigorous study than most was conducted with offenders in Oregon's chemical castration treatment program. Three groups were studied: men judged to need the chemical treatment and who actually received it; men recommended for the treatment but, for a variety of reasons, did not receive it; and men deemed not to need the treatment. Results of the study found significant differences among the groups, with men actually receiving the treatment committing no new sexual offenses and also committing fewer overall offenses and violations compared with the other two groups (Maletzky, Tolan, & McFarland 2006). Results such as these suggest that at least some versions of technological incapacitation of male sex offenders may hold promise for the future.

some sex offenders are motivated by anger, hatred, or power rather than by sex. Those people will not be affected by chemical castration because their crimes do not rely on sexual urges or fantasies

▶ *Rehabilitation*

Some people do not consider rehabilitation as either a form of or justification for punishment. It just does not seem right to think of efforts to "restore someone to good health" as being a type of punishment. But consider the point raised by Weihofen (1971), who argues that any measure that deprives people of their liberty against their will is essentially punitive in nature, no matter how well intentioned are the authorities who administer the measure. When the choice of where and how you will spend Wednesday afternoons for the next nine months is your probation officer's rather than yours, it makes the sentences no less punitive just because the goal is to help you earn a high school equivalency diploma. The point is, someone else is making the choice for you. So, let's consider how rehabilitation operates as a punishment rationale.

The idea of punishment for purposes of rehabilitation is possibly the newest of the five punishment rationales. This newcomer has a lengthy history, from the Quakers' desire to reclaim the offender's soul to the contemporary version of rehabilitation as way to reintegrate the offender back into society.

The contemporary approach to rehabilitation is likely linked to what Travis (2005, 64) calls the **iron law of imprisonment**: "Except for those few who die in custody, all prisoners come back to live in the free society." The extensive use of imprisonment since the 1980s has resulted in a dramatic increase in the number of prisoners flowing back into the community after their release from prison. In fact, in recent years prisons have released about as many prisoners each year as they have admitted (see Figure 2.6). As the reality of the iron law of imprisonment sinks in, community members seem increasingly concerned about the type of neighbors these former prisoners are going to make. The community is, in other words, interested in having as neighbors people who have been rehabilitated from their previous law-violating ways. However, contemporary rehabilitation seems less treatment-based and more reentry-based—that is to say, whereas traditional rehabilitation followed a medical model that focused on the offender's diagnosis and treatment plan, reentry programs focus on both offender and community to provide programs geared toward reintegration or restoration of the offender into the community.

The need for this emphasis on rehabilitation as reentry becomes apparent upon seeing statistics showing that prisoners today are ill-prepared for life on the outside. The Justice Policy Center at the Urban Institute, which is actively involved in conducting and reporting on prisoner reentry research, notes that the challenges confronting men and women when they enter prison remain—and may even be worse—upon their release. For example, despite the need for employment assistance few prisoners receive employment-related training in prison. Similar problems are found in the lack of adequate mental and physical health care either in prison or after release, and in the limited or temporary living options available to returning prisoners (Urban Institute 2006).

Even as the realization that inmates must be prepared for postincarceration life gathers momentum, there remains the feeling that offenders must also be punished for having committed a crime in the first place. It can be argued that this desire to punish a wrongful act is a basic aspect of society. And that point brings us to the punishment philosophy called retribution.

LEARNING OUTCOMES 4 Summarize rehabilitation's development from a reclamation focus to a reentry emphasis.

GLOSSARY

iron law of imprisonment The realization that almost all prisoners will return to free society.

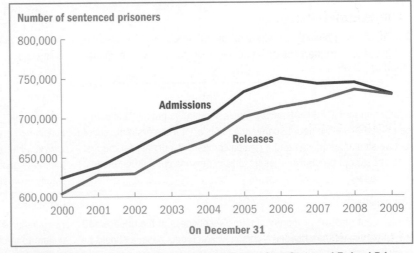

Number of sentenced prisoners

Admissions

Releases

On December 31

FIGURE 2.6 Sentenced Prisoners Admitted and Released from State and Federal Prisons, 2000–2009.

Source: West, H. C., Sabol, W. J., & Greenman, S. J. (2010). Prisoners in 2009(NCJ 231675). Figure 5, page 4. Retrieved from Bureau of Justice Statistics website: http://bjs.ojp.usdoj.gov/index.cfm?ty=pbdetail&iid=2232.

The History of Rehabilitation as a Punishment Philosophy

Late Eighteenth Century	Late Nineteenth Century	Twentieth Century (especially 1960s & 1970s)	Twenty-First Century
Rehabilitation as reclamation aimed to rescue wrongdoers from the evil that had overcome them. Pennsylvania Quakers believed imprisonment would bring the offender back to the correct way of living.	**Rehabilitation as reformation** saw offenders as responsible for changing themselves. Society should provide opportunities from among which offenders must select those most helpful to them.	**Rehabilitation as individualized treatment** viewed criminal behavior as similar to a treatable illness. Following a medical model, the offender was examined, diagnosed, and then treated.	**Rehabilitation as reentry** is a contemporary view that focuses less on offender treatment and more on how the offender can be reintegrated into the community.

▶ *Retribution*

Retribution is sometimes mistakenly assumed to be the same as revenge. The two concepts, though related, actually differ in several key ways. Because of those differences retribution is considered a legitimate penal philosophy, but revenge is not.

In addition to distinguishing retribution and revenge, we can also set retribution apart from the other punishment philosophies by noting retribution's lack of interest in preventing crime. Deterrence, incapacitation, and rehabilitation all have a utilitarian aspect—that is, each hopes that punishment will achieve some goal, have some utility. Retributivists, however, do not care if criminals or others are deterred, if society is safer while a criminal is locked up, or whether offenders are rehabilitated. Their concern is simply that society carries out its moral obligation to punish people who commit a crime. To be fair, it should be noted that retributivists certainly do not mind if punishment results in crime prevention. However, any prevention that occurs as a result of imposing punishment on an offender is simply a secondary result that is welcome but was neither sought nor intended.

Probably the most difficult problem presented by a retributive philosophy of punishment is determining exactly what the just punishment is for a particular offense. Ellis and Ellis (1989) note that both the crime and the penalty must somehow be measured—crime for its seriousness and penalty for its desert. Of course, deterrence theorists had a similar problem because that philosophy also required a correspondence between crime and penalty—that is,

> *Retribution is sometimes mistakenly assumed to be the same as revenge.*

TABLE 2.1 | What Retribution Is and Isn't.

In its more crude form, retribution was the revenge exhibited in feuds between individuals and families. Today, retribution—but not revenge—is considered a legitimate punishment philosophy because it includes three key elements: formal penal sanction, equity, and just deserts.

Elements of Retribution	How It Differs from Revenge
Formal penal sanction	Informal sanction
Retribution is applied in the name of the public when a law has been violated. For example, a judge sentences Lynn to prison for committing theft.	Revenge is applied individually in retaliation for a perceived wrong. For example, Laura spreads rumors about Lynn as payback for Lynn snubbing Laura.
Equity	Irregular
Retribution maintains that similar crimes and similar criminals should be treated alike. Two people committing burglary for the first time should receive similar sentences and a person committing burglary for the first time should not be punished as harshly as persons committing their third burglary.	When revenge is sought, there can be considerable variation in what is considered appropriate retaliation for similar wrongs. Even the mistreated individual may retaliate differently to separate wrongdoers. Both Scott and Mary push Tammy into the mud, but Tammy pushes Scott back and simply frowns at Mary.
Just deserts	Unbalanced
Punishment must be proportional to the seriousness of the offense and the culpability of the offender. A person who commits assault should be punished more severely than one who damages property, and a person who purposefully struck another in the head with a beer bottle should receive a harsher penalty than one who recklessly ran toward a door and unintentionally hit another in the face with a book.	The person seeking revenge often favors a punishment that is disproportionate to the harmful act. Steal my neighbor's car and I think you should be placed on probation; steal my car and I want you to be put in jail for three years.

for deterrence to occur, the penalty had to be fixed at a level just harsh enough to convince the offender, or potential offender, that the pain would outweigh the pleasure. There is a difference, however, between the deterrence and retribution view of how a crime and its appropriate penalty are linked. Where deterrence requires correspondence in order to accomplish a goal of crime prevention or reduction, retribution requires correspondence in the sense that an offender justly deserves a certain severity of punishment (Ellis & Ellis 1989). So, we are back to the problem of deciding which penalty a crime deserves or merits.

Retribution:
Punishment is applied because it is the right thing to do, not because it will achieve some end.

The Purpose of Punishment

Deterrence:
Punishment either keeps criminals from reoffending or prevents others from committing a crime in the first place.

Incapacitation:
Punishment protects society by restricting the offender's access to people and their property.

Rehabilitation:
Punishment can change people from criminals to law-abiding citizens.

FIGURE 2.7 **Retribution as Non-Utilitarian.** Retribution is unique among the punishment philosophies in its non-utilitarian nature. The other philosophies view punishment as having some purpose or achieving some goal. For retributionists, punishment is simply the necessary response to crime. Criminals are punished because they deserve to be.

Determining when a penalty has provided criminals with their just deserts is no small task. We could ask the public to rate the unpleasantness of a given penalty or to rank penalties according to their level of severity. Neither of these techniques accounts for the individual differences that certainly arise when one person's penalty is another person's mere inconvenience. But more importantly, these approaches seem better suited to deterrence purposes when trying to find a penalty to prevent or reduce crime. What is really needed is a way to determine what kind (type, level, etc.) of penalty a particular criminal act deserves.

LEARNING OUTCOMES 5 Explain the keys ways in which retribution differs from revenge.

GLOSSARY

lex talionis The law of retaliation.

So far, the closest retributivists have come to matching the penalty to the crime is the principle of **lex talionis**, or the law of retaliation. The classic example of this principle is stated in the Bible: "And if any mischief follow, then thou shalt give life for life, eye for eye, tooth for tooth, hand for hand, foot for foot, burning for burning, wound for wound, stripe for stripe" (Exodus 21:23–25). A similar principle is stated in the Koran: "And [as for] the man who steals and the woman who steals, cut off their hands as a punishment for what they have earned" (5:38).

This goal of having a punishment equivalent to the crime is infrequently found in U.S. jurisdictions today. The death penalty for homicide is the best example, but more often retribution seeks proportional rather than equivalent punishment.

Nigel Walker (1991) has succinctly described, in the form of two ladder-like scales whose rungs correspond, how retributivists conceive of proportionality (see Figure 2.8). On the penalty ladder, each rung indicates different levels of severity increasing in order from the lowest rungs to the higher ones. Unfortunately, we cannot assume that the distance between each rung indicates any standard progression. In this manner, the third rung might indicate a fine, the fourth could mean a probation sentence, and the fifth could require nine months in jail. But is the progression of severity between the third and fourth rungs, or even between the fourth and fifth, of similar degree? Possibly more important, is a jail sentence always more severe than a fine or probation? Maybe an offender would actually choose confinement in order to avoid financial hardship. In other words, the ladder's rungs are not only loose, but they may also be interchangeable.

The other ladder is a harm ladder, in which the rungs are well-defined harms. But this ladder remains poorly defined by retributivists. Instead, the second structure more often is a crime-seriousness ladder. Its rungs consist of offenses distinguished by their legal definitions: murder, robbery, theft, and so on. Again, the rungs may imply a rank order of seriousness (though, as on the penalty ladder, individuals may differ in their assessment of seriousness), but the distance between rungs cannot be taken to show similar degrees.

To achieve proportionality according to the retributivist, the two ladders are fitted together so that a rod of proportionality

Think About It...

In some jurisdictions following Islamic criminal law, the concept of equivalent punishment is practiced for the crime of theft by amputating the thief's right hand. If America adopted a similar punishment for theft, do you think we would see a decrease in theft? Is the amputation of a thief's hand a good example of retributive justice or does it violate the concept of proportionality?

Source: TORSTEN BLACKWOOD/ AFP/Getty Images

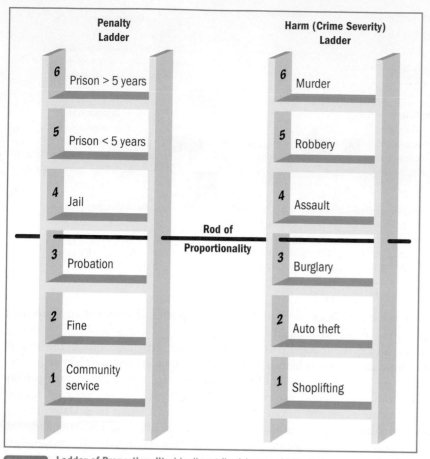

Penalty Ladder

6 — Prison > 5 years
5 — Prison < 5 years
4 — Jail
3 — Probation
2 — Fine
1 — Community service

Harm (Crime Severity) Ladder

6 — Murder
5 — Robbery
4 — Assault
3 — Burglary
2 — Auto theft
1 — Shoplifting

Rod of Proportionality

FIGURE 2.8 **Ladder of Proportionality.** Ideally, retributivists would like to have proportionality between the punishment and the crime. This might be possible if one could truly determine equivalence between a particular penalty (typified by a rung on the penalty ladder) and a particular crime (a rung on the harm ladder). But, unlike the nicely balanced rod of proportionality shown here, the rungs on each ladder are not so easily aligned.

could be balanced on corresponding rungs of the two ladders. In this way, the punishment (penalty rung) will match the offense (harm rung). But because of problems such as inconsistent intervals among rungs within and between the ladders, the best a retributivist can claim is that the ladders provide consistency among judges using the ladders—that is, when several judges use the coupled ladders to determine sentences, the penalties will be similar as the harm rung and penalty rung match up. But consistency is not the same as proportionality, and Walker suggests the retributivists have been unable thus far to provide a way to measure both crimes and penalties in order to ensure offenders get their just deserts.

Another aspect of retributive philosophy deserves mention. It is possible to view the norm of reciprocity as trying to restore equilibrium. Just as the balance is unequal when your friend has invited you to dinner but you have not yet returned the favor, so is it unequal when a criminal has caused the victim harm to his or her person or property and the criminal has not been held accountable. Punishment, in its reciprocal role, can help restore the balance that the criminal has upset. When punishment is considered in this light, a new aspect of the sanction and a new rationale under which it can be discussed emerge as the fifth, and last, punishment philosophy: restoration.

▶ *Restoration*

The focus of punishment philosophies thus far has been on either the offender (rehabilitation) or the crime (deterrence, incapacitation, and retribution). Increasingly in U.S. jurisdictions, calls are made for a penal philosophy that considers the harm done to the victim when deciding an appropriate punishment for the offender. Restoration is a punishment rationale that attempts to make the victim and the community "whole again" by restoring things, as much as possible, to how they were before the crime occurred. This return to equilibrium provides a link between retribution and restoration because each philosophy is based on the **norm of reciprocity** wherein punishment is a natural response, or reciprocation, to a wrongful act (Newman 1985). In addition, restoration incorporates reentry (rehabilitation) as a key ingredient for achieving equilibrium.

There is increasing indication that a penal philosophy of restoration will take a prominent role in the twenty-first century. The label attached to this philosophy is **restorative justice** or community justice, and its initial proponents include people such as Howard Zehr (1985), Mark Umbreit (1989), and Martin Wright (1991). Although the terms *restorative justice* and *community justice* are used interchangeably in many U.S. communities, this book prefers *restorative justice* since the philosophy is applied in both community and incarceration settings.

Restorative justice principles are used today for sentencing, during community supervision of the offender, and even in prison. At the sentencing stage, mediation sessions involving both offender and victim take the place of traditional sentencing by a judge. These **victim-offender mediation** programs are most often used with misdemeanor offenses or felony property offenses—especially when the offender is a juvenile or first-time adult offender (Umbreit, Vos, Coates, & Brown 2003). A unique example of this type of restorative justice is the sentencing circle based on the customs of Native American and Canadian tribal peacemaking. Forming the circle are the offender, victim, family, friends, and coworkers of both the offender and the victim; social service personnel; juvenile justice personnel; and interested community members. The judge, prosecutor, and defense attorney may even be present. The group discusses the event and eventually comes to an agreement regarding the best resolution. The "sentence" is either accepted within the group or recommended to the judge at the next court appearance (Kurki 1999).

Restorative justice programs are used in the community in both postconviction (for example, community reparation) and prisoner reentry (for example, citizens circles) formats. An example of the postconviction type is Vermont's state-wide **reparative probation program** (one form of probation in

Vermont), which combines a suspended probation sentence by the court with elements of community reparation boards. Those boards, numbering 76 across the state, draw on citizen volunteers and corrections employees to place less serious offenders in a situation where they come to understand the consequences of their actions and move toward restoring the community. As long as the probationer completes the reparation board's contract terms and conditions and stays out of trouble for a specified time, the probationer's sentence will be expunged. If an offender does not complete the reparation board conditions, he or she is referred back to court for an executed sentence of probation that remains permanently on his or her criminal record (Humphrey, Burford, & Huey 2007; Vermont Department of Corrections 2010).

Prisoner reentry under restorative justice is the process by which incarcerated prisoners get reacquainted with living a regular life in the larger society. Reentry is not an easy process, so restorative justice methods can be used to help ease that transition. In Ohio, **citizen circles** developed with the goal of community collaboration with offenders during their supervision. Parole officers lead the circles, which are comprised of the offender, the offender's family, ex-convicts, employers, victims, the police, and faith-based staff. The thinking behind this is that ex-convicts are less likely to return to crime if they feel accepted by their community rather than shunned. Like all other restorative justice programs, the offender must voluntarily participate and be willing to set goals that focus on productive legitimate behavior. The community board assists the offender in employment opportunities and positive social support. In turn, the offender comes

There is increasing indication that a penal philosophy of restoration will take a prominent role in the twenty-first century.

to understand that being a positive community member demands responsibility and obligation (Rhine, Matthews, Sampson, & Daley 2003; State of Ohio 2007).

Many predatory criminals who commit violent crimes are able to victimize other people because they reduce them to objects or in some way justify that the crime has little impact on the victim (for example, the victim is insured, the victim deserved it, etc.). A common complaint of traditional methods of punishment for violent crimes is that offenders rarely understand how their actions affected the victims' lives and their loved ones. Restorative practices in prison attempt to remedy these concerns by encouraging or requiring that prisoners attend victim impact classes while incarcerated. The session leaders are violent crime survivors and have agreed to come forward in an educator role to share their experiences with groups of offenders in hopes that their story will make a difference in offenders' lives. Although the victims may not be necessarily matched with their actual offender, the participants represent all crime survivors and their families.

More than 70 percent of U.S. jurisdictions have victim impact classes in place and the effects of these programs are quite promising. Participation in Connecticut Department of Corrections victim impact classes showed significant improvement in offenders' understanding of victimization facts, knowledge of victims' rights, and sensitivity to the plight of victims when compared with a matched control group that did not attend the classes. A separate study in Iowa and another that involved four states (California, Ohio, Tennessee, Virginia) had similar results leading researchers to believe the classes are reinforcing the message that being victimized is a traumatic experience (Office for Victims of Crime 2010).

> **LEARNING OUTCOMES 6** Describe how restorative justice principles are used in sentencing, during community supervision, and in prison.
>
> **GLOSSARY**
>
> **norm of reciprocity** The view of punishment as a natural response, or reciprocation, to a wrongful act.
>
> **restorative justice** The process, also called community justice, wherein victim, offender, and community representatives determine a fair or just way to restore the balance that the crime had upset.

Restorative Practices in Sentencing

- **Victim-offender mediation**
  - This is a process wherein the victim, offender, and community representative work out their version of what would be a fair or just way to restore the balance that the crime upset. The emphasis is less on the sanction (for example, apology, financial compensation, community service) than on getting the offender to take responsibility, express remorse, and repair the damage.

Restorative Practices in the Community

- **Community reparation boards**
  - This is a postconviction use of restorative justice wherein board members meet with the offender and victim to determine how the offender will repair the harm done and to identify strategies for reducing future offending. These trained board members also monitor and supervise the offender's progress.

- **Citizen circles**
  - During parole, a group comprised of the offender, the offender's family, ex-convicts, employers, victims, the police, and faith-based staff, joins to assist in the reentry process by providing employment opportunities and positive social support.

Restorative Practices in Prison

- **Victim impact classes**
  - These are sessions attended by prisoners while incarcerated where violent crime survivors share their experiences with the hope of effecting positive change in the offender.

FIGURE 2.9 Examples of Restorative Justice Practices.

Research Supporting Restorative Justice Programs

Communities in Vermont have collaborated with the Vermont Department of Corrections to provide restorative justice in the form of reparative probation boards. The program seems to be proving that low-level offenders are less likely to reoffend when they have been required to make direct amends to the community and to their victims for their harmful acts. Humphrey, Burford, and Huey (2007, 2) report that offenders who are placed on reparative versus standard probation are significantly less likely to commit a new offense while either on probation or during the five year period following the imposition of the original probation sentence.

victim-offender mediation An application of restorative justice principles at the sentencing stage by having mediation sessions involving both offender and victim take the place of traditional sentencing by a judge.

reparative probation program A Vermont restorative justice program at the postconviction stage that combines a suspended probation sentence with elements of community reparation boards.

citizen circles An Ohio restorative justice program at the prisoner reentry stage that encourages community collaboration with offenders during their supervision in the community.

victim impact classes Restorative justice program, typically offered in prison, wherein prisoners hear violent crime survivors share their experiences with the hope of effecting positive change in the offender.

Criticism of Restorative Justice

It is appropriate to briefly note here some of the criticisms directed at the restoration philosophy. For example, retributivists often see it as too lenient, proponents of deterrence do not think it can deter (either specifically or generally), and those favoring incapacitation fail to see how society is protected from continued harm. Some people are concerned that restorative justice will unnecessarily increase the number of people brought under the net of social control. That situation—referred to as net widening—expresses a concern that programs designed as alternatives to the traditional process actually end up bringing more people into the system.

Another criticism of restorative justice is that it can promote discrimination. Some critics of the restorative process warn that it may perpetuate existing social inequities when one party has greater economic, intellectual, political, or physical power than the other. Proponents respond that the restorative process relies on all participants negotiating in good faith and not using mediation to legitimize an unfair solution. Critics feel relying on good faith and achieving fairness are not always compatible.

People in a weaker or subordinate position (such as students to school officials or employees to employers) may be under pressure to accept too little in the hope of obtaining an agreement and being left alone. Or weaker parties (such as persons with fewer financial resources) may argue for what they think they can get rather than what they think is fair. In other words, weaker parties, whether victim or offender, may accept agreements that give them much less than they could have obtained if the power imbalance did not exist. Even mediators could influence the outcome if they are of a higher social standing than one or both participants. As Merry puts it, "Mediation can end up a new forum in which the predominantly middle-class helping professionals are invited to supervise and control the private lives of the working class" (1989, 239).

These are valid concerns, and restorative justice proponents note that the programs and procedures must be continually evaluated to make sure they are operating in as nondiscriminatory a fashion as possible. Some authors have also noted that restorative justice is certainly no more likely to discriminate than is the traditional formal justice process. In fact, it may even have the potential to be more responsive to cultural diversity. Maxwell and Morris (1996), for example, suggest that restorative justice processes may challenge misconceptions in cases involving racial strife and could even increase understanding among different subcultures—goals the traditional justice system does not even attempt.

As Bright (1997) reminds us, social injustices in society are bound to influence any system of justice, including restorative justice. However, because restorative justice involves the community members in an attempt to resolve the problem, the possibility for engagement and interaction may provide opportunities to address even broader issues such as inequalities, discrimination, and prejudice.

Despite those valid concerns, restorative justice has its proponents and has been shown to have positive outcomes. Also, its ability to incorporate aspects of retribution and rehabilitation suggest to some that the restorative philosophy may foretell the twenty-first century's response to the question "Why do we punish?"

Think About It...

A criticism of restorative justice is that it may not work when one person is in a subordinate position. For example, weaker victims may be under pressure to accept too little in the hope of quickly obtaining an agreement and being left alone—or, may argue for what they think they can get rather than what they think if fair. Is this a legitimate criticism of restorative justice? What procedures could be used to lessen the likelihood that weaker parties may accept agreements that give them less than they could have obtained if the power imbalance did not exist?

Source: Photodisc/ Valueline/Thinkstock

Did Charles Manson Text You?

In 2010, notorious California prisoner Charles Manson was caught with a flip phone under his prison mattress. Officials said Manson made calls and sent text messages to people across the country for reasons still unknown. Earlier the same year, two escapees from a minimum-security work detail at California's Folsom prison used a contraband cell phone to arrange for a friend to pick them up.

Cell phones have troubled prison officials for several years, but smartphones present even more serious problems. With Internet access, prisoners can—at a minimum—continue to direct the criminal activity of others from inside prison or even directly participate in criminal behavior while locked up. At the end of 2010, Georgia prisoners used e-mail lists and smartphones to coordinate simultaneous protests and work-stoppages among inmates at several Georgia prisons. Then, using pseudonyms, they shared hour-by-hour updates with followers on Facebook and Twitter while holding news media interviews and monitoring the coverage of their protest (Dolan 2010; Severson & Brown 2011).

1. Criminals are put in prison in order to restrict their ability to harm citizens and their property. This incapacitation, or restricting freedom of movement, is an important goal when punishing offenders. But what if a prisoner is able to continue interacting in the community even from a prison cell? *Is incapacitation still a reasonable punishment goal when prisoners can continue to interact with people outside the prison walls?*

2. Even when meeting the goal of incapacitation, it is possible to seek the goal of rehabilitation. Prisoner-rights advocates argue that cell phones let prisoners stay in touch with family and friends while they are in prison. Such contact is crucial, advocates argue, to successful reintegration after the prisoner's release. For example, when he's not counting down on his Facebook page the remaining days of his three-year prison sentence, a Georgia prisoner uses his smartphone to play FarmVille and Street Wars. *Rather than being seen as a problem, could cell phones be a way to promote rehabilitation and reintegration by allowing prisoners to maintain normal social interaction with nonprisoners?*

3. Prison officials across the county report increasing numbers of contraband cell phones. Administrators have asked for the authority to jam cell phone signals on prison grounds, but so far the Federal Communications Commission has refused—jamming is not precise, so legitimate cell phone users near prisons may be denied service. *How can we balance the desire to remove offenders from society without inconveniencing law-abiding citizens?*

Source: ASSOCIATED PRESS

LEARNING OUTCOMES 1

Name and describe the five primary punishment philosophies.

The five punishment philosophies—or reasons for punishment—are deterrence (both specific and general), incapacitation (both selective and general), rehabilitation, retribution, and restoration.

1. Which punishment philosophy is being used when a judge sentences a thief to three years in prison as a way to discourage other people from stealing?

2. Which punishment philosophies are reflected in the court rules for California?

3. Which punishment philosophy does Vermont emphasize that is not so clearly found in Alabama, California, Colorado, or Texas?

deterrence Discouraging future criminal acts by both the offender and others in the population.

incapacitation Restricting an offender's freedom of movement through isolation from the general population.

rehabilitation Providing the offender with skills, attitudes, and norms that enable him or her to be law-abiding.

retribution Just and adequate punishment.

restoration Restoring the victim, community, and offender through accountability, respect for the law and the legal process, and attention to victim needs.

LEARNING OUTCOMES 2

List and summarize the three key elements for effective deterrence.

In order for a punishment to deter an offender or others from committing a crime, the punishment must be certain, severe, and swiftly applied.

1. How does specific deterrence differ from general deterrence?

2. Why would certainty of punishment require constant monitoring of people?

3. If one person views probation as a minor nuisance and another person sees it as a major inconvenience how can severity be achieved in sentencing?

4. Is it possible for punishment to be swift and still protect the rights of suspects and defendants?

5. Publicity is considered an important, but not a key, element for successful deterrence. Should it be given greater weight and actually be a fourth key element? Why?

specific deterrence Seeks to prevent crime by using punishment to discourage that person from committing additional crimes.

general deterrence Seeks to prevent crime by using punishment to discourage people from committing a crime in the first place.

LEARNING OUTCOMES 3

Compare and contrast selective and general incapacitation.

Selective incapacitation relies on characteristics of the criminal to identify which offenders need to be in prison, whereas general incapacitation emphasizes crime characteristics when sentencing to prison.

1. What is the common premise upon which both selective and general incapacitation is based?

2. Name five personal characteristics you believe many or most criminals have in common. If these characteristics were used to identify people who should be sentenced to prison could sentencing end up being unfair to a particular segment of society?

3. Would justice be served by using technological incapacitation to temporarily disable (for example, make blind or deaf, or confine to a wheelchair) a person as punishment for a crime?

selective incapacitation Imprisonment is reserved for those very few offenders who must truly be locked away for society's protection.

general incapacitation Imprisonment is acceptable and desirable on an extensive scale for a wide range of offenders as a means of crime prevention.

technological incapacitation Using technologies such as critical organ surgery, chemical treatment, and electronic monitoring to restrict an offender's freedom of movement.

LEARNING OUTCOMES 4

Summarize rehabilitation's development from a reclamation focus to a reentry emphasis.

The concept of rehabilitation began with an eighteenth century belief that criminals had to be rescued from evil ways, then progressed through nineteenth century views of offenders as responsible for reforming themselves and twentieth century ideas that criminals were ill and needed individualized treatment. Today's view is that rehabilitation should focus on how the offender can be reintegrated in the community.

1. How did the belief in reclamation differ from the idea of reformation?

2. How could one argue that the twentieth-century view of rehabilitation followed a medical model?

3. What is the "iron law of imprisonment" and is it likely to always be true?

4. Is it possible to achieve the goal of rehabilitation while implementing the goal of incapacitation?

iron law of imprisonment The realization that almost all prisoners will return to free society.

LEARNING OUTCOMES 5

Explain the keys ways in which retribution differs from revenge.

Although closely related, retribution is distinguished from its better known cousin by noting that retribution, but not revenge, is a legitimate punishment philosophy requiring formal penal sanction, equity, and just deserts.

1. Should revenge, rather than retribution, be a punishment philosophy? Why or why not?

2. Design your own ladder of proportionality and describe how you matched the rungs on the harm ladder with the proportional rung on the penalty ladder.

3. Some people argue that retributionists must favor the death penalty for homicide. Others suggest that as long as society's most severe penalty is applied to its most serious crime, retribution is achieved. That could mean that a retributionist favors life imprisonment rather than death as a proportional punishment if society chose life imprisonment as its most severe penalty. Do you agree with this assessment of retribution?

lex talionis The law of retaliation.

LEARNING OUTCOMES 6

Describe how restorative justice principles are used in sentencing, during community supervision, and in prison.

Restorative justice can be found at every stage in the justice process since it can be used to determine the appropriate penalty (as is done in mediation sessions), while an offender is at liberty in the community (reparative probation programs are an example), or even when the offender is in prison (as is shown with victim impact classes).

1. Explain the norm of reciprocity.

2. Why is restorative justice said to place more emphasis on the victim than other punishment philosophies?

3. Why is victim-offender mediation considered a good way to achieve restorative justice?

4. In what way can the use of restorative justice principles help make the community whole again after a crime has occurred?

5. What is net widening and do you think it is a legitimate concern?

6. Describe how restorative justice could be used even in situations where one of the involved parties is in a subordinate position to the other.

norm of reciprocity The view of punishment as a natural response, or reciprocation, to a wrongful act.

restorative justice The process, also called community justice, wherein victim, offender, and community representatives determine a fair or just way to restore the balance that the crime had upset.

victim-offender mediation An application of restorative justice principles at the sentencing stage by having mediation sessions involving both offender and victim take the place of traditional sentencing by a judge.

reparative probation program A Vermont restorative justice program at the postconviction stage that combines a suspended probation sentence with elements of community reparation boards.

citizen circles An Ohio restorative justice program at the prisoner reentry stage that encourages community collaboration with offenders during their supervision in the community.

victim impact classes Restorative justice program, typically offered in prison, wherein prisoners hear violent crime survivors share their experiences with the hope of effecting positive change in the offender.

MyCJLab

Go to the Chapter 2 section in *MyCJLab* to test your understanding of this chapter, access customized study content, engage in interactive simulations, complete critical thinking and research assignments, and view related online videos.

Additional Links

Go to **http://topics.law.cornell.edu/wex/table_criminal_code** and click on the link for your state. Try to find a section that explains the punishment philosophies that should be guiding sentencing.

Psychology students at California State University Northridge have identified helpful sources that support **www.csun.edu/~psy453/crimes_y.htm** and oppose **www.csun.edu/~psy453/crimes_n.htm** chemical castration for male sex offenders.

Visit **www.urban.org/reentry_mapping/index.cfm** where the Urban Institute provides interesting information about reentry mapping, which helps in understanding the spatial dynamics of incarceration and prisoner reentry.

The Victim Offender Mediation Association (VOMA) has a lot of information about restorative justice in general—and mediation more specifically—on its website at **www.voma.org**.

Correctional Practices from Ancient to Contemporary Times

1 Describe key features of the Code of Hammurabi, Mosaic Law, Roman Law, and law during the Middle Ages.

2 Identify the two important themes in the development of imprisonment as punishment and explain the link between hospice facilities and houses of corrections to those themes.

3 Compare and contrast the Pennsylvania and Auburn prison systems in terms of their architecture, orienting strategies, and advantages/disadvantages.

4 Describe how men's and women's prisons differed during the reformatory movement of the nineteenth century.

5 Explain how penal systems in the South and West differed from those in the East and summarize reasons for those differences.

6 Summarize the development of prison programs and the treatment of women and other minorities during the early, middle, and late twentieth century.

7 Explain how public opinion about crime and punishment in the twenty-first century seems to be influencing the use of imprisonment and prison alternatives.

3

SENTENCE FOR SHOPLIFTING? A TRIP TO THE COLONIES!

On January 16, 1760, Joseph Tedar, 32 years old, was tried at London's Old Bailey. He was charged with stealing one pair of silver shoe buckles worth 10 shillings from Robert Parr's shop. The shop clerk explained to the court that Tedar asked to be shown some silver buckles: "I shew'd him some, and he chose out a pair. . . He stood at the door some time to look at them, then put them into his pocket, and went away with them. . . I went out from behind the counter and cry'd stop thief." Tedar was caught and found guilty of shoplifting and sentenced to be transported (Old Bailey Proceedings Online).

Most likely, Tedar would have ended up in Virginia Colony or Maryland Colony. At either location he would have been sold as a convict servant to private individuals soon after he landed. Buyers were typically plantation

DISCUSS Is there a place in today's society for such punishments as transportation and banishment?

owners looking for persons with skill sets that would prove useful on the plantation. Since most convicts had no identifiable skills, they were generally forced to work as common field hands alongside slaves or laboring in the iron mines. Since Tedar announced in court that he had been a sailor, he may have been more fortunate and ended up on a boat (Vaver 2009).

The American colonists did not have transportation available to them as a way to handle criminal offenders. They did, however, make use of the other common British sentences: corporal and capital punishment. But this chapter is mostly concerned with punishments such as long-term imprisonment that were developed in nineteenth century America and how those developments influenced what has come since.

Concepts of crime and punishment have evolved over the centuries from the ancient blood feuds sparked by harm done to a person or property to today's complex legal systems that distinguish among categories of crime and varieties of punishment. A key point in this developmental process occurred when responsibility for punishing antisocial behavior moved from being an obligation of the harmed person or family to being the responsibility of the entire community. As Roth (2011) explains, the mode of revenge was taken from a victim and placed in the collective hands of the community. This process is typically established with a written code describing desirable behavior and specifying punishment for those not complying. Key features of law in ancient Babylonia, Hebrew law, Roman law, and law during the medieval period provided the basis for society's response to criminal offenders in modern times.

▶ Corrections in the Ancient and Medieval World

The **Code of Hammurabi**, for example, provided the basis for criminal and civil law, and defined procedures for commerce and trade. It also introduced the concept of *lex talionis*, which is commonly known as "eye for an eye" justice. The Hebrew legal system (**Mosaic Law**) started when God gave Moses two stone tablets containing the Ten Commandments. Those religious and moral imperatives are recorded in the book of Exodus, which—along with Genesis, Leviticus, Numbers, and Deuteronomy—make up the first five books of the Bible. Those books, known as the Torah to Jewish people, provided the base for the Hebrew legal system. Mosaic Law continued the principle of *lex talionis* with such proclamations as "life for life, eye for eye, tooth for tooth" (Exodus 21:23–24), but expanded it to include the concept of proportionality (recall Chapter 2's discussion

of proportionality as a key aspect of retribution). Rather than literally requiring an eye for an eye, scholars of Jewish law understand the proclamation as setting forth a commandment that punishment should be no more severe than the crime. In that manner, "an eye for eye, or a tooth for a tooth" is seen as limiting what kind of response the injured party could give (Roth 2011).

The earliest form of written Roman law dates to about 450 BCE, when a council of ten men inscribed the rights of Roman citizens on twelve bronze tablets. The **Twelve Tables**, which provided the basis for private rights of Roman citizens, consisted mainly of ancient custom and concerned procedure more than substantive law. Nevertheless, it added to the legal base and punishment

Rather than literally requiring an eye for an eye, scholars of Jewish law understand the proclamation as setting forth a commandment that punishment should be no more severe than the crime.

LEARNING OUTCOMES 1 Describe key features of the Code of Hammurabi, Mosaic Law, Roman Law, and law during the Middle Ages.

GLOSSARY

Code of Hammurabi The first known body of law, established by King Hammurabi about 4,000 years ago, lays out the basis of criminal law.

Mosaic Law The Hebrew legal system, which started when God gave Moses two stone tablets containing the Ten Commandments.

Twelve Tables The earliest form of written Roman law, which provided the basis for private rights of Roman citizens.

1800–1600 BCE	1200 BCE–100 CE	500 BCE–550 CE	400–1400 CE
Legal Systems in Babylonia King Hammurabi (reign circa 1792-1750 BCE) provides one of the first known bodies of law. The Code of Hammurabi introduces the concept of *lex talionis* (the law of retaliation).	**Mosaic Law** Moses receives from God two stone tablets containing the Ten Commandments and these along with the entire Torah provide a base for the Hebrew legal system. Mosaic Law continues the principle of *lex talionis*, but expands it to include the concept of proportionality.	**Roman Law** The Twelve Tables (451–450 BCE) provide the basis for private rights of Roman citizens. Prescribed punishments include the death penalty, early forms of imprisonment, and some compensation penalties.	**Law in the Medieval Period** Increased attempts to move conflict resolution out of the hands of individuals and into the courts. This is reflected in the increased importance of the British justices of the peace, who are authorized to hear misdemeanor cases and the occasional felony.

types for what eventually became sophisticated legal systems and a greater variety of punishments. Developments continued into the Middle Ages as societies struggled to establish just systems for responding to law violators and experimented with other punishment types.

The Middle Ages, the medieval period from the fifth century to the early fifteenth century, saw changes to crime and punishment throughout Europe. Developments in England were especially important to the correctional systems in the United States because colonial America was heavily influenced by British custom and practice. Upon his arrival in England, William the Conqueror (reigning from 1066 to 1087) established a system of royal courts with primary interest in settling disputes of landholders. By the mid-1300s, the justice of the peace was becoming the cornerstone of British law and played a major role in maintaining law and order. Punishments during this period moved away from capital punishment and toward mutilation, although convicted offenders often still died from such punishments as having their eyes put out or their testicles cut off (Roth 2011). By the end of the Middle Ages, punishment became less cruel and there was a movement toward exhibitory punishments, such as stocks and pillories and other shame punishments.

▶ Corrections in Seventeenth and Eighteenth Century England

Many histories of American correctional practices begin with happenings in seventeenth-century Europe because that is when we start seeing punishment types that are more familiar to us today. Early attempts to protect society by removing offenders from the community (**transportation**, for example) and confinement while awaiting punishment (such as jails) served as forerunners to what would become long-term imprisonment.

There are examples of imprisonment being used as punishment in ancient times, but secure confinement was more typically used to prepare offenders for the torture that would soon extract a confession, to await their execution or banishment, or even to coerce payment of debts. The idea of using long-term imprisonment in a secure facility as a punishment for convicted felons did not fully occur until the nineteenth century. But the pre-nineteenth-century institutions serving as forerunners to

The idea of using long-term imprisonment in a secure facility as a punishment for convicted felons did not fully occur until the nineteenth century.

the modern penitentiary provided important philosophies and practices that continue to have an impact today. Notable examples of those forerunners include **hospice facilities** and **houses of correction**. Together these institutions gave rise to two important themes in the development of imprisonment as punishment. One was the idea that convicts should be isolated and a second theme was that prisoners should be required to work. These themes had parallel development during the sixteenth and seventeenth centuries and can be traced through the hospice facilities (representing the isolation theme) and the houses of correction (representing the work theme).

With the procedures developed at the hospice facilities and the houses of correction providing the ideas of separating prisoners and putting them to work, the concept of punishment through imprisonment was ready to move to the next stage. In England this

LEARNING OUTCOMES 2 Identify the two important themes in the development of imprisonment as punishment and explain the link between hospice facilities and houses of corrections to those themes.

GLOSSARY

transportation The removal of criminals to a remote location where they could be used as laborers.

hospice facilities Late-sixteenth and early-seventeenth century institutions that promoted the idea of isolating offenders from each other.

houses of correction Sixteenth-century institutions for offenders that emphasized the importance of hard work at disagreeable tasks.

prison hulks Eighteenth-century British merchant and naval ships converted into floating prisons.

1779 Penitentiary Act Passed by the English Parliament, this act relied on John Howard's ideas to make significant reforms to the prison system.

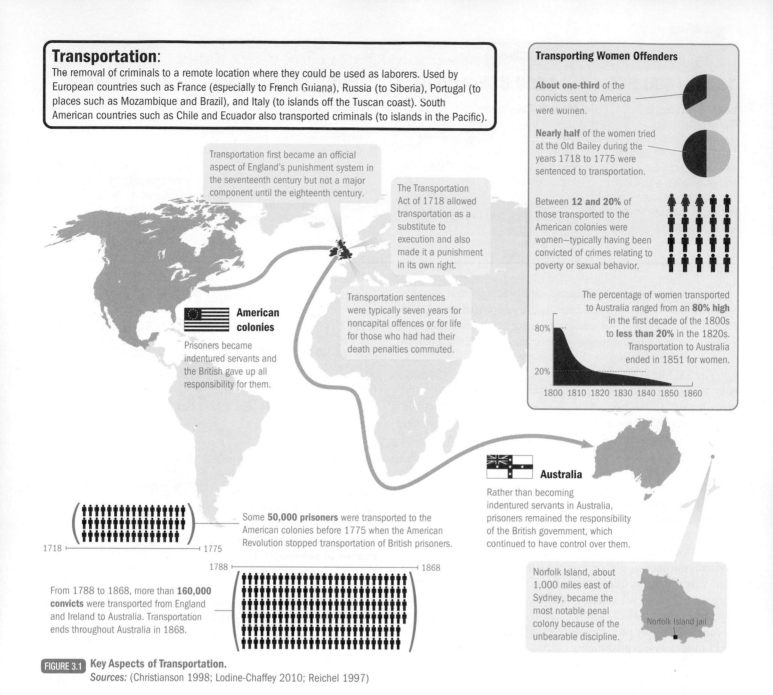

Transportation:

The removal of criminals to a remote location where they could be used as laborers. Used by European countries such as France (especially to French Guiana), Russia (to Siberia), Portugal (to places such as Mozambique and Brazil), and Italy (to islands off the Tuscan coast). South American countries such as Chile and Ecuador also transported criminals (to islands in the Pacific).

Transportation first became an official aspect of England's punishment system in the seventeenth century but not a major component until the eighteenth century.

The Transportation Act of 1718 allowed transportation as a substitute to execution and also made it a punishment in its own right.

Transporting Women Offenders

About one-third of the convicts sent to America were women.

Nearly half of the women tried at the Old Bailey during the years 1718 to 1775 were sentenced to transportation.

Between **12 and 20%** of those transported to the American colonies were women—typically having been convicted of crimes relating to poverty or sexual behavior.

American colonies

Prisoners became indentured servants and the British gave up all responsibility for them.

Transportation sentences were typically seven years for noncapital offences or for life for those who had had their death penalties commuted.

The percentage of women transported to Australia ranged from an **80% high** in the first decade of the 1800s to **less than 20%** in the 1820s. Transportation to Australia ended in 1851 for women.

Australia

Rather than becoming indentured servants in Australia, prisoners remained the responsibility of the British government, which continued to have control over them.

1718 — 1775

Some **50,000 prisoners** were transported to the American colonies before 1775 when the American Revolution stopped transportation of British prisoners.

1788 — 1868

From 1788 to 1868, more than **160,000 convicts** were transported from England and Ireland to Australia. Transportation ends throughout Australia in 1868.

Norfolk Island, about 1,000 miles east of Sydney, became the most notable penal colony because of the unbearable discipline.

Norfolk Island jail

FIGURE 3.1 **Key Aspects of Transportation.**
Sources: (Christianson 1998; Lodine-Chaffey 2010; Reichel 1997)

was accomplished through the efforts of John Howard, who is credited with formalizing the penitentiary system.

In 1773 John Howard, often considered the greatest prisoner reformer of modern times, was elected high sheriff of Bedfordshire, England. Through this position, he was made aware of the deplorable conditions existing in the English gaols (jails) and **prison hulks** of his day. The hulks, which were old merchant and naval ships that had been converted into floating prisons, came into use after the American colonies declared their independence from England and closed their ports to British prisoner transportation ships. Although envisioned as a temporary measure, the act authorizing use of prison hulks lasted for 80 years and many prisoners served their entire sentence on the hulks. Most of the 6,000 convicts imprisoned on hulks at any given time during the 80-year period were taken off the ships by day to perform hard labor. Hygiene standards on

the hulks were so poor that disease spread quickly and mortality rates of around 30 percent were quite common (PortCities London, n.d.).

Because of Howard's attacks on the prevailing system, in 1774 Parliament corrected some abuses and tried to improve the sanitary conditions of the gaols. Howard, however, believed there still had to be better ways to house offenders. In 1775 he visited institutions in Paris, Amsterdam, Mannheim, Ghent, and Rome to see what could be learned from the institutions operating there. In some parts of Europe, he found conditions that were as bad as those in England, but other places impressed him with their treatment of the convicts.

In one European house of correction, for example, Howard noted that prisoners' cells had a sleeping bench and appropriate bedding, and that the prisoners themselves were given adequate food, were allowed to perform work, and could attend daily

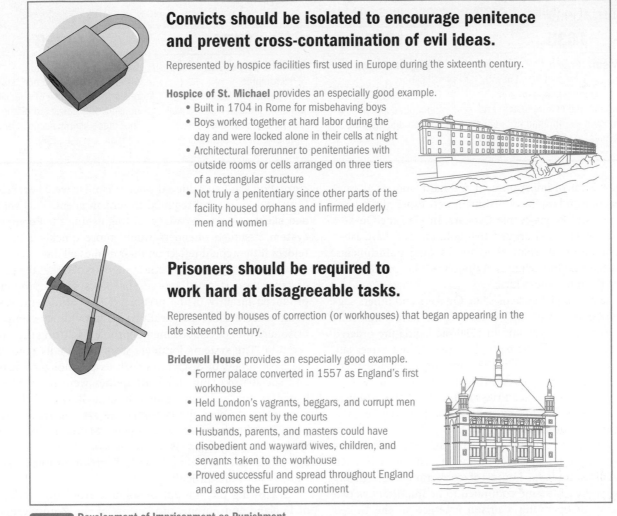

Convicts should be isolated to encourage penitence and prevent cross-contamination of evil ideas.

Represented by hospice facilities first used in Europe during the sixteenth century.

Hospice of St. Michael provides an especially good example.
- Built in 1704 in Rome for misbehaving boys
- Boys worked together at hard labor during the day and were locked alone in their cells at night
- Architectural forerunner to penitentiaries with outside rooms or cells arranged on three tiers of a rectangular structure
- Not truly a penitentiary since other parts of the facility housed orphans and infirmed elderly men and women

Prisoners should be required to work hard at disagreeable tasks.

Represented by houses of correction (or workhouses) that began appearing in the late sixteenth century.

Bridewell House provides an especially good example.
- Former palace converted in 1557 as England's first workhouse
- Held London's vagrants, beggars, and corrupt men and women sent by the courts
- Husbands, parents, and masters could have disobedient and wayward wives, children, and servants taken to the workhouse
- Proved successful and spread throughout England and across the European continent

FIGURE 3.2 **Development of Imprisonment as Punishment.**
Sources: (Barnes & Teeters 1943; Dobash, et al. 1986; Eriksson 1976; Johnston 1973; Spierenburg 1995)

religious services. Such procedures stood in stark contrast to conditions in England, where Howard had found prisoners being forced to sleep on damp dungeon floors or required to go hungry because they could not afford to buy food from their jailer. At the Hospice of St. Michael, Howard was quite taken with the monastic philosophy of doing penance in seclusion. He returned to England with a wealth of new information and immediately set about advocating changes to the operation of English gaols and prisons.

In 1777 Howard published a book entitled *The State of Prisons in England and Wales.* Eventually the English Parliament used Howard's book to provide the basic principles underlying the **1779 Penitentiary Act** (Barnes & Teeters 1943; Dobash, Dobash, & Gutteridge 1986):

- Prisoners should be housed in secure and sanitary facilities.
- Those facilities should undergo systematic inspection.
- Fees for basic needs and services, such as food, should be abolished.
- Discipline at the facilities should follow a reformatory regime.
- The facilities should be built for solitary confinement and operated on the basis of silent contemplation and continuous labor.

Those basic principles brought positive change in England and would also influence the development of corrections in the American colonies.

▶ Corrections in Eighteenth and Nineteenth Century America

Corporal and capital punishment remained the primary sentence types well into eighteenth century America. Legislators in the new country were hesitant to replace those tried and true methods with the untested idea of long-term imprisonment as punishment. Rather than completely changing the criminal codes to make imprisonment the only punishment option, incarceration was more often an alternative to, rather than a replacement for, the old corporal punishments. For example, when Massachusetts established Castle Island as the state prison, the sanction of imprisonment and hard labor was often just one of several options available to the judge. Arson against a building other than a dwelling, for example, had always been punished by whipping. The revised statute of 1785 allowed sentences to include hard labor (either for life or a specified number of years), the pillory, whipping, imprisonment, a fine, or some combination of these (Hirsch 1992, 57).

A Timeline of Early American Jails and Prisons

1635	**1773**	**1776**	**1785**
Boston Prison (Boston, Massachusetts)—Operates as a jail with both criminal (holding prisoners and persons awaiting trial or sentencing) and civil (holding persons who had not paid a debt, taxes, fines, or court costs) functions.	**Newgate Prison** (Simsbury, Connecticut)—Located in an old copper mine with an underground dormitory for prisoners.	**Walnut Street Jail** (Philadelphia, Pennsylvania)—Houses petty offenders and debtors as well as more serious offenders awaiting trial or sentencing.	**Castle Island** (Boston, Massachusetts)—The first "state prison" in the sense of a facility housing only convicted offenders (not those simply accused of crime) from all over the state.

The new ideas of imprisonment and hard labor as alternatives to corporal and capital punishment were especially evident in the activities of **Pennsylvania Quakers**. In 1787 the Quakers (the Society of Friends) argued that solitude and hard labor were humanitarian alternatives to the existing punishments. And they believed Philadelphia's Walnut Street Jail provided the perfect setting to test those ideas.

With the new penal code of 1786, Quakers and others suggested the **Walnut Street Jail** be expanded to have a new role. The pleas were successful, and in 1790 the legislature ordered that a special block of cells be built at the Walnut Street Jail. Construction was completed in 1792, and the new penitentiary house confined the most hardened criminals in single cells. In theory, if not in practice (see Eriksson 1976, 46), the prisoners were kept strictly isolated from each other and from other prisoners and were made to work at hard labor.

As the eighteenth century came to a close, the dual themes of solitude and labor—first seen in the English and European hospice facilities and the houses of correction—were firmly established and each theme continued to be important as two parallel views of operating a prison emerged in the United States. Both were based on the idea that regimens of silence and penitence would prevent cross-infection and encourage positive changes in behavior. The systems' names come from the first locations of their use: Pennsylvania and Auburn (New York).

The Pennsylvania System

Eastern State Penitentiary opened in 1829 in Philadelphia, Pennsylvania. It was designed with seven cell blocks radiating from a hublike center. A corridor ran down the center of each cell block, with the cells positioned on each side of the corridor. Each cell had a back door to a small, uncovered yard where prisoners were allowed to exercise for two brief periods each day. The prison's design was important to the idea that

correction was best achieved when prisoners were kept separate from each other and required to remain silent. This **separate and silent** strategy, key words distinguishing the **Pennsylvania system**, assumed offenders would more quickly repent and reform if they could reflect on their crimes all day.

Critics of the Pennsylvania system argued that the practice of separation (termed *solitude* by the system's proponents) produced insanity in the prisoners. This argument was difficult to refute because reality kept providing examples of prisoners who developed mental problems during their incarceration. The system's founders were admittedly ignorant of the basic tenets of disciplines such as psychology, sociology, and social work. But those disciplines were not well established in the early and mid-1800s, so it is probably more appropriate to view the Pennsylvania system backers as well intentioned rather than as inhumane. Mental retardation and mental disease were considered the same by most laypeople, and attempts to explain how either version of this "insanity" came about were difficult.

Borrowing the concept of solitude from the workhouses of England and Europe, proponents of the Pennsylvania system had hoped to stop what they saw as the training in

Think About It . . .

Eastern State Penitentiary was designed with cell block spokes jutting from a central hub. During its earliest days, the rule of silence was strictly followed as inmates were not allowed to see or talk with each other. The idea was, in part, to prevent cross-contamination among the prisoners—that is, preventing them from sharing criminal values and techniques. However, maintaining complete separation and silence quickly became impossible for prison administrators. If complete and continued solitude and silence could be achieved in prisons today, do you think the result would have more positive or negative consequences?

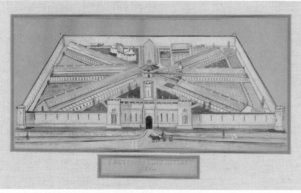

Source: © Judith Miller/Dorling Kindersley/Freeman's

Source: Library of Congress, Historic American Buildings Survey/Historic American Engineering Record/Historic American Landscapes Survey, HABS PA,51-PHILA,354-134

Walnut Street Jail's Penitentiary House
(Philadelphia, Pennsylvania)—Special block of cells constructed to confine the most hardened criminals under a "separate and silent" system.

Virginia and Kentucky Prisons
(Richmond, Virginia, and Frankfort, Kentucky)—These states, the first in the South to open prisons, are unusual in this region of the country where justice and punishment tends to be handled more at the local level.

Auburn Prison (Auburn, New York)—After an unsuccessful attempt to implement the "separate and silent" system borrowed from the Walnut Street Jail's Penitentiary House, Auburn turns (in 1821) to a "congregate and silent" model that came to be known as the Auburn system.

Source: © Everett Collection Inc/Alamy

Think About It...

Segregation of the sexes into separate cells began occurring with some regularity in the 1820s, but it was not until the 1830s that separate facilities became more standard. When Belle Starr (shown here) was convicted in 1883 for horse theft in Indian Territory, she was sentenced to the women's unit of the Detroit House of Corrections. However, placing women in facilities built for men presented a variety of problems for those women. Issues of privacy were foremost, but what other problems can you think of? Loneliness? Sexual exploitation? Access to medical care? Were problems eliminated with segregation into separate cells or facilities?

crime that prisoners received at those institutions where inmates had close and constant contact with each other. But, as Barnes and Teeters (1943) note, it was physically impossible to keep prisoners entirely apart. Inmates developed ingenious methods to communicate with each other (such as tapping out codes on the water pipes within the cells), but even such shrewdness was soon unnecessary because the officials themselves provided contact among the prisoners. From the beginning, convicts were used as servants in the warden's home, and very soon two men were put in each cell so that one might learn a trade from the other. Possibly most important in affecting how the prison was made to operate, the legislature's building appropriations never kept pace with the ever-increasing prison population, so that doubling of prisoners in single cells became necessary. The separate and silent system soon proved a failure, although some could argue it never received a fair chance.

Criticism that the separate and silent system caused mental problems in the inmates and the inability to maintain separation of prisoners were important factors in the Pennsylvania system's demise. But another criticism seemed to take priority in the debates between its champions and its critics: The separate and silent system was very costly. As the system developed at Eastern State Penitentiary, prisoners were allowed to

work in their cells at various handicrafts. They made shoes, caned chairs, and knitted hose, but the cell size (18-feet long, 8-feet wide, and 16-feet high) made it difficult to get much production from its single occupant. Even when two prisoners were working in the cell, the profits that could be gained by the prison for their labor were small. Fortunately, for those wanting an economically self-supporting prison, another option was developing in Auburn, New York.

The Auburn System

The Auburn prison opened in 1817 in Auburn, New York. In 1821 Auburn officials borrowed the separate and silent strategy from the Walnut Street Jail for use at the new prison. This meant the Auburn prison actually used the Pennsylvania system before the Eastern State Penitentiary even opened, but it did not prove very successful in New York. The Auburn design, with cells built back-to-back on five tiers within a hollow building and doors opening out on galleries, did not allow for individual exercise yards. Continual

> *The separate and silent system soon proved a failure, although some could argue it never received a fair chance.*

LEARNING OUTCOMES 3 Compare and contrast the Pennsylvania and Auburn prison systems in terms of their architecture, orienting strategies, and advantages/disadvantages.

GLOSSARY

Pennsylvania Quakers Members of the Society of Friends who, in 1787, argued that solitude and hard labor were humanitarian alternatives to the existing punishments.

Walnut Street Jail Opened in Philadelphia in 1776 to house petty offenders, debtors, and serious offenders and operated only as a jail until 1792 when a penitentiary addition was completed.

separate and silent Key words distinguishing the Pennsylvania system, which sought to keep prisoners separate from each other and required them to remain silent.

Pennsylvania system Prison system established with the Eastern State Penitentiary in 1892 in Philadelphia that assumed offenders would more quickly repent and reform if they could reflect on their crimes all day in silence and separated from others.

1825	1828	1829
Auburn Prison's Women's Unit (Auburn, New York)—Female offenders are accepted in Auburn but are confined to a third-floor attic above the prison kitchen.	**Sing Sing** (Sing Sing, New York)—Built by convict labor, Sing Sing refines the Auburn system into an especially repressive disciplinary regimen.	**Eastern State Penitentiary** (Philadelphia, Pennsylvania)—Built to implement the "separate and silent" system, which came to be called the Pennsylvania system and found greater success than it had at Auburn prison.

congregate and silent Key words distinguishing the Auburn system, which required prisoners to remain silent, even while working and eating together.

Auburn system Prison system established with the Auburn Prison in New York, which used a modified version of the Pennsylvania system wherein prisoners were kept separate from each other at night but allowed work and eat together, in silence, during the day.

reformatory A system of prison discipline that incorporates a more humanitarian approach to confinement and has an interest in preparing inmates for their eventual return to the community.

confinement in their cells without access to an outside area and without the distractions of work created mental and physical problems for the inmates. Officials soon decided the separate and silent strategy from Pennsylvania was not working and the experiment was abandoned as a failure in 1823.

The alternative that Auburn officials turned to was a modification of the Pennsylvania system in which inmates were locked in separate cells at night but allowed to work and eat together, in silence, during the day. This **congregate and silent** policy, which was often enforced with flogging, distinguished the **Auburn system**. The spread of evil ideas among prisoners could be prevented, Auburn proponents argued, by separating prisoners at night and enforcing strict silence in the shops and dining hall during the daytime. That silence was enforced through regulations such as lockstep marching, downcast eyes, constant activity when out of the cells, and prohibitions against prisoners ever being face-to-face (Barnes & Teeters 1943). Eventually, the Auburn model was adopted in states across the country because it produced more money for the state. The craft-oriented labor at Eastern State Penitentiary was considered an outdated labor system when compared with the factory-oriented labor at Auburn.

By the mid-1800s, long-term imprisonment as designed in the United States was influencing the spread of penitentiaries in Europe and other parts of the world. However, the next steps for America's penal system were heavily influenced by activities in European countries. There were, of course, homegrown efforts as well, but the reformatory movement in America owes a great deal to activities that first occurred in other countries.

The Reformatory Movement

The United States was at the forefront of putting into operation the first penal philosophies for long-term imprisonment. But after about 50 years of little more than debate about the merits of the Auburn and the Pennsylvania systems, things were stagnating in the United States and some prison reformers began looking for new approaches. It soon became apparent that since the 1830s, some people had focused their attention less on handling the prisoner in confinement and more on ways to prepare the prisoners for their eventual return to the community. This new focus, which was appealing to many in post–Civil War America, featured an approach that came to be called the reformatory movement.

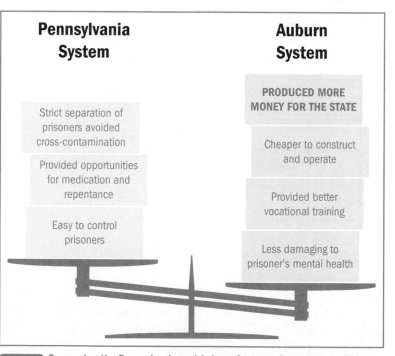

FIGURE 3.3 **Comparing the Pennsylvania and Auburn Systems.** Between the 1820s and 1860s the merits of the Pennsylvania and Auburn systems were hotly debated. Proponents of the Pennsylvania strategy claimed it was superior because it was easier to control prisoners, it provided more opportunity for meditation and repentance, and it avoided cross-contamination of prisoners by maintaining strict separation. Supporters of the Auburn system claimed it was superior because it was cheaper to construct and operate, it provided better vocational training, it was less damaging to the prisoner's mental health, and it produced more money for the state. **This last point tipped the balance in favor of the Auburn system** and it was adopted in most states in the hope that convict labor could help defray institutional expenses and possibly earn a profit for the state.

1839	**1873**	**1876**
Sing Sing Women's Unit (Sing Sing, New York)— Women offenders are placed in a separate cell block in a partially isolated corner of the yard at Sing Sing. (Some sources use 1835 as the date this occurred).	**Indiana Reformatory Institution for Women and Girls** (Indianapolis, Indiana)—The first completely independent and physically separate prison for women in the United States.	**Elmira Reformatory** (Elmira, New York)—Specifically built to implement the progressive ideas, known collectively as the Irish system, of people such as Alexander Maconochie and Sir Walter Crofton.

Source: From p. 72 in "A Timeline of Early American Jails and Prisons" from CORRECTIONS: Philosophies, Practices, and Procedures 2nd ed. by Philip L. Reichel. Copyright © 2001. Printed and electronically reproduced by permission of Pearson Education, Inc., Upper Saddle River, New Jersey.

When reviewing the history of penal institutions, the term **reformatory** refers to a system of prison discipline that incorporates a more humanitarian approach to confinement and has an interest in preparing inmates for their eventual return to the community. Reformatory procedures and institutions called *reformatories* presented different views about prison discipline and administration than were found in the penitentiaries that developed in the first half of the nineteenth century. The first American reformatory, which was in Elmira, New York, opened in 1876 and received offenders ranging from 16 to 30 years old who were serving their first prison term.

The reformatory differed from existing prisons by

- Using indeterminate sentences with fixed minimum terms
- Allowing the possibility of early release on parole
- Placing greater emphasis on reforming the inmates
- Providing more extensive trade training
- Increasing opportunities for academic education

Inmates were placed into one of three classes depending on their achievement and conduct. They entered at the second grade and after six months were demoted to third grade for bad conduct or promoted to first grade as they earned marks. Only those at first grade were eligible for parole. Paroled inmates remained under the jurisdiction of reformatory authorities for another six months.

That emphasis on education and trade training, indeterminate sentences, and early release from prison came to the attention of Americans by way of Ireland and, as such, they comprised what came to be known as the Irish system— which, in turn, resulted from the work of Scotsman Alexander Maconochie and Irishman Walter Crofton. These men are discussed more fully in Chapter 10 since their efforts were especially relevant to the development of discretionary parole.

In 1870, Americans got a chance to hear firsthand about the Irish system when the American Prison Association (now the American Correctional Association) met in Cincinnati for its first National Prison Congress. One hundred thirty delegates from twenty-four states heard some forty papers presented by penal reformers and administrators. As one of the presenters, Crofton's arguments were well received and they clearly influenced both the direction of the meeting and the development of a reformatory philosophy in the United States.

Another presenter, Zebulon Brockway, also made quite an impact on the delegates at the Congress. Since 1861,

Brockway had been director of the Detroit House of Correction, which several people had commented as being a praiseworthy institution. Brockway advocated classification of prisoners by age, sex, and offense and saw great benefit in the use of indeterminate sentences. By the meeting's end, the views of people such as Crofton and Brockway had been adopted in a declaration of principles and the view that society should take responsibility for its criminals and their rehabilitation began to take hold. The reformation of offenders would be achieved "through religion, education, industrious work habits, and the aid and supervision of convicts after discharge" (Sullivan 1990). The enthusiasm generated at the meeting resulted in the 1876 opening of a facility in Elmira, New York, specifically built to carry out the progressive ideas from Maconochie and Crofton.

▶ *Segregating the Sexes*

As the reformatory movement began taking hold in the 1860s, there was an interest in reforming female as well as male prisoners. Feminists of the time worked hard to get all-male legislatures to fund separate reformatory prisons for women. The call was for different responses to women and men prisoners. Women were worthy of reform, they argued, and that reform was best achieved in separate facilities operated by women. There were certainly opponents to such a change, but prisons or reformatories specifically for women began operating when Indiana opened the Women's Prison in 1873 and Massachusetts

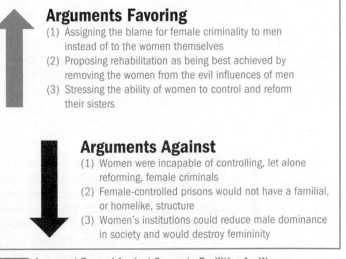

Arguments Favoring

(1) Assigning the blame for female criminality to men instead of to the women themselves

(2) Proposing rehabilitation as being best achieved by removing the women from the evil influences of men

(3) Stressing the ability of women to control and reform their sisters

Arguments Against

(1) Women were incapable of controlling, let alone reforming, female criminals

(2) Female-controlled prisons would not have a familial, or homelike, structure

(3) Women's institutions could reduce male dominance in society and would destroy femininity

FIGURE 3.4 **Argument For and Against Separate Facilities for Women** (Freedman 1974).

GLOSSARY

differential response Term applied to society's response to women offenders when emphasis was on having separate and different-style prisons, different programs, and different sentencing practices for women offenders.

opened the Reformatory Prison for Women in 1877. The women reformers who had argued for these facilities often became administrators in the new reformatories. In doing so, they were able to put into practice the principles they had argued in the legislatures—women inmates should be treated differently from male prisoners.

The new women's facilities differed from those for men in four important ways (Freedman 1974; Rafter 1990 and 1993):

1. **Architectural style:** The women's reformatories were built in a cottage plan with inmates living in relatively small individual units (cottages) that created an atmosphere more like a home than a cell block. The cottages themselves could be set up in dormitory style or with individual rooms having windows, bedspreads, rugs, and wooden doors instead of iron bars. The goal was to project a domestic atmosphere that would focus the women's attention and interests on their expected role in society.

2. **Programs:** Programs for women were consistent with the cottage atmosphere by emphasizing domesticity. In their new reformatories, the women prisoners mainly received training in sewing, cooking, washing and ironing clothes, gardening, and farming. The reformers, who were primarily middle-class women, seemed intent on putting female offenders into a homemaker mold despite the fact that most of the prisoners would have to support themselves after release from prison.

3. **Sentencing disparity:** For the reform efforts to be successful, it was necessary to have access to the offenders over a long time. As a result, the legislation establishing women's reformatories allowed them to hold misdemeanor offenders on sentences that were equivalent to those given to felons serving time at the state prison.

4. **Racial bias:** The reformers establishing the new reformatories were not much interested in dealing with felons. Those serious offenders, many of whom were black, did not draw much empathy from the middle-class and essentially white women reformers. The "preferred" clientele for reform

Although the lack of clear records makes it hard to substantiate, there is good reason to suspect that black women prisoners did not benefit as much from the reformatory movement.

efforts were white women convicted of misdemeanors. Although the lack of clear records makes it hard to substantiate, there is good reason to suspect that black women prisoners did not benefit as much from the reformatory movement. Nineteenth-century women's reformatories may have accepted only white women, leaving black female offenders to serve their sentence in the women's—and sometimes men's—custodial prisons. In the twentieth century, black women were more likely to be admitted to reformatories but were usually segregated in cottages of their own.

Separate and different-style prisons, different programs, and different sentencing practices are just some of the areas indicating a **differential response** to women offenders during the reformatory movement. In many ways the result was a clear improvement over the neglect and mistreatment women prisoners suffered when they were housed in male-dominated prisons. But in highlighting the special needs of women prisoners and in encouraging a different response, reformers "created a new set of problems by assuming that all women inmates, as women, could be treated alike, by methods aimed at reinforcing true womanhood in an era in which a new woman was emerging" (Freedman 1974, 90).

By the end of the nineteenth century, enthusiasm for the reformatory concept had been dampened. One reason the reformatory ideals had trouble was the setting in which they were being tried. The first three reformatories (Elmira, New York; Concord, Massachusetts; and Huntingdon, Pennsylvania) were all opened in buildings that were originally built as maximum-security prisons for adult felons. The economic benefits of using existing structures meant that many states tried the reformatory ideas in settings that were more conducive to tight security and hard labor than to progressive stages and vocational training. Barnes and Teeters (1959) attribute the decay of the reformatory program to the forbidding atmosphere of steel cages and high, gloomy walls that made it impossible to develop true reformatory ideals. Reformatories became more

Think About It...

Over the years, the male model of imprisonment has become the measuring rod for what is considered equal treatment of women offenders. That is, if the standard punishment for male offenders is imprisonment, equal treatment makes imprisonment the standard for female offenders. Some critics of equalization argue that an undesirable consequence has been few non-prison alternatives for women. What arguments can be made for treating women offenders differently than men offenders? Can an equitable response to both men and women offenders be a "fair" response yet not necessarily the same response?

like junior prisons than the enlightened alternative proposed by reformers at the Cincinnati Congress. As the century ended, vocational training was about the only aspect of the reformatory philosophy that officials stressed—but even that survived less for purposes of education and training than as a way for the prison to make a profit.

▶ *Prison Development in the South and West*

The history of America's prison development was not restricted to the northeastern part of the country. Obviously, the rest of the country did not just wait around for the northeastern states to decide what form U.S. imprisonment would take. The other states and territories were certainly influenced by what was happening in places such as Massachusetts, New York, and Pennsylvania, but they also realized there were unique circumstances at home that often required modification, replacement, and even rejection of the prison systems developing in the Northeast. In this section, we consider the history of state prisons in the South and the West.

Developments in the American South

By 1835, most of the states had revised their criminal codes to substitute imprisonment for the traditional corporal punishments. But in many of those jurisdictions, the administration of justice was left to local authorities instead of being centralized at the state level. The reliance on local authority was especially entrenched in the South, where the role of county government and the position of sheriff were of greater consequence than either was in the North. A few states tried the penitentiary idea, with Virginia, Kentucky, and Maryland opening state prisons during the first decade of the nineteenth century. Georgia established a prison in 1817, Tennessee in 1831, and Louisiana in 1835, but by the mid-1800s, state prisons in the South were still more talk than reality (Colvin 1997). The South still preferred to have justice and punishment dispensed at the county rather than the state level.

But the principle of **decentralization** was not the sole or even primary cause of differences between southern and northern penal developments. Religion also played a role—with groups such as the Quakers in the North supporting penitentiaries and religious beliefs in the South being more inclined to follow the Bible's lead and rely on corporal and capital punishment.

Finally, economic differences between the North and the South influenced developments in punishment (Colvin 1997; McKelvey 1977). While the industrial North put its prisoners to work under labor systems designed to produce a product, the agricultural South was making greater use of a **lease system** that provided labor to plantation owners and others. In fact, arguments have been made that imprisonment in the postwar South quickly came to take the place held by slavery in the antebellum South (Colvin 1997; Hindus 1980). Statistics showing that African-Americans soon made up over 90 percent of the total criminal population in the Deep South help to support that thesis. The lease system put convicts in the role of exploited laborer and prison wardens in the role of slaveholder. By 1880, all the former Confederate states and Kentucky had leased out a major portion of their criminal populations. When reformers sought to end leasing, the taxpayers prevented any change. The tragic system continued as former slaves "awoke from rosy dreams of freedom and forty acres and a mule to find themselves shackled to the task of rebuilding the wealth of the South in hopeless penal slavery" (McKelvey 1977, 207).

Leasing's end was brought about not so much by new humanitarian concerns as by reduced profits. By the end of the nineteenth century, states were finding that other labor systems were proving beneficial. Experiments with penal plantations were especially encouraging. Louisiana, Mississippi, and Texas were among the first states to experiment with the use of

LEARNING OUTCOMES 5 Explain how penal systems in the South and West differed from those in the East and summarize reasons for those differences.

GLOSSARY

decentralization A principle popular in the South during the first half of the nineteenth century wherein the administration of justice was left to local authorities instead of being centralized at the state level.

lease system Prison officials lease a prisoner to a private contractor to do labor for a specified sum and for a fixed time.

TABLE 3.1	Corrections in the Nineteenth-Century South.
	While penitentiaries and reformatories were developing in the North during the nineteenth century, the South found little advantage to building large prison facilities—whether based on the Pennsylvania, Auburn, or reformatory model. Explanations for the lack of interest in penitentiaries are summarized here.
Southern reliance on decentralization to local authorities	Political authority in the South was spread more across rural areas than centralized at the state level. As a result, justice and punishment was dispensed at the county rather than state level.
Absence of religious support in the South	Several religious groups in the North promoted penitentiaries as a means of salvation, but southern evangelicals preferred instead the application of corporal and capital punishment—as directed in the Bible.
Southern agricultural economy	Agricultural labor such as farm work, road construction, and turpentine extraction required that workers be dispersed over a wide area. Rather than being conveniently housed in a big building, prisoners needed to be where the crops were grown, the roads built, and the pine trees sapped. Rather than putting prisoners in a single state penitentiary it was more reasonable and economical to have smaller work camps from which prisoners could be transported to the work site each day.

prisoners on large farms and plantations. These states began purchasing farmland and buying plantations where prisoners would work for the state rather than for private contractors or lessees. The penal plantation became entrenched in southern penology and influenced the direction imprisonment would take in the twentieth-century South.

Developments in the American West

The earliest prisons in the West were not strongly influenced by the developments in New York and Pennsylvania. California opened San Quentin prison in 1852 and Folsom in 1880 and the total prison population was soon double capacity. But as bad as the crowding in California prisons was, the conditions to the north were of even greater concern. To handle its law violators, the Washington Territory started leasing prisoners to a mill owner who worked the prisoners during the day and then herded them through a trapdoor into a log pit to spend the nights. Conditions in the pit were so terrible that the "structure was possibly the worst prison in America since the closing of Connecticut's old copper mine nearly a century before" (McKelvey 1977, 229).

One explanation for California's overcrowding was the lack of satisfactory classification procedures. Because of inadequate classification, California tended to place a larger portion of its lesser offenders into prisons than was the practice in the East. Problems were aggravated when the criminally naïve were mixed with the more hardened offenders and no system of correctional discipline was used to control, reward, or encourage the inmates.

Some of the territories chose to transfer their criminals to other states rather than build their own prisons. Wyoming Territory contracted first with the Nebraska state prison, and then with the Illinois prison at Joliet, to house its criminals. Oklahoma's criminals—who multiplied even more rapidly than its citizens (McKelvey 1977)—were sent off to the penitentiary in Kansas, where they were jammed into crowded cells when they were not digging coal in the mine pits.

Possibly the most successful states to develop stable prison systems in the West were Colorado, Utah, and the Dakotas. McKelvey (1977) suggests the success of these states was due to their ability to keep open the channels of eastern influence and their participation in the congresses of the National Prison Association. From each source, these Western states were kept informed about Eastern debates, experiments, and theories regarding penal administration. For example, when the National Prison Association held its 1895 Congress in the Rocky Mountain west, Colorado officials were able to brag about having the first adult reformatory, the first board of charities, the only separate prison building for women, the only effective parole law, and the only genuine grading system west of the Mississippi River.

During the twentieth century, other western states, most notably California, came to play a prominent role in directing penal policies and procedures across the nation. The East no longer had a hold on innovation, and both independent and collaborative efforts by each of the 50 states created facets of the U.S. penal system. But while this brief history is informative, its importance for this chapter is to remind us about the cycle of history. Problems of crowding, complaints about prison conditions, and concerns over prison labor systems are not new in American history. Although it would be nice to explain that society has learned from history and can now handle these problems with efficiency and expertise, it is more accurate to say that society has not. Contemporary problems are typically seen by the media, the public, legislators, and even corrections professionals as being unique to this time.

▶ Corrections in the Twentieth Century

In the 1890s, a general reform movement known to history as **progressivism** began sweeping the country. For the next 30 years, America would undergo dramatic changes to the nation's political, social, and economic arenas. By the end of the progressive era, women had won the right to vote, child labor was restricted, general working conditions were improved, citizens had more direct control over their government, business practices were better regulated, and the sale of alcohol was prohibited. The efforts of progressives to reform institutions for delinquent youth, the mentally ill, and prisoners are especially relevant for our purposes.

The reformatories, asylums, and prisons that had been established as mechanisms of social control were viewed by the

TABLE 3.2	Correctional Problems and Possibilities in the Nineteenth-Century West.
	Penal policy in the West reflected a potpourri of influences from Spain and the American East to the independent spirit of the gold rush. As a result, conditions for prisoners ranged from what some describe as among the worst in the country to others that were cited as shining stars. Examples of the extremes are summarized here.
Poor prison accommodations	Prisons built in California and the Washington Territory in the middle to late 1800s were inadequate for the number of prisoners.
Poor classification procedures	An inadequate classification process resulted in California putting more low-level offenders in prison than happened in the East and in an inappropriate mixing of the less serious with the more hardened.
Outsourcing	Rather than spending money on their own prisons, some territories transferred their criminals to other states under contract arrangements.
Learning from others	The successful and stable prison systems in the West were those that kept informed about happenings in the East and approached imprisonment from a more professional perspective.

	Early Century	Mid Century	Late Century
Prison Architecture	• Prison camps and farms continue to dominate in the South. • Some states build "big house" prisons holding more than 2,500 inmates (for example, Stateville prison in Illinois and San Quentin prison in California).	• Most southern states had at least one centrally located penitentiary, but most prisoners were still on large prison farms. • "Telephone pole" prison design flourished (for example, Vacaville, CA and Ferguson Unit, TX).	• Super-maximum security prisons (known as super-max prisons) are built by the federal government (for example, in Florence, CO) and by some states (for example, California's Pelican Bay state prison).
Prison Programs	• Social and behavioral scientists are introduced in the prison environment to help implement basic concepts of classification. • Educational and vocational training programs are introduced in prisons. • The Federal Bureau of Prisons is established in 1930 and quickly takes the lead in new methods and programs (for example, improved training of correctional officers and enhanced vocational training).	• Classification of inmates is implemented throughout the country's prisons. • Diagnosis is added to the classification process to determine appropriate treatment plans.	• The rehabilitation model falls out of favor and a new reliance on incapacitation turns to warehousing serious offenders as a way to protect society. • Restorative justice procedures receive increased attention as a way to recognize concerns of victims.
Women Offenders	• As male inmates were providing prison labor that gave them some marketable skills and had economic advantage for the prison, female inmates were delegated to domestic chores and training that resulted in neither economic advantage for the prison nor for the inmate upon her release.	• Calls are made, and action taken, toward equal treatment of male and female inmates in such areas as opportunities to participate in similar vocational and treatment programs.	• A new approach to female offenders recognizes differences between women and men and argues for deciding appropriate responses toward women offenders from a female orientation. For example, since women present low risk to public safety they should receive greater consideration for community-based sentences.
Race/Ethnicity Disparity	• Although making up only about 9% of the American adult population in the mid-1920s, African-Americans comprise 31% of the prison population.	• Foreign-born Caucasian immigrants are increasingly rare in prisons, but the proportion of African-Americans, Hispanics, and Native Americans grows.	• African-Americans comprise about 12% of the national population but represent more than 40% of the total prison population.
Key Developments	• The number of inmates employed in prison industries declines as organized labor argues that prisoner labor creates unfair business competition.	• The 1960s civil rights movement includes an interest in prisoner rights and federal courts start taking a more active role in how states treat prisoners.	• Mandatory sentencing and increased severity of drug penalties requires more jails and prisons to handle bigger prison population.

FIGURE 3.5 **Key Features of Corrections in the Twentieth Century.**
Sources: (Chesney-Lind & Pollock 1995; Christianson 1998; Kurshan 1992; Rafter 1990; Roth 2011)

Progressives as misguided. Instead, these benevolent and optimistic social reformers believed that people could be cured of delinquency, insanity, and crime through an individualized program of treatment (Smith 1997). These reformers differed from those in earlier decades by being professional experts rather than amateur volunteers. As such, the Progressives collected and analyzed data using social science methods and made treatment decisions based on scientific understanding of the time. The belief that criminal behavior is influenced by sociological, psychological, and biological factors—rather than simply the result of misdirected free will on the part of the criminal—came to define the correctional practices during much of the twentieth century.

One of the clearest examples of progressivism's influence during the twentieth century is seen in the general development of prison programs and the specific influence of the rehabilitation philosophy. The progressive reformers saw themselves as

Progressives collected and analyzed data using social science methods and made treatment decisions based on scientific understanding of the time.

| **Examination** A case history is developed to identify causes or sources of the illness | **+** | **Diagnosis** A particular version of the illness is identified and the offender is assigned to groups with similar problems | **=** | **Treatment** A plan is proposed that allows the offender to "get well" and return to the community as a law-abiding citizen |

FIGURE 3.6 **Medical Model.** Using these stages, imagine an offender who professionals conclude has committed a crime because he or she came from a dysfunctional family (the source of the illness) and then dropped out of school and began using drugs (placing him or her in a category holding other offenders with similar "symptoms"). Such an offender may be assigned to a treatment program that includes academic instruction and therapy for substance abuse.

impartial experts gathering and analyzing social data that would allow them to uncover laws of human behavior. Newfound knowledge in medicine, such as the germ theory of disease, bolstered the idea that individuals are not totally responsible for what happens to them. Illness began to replace free will as an explanation as to why antisocial behavior occurs.

Reforms initiated by the Progressives at the century's start gave rise in the 1930s to a medical model that presented criminal behavior as pathological. Criminals were not so much "bad" as they were "ill." Because of that, offenders should be referred to as people who are sick (physically, mentally, and/or socially), and their crimes are symptoms of their sickness. This **medical model** approach argued that society's response to the criminal should include three stages of examination, diagnosis, and treatment (Abadinsky 1994). Following these stages, professionals could identify and respond to the underlying causes of criminality.

Many types of treatment programs were developed during the 1950s and 1960s. Academic programs treated persons lacking basic educational abilities, whereas vocational training was the remedy for those presumably choosing a career in crime because they did not have marketable job skills. Others, it was argued, engaged in criminal acts because they were morally deficient (treatment = religious training), abused a variety of substances (treatment = therapy groups), or had mental health problems (treatment = group and individual counseling).

The medical model with rehabilitation as individualized treatment began falling out of favor in the 1970s. However, many of the innovations from that period continue to influence prison programs today. The major difference is that they are no longer a central theme around which prisons are organized. Basic vocational and academic education remain popular programs in contemporary prisons. Similarly, programs focused on alcohol and drug treatment are widespread.

▶ Corrections at the Start of the Twenty-First Century

At the start of the new century, the United States had the highest incarceration rate of any country in the world, but by 2010 there were signs the prison boom may be slowing. Attention was increasingly focused on prison alternatives and on evidence-based practices. Measures of public opinion showed that voters recognize the important role probation and parole can play in reducing crime, and strong support was found for a reduced emphasis on prison (Pew Center on the States 2010). This chapter concludes with a look at the changing public opinions and the affect those opinions and budget considerations are likely to have on prisons.

Public Opinion in 2010

According to results of a nationwide public opinion survey conducted in 2010, the American public favors sending fewer low-risk, nonviolent offenders to prison—or reducing their prison terms—and reinvesting some of the savings in creating a stronger probation and parole system that holds offenders accountable for their crimes (Pew Center on the States 2010, 2). Importantly, support for reducing prison sentences or time comes from all political perspectives and across all regions of the country.

The opinions found in the 2010 survey were not new. At the start of the decade a multiphase research project designed to gauge public opinion on crime and corrections found a

At the start of the new century, the United States had the highest incarceration rate of any country in the world, but by 2010 there were signs the prison boom may be slowing.

 LEARNING OUTCOMES 6 Summarize the development of prison programs and the treatment of women and other minorities during the early, middle, and late twentieth century.

GLOSSARY

progressivism Reform movement that began in the 1890s and resulted in widespread, significant political and social reforms in many social institutions, including prisons.

medical model An orienting philosophy that views criminals not so much "bad" as "sick" and in need of treatment.

preference for tackling the root cause of crime rather than its symptoms and a reconsideration of harsh prison sentences as a primary crime-fighting tool, especially for non-violent offenders (Peter D. Hart Research Associates 2002). Specific examples of a preference for non-prison sanctions are reflected in only 38 percent support for mandatory prison sentences (down from 55 percent support in 1995) and a view of drug abuse as a medical problem needing counseling and treatment (63 percent) rather than as a serious crime to be handled by the courts and prison system (31 percent).

With the twenty-first century public being more supportive of a reduction in the use of prisons, we should begin seeing crime control policy moving away from primary reliance on imprisonment and toward greater reliance on prevention and rehabilitation—and, in fact, we have.

Decreased Reliance on Prisons

In November 2000, California voters passed Proposition 36, which allows people convicted of first- and second-time nonviolent, simply drug possession to receive drug treatment instead of imprisonment. In 2002, Michigan legislators repealed almost all of the state's mandatory minimum drug statutes and replaced them with sentencing guidelines that give discretion back to judges. In 2003, Colorado reduced the maximum sentence for schedule I (for example, heroin) or II (for example, cocaine) substances from three years in prison to eighteen months in prison (plus mandatory parole periods).

LEARNING OUTCOMES 7 — Explain how public opinion about crime and punishment in the twenty-first century seems to be influencing the use of imprisonment and prison alternatives.

These examples foretold a new response to offenders—drug offenders, at least—that moved away from reliance on imprisonment.

On January 1, 2010, the results of that decade-long change in approach were becoming more apparent. On that day, there were 0.3 percent fewer prisoners under the jurisdiction of state prison authorities than there had been a year earlier. It was the first year-to-year decline in the state prison population since 1972 (Pew Charitable Trusts 2010).

The likelihood of an overall decline was apparent even by mid-year 2009 (West 2010). Some have wondered why the drop took so long since crime rates had declined for more than a decade and public attitudes had been supportive of less reliance on imprisonment. Some

0.3% On January 1, 2010, there were 0.3 percent fewer prisoners under the jurisdiction of state prison authorities than there had been a year earlier.

possible explanations include the following (Pew Charitable Trusts 2010):

- **State budget deficits have forced states to reduce prison populations in an attempt to save money.** The fiscal crisis clearly prompted states to reconsider their sentencing and release policies, but financial pressures alone cannot explain the decline in state prison populations.

- **Fewer prison admissions.** A drop in prison admissions actually began in 2007—well before the economic collapse—and occurred again in 2008. The admissions decline was driven by a reduction in the number of people sent to prison for new crimes rather than admissions for probation or parole violations.

- **More prison releases.** The number of inmates released from state prisons grew for the seventh straight year in 2008.

- **States began to realize they could get taxpayers a better return on their public safety dollars.** Several

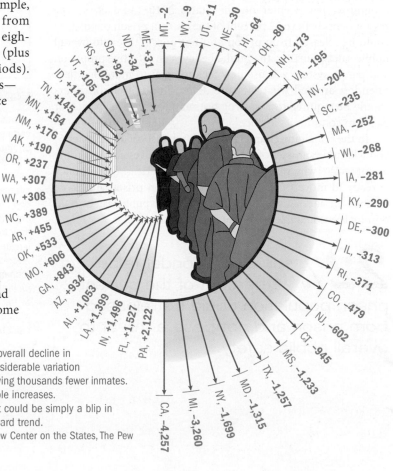

FIGURE 3.7 **Prison Count Drops in 26 States.** Although there was an overall decline in state prison population from 2008 to 2009, there was considerable variation among the states. The population dropped in 26 states with some having thousands fewer inmates. The population grew, however, in the other 24 states—some with notable increases.

Because the drop in 2009 was the first in nearly four decades, it could be simply a blip in continued growth or could signal the beginning of a sustained downward trend.

Source: Based on data from PUBLIC SAFETY PERFORMANCE PROJECT, Pew Center on the States, The Pew Charitable Trusts. Reprinted by permission.

states, including those with the largest prison population declines (for example, California, Michigan, Texas), have enacted reforms that reduced the number of prisoners without sacrificing public safety. Texas, for example, invested in residential and community-based treatment and diversion programs to provide non-prison options for probation violators, whereas Mississippi implemented a new risk assessment tool that helps distinguish between inmates who can be safely paroled and those needing to remain behind bars.

The widespread support for reducing prison time is linked to having offenders participate in programs aimed at reducing recidivism, including literacy and substance abuse treatment programs (Pew Center on the States 2010). In fact, survey respondents believe 22 percent of the current prison population could be released from prison and not pose a threat to overall public safety. Further, the public believes an effective probation and parole system will use new technologies to monitor where offenders are and what they are doing. In addition, offenders should be required to pass drug tests and to either keep a job or perform community service.

In the remaining chapters of this book (especially Chapter 5) you will find examples of these prison alternatives and will come to appreciate why many people believe American crime policy is ready to move toward less dependence on prison and more reliance on alternatives that will provide for public safety, hold criminals accountable, and reduce recidivism.

22% survey respondents believe 22 percent of the current prison population could be released from prison and not pose a threat to overall public safety.

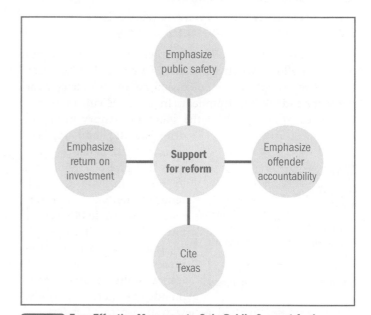

FIGURE 3.8 **Four Effective Messages to Gain Public Support for Less Prison.** Even though the public seems supportive of reducing reliance on imprisonment, reform efforts should be presented with certain things in mind to assure success of those reforms. In its report on public attitudes about crime and punishment, the Pew Center on the States (2010) included four effective messages that politicians and policymakers can use as they garner support when moving toward prison alternatives. For example, public safety and offender accountability should be emphasized since those are primary voter concerns. Similarly, voters are impressed with language suggesting they could get a better return on their taxpayer dollars. Terminology is also important, especially when the language emphasizes public safety. For example, voters respond more favorably to "mandatory supervision" to describe prison alternatives than "community corrections" or other phrases that suggest the criminals will be in their neighborhoods. Finally, the survey respondents were impressed by the fact that Texas is shifting its emphasis away from prison. If Texas, with its strong law-and-order reputation, is relying less on prison then it must be an idea worth considering.

From Eastern State Penitentiary to Alcatraz of the Rockies

What do a shoe bomber, the Unabomber, a 9/11 conspirator, and an FBI agent turned Russian spy have in common with prisoners serving time at Eastern State Penitentiary in the 1830s? They have all experienced prison under the separate and silent system.

The Administrative Maximum (ADX) facility in Florence, Colorado, is the most secure facility in the federal prison system—and possibly the most secure in the world. Called Supermax, or Alcatraz of the Rockies, some of the country's most notorious prisoners are housed here, including would-be airline shoe bomber Richard Reid, "Unabomber" Ted Kaczynski, the self-confessed al-Qaeda operative Zacarias Moussaoui, and former FBI agent turned Russian spy Robert Hanssen.

These and the other inmates housed at ADX find themselves for 23 hours a day in a 7' × 12' soundproofed cell furnished with a poured concrete bed slab where they can sleep on a thin green mattress or lay to watch selected programs on a 12" black and white television set. Or, they can sit on a poured cement stool to read books or write letters at a concrete desk. Stainless steel toilets and sinks provide what is probably a welcome color and texture contrast. Each cell has a slit window, only a few inches wide, providing a view of an inner courtyard and maybe a patch of sky—but no one has a view of the surrounding Rocky Mountains (Cohen 2007; Schuster 2007).

Inmates who have been abiding by the rules may get about ten hours per week of outside recreation in an area that Olympic Park bomber Eric Rudolph describes as a large empty swimming

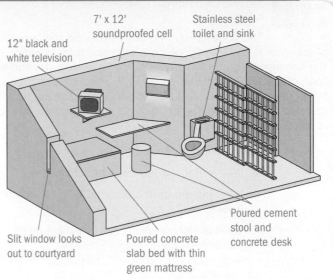

7' x 12' soundproofed cell · **12" black and white television** · **Stainless steel toilet and sink** · **Slit window looks out to courtyard** · **Poured concrete slab bed with thin green mattress** · **Poured cement stool and concrete desk**

Zacarias Moussaoui—the only person who has been tried in a United States court on charges of involvement in the September 11, 2001, attacks—pleaded guilty in 2005 on charges of involvement in the strikes. In 2006 he was taken to ADX Florence to begin serving a life sentence. The graphic shows a typical cell at ADX Florence.

pool divided into dog-kennel style cages (Rappold 2006). Other inmates are under Special Administrative Measures (SAMs) and they may get only 90 minutes of exercise five days a week in a caged courtyard.

1. **ADX inmate Eric Rudolph wrote to a Colorado Springs newspaper that Supermax was designed to isolate inmates from social and environmental stimuli, with the ultimate purpose of causing mental illness and a variety of physical ailments (Rappold 2006). Similar arguments were made by detractors of the Eastern State Penitentiary's version of separate and silent. *Do you think such descriptors are exaggerations or reasonably accurate? Is a separate and silent regimen cruel and unusual punishment?***

2. **ADX officials point out that although the prisoners have no authorized contact with each other, they are in contact with prison staff during the day. *Should contact with prison staff be sufficient to counter criticism that ADX is creating a situation of sensory deprivation?***

Source: Hernan H. Hernandez A./Shutterstock.com

LEARNING OUTCOMES 1

Describe key features of the Code of Hammurabi, Mosaic Law, Roman Law, and law during the Middle Ages.

The Code of Hammurabi introduced the concept of *lex talionis* and Mosaic Law expanded on it by including the concept of proportionality. The Twelve Tables, the earliest form of written Roman law, provided the basis for private rights of Roman citizens. During the Middle Ages, courts rather than individuals began taking a greater role in conflict resolution.

1. Explain the principle of *lex talionis*.

2. Why is Hebrew law called Mosaic Law?

3. What serves as the earliest form of written Roman law?

4. What are some examples of exhibitory punishments?

Code of Hammurabi The first known body of law, established by King Hammurabi about 4,000 years ago, lays out the basis of criminal law.

Mosaic Law The Hebrew legal system, which started when God gave Moses two stone tablets containing the Ten Commandments.

Twelve Tables The earliest form of written Roman law, which provided the basis for private rights of Roman citizens.

LEARNING OUTCOMES 2

Identify the two important themes in the development of imprisonment as punishment and explain the link between hospice facilities and houses of corrections to those themes.

The sixteenth century ideas that prisoners should be isolated (taken from hospice facilities) and should be required to work (taken from houses of correction) provided themes that would continue to influence penal philosophy into the nineteenth century.

1. What are some countries besides England that used transportation?

2. Transported prisoners to Australia remained the responsibility of the British government. How did that differ for the transported prisoners to the American colonies?

3. What were "prison hulks"?

4. Explain three of the basic principles underlying the 1779 Penitentiary Act.

5. Are the themes that prisoners should be isolated and prisoners should work still important today? In what way, or why not?

transportation The removal of criminals to a remote location where they could be used as laborers.

hospice facilities Late-sixteenth and early-seventeenth century institutions that promoted the idea of isolating offenders from each other.

houses of correction Sixteenth-century institutions for offenders that emphasized the importance of hard work at disagreeable tasks.

prison hulks Eighteenth-century British merchant and naval ships converted into floating prisons.

1779 Penitentiary Act Passed by the English Parliament, this act relied on John Howard's ideas to make significant reforms to the prison system.

Compare and contrast the Pennsylvania and Auburn prison systems in terms of their architecture, orienting strategies, and advantages/disadvantages.

The Pennsylvania system was used at Eastern State Penitentiary, which followed a separate and silent strategy. The prison, which was built with this strategy in mind, had individual cells with small outside recreation yard for each prisoner. Auburn prison, on the other hand, followed a congregate and silent strategy since its architecture was better suited for prisoners to leave their cells and work together during the day. The Pennsylvania system allowed easier control of the prisoners and had the advantage of avoiding cross-contamination since prisoners had no contact with each other. It also provided more opportunities for meditation and repentance. The Auburn system was more widely adopted by other states because it was deemed less damaging to prisoner's mental health, provided better vocational training, was cheaper to construct and operate, and—most importantly—produced money for the state.

1. What role did the Pennsylvania Quakers play in having long-term imprisonment as an alternative to corporal and capital punishment?

2. Highlight what you consider to have been the major advantages of both the Pennsylvania and Auburn systems.

3. Why did most American states choose to follow the Auburn model rather than the Pennsylvania model?

4. In what way was the 1870 meeting of the American Prison Association important for the development of American corrections?

5. What were the key characteristics of the reformatory movement?

Pennsylvania Quakers Members of the Society of Friends who, in 1787, argued that solitude and hard labor were humanitarian alternatives to the existing punishments.

Walnut Street Jail Opened in Philadelphia in 1776 to house petty offenders, debtors, and serious offenders and operated only as a jail until 1792 when a penitentiary addition was completed.

separate and silent Key words distinguishing the Pennsylvania system, which sought to keep prisoners separate from each other and required them to remain silent.

Pennsylvania system Prison system established with the Eastern State Penitentiary in 1892 in Philadelphia that assumed offenders would more quickly repent and reform if they could reflect on their crimes all day in silence and separated from others.

congregate and silent Key words distinguishing the Auburn system, which required prisoners to remain silent, even while working and eating together.

Auburn system Prison system established with the Auburn Prison in New York, which used a modified version of the Pennsylvania system wherein prisoners were kept separate from each other at night but allowed to work and eat together, in silence, during the day.

reformatory A system of prison discipline that incorporates a more humanitarian approach to confinement and has an interest in preparing inmates for their eventual return to the community.

Describe how men's and women's prisons differed during the reformatory movement of the nineteenth century.

Rather than following the architectural style of big prisons, women's reformatories were built in a cottage plan wherein small individual units created a more home-like than cell-like atmosphere. The programs for women were consistent with the cottage atmosphere and emphasized domestic activities rather than vocational training. In order to have more time to reform women offenders, state laws allowed them to be put in the reformatories for less serious crimes than required for men to be sent to prison. That disparity was even more apparent for black women, who were more likely to be put in custodial prisons than in the reformatory.

1. What were three arguments favoring separate prison facilities for women in the nineteenth century?

2. What were three arguments against separate prison facilities for women in the nineteenth century?

3. What are the four ways in which women's facilities differed from men's during the reformatory movement?

differential response Term applied to society's response to women offenders when emphasis was on having separate and different-style prisons, different programs, and different sentencing practices for women offenders.

Explain how penal systems in the South and West differed from those in the East and summarize reasons for those differences.

While the northern states were developing large central prison facilities to hold offenders from throughout the states, southern states relied on prison farms distributed in rural locations across the states. The large penitentiaries did not catch on in the South because of the South's preference to let local authorities handle issues of justice and punishment and because the South's rural economy made prison farms and work camps more convenient sites for convict labor. In addition, there wasn't religious support for penitentiaries in the South as there was in the North. The penal system in the West often suffered from overcrowding to a greater extent than was present in the East, and some of that was the result of inadequate classification procedures that put low-level offenders into prison. The western states that had stable prison systems were those that kept informed about what was happening in the East and were willing to implement those more professional procedures.

1. Religion was important in both the North and the South, but the result in terms of penal philosophy was different. Why?

2. How did economic differences between the North and the South influence the resulting punishments in each region?

3. Do you think that imprisonment took slavery's place in the post–Civil War South? Explain.

4. In what ways did classification procedures affect imprisonment in California during the nineteenth century?

5. What explanations are offered for why Colorado, Utah, and the Dakotas had reasonably stable prison systems in the late 1800s?

decentralization A principle popular in the South during the first half of the nineteenth century wherein the administration of justice was left to local authorities instead of being centralized at the state level.

lease system Prison officials lease a prisoner to a private contractor to do labor for a specified sum and for a fixed time.

Summarize the development of prison programs and the treatment of women and other minorities during the early, middle, and late twentieth century.

During the twentieth century, prisons began using information from the social and behavioral sciences to provide for basic classification of prisoners and to introduce more educational and vocational training. Classification became more sophisticated as the century progressed and rehabilitation took hold as the orienting philosophy. But by late century, rehabilitation had fallen out of favor and a preference for warehousing offenders took priority. Vocational training throughout the century was geared primarily toward male offenders, whereas women prisoners received domestic training at the century's start and were only able to participate in some of the more marketable training in middle and late century. By the 1990s arguments were being made for providing more non-prison sanctions for women offenders. Throughout the century African-Americans, Hispanics, and Native Americans were disproportionately represented in the nation's prison population.

1. What was progressivism?

2. What role did the Federal Bureau of Prisons play in moving prison programs forward in the early twentieth century?

3. Is there any advantage to providing women offenders with vocational training in nondomestic skills when they are in prison? Explain.

4. In what ways, if any, did racial disparity in imprisonment change from early to late twentieth century?

5. Using information from other classes in sociology, psychology, criminal justice, and social work, what are some arguments supporting the basic concepts of the medical model?

progressivism Reform movement that began in the 1890s and resulted in widespread, significant political and social reforms in many social institutions, including prisons.

medical model An orienting philosophy that views criminals not so much "bad" as "sick" and in need of treatment.

LEARNING OUTCOMES 7

Explain how public opinion about crime and punishment in the twenty-first century seems to be influencing the use of imprisonment and prison alternatives.

During the first decade of the twenty-first century, opinion polls indicated the American public was interested in strengthening the probation and parole system and in decreasing reliance on prisons—especially for low-risk, nonviolent offenders. Legislators are responding to the public's interest in prison alternatives—and to state budget deficits—by reducing the number of people being sent to prison and increasing the number of inmates released from prison.

1. Why does the United States have the highest incarceration rate of any country in the world?

2. Was the 2010 public opinion survey showing Americans favoring less reliance on imprisonment a fluke or the start of an ongoing trend?

3. Do you think treatment in the community or imprisonment is a better response to drug offenders? Why?

4. Looking at the three states that had the greatest drop in prison populations from 2008 to 2009 and the three states with the greatest increases, what cultural or social differences in those states might explain the differences?

5. Do you agree that as much as 22 percent of the current prison population could be released from prison without jeopardizing public safety? Is that reason enough to release those people?

MyCJLab

Go to the Chapter 3 section in *MyCJLab* to test your understanding of this chapter, access customized study content, engage in interactive simulations, complete critical thinking and research assignments, and view related online videos.

Additional Links

Visit **www.earlyamerica.com/review/2010_winter_spring/female-convicts-tables.html** to learn more about the crimes and sentences that resulted in women being transported to the American colonies.

Search the records of the Old Bailey, London's central criminal court, from 1674 to 1913 at **www.oldbaileyonline.org/**. Maybe you'll find some ancestors who were transported to the American colonies.

The official website of the historic Eastern State Penitentiary **www.easternstate.org/** includes a virtual tour of the prison and many other items of interest.

See the PEW Center report on public attitudes toward crime and punishment at **www.pewcenteronthestates.org/initiatives_detail.aspx?initiativeID=60775**.

Get the most recent mid-year report on jail and prison populations at **http://bjs.ojp.usdoj.gov/index.cfm?ty=pbse&sid=38** to see if the 2009 decline continued.

Watch the CBS *60 Minutes* episode "Supermax: A Clean Version of Hell" about the Administrative Maximum (ADX) federal penitentiary at Florence, CO (Supermax) at **www.cbsnews.com/video/watch/?id=5101352n**.

Sentencing

"Injustice anywhere is a threat to justice everywhere."

—Martin Luther King, Jr. (1929–1968) Civil Rights Leader

1 Identify the various types of sentences and explain the problems of comparing them in terms of severity.

2 Explain the two basic sentencing structures used in the United States.

3 List and explain three sentencing practices.

4 List and describe three techniques used to reduce the length of a sentence.

5 Give examples of specific measures that evidence-based sentencing suggests judges should follow during the sentencing process.

6 Describe two types of sentencing injustice.

4

INTRO   PRISON FOR TAX EVASION

In December 2010, actor Wesley Snipes (the Blade trilogy and other movies) entered a federal correctional institution and began a three-year prison sentence after his conviction in 2008 on three misdemeanor counts of failing to file tax returns. The prosecuting attorney for the Justice Department's Tax Division said that Snipes's long prison sentence should send a clear message to all tax deniers that they face similar sanctions. Prosecutors claimed that Snipes made close to $14 million between 1999 and 2004 and owed nearly $3 million in back taxes. Snipes claimed that he was unfamiliar with the science of law and finance and that his prison sentence was excessive. Prosecutors countered that the prison term was justified because Snipes had tried to hide his income using corporate shells and offshore financial accounts (Bluestein 2010; Itzkoff 2010; Phillips 2008). In January 2011, entertainment website TMZ reported that Snipes had requested yoga mats for himself and a few other prisoners, and was teaching yoga at the McKean Federal Correctional Facility in Pennsylvania (TMZ Staff 2011).

In his appeal (which was denied) of the prison sentence, Snipes argued for house arrest or probation instead of a prison sentence. In an interview with CNN's Larry King, Snipes claimed his prison

Actor Wesley Snipes leaves the Federal Court building in Ocala, Florida, where he was convicted on three misdemeanor counts of failing to file tax returns.

Source: m63/m63/ZUMA Press/Newscom

sentence was influenced by his race (Hodgson 2010).

This chapter is concerned with the topic of **sentencing**, which refers to the process of a court imposing a penalty on a person convicted of a crime. There are a variety of penalties or punishments that a judge might apply, and that makes sentencing policy very complex. Sanctions can include fines, community service, probation, electronic monitoring, imprisonment, and several others—including combinations of the penalties. Adding to that complexity, the perceived severity of various sentences is not easily determined. This makes it difficult, for example, to decide whether a particular punishment will be considered severe enough by an offender to deter his or her continued criminal behavior.

DISCUSS Would a different sentence have been more appropriate? Is his sentence an example of sentencing disparity?

▶ Sentence Severity and Types

Presumably, the penalty applied to a convicted offender will be of increasing severity as the seriousness of the offense increases. We say "presumably" because punishment continuums are proposed by legislators and practitioners rather than being based on the experiences of people who actually serve the sentence. In fact, several studies (see, for example, Wodahl, Ogle, Kadleck, & Gerow 2009) suggest that imprisonment is not always viewed as the most punitive sanction. In fact, some offenders prefer time in jail to such community-based sanctions as electronic monitoring and time in prison to such alternatives as boot camp. Maybe some offenders view a relatively short jail sentence as a welcome break from the stressors of employment and family obligations. Possibly other offenders prefer the structure and clear-cut expectations of prison to having to put forth the greater personal responsibility needed to successfully complete a community-based penalty.

The research on punishment ranking is careful to point out that people receiving identical punishments may perceive the severity of that punishment very differently. May and Wood (2010) explain that factors such as age (for example,

DISCUSS *Meet with 3-4 other students and build your own ranking of sentence types from most to least serious. What arguments were used when people disagreed on the rankings?*

people receiving identical punishments may perceive the severity of that punishment very differently

older offenders perceive brief imprisonment as less severe than community-based sanctions of longer length) and experiences in the system (for example, those with experience serving time in prison are more likely than those without prison experience to view a jail term as less severe than a longer time of close supervision in the community) will affect one's punishment ranking. Also, race, ethnicity, and gender are found to influence views about the severity of various punishments. In several studies, blacks have been found to be more likely than whites to choose prison over community-based sanctions (see May & Wood 2010, 63). One explanation for this might be that blacks perceive prison alternatives such as boot camp, halfway houses, and even day reporting as too much of a hassle (for example, abusive program officers and rules that are too hard to follow) compared with prison. But, regardless of the reason, the important point made by punishment ranking research is that common assumptions about imprisonment being the most

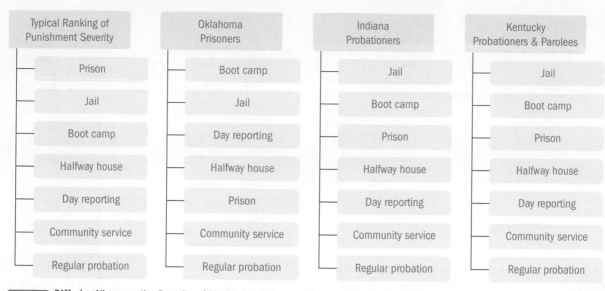

Typical Ranking of Punishment Severity	Oklahoma Prisoners	Indiana Probationers	Kentucky Probationers & Paroxees
Prison	Boot camp	Jail	Jail
Jail	Jail	Boot camp	Boot camp
Boot camp	Day reporting	Prison	Prison
Halfway house	Halfway house	Halfway house	Halfway house
Day reporting	Prison	Day reporting	Day reporting
Community service	Community service	Community service	Community service
Regular probation	Regular probation	Regular probation	Regular probation

FIGURE 4.1 **Differing Views on the Severity of Punishment.** The punishments listed in the first column will be seen by many people as clearly progressing from the most severe to the least severe. However, that is not necessarily how offenders view the same penalties. May and Wood (2010) surveyed three categories of offenders (prisoners in Oklahoma, probationers in Indiana, and both probationers and parolees in Kentucky) and found rather different views about punishment rankings. Despite general agreement by lay public and offenders that community service and regular probation are not very severe punishments, the offenders saw jail and boot camp as being more severe penalties than prison.

Source: Table 3.11, p. 41, adapted from RANKING CORRECTIONAL PUNISHMENTS: Views from Offenders, Practitioners and the Public by D. C. May & P. B. Wood. Copyright © 2010 by David May and Peter B. Wood. Published by Carolina Academic Press. Reprinted by permission of the publisher. All rights reserved.

severe penalty and community-based punishment being less severe, might be incorrect—at least in the calculation of some offenders. It will be helpful to keep this in mind as various punishment types are discussed and the sentencing process is reviewed.

Although there may be restrictions placed on the options a judge has when sentencing an offender (such as those mentioned later in this chapter), judges typically have some discretion in the sentencing process. Importantly, judges are not restricted to using just one sentence type. Some types obviously cannot occur together (for example, a person could not be executed and placed on probation), but for the most part several different sentence types can be included as part of the actual sentence. Consider Keith's case, for example. After Keith's conviction for burglary, Judge Swanson requests a presentence investigation from the probation department. The results of that investigation tell Judge Swanson that this is Keith's second conviction for burglary in the past three years. For the first conviction Keith was placed on probation for nine months, and he successfully completed that sentence without incident.

LEARNING OUTCOMES 1 Identify the various types of sentences and explain the problems of comparing them in terms of severity.

GLOSSARY

sentencing When a court imposes a penalty on a person convicted of a crime.

presentence investigation report A report developed from information derived through a presentence investigation that is provided to the judge to assist in sentencing decisions.

presentence investigation An inquiry interview and data-collection method used by a probation officer to summarize information about a convicted offender.

Believing that this second conviction requires a harsher punishment, Judge Swanson sentences Keith to probation again, but with the special condition that he reside at the local halfway house. The sentence also requires Keith to perform 50 hours of unpaid labor that will benefit his community. This sentence, which uses probation, residential community corrections, and community service, is a reasonable example of combining sentence types. For a more complete understanding of how the sentencing process works, we will begin with that presentence investigation that Judge Swanson ordered.

Presentence Investigation Reports

In order to determine the most appropriate sentence type, it is vital that sentencing judges have access to information about the crime and the offense. The **presentence investigation report** is an important informational source on which judges base their sentencing decision for adult felony offenses. Writing a presentence report first requires a **presentence investigation (PSI)**, which is an inquiry interview and data-collection method used by a probation officer to summarize information about a convicted offender. The officer uncovers the offender's prior record as well as relevant personal and family data and compiles the report prior to the sentencing hearing. That information is then compiled into an eight to ten page report with a concluding summary wherein the probation officer recommends a sentence to the judge.

One study in Ohio found that sentencing judges followed the probation officer's recommendation in 66 percent of the cases when prison was recommended and in 85 percent of the cases when probation was recommended. Another study in Utah found that the court agreed with the probation officer's

TABLE 4.1

TABLE 4.1 | **Types of Punishment.**
Although there may be disagreement about how various penalties rank in severity, there is general agreement as to what each type involves. The primary sentences are briefly described here although each receives greater attention in other chapters.

Boot Camp

A form of short-term imprisonment that emphasizes a military-like philosophy and includes a combination of hard work, physical conditioning, and treatment

Jail

A sentence to confinement in a city or county facility (typically for one year or less) that could be under minimum-, medium-, or maximum-security supervision conditions

Halfway House

Community-based residential facilities that house offenders and serve as midpoints between liberty in the community and deprivation of liberty in a prison

Community Service

Requirements for the offender to do unpaid work for the general good of the community

Electronic Monitoring

Community-based sanction that requires the offender to wear an electronic device that can be used to monitor the offender's location and help ensure compliance with conditions of probation

Prison

A sentence to confinement in a state or federal facility (typically for more than one year) that could be under minimum-, medium-, or maximum-security supervision conditions

Day Reporting

A nonresidential community-based sanction that blends high levels of supervision with the delivery of specific services needed by the offender

Intensive Supervision Probation

A form of probation that requires closer supervision of the offender under increased rules and regulations governing the offender's movement and behavior

Regular Probation

Community supervision of an offender under court-imposed conditions for a specified time period during which the court can modify conditions as needed

Fines

A financial penalty that requires the offender to pay a specified sum of money within limits set by law

---

recommendation about 91 percent of the time in felony and misdemeanor cases (Norman & Wadman 2000). Such a high level of concurrence may be influenced by factors such as probation officers recommending what they have learned over time, what a particular judge is likely to do anyway, or by the probation officer conforming to a plea agreement that was struck with the prosecutor. But in fairness to the hard work and dedication of probation officers charged with producing PSI reports, it must also be acknowledged that judges recognize those efforts and express their confidence in the probation officers by agreeing with

91% the court agreed with the probation officer's **recommendation about 91 percent of the time**

recommended sentences. While keeping in mind the purposes of punishment, judges are influenced by the presentence investigator's report along with the wishes of the victim, prosecutor, and the defense attorney.

Although the PSI report's primary use is to assist judges in determining the most appropriate sentence for a particular offender, it is also helpful to probation officers charged with supervising the offender in the community. Probation and parole supervisors use the PSI when assigning offenders to officers' caseloads. Field probation and parole officers use the PSI when writing a treatment or program plan (Norman & Wadman 2000).

Despite its importance in the process, the use of the PSI at sentencing for felony crimes has declined in many states due to funding

Information about harm or losses suffered by the victim

Criminal background check

Presentence Investigation Report

Interview information from the offender (for example, home environment, family life, work history, education, substance abuse history, physical and mental health, and finances)

FIGURE 4.2 **PSI (Presentence Investigation).** The PSI requires the probation officer to gather information that might influence the sentencing decision but was not available to the judge during the plea bargaining or trial proceedings. Because of the wealth of information, most well-researched PSIs for state cases are between eight to ten pages, with federal PSIs standardized at about fifteen to twenty pages in length.

1/2 About half of all states required a presentence investigation in all felony cases

of all states required a presentence investigation in all felony cases, while a PSI was discretionary in sixteen states and non-existent in ten states (Petersilia 2002). Probation officers in jurisdictions that do not have PSIs (for example, Minnesota) complete a guidelines or sentencing worksheet to calculate the sentence based solely on prior criminal history and severity of current offense. This short form unfortunately deprives correctional agencies of valuable information about the offender.

▶ Basic Sentencing Structures

Describing how sentencing is accomplished across the country is not easily done. Each state and the federal government have developed their own specific procedures for determining and assigning the type and severity of punishment given to convicted offenders. Rather than trying to describe 51 different systems, the various approaches are typically grouped into one of two basic structures—but with the important caution that there are hybrids within each of the two structures making it difficult to flatly say that a particular state is a pure example of one structure or the other. The two broad approaches are **indeterminate sentencing** and **determinate sentencing**.

During the first hundred years of sentencing in the United States, the various states took the position that offenders should be sentenced to a specific penalty (a determinate sentence). Typically, that sentence was either corporal or capital punishment. With the growing use of prisons for punishment, the idea of specific penalties remained and offenders were sentenced to prison for a definite time period. A prisoner was released from confinement only when he or she had completed the years, months, and days stipulated in the judge's sentence. By the mid-nineteenth century some prison officials were convinced that a fixed penalty prevented the reformation of offenders by keeping prisoners confined regardless of their efforts toward improvement. A new sentencing strategy—indeterminate sentencing—developed that allowed people other than a judge to determine when a prisoner should be released from confinement. Although it followed determinate sentencing in U.S. history, indeterminate sentencing

LEARNING OUTCOMES 2 Explain the two basic sentencing structures used in the United States.

GLOSSARY

indeterminate sentencing A system wherein the convicted offender receives a sentence that covers a time range rather than a fixed period.

determinate sentencing A system wherein the convicted offender receives a sentence to a specific time period rather than a time range.

statutory penalties Sentences linked via legislation to specific crimes, or to specific classes of felonies or misdemeanors, with a minimum and maximum time period.

cuts and the increased use of determinate sentencing. Approximately 64 percent of all felony cases nationwide included a PSI prior to sentencing. About half

A judicial sentence must fall within the statutory penalty set by the legislature.

provides the background for an understanding of today's resurgence of fixed or specific penalties, so we begin with the indeterminate type.

Indeterminate Sentencing

Indeterminate sentencing is linked more to rehabilitation and behavioral change while incarcerated, with release determined by a parole board as to when the board thinks the offender is ready. Although the judge specified the minimum and maximum indeterminate sentence length (which in many cases prior to the 1980s, the maximum was left open with no date), the offender's fate would rest with parole officials who would determine the true length of sentence by means of the release date. Conceivably, one burglar could be released after one year, while another offender convicted of a similar crime could spend his or her entire life in prison. Today, both state legislatures and judges provide limits to indeterminate sentencing in the United States. State legislatures are responsible for enacting criminal laws and penalties in their respective jurisdictions, and the resulting **statutory penalties** are linked to specific crimes or to classes of felonies or misdemeanors. With the state legislatures typically identifying a minimum and maximum time period, a person convicted of auto theft, for example, may be sentenced to at least one year but no more than five years. A statutory maximum is defined as the maximum amount of time a judge may impose given the facts reflected in the jury verdict or those facts admitted by the defendant (*Blakely* v. *Washington* 2004). A judicial sentence must fall within the statutory penalty set by the legislature. If, for example, the statutory penalty requires that an auto thief receive a punishment between one and five years, the judge must impose a minimum and maximum somewhere between those numbers. Once the sentence is given, its termination is determined by a parole board on the basis of the offender's rehabilitation.

Determinate Sentencing

Dissatisfaction with indeterminate sentencing first surfaced in the early 1970s, when the American Friend's Service Committee (AFSC) published an attack on indeterminate sentencing and parole. The criticism struck at the very heart of indeterminate

DISCUSS *The assumption underlying indeterminate sentencing is that corrections personnel, such as paroling authorities, are better able to determine when an offender is ready to be released than is a judge. Does that mean it would be even better to simply sentence a person to prison without any minimum or maximum and leave sentence termination entirely up to corrections officials? The result, of course, could mean some offenders could be released after only a few days or weeks in prison whereas others would never be released.*

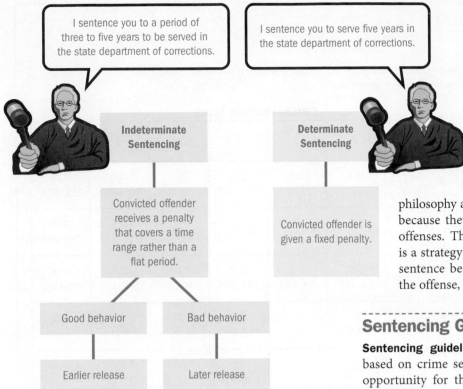

I sentence you to a period of three to five years to be served in the state department of corrections.

I sentence you to serve five years in the state department of corrections.

Indeterminate Sentencing

Determinate Sentencing

Convicted offender receives a penalty that covers a time range rather than a flat period.

Convicted offender is given a fixed penalty.

Good behavior

Bad behavior

Earlier release

Later release

FIGURE 4.3 **Determinate and Indeterminate Sentencing.**

sentencing—the idea of individualized sentences. Although the proponents of indeterminate sentencing praised the notion that sentences should vary according to individual needs, the AFSC complained that poverty was ignored and discrimination was rampant. Furthermore, despite their best efforts, behavioral sciences had not advanced to the point that a parole board could tell when a person had been rehabilitated and, therefore, was ready for release to the community.

The attack on rehabilitation programs, excessive discretion by parole boards, and apparent sentencing inequalities seemed to leave indeterminate sentencing with few supporters. People on the political right asserted that the parole boards were releasing prisoners too early. Those on the political left said persons convicted of the same crime received very different sentences. The result was a return in many states to determinate sentencing in which the judge sentenced offenders to a fixed period of time within narrow statutory limits determined by the legislature, with release determined by percent of sentence completed rather than whether a person has been rehabilitated. Under determinate sentencing, judges impose a flat sentence for a specific amount of time. For example, if the statutory penalty is two to five years, sentences such as two-and-a-half years' probation or four years' imprisonment would be acceptable. Sentences of one year or of five and a half years would not be possible because the time falls outside the statutory penalty. Several states have found determinate sentencing to be a satisfactory way to restore justice by reducing discretion and increasing the likelihood that the length of time actually served is closer to the time imposed by the courts.

▶ Sentencing Practices

Variation among the sentencing procedures is the result of how jurisdictions modify their indeterminate or determinate sentencing structure using one or more special sentencing practices. The specific practices covered here are sentencing guidelines, mandatory sentencing, and aggravating/mitigating factors. The first two are tied to a just deserts philosophy and to general incapacitation (see Chapter 2) because they require similar sentences for comparable offenses. The use of aggravating or mitigating factors is a strategy that allows judges to increase or decrease a sentence because of special conditions associated with the offense, the offender, or the victim.

Sentencing Guidelines

Sentencing guidelines impose a predefined sentence length based on crime severity and prior criminal history, with the opportunity for the judge to depart (impose a greater or a lesser sentence) from the guidelines when circumstances warrant. When indeterminate sentencing states use guidelines that retain a parole board, the judge is recommended to use a range of years deemed appropriate for the case at hand. When guidelines are used in determinate sentencing jurisdictions, the judge sets a very narrow range or fixed sentence.

The two types of sentencing guidelines are voluntary and presumptive. Eight states have **voluntary sentencing guidelines** in that they simply suggest possible sentences to judges but do not require their usage. In twelve **presumptive sentencing guidelines** states, judges are required to issue a sentence that falls in a range established for a particular crime; they may even be required to provide written reasons for deviating beyond the customary limits. Only six states with sentencing guidelines have also built in or linked these guidelines to prison population capacities or adequate resources.

One study sought to evaluate the impact of mandatory sentencing guidelines between 1975 and 1998, comparing states that linked their guidelines to correctional resources with states that did not. Findings indicated that states with guidelines that were linked to resources *decreased* the prison admission rate by an average of 30 inmates per 100,000 citizens per year. States that did not link guidelines to resources experienced an increase of 14 inmates per year per 100,000 citizens (Nicholson-Crotty 2004).

Minnesota provides a good example of presumptive sentencing guidelines and can be used to explain how they are used by judges. For example, looking at the grid in Figure 4.4 consider a robbery involving two offenders with similar criminal histories: If offender "A" (the leader/instigator) had a criminal history score of 2 and was convicted of aggravated robbery, he could receive a sentence of between 58 and 81 months in prison. The accomplice, offender "B" with a criminal history score of 2, is convicted of simple robbery because she had a minor role

IV. SENTENCING GUIDELINES GRID

Presumptive Sentence Lengths in Months

Italicized numbers within the grid denote the range within which a judge may sentence without the sentence being deemed a departure. Offenders with non-imprisonment felony sentences are subject to jail time according to law.

SEVERITY LEVEL OF CONVICTION OFFENSE (Common offenses listed in italics)		CRIMINAL HISTORY SCORE						
		0	1	2	3	4	5	6 or more
Murder, 2nd Degree (intentional murder; drive-by-shootings)	XI	306￼ *261–367*	326￼ *278–391*	346￼ *295–415*	366￼ *312–439*	386￼ *329–463*	406￼ *346–480[2]*	426￼ *363–480[2]*
Murder, 3rd Degree Murder, 2nd Degree (unintentional murder)	X	150￼ *128–180*	165￼ *141–198*	180￼ *153–216*	195￼ *166–234*	210￼ *179–252*	225￼ *192–270*	240￼ *204–288*
Assault, 1st Degree Controlled Substance Crime, 1st Degree	IX	86￼ *74–103*	98￼ *84–117*	110￼ *94–132*	122￼ *104–146*	134￼ *114–160*	146￼ *125–175*	158￼ *135–189*
Aggravated Robbery, 1st Degree Controlled Substance Crime, 2nd Degree	VIII	48￼ *41–57*	58￼ *50–69*	68￼ *58–81*	78￼ *67–93*	88￼ *75–105*	98￼ *84–117*	108￼ *92–129*
Felony DWI	VII	36	42	48	54￼ *46–64*	60￼ *51–72*	66￼ *57–79*	72￼ *62–84[2]*
Controlled Substance Crime, 3rd Degree	VI	21	27	33	39￼ *34–46*	45￼ *39–54*	51￼ *44–61*	57￼ *49–68*
Residential Burglary Simple Robbery	V	18	23	28	33￼ *29–39*	38￼ *33–45*	43￼ *37–51*	48￼ *41–57*
Nonresidential Burglary	IV	12[1]	15	18	21	24￼ *21–28*	27￼ *23–32*	30￼ *26–36*
Theft Crimes (Over $5,000)	III	12[1]	13	15	17	19￼ *17–22*	21￼ *18–25*	23￼ *20–27*
Theft Crimes ($5,000 or less) Check Forgery ($251–$2,500)	II	12[1]	12[1]	13	15	17	19	21￼ *18–25*
Sale of Simulated Controlled Substance	I	12[1]	12[1]	12[1]	13	15	17	19￼ *17–22*

Presumptive commitment to state imprisonment. First-degree murder has a mandatory life sentence and is excluded from the guidelines by law. See Guidelines Section II.E., Mandatory Sentences, for policy regarding those sentences controlled by law.

Presumptive stayed sentence; at the discretion of the judge, up to a year in jail and/or other non-jail sanctions can be imposed as conditions of probation. However, certain offenses in this section of the grid always carry a presumptive commitment to state prison. See, Guidelines Sections II.C. Presumptive Sentence and II.E. Mandatory Sentences.

[1] One year and one day

[2] M.S. § 244.09 requires the Sentencing Guidelines to provide a range for sentences which are presumptive commitment to state imprisonment of 15% lower and 20% higher than the fixed duration displayed, provided that the minimum sentence is not less than one year and one day and the maximum sentence is not more than the statutory maximum. See, Guidelines Sections II.H. Presumptive Sentence Durations that Exceed the Statutory Maximum Sentence and II.I. Sentence Ranges for Presumptive Commitment Offenses in Shaded Areas of Grids.

Effective August 1, 2010

FIGURE 4.4 **Minnesota Sentencing Guidelines Grid: Presumptive Sentence Lengths in Months.**
Source: "Sentencing Guidelines Grid/State of Minnesota" www.msgic.state.mn.us/guidelines/grids/grid_2010.pdf.

> *proponents of general incapacitation believe that an increase in the use of prison will lead to a decrease in crime rates*

of driving the getaway car; she could receive a sentence of 28 months probation.

Guidelines in other states vary with respect to the offense severity ranking and also the way the criminal history score is calculated. There are also different regulations that govern the circumstances in which a judge may depart from the guideline ranges.

Mandatory Sentencing

The possibility of a judge imposing probation or some other form of community-based sentence rather than prison time did not always agree with "get tough on crime" supporters, who often criticized judges' decisions to impose a nonprison sentence on offenders who were viewed as deserving or needing prison. Complaints were especially forceful in indeterminate sentencing states because those judges had the most discretion. Lawmakers responded by passing legislation to make a prison sentence mandatory for some crimes and offenders.

The theory behind **mandatory sentencing** is crime prevention through the use of general incapacitation and "just deserts" sentencing. According to Alarid (2004), proponents of general incapacitation believe that an increase in the use of prison will lead to a decrease in crime rates. All states and the District of Columbia presently employ some version of mandatory sentencing laws. Mandatory sentencing is most commonly used for repeat or habitual offenders (40 states), crimes committed using a deadly weapon (38 states and the District of Columbia), drug possession/trafficking (36 states and the District of Columbia), and, in 31 states, drunk driving (Bureau of Justice Assistance 1998).

Two specific sentencing practices that are linked to mandatory sentencing are truth-in-sentencing and

"three strikes and you're out" laws. **Truth-in-sentencing** (TIS) guarantees how long an incarcerated offender will spend in prison, but because of plea bargaining, truth-in-sentencing *does not guarantee that a person will go to prison in the first place*. The U.S. Congress came to the states' assistance in 1994 by authorizing funding to construct or renovate state prisons and jails so that more violent prisoners could be confined for a greater percentage of their sentence. To receive the early Violent Offender Incarceration and Truth-in-Sentencing Incentive (VOI/TIS) grants, states had to guarantee that within three years of accepting the money, persons convicted of *Uniform Crime Report Part I* violent crimes (that is, homicide, aggravated assault, forcible rape, or armed robbery) would serve no less than 85 percent of the prison sentence (Ditton & Wilson 1999). Two years later, the federal government relaxed its rules, allowing states with indeterminate sentencing structures to apply for federal aid and not holding states to the initial 85 percent requirement. Only nine states introduced new laws and eleven made small modifications as a result of the federal money. Twenty-one states had already enacted mandatory minimum-type laws. There were an additional nine states that chose against enacting any TIS laws (Rosich & Kane 2005).

In addition to the goal of attaining a closer match between sentence given and time served, TIS laws allowed states to forecast the effect of sentencing policies on the numbers of people incarcerated. Although a handful of states has successfully developed sentencing guidelines while keeping space allocation in mind, many states may have adopted TIS policies that created state fiscal problems because they have no "overcrowding release valve," such as good time or early release, to account for the new prison admissions that may enter faster than the number of available beds. One unique response to such fiscal problems is reflected in Missouri's policy of informing

GLOSSARY

sentencing guidelines Impose a predefined sentence length based on crime severity and prior criminal history, with the opportunity for the judge to depart from the guidelines when circumstances warrant.

voluntary sentencing guidelines Suggested, rather than required, guidelines that stipulate a time range for a judge to use when deciding a sentence.

presumptive sentencing guidelines Required, rather than suggested, guidelines for a judge to use when deciding a sentence.

mandatory sentencing Requires a prison sentence for some crimes and some offenders.

truth-in-sentencing When the length of time served in a sentence is close to the time imposed by the courts.

three strikes and you're out Laws that authorize, or mandate in some cases, longer periods of incarceration after a certain number of prior convictions ("strikes").

aggravating circumstances An event or condition that makes an offense more serious than it might otherwise be.

mitigating circumstances An event or condition that makes an offense less serious than it might otherwise be.

Truth-in-Sentencing
This guarantees that offenders who receive a prison sentence will serve at least 85% of that sentence.

Three Strikes and You're Out
These laws authorize or mandate longer periods of incarceration for persons convicted of subsequent crimes.

Mandatory Sentencing
This makes a prison sentence mandatory for some crimes and for some offenders. It is the result of such practices as truth-in-sentencing and three strikes laws.

FIGURE 4.5 Examples of Mandatory Sentencing.

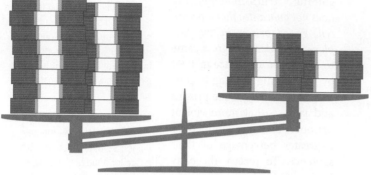

Using cost of punishment is an irrelevant consideration when deciding a criminal's fate, and there is a risk of overlooking the larger social costs of crime.

Using cost when deciding on punishment is an overdue tool that will force judges to ponder alternatives to prison more seriously.

FIGURE 4.6 **Considering Cost When Deciding Punishment.** Under Missouri's sentencing procedure a judge can learn that it could cost $37,000 to impose a prison sentence on someone convicted of endangering the welfare of a child whereas probation would cost $6,770. A second-degree robber, the judge might be told, would carry a price tag of less than $9,000 for five years of intensive probation, but more than $50,000 for a comparable prison sentence and parole afterward (Davey 2010).

DISCUSS *Defense lawyers and fiscal conservatives lean toward the "overdue tool" position, whereas prosecutors are more likely to support the "cost is irrelevant" side. Which do you believe is the stronger argument?*

judges about the cost of a particular punishment. The idea is to encourage judges to consider punishments that are less costly than imprisonment.

A second practice linked to mandatory sentencing is popularly known as **three strikes and you're out** legislation. The first "three strikes" law was passed in Washington State (1993), then a few months later in California (1994). Currently, 25 states have enacted laws specifically addressing repeat and habitual offenders, 11 of which impose mandatory life without parole. The "three strikes and you're out" moniker is more a catchy phrase than a helpful descriptor because the states vary widely on its meaning (in some states, two strikes are sufficient for a longer prison sentence) and implementation. Despite the differences, all three-strikes laws authorize, or in some cases mandate, longer periods of incarceration for violent felonies such as murder, rape, robbery, arson, aggravated assault, and carjacking (Clark, Austin, and Henry 1997). Less common are longer prison sentences for

reducing judicial discretion is a way the legislature can have greater impact on sentencing and presumably assure its constituents that stiff penalties will be imposed when necessary.

drug sales (for example, California, Indiana, and Louisiana), escape (Florida), treason (Washington), and embezzlement and bribery (South Carolina).

Eleven of the twenty-five states that follow three-strikes legislation do not allow parole, and three states allow for parole only after a minimum amount of time is served, varying from 40 years in Colorado down to 25 years in California. All but one of the states (Kansas) had preexisting laws that targeted repeat violent offenders, so the breadth of those preexisting statutes will to a large extent determine the impact of the new laws in each state. All of the statutes either increased the period of incarceration for violent crime, expanded the number of crimes that are included in the violent crime category, or both (Clark, Austin, & Henry 1997).

California's three-strike laws are the most inclusive, so the effect is dramatic in terms of prison admissions and cost. About 10,000 offenders each year are admitted to the California Department of Corrections (CDC) under three-strikes legislation (Caulkins 2001). In six of seven objective research studies evaluating California's three-strikes law, the research has shown that three strikes has had a minimal deterrent impact on reducing rape, robbery, assault, burglary, larceny, auto theft, and petty theft. One national study found that three strikes increased the homicide rate (Kovandzic, Sloan, & Vieraitis 2004). Only one study found a deterrent effect (Shepherd 2002).

Aggravating and Mitigating Circumstances

A goal of sentencing guidelines and mandatory sentencing is to reduce the discretion of judges. That is partly an attempt to achieve fairness in sentences given to different offenders convicted of similar crimes, and in sentences given by different judges throughout a jurisdiction. In addition, reducing judicial discretion is a way the legislature can have greater impact on sentencing and presumably assure its constituents that stiff penalties will be imposed when necessary. But in most jurisdictions the judges still have some discretion available since they are often allowed to take aggravating and mitigating circumstances into consideration.

Legislatures have realized that they cannot anticipate all the different aspects of a particular case. Deciding that all convictions of robbery with a weapon will require a prison term of eight years may sound reasonable as a general principle. But what happens when the convicted robber not only carried a weapon but also repeatedly kicked the victim while the victim was lying face down on the sidewalk? Is the mandatory eight-year sentence harsh enough for this case? On the other hand, what if the convicted robber had no prior criminal record and engaged in this crime only at the urging of his older brother, who has two

DISCUSS *Should mitigating and aggravating circumstances be used for all types of crimes and criminals? For example, should sentencing in death penalty cases be influenced by mitigating and aggravating circumstances? For what other types of crimes or criminals might the use of mitigating and aggravating circumstances be controversial? (See Figure 4.7.)*

TABLE 4.2   Pros and Cons of Three-Strikes Legislation.

Pros	Cons
One of the fundamental principles of criminal justice is that the punishment should fit the crime. That principle is abandoned when a life sentence is automatically imposed for a third felony—whether that felony is serious and violent, or minor and nonviolent. Because there is only one sentence possible for many kinds of crimes, it follows that the sentence does not necessarily correspond to the seriousness of the offense.	It is a primary obligation of the criminal justice system to establish clear and certain penalties for crime. The three-strikes laws offer such clarity, and their mandatory nature makes punishment certain. These laws prevent inconsistency in the criminal justice system.
It often happens that the third felony—that is, the one that triggers the automatic sentence—is relatively minor. For example, a life sentence has been imposed on someone for the attempted shoplifting of videotapes. A life sentence for such a crime is "cruel and unusual," and, as such, is forbidden by the Eighth Amendment to the U.S. Constitution.	Historically, judges have abused the discretion that they have been given by the criminal justice system. Too often, judges have imposed light sentences on criminals, even when those criminals have been repeat offenders. The mandatory sentences imposed by three-strikes laws ensure that recidivists (repeat offenders) are punished appropriately.
Historically, judges have had discretionary powers when sentencing criminals; this practice recognizes that sentencing should take into account the circumstances of the crime, the character of the criminal, and the amount of harm caused by the crime. Mandatory sentences rob judges of those discretionary powers that are properly theirs. Indeed, mandatory sentences are imposed, in effect, by the politicians of the legislative branch of government—thus violating the independence of the judiciary and the separation of powers outlined in the Constitution.	The fundamental purpose of the criminal justice system is to protect the rights and the safety of law-abiding citizens. But these citizens are not protected by "revolving door justice," which allows criminals back on the street after repeat offenses. Three-strikes laws remove repeat offenders from society, and prevent them from committing further crimes.
Defenders of the three-strikes laws claim that these laws have a powerful deterrent effect, and reduce the occurrence of crime. Statistics show, however, that recidivism has not been reduced by the presence of such laws, and the general reduction in crime, when and where it has occurred, is due to effective policing, rather than to harsh sentencing.	Since three-strikes laws have been introduced across the nation, crime has dropped dramatically. The reason for this decline is obvious: Convicted recidivists are not free to commit more crimes, and felons with one or two strikes on their records are deterred by the punishment that they know will follow a third offense.
The three-strikes laws are, in effect, *ex post facto* laws: That is, criminal sentences can take into account—as first and second strikes—crimes that were committed before the law was passed. Moreover, the imposition of mandatory maximum sentences because of past history constitutes "double jeopardy": Criminals are being punished again for crimes for which they already served time.	Opponents of three-strikes laws claim that these laws give criminals no chance to rehabilitate and redeem themselves. But studies have shown that rehabilitation is highly unlikely for recidivists. Someone who has committed three felonies is not likely to reform; rather, it is the destiny of the recidivist to keep committing crimes.
One effect of mandatory sentencing, and of three-strikes laws in particular, is the rapid growth of the prison population. The United States now locks up a higher proportion of its population than any comparable developed nation, yet many of those imprisoned for a great many years are nonviolent offenders convicted of relatively minor drug offenses or shoplifting. All of this comes at a very high cost to the taxpayer and is rapidly becoming unaffordable in a period of economic hardship. It is also notable that prison guard unions have spent heavily in favor of such mandatory sentencing, which favors the narrow economic interest of their members rather than the society they are meant to serve.	The growth of the prison population has occurred alongside the decline in the crime rate; the two are clearly linked. Because those imprisoned under three-strikes laws are habitual criminals, the extra cost of holding them in prison has to balance against the economic savings to society from fewer robberies, burglaries, vandalism, violent crime (resulting in expensive hospital treatment), drug addicts, and so forth.

Source: "Pros and Cons of Three Strikes Legislation" in THREE STRIKES by W. J. Driscoll. Copyright © 2009 by International Debate Education Association. Reprinted by permission. www.idebate.org/debatabase/topic_details.php?topicID+93.

prior robbery convictions? Should the younger brother receive the same eight-year sentence as his older brother?

Because some cases are more serious or less serious than the standard incident, legislatures often allow judges to vary from the determinate or presumptive sentence when either aggravating or mitigating circumstances are present. **Aggravating circumstances** refer to situations that require a tougher sentence, whereas

mitigating circumstances are situations requiring a lighter sentence. Similarly, under sentencing guidelines the judge is often allowed to impose a sentence outside the guidelines if circumstances of the case warrant such departure. When aggravating or mitigating circumstances lead a judge's sentence to depart from the determinate or guideline sentence, many jurisdictions require the judge to provide written justification for the deviation.

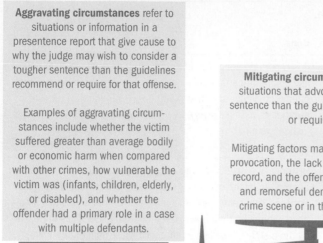

Aggravating circumstances refer to situations or information in a presentence report that give cause to why the judge may wish to consider a tougher sentence than the guidelines recommend or require for that offense.

Examples of aggravating circumstances include whether the victim suffered greater than average bodily or economic harm when compared with other crimes, how vulnerable the victim was (infants, children, elderly, or disabled), and whether the offender had a primary role in a case with multiple defendants.

Mitigating circumstances are situations that advocate a lighter sentence than the guidelines suggest or require.

Mitigating factors may involve victim provocation, the lack of a prior arrest record, and the offender's prosocial and remorseful demeanor at the crime scene or in the courtroom.

FIGURE 4.7 How Aggravating or Mitigating Circumstances Affect a Sentence.

▶ *Reducing Sentence Time*

Practices such as sentencing guidelines, truth-in-sentencing, three strikes, and aggravating circumstances have resulted in crowded prisons in many jurisdictions. As a counterbalance to those population-increasing factors, most states use little "tricks of the trade" to help make sure there is room for newly sentenced prisoners.

Pretrial Jail Time

Pretrial detainees may receive credit off their sentence for time served before their conviction. For defendants pleading not guilty to the charges brought against them, the Speedy Trial Act of 1974 requires the federal government to hold a trial within 100 days of the arrest. State jurisdictions have restrictions ranging from those such as Minnesota's 60 days from the date a trial is demanded by the defendant to Massachusetts's 12 months between arrest and trial. The most frequent time limit is six months, either from arrest to trial or indictment to trial (cf. Zawitz 1988).

Six months may seem a long time to wait for a trial, but the actual time is often even longer.

190 In 1994, the average time between arrest and sentencing was 190 days for defendants pleading guilty and 269 days for defendants going to trial

Speedy trial limits can be ignored in certain situations, such as when the delay is caused by requests from the defense. In 1994, the average time between arrest and sentencing was 190 days for defendants pleading guilty and 269 days for defendants going to trial (Maguire & Pastore 1998). After conviction, felony prisoners may also spend time in a county jail waiting to be transferred to prison. Most states have decided that all or some of this **pretrial jail time**—either pretrial or after conviction—should be counted toward their sentence. In other states the offender does not receive credit for that jail time.

Good Time

The concept of **good time** refers to a reduction of days from a sentence as a result of statutory provisions, the offender's good behavior, or extra work done by the offender. Good time typically falls into three categories: statutory good time, earned good time, and meritorious good time. **Statutory good time** is usually given automatically when inmates serve their time as a prison management tool to relieve overcrowding. Although good-time deductions were originally given only after a period of good behavior, many states automatically deduct the good time the day the offender arrives at prison (Davis 1990). Some states have fluctuating good-time days that depend solely on how full the county jails and prisons become—once facilities become crowded, prisoners earn more good-time days until the prison population decreases.

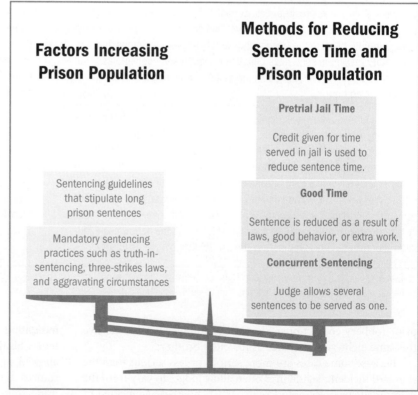

Factors Increasing Prison Population

Sentencing guidelines that stipulate long prison sentences

Mandatory sentencing practices such as truth-in-sentencing, three-strikes laws, and aggravating circumstances

Methods for Reducing Sentence Time and Prison Population

Pretrial Jail Time

Credit given for time served in jail is used to reduce sentence time.

Good Time

Sentence is reduced as a result of laws, good behavior, or extra work.

Concurrent Sentencing

Judge allows several sentences to be served as one.

FIGURE 4.8 **Reducing Sentence Time.** With the aid of jail time, good time, and concurrent sentencing, justice officials can reflect a just deserts response to criminals (lock 'em up) while still allowing the system to operate (let 'em out) in a reasonably efficient manner.

Earned good time is when inmates receive good-time credit as the result of good behavior or through participation in work or education programs. Earned time is a prison management tool to encourage compliance with institutional rules and to keep prisoners occupied. For example, prisoners from the District of Columbia are able to earn "educational good-time credits" of up to five days per month (for a maximum of 150 days) if they complete an approved educational program while in custody. When inmates misbehave, the good-time days may be withheld for that month and for future months.

Jurisdictions vary as to whether good time, once earned, can be taken away. Wisconsin has "bad time," which allows the adding of time to the mandatory release date (Bureau of Justice Assistance 1998). The prisoner's release date is figured from the actual sentence less the good time earned. In this way, prisoners are also encouraged to remain free of prison violations and may have the opportunity to decrease their sentence length through good-time deductions or credits.

A few states reward **meritorious good time** to inmates who perform exceptional acts or services such as firefighting or working in emergency conditions (Davis 1990). For example, whereas qualified California inmates in any of the state's facilities and programs might potentially perform a heroic act suitable for a meritorious time reduction, those assigned to the Conservation Camp program have increased opportunities to be heroic. The men and women in that program live and work in some of the state's most secluded wilderness areas and provide a large force of trained crews for wild land firefighting and other natural disasters, and for search and rescue missions.

LEARNING OUTCOMES 4 List and describe three techniques used to reduce the length of a sentence.

GLOSSARY

pretrial jail time Time spent in jail, either pretrial or after conviction, that could be counted toward a convicted offender's sentence.

good time Reduction of days from a sentence as a result of statutory provisions, the offender's good behavior, or extra work done by the offender.

statutory good time Reduction of days from a sentence usually given automatically as a prison management tool to relieve overcrowding.

earned good time Good-time credits resulting from good behavior or through participation in work or education programs.

meritorious good time Good-time credits given to inmates who perform exceptional acts or services such as firefighting or working in emergency conditions.

concurrent sentencing Allows an offender convicted of multiple offenses to serve those offenses at the same time.

FIGURE 4.9 **Meritorious Good Time.** The California Department of Forestry has handpicked inmate crews that receive meritorious good time for their work. Shown here are rescue workers searching in the aftermath of a mudslide in the San Bernardino Mountains.
Source: ROBYN BECK/AFP/GETTY IMAGES/Newscom

sentencing works: If Anna is convicted of trespassing (one year), burglary (four years), and theft (two years), she serves only a total of four years on a concurrent sentence for all three crimes because the time clock starts simultaneously. Anna will still have three convictions on her record, but her time is increased dramatically if the judge decides to make her sentence *consecutive*, where she must serve each sentence one at a time for each offense. In this case, Anna would have to serve up to seven years in prison.

Jail time, good time, and concurrent sentencing give legislators, judges, and prison officials ways to help control the number of inmates in prison. Furthermore, especially in the case of good time, control can also be exerted over the inmates' behavior while in prison. All of these techniques have been around for decades, but they have become especially helpful under determinate and presumptive sentencing.

Concurrent Sentencing

Both jail time and good time are techniques that effectively reduce the time offenders must serve on their sentences. A third way to reduce sentence time is through **concurrent sentencing**, which allows offenders convicted of multiple offenses to serve those offenses at the same time. Here is the way that concurrent

Jail time, good time, and concurrent sentencing give legislators, judges, and prison officials ways to help control the number of inmates in prison.

▶ Evidence-Based Sentencing

Sentencing policies beginning in the 1970s relied on incapacitation as the primary punishment philosophy and those policies resulted in overcrowded prisons and skyrocketing corrections costs—second only to growth in state expenditures for Medicaid (Casey 2010; Warren 2007). Criminal justice practitioners, legislators, and the general public are becoming increasingly dissatisfied with the burgeoning prison populations and their accompanying costs to state budgets. The overreliance on incarceration is increasingly viewed as having limited and diminishing effectiveness as a crime-control strategy. An especially promising response is the increased reliance on evidence-based sentencing (EBS).

Evidence-based practices in corrections are those practices that have been proven through scientific research to reduce offender recidivism (Warren 2007, 26). **Evidence-based sentencing**, then, involves the use of scientific research to improve the quality of judicial decision making when determining sentences and sentencing conditions (cf. Redding 2009). In the past, judges relied on gut instinct, experience, or guidelines set by legislators when deciding an offender's sentence. Redding argues that instead of those unscientific measures, judges should be selecting the sentencing options that will best reduce recidivism through deterrence, incapacitation, or rehabilitation. Doing so makes sentencing a scientific question rather than one based on instinct, experience, or legislative mandate.

Drawing on the results of evidence-based practices, we can identify some specific measures the judge should follow during the sentencing process (Warren 2007):

- The judge, like the probation officer, should act as a change agent to reinforce the importance of the offender's voluntary compliance, not merely to enforce compliance.

- Judges have the opportunity to maximize the positive effect and minimize any negative effect of court processes by the way they interact with people coming before them.

- The more offenders feel they have been treated fairly, the more likely they will be to obey the law in the future.

- To achieve multiple sentencing objectives (for example, deterrence, rehabilitation, restoration), effective treatment programs must be successfully integrated with other sentencing requirements.

Evidence-based sentencing is seen as a means to smarter and more individualized sentencing and corrections policies that allow targeting of individual offenders who should be imprisoned and those who are appropriate candidates for effective treatment, intermediate sanctions, or community

WHAT WE KNOW

Evidence-based practices research has provided important information that can help judges make sentencing decisions. The following conclusions can be drawn from that research and sentences based on the findings can reduce recidivism of felony offenders and, as a result, represent significant savings in corrections costs and the avoidance of future crime (Casey 2010; Warren 2009):

- Effective recidivism-reduction programs must target moderate- and high-risk offenders. Offenders in these risk categories have reduced recidivism when correctional interventions are provided with appropriate supervision and treatment services.

- Low-risk offenders need less supervision and fewer services. Placing low-risk offenders in structured treatment and supervision programs with higher-risk offenders may actually increase recidivism among the low-risk offenders.

- Cognitive-behavioral programs that are rooted in social learning theory and address offender attitudes and thought processes are the most effective in reducing recidivism. Examples of such programs include Moral Reconation Therapy and Thinking for a Change (Milkman & Wanberg 2007, 41–47).

- Positive reinforcement is more effective than negative sanctions. Offenders respond better, and maintain newly learned behaviors longer, when approached with "carrots" rather than "sticks," rewards rather than punishments. Research indicates that a ratio of four positive reinforcements to every negative reinforcement is effective in changing offender behavior (Crime and Justice Institute 2004).

- Sentencing to some programs should be avoided. For example, adult boot camps, wilderness programs, domestic violence education, and life skills education typically do not reduce recidivism. Some programs, such "scared straight," actually increase recidivism. Ineffective programs tend not to be sufficiently individualized and are often based on inappropriate or unproven treatment approaches or are improperly implemented (National Center for State Courts 2009; Redding 2009, fn. 26).

LEARNING OUTCOMES 5 Give examples of specific measures that evidence-based sentencing suggests judges should follow during the sentencing process.

GLOSSARY

evidence-based sentencing Involves the use of scientific research to improve the quality of judicial decision making when determining sentences and sentencing conditions.

corrections programs (Warren 2007). Increasingly, states are incorporating evidence-based practices into their probation and community corrections systems as a way to determine appropriate supervision and recidivism-reduction strategies. Such state courts as those in Arizona, California, Idaho, Iowa, Texas, and Wisconsin are using or exploring how to use evidence-based practices to increase the effectiveness of their sentences (Casey 2010).

▶ Unjust Justice

As Dr. Martin Luther King, Jr., observed in his oft-quoted phrase, "Injustice anywhere is a threat to justice everywhere." Unfortunately, examples of injustice can be found in both the factors used when determining a sentence and in the wrongful conviction of innocent people. This first of these injustices involves sentencing disparity; that difference in sentencing may be attributed to extra-legal factors such as gender and race or ethnicity, rather than by the appropriate factors such as offense severity and prior criminal record.

the drug war may have affected female offenders more than male offenders.

Sentencing Disparity

Today's sentencing policies do not openly target any specific groups of people, but many changes in sentencing policy have increased the disproportionality of Latinos, Native Americans, and African-Americans who are sentenced to prison throughout the country. This disproportionate representation in prison is an example of **sentencing disparity**. For example, enhanced penalty or mandatory drug laws for drug possession or distribution in public housing is more likely to target poor people living in those communities, a disproportionate number who also happen to be Latino or African-American. Furthermore, police and prosecutors pursue violent crimes and nonviolent property and drug crimes more fervently than white-collar crimes. If actions are taken against white-collar offenders, most cases are pursued in civil rather than criminal court.

Although many state sentencing guidelines have been shown to decrease racial disparity effectively, disparity has not been eradicated. The American Bar Association Justice Kennedy Commission report (2004b) perhaps said it best:

What proponents of determinate sentencing did not fully realize was that the elimination of judicial discretion at the sentencing stage would not eliminate disparities as long as police and prosecutors continued to exercise discretion at the arrest, charging, and plea bargaining stages of the process. (p. 17)

Sentencing disparity is also found when gender is considered. Past beliefs about women criminals were that they were more amenable to rehabilitation than men but also seemed to have more problems than men, thus women should actually spend *more* time in prison for the same crime. Following the 1970s, statutes that provided harsher maximum sentences for women than for men were consistently overturned by the courts, and today those kind of disparate sentencing laws no longer exist. Today's sentencing policies might still be affecting women differently than they do men—even though no gender-based differences are explicitly identified in the statutes.

Consider for a moment that the drug war may have affected female offenders more than male offenders. There are several reasons for this.

FIGURE 4.10 The Fair Sentencing Act of 2010. In August 2010, President Obama signed legislation that reduced, but did not eliminate, longstanding federal sentencing disparities between those caught with crack and those arrested with powder cocaine. Under the old law, a person caught with five grams of crack received a mandatory sentence of five years in prison, while a person caught with powder cocaine had to have 500 grams to merit the same term. The new law reduces the 100-to-1 disparity to 18-to-1. A crack defendant would have to have 28 grams to trigger the five-year mandatory minimum sentence, or roughly the amount that authorities presume would indicate a dealer rather than a casual user.
Source: Owen/Owen/Black Star/Newscom

First, women's drug use is more likely linked to their criminal behavior. Research shows a more consistent and significant link between drug use and female offenders than drug use and male offenders at time of arrest (Merlo 1995; Pollock 1999). A similar profile is found for women in prison, particularly for the disproportionate number of African-American and Hispanic women sentenced to prison for a drug offense. Reports on drug use history find that female prisoners used more drugs than did male prisoners (Greenfeld & Snell 1999). If female offenders are more likely to have drugs linked to their criminal behavior, sentencing policies that inadvertently incarcerate small-time drug users and dealers are more likely to affect women (Mauer, Potler, & Wolf 1999).

In mixed-gender crime partnerships, men offenders tend to operate in higher positions and in more primary criminal roles than women (Alarid, Burton, Cullen, Marquart, & Cuvelier 1996). This line of reasoning should not be confused with leniency, only to suggest that women may receive less time than men because they play a secondary role in the same criminal incident and are sentenced accordingly. Roles played in crime may not be available to sentencing researchers who are merely examining time served for various types of crime.

The courts are interested in maintaining the family unit and not punishing dependents for the actions of one offender. In larger society, women tend to be the primary caretakers of dependent children, in terms of spending more time caring for children and being involved in domestic duties. Daly called this "familial paternalism" in which the identified primary caretaker may receive a more lenient sentence (particularly in state courts) than an offender without family or dependents. So in some courts, being a caretaker of dependent children, and assuming that the crime was not related to parental ability, judges may give leniency for this reason. The federal courts eliminated the consideration of family at the time of sentencing, which has disadvantaged primary caretakers. However, the federal sentencing guidelines do allow a very small number of women to receive more lenient sentences as a result of their family responsibilities (Morash & Schram 2002).

Gender of the victim even makes a difference in the sentence lengths for homicide, robbery, and assault. For example, in Texas, while gender did not affect the incarceration decision, prison sentences were significantly longer for men who victimized women and when the victim suffered extensive injuries. Age and race/ethnicity had no effect on sentencing outcome or sentence length for these same crimes (Curry, Lee, & Rodriguez 2004).

Ironically, laws that were changed to protect racial minorities and women from disparity result in further oppressing them. Individuals have different situations and needs that must be considered at the time of sentencing; at the same time, it is important to establish equitable sentences between the sexes and among various racial and ethnic groups.

Defendant: Rapper Snoop Dogg
Crime: Felony possession of a dangerous weapon at an airport
Sentence: 160 hours of community service, three years' probation, $1,000 in fines and court costs, mandatory $10,000 donation to charity

Defendant: Actress Lindsay Lohan
Crime: Stealing a necklace from a jewelry store
Sentence: Probation with five weeks of home confinement followed by 480 hours of community service

Defendant: Financier Bernard Madoff
Crime: Fraud for giant Ponzi scheme, which judge called "extraordinarily evil"
Sentence: 150 years (thrice the length asked by the federal probation office)

FIGURE 4.11 **Sentencing Disparity and Celebrities.** In addition to sentencing disparity issues related to such extra-legal factors as race, ethnicity, and gender, an argument might be made that celebrities receive sentences that are both less and more harsh than is typical based, in part, on their celebrity status.
Sources: ROBYN BECK/AFP/Getty Images/Newscom; © Everett Collection Inc/Alamy; © Mikael Karlsson/Alamy

Wrongful Convictions

A second type of injustice is the wrongful conviction of an innocent person. Whether you agree with William Blackstone's ratio of "better that ten guilty persons escape than that one innocent suffer" or have some other proportion in mind, it is likely that you at least agree with the principle of punishing the guilty rather than the innocent.

Wrongful convictions can be the result of several types of missteps or misbehavior in the criminal justice system. The Center on Wrongful Convictions (www.law.northwestern.edu/wrongfulconvictions) lists erroneous eyewitness identification, false confessions, ineffective defense counsel, and police or prosecutorial misconduct as examples of such problems. Of those, erroneous eyewitness identification and false confessions are generally considered to account for the majority of wrongful convictions.

Erroneous eyewitness identification, whether offered in good faith or perjured, is the single greatest cause of wrongful convictions in the U.S. criminal justice system (Northwestern University School of Law 2010). Fortunately, this problem is receiving increased attention and police departments across the country are revising procedures in an attempt to lessen the likelihood of mistaken eyewitness identification.

A wrongful conviction based on a false confession may be even more difficult to understand than is erroneous eyewitness identification. The largest category of falsely confessing

> *Erroneous eyewitness identification, whether offered in good faith or perjured, is the single greatest cause of wrongful convictions in the U.S. criminal justice system*

suspects consists of the mentally impaired, the mentally ill, the young, and the easily led. It is not uncommon that a confession—later determined to have been false—may include a detailed and accurate account of what occurred. However, Garrett (2010) explains that such details may actually have been introduced, whether intentionally or not, by the police during interrogation.

Three decades of research has led psychologists to suggest the following steps as ways to lessen the likelihood of erroneous eyewitness identification during police lineups (Dittmann 2004).

- Select fillers to appear in lineups that fit a witness's description of the perpetrator.

- Instruct witnesses that the person who committed the crime may not be in the lineup.

- Do not say anything that may influence the witness's decision in identifying a person from the lineup, such as by providing any information about lineup members.

- Use a sequential method by presenting photographs one at a time to witnesses and having them make a decision about a photo before viewing the next.

- Record in writing both identification and nonidentification lineup results, including witnesses' statements—in their own words—about their identification certainty.

Steal Shoes, Get Life

California's three-strikes law is considered to be the country's harshest noncapital sentencing law. The law's main feature is the imposition of a life sentence for any felony conviction, no matter how minor, if the defendant has two prior serious felony convictions.

Because the third-strike offense can be any felony, including simple drug possession or petty theft, it is possible for nonviolent offenders to receive a life sentence. For example, within a few years of the law's passage, Vincent Rico was sentenced to life for the petty theft of two pairs of children's shoes from Ross Dress for Less and Alex Maese received a life sentence for possession of a cotton ball fragment containing 0.029 grams of heroin. In 2008, Maese had his sentence reduced to the 11 years he had already served, and in 2009 Rico's sentence was reduced and he too was released from prison. The sentence reductions were the result of efforts by students with the Stanford Three Strikes Project, which represents inmates sentenced to life for nonviolent crimes (www.law.stanford.edu/program/clinics/threestrikesproject/).

1. The sentence reductions for Rico and Maese were granted by California courts upon hearing new evidence gathered by the Stanford Three Strikes Project. Documentation was found showing Rico likely suffered from post-traumatic stress that resulted from being subjected to gang violence as a child and Maese suffered from combat-induced post-traumatic stress disorder resulting from his service in Vietnam. These conditions had not been presented during the original trials and were believed by the rehearing judges to present mitigating circumstances that would have likely resulted in non–life sentences. *Did these circumstances simply provide justifiable reasons for judges to correct what was excessive punishment?*

2. Nearly 4,000 California prisoners are serving life for a third strike that was neither violent nor serious, according to the legal definition. That is more than 40 percent of the total third-strike population of about 8,500 (Bazelon 2010). *Since the first two strikes had to be for serious felonies, does the seriousness of the third offense make any difference?*

3. One "three-striker" who has not received a reduced sentence is Gary Ewing. He was sentenced to life for shoplifting three golf clubs. Today he is blind, wheelchair-bound, and suffers from numerous medical ailments. After losing his eyesight following an unsuccessful medical procedure several years ago, Ewing fell out of bed (a top bunk—his request for a lower bunk had been denied) and complications from the fall prevent him from walking or standing for extended periods (Bierman & Dorenbaum 2010). *Since the three-strikes law is meant to protect the public from repeat offenders, should medical conditions arising while incarcerated be considered when deciding if a person should be released from a life sentence?*

Source: © Mikael Karlsson/Alamy

Identify the various types of sentences and explain the problems of comparing them in terms of severity.

Sentence types include ones as simple as fines and community service and as disruptive as jail and prison. Others, such as boot camps and halfway houses can be alternatives to prison, whereas additional ones are considered more community-based sanctions (for example, day reporting, regular and intensive supervision probation, and electronic monitoring). It is difficult to rank these sanctions by severity since the consequences of each are perceived differently depending on the individual.

1. Make an argument for one year on regular probation being a more severe punishment than three months in jail.

2. If you were a judge, what information would you want to have in a Presentence Investigation Report to help you decide an appropriate sentence?

3. How does regular probation differ from intensive supervision probation?

4. Could fines be made so punitive that the public would accept them as an alternative to probation or jail? What are some problems when using fines in that way?

sentencing When a court imposes a penalty on a person convicted of a crime.

presentence investigation report A report developed from information derived through a presentence investigation that is provided to the judge to assist in sentencing decisions.

presentence investigation An inquiry interview and data-collection method used by a probation officer to summarize information about a convicted offender.

Explain the two basic sentencing structures used in the United States.

The basic sentencing structures found in the United States are indeterminate and determinate sentencing. Under indeterminate sentencing, the judge can impose a range of years (for example, two to four years in prison), but determinate sentencing requires imposition of a specific penalty (for example, five years in prison).

1. Some of the strongest proponents of determinate sentencing are prisoners. Why?

2. State legislators set minimum and maximum penalties for crimes, but judges must determine particular sentences for individual offenders. Wouldn't it make more sense to allow judges complete authority to determine a sentence?

indeterminate sentencing A system wherein the convicted offender receives a sentence that covers a time range rather than a fixed period.

determinate sentencing A system wherein the convicted offender receives a sentence to a specific time period rather than a time range.

statutory penalties Sentences linked via legislation to specific crimes, or to specific classes of felonies or misdemeanors, with a minimum and maximum time period.

LEARNING OUTCOMES 3

List and explain three sentencing practices.

Three sentencing practices used today are sentencing guidelines, mandatory sentencing, and aggravating/mitigating circumstances. All of these can be used under either a determinate or indeterminate sentencing structure and each provides a way to modify that basic structure. For example, sentencing guidelines encourage or require a judge to impose a sentence within an established range. Mandatory sentencing—exemplified by three-strikes and truth-in-sentencing laws—requires prison sentences for some crimes and offenders. Aggravating and mitigating circumstances allow sentences to be increased or decreased due to particular circumstances.

1. What two factors are used in the Minnesota sentencing guidelines to calculate a sentence?

2. What could be some key issues raised by persons wanting to show that three-strikes laws violate either the Eighth or Tenth Amendments to the U.S. Constitution?

3. What are some pros and cons of three-strikes laws?

4. Why are truth-in-sentencing and three-strikes laws examples of mandatory sentencing?

5. What are some arguments for why judges should be allowed to take aggravating and mitigating circumstances into consideration when imposing a sentence? What are some arguments for why they should not?

sentencing guidelines Impose a predefined sentence length based on crime severity and prior criminal history, with the opportunity for the judge to depart from the guidelines when circumstances warrant.

voluntary sentencing guidelines Suggested, rather than required, guidelines that stipulate a time range for a judge to use when deciding a sentence.

presumptive sentencing guidelines Required, rather than suggested, guidelines for a judge to use when deciding a sentence.

mandatory sentencing Requires a prison sentence for some crimes and some offenders.

truth-in-sentencing When the length of time served in a sentence is close to the time imposed by the courts.

three strikes and you're out Laws that authorize, or mandate in some cases, longer periods of incarceration after a certain number of prior convictions ("strikes").

aggravating circumstances An event or condition that makes an offense more serious than it might otherwise be.

mitigating circumstances An event or condition that makes an offense less serious than it might otherwise be.

LEARNING OUTCOMES 4

List and describe three techniques used to reduce the length of a sentence.

Sentence length can be reduced by giving credit for time spent in jail while awaiting trial (pretrial jail time), for good behavior while in prison (good time), and serving multiple sentences all at the same time (concurrent sentencing).

1. What are some factors leading to the increase in prison populations?

2. How might correctional workers and administrators benefit from good-time credits being given to prisoners?

3. Should offenders be given time off their sentence for good behavior?

4. Is it fair to crime victims when offenders serve multiple sentences concurrently?

pretrial jail time Time spent in jail, either pretrial or after conviction, that could be counted toward a convicted offender's sentence.

good time Reduction of days from a sentence as a result of statutory provisions, the offender's good behavior, or extra work done by the offender.

statutory good time Reduction of days from a sentence usually given automatically as a prison management tool to relieve overcrowding.

earned good time Good-time credits resulting from good behavior or through participation in work or education programs.

meritorious good time Good-time credits given to inmates who perform exceptional acts or services such as firefighting or working in emergency conditions.

concurrent sentencing Allows an offender convicted of multiple offenses to serve those offenses at the same time.

LEARNING OUTCOMES 5

Give examples of specific measures that evidence-based sentencing suggests judges should follow during the sentencing process.

Findings from evidence-based practices suggest that during the sentencing process judges should act as a change agent, rather than merely enforcing compliance, to minimize any negative effect of the court process on the offender. Further, the judge should work to assure that offenders believe they have been treated fairly and should integrate effective treatment programs with other sentencing requirements.

1. What are some things a judge can do during the sentencing process to have a positive effect on the person being sentenced?

2. Why is recidivism increased among low-risk offenders when they are put in programs designed for moderate- and high-risk offenders?

3. Why are cognitive-behavioral programs especially effective in reducing recidivism?

4. Why do some people support the use of boot camps even if they cannot be shown to reduce recidivism?

evidence-based sentencing Involves the use of scientific research to improve the quality of judicial decision making when determining sentences and sentencing conditions.

LEARNING OUTCOMES 6

Describe two types of sentencing injustice.

Unjust sentencing is reflected in instances of sentencing disparity wherein members of minority groups are subject to harsher penalties, and in instances of wrongful convictions that result in innocent people being punished for crimes they did not commit.

1. What are some steps that can be taken to lessen the likelihood of erroneous or mistaken eyewitness identification during a police lineup?

2. Generally speaking, are celebrities treated differently at sentencing?

3. What would you consider to be just compensation for someone who was wrongfully convicted of a crime?

sentencing disparity A type of injustice wherein sentencing policy has the unintended effect of targeting a population group—often minority—and resulting in members of that group being disproportionately represented among persons in the correctional system.

wrongful convictions A type of injustice wherein a person is convicted and punished for a crime he or she did not commit.

MyCJLab

Go to the Chapter 4 section in *MyCJLab* to test your understanding of this chapter, access customized study content, engage in interactive simulations, complete critical thinking and research assignments, and view related online videos.

Additional Links

California is considered to have the toughest three-strikes legislation in the country. Read the basics of that law at **www.law.stanford.edu/program/clinics/threestrikesproject/#three_strikes_basics**.

The Pew Center works with states to achieve better returns on public safety investments. Visit **www.pewcenteronthestates.org/initiatives_detail.aspx?initiativeID=48884** and select one of the links to read state-specific examples of sentencing programs.

Visit **www.innocenceproject.org/** to read about an organization dedicated to assisting prisoners who could be proven innocent through DNA testing.

Community Supervision

"Few things help an individual more than
to place responsibility upon him, and to let
him know that you trust him."

—Booker T. Washington, Educator, 1856–1915

1 Explain the key ways in which community supervision is beneficial to the offender, the community, and the victim.

2 Describe how probation supervision works.

3 Identify the ways that court-ordered sanctions can be reparative to the victim and community.

4 List and summarize the community programs that address minimizing risk to public safety.

5 Describe the most typical community-based programs that address root causes of defendants' problems with crime.

5

Source: © Mikael Karlsson/Alamy

SHOULD OFFENDERS BE SUPERVISED ON PROBATION FOR CRIMES OF VIOLENCE?

Charles Clements, a 69-year-old retired bus driver and former Marine, was quite particular about his front lawn; so much so that he killed his neighbor over it. Joshua Funches, age 23 and father of two, was walking his fox terrier when the 5-month-old puppy urinated on Clements' lawn. Clements followed Funches home, and pulled out a .45 caliber pistol to confront his neighbor. Funches allegedly cursed Clements during the argument. Clements then shot

DISCUSS What are the ramifications of allowing Clements to remain on probation in his community? What possible difficulties or risks might exist? Should violent offenders be supervised on probation?

Funches once in the abdomen saying that he feared Funches would further harm him. Neighbors reported that Clements has always been concerned about disorder and has helped police with investigations, while other neighbors said that he previously threatened anyone who stepped on his lawn. Clements, who had no prior arrests, was sentenced in 2010 to four years' probation for second degree murder despite opposition by the victim's family (Rozek 2011).

▶ A Need for Community-Based Sentences

Nearly 70 percent of offenders (over 5 million) serve at least a portion of their correctional sentence through some form of community supervision and treatment. Of this number, 4.2 million are on **probation** (Glaze & Bonczar 2010). Community supervision is not only less expensive than jail or prison, but it also provides an opportunity for individuals to continue working or going to school while completing their court-ordered **standard conditions**. Probation forms the foundation of most community-based sentences and will be discussed in this chapter, along with additional penalties such as community service, fines, or restitution. These add-on conditions are based on each individual's life circumstances, the victim's needs, and the local community. While on probation, an offender most often lives at home, but can also serve a portion of his or her sentence in a residential community correctional facility, day reporting center, or drug therapy program. A probationer may be on house arrest or electronic monitoring. For this reason, probation is the most common community sentence.

The use of community sanctions is favored for women offenders because they are generally less likely to present a risk to the general public compared to men, and women offenders generally have less serious prior records. However, the vast majority of people on community

LEARNING OUTCOMES 1 Explain the key ways in which community supervision is beneficial to the offender, the community, and the victim.

GLOSSARY

probation The court-ordered community supervision of an offender by an officer who enforces conditions for a specified length of time.

standard conditions Commitments every probationer agrees to abide by in return for remaining at liberty in the community.

> *Nearly 70 percent of offenders (over 5 million) serve at least a portion of their correctional sentence through some form of community supervision and treatment.*

supervision are men, primarily because men are arrested for crimes far more often than women.

Various times when probation can be used are up to the judge, and may include during pretrial supervision, diversion/deferred adjudication, or following the sentencing of a convicted offender.

From Shoemaker to Third Party Surety

Boston shoemaker John Augustus devoted his life as a third-party surety in recognizance cases to provide aid and supervision to offenders released to his care. Augustus assured the court that the defendants would return for the sentencing hearings, in return for the court releasing the defendants to him instead of throwing them in jail. As a result of his devotion over ten years, Augustus is considered the first bail bondsman and the founder of American probation. Augustus was able to help defendants find homes, secure employment, ensure school attendance, and soothe family problems. Augustus claimed that only one person forfeited bond (Vanstone 2004). The biggest problem with simple recognizance or suspension of sentence was, at that time, the absence of any effective control over the offenders who were released to the community. So, various probation

> *As a result of his devotion over ten years, Augustus is considered the first bail bondsman and the founder of American probation.*

1000–1827	1275	1700s and 1800s	1700s	1700s
Benefit of clergy meant that ordained priests, monks, and nuns accused of violating common law had their cases transferred to the bishop's church court for leniency.	**Statute of Westminster** limited the offenses for which sheriffs could mandate bail (sheriffs had complete authority on the bail amounts and release decision).	A person who had pled or been found guilty and was waiting for a pardon from the Crown could receive a **Judicial reprieve** or temporary suspension of the prison sentence.	**Recognizance**—As an alternative to bail, defendant promises to appear in court at a specified time while the court allows the defendant to remain at liberty in the community.	**Surety**—Defendant's release is backed by a third party who is responsible for the defendant's next court appearance and has the duty to return the offender to court if a new offense is committed.

Source: From SUPERVISING OFFENDERS IN THE COMMUNITY by Maurice Vanstone. Copyright © 2004.

laws were enacted to make probation a permanent part of court proceedings.

As you learned about earlier, judges impose the actual length of a probation sentence, which is often less than statutory limits if the offender were sent to prison. Judges rely heavily on the defendant's prior record, along with other factors such as his or her risk to the community, demeanor and cooperativeness, and community ties when deciding whether probation is appropriate. Judges may further modify the length of probation after initial sentencing as the offender shows improvement or digresses. For example, the probationer is showing improvement but the probation officer wants to keep him or her on probation until a new treatment program is

65% About 65 percent of probationers complete supervision successfully

completed—some jurisdictions allow judges to extend the probation term before sentence expiration. About 65 percent of probationers complete supervision successfully and some may be discharged early and have their probation term reduced. An increase in these early discharges has recently contributed to a 0.9 percent decline in the probation population (Glaze & Bonczar 2010).

BENEFITS	PROBLEMS
• Offender continues to pay taxes, work, and/or go to school.	• Financial obligations and appointment responsibilities may be overwhelming for offenders to meet.
• The offender retains important family ties and continues to support dependent children.	• The arrangement intrudes on civil liberties of family members who are living in the same household as a person on correctional supervision.
• Offender is able to live at home.	• If family problems exist or if the family does not agree to have the offender live in the household, finding permanent housing is difficult.
• Offender avoids corrupting influences, stigmatizing effects, and physical and psychological damage that might accompany a stay in jail or prison.	• Public safety may be jeopardized by the presence of the offender in the community.
• There are cost savings to taxpayers over jail or prison.	• Net widening—Some offenders are in programs that are more restrictive than needed.
• There are more treatment options for offender rehabilitation than for jails and prisons.	• Transportation and child-care issues constantly hamper the offender's ability to meet treatment obligations.
• There is an increased chance that the offender will pay back restitution to victims, if any is owed.	• Victims may not receive restitution if the offender has too many other financial obligations.

FIGURE 5.1 Benefits and Problems of Community-Based Sanctions.

1830	1841–1859	1878	1891	1925	1956
Judge Oxenbridge Thacher first used **recognizance** in the Municipal Court of Boston. The practice, known as "release on recognizance" is still used today, but only before a guilty plea/verdict.	**John Augustus** helped men and women stay out of jail by providing surety bonds to the Boston court. His efforts inspired other volunteers and philanthropic organizations to help.	First probation law enacted by the Massachusetts legislature permitted hiring paid presentence investigation advisors to investigate cases and recommend probation, as appropriate, to the judge.	Massachusetts law mandated statewide salaried probation officers to supervise all offense levels.	Federal statute authorizing probation in federal courts was passed.	All states had enacted probation statutes for juveniles and adults.

Source: From SUPERVISING OFFENDERS IN THE COMMUNITY by Maurice Vanstone. Copyright © 2004.

20% National data indicate that nearly 20 percent of all offenders on probation have been convicted of a violent offense against a person, such as assault, domestic violence, sexual offense, or murder

Evidence-Based Principle #1: Assess Offender Risk and Needs

At the first meeting, offenders are typically assessed by a trained officer using a reliable and objective assessment instrument to identify the potential threats or problems that the offender may pose, along with the needs that might be addressed through treatment. Objective instruments that are typically used for community supervision are the Level of Service Inventory (LSI-R) and COMPAS.

Evidence-Based Principle #2: Use Motivational Interviewing Techniques

After the initial interview and screening, individuals on probation are assigned to a particular officer's **caseload** depending on the nature of the case and intensity of supervision required. Individuals requiring more individualized attention are assigned to an officer with a smaller caseload (between 25–50 offenders), whereas individuals requiring minimal supervision may be assigned to an officer with a caseload

of 200–300 people. Through **motivational interviewing**, each officer uses the risk/needs assessment score to devise an individualized case plan with the offender—one that the offender agrees to do.

National data indicate that nearly 20 percent of all offenders on probation have been convicted of a violent offense against a person, such as assault, domestic violence, sexual offense, or murder, as you read about at the beginning of the chapter (Glaze & Bonczar 2010). This surprises some people who think that offenders who have committed a violent act are in prison, while nonviolent offenders are on probation. It is also commonly assumed that offenders convicted of a violent crime automatically pose a greater risk than other types of offenders. This is also not true, as even various types of sex offenders pose different

LEARNING OUTCOMES 2 Describe how probation supervision works.

GLOSSARY

caseload The number of individuals that one probation officer can effectively supervise based on predefined risks and needs posed.

motivational interviewing A style of personal interaction between the officer and client that involves rapport, trust, and persuasion to help bring about positive behavior change.

legal violation When a probationer commits a new criminal act, and the original probation sentence can be revoked.

technical violation When a probationer repeatedly fails to abide by conditions of probation, and the probation sentence can be revoked.

special conditions Requirements in addition to the standard conditions, such as paying fines or undergoing electronic monitoring.

| **Pretrial Supervision**: When courts impose supervision *before* a guilty plea so that a defendant can better assist in case preparation, and the court is assured the defendant will appear. | **Diversion/Deferred Adjudication Probation**: When defendants enter into an agreement with the court to complete various conditions so that if successfully completed, the charges will be dismissed without a conviction. If a defendant on deferred adjudication is noncompliant or commits a new crime during supervision, the courts will sentence the offender and the defendant's conviction will be permanently on record. | **Misdemeanor/Felony Probation**: Community supervision of a convicted offender under court-imposed conditions for a length of time according to offense severity and completion of treatment or other court-ordered condition. | **Intensive Probation/ Specialized Caseload**: More frequent contact between a convicted offender and the supervision officer, along with greater restrictions (curfew, home visits) due to a special risk or specialized needs. |

FIGURE 5.2 Four Types of Probation Supervision.

Examples of Standard Probation Conditions from Various Jurisdictions

- Obey all local, state, and federal laws.
- Answer all reasonable inquiries by the probation officer, and follow officer directives.
- Remain within the jurisdiction (county or state) at all times. Leaving the jurisdiction requires permission in advance.
- Pay all probation supervision fees, fines, and restitution as ordered by the court. Complete any court-ordered community service.
- Refrain from possessing any firearms, or any other dangerous weapon without written permission from the court.
- Refrain from using or possessing controlled substances or dangerous drugs unless with a medical doctor's prescription. Refrain from alcohol use if under supervision for an alcohol-related offense.
- Submit to testing for controlled substances (and alcohol testing if under supervision for an alcohol-related offense).
- If there is a history of substance abuse, participate in a substance abuse evaluation and complete treatment as directed.
- Maintain suitable employment and/or educational/vocational training and notify third parties of your criminal record, as directed by the probation officer.
- Promptly inform the probation officer of any changes in residence, employment, educational status, or any contact with law enforcement.
- Allow the probation officer access to your home and workplace at reasonable times. Consent to the search of person, vehicle, or premises if the supervising officer has reasonable grounds to believe that evidence of a violation will be found.
- Support your dependents, including keeping current on any child support obligations.
- If under supervision for a sex offense, participate in an evaluation, submit to polygraph examinations, register with local law enforcement, and if directed, successfully complete an approved sex offender treatment program.

noncompliance was a more important predictor of probation failure than type of victim for aggressive offenders (Stalans, Yarnold, Seng, Olson & Repp 2004).

To carry out all the expectations of a community-based sentence, probation officers have multiple roles that in some ways conflict with each other. On one hand, they are expected to be a supportive confidante to turn to for advice or to help offenders obtain jobs, education, or re-apply for other government benefits for which they are eligible. On the other hand, the probation officer is the court's representative, charged with enforcing the conditions of the offender's sentence and with bringing violations of those conditions to the court's attention—thereby placing the offender at risk of losing his or her liberty. It is not easy to serve simultaneously as advisor and enforcer.

If an offender on community supervision commits a new crime, it is known as a **legal violation**. In this case, the local prosecutor has the authority to charge and prosecute the offender on that new crime but cannot order the offender's probation revoked. Prosecutors may be willing to avoid prosecution of the new crime in exchange for the offender having probation revoked and being sent to prison for the crime for which he or she was originally placed on probation.

If the probationer repeatedly fails to abide by any of the court-ordered standard (or special) conditions of probation, this is considered a **technical violation**, which is the more common of the two. Probation officers report the infractions to the court and recommend a course of action. The judge makes the final decision regarding the revocation, choosing to retain the original sentence with modifications, or revoke probation completely and incarcerate.

In addition to the standard conditions of probation, **special conditions** may be required by the court that repair the harm caused to the victim or the community. This may

levels of risk in the community (Hepburn & Griffin 2004). It is unfair therefore to assume that all sex offenders will recidivate. Offenders are too often defined solely by their offense rather than going deeper into other possible factors that may offer causation clues. For example, treatment

Think About It...

2% Only 2 percent of sex offenders on probation committed another sex offense while on probation (Hepburn & Griffin 2004). Sex offenders who were more likely to fail tended to be unmarried, unemployed, and had drug and alcohol problems. Would you advocate for probation for sex offenders based on this one study? Why or why not?

1. **Presentence investigator**: Interviews convicted felons and gathers information prior to court sentencing to determine the offender's suitability for probation.

2. **Caseworker**: Provides mentoring and advice to clients in areas such as time management, talking to other family members, and budgeting. Most prevalent in juvenile probation.

3. **Broker of Services**: Refers offenders to court-ordered services such as anger management, drug and alcohol treatment, and parenting classes.

4. **Surveillance**: Monitors the whereabouts of the probationer and ensures that the conditions of probation are being followed. In some jurisdictions, the officer carries a firearm.

FIGURE 5.3 Four Hats a Probation Officer Wears.

Services to Assist Offenders	Description
Navigating basic services offered by the government and nonprofit organizations	Offenders may need help applying for welfare, food stamps, or to make arrangements for emergency temporary housing and financial assistance for the purchase of necessities, such as food, clothing, medicine, and child care. In addition, referrals may be made for transportation to treatment facilities, medical visits, or other placement programs.
Employment assistance	Probation officers may refer offenders for testing and work skills evaluations, preemployment training, skill-development, or directly to certain employers or job placement agencies.
Literacy, education, and vocational training	Literacy, General Educational Development (GED), and vocational training programs are available, as is access to higher education institutions.
Diagnostic assessments	Assessments may be conducted by a licensed professional for substance abuse, mental health, and/or developmental disabilities. The assessment is followed by a prognosis report and treatment plan.
Detoxification	Probation officers may request inpatient and outpatient detoxification services. Such services may include, for example, a physical examination and report; medication, such as methadone, Antabuse®, or naltrexone hydrochloride; laboratory work; and a residential placement.
Substance abuse treatment	This includes substance abuse prevention and treatment readiness groups; individual, family, and group substance abuse counseling; intensive outpatient group or individual treatment; short-term residential treatment; longer-term placement in a therapeutic community setting; and methadone maintenance.

Source: Ekstrand, L. E. & Burton D. R. (2001). *Prisoner releases: Trends and information on reintegration programs.* GAO-01-483. Washington, DC: U.S. General Accounting Office, 40–41.

include community service, restitution, and payment of fines. Other special conditions may be related to reducing the risk to public safety through increased surveillance, such as community-based residential facilities, and electronic monitoring. A third reason for special conditions are specific to the offender's problems as related to his or her crime. These conditions require the offender to enroll and pay for mental health evaluations, counseling, substance abuse treatment, and parenting classes. All of these special conditions described next can be mandated for diversionary programs or for any community supervision program as add-ons to probation or graduated sanctions when the offender fails to comply with the original sentence.

▶ Special Conditions that are Reparative to the Victim or Community

Community Service

In its most general meaning, **community service** mandates that offenders labor in unpaid work for the general good of the community. As early as the seventeenth century, community work was used in Germany as a separate sentence and as the default for an unpaid fine (van Kalmthout & Tak 1988). However, it was not until 1966 in California that community service appeared in the United States as a sanction receiving serious attention for traffic offenders, misdemeanants, and juvenile delinquents.

Community service is underutilized in most jurisdictions, with judges requiring community service of about 25 percent of felons on probation (Bonczar 1997). Of the judges who order community service, offenders labor between 40 and 1,000 hours before their service is considered complete. The most common problem is failure to show up and failure to complete community service hours, both of which may constitute a technical violation of probation. Completion rates vary from 50 to 85 percent, depending on how well community service is enforced (Anderson 1998). Community service orders had no significant effect on recidivism, but the programs are cost-effective. If we consider minimum wage rates, offenders in Florida completed the equivalent to over $3.3 million in wages in a single year (Harris & Lo 2002).

Restitution

Compensating crime victims is one of the oldest principles of justice, dating back to the Old Testament and to ancient codes such as the Code of Hammurabi. In the mid-1800s in the United States, Quaker prison reformer Elizabeth Fry viewed repaying the victim as a step toward offender rehabilitation, and was known as **restitution**. However, widespread enforcement of restitution did not occur until the 1970s due to more active victim advocacy efforts. Yet, victims forfeited restitution if offenders went to prison. That changed when a

Community service is underutilized in most jurisdictions, with judges requiring community service of about 25 percent of felons on probation

series of federal acts in the 1980s broadened the use of restitution to include offenders who went to prison and those who owed back child support. Restitution also became mandatory in crimes such as sexual abuse, sexual exploitation of children, domestic violence, and Title 18 property offenses (Dickman 2009).

In restorative justice cases, restitution amounts are determined at victim-offender mediation sessions. In conventional misdemeanor and felony courts, judges order restitution at the time of sentencing. The more active that victims were about demanding restitution, the more likely that it was ordered (Ruback, Schaffer, & Logue 2004). Restitution amounts are based on the following:

- The crime for which an offender is formally convicted
- The cost of replacement value or actual losses suffered
- Amounts do not involve money for "pain and suffering"

GLOSSARY

community service Court-ordered special condition that mandates that offenders complete unpaid work for nonprofit organizations.

restitution A court-ordered cash payment that an offender makes to the victim to offset some of the losses incurred from the crime.

victim compensation A general fund by which state governments disperse money to qualifying victims of violent crimes for payment of bills and lost wages.

fines A fixed financial penalty imposed by the judge, with the amount determined by the severity of the offense.

Just because restitution is court ordered does not mean that a victim will necessarily receive restitution. Part of the problem lies with probation officers enforcing its collection from the offender while on community supervision. Indigence does not entitle the offender to immunity from restitution, but failure to pay restitution because of indigence by itself is not a jailable offense. The court differentiates *inability* to pay from *unwillingness* to pay (*Bearden* v. *Georgia* 1983).

In cases where the losses incurred by the victim are substantial, the state attorney general provides money to qualifying victims of violent crimes through a **victim compensation** fund. A victim

BENEFITS OF COMMUNITY SERVICE

Labor for nonprofit organizations that lack money or personnel

An important function in areas that may lack city services or need relief efforts

Allows offender to restore damages and feel he or she has helped someone in need—leading to an increase in an offender's self-esteem

Appropriate for wealthy offenders whose financial resources are so great that fines or fees have no punitive effect

Alternative sanction for indigent offenders who are unable to afford payment

FIGURE 5.4 Benefits of Community Service.

could potentially obtain both compensation and restitution if the victim agrees to prosecute. For example, in a sexual assault case, potential costs incurred may include hospital bills for physical injuries, lost income from work, court transportation, child care during litigation, counseling sessions, sexual assault exams, HIV testing, rehabilitative therapy, and moving expenses (Office for the Victims of Crime 2010).

Fines

Another monetary sanction that the offender typically pays is a fixed **fine**. Fines are determined by the severity of the offense and, like restitution, can be paid in installments. The idea of punishing offenders financially predates the Code of

Source: Dmitriy Shironosov/Shutterstock

Think About It...

To increase community service completion rates, some counties have opted to allow misdemeanor offenders the option to donate an amount of money equal to the number of service hours multiplied by the minimum wage. The offender merely buys a new product from a pre-approved list and brings in the purchases with receipts to fulfill community service hours (Dunn 1999). Do you think charitable donations should substitute for community service?

Ruback and colleagues (2004) found that while on supervision, likelihood of rearrest lessened as the proportion of restitution paid increased, but it was difficult to determine which was the cause and which was the effect. In another study, offenders with strong community ties to employment, school, and the neighborhood were more likely to fully pay restitution than offenders without such ties (Davis et al. 1991). Based on these two conclusions, how does payment of restitution lower recidivism?

Source: corepics/Shutterstock

Hammurabi and is widely used in many countries throughout the world as the primary means of punishment. While U.S. jurisdictions use the fine as a sole sanction for most traffic offenses and ordinance violations, fines for misdemeanors and felonies, if used at all, are typically an add-on to probation (Vigorita 2002). Morris and Tonry (1990, p. 111) stated that it is ironic that "a society that relies so heavily on the financial incentive in its social philosophy and economic practice should be so reluctant to use the financial disincentive as a punishment of crime."

Fines average $1,000 for felony cases and $100 for misdemeanor cases and are largely based on the defendant's ability to pay (Vigorita 2002). This means that the courts consider employment status at arrest, future employment status, current financial status, and future bills.

▶ *Community Programs that Reduce Risk to Public Safety*

Some community conditions ordered by the court may require more surveillance than probation alone, so intermediate sanctions were created to fill that gap to reduce the risk to public safety. Increased surveillance programs discussed in this section include residential community corrections facilities, electronic monitoring, and day reporting centers.

it is ironic that "a society that relies so heavily on the financial incentive in its social philosophy and economic practice should be so reluctant to use the financial disincentive as a punishment of crime."

Residential Community Corrections Facilities

In the mid-1800s, halfway houses first opened to assist men and women who were released from jails and prisons with housing and clothing, until they found more permanent jobs and were able to transition out to living independently (Goldfarb & Singer 1973). Many of the earlier facilities were nonprofit and supported through private donations and faith-based organizations.

$$$ Fines average $1,000 for felony cases and $100 for misdemeanor cases

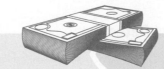

BENEFITS	PROBLEMS
• Fines can be combined with other sanctions when multiple sentencing goals are sought.	• There are possible credibility issues in the public's eyes.
• Fines can be tailored to the offender's assets and income to make up roughly comparable financial burdens.	• This is a form of discrimination against the poor.
• Fines can be collected with the same vigor and ruthlessness that characterize finance companies.	• Collecting small fines is more trouble than it is worth.
• Fines do not necessarily undermine the offender's ties to family and community.	• Debt might be shared by others in the household who had nothing to do with the crime but who combine their assets with the offender.

FIGURE 5.5 Benefits and Problems of Fixed Fines.
Source: Derived from BETWEEN PRISONS AND PROBATION: Intermediate Punishments in a Rational Sentencing System by N. Morris & M. Tonry (1990) Oxford University Press.

List and summarize the community programs that address minimizing risk to public safety.

GLOSSARY

residential community correction facility (RCCF) A modern term for *halfway house*; community-based correctional center in which the offender lives under supervision and must obtain permission to leave for work and leisure.

levels system A behavior modification program that increases a client's community freedom with good behavior.

electronic monitoring When a probationer or parolee is monitored in the community by wearing an electronic device that tracks his or her location.

home detention Requires offenders to remain at home at all times, except for such purposes as employment, school, treatment, medical emergencies, or approved shopping trips.

day reporting center A non-residential community corrections sanction that blends high levels of control with the delivery of specific services needed by offenders.

Beginning in the 1960s with federal support, halfway houses expanded their mission to include an intermediate sanction option for probationers who needed increased surveillance. Today, halfway houses are called **residential community correction facilities (RCCFs)** and are places in which the offender lives under supervision and must obtain permission to leave for work, treatment, and occasional leisure passes. RCCFs exist at the federal, state, and local levels and include profit-oriented companies that contract with the government. At the federal level alone, there were 183 active community corrections centers/residential reentry centers for juveniles or adults (Bureau of Prisons 2010). RCCFs are considered to be a type of minimum-security facility with large, open, dormitory-style rooms where clients can freely interact. Others have private rooms where prisoners are allowed keys to their own rooms.

183 At the federal level alone, there were 183 active community corrections centers/residential reentry centers for juveniles or adults

The exact number of RCCFs at the state and local level is unknown, but any facility classified as work release, prerelease, a restitution center, or a community facility for mothers and infants is a type of RCCF. The most promising intervention strategies for female offenders are skill building to teach economic and emotional independence (van Wormer 2010). One example of an RCCF for women leaving prostitution is called "Safe House." Women can stay for up to 18 months and are provided with job skills training, food, and counseling for domestic violence, drug abuse, and sexual assault victimization (Tsenin 2000). Some programs are culturally focused to meet the needs of African-American and Latina clients.

When not working, residents at all RCCFs have assigned chores, and some perform community service and attend drug-treatment programs if court ordered. Residents submit to random drug testing, breathalyzers, and subsidize some of the daily costs by paying rent. Most RCCFs operate on a **levels system**, which is a behavior modification program that increases a client's community freedom depending on the amount of time spent in the program, the client's behavior, employment status, and amount of money saved. Preapproved daytime visits to a pass address (a family member's home) are allowed, provided the clients return to check in at the RCCF after work. Clients out on pass must be available by phone at all times and must produce receipts to verify their whereabouts. Clients who receive a disciplinary report for misconduct or who fall behind on making rental payments to the facility will lose privileges and their level changes.

Employment Verifications

• Probation officers may periodically verify employment through talking to employers and by monitoring pay stubs/paychecks.

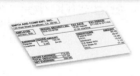

Drug and Alcohol Detection

• Probation officers and service providers may collect urine specimens or use portable drug testing devices, breathalyzers, and saliva swabs. Some use vehicle ignition locks, which link a breathalyzer to an offender's vehicle so that the ignition cannot be started unless the offender blows into the device and registers a breath alcohol content level below legal limits.

Community and Home Confinement

• Probation officers may recommend that the court require an offender to reside in a community corrections center or remain in his or her residence for all or part of the day. Both of these options are used as alternatives to incarceration, permitting the officer to work with the offender in the community.

FIGURE 5.6 **Supervision Strategies Used for Community-Based Sanctions.**
Source: Ekstrand, L. E. & Burton, D. R. (2001). *Prisoner releases: Trends and information on reintegration programs.* Publication GAO-01-483. Washington, DC: U.S. General Accounting Office, 40–41.

Electronic Monitoring

Technological advancements in the last several decades have encouraged people to think of how limited movement can be accomplished in the community without the use of high walls or razor-wire fences. **Electronic monitoring (EM)** is a community-based tool that is increasingly used in a wide variety of situations, such as during pretrial release, as a condition of

Characteristic	Level 5	Level 4	Level 3	Level 2	Level 1
Minimum time residing at RCCF to be at this level	Client placed on hold for up to 24 hours	Two weeks	Four weeks	Six weeks	Eight weeks
Requirements client must meet to be on this level	Complete intake assessment with case manager	Part-time or full-time employment	Full-time employment; no disciplinary reports for two weeks	Full-time employment; no disciplinary reports for two weeks; rent is current	Full-time employment; no disciplinary reports for two weeks; rent is current; $200 in savings
Reasons client could leave RCCF	N/A—client cannot leave facility	Work/school, treatment, medical/doctor, religion	Work/school, treatment, medical/doctor, religion, store, leisure/family	Work/school, treatment, medical/doctor, religion, store, leisure/family	Work/school, treatment, medical/doctor, religion, store, leisure/family
Length of daily leisure pass with family	N/A	N/A	Four hours	Six hours	Eight hours
Weekday curfew	N/A	N/A	10:00 PM	11:00 PM	11:59 PM
Weekend furlough	No	No	No	No	6:00 PM Friday to 11:59 PM Sunday
Driving privileges	No	No	No	No	Yes

diversion, or following sentencing. Sentences may include EM as a condition for a placement on work release, furlough, at a residential facility, or as a parole condition following a prison sentence.

While there are several types of EM, all EM devices have a unique transmitter device that is permanently attached to the offender (usually

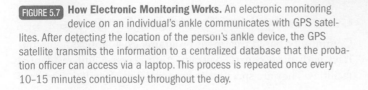

The advent of global positioning system (GPS) technology changed the face and the capabilities of EM technology.

around the ankle) that emits a continuous signal to a receiving device. For radio frequency devices, the receiver is attached to the offender's home telephone and can only detect transmissions when the offender is within 500 feet. Radio frequency devices are used for offenders who are court ordered to **home detention**. When enforced with EM, home detention is stricter than curfew and affords greater control over offenders' activities.

If the signal is not received when it should be, a computer sends a report of the violation to a central computer accessed by corrections officials. Other devices emit a signal only in response to a random computer phone call. The offender verifies his or her presence at home by placing the transmitter on the verifier box. Alternative methods of confirmation allow the offender to provide voice verification or visual verification by still-picture video phone.

The advent of global positioning system (GPS) technology changed the face and the capabilities of EM technology. Instead of limiting tracking to the home, GPS technology uses military satellites to pinpoint locations anywhere in the world using specific data coordinates that communicate with each receiver (Greek 2002). The newest technology has

FIGURE 5.7 **How Electronic Monitoring Works.** An electronic monitoring device on an individual's ankle communicates with GPS satellites. After detecting the location of the person's ankle device, the GPS satellite transmits the information to a centralized database that the probation officer can access via a laptop. This process is repeated once every 10–15 minutes continuously throughout the day.

the transmitter and receiver built in the same ankle device, as opposed to being two separate devices. The microprocessor also allows the probation officer to program in places where the offender is not allowed, such as near a victim's house or near a school. The newer systems allow authorities to know an offender's whereabouts at all times (Gowen 2001; Greek 2002). The main drawback to GPS technology is the occasional loss of GPS signal and "dead spots," the offender's receiver is unable to make the repeated cell phone calls to the central station with updates (Gowen 2001). As the number of dead spots increase and technology costs decrease in the future, GPS technology will likely be expanded to other types of offenders.

Day Reporting Centers

The **day reporting center (DRC)** is a nonresidential alternative to incarceration that blends high levels of control with the delivery of specific services needed by offenders. Officials in Connecticut and Massachusetts initially adopted the idea in the 1990s from England. DRCs are typically used as a "graduated sanction" for probationers who violate conditions of supervision, most commonly for drug use, but need to be in a treatment program or kept in the community. Clients report to the DRC five days during the workweek and attend classes such as anger management and cognitive behavior modification. DRCs are currently revising their risk assessment and classification scheme to more fully embrace evidence-based practices (Kim, Joo, & McCarty 2008).

▶ Community Supervision Conditions that Address Root Causes

Court-ordered conditions in the community that seek to address **substance abuse** are problem-solving courts and community drug treatment programs. Of course, the degree of abuse (occasional, moderate, severe), length of abuse, and the type of substances vary greatly. Individuals who committed a crime to support a drug habit or criminals who were heavily under the influence of drugs when they committed their crime

Characteristics of Day Reporting Centers

- Provide treatment and other services on-site to address clients' employment, education, and counseling needs and to reduce jail or prison crowding.
- Accept probation or parole violators for an average duration of five months.
- Three phase system: During the most intensive phase, offenders report daily and are tested for drug use about once per week. Offenders monitored for 70 hours per week.
- Offenders are required to perform community service.
- Offenders are progress with increasingly less-stringent requirements.

FIGURE 5.8 **Characteristics of Day Reporting Centers.**
Source: EXPLORATORY ANALYSIS OF CLIENT OUTCOMES, COSTS AND BENEFITS OF DAY REPORTING CENTERS _ FINAL REPORT by A. Craddock (2000) Federal Grant 97_IJ_CX_0006, National Institute of Justice.

qualify at some level. It is estimated that over 70 percent of all convicted offenders have a substance abuse or dependency problem (Karberg & James 2005). However, disproportionately few treatment programs exist in jails and prisons, so most offenders with substance abuse problems are more likely to receive treatment in the community.

Problem-Solving Courts

One of the noted problems with our criminal justice system is the long period of time that passes from arrest to sentence, and then another delay from sentencing until court-ordered treatment commences. **Problem-solving courts** are an alternative process to traditional criminal court for people who have been arrested for a nonviolent crime and have a history of alcohol or drug abuse, or who have committed a crime and have a mental illness. The most common courts are drug courts, DWI courts, and mental health courts. The primary goals of these courts are to reduce recidivism, increase treatment services, and stabilize clients. Each court involves a specially trained team for each particular issue (either addiction or mental illness) and consists of collaborative efforts by the judge, prosecutor, defense attorney, probation officer, and various treatment providers who all act in the client's best interest. All clients in a problem-solving court sign a contract to agree to the treatment or medication. Problem-solving courts can be pre-plea/diversionary, or they can be post-plea and carry a conviction. Both types of courts seek to avoid jail and obtain treatment as quickly as possible. The court team reviews the progress of each individual case every two to four weeks, and decides when the client has earned the privilege to progress to the next level (Thompson, Osher, & Tomasini-Joshi 2008). Mental health courts frequently address **co-occurring disorders**.

LEARNING OUTCOMES 5 Describe the most typical community-based programs that address root causes of defendants' problems with crime.

GLOSSARY

substance abuse When the use of one or more chemical substances disrupts normal living patterns.

problem-solving courts An alternative court process for people who get arrested and have a history of alcohol or drug abuse, or a mental illness.

co-occurring disorders A client with a mental disorder and a substance abuse problem.

detoxification A process of sudden withdrawal from all drugs and alcohol so that treatment can begin.

therapeutic communities Long-term peer-led programs for chronic addicts using group confrontational methods.

short-term inpatient residential programs Drug treatment programs of three to six months in length for less severe drug abusers.

outpatient treatment Drug treatment programs for participants who live and work independently in the community.

Community Drug Treatment Programs

Community-based treatment programs exist alongside or contract with drug courts, day reporting centers, and residential facilities. They are specifically for convicted offenders who have abused drugs and alcohol. Some modalities exist exclusively in the community, while others begin in prison and continue out in the community. Certain treatments are residential (in-patient), which means that a resident lives at the facility during the most crucial treatment periods and gradually transitions out. Other treatment facilities and modalities are nonresidential where the client lives at home and comes to the facility for meetings and treatment. Community drug treatment modalities include the following:

1. **Detoxification** is an entry-point measure for chronic drug users where the body is cleansed of drugs so that treatment while sober can begin.

2. **Therapeutic communities (TCs)** are long-term peer-led programs that force chronic addicts to face their addiction using group confrontational methods. TCs are based in the community and in prison, with 9–12 months residential followed by outpatient treatment. Confrontational style peer-led encounter groups are the hallmark for clients to learn how to express their feelings constructively and to improve their interpersonal skills. As individuals progress through the program, they become role models for newer members.

3. **Short-term inpatient residential programs** are three to six months in length and are for less severe drug abusers. These programs can exist in both the community and behind the walls. In the community, the most well-known example is Treatment Alternatives to Street Crime (TASC), which has about 130 programs in 25 states.

4. **Outpatient treatment** is where participants are involved in activities while they live and work independently in the community. Outpatient treatment may be used during transition from inpatient drug treatment, transition from prison, or solely as a part of probation conditions. Forms of outpatient treatments include one or more (in combination) of the following:

- **Methadone or naltrexone maintenance**: a prescribed substance to help fight cravings for illegal opiate drugs

- **Antabuse**: a prescribed substance that deters alcoholics from ingesting alcohol

- **Relapse prevention**: a form of aftercare for recovering addicts who have completed a TC or other residential program that continues enforcing the principles of the previous treatment modality

- **Alcoholics Anonymous/Narcotics Anonymous meetings**: a support system of recovery using a designated sponsor and integrating faith-based beliefs with a 12-step program of taking responsibility for actions

- **Drug education classes**: teaching the recreational or occasional drug user on probation the effects and dangers of using various illegal drugs through 25–35 contact hours (Welsh & Zajac 2004)

Long-term programs for addiction have been in prisons since the late 1960s. This sounds impressive until we point out that less than 15 percent of offenders who have a problem actually receive treatment while incarcerated (Welsh & Zajac 2004). Available drug treatment is not near enough to cover the offenders in correctional facilities with alcohol or drug-related problems, making community-based interventions crucial for offenders as a part of their probation (or parole conditions once they leave prison). As you can see, there are several options available for drug treatment. This is because some modalities are more effective for chronic abusers, while others are tailored for occasional users. The type of drug used or abused, along with the reasons behind the drug abuse, may dictate the treatment modality as well.

Applying Evidence-Based Practices in a Community-Based Therapeutic Community

Lisa M. is 22 years old and has been using drugs since age 14. She began with alcohol and inhalants, but switched to methamphetamine by the age of 18 to stay awake. Lisa was sexually abused by her father at the age of 13 and when she confronted her mother about the situation, Lisa was called a liar. Lisa ran away multiple times between the ages of 13 and 15 to minimize the abuse. She dropped out of school in her senior year when she moved in with an older man who was her boyfriend. Within a year, he turned her on to methamphetamine. Lisa was arrested and jailed for prostitution multiple times between the ages of 18 and 21—yet, her chronic drug habit made relapse likely.

On Lisa's latest arrest, an understanding judge ordered her to treatment for the first time at an all women's community-based residential therapeutic community. The TC was regimented, highly structured, and led by ex-addicts and licensed counselors so that clients could identify with someone who had been through the same experience. Treatment was based on cognitive-behavioral components and encounter groups, where others confront Lisa's thinking patterns and behaviors (Greenfield, Brooks, Gordon, Green, Kropp, McHugh, Lincoln, Hien & Miele 2007).

As she progressed through the program, Lisa began to understand that she turned her anger inward and became severely depressed about abandonment, but covered those feelings with drugs. Lisa learned that she was also acting in a "codependent" role—she allowed her boyfriend to continue using by taking on his problems as her own and prostituting herself to support both of them, never asking that he help. Lisa learned how her situation led to a greater likelihood of arrest and how she could break the cycle. After eight months, Lisa is still learning how to express her feelings constructively and hopes to soon become a role model for newer clients. But first, she must transition out on her own and learn how to use her new skills in the real world.

TCs have shown through evidence-based research to significantly reduce relapses and return to criminal behavior. Treatment programs that address these issues in a single-sex environment have a greater likelihood of retention and completion than in a co-ed program (Grella 1999). An eight-month stay in a community-based TC costs about $21,000 per year per person (French, Popopvici, & Tapsell 2008).

Lisa's situation raises several interesting questions:

1. Researchers found that women are actually less likely over their life to enter treatment compared to men. Like Lisa, many women enter through a court order. What other efforts could be made to encourage women to seek community-based treatment?

2. In order for the TC to be effective, Lisa must assume responsibility for her own actions. Do you think the community-based TC was an appropriate placement, or should she have gone to jail?

3. Do you think that treatment for substance abuse in community settings can work to reduce reoffending?

4. Using the "Possible Outcomes of EBPs in Corrections" box from Chapter 1 to guide you, what evidence-based techniques were incorporated into Lisa's experience?

Source: © Mikael Karlsson/Alamy

LEARNING OUTCOMES 1

Explain the key ways in which community supervision is beneficial to the offender, the community, and the victim.

Offenders continue to be productive, retain family ties, continue to support dependent children, and avoid corrupting influences, stigmatizing effects, and physical and psychological damage that might accompany a stay in jail or prison. Taxpayers enjoy cost savings and victims are more likely to receive restitution.

1. Which standard probation conditions emphasize deterrence?

2. Which standard conditions have a rehabilitative aspect?

3. Which probation conditions are incapacitative, in the sense that they limit the offender's freedom while in the community?

4. Who benefits most from a community-based sentence, and why?

probation The court-ordered community supervision of an offender by an officer who enforces conditions for a specified length of time.

standard conditions Commitments every probationer agrees to abide by in return for remaining at liberty in the community.

LEARNING OUTCOMES 2

Describe how probation supervision works.

Offenders are assessed for their risks and needs, and assigned to a caseload to best meet these needs. A case supervision plan is drafted to incorporate the special conditions.

1. Why is assessing offender risk important to community supervision?

2. If the courts already order the treatment programs, why are offender needs still assessed?

3. If a crime wasn't committed, why do probation officers report technical violations to the court?

caseload The number of individuals that one probation officer can effectively supervise based on predefined risks and needs posed.

motivational interviewing A style of personal interaction between the officer and client that involves rapport, trust, and persuasion to help bring about positive behavior change.

legal violation When a probationer commits a new criminal act, and the original probation sentence can be revoked.

technical violation When a probationer repeatedly fails to abide by conditions of probation, and the probation sentence can be revoked.

special conditions Requirements in addition to the standard conditions, such as paying fines or undergoing electronic monitoring.

LEARNING OUTCOMES 3

Identify the ways that court-ordered sanctions can be reparative to the victim and community.

Offenders are responsible for repaying the harm caused through unpaid labor to nonprofit organizations, payment of fines to reimburse the court for some of the expenses the system incurs, and payment of restitution to directly compensate the victim.

1. What ideas do you have for how restitution rates can be increased to make completing the payment more attractive?

2. How can community service hours be more readily completed?

3. Should the victim compensation fund be expanded for victims in other types of crimes? If so, what types of crime, and how would you decide who is eligible?

community service Court-ordered special condition that mandates that offenders complete unpaid work for nonprofit organizations.

restitution A court-ordered cash payment that an offender makes to the victim to offset some of the losses incurred from the crime.

victim compensation A general fund by which state governments disperse money to qualifying victims of violent crimes for payment of bills and lost wages.

fines A fixed financial penalty imposed by the judge, with the amount determined by the severity of the offense.

LEARNING OUTCOMES 4

List and summarize the community programs that address minimizing risk to public safety.

Reducing the risk to public safety while keeping an offender in the community requires more surveillance through intermediate sanctions such as residential community corrections facilities, electronic monitoring, and day reporting centers.

1. What are some of the graduated sanction options available for probation violators?

2. How can residential community corrections facilities use technological advances to monitor offenders when they leave the facility?

3. Do you believe that monitoring using GPS may one day replace prisons? Why or why not?

residential community correction facility (RCCF) A modern term for *halfway house*; community-based correctional center in which the offender lives under supervision and must obtain permission to leave for work and leisure.

levels system A behavior modification program that increases a client's community freedom with good behavior.

electronic monitoring When a probationer or parolee is monitored in the community by wearing an electronic device that tracks his or her location.

home detention Requires offenders to remain at home at all times, except for such purposes as employment, school, treatment, medical emergencies, or approved shopping trips.

day reporting center A nonresidential community corrections sanction that blends high levels of control with the delivery of specific services needed by offenders.

LEARNING OUTCOMES 5

Describe the most typical community-based programs that address root causes of defendants' problems with crime.

Community-based treatment programs focus primarily on reducing substance abuse and stabilizing persons who have mental illnesses to break the cycle of recidivism.

1. Attend a session of drug court and compare it to a session in a regular criminal court. What main differences do you observe?

2. If a treatment is court ordered, is it truly voluntary? Is court-ordered treatment implemented against a person's free will?

3. For an offender who is nonviolent and has a substance abuse problem, how many chances do you think would be acceptable to provide him or her another chance to reenter treatment and get clean?

4. For an offender who has violent tendencies while inebriated, how many chances do you think would be acceptable to provide him or her another chance to reenter treatment and get clean?

5. How do you define "relapse"? How is relapse similar to "recidivism"?

substance abuse When the use of one or more chemical substances disrupts normal living patterns.

problem-solving courts An alternative court process for people who get arrested and have a history of alcohol or drug abuse, or a mental illness.

co-occurring disorders A client with a mental disorder and a substance abuse problem.

detoxification A process of sudden withdrawal from all drugs and alcohol so that treatment can begin.

therapeutic communities Long-term peer-led programs for chronic addicts using group confrontational methods.

short-term inpatient residential programs Drug treatment programs of three to six months in length for less severe drug abusers.

outpatient treatment Drug treatment programs for participants who live and work independently in the community.

MyCJLab

Go to the Chapter 5 section in *MyCJLab* to test your understanding of this chapter, access customized study content, engage in interactive simulations, complete critical thinking and research assignments, and view related online videos.

Additional Links

Visit the National Center on Institutions and Alternatives, a nonprofit policy and research organization for more information on community sanctions: **www.ncianet.org/**.

Listen to the debate surrounding community supervision by tuning in to National Public Radio's show *Justice Talking*, "Probation and Parole—In Need of a Big Fix?": **www.justicetalking.org/**.

To examine the features of COMPAS offender risk assessment instruments, visit **www. northpointeinc.com/compas-core.aspx**.

Visit the Arkansas Department of Community Correction for services and programs in each county: **www.dcc.arkansas.gov/programs_services.html**.

Go to the Office for the Victims of Crime website, **http://ovc.ncjrs.gov/HelpVictim.aspx**, and scroll down to the video entitled, "Recovering From Your Crime-Related Injuries" or access the 12-minute video directly to find out more information about victim compensation: **http://ovc.ncjrs.gov/videos/wmv/musc_ncv_web.wmv**.

Examples of residential facilities in Colorado can be found here: **http://denvergov.org/communitycorrections/Programs/tabid/424170/Default.aspx**.

An example of an Electronic Monitoring Program in Michigan can be found at **www.michigan.gov/corrections/0,1607,7-119-1435-5032--,00.html**.

For a report about various instruments that assist in screening inmates for drug and alcohol problems, go to **www.ncjrs.org/pdffiles1/nij/grants/198805.pdf**.

Jails and Pretrial Release

"In jail I was just like everybody else, I was sitting there praying, feeling caged."

Dennis Rodman—Professional Basketball Player

1 Explain the two basic types of pretrial release and provide examples of each type.

2 Distinguish jails from prisons and list at least three purposes served by jails.

3 Describe the general characteristics of the jail population and then summarize the characteristics of females in jail, jails in Indian Country, and the mentally ill in jail.

4 Compare and contrast jail design and inmate supervision in new generation jails to those operating before the mid-1970s.

6

AMERICA'S TOUGHEST SHERIFF

That's how Sheriff Joe Arpaio of Maricopa County, Arizona, is introduced on radio and television shows—and how he identifies himself on the sheriff's office website (www.mcso.org/). At that same website one finds a link to the Deadbeat Parents Hall of Shame where you are directed to "choose the deadbeat parent you would like to view" (including a photo and notice of the amount owed) and another link to mug shots of people booked into the jail within the last three days.

Sheriff Joe's "tough on crime" philosophy is probably best known from his operation of the county's jails—especially the internationally known Tent City Jail that opened in 1993. Vowing to not release any inmates due to jail overcrowding, Sheriff Joe obtained surplus military tents and set them up in an area adjacent to one of the existing county jails. The Tents Jail can currently hold up to 2,000 inmates.

Inmates range from persons awaiting their trial to convicted celebrities such as former world heavyweight boxing

> **DISCUSS** Do you think persons who spend time in a Maricopa County jail are less likely to commit another crime because of the conditions Sheriff Joe imposes on the inmates?

champion Mike Tyson who was sentenced in 2007 to three years' probation and 24 hours at Tent City Jail for drug possession and driving under the influence. Whether unconvicted or convicted, all the inmates wear black and white striped uniforms with pink underwear. They will eat two meals a day that cost the taxpayers about 35 cents each—tasting as one would expect a 35 cent meal to taste. However, inmates can pay 40 cents for a condiment packet (salt, pepper, mustard, mayonnaise, ketchup) if they would like to enhance the flavor. Inmates are entertained by watching TV (as long as it is on a network such as the Disney Channel and C-SPAN) or the occasional "Inmate Idol" extravaganza. The first idol show was held in 2007 (including Alice Cooper as a judge) and another was held in December 2010 with a Christmas caroling contest. The Christmas winner (Jodi Arias, who was awaiting trial for the alleged murder of her boyfriend) received a full turkey dinner with all the trimmings for herself and her entire housing unit.

This chapter focuses on jail as a key feature of the American justice system and the correctional process. Some suspects and defendants, however, never see much more of a jail than the booking area. That is because not everyone who has been arrested or is awaiting trial is required to stay in jail. Instead, the majority of persons arrested technically have the opportunity to remain at liberty in the community while their case is prosecuted. It's important to note, however, that those defendants released to the community are increasingly being monitored by justice officials rather than simply roaming at will. It seems appropriate, therefore, to consider the topic of pretrial release before concentrating on the jail and its place in American corrections.

▶ Pretrial Release

When authorities arrest a person suspected of having committed a crime, two conflicting goals are put in motion: those of the community and those of the suspect. The community, which believes it has been harmed by the suspect, is interested in ensuring that the suspect will appear for trial and, meanwhile, will refrain from harming members of the public and their property. The suspect is, among other things, interested in preparing a defense against the charges brought by the community and in avoiding damage to such areas as employment, school, and family life. The community's goals seem best achieved if the suspect is confined in a jail or is at least closely monitored in the community. The suspect's goals are most easily realized if he or she has complete freedom of movement and choice of associates. The resulting dilemma has forced jurisdictions to develop systems of pretrial release and pretrial detention that try to balance the interests of both the community and the suspect. This section looks at approaches that have been tried, discarded, modified, or proposed to accomplish those goals.

Types of Pretrial Release

According to a national sample of state felony cases, 58 percent of all defendants were released before case disposition and 42 percent were detained (Figure 6.1). The released

defendants returned to the community as the result of incurring some financial obligation (33 percent) or because they simply promised to return to court for all required appearances (25 percent). Those who were not allowed to remain in the community were kept in jail because they were unable to meet the required financial obligation (37 percent) or because the court had denied their release (5 percent). We consider first those who are released to the community.

Pretrial release occurs when efforts to balance community and suspect interests result in the suspect's release in the community. Under pretrial release, the suspect is released from custody for all or part of the time before or during prosecution. That release is conditional upon the defendant's agreement to return to court at the appointed day and time. When the

58% of all defendants were released before case disposition and 42 percent were detained

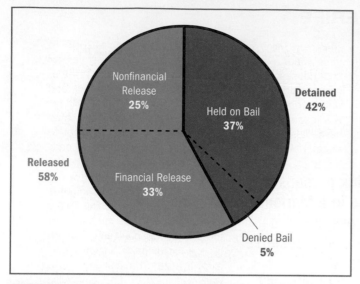

FIGURE 6.1 Types of Pretrial Release or Detention.
Source: Data from T.H. Cohen & T.K. Kyckelhahn. (2010). Felony defendants in large urban counties, 2006 (NCJ 228944).Washington, DC: Bureau of Justice Statistics, Table 6.

Pretrial release occurs when efforts to balance community and suspect interests result in the suspect's release in the community.

agreement is backed by a financial obligation, it involves a **bail bond**, which is a written agreement by the defendant to pay cash or relinquish property to the court if the defendant fails to attend required court appearances. Because not all defendants have the money or property necessary to secure bail, another person, acting as surety, is allowed to pay the money or put up the property for the defendant. Of

course, just as the defendant may not have the necessary money or property, neither may the defendant's family or friends. In those cases it may be possible for a bail bondsman to secure the defendant's release by telling the court that the bondsman will pay the required sum if the defendant fails to appear. Bondsmen make money this way because the defendant must pay the bondsman (usually 10 percent of the bail amount) to gain the bondsman's financial support.

The most frequent nonfinancial release procedure is **release on recognizance (ROR)**, which is based only on the defendant's promise to appear for trial (not backed with money or property). The other primary type of nonfinancial pretrial release is **conditional release**, wherein the defendant is released on a promise to fulfill some requirement such as staying employed, maintaining a curfew, or participating in a treatment program. In some jurisdictions defendants may be released without having to make any payment but are liable for the full bail amount if they fail to appear (called release on an **unsecured bond**).

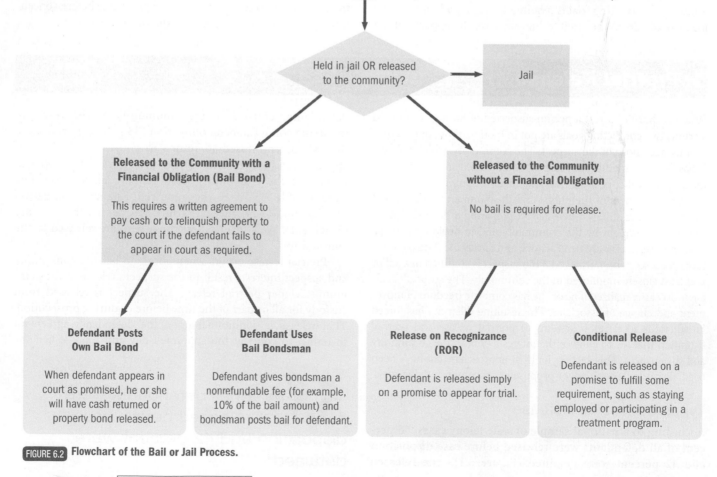

FIGURE 6.2 Flowchart of the Bail or Jail Process.

Think About It...

The commercial bail system is criticized as discriminating against low-income people. Poor defendants may be required to stay in jail simply because they lack financial means for release on bail rather than because of any danger they present to the community. Arguments against bail bondsmen include requiring persons presumed innocent to pay a nonrefundable fee to a private business even when that person turns up for every court appearance. An argument for commercial bail bonds is that commercial bail clients are more likely than those released under other forms of supervision to appear for court in the first place. Which side do you believe has the more persuasive argument?

Behavior of Pretrial Release Defendants

As noted at this section's start, the community's goals when considering pretrial release are (1) that the defendant refrain from causing further harm in the community and (2) that the defendant appear in court at the required time. Whether the pretrial release procedures are effective in achieving those goals of community safety and court appearance depends on how much compliance is expected. Data from a sample of state court felony cases show that 82 percent of defendants who were released prior to case disposition made all scheduled court appearances and had no pretrial misconduct, such as being arrested for a new offense. Of the defendants who were rearrested for a new offense (18 percent of all released defendants) while they were on pretrial release, the majority (63 percent) were arrested for a new felony (Cohen & Kyckelhahn 2010).

LEARNING OUTCOMES 1 Explain the two basic types of pretrial release and provide examples of each type.

GLOSSARY

bail bond A written agreement by the defendant to pay cash or relinquish property to the court if the defendant fails to attend required court appearances.

release on recognizance Pretrial release based only on the defendant's promise to appear for trial (not backed with money or property).

conditional release The return of prisoners to the larger community with a brief period of supervision with rules such as curfew, treatment completion, and maintaining employment. Can be used either pretrial or postconviction.

unsecured bond When a defendant is released without having to make any payment but is liable for the full bail amount if required court appearances are missed.

There is no agreed upon percentage for determining successful pretrial release policies. As a result, some people will focus on the 18 percent who missed their court appearance and the 18 percent who were rearrested for new crimes and determine that pretrial release is not meeting court appearance or community safety needs. Others will view the 82 percent court appearance rate and the 82 percent who did not get rearrested while on pretrial release as proportions representing an acceptable risk. These people argue that in exchange for living in a society where persons merely accused of a crime have the ability to maintain their family, work, and community ties while assisting in the preparation of their defense, citizens must be willing to accept a procedure that is less than 100 percent effective—although we should always strive to do better. This is where programs and services designed to further reduce the community's risk come into play.

Pretrial Services

Pretrial service programs are designed to achieve two goals (Stevenson & Legg 2010; VanNostrand 2007):

1. **Pretrial Assessment**: Intended outcome is to reduce the number of pretrial defendants who fail to make required court appearances by providing the court official who is making the pretrial release decision with information about the defendant. That information should help the judicial officer decide whether release in the community or detention in jail is more appropriate.

2. **Pretrial Supervision**: Provide pretrial service workers with information that will assist in monitoring and supervising pretrial defendants who are released pending trial.

For the pretrial assessment, a team of workers gathers information from and about a defendant and then evaluates the defendant in terms of the risk of failure to appear in court and the danger he or she poses to the community during the pretrial stage. Typically the risk assessment is accomplished using an objective and research-based instrument that evaluates the defendant on the basis of factors shown to be good predictors of court appearance and/or danger to the community (for example, whether the person is currently on probation or some other form of community supervision).

The supervision goal of pretrial services provides an opportunity to motivate offenders to make behavioral changes while assuring court appearances and community safety. During this period of pretrial release in the community, offenders may participate in treatment programs, hold down a job, attend classes, take anger management classes, and generally show themselves to be capable of responsible behavior. At the other extreme, they could fail to make required court appearances, ignore any treatment referral suggestions, and basically present themselves as uncooperative. In either case, the pretrial case managers will be able to provide sensible and practical sentencing recommendations to judges, prosecuting attorneys, and the offender's defense attorney (Stevenson & Legg 2010).

82% of defendants who were released prior to case disposition made all scheduled court appearances and had no pretrial misconduct

- Current charges
- Outstanding warrants at time of arrest
- Pending charges at time of arrest
- Active community supervision at time of arrest (for example, pretrial release, probation, parole)
- History of criminal convictions
- History of failure to appear
- History of violence
- Residence stability
- Employment stability
- Community ties
- History of substance abuse

DISCUSS *Using at least seven of these factors, describe a person you think would be a good candidate for pretrial release. If that person were granted pretrial release and you were his or her case manager, what pretrial supervision conditions would you recommend?*

Positive pretrial performance reports may lead to opportunities for non-prison sanctions, whereas negative reports could bolster arguments for incarceration or close supervision in the community.

In the United States, six states have state jail systems rather than the more typical local jail systems.

Jail Function and Purposes

Jails, which are distinguished from prisons in several important ways, are confinement facilities usually operated by city or county governments and typically managed by that government's law enforcement agency. For example, the city police department administers the city jail, and the county sheriff manages the county jail. Not all cities and counties operate their own jails, but those that do not have made some arrangement with another entity for jail services. The Federal Bureau of Prisons operates nine jails (called federal detention centers or metropolitan detention centers) in locations around the country and in Puerto Rico, but those facilities typically are not included in reports and statistics on jails.

In the United States, six states have state jail systems (also called **integrated jail–prison systems**) rather than the more typical local jail systems. In those states—Alaska, Connecticut, Delaware, Hawaii, Rhode Island, and Vermont—the state government is responsible for the administration and operation of jails located throughout the state (West, Sabol, & Greenman 2010).

You might think of jails only as places where persons are held awaiting trial or are serving short-term confinement sentences, but contemporary jails serve many purposes, including the following:

- Receive individuals pending arraignment and hold them while awaiting trial, conviction, or sentencing
- Readmit probation, parole, and bail-bond violators and absconders
- Temporarily detain juveniles pending transfer to juvenile authorities
- Hold mentally ill persons pending their movement to appropriate health facilities
- Hold individuals for the military, for protective custody, for contempt, and for the courts as witnesses
- Release convicted inmates to the community upon completion of sentence

JAILS	PRISONS
• Operated by local government (except in AK, CT, DE, HI, RI, and VT)	• Operated by the state or federal government
• Hold convicted misdemeanants (usually on sentences up to one year)	• Hold convicted felons (usually on sentences of one year and more)
• Typically hold males and females in separate units of the same facility	• Typically hold males and females in separate facilities
• Serve as a detention facility for persons not yet convicted of a crime	• Serve as a custody facility for persons already convicted and sentenced

FIGURE 6.3 **Some Differences between Jails and Prisons.**

- Transfer inmates to federal, state, or other authorities

- House inmates for federal, state, or other authorities because of crowding of their facilities

- Sometimes operate community-based programs as alternatives to incarceration(Minton 2010)

GLOSSARY

jails Confinement facilities usually operated by city or county governments and typically managed by that government's law enforcement agency.

integrated jail–prison systems A state government, rather than the more typical local government agency, is responsible for the administration and operation of jails located throughout the state.

As that list suggests, a person in jail could be unconvicted and awaiting trial, waiting for a transfer to another agency or jurisdiction, or being held for possible revocation of his or her probation or parole. Similarly, a jail resident could be convicted but not yet sentenced or convicted and waiting for transfer to a prison. It is clear that jails hold persons under a variety of statuses, but they can be described according to particular characteristics.

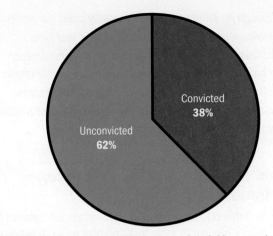

FIGURE 6.4 **Jail Population Is Mostly Unconvicted.** Most people in jail have not been convicted of anything: 62 percent of the nation's adult jail inmates are unconvicted (awaiting court action on their current conviction) and the other 38 percent are serving a jail sentence, awaiting sentencing, or serving time for probation or parole violation (Minton 2010).

► Characteristics of the Jail Population

About 40 percent of the nearly 2,900 local jails around the country today are rather small (holding fewer than 50 inmates) but almost 6 percent are **"mega" jails**, holding over 1,000 people. The nation's two largest local jail jurisdictions, Los Angeles County and New York City, together held about 33,000 inmates in 2009—about 4 percent of the national total (Minton 2010; Sabol & Minton 2008).

The number of inmates held in the nation's jails has surpassed 750,000 each year since 2006. However, the growth of the U.S. jail population has slowed since 2005 and between 2008 and 2009 there was actually a decline by about 18,000 inmates. This was the first actual decline in the jail population since the Bureau of Justice Statistics began collecting the data in 1982 (Minton 2010). Most of the local jail inmates are African-American and Hispanic males. However, Table 6.1 shows that these characteristics have changed gradually since 1990.

In addition to the inmates held in jail, there are others under jail supervision but they are supervised outside of a jail facility. In 2009, there were about 70,000 people in this category across the country and most of them were doing community service under the supervision of jail authorities (Minton 2010).

CONSEQUENCES OF THE JAIL-VERSUS-BAIL DISTINCTION

About 40 percent of defendants are kept in jail while awaiting their case disposition. That pretrial detention will obviously affect such things as a person's work, school, family life, and—even under the best of jail conditions—their physical and psychological well-being. But, there seems to be another negative consequence of pretrial detention in comparison with being released in the community to await trial: *Those detained are more likely to be convicted and incarcerated.*

Data from several sources consistently show that detained defendants are more likely to be convicted than are released defendants, and, when convicted, are more likely to receive a jail or prison sentence (Cohen & Reaves 2006, 2007; Phillips 2008). Of course, the higher conviction rate and increased likelihood for incarceration may simply reflect a more serious criminal history or a more serious felony charge for the detained defendants. However, Phillips found that detention had an adverse effect on outcomes in felony cases beyond that

explained by such variables as criminal history, offense type, and charge severity. The implication is that persons who were detained in jail suffered more negative consequences as a result of that detention than did similarly situated defendants who were released to the community to await trail.

DISCUSS *What is it about detention that could explain the harsher penalties? Might a jailed defendant be more likely to plead guilty than a defendant under pretrial release—thereby explaining the greater likelihood of conviction? Do released defendants benefit from being able to show the judge that they can hold a job and stay out of trouble—thereby getting a probation sentence rather than a jail or prison sentence?*

Although jail inmates are predominantly male, the adult female jail population has increased each year (see Table 6.1). What explanations can you offer for this phenomenon? More than half of the jail inmates are members of racial or ethnic minorities. However, since 1990 the percentage of non-Hispanic African-Americans has declined whereas the percentage of Hispanics has increased. Why?

Females as an Increasing Percentage of Jail Inmates

As shown in Table 6.1, the percentage of women jail inmates has increased from 9 percent in 1990 to 12 percent today. It is becoming more difficult for jails to ignore the problems associated with female inmates. Their numbers are increasing too rapidly for administrators to maintain the "head-in-the-sand" response that identifies many jails. Although there are several gender-specific concerns associated with female inmates (for example, high rates of substance abuse and mental illness, physical health problems, and parenting and child-care issues), problems associated with histories of physical and sexual abuse are often highlighted in the literature.

Veysey, De Cou, and Prescott (1998) suggest that the coercive environment and procedures in jails present particular problems for women inmates who have histories of abuse. This is because those women may perceive the environment and procedures as dangerous and threatening. In response to that misperception, the women may withdraw, fight back, experience a worsening

Because they were created with male inmates in mind, the security and treatment practices in jails may unintentionally create crisis situations for female inmates.

of psychiatric symptoms or physical health problems, engage in self-injury, or find access to illegal substances. Veysey et al. argue that it behooves jail administrators to understand the genesis of these behaviors in order to respond appropriately or, better yet, reduce the likelihood they will even appear.

Because they were created with male inmates in mind, the security and treatment practices in jails may unintentionally create crisis situations for female inmates. Examples of standard procedures that are harmless, even if irritating, for male inmates but that may remind women of prior experiences of abuse might include intimate touching (for example, strip searches); threatened use of force (for example, crisis response teams); observing threats, assaults, or use of physical force (for example, inmate–inmate or inmate–staff violence);

12% the percentage of women jail inmates has increased from 9 percent in 1990 to 12 percent today

---

TABLE 6.1 — Characteristics of Inmates in Local Jails, Midyear 1990–2009.

	Percentage of Jail Inmates				
Characteristic	1990	1995	2000	2005	2009
Total	100	100	100	100	100
SEX					
Male	91	90	89	87	88
Female	9	10	11	13	12
STATUS					
Adult	99	98	99	99	99
Juvenile*	1	2	1	1	1
RACE/ORIGIN					
White, non-Hispanic	42	40	42	44	43
Black/African-American, non-Hispanic	43	44	41	39	39
Hispanic	14	15	15	15	16
Other**	1	2	1	2	2

* Includes juveniles held as adults and juveniles held as juveniles in adult jail.

** Includes American Indians, Alaska Natives, Asians, Native Hawaiians, other Pacific Islanders, and—for 2005 and 2009—those self-identifying as "two or more races."

Source: Data for 1990 (Gilliard 1999). Data for 1995 (Harrison & Beck 2006). Data for 2000, 2005, and 2009 (Minton 2010).

isolation (for example, administrative or medical isolation); and locked rooms or spaces and the use of restraint devices (for example, handcuffs or shackles). Add to those jail features the appearance of uniforms and male officers and the presence of fear based on lack of information, and it is not surprising that women with histories of physical and sexual abuse experience increased stress and vulnerability. When the response to these triggers is turned outward, there may be an escalation of violence in the women's unit of the jail.

Jails in Indian Country

U.S. law recognizes as **Indian Country** the land within an Indian reservation or land that is technically owned by the federal government but held in trust for a tribe or tribal member. Law enforcement services in Indian Country, which consists of some 56 million acres of land in 35 states, is provided by the Bureau of Indian Affairs (BIA) through direct assistance to tribes on reservations (U.S. Department of the Interior 2004).

As part of those law enforcement services, the BIA operates or funds detention facilities throughout Indian Country and, unfortunately, those jails are among the worst in the nation. A U.S. Department of the Interior report (2004) that evaluated these facilities was titled "Neither safe nor secure" and declared the BIA detention program to be a national disgrace. Many facilities had conditions comparable to those found in third-world countries and were considered a hazard to both inmates and staff alike (p. 1).

This issue of facility safety and security is important not only on its own merits but also because of the increasing number of people held in these jails. The number of inmates in Indian Country jails increased 25 percent from 2004 to 2009, and from 2008 to 2009 the average daily jail population increased by 12 percent (Minton 2011). The majority of inmates was held in Indian Country jails in Arizona, New Mexico, North Dakota, South Dakota, Washington, and Wisconsin.

Two types of Indian offenders are detained in Indian Country jails—those who have committed crimes under federal law and those who have committed crimes under tribal law (Summerill 2005). The federal law offenses

LEARNING OUTCOMES 3 Describe the general characteristics of the jail population and then summarize the characteristics of females in jail, jails in Indian Country, and the mentally ill in jail.

GLOSSARY

mega jails The country's largest jails holding over 1,000 people.

Indian Country Land within an Indian reservation or land that is technically owned by the federal government but held in trust for a tribe or tribal member.

A U.S. Department of the Interior report declared the BIA detention program to be a national disgrace.

ACCOMMODATING THE NEEDS OF WOMEN IN JAIL

Jails have a mandate to provide secure and humane conditions of confinement, but doing so for female inmates may require modifying the jail environment and procedures. Veysey and her colleagues (1998, pp. 52–53) offer a few suggestions for how this might be accomplished.

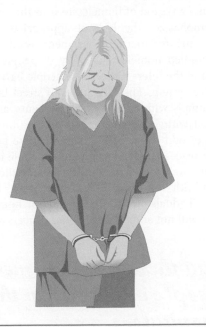

Information disclosure. Both women and men should have a detailed understanding of what will happen during their time of incarceration, but jail administrators should be aware that each group may need different kinds of information. For example, female inmates especially will want information regarding their children and what child-care arrangements have been made.

Regimentation, lack of privacy, and unquestioned response to authority. Jails must provide a secure environment for the safety of both inmates and staff. However, security measures developed to control male inmates may not be necessary or appropriate for female inmates. Because most female offenders are arrested for nonviolent crimes, they may not need the same high-security supervision that men require. Keeping cell doors unlocked or open, allowing greater interaction among the women inmates, and training staff in nonthreatening management techniques may actually result in a more tranquil women's unit.

Treatment services. Incarcerated women, more so than incarcerated men, report that they want someone to talk to—not necessarily someone to solve their problems, just someone who will listen. Women inmates, especially those who are victims of abuse, also tend to find single-gender group treatment activities preferable to mixed-gender groups. Recognizing and responding to these preferences may allow jail staff to provide a more effective treatment response to their female inmates.

mental health disorder A broad category used to identify convicted offenders who are considered to have mental health problems as a result of self-reported clinical diagnosis or treatment by a mental health professional.

serious mental illness A narrow category used to identify convicted offenders suffering from such conditions as bipolar disorder, schizophrenia spectrum disorder, or major depression.

are more serious crimes (for example, murder, rape, aggravated assault) and the tribal law violations are less serious acts that are subject to a maximum $5,000 fine or one year incarceration. Most of those in jail are adult males (81 percent) who have been convicted of a crime (69 percent). Assault, domestic violence, and DWI/ DUI offenses are most typical, although confinement for domestic violence declined from 20 percent in 2007 to 12 percent in 2009(Minton 2011). The decline of domestic violence is especially promising since American Indian women residing on Indian reservations suffer domestic violence and physical assault at rates far exceeding women of other ethnicities and locations. In fact, 39 percent of American Indian women report being victims of domestic violence (Fletcher 2009). Hopefully, the Tribal Law and Order Act (signed into law in 2010) will help address this crime and others in Indian Country.

Jailing the Mentally Ill

Today there are more mentally ill people in jails than there are in hospitals. Specifics vary depending on the definition of mental illness that is used in the study, but there is general agreement that America's jails and prisons have become our new mental hospitals. Torrey and his colleagues put this in historical perspective by noting that we have returned to the early nineteenth century, when mentally ill people filled our jails and prisons (2010, p. 1).

The rate of mental illness in America's state prisons and local jails is at least three times the rate in the general population. Los Angeles County Jail alone holds more people with mental illness than does any state hospital or mental health institution in the United States (Council of State Governments 2002, xii–xiii). Using the broad criterion of self-reported mental health problems—including clinical diagnosis or treatment by a mental health professional—64 percent of jail inmates had symptoms of a **mental health disorder** (James & Glaze 2006). Using a more stringent definition, 17 percent of jail inmates suffer from a **serious mental illness** (bipolar disorder, schizophrenia spectrum disorder, major depression).

3x The rate of mental illness in America's state prisons and local jails is at least three times the rate in the general population.

With either definition, the problem is obvious since our nation's jails were not designed as mental health facilities. The number of people with serious mental illness or mental health problems is substantial and these individuals require complex treatment, services, and supervision that jails were neither designed nor equipped to provide (Council of State Governments n.d.).

The high rate of mental health disorder among jail inmates simply reflects the role of local jails in today's criminal justice system. As locally operated facilities, jails hold—along with other offenders—mentally ill persons pending their movement to appropriate mental health facilities. The percentage of jail inmates identified as having a mental health problem was especially high for white non-Hispanics (71 percent), females (75 percent), and persons age 24 or younger (70 percent). In addition, inmates with a mental health problem were more likely than those without a mental health problem to have been homeless in the year before their incarceration and to have lived in a foster home, agency, or institution while growing up (James & Glaze 2006).

Having a period of homelessness in the year prior to their arrest emphasizes the lack of appropriate facilities in the United States for many of our mentally ill citizens. Belcher (1988) studied homeless mentally ill people in an effort to understand the interactions those people have with the criminal justice system. The difficulties of street life, the tendency not to comply with aftercare arrangements, and the problems associated with impaired mental functioning often result in displays of odd behavior by many of these people. That odd behavior places homeless mentally ill people in direct conflict with many societal norms, and as a result, they are frequently involved with the criminal justice system. In many states, unless individuals are overtly suicidal or homicidal, the state hospitals will not admit them. Police officers are left to decide

Today there are more mentally ill people in jails than there are in hospitals.

Why the Disproportionate Number of Mentally Ill People in Jail?

Some studies have found persons with mental illnesses to be slightly more likely than other offenders to have committed violent offenses, but that does not explain their overrepresentation in jail. More likely explanations include (Council of State Governments n.d.; Ditton 1999):

- The behavior resulting in arrest and jail is often less indicative of criminal behavior than it is of untreated mental illness (for example, experiencing delusions, immobilized by depression, suffering the consequences of inadequate treatment).

- People with serious mental illness have high rates of co-occurring substance use disorders and are therefore more likely to be arrested for drug-related crimes.

- People with serious mental illness are often unable to access affordable housing and homelessness is frequently associated with arrest.

- Many people with mental illness have no health insurance and cannot access community care.

- Police may find it easier to catch mentally ill offenders, juries might be more willing to convict them, and judges may be more inclined to sentence them to jail or prison than to release them on probation.

DISCUSS *Which of these explanations do you find most persuasive? What other explanations can you think of for why the mentally ill are overrepresented in the jail population?*

---

providing jail-based mental health programming services for inmates with mental illness can stabilize psychiatric symptoms and support effective jail operations

health programming services for inmates with mental illness can stabilize psychiatric symptoms and support effective jail operations (Hagar, Ludwig, & McGovern 2008).

▶ New Generation Jails

For more than 200 years, America's jails were designed in a consistent style and the inmates were managed in a common manner. The typical architectural design had cells placed sequentially along a hallway. Inmates were monitored by correctional officers patrolling the hallway and looking into each cell. These two key features of jail management—facility design and inmate supervision—began changing in the mid-1970s when the Federal Bureau of Prisons opened three detention centers that featured a more residential type design and operated under a management system that gave correctional officers more direct contact with inmates (Wener 2005).

This innovative design and supervision model was adopted by some cities and counties and by 1995 the National Institute of Corrections had identified 199 jails across the country that used the new model. Today, the more than 350 jails implementing this design and supervision philosophy are known as **new generation jails** (National Institute of Corrections 2006). The two key ingredients of the new generation approach are architectural design and inmate supervision.

Architectural design may seem like a strange thing to concentrate on, but it has been accepted as an integral part of jail and prison construction since the nineteenth century. Also, some people may view inmate supervision as being little more than a couple of guards watching a group of prisoners. But, like architectural design, inmate supervision is more complicated than it first appears. Although new generation jails are identified by the integration of both design and supervision aspects, we separate them here for discussion purposes.

Jail Design

Prior to the mid-1970s, jails throughout the United States had much in common with their historical ancestors—in fact, some of them were old enough to have been those very ancestors. A jail reform movement was attempted in the 1970s when 1,000 new jail facilities were built (Zupan 1991). But the design of those facilities was basically the same as the jails built in the eighteenth century, and the end result was more of the same rather than the beginning of a new era. Specifically, jails were configured as **linear facilities** in which single- or multiple-occupancy cells are aligned along corridors—similar to a hospital in which long rows of rooms are placed along a hallway.

whether to let the people wander back to the void of street life or detain them in jail.

The jail may be a refuge for the homeless mentally ill, but it is a refuge without treatment or even prolonged shelter because these people are quickly released—55 percent of convicted jail inmates with mental problems serve six months or less (James & Glaze 2006). As Belcher puts it, "Wandering aimlessly in the community, psychotic much of the time, and unable to manage their internal control systems, these [chronically homeless mentally ill people] found the criminal justice system was an asylum of last resort" (1988, p. 193). Unfortunately, the jail serves more as a shelter for these people than a treatment facility. James and Glaze (2006) report that only one in every six jail inmates with a mental health problem had received treatment since their admission to jail.

Bleak as this may sound, there is reason for hope. One option is to divert people with mental illness from jail to community-based services—and doing so has had positive results. A multisite national study of persons who participated in postbooking jail diversion programs found that persons with serious mental illness who are diverted to community-based services experience fewer arrests and days in jail in the 12 months following their diversion than in the prior 12 months (Case, Steadman, Dupuis, & Morris 2009). Another option is to provide jail-based treatment programs. Although such programs are infrequently found and those that are operating need additional study, an evaluation of a therapeutic program for mentally ill adult male inmates in the Broward County (Florida) Jail suggests that providing jail-based mental

Compare and contrast jail design and inmate supervision in new generation jails to those operating before the mid-1970s.

GLOSSARY

new generation jails Facilities using a specific architectural design and inmate supervision model in order to reduce violent and destructive behavior by the inmates.

linear facilities Jails and prisons designed with single- or multiple-occupancy cells aligned along corridors that, in turn, are often stacked in tiers.

intermittent supervision Inmate supervision method wherein custodial staff are able to observe or interact with inmates only on an irregular or sporadic basis.

indirect supervision Inmate supervision method wherein custodial staff observe and interact with inmates remotely by watching through windows and listening via microphones.

direct supervision Inmate supervision method wherein custodial staff members are placed—for their entire shift—in the inmates' living area.

Security in the linear jails relied on physical containment rather than active supervision and management of inmates. Heavy metal doors, bars, and other security devices were considered necessary to prevent inmate escapes and assaults on staff. To observe inmates, the officer had to patrol the hall and look into individual rooms. The result was infrequent inmate supervision making it difficult to monitor inmate behavior and to anticipate problems. The absence of active supervision resulted in such problems as assaults on inmates and staff, introduction of dangerous contraband, and inmate disregard for staff-imposed rules (Bowker 2002).

New generation jails take a dramatically different approach to architectural design. Specifically, they use a layout consisting of a triangular or pie-shaped pod that has its walls lined with cells or rooms arranged around a common area. That common area, or dayroom, is where the inmates converge to watch television, play board games, and socialize. In many podular jails, inmate meals are delivered to the dayroom rather than having to move the inmates to a remote location three times a day.

The living area and cells in new generation jails are likely to have comfortable furniture, tile or carpet floors, access to telephones, and basically a normalized living environment when compared with linear facilities. The goal is to provide an incentive for inmates to behave—since misbehavior results in placement in a less desirable part of the jail with fewer privileges. In fact, studies have found a decrease in property destruction and reduced levels of vandalism in new generation jails (Senese 1997; Wener 2006).

With the elimination of the old physical barriers the inmates and officers can now intermingle in relative freedom. In this way, control lies in the hands of institutional staff rather than with the inmates, as it often does when officials rely too much on things (bars, indestructible furniture, etc.) rather than people (correctional staff) to control inmate behavior.

Inmate Supervision

The linear facility design made it difficult—impossible, even—for custodial staff to continuously supervise inmate activities. Inmate supervision in such facilities is described as being **intermittent**, since jail staff could observe or interact with inmates only on an irregular or sporadic basis. As a result, the inmates were left unsupervised for long periods. In addition, inmates had to be moved from their cells to other locations for various activities. For example, it would not be unusual to have hundreds of inmates gather together on the "big yard" for recreation or in the mess hall for meals—and both of those locations could become dangerous places for inmates and staff.

In addition to a unique architectural design, the new generation jails provide an alternative to the intermittent supervision model. Initially the podular design included an observation area (typically at the hub from which the various pods flow out) where correctional officers engaged in remote observation and supervision of the inmates (for example, issuing commands to the inmates in each pod via an intercom system). This system of podular **indirect supervision** (also called remote supervision) increased visual surveillance over what was possible in linear facilities but allowed less frequent verbal interaction with the inmates. Watching through windows (typically one-way) and listening via microphones in the living area, the officers monitor inmate behavior and conversation.

Beginning in the 1970s, design and supervision was further refined, and the result is today's podular **direct supervision** wherein custodial staff are placed—for their entire shift—in the inmates' living area. In this way, the officer has immediate visual observation of inmates and has the ability to interact freely with them. This style of inmate supervision provides for continuous rather than intermittent or indirect supervision. By placing the officer in the pod,

Source: Philip Reichel

Think About It...

Incorporating ideas from social and environmental psychology, new generation jails are designed to maximize the power of expectations as a way to encourage positive behavioral norms (Wener 2005). The idea is that rather than challenging someone to break or damage an item designed to be unbreakable, surround them instead with more normal furnishings that provide no challenge or gratification when vandalized. So, a well-lit and colorful area with carpeting and upholstered furniture should encourage caretaking among the inmates. Do the potential benefits of putting inmates in a less-institutionalized setting outweigh any retributive or deterrent benefit that might result from placing them in a harsher environment?

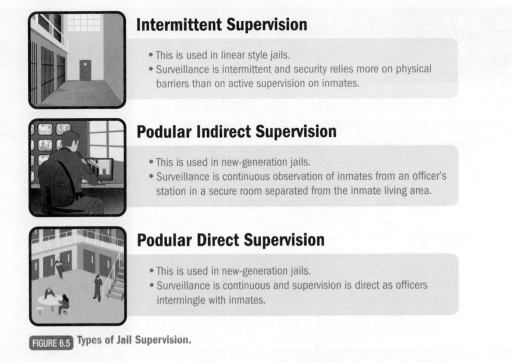

Intermittent Supervision

- This is used in linear style jails.
- Surveillance is intermittent and security relies more on physical barriers than on active supervision on inmates.

Podular Indirect Supervision

- This is used in new-generation jails.
- Surveillance is continuous observation of inmates from an officer's station in a secure room separated from the inmate living area.

Podular Direct Supervision

- This is used in new-generation jails.
- Surveillance is continuous and supervision is direct as officers intermingle with inmates.

FIGURE 6.5 Types of Jail Supervision.

> *By placing the officer in the pod, there is an increased awareness of the behaviors and needs of the inmates.*

there is an increased awareness of the behaviors and needs of the inmates. This creates a safer environment for both staff and inmates. Since interaction between inmates is constantly and closely monitored, dissension can be quickly detected before it escalates. Inmates who show signs of becoming unruly also can be quickly identified and moved to a more secure living unit/pod(Beck 2006).

The confinement function provided by jails is certainly important, but when the general public thinks of incarceration it is probably the prison that comes to mind. We turn to prisons in the next chapter as we consider the facilities designed for long-term confinement and some of the issues faced by officials charged with the management of those facilities and their prisoners.

EVIDENCE-BASED PRACTICE—DOES IT WORK?

Direct Supervision

Assuming that jail staff have received the appropriate training and have the necessary interpersonal and communication skills to successfully implement direct supervision—admittedly, not always a safe assumption—we should expect new generation jails to be a safer environment for both staff and inmates. For the most part, research supports this expectation. In his review of some 20 years of direct supervision literature, Wener (2006) concludes that direct supervision design and management results in reduced levels of serious and violent incidents, fewer inmate assaults on staff, and a diminished number of inmate–inmate assaults. However, there are mixed results regarding the quality of the working environment (for example, stress levels and job satisfaction) among jail staff in new generation jails (Wener 2006), and one study suggests direct supervision can be used without negative effects on staff regardless of the facility's architectural design (Applegate & Paoline 2007). Another study found that suicide may be more affected by the institutional living environment than by the use of direct supervision (Tartaro & Levy 2010). Despite the mixed results, we believe the research to date indicates that direct supervision looks promising.

Do People with Mental Illness Belong in Jail?

A Harris County (Texas) Jail inmate sat at a picnic table and explained to a reporter that he is extremely mentally ill and extremely intelligent. The *New York Times* reporter describes the inmate as veering in and out of reality during the interview. Sometimes he talked lucidly about taking medication for his severe bipolar disorder; at other times he described how Vice President Joseph Biden spoke to him through the television or explained that Pope Benedict XVI is his grandfather (Grissom 2011).

The Harris County Jail houses more than 10,000 inmates and about 2,400 of them are taking psychotropic medications. Some of the inmates with mental health problems say the jail—which is essentially the largest mental institution in Texas—provides the best mental health care available to them in the Houston area. Community mental health care suffered major cuts in 2003 as a result of the state budget crisis and more cuts seem likely under the current crisis. The situation is not much different in other states, and across the country more mentally ill people are likely to end up on the streets or behind bars.

1. It is important for public safety that persons with mental illness who commit serious crimes be held responsible for their actions. However, many people with mental illness who wind up in jail have committed low-level, nonviolent crimes, often as a result of their untreated mental illness or co-occurring substance abuse. Both jail officials and community-based treatment providers will often agree that the jail environment is not the best treatment setting for persons with mental illness. *Do you think people with mental illnesses belong in jail? If budget cuts continue to reduce community-based mental health programs, might jail be the best available option?*

2. The proportion of women with serious mental illness in jails is double that of men (Steadman, Osher, Robbins, Case, & Samuels 2009). The cause of the disparity awaits additional research, but some have suggested that early childhood experiences and higher rates of trauma exposure may explain some of the variation (Council of State Governments, n.d.). *Might experiences with physical or sexual abuse be a factor? Are men and women affected differently by such childhood experiences as growing up in homes where a parent or guardian abused alcohol or drugs? What other childhood experiences might explain the phenomenon?*

Source: Lou Oates/Shutterstock.com

LEARNING OUTCOMES 1

Explain the two basic types of pretrial release and provide examples of each type.

Pretrial release can be of either a financial or a nonfinancial type. When release is backed by a financial obligation it involves an agreement to pay cash or relinquish property to the court if the defendant fails to make required court appearances. Under nonfinancial release, the defendant either makes a simple promise to appear for trial or may be released under specific conditions such as a promise to participate in a treatment program.

1. Four states (Illinois, Kentucky, Oregon, and Wisconsin) have abolished commercial bail bonds and rely on the defendant's promise to return for trial or on deposits to courts instead of payments to private businesses. What are some pros and cons of abolishing commercial bail?

2. Eighty-two percent of defendants on pretrial release made all scheduled court appearances and had no pretrial misconduct. Eighteen percent of defendants on pretrial release missed court appearances or were rearrested for new crimes. Which of those statistics is more important to you when deciding whether to support pretrial release?

bail bond A written agreement by the defendant to pay cash or relinquish property to the court if the defendant fails to attend required court appearances.

release on recognizance Pretrial release based only on the defendant's promise to appear for trial (not backed with money or property).

conditional release The return of prisoners to the larger community with a brief period of supervision with rules such as curfew, treatment completion, and maintaining employment. Can be used either pretrial or postconviction.

unsecured bond When a defendant is released without having to make any payment but is liable for the full bail amount if required court appearances are missed.

LEARNING OUTCOMES 2

Distinguish jails from prisons and list at least three purposes served by jails.

Whereas jails are operated by local governments, detain persons not yet convicted of a crime, and hold convicted misdemeanants, prisons are operated by the state or federal government, hold only persons already convicted and sentenced, and provide custody for convicted felons. Jails typically hold both males and females in separate units of the same facility, but prisons usually hold males and females in separate facilities. Jails serve several purposes including detention of persons awaiting trial and the temporary holding of persons awaiting transfer to other agencies or facilities.

1. What are some pros and cons of having jails operated by the local government rather than the state government?

2. Many of the people in jail have not been convicted of anything. Should those who are awaiting trial be treated differently while in jail than those who have been convicted? Do people who have not yet been found guilty have more "rights" than those who have been found guilty?

3. Should governments invest in separate jail facilities for men and women rather than simply have separate units within the same facility? What would be advantages and disadvantages of doing that?

jails Confinement facilities usually operated by city or county governments and typically managed by that government's law enforcement agency.

integrated jail–prison systems A state government, rather than the more typical local government agency, is responsible for the administration and operation of jails located throughout the state.

Describe the general characteristics of the jail population and then summarize the characteristics of females in jail, jails in Indian Country, and the mentally ill in jail.

Most jail inmates are African-American and Hispanic males, but the percentage of females has increased since 1990 and along with that increase comes a need for greater attention to such gender-specific concerns, such as high rates of substance abuse, mental illness, and problems associated with physical and sexual abuse. The number of inmates in Indian Country jails has also increased in recent years and they are often kept in facilities that are neither safe nor secure. Most of the inmates are adult males convicted of assault, domestic violence, and DWI/DUI offenses. There are more mentally ill people in jail today than in hospitals. Some 17 percent of jail inmates suffer from a serious mental illness and as many as 64 percent have symptoms of a mental health disorder.

1. What are some explanations for the gender, racial, and ethnic characteristics of jail inmates?

2. Why is the percentage of female jail inmates increasing?

3. Veysey et al. (1998) have suggested modification to the jail environment that can better accommodate the special needs of women detainees and convicts. Argue for why such modifications should be done? Why should they not be done?

4. Why are jail facilities in Indian Country in such poor condition? Why should we care?

5. Discuss the extent to which you believe homeless mentally ill people in your community are involved with the criminal justice process. What options should the police have when dealing with such people?

mega jails The country's largest jails holding over 1,000 people.

Indian Country Land within an Indian reservation or land that is technically owned by the federal government but held in trust for a tribe or tribal member.

mental health disorder A broad category used to identify convicted offenders who are considered to have mental health problems as a result of self-reported clinical diagnosis or treatment by a mental health professional.

serious mental illness A narrow category used to identify convicted offenders suffering from such conditions as bipolar disorder, schizophrenia spectrum disorder, or major depression.

LEARNING
OUTCOMES
4

Compare and contrast jail design and inmate supervision in new generation jails to those operating before the mid-1970s.

Prior to the mid-1970s, jails were designed in a linear style with inmate supervision being only intermittent as officers strolled the cell block. With the advent of new generation jails, designs were based on pie-shaped pods with cells arranged in tiers around a central living area. This design allows inmate supervision to be either indirect (from an observation point separated from the living area) or direct (officer stays in the living area with the inmates).

1. How are the concepts of jail design and inmate supervision interrelated?

2. Why is it said that control lies in the hands of inmates in linear facilities, but in the hands of officers in new generation facilities?

3. Distinguish between indirect and direct supervision.

4. Do you accept or reject the idea that jail inmates are less likely to damage more normal furnishings than items designed to be unbreakable? Why?

5. If you were a jail correctional officer, which work environment would you prefer: a linear facility, a podular facility with indirect supervision, a podular facility with direct supervision? Why?

new generation jails Facilities using a specific architectural design and inmate supervision model in order to reduce violent and destructive behavior by the inmates.

linear facilities Jails and prisons designed with single- or multiple-occupancy cells aligned along corridors that, in turn, are often stacked in tiers.

intermittent supervision Inmate supervision method wherein custodial staff members are able to observe or interact with inmates only on an irregular or sporadic basis.

indirect supervision Inmate supervision method wherein custodial staff observe and interact with inmates remotely by watching through windows and listening via microphones.

direct supervision Inmate supervision method wherein custodial staff are placed—for their entire shift—in the inmates' living area.

MyCJLab

Go to the Chapter 6 section in *MyCJLab* to test your understanding of this chapter, access customized study content, engage in interactive simulations, complete critical thinking and research assignments, and view related online videos.

Additional Links

Watch the slide show and listen to the audio file about a bail bondsman at **www.nytimes.com/packages/html/us/20080128_BAIL_FEATURE/index.html**.

Visit the National Institute of Corrections Jails Division **http://nicic.gov/JailsDivision** and look at some of its initiatives and training programs.

The American Jail Association (AJA) **www.aja.org/** is a national, nonprofit organization dedicated to supporting those who work in and operate our nation's jails.

Read the Bureau of Justice Statistics report on *Jails in Indian Country, 2009* **http://bjs.ojp.usdoj.gov/index.cfm?ty=pbdetail&iid=2223**.

Visit the website for *The Released*, a PBS Frontline show about mentally ill offenders struggling to make it on the outside **www.pbs.org/wgbh/pages/frontline/released/**.

Managing Prisons and Prisoners

"Corrections must ... pursue a balanced program of humaneness, restoration, rehabilitation and the most appropriate sanctions consistent with public safety."

—American Correctional Association, "Justice" Principle

1 Outline the development and organization of the federal prison system.

2 Outline the development and organization of the state prison systems.

3 Explain how prisoners are classified and assigned in prisons.

4 Describe the various jobs and functions of prison staff.

5 Summarize the privatization of prisons.

7

Source: Donald R. Neudecker/Shutterstock.com

"As we pulled up to the prison, I wasn't sure what I was feeling. I tried not to show I was scared, but I was. I tried to act like I was just going to the mall. I wanted so much to be somewhere else, but I couldn't go. I guess I deserved all that I got. I don't even want to relive the experience as I tell you about it, but it is as vivid today as it was then. It was a traumatic day .... As we neared the entryway, you could see the razorwire on the fences that surrounds the place, and you could have heard a pin drop inside that bus. Nobody made a sound" (ADMIN 2011).

That is how "John"—convicted of murder at age 30 and given a 15 year to life sentence—describes his initial reactions as he arrived at the state reception facility to be processed into the prison system. "John" will stay at this initial facility where he will be interviewed

and tested before being sent to the state prison where he will begin his sentence. As "John" explains it,

You will be in this Receiving Center for a few weeks. One day they will inform you (after lockdown for the day) that you'll be leaving in the morning for whatever institution that they have decided to send you. Don't try to fight it. You might as well know right now that you can't fight them. They make all of your decisions for you now. If you make a fuss, you're still going to the institution of their choice. The only difference is, if you fight them, you'll go from the hole and once you get to your Parent Institution, you'll go to the hole there as well. It's better to start out at your Parent Institution with a clean record, don't you think?

DISCUSS Does the prison, or any specific prison employee, have an obligation to help newly arrived prisoners feel less anxious and to adjust as quickly as possible to the new environment? Or, could it be to the prison's advantage to keep newly arrived prisoners as nervous as possible? Why or why not?

Contemporary prisons have two primary purposes. First, they must provide security to the general public by keeping the prisoners confined, but must also provide a safe environment for the staff and inmates working and living there. Second, most prisons try to provide inmates with opportunities to change and thereby reduce the likelihood of them continuing their criminal behavior. The second goal is the more controversial (some people would prefer that prisons do no more than incapacitate or provide an experience that serves as a deterrent), but we see in this chapter that prisons mostly accept both security and treatment obligations.

This becomes apparent as we see the importance of both security and treatment in the federal and state prison systems, and especially when we consider the importance of inmate classification in meeting prison security and treatment goals. The chapter continues with attention to the prison staff members who have responsibility for the security and treatment tasks and concludes with a look at how private prisons are taking over some of the responsibilities previously held by the government.

▶ The Development and Organization of the Federal Prison System

The Federal Bureau of Prisons (BOP) was established in 1930 as part of the Department of Justice. The bureau had three goals:

1. To ensure consistent, centralized administration of the federal prison system

2. To professionalize the prison service

3. To provide more progressive and humane care for federal inmates

For more than 80 years, the BOP has sought to achieve these goals and in doing so has often served as a model for state correctional systems (Bureau of Prisons 2011, April 23).

A Brief History of the BOP

Prior to the creation of the BOP, most offenders convicted of violating federal laws were placed in state prisons and county jails. After the Civil War, the number of federal offenders began expanding, and the states and counties increasingly complained about the burden of housing federal criminals. In 1891, Congress responded by authorizing the construction of three

federal penitentiaries for men: one in Atlanta, Georgia; one in Leavenworth, Kansas; and one in McNeil Island, Washington. Later, a detention center, a youth facility, and the first federal women's reformatory opened as part of the federal prison system under the authority of the Justice Department.

By the 1920s the federal prisons were experiencing crowding problems and were plagued by inconsistent, haphazard administration. Much of the blame for that condition was due to the wardens, who were political appointees operating with no central direction as they applied their individual policies and procedures. Finally, in 1930, Congress decided to provide the needed centralization by establishing the BOP to manage and regulate all federal prisons. The new bureau quickly began to build or acquire new institutions in an attempt to relieve the crowding—including abandoned military barracks on Alcatraz Island.

The first federal women's reformatory officially opened in 1928 in Alderson, West

LEARNING OUTCOMES 1 — Outline the development and organization of the federal prison system.

Virginia. Dr. Mary B. Harris was the first warden who insisted that this showcase prison's goal was not to punish but to maximize rehabilitation. Sixteen redbrick cottages, each with separate kitchens and sewing areas, were situated in the mountains of rural West Virginia on beautiful grounds that resembled a college campus. The prison had no fences, no walls, and no armed guard towers, but successful escape was difficult because of the remote location. Over time, as the redbrick cottages became too expensive to keep repairing, a new four-story facility replaced the cottages. Alderson now holds approximately 1,000 women and remains a minimum-security facility.

Today there are 28 facilities that house federal female inmates. The "Big Seven"—Alderson, Bryan, Carswell, Danbury, Dublin, Tallahassee, and Waseca—house only women (although Dublin and Tallahassee each have a small male detention unit), but all the others are mixed men and women facilities (Bureau of Prisons 2011).

FIGURE 7.1 Rise and Fall of the U.S. Penitentiary at Alcatraz.
Source: Tomasz Szymanski/Shutterstock.

The BOP Today

Today, the BOP consists of 116 institutions and 22 community corrections offices and is responsible for more than 200,000 prisoners. Those prisoners, which are primarily white males with U.S. citizenship, are dealt with by a staff that is also mostly white

116 the BOP consists of 116 institutions and 22 community corrections offices and is responsible for more than 200,000 prisoners

TABLE 7.1	Quick Facts about the Bureau of Prisons.*		
Inmates by gender	Male: 93.5%	**Staff by gender**	Male: 72.4%
	Female: 6.5%		Female: 27.6%
Inmates by race	White: 58%	**Staff by race/ethnicity**	White (Non-Hispanic): 64%
	Black: 38%		African-American: 21%
	Native American: 2%		Hispanic: 11%
	Asian: 2%		Asian: 2%
			Native American: 2%
Inmates by ethnicity (could be any race)	Hispanic: 34%		
Inmates by citizenship	United States: 73%		
	Mexico: 18%		
	Remainder: 9%		
Inmates by offense	Drug Offenses: 51%		
	Weapons, Explosives, Arson: 15%		
	Immigration: 12%		
	Extortion, Fraud, Bribery: 5%		
	Sex Offenses: 5%		
	Robbery: 4%		
	Burglary, Larceny, Property Offenses: 4%		
	Homicide, Aggravated Assault, and Kidnapping Offenses: 3%		
	Other: 1%		

Source: Modified from Bureau of Prisons. (2011). Quick facts about the Bureau of Prisons. (April 23). Retrieved from www.bop.gov/news/quick.jsp.
*All data as on April 23, 2011.

The security level of a prison is determined by such features as the prison's design, perimeter, and staff-to-inmate ratio.

and male. From the bureau's central office in Washington, DC, the director and assistant directors oversee BOP activities around the nation. For management purposes, the country is divided into six geographic regions, each with a regional director.

An indication of the changing nature of federal corrections is the influx of persons linked to terrorism. In 2009, the BOP housed more than 300 persons with a history of or connection to international or domestic terrorism. Management of these offenders is comprehensive and includes such things as coordinated information sharing with relevant agencies, close monitoring of general correspondence and social telephone calls,

and staff training on identifying recruitment and radicalization activities. Although there have been no indications of organized recruitment or radicalization efforts, BOP recognizes the need for continued vigilance so pockets of concern can be quickly identified and managed (Bureau of Prisons 2009).

To assist the BOP in policies, programs, and protocols related to terrorism, the Counter-Terrorism Unit (CTU) was established in 2006. CTU responsibilities include identifying and validating inmate involvement in terrorist activities, monitoring and analyzing terrorist inmate communications, and providing counter-terrorism training (Bureau of Prisons 2009).

Security Levels at Federal Facilities

The security level of a prison is determined by such features as the prison's design, perimeter, and staff-to-inmate ratio. The more elaborate a prison's design and perimeter, and the higher its staff-to-inmate ratio, the more secure the prison is said to be. The BOP classifies its prisons by five security levels (minimum, low, medium, high, and administrative). Administrative facilities (which include those with special missions, such as detaining pretrial offenders or offenders with serious medical problems) can actually hold inmates in all security levels. An exception is the administrative-maximum penitentiary, which is an administrative facility but holds only those inmates that are extremely dangerous, violent, or escape-prone. As such, these inmates are under the tightest security available in the BOP.

In addition to the more distinctive facility types, the BOP also operates satellite camps that are small, minimum-security units adjacent to a main facility with a higher security rating. Inmates at these camps provide labor to the main institution and to off-site work programs. For example, the Federal Correctional Institution in Jesup, Georgia, is a medium-security

Minimum Security facilities, also called Federal Prison Camps (FPC), have dormitory housing, limited or no perimeter fencing, and a relatively low staff-to-inmate ratio. FPCs are work- and program-oriented and their inmates often work at nearby military bases or at other federal prisons.

Low Security Federal Correctional Institutions (FCIs) have double-fenced perimeters. Most use dormitory or cubicle housing and include strong work and program components. The staff-to-inmate ratio is higher than in FPCs.

Medium Security FCIs and some U.S. Penitentiaries housing medium-security inmates use this security level. These facilities have double fenced perimeters with electronic detection systems and use mostly cell-type housing. They have a higher staff-to-inmate ratio and provide a variety of work and treatment programs.

High Security institutions are called U.S. Penitentiaries (USPs) and they have highly secured perimeters featuring walls or reinforced fences. Inmate housing is in multiple- or single-occupant cells and the staff-to-inmate ratio is the highest of all facilities.

Administrative facilities are institutions with special missions, such as the detention of pretrial offenders (for example, Metropolitan Detention Centers), treatment of inmates with serious medical problems (Federal Medical Centers), or for holding extremely dangerous or escape-prone inmates (Administrative Max USP).

FIGURE 7.2 The Five BOP Security Levels.
Source: Federal Bureau of Prisons.

facility housing male offenders. It has one adjacent low-security satellite facility and a minimum-security prison camp, both housing male inmates.

A final type of BOP facility to mention is actually a grouping of facilities. In 1991 the BOP began constructing the first Federal Correctional Complex (FCC). The complex, located in Florence, Colorado, used a new design concept with several correctional facilities of different security levels at a single site. Benefits of the complex include the obvious financial savings like lower construction and operating costs, but also have personnel advantages, since staff members can have career mobility without making geographic moves. Today there are 14 such complexes located across the country, each with at least two main facilities.

▶ The Development and Organization of State Prison Systems

State prison systems are typically operated by the state's **department of corrections** (DOC) or a state agency with a similar name (for example, Hawaii's Department of Public Safety, New York State's Department of Correctional Services, and Ohio's Department of Rehabilitation and Correction). Each state's DOC manages at least the state's adult prison facilities and may also be responsible for parole services and community corrections.

At the time of the last national census of state correctional facilities (Stephan 2008), there were about 1,700 state correctional facilities with nearly 1,200 identified as confinement facilities (for example, prisons, penitentiaries, work camps) and about 500 as community-based facilities (for example, halfway houses, restitution centers, residential treatment centers). Some states have as few as 6 or 7 correctional facilities (for example, Maine, Rhode Island, South Dakota, Utah, and Wyoming) whereas others have 100 or more (California, Florida, and Texas). Most state correctional facilities hold fewer than 500 inmates although some have a daily population exceeding 2,500 prisoners (examples include some prisons in California, Florida, Pennsylvania, and Texas).

Overcrowding is a problem in most states, with state correctional facilities operating at an average of 114 percent of **design capacity** (the number of inmates that facility planners or architects intended for the facility) and 108 percent of **rated capacity** (the maximum number of beds or inmates allocated by a rating official to institutions in the states). The problem is especially notable in Alabama and California where prisons are at more than 170 percent of design capacity and in California, Illinois, and Washington, where prisons operate at more than 130 percent of rated capacity (Stephan 2008).

500 Most state correctional facilities hold fewer than 500 inmates although some have a daily population exceeding 2,500 prisoners

Security Levels at State Facilities

The actual terms used to designate the security levels of state correctional facilities vary by state, as does the number of levels used. In order to provide a summary of facility security levels, the census of correctional facilities (Stephan 2008) uses the most basic of distinctions: minimum (including low or no security designations), medium, or maximum (including those identified in some states as super maximum, close, or high security). Some facilities mix several security levels, while others house a single level. Most of prisoners held in the country's state prisons are in medium-security facilities (43 percent), followed by those in maximum-security facilities (38 percent) and minimum-security facilities (19 percent).

Inmates assigned to **minimum-security facilities** have the most freedom and privileges afforded any state prisoner. These facilities, some of which resemble residential houses and even college campuses, are typically dormitory-style, barracks, or small rooms for which inmates have their own key. The absence of walls, fences, guarded towers, and obvious physical barriers is not unusual. Such facilities are desirable for offenders who have earned a transfer there based on good behavior and who show little threat to themselves or others. Minimum-security facilities are often used for inmates nearing their release date and who are eligible to participate in work- or education-release programs to help prepare them for return to the community.

Prisoners at **medium-security facilities** are not allowed to leave the institution grounds without an escort. The perimeter is lined with chain-link fences, razor wire, and electronic sensors, and the staff-to-inmate ratio is higher than in

LEARNING OUTCOMES 2
Outline the development and organization of the state prison systems.

GLOSSARY

department of corrections The state agency responsible for managing and operating the state's adult prison system.

design capacity The number of inmates that facility planners or architects intended for the facility.

rated capacity The maximum number of beds or inmates allocated by a rating official to institutions in the states.

minimum-security facility Institutions where inmates have considerable personal freedom and more relaxed supervision.

medium-security facility Institutions where inmates receive more supervision than at minimum-security prisons, but still have considerable freedom to move around to work assignments and programming activities.

maximum-security facility Designed for the fullest possible supervision, control, and surveillance of general population inmates. Also known as *close-security prisons*.

supermax prison Prisons at the highest security level, with prisoners isolated from the general population and from each other. Also known as *control units* or *secured housing units*.

dispersion approach Prison administrators spread troublemakers to prisons throughout the system or in various units of the prison.

concentration approach Prisoners are grouped together in special prisons or special units within a prison, and their activities and movements are severely restricted and highly monitored.

Minimum

Minimum security includes both institutional and community-based institutions, such as prerelease/work-release centers, restitution centers, trusty units, large drug rehabilitation centers, community corrections facilities, forestry or wilderness camps, and honor camps. Inmates have considerable personal freedom and are often given opportunities on a time-restricted basis for work furloughs and educational release outside the institution.

Medium

These prisons may resemble higher-security prisons from the outside, but inmates in a medium-security facility have more freedom of movement inside the walls. Although most prisoners spend most of the day outside their housing area, they are still locked in their housing area at night after curfew.

Maximum

The "Big House," as the nineteenth-century maximum-security prisons were often called, was designed for the fullest possible supervision, control, and surveillance of inmates. Contemporary maximum-security prisons forego the high walls and rely instead on fenced perimeters with electronic sensing devices and video surveillance to alert officials about perimeter breaches.

FIGURE 7.3 **Three General Security Levels for State Facilities.**
Source: Federal Bureau of Prisons.

minimum-security facilities. However, there is relatively free movement of the inmates within the confines of the prison itself as they move around the living quarters, walk to work assignments, and visit to programming areas.

Traditionally, **maximum-security prisons** were built as fortress-like structures with high stone walls surrounding groupings of buildings that serve as cell blocks, chow halls, auditoriums, laundry rooms, gymnasiums, and chapels. Guard towers were attached to the walls at the corners and other strategic places, such as at the front and back entrances. Although some of those early prisons still exist, the more recently constructed maximum-security prisons tend to rely on a double-fence perimeter (usually including coiled razor wire) or an electric fence rather than high walls. Prisoners are housed in single or double cells, and time out of the cell is structured and controlled with passes for a specific purpose. Security takes priority over rehabilitation, so fewer treatment and work programs are present. The theory behind this is that maximum-security inmates have

the more recently constructed maximum-security prisons tend to rely on a double-fence perimeter (usually including coiled razor wire) or an electric fence rather than high walls

shown through their attitudes and behavior that they need more regulation in their daily lives.

A small number of prisons at the highest security level are known as **supermax prisons**, or what some states call "control units" or "secured housing units." The first supermax prison was the U.S. Penitentiary at Marion, Illinois, which converted to permanent lockdown status in 1983 due to the murder of two correctional officers. Since then, many states have followed the federal lead and have modified existing prisons or built new ones to allow implementation of the control-unit philosophy. Because Marion was not built as a lockdown facility (but was being used as one), the federal government eventually constructed an administrative/maximum penitentiary (ADX) prison in Florence, Colorado, that was specifically designed as a supermax facility.

A supermax facility can be either an administrative segregation housing unit within a maximum-custody facility or the entire facility can consist of prisoners at the highest custody level who are isolated from the general population of prisoners and from each other. Inmates assigned to these units are believed to pose a threat to other prisoners and/or correctional officers based on gang membership or behavior while incarcerated. Supermax prisoners may have killed someone while in custody, have a pattern of assaulting other officers, have attempted or completed escape from a high-custody facility, or have incited or threatened to incite a disturbance in a correctional facility.

The growth of supermax facilities for troublesome inmates indicates a prison management trend away from a **dispersion approach** and toward a **concentration approach**. In the dispersion approach, prison administrators spread troublemakers around the system or in various units of the prison. Sometimes they might even be sent to other states or to the Federal Bureau of Prisons. The goal was to prevent troublemakers from collaborating, and it enabled officials to break up cliques and gangs. In most cases, the dispersion approach backfired and actually assisted prison gang recruitment—leaders started a chapter in each new location.

Under a concentration approach, prisoners are grouped together, and their activities and movements are severely restricted and highly monitored. As a result, the general prison population is more easily and safely managed because the most ardent troublemakers have been removed.

▶ Inmate Classification

When the courts sentence offenders to imprisonment, the judge has no control over the facility at which the offenders will serve time or the treatment programs in which they will

When the courts sentence offenders to imprisonment, the judge has no control over the facility at which the offenders will serve time or the treatment programs in which they will participate.

participate. Those tasks belong to a team of correctional experts that specializes in determining the risk each offender poses to the community and within the prison, as well as the offender's treatment needs. The process and procedures by which this accomplished is called **classification**.

Classification in the Early Years

The earliest versions of classification were to separate prisoners on the basis of such simple and obvious criteria as gender, age, and offense seriousness. It was not until the twentieth century that classification was viewed as a crucial element in prison management. This began in the late 1920s with the efforts of F. Lovell Bixby, a psychologist in charge of the classification division for New Jersey's prisons.

In the late 1920s, Bixby developed a classification procedure that standardized the testing of newly sentenced offenders throughout New Jersey's diverse prison facilities. He prepared various reporting forms in order to standardize information that had been gathered on each new arrival and tried to identify some of their personality traits, work skills, and educational needs. Using the collected data for each prisoner, Bixby divided them into groups requiring minimum, medium, or maximum security (McKelvey, 1977). By the 1950s, classification was being implemented throughout the country's prisons as a way of separating inmates based on the security risk they presented and to determine what treatment programs might benefit them the most.

Although the classification process provided more standardization in prisoner placement, the procedures remained primarily subjective in nature. Decisions about which prisoners needed what services were made in the "professional opinion" of treatment personnel, whereas decisions about offender custody level were based on the "experiences" of the security staff. In the mid-1970s a move toward greater objectivity in classification helped bring the process into the modern era.

Increasing Objectivity in Classification

As the concept of rehabilitation was increasingly criticized and as the focus shifted to public safety and victims' rights, classification was also modified to better fit the changing penal philosophies. Classification procedures used in prison and in community corrections were increasingly concerned with the risk that offenders posed to public safety and to other prisoners. Treatment needs were of secondary concern.

In the latter half of the 1970s, court decisions directed prison officials to make significant changes in the classification process. Federal courts ruled that classification, though not constitutionally required (*French* v. *Heyne* 1977), must be rational and reasonable rather than arbitrary and capricious (*Kelley* v. *Brewer* 1975; *Laaman* v. *Heigemore* 1977; *Pugh* v. *Locke* 1976).

In the 1980s the courts continued to agree that there was no constitutional requirement for a classification system, but they also recognized that there may be times when classification is necessary to ensure inmates' constitutional rights to a safe and secure living environment (*Grubbs* v. *Bradley* 1982). The rational and reasonable requirement did not provide specific criteria that prison officials could use to meet those conditions, but the implication was that procedures should be more objective than subjective—and that is exactly the direction in which the states moved.

LEARNING OUTCOMES 3 Explain how prisoners are classified and assigned in prisons.

GLOSSARY

classification The process and procedures by which prison officials determine the risk posed by each offender and the offender's individual treatment needs.

objective classification system Classification procedures that have a factual, impartial, and observable base rather than the intuitive footing of subjective systems.

external classification A stage in the classification process wherein a prisoner's custody level is determined and, based on that custody level, in which the prison inmate begins serving the sentence.

internal classification Establishes the prisoner's housing, program, and work assignments within the prison.

prison risk assessment A determination of the risk an offender poses to escape or to be a management problem for prison officials.

public risk assessment A determination of the risk posed by an offender to the general public.

static factors Individual characteristics that are constant or happened in the past and cannot be changed; such as a person's gender, age at first arrest, or number of prior arrests.

(**Think About It...**

Classification committees have operated in federal and state prisons since the mid-twentieth century. Composed of professionals representing a variety of areas, the committee members review reports on newly arrived inmates and decide such things as the inmate's work area, treatment programming, and security level. What disciplines do you think should be represented on a classification committee? What would people with undergraduate majors in sociology, criminal justice, psychology, rehabilitation, education, religion, or other areas be able to add to the discussion about the most appropriate custody level and treatment program for an inmate?

TABLE 7.2 | Four Generations of Risk/Needs Assessment.

First Generation Assessments	The assessment of risk/needs relied on subjective experiences or professional opinion.
Second Generation Assessments	Using mathematical and statistical tools to assess risk, these methods predicted the likelihood of recidivism based on measurable static factors such as age, gender, prior convictions, and the nature of the present offense. These tools were 4–6 times more effective than professional judgment alone in predicting recidivism.
Third Generation Assessments	These instruments include an assessment of dynamic risk factors but predict recidivism no better than do second generation tools. However, unlike second generation tools, these provide guidance as to how recidivism can be reduced by addressing criminogenic needs.
Fourth Generation Assessments	These most recent assessment tools build on the third generation instruments by incorporating recommendations for case management and supervision plans.

Source: Developed from National Center for State Courts. http://contentdm.scsconline.org/cdm4/item_viewer.php?CISOROOT=criminal&CISOPTR=185&REC=3.

TABLE 7.3 | Distinguishing Features of an Objective Classification System.

Reliability and Validity	The use of criteria that have been proven through research to use both reliable and valid factors to assess a prisoner's custody level
Professionalism	A centralized classification unit that is adequately staffed with well-trained professional personnel who have control over all inter-agency transfers
Continuity	A centralized classification unit that is responsible for monitoring the classification unit and preparing all policies and procedures that pertain to classification
Transparency	A fully automated classification system such that each classification decision, and the factors used to make each decision, is recorded and available for analysis
Reclassification	An initial and reclassification process where all prisoners are reviewed at least annually to update and possibly modify the prisoner's current classification level
Discretion	The use of overrides to allow staff to depart from the scored classification level for reasons approved by the agency

Source: Austin, J. (2003). Findings in prison classification and risk assessment. Retrieved from National Institute of Corrections Library website: http://nicic.gov/Library/018888.

Objective classification systems are ones that have a factual, impartial, and observable base rather than the intuitive footing of subjective systems. The goals of classification remain the same—determining risk and needs. The classification procedures are often described as falling into two stages: external prison classification and internal prison classification. **External classification** determines a prisoner's custody level, which in turn determines the prison where the inmate begins serving the sentence. **Internal classification** establishes the prisoner's housing, program, and work assignments. Both of these classification systems deserve some elaboration.

External Prison Classification

Upon receiving a prison sentence, felony offenders are transferred to a facility where they are officially turned over to the state's DOC. This facility, which is typically called a reception and diagnostic unit or reception and orientation unit, will house the newly sentenced prisoners for several weeks as they undergo a variety of tests and interviews. The tests may include those measuring intelligence quotient (IQ), reading comprehension, and the grade level at which the inmate is operating. Complete medical and dental exams will be conducted along with a determination of any medicine that must be continued or should be started. Interviews with psychologists, clergy, vocational rehabilitation professionals, and others are also likely.

Of particular importance at this stage is determining the risk posed by the inmate. Austin (2003) points out that the risk being assessed here (**prison risk assessment**) is different from that which may have been assessed earlier (**public risk assessment**). For example, when probation officials were making a sentence recommendation the concern was with the level of risk the offender posed to the public. That is, was this person likely to continue engaging in criminal behavior if allowed to remain in the community? Prison risk assessment, however, is less interested in the risk posed to the public (given the offender's removal from

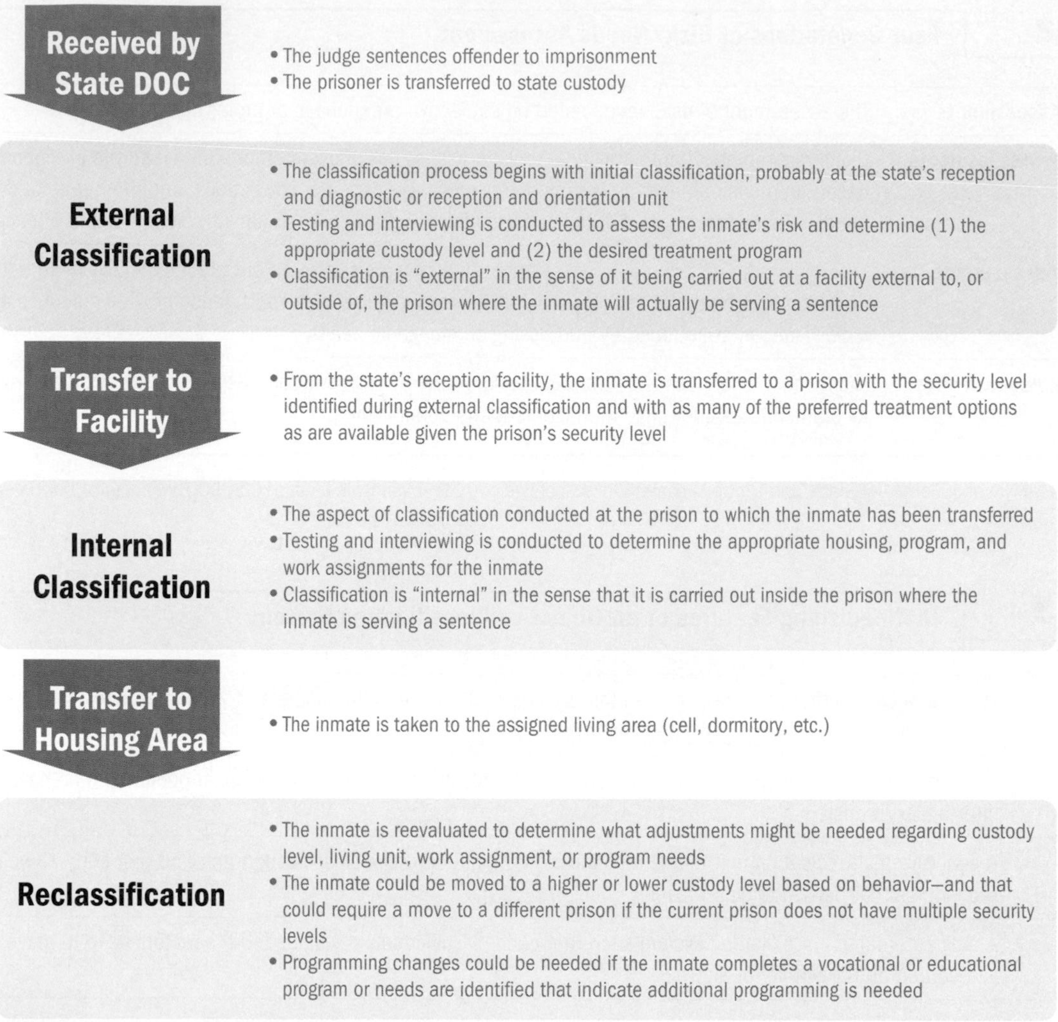

Received by State DOC
- The judge sentences offender to imprisonment
- The prisoner is transferred to state custody

External Classification
- The classification process begins with initial classification, probably at the state's reception and diagnostic or reception and orientation unit
- Testing and interviewing is conducted to assess the inmate's risk and determine (1) the appropriate custody level and (2) the desired treatment program
- Classification is "external" in the sense of it being carried out at a facility external to, or outside of, the prison where the inmate will actually be serving a sentence

Transfer to Facility
- From the state's reception facility, the inmate is transferred to a prison with the security level identified during external classification and with as many of the preferred treatment options as are available given the prison's security level

Internal Classification
- The aspect of classification conducted at the prison to which the inmate has been transferred
- Testing and interviewing is conducted to determine the appropriate housing, program, and work assignments for the inmate
- Classification is "internal" in the sense that it is carried out inside the prison where the inmate is serving a sentence

Transfer to Housing Area
- The inmate is taken to the assigned living area (cell, dormitory, etc.)

Reclassification
- The inmate is reevaluated to determine what adjustments might be needed regarding custody level, living unit, work assignment, or program needs
- The inmate could be moved to a higher or lower custody level based on behavior—and that could require a move to a different prison if the current prison does not have multiple security levels
- Programming changes could be needed if the inmate completes a vocational or educational program or needs are identified that indicate additional programming is needed

FIGURE 7.4 The Classification Process from Intake to Reclassification.

the public) and more interested in identifying those prisoners who pose a risk to escape or may cause management problems. As a result, the purpose of prison risk assessment is to determine the custody level to which a prisoner should be initially assigned. That assignment allows officials to match the inmate's custody level with a prison's security level—for example, a minimum-custody prisoner goes to a minimum-security prison whereas a close-custody prisoner will go to a high-security prison.

Many of the assessment instruments used to determine prison risk during the external classification process are the same as those used to determine public risk. The LSI-R, mentioned in Chapters 1 and 5, is a good example, but Austin (2003) notes that several factors important for public risk assessment are irrelevant for prison risk assessment (for example, current employment status, current marital status) or have no predictive value regarding prison conduct (for example, age at first arrest, associations with criminal peer groups). As such, work is needed on developing assessment instruments for prison risk specifically.

Internal Prison Classification

Once custody level has been determined and the prisoner has been transferred to a prison with the appropriate security level, another type of classification becomes important. This internal classification system governs facility-specific decisions such as where and with whom the prisoner will be housed, the types of

Prison risk assessment is less interested in the risk posed to the public and more interested in identifying those prisoners who pose a risk to escape or may cause management problems.

dynamic factors Individual characteristics that can be changed, such as antisocial attitudes, values, and beliefs, poor self-control, criminal peers, and criminal thinking patterns.

criminogenic Factors that cause or tend to cause criminal behavior.

responsivity The process in which prisoners are assigned to treatment programs designed to address their particular set of dynamic criminogenic needs.

reclassification A stage in the classification process wherein an inmate's custody level, treatment program, or work assignment is reevaluated to be sure they are still appropriate.

Classifying Women with the LSI-R

The Level of Services Inventory-Revised (LSI-R) is a highly regarded classification tool that is used in both community corrections and institutional settings to identify such things as the supervision or custody level that is most appropriate for an offender. However, the LSI-R, as with most such instruments, was developed based on data from males and may not be valid when applied to females. That is because some criminologists believe that men and women get involved in crime differently (that is, the pathways to crime are "gendered") and that men and women are exposed to different risk factors (for example, factors such

as victimization, abuse, and low self-esteem may have greater impact on women). When classification tools that ignore or avoid these points are used to determine needed supervision levels and service types, the result may not be accurate for women offenders.

Vose and her colleagues (2009) tested the LSI-R's applicability to women offenders in terms of the LSI-R's ability to accurately predict recidivism (higher LSI-R scores are considered to predict persons most likely to recidivate). Their results indicate that the LSI-R is a valid instrument for predicting recidivism with both male and female offenders and should be considered a useful resource in corrections.

---

programs and services to be made available to the prisoner, and the prisoner's work assignment.

As with the assessment instruments used for external classification purposes, those that provide objectivity for internal classification remain rather closely tied to instruments designed more for community corrections than for institutional placement. Exceptions include the Adult Internal Management System (AIMS), which identifies inmates who are likely to be incompatible in terms of housing and those most likely to pose risk to the safety and security of the facility.

Identifying the prisoner's program needs can also rely on evaluation instruments used for community corrections, but an obvious weakness of doing so is that many programs available in the community are not available in the confines of a prison. The Case Needs Identification and Analysis (CNIA) instrument is designed to assess inmate needs at admission and the Prison Inmate Inventory (PII) measures such items as truthfulness, self-esteem, and stress-coping abilities in order to identify inmate needs. These and other reliable and valid classification instruments are careful to address dynamic

rather than static factors since the dynamic factors are those to which treatment programs are most effectively directed. This focus on dynamic factors is best understood in the context of criminogenic needs.

Criminogenic Needs

Research has identified a variety of factors that predict recidivism—the likelihood that an offender will repeat his or her criminal behavior. Among those predictors are the person's gender, age at first arrest, number of prior arrests, and alcohol/substance abuse history. An interesting thing about those factors is that they are all constant or happened in the past and cannot be changed. They are, in other words, **static factors**. Developing treatment programs that try to affect these unchangeable factors are, of course, useless. But there are also other predictors of recidivism, such as antisocial attitudes, values and beliefs, poor self-control, criminal peers, and criminal thinking patterns. These are **dynamic factors** because they can be changed.

TABLE 7.4	Recommendations for Effective Classification of Women Offenders.
	Much like prisons themselves, prison classification systems were developed with male offenders in mind. Some of those systems were valid for women, but some were not. Attention to recommendations such as the following could make classification more gender-responsive.

Ensure the validity of classification systems for women offenders.	In some states, the external classification process is the same for both men and women despite validation studies showing that the systems are invalid for women. A common result is that prison staff members make extensive use of overrides wherein the staff member's subjective opinion is relied upon rather than an objective instrument to determine a woman prisoner's custody level.
Modify current risk factors and/or scale cutoff points to reflect the differences between women and men.	Validation studies often find statistically significant differences in the predictive power of risk factors for men and women offenders. For example, criminal history factors are poor predictors of prison adjustment for women offenders and education factors appear to be an indicator of stability among men but not women offenders. Classification systems that ignore such gender differences will not provide accurate custody predictions for women prisoners.
Include gender-specific needs in screening and assessment.	Current assessment scales do not include risk and need factors that may be especially relevant to women offenders. These may include needs related to abuse, relationships, parenting, self-esteem, and victimization. Omitting such factors may result in the absence of essential programs for women—although see this chapter's Evidence-Based Practice box.

Sources: From Hardyman & Van Voorhis (2004); Van Voorhis, et al., 2010.

Major Risk/Need Factor	Characteristics	Dynamic Criminogenic Need
History of Antisocial Behavior	Early and continuing involvement in a number and variety of antisocial acts in a variety of settings	Build up low-risk noncriminal alternative behavior in risky situations
Antisocial Personality Pattern	Adventurous pleasure seeking, weak self-control, restlessly aggressive, callous, and disagreeable	Build problem-solving skills, self-management skills, anger management and coping skills
Antisocial Cognition	Attitudes, values, beliefs, and rationalizations supportive of crime, and cognitive emotional states of anger, resentment, and defiance Criminal/reformed criminal/anticriminal identity	Reduce antisocial cognition; recognize risky thinking and feeling; build up alternatives, less risky thinking and feeling; adopt reform/anticriminal identity
Antisocial Associates	Close association with criminal others and relative isolation from anticriminal others; immediate social support for crime	Reduce association with criminal others; enhance association with anticriminal others

DISCUSS *Imagine that you are a counselor working with a prison inmate who has been identified in the classification process as having all four of the major risk/need factors shown. Select one of those factors and provide some specific examples of what you could do to implement the suggested action under the dynamic criminogenic need column.*

Source: Modified from Table 2 in Andrews, D. A., & Dowden, C. (2007). The risk–need–responsivity model of assessment and human service in prevention and corrections: Crime-prevention jurisprudence. *Canadian Journal of Criminology & Criminal Justice, 49*(4), 439–464.

Both static and dynamic factors can be **criminogenic** in the sense that they cause or tend to cause criminal behavior. The interviews, tests, and evaluation instruments used during the internal classification process help identify these criminogenic factors or needs. Prisoners are then assigned to treatment programs designed to address their particular set of dynamic criminogenic needs—a process called **responsivity** (see Table 7.5).

Reclassification

Because criminogenic needs are dynamic, the classification process must include procedures to keep pace with changing risks and needs of prisoners. The **reclassification** procedures provide an opportunity to reevaluate the inmate's prison risk assessment (possibly, good behavior may allow a custody level change from medium to minimum) and current needs assessment (maybe the inmate completed his or her GED and can now enter a vocational training program).

Austin (2003) suggests that no later than 12 months after prison admission, a reclassification form should be used to score the prisoner on factors such as the type and number of misconduct reports lodged against the prisoner, the prisoner's participation in treatment programs, and the prisoner's work performance. In this way, the inmate's risk status (custody level) and programming needs are kept current and relevant.

Because criminogenic needs are dynamic, the classification process must include procedures to keep pace with changing risks and needs of prisoners.

Prisons Staff

A prison operates only through the efforts of people in a wide variety of occupations. Even in smaller facilities, the warden manages employees with responsibilities in areas ranging from laundry and food services to facility maintenance and recreation. As facility size increases, there may be positions related to prison industries and the need for medical services. We cannot give the deserved attention to all these staff members, so instead we concentrate on those linked to the two more well-known aspects of prison work: employees responsible for security and employees responsible for treatment.

Correctional Officers

Correctional officers (COs) maintain order within the institution and enforce rules and regulations. In this way they are responsible for public safety (ensuring that criminals confined to an institution stay there) and institutional security (guaranteeing that prisoners and staff members are safe while in the institution). Although they have no law enforcement responsibilities outside the institution where they work, COs maintain security and inmate accountability in prisons to prevent disturbances, assaults, and escapes.

This occupational group, which accounts for more than 60 percent of prison

 LEARNING OUTCOMES 4 Describe the various jobs and functions of prison staff.

GLOSSARY

correctional officer The person responsible for maintaining order within the institution and enforcing prison rules and regulations.

mental health screening An examination performed on each newly admitted inmate that usually includes a review of the medical screening, behavior observations, an inquiry into any mental health history, and an assessment of suicide potential.

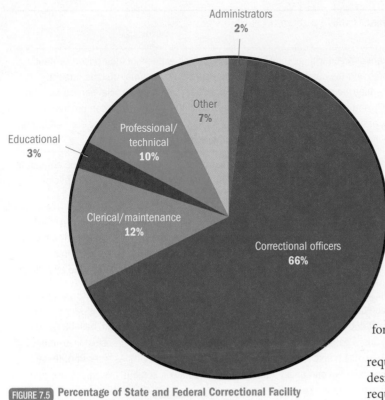

Other
7%

Professional/
technical
10%

Educational
3%

Clerical/maintenance
12%

Correctional officers
66%

FIGURE 7.5 **Percentage of State and Federal Correctional Facility Employees by Occupational Category.**

Source: Chart developed from data in Table 4 (p. 4) of Stephan, J. J. (2008). Census of state and federal correctional facilities, 2005.(NCJ 222182). Retrieved from Bureau of Justice Statistics website: http://bjs.ojp.usdoj.gov/index.cfm?ty=pbdetail&iid=530.

Correctional officers (COs) maintain order within the institution and enforce rules and regulations.

The unskilled perception is unfortunate and inaccurate because today's CO must be intelligent, well-trained, and have extensive interpersonal skills. Unfortunately, the poorly paid part seems to be true. Using salary averages from the Bureau of Labor Statistics (2011), in 2010 correctional officers nationally had an average salary of $43,000 compared with $56,000 for the police and sheriff patrol officer category. Salary amounts continue to increase for these occupation categories, but until the gap between correctional officer and police officer earnings closes, it seems unlikely that college graduates will pursue CO positions with the same enthusiasm they have for police officer positions.

Lack of interest in becoming a CO means the entry-level requirements for the position might be less stringent than is desirable. To encourage a larger pool of applicants, education requirements tend to be high school graduate (or GED) rather than any college credits or degrees. In those states requiring prehire testing, applicants must pass physical agility, psychological evaluation, reading comprehension, report writing, and drug screening tests. Oral interviews and background checks are also typical (American Correctional Association 2008a).

Treatment Staff

Correctional officers may be expected to actively support treatment goals as they ensure a safe and secure environment; however, persons more directly charged with carrying out treatment duties range from full-time psychiatrists, psychologists, and social workers to other professionals working with prisoners on health, ethical, educational, vocational, and recreational issues. The programs through which treatment objectives are achieved are also quite varied. A more complete understanding of treatment in a prison environment is found in Chapter 9, but in this chapter we briefly consider the people

staff at both state and federal levels, is mostly white non-Hispanic males (Bureau of Prisons 2011, April 23; Camp 2003). Exceptions (American Correctional Association, 2007) include Mississippi where more than 60 percent are female and a few states where the majority of COs are minority group members. For example, in Hawaii more than 80 percent are "Other" (presumably, Asian-Pacific Islanders) and in Alabama, Arkansas, Georgia, Louisiana, Mississippi, and South Carolina where the majority of COs are African-American.

Seiter (2002) notes that many people receiving a two- or four-year college degree do not seriously consider CO positions because they are viewed as unskilled and poorly paid.

TABLE 7.6	**Frequently Asked Questions about Female Correctional Officers.**
When did female COs first come on the scene?	The earliest prisoners, both male and female, were guarded by men. The first female prison "guards" (as they were called) were hired in 1832 to work in the women's wing of Auburn Prison (Zupan 1992).
Are female COs allowed to work in male prisons?	Sex-based employment discrimination by public employers is prohibited by Title VII of the 1964 Civil Rights Act. As a result, the courts have generally upheld a woman's right to employment in all-male institutions. In 1984, a federal court (Grummet v. Rushen) recognized a woman's right to employment as taking precedence over inmates' rights to privacy.
Is safety compromised when female COs are on duty?	Several studies have consistently found that female COs are not assaulted more frequently or more seriously than male officers. Nor is there any evidence that male COs are assaulted more frequently when there are more women working in the prison. In fact, there is reason to believe that women officers have a calming effect on male prisoners and that the presence of female COs reduces tension and hostility in the institution (Lawrence & Mahan 1998).

TABLE 7.7 | Primary Treatment Staff Positions.

Case managers	Case managers, also called caseworkers, are charged with guiding inmates through all aspects of their prison sentence and may serve as a liaison between inmates and the outside community. More specific duties may include inmate classification (if that is the only or primary duty, the position may be called *classification officer*), social service support (for example, facilitating contact with family and appropriate others in the outside community), institution program planning (for example, assisting with work assignments, educational/vocational classes, group counseling sessions), and release preparation (for example, helping inmates with postrelease living and employment arrangements).
Correctional educators	All correctional educators must be certified to provide instruction in either academic or vocational areas. These educators provide instruction in such areas as literacy, secondary education, GED preparation, vocational training, and special education.
Counseling staff	Members of the counseling staff include those working with prisoners having mental health problems or simply needing assistance working through problems such as poor life skills, alcohol and drug dependence, or employment related issues. The mental health counseling is provided by employees who may be psychiatrists, licensed professional counselors, clinical social workers, psychologists, and others. More general counseling and/or assistance could be provided by college graduates with degrees in criminal justice, sociology, and other social sciences.
Recreation staff	Members of the recreation staff provide recreation programs that teach and develop the social skills necessary for participation in free society. They organize outdoor group intramural activities (for example, flag football, baseball), indoor group activities (for example, card games, board games), individual activities (for example, playing musical instruments, making crafts, performing in talent shows), and club activities (for example, Jaycees, stamp club). As a result of these efforts, inmates learn the value of teamwork, fair play, and anger management, and have a constructive way to use idle time and relieve the stress and tension of incarceration (Kahler 1999).
Religious staff	Religious staff members provide religious services, counsel troubled inmates, and advise inmates of "bad news" from home or from prison authorities. More recently, their role has expanded to include organizing volunteers, facilitating religious furlough visits, contracting for outside religious services, and training prison staff about the basic tenets and rituals of the different faith groups, especially the nontraditional ones about which some staff members may have limited or no knowledge (Dammer 1996; Schwartz & Fewell 1999).

responsible for implementing the treatment programs. Those people, after all, may play a key role in reducing recidivism. For our purposes, treatment staff members include those persons in positions related to counseling, recreation, religion, and education.

Members of the counseling staff are responsible for providing such programs as cognitive behavioral therapy, anger management, substance abuse therapy, and others. These prison employees will typically have specific training (received as part of a graduate education in such disciplines as psychology or social work, or as part of a prison's in-service training program for employees interested in broadening their education and expertise) that enables them to provide particular treatment modalities.

Some prison counselors work specifically with prisoners having mental health problems—an increasingly important

and time-consuming inmate category. Adams and Ferrandino (2008) note that the problem of mentally ill prisoners is serious and substantial and by all indications is likely to worsen. The first steps in working with these inmates are to identify which ones may need mental health services and to link them with appropriate staff. A national survey (American Correctional Association 2008b) found that all prison systems do **mental health screening** (80 percent do this at intake and the remainder within 24 hours to 14 days of intake), but the bigger problem is having sufficient numbers of staff qualified to work with the mentally ill. The same survey found that most prison systems consider their number of staff dealing with mentally ill offenders to be inadequate.

Recreation is an essential part of prison operations, and a well-run recreation program is an important goal of every

Think About It...

Should religious instruction and practices be allowed in prison? Some people argue that if the offenders were all that religious to begin with, they wouldn't be in prison. And, if you allow some religions, won't you have to allow all of them—including Satanism, Wicca, and others outside the mainstream?

Source: SHERRY LAVARS/MCT/Newscom

People in prisons are among the most educationally disadvantaged groups in the nation

prison or jail administrator (Kahler 1999). That position may seem at odds with media reports and legislator comments that purport to reflect public dissatisfaction with inmates being allowed to lift weights, attend movies, participate in sporting events, and make ceramic pottery. "Where is the punishment in such coddling?" voters seem to ask. But corrections professionals have a more supportive view of recreation programs and are more appreciative of the staff providing those programs. As Kahler (1999) notes, it might be appropriate to question prison recreation programs if they were solely for the benefit of inmates. However, most correctional managers support these programs and consider them to be important management and rehabilitation tools that benefit the inmates as well as the staff and even the public.

Members of the clergy were probably the first non-guard occupation group to work regularly in prisons. Dammer (1996) explains that most state and federal correctional institutions provide support for the four traditional religious denominations—Catholic, Protestant, Muslim, and Jewish. Regional variation and inmate interest also result in representation in some prisons by faiths such as Buddhist, Rastafarianism, Jehovah Witness, Native American Church, Moorish Temple, and Black Hebrew Israelite Nation. The chaplains, volunteers, and spiritual advisers representing the various faiths may be assigned to the prison facility itself (especially for the major denominations) or might be regular visitors from the outside (for those denominations with fewer adherents in the prison).

Inmates have a variety of reasons for involvement in religious activities while in prison (Dammer 1996). In some cases the inmates believe that religion provides direction and meaning for their lives and is a source of hope that their future holds more promise than their past. Inmates also report that religion improves their self-concept because the core of many religious beliefs is acceptance and love from a higher being and from members of the faith group. Still others (sex offenders, for example) affiliate with faith groups as a way to gain protection. For some, religious involvement is a way to access things that would otherwise be too difficult or costly to obtain (such as free food and coffee, holiday items, and even musical instruments).

People in prisons are among the most educationally disadvantaged groups in the nation, and the important task of providing academic and vocational education typically falls to correctional educators. Their efforts are not in vain since the research shows that correctional education reduces recidivism and enhances postrelease employment (Gaes 2008). Academic education programs in prisons may be accredited through affiliation with local school districts, community colleges or universities, or a private educational agency. In some instances the correctional system is large enough to be legislated as a distinct school district.

▶ Private Prisons

The last topic for this chapter is actually a variation on the management theme. Prison management in the twentieth century was primarily carried out by public employees in public facilities. In the twenty-first century, it appears that prison management increasingly may be the responsibility of corporate employees in private facilities.

In other books, you have read about the volunteer and private law-enforcement techniques that preceded modern policing and the early reliance on victims or privately run prosecution societies to prosecute offenders. You may also have read about the historical and continued role of private bondsmen and the early use of the jail as a way for keepers to earn fees for providing services such as bedding and food. In this book we reviewed examples of the important role that private groups, such as the Quakers in Pennsylvania, played in developing the new sanction of long-term imprisonment and the significance of private businesses' role in influencing a preference in the United States for the Auburn-style prison philosophy. Specific aspects of penal philosophies have been linked to prison labor, which in turn has ebbed and flowed as support from private businesses fluctuates. In the area of intermediate sanctions, the direct tie to private individuals (for example, John Augustus in Boston) makes clear the widespread impact of private individuals, associations, and businesses in the area of corrections. This reminds us that privatization in corrections is much more an old concept than a new one, but is certainly one of growing importance.

> **LEARNING OUTCOMES 5** Summarize the privatization of prisons.

> **GLOSSARY**
>
> **private prison** A correctional facility operated by a nongovernmental organization that is under contract with federal or state authorities to provide security, housing, and programs to adult offenders.

Privatization in the United States Today

A **private prison** is a correctional facility operated by a nongovernmental organization that is under contract with federal or state authorities to provide security, housing, and programs to adult offenders. The organization is often a for-profit company using facilities built by the company to house the prisoners and using its own employees to provide the needed security and programming. One of the largest private prison companies is Corrections Corporation of America (CCA), which specializes in the design, construction, expansion, and management of prisons, jails, and detention facilities. The importance of this type of business arrangement wherein public agencies partner with private enterprises to provide correctional services is apparent upon noting that CCA is now the fifth-largest corrections system in the nation, behind only the federal government and three states (Corrections Corporation of America 2008).

About 130,000 state and federal prisoners are held in privately operated corrections facilities (West, Sabol, & Greenman 2010). That is 8 percent of all prisoners—up from 6 percent in 2000—with the biggest increase found in the federal system

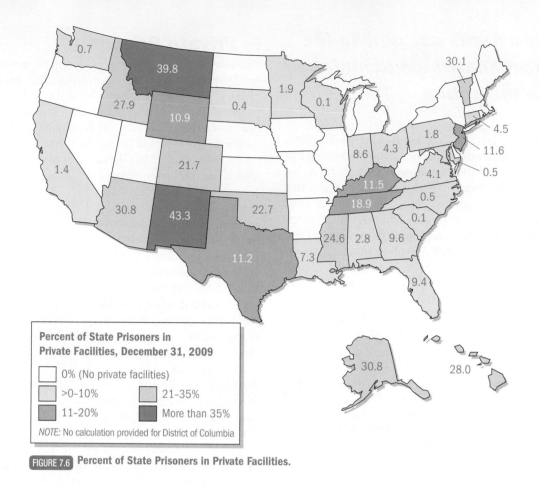

Percent of State Prisoners in Private Facilities, December 31, 2009

0% (No private facilities)

>0–10%   21–35%

11–20%   More than 35%

NOTE: No calculation provided for District of Columbia

FIGURE 7.6 Percent of State Prisoners in Private Facilities.

130k About 130,000 state and federal prisoners are held in privately operated corrections facilities

(West 2010). Of the many issues to discuss in relation to privatization, we look at where privatization is especially popular, the characteristics of persons held in private facilities, and the issue of cost savings.

Privatization has certainly increased over the last several decades, but much of the growth has been in particular geographic areas (see Figure 7.6). About 18 states have no prisoners in private facilities; however, ten states have at least 20 percent of their prison population housed in private facilities. At the end of 2009 (West et al. 2010), approximately two in three inmates held in private facilities were held in six states—Texas (19,000), Florida (9,800), California (9,000), Oklahoma (6,000), Georgia (5,100), and Tennessee (5,100)—or in private facilities under contract with the Federal Bureau of Prisons (34,000).

90% of the nation's privately held state prisoners are in southern and western states

This geographical distribution of the private prison population (90 percent of the nation's privately held state prisoners are in southern and western states) is consistent with the historical evolution of private prisons, which was in the South and West. The lack of private prisons in the Midwest and Northeast is, according to Austin and Coventry (2003), directly related to the strength of labor unions in those regions and their successful resistance to any significant attempts to privatize.

The characteristics of persons held in private prisons are generally consistent with those in public prisons. Blakely and Bumphus (2004) found that both private and public facilities house a large percentage of African-American offenders (43 percent for private and 47 percent for public). However, more females were in private sector facilities (10 percent) than in the public sector (6 percent), the average length of sentence for all offenders was less in private facilities (11 months versus 28 months in public facilities), and the custody level was generally lower in private facilities—90 percent of the private sector's inmates were at the medium- or minimum-security levels compared with 69 percent at the same levels in the public sector. This point of private facilities tending to have more females and having prisoners with lower average sentences and custody levels has led to charges that comparing the cost effectiveness of private facilities with public facilities is unfair (Oppel 2011). "Give us prisoners with the same characteristics and we'll look more cost effective too," say the public facilities.

Why spend time debating the merits of private and public prisons? Both are designed for the same purpose and in a similar manner, neither has been shown to have significantly lower recidivism rates, and neither has a unique management system. In fact, many people who were wardens in public prisons are now managing private facilities. Should we expect private prisons to be very different from public ones? Instead of debating which type of incarceration facility or system is cheaper or better, would our efforts be better spent in questioning the need for relying so heavily on imprisonment?

Source: Angelo

Private prisons have greater flexibility and can respond quickly to problems and opportunities because they are not encumbered by government "red tape"

The use of private prisons reduces the pressure and costs of overcrowding in the public sector

As a private enterprise, private prisons can be more creative and innovative

Private prisons are motivated to provide good quality at a reasonable cost in order to secure repeat contracts

Punishing criminal offenders is a core function of government and should be administered only by government agencies

Contracting with private business is more expensive because it adds a profit margin to all other costs

Sentencing- and prison-related legislation may be influenced by private companies wishing to improve their profit margin

Contracting diffuses responsibility allowing government and private entities to blame each other

FIGURE 7.7 **Debating Private Prisons.**

 DISCUSS *Which arguments (name one or two) do you find most compelling? Why?*

The cost-effectiveness argument is especially relevant because cost savings to tax payers is a primary claim made by supporters of privatization. Presumably, private firms can finance and construct prisons more quickly than can the government; are more likely to design efficient operations; and are freed from the cumbersome bureaucracy, restrictive personnel policies, and union contracts that add expenses for government agencies (Austin & Coventry 2003; Logan 1990). There are, however, a variety of methodological problems that make it very difficult to compare cost savings. For example, because private prisons have not been used to any significant extent in those states with the more expensive prison systems (that is, the Midwest and Northeast), it has been difficult to clearly determine if there can actually be cost savings with privatization (Austin & Coventry 2003). Similarly, deciding how—or even if—to count indirect costs (for example, contract writing, financial liability) and some direct costs (for example, medical care, construction, renovation) makes study comparison problematic.

After reviewing more current studies on cost savings from privatization, Austin and Coventry (2003) found little, if any, evidence that private prisons are cheaper to operate. Even studies that found cost-effectiveness have shown only minimal savings (5 to 15 percent), so it is difficult for there to be any significant impact on a state prison budget when private prisons continue to reflect such a small proportion of the overall prison population. A meta-analysis by Lundahl and his colleagues (2007) led to a similar conclusion (that is, "cost savings from privatizing prisons are not guaranteed and appear minimal") and most recently, an Arizona report found that it can often be more expensive to house inmates in private than in state prisons (Newton, Rough, & Hensley 2010).

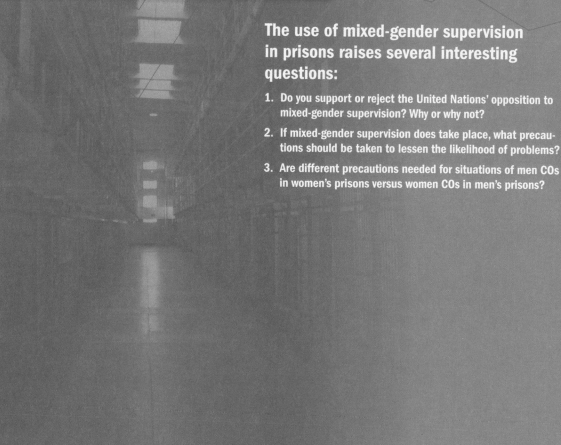

Correctional Officer Barbara Williams tells a journalist of a male inmate's comment about the way Williams's hips swayed beneath her blue uniform. He said, "Damn! You remind me of a pantyhose commercial." The comment came early in her career and Williams quickly saw that she'd have to change her demeanor, be more forceful, and harden herself. She went home that evening and practiced stiffening her walk in front of a mirror (Hauser 2008).

Since that event, Williams's nearly 20 years of experiences as a correctional officer (CO) include being trapped in a mess hall with rioting inmates and being thrown against an iron gate by a man twice her size. She tells her daughters, "In life, you have to know when to be a woman and when to be a lady." She doesn't believe ladies belong in jail so she says she leaves that softer part of her outside the walls.

Women COs have an increasing presence in jails and prisons around the country, but it has not occurred without controversy. Not the least among those organizations expressing concern is the United Nations (UN), which generally opposes having male COs in women's prisons and women COs in men's—that is, mixed-gender supervision (United Nations Office on Drugs and Crime 2008, p. 36). Although noting that having women COs in men's prisons has the advantages of changing the male dominated prison culture and having a positive effect on men, the same does not seem to be true when male COs are in women's prisons. In those cases, the UN argues, risks outweigh any advantages. Lawsuits in 2009 by women inmates in Michigan prisons who were raped and molested by male COs would certainly support the UN's argument (Seidel 2009).

The use of mixed-gender supervision in prisons raises several interesting questions:

1. Do you support or reject the United Nations' opposition to mixed-gender supervision? Why or why not?

2. If mixed-gender supervision does take place, what precautions should be taken to lessen the likelihood of problems?

3. Are different precautions needed for situations of men COs in women's prisons versus women COs in men's prisons?

Source: Donald R. Neudecker/Shutterstock.com

LEARNING OUTCOMES 1

Outline the development and organization of the federal prison system.

Although the federal government operated prisons beginning in the 1890s, it was not until the Bureau of Prisons (BOP) was created in 1930 that a true federal prison system began. Since that time the BOP has grown to an organization with more than 100 institutions responsible for more than 200,000 prisoners. The BOP's central office is in Washington, DC, but for management purposes the country is divided into six geographic regions, each with a regional director for all facilities in that region. Federal facilities are identified by their security level, which will be minimum, low, medium, high, or administrative.

1. What are the top three offenses for which persons are in a federal prison?

2. After the United States, of which country are federal prisoners most likely to be citizens?

3. Describe characteristics of prisons at each of the five federal prison security levels.

4. What role is the BOP playing in the fight against terrorism?

LEARNING OUTCOMES 2

Outline the development and organization of the state prison systems.

State prisons are operated by a state agency (usually called the Department of Corrections) that manages all prisons in the state and may also be responsible for community corrections and parole services. There are about 1,700 state correctional facilities across the country, but the number in each state varies considerably from as few as 6 or 7 in some states to more than 100 in others. As in the federal prison system, state prisons identify their facilities by security level. The level names and the number of levels vary by state, so it is easiest to simply refer to state security levels as being minimum, medium, and maximum. There are, however, some state prisons identified as supermax because they house the most dangerous or troublesome prisoners in the tightest security available in the state.

1. Of the 1,700 state correctional facilities across the country, about how many of them are community-based facilities?

2. Distinguish between design capacity and rated capacity. What do you suppose are some reasons for having two types of prison capacity?

3. Describe characteristics of prisons at the minimum, medium, and maximum levels.

4. What is meant by saying that the growth of supermax facilities indicates a trend away from a dispersion approach and toward a concentration approach for handling troublesome inmates?

department of corrections The state agency responsible for managing and operating the state's adult prison system.

design capacity The number of inmates that facility planners or architects intended for the facility.

rated capacity The maximum number of beds or inmates allocated by a rating official to institutions in the states.

minimum-security facility Institutions where inmates have considerable personal freedom and more relaxed supervision.

medium-security facility Institutions where inmates receive more supervision than at minimum-security prisons, but still have considerable freedom to move around to work assignments and programming activities.

maximum-security facility Designed for the fullest possible supervision, control, and surveillance of general population inmates. Also known as *close-security prisons*.

supermax prison Prisons at the highest security level, with prisoners isolated from the general population and from each other. Also known as *control units* or *secured housing units*.

dispersion approach Prison administrators spread troublemakers to prisons throughout the system or in various units of the prison.

concentration approach Prisoners are grouped together in special prisons or special units within a prison, and their activities and movements are severely restricted and highly monitored.

LEARNING OUTCOMES 3

Explain how prisoners are classified and assigned in prisons.

In order to achieve their security and treatment obligations, prison systems must have a way to identify how much risk an inmate presents and what needs the inmate has that can be addressed in the prison environment. In the past those decisions were made very subjectively but today there is increased reliance on objective classification methods that allow for more accurate assessment of both risk and needs.

1. Describe the four generations through which risk/needs assessments have passed.

2. How do objective classification procedures differ from subjective ones?

3. List and explain at least three features of an objective classification system.

4. Distinguish between external and internal prison classification systems.

5. Explain how both static and dynamic factors can be criminogenic, but successful treatment programs need to focus on dynamic factors.

6. What is meant by the term reclassification? Do you think it is necessary to do on a regular basis or could it be done only upon request from the prisoner or treatment staff?

classification The process and procedures by which prison officials determine the risk posed by each offender and the offender's individual treatment needs.

objective classification system Classification procedures that have a factual, impartial, and observable base rather than the intuitive footing of subjective systems.

external classification A stage in the classification process wherein a prisoner's custody level is determined and, based on that custody level, in which the prison inmate begins serving the sentence.

internal classification Establishes the prisoner's housing, program, and work assignments within the prison.

prison risk assessment A determination of the risk an offender poses to escape or to be a management problem for prison officials.

public risk assessment A determination of the risk posed by an offender to the general public.

static factors Individual characteristics that are constant or happened in the past and cannot be changed, such as a person's gender, age at first arrest, or number of prior arrests.

dynamic factors Individual characteristics that can be changed, such as antisocial attitudes, values and beliefs, poor self-control, criminal peers, and criminal thinking patterns.

criminogenic Factors that cause or tend to cause criminal behavior.

responsivity The process in which prisoners are assigned to treatment programs designed to address their particular set of dynamic criminogenic needs.

reclassification A stage in the classification process wherein an inmate's custody level, treatment program, or work assignment is reevaluated to be sure they are still appropriate.

LEARNING OUTCOMES 4

Describe the various jobs and functions of prison staff.

Of the many occupational areas represented by prison staff, two are of particular importance in this chapter. Prison staff members responsible for security are the correctional officers (COs) who maintain order and enforce prison rules and regulations. Nationwide, this group is mostly white non-Hispanic and male, but in some states women and minorities represent a large proportion of COs. The second group of prison staff highlighted in this chapter is made up of members of the treatment staff. These people are responsible for such areas as counseling, recreation, religion, and education.

1. About what percentage of prison staff members are correctional officers (COs)?

2. Would you consider a career as a CO? Why or why not?

3. Under what legal precedents are women allowed to work as COs in a men's prison?

4. Do, or should, COs have a treatment role in addition to their security role?

5. Describe the possible benefits of having education, religious, and recreation programs in a prison environment.

correctional officer The person responsible for maintaining order within the institution and enforcing prison rules and regulations.

mental health screening An examination performed on each newly admitted inmate that usually includes a review of the medical screening, behavior observations, an inquiry into any mental health history, and an assessment of suicide potential.

LEARNING OUTCOMES 5

Summarize the privatization of prisons.

Traditionally prison management has been carried out by public employees in public facilities, but that is changing in the twenty-first century. Not all, but most states today have some prison facilities operated by private for-profit companies. The companies make money by contracting with federal, state, or local government to provide the housing, security, and programming for prisoners. About 8 percent of all prisoners in the country are now held in private facilities. A major argument for privatization is that private prisons are cost-effective, but some research suggests there is little evidence that private prisons are cheaper to operate.

1. Define private prison.

2. Why have private prisons been more accepted in some regions of the country than others?

3. Give two arguments favoring and two opposing the use of private prisons.

private prison A correctional facility operated by a nongovernmental organization that is under contract with federal or state authorities to provide security, housing, and programs to adult offenders.

MyCJLab

Go to the Chapter 7 section in *MyCJLab* to test your understanding of this chapter, access customized study content, engage in interactive simulations, complete critical thinking and research assignments, and view related online videos.

Additional Links

Read about a prisoner's first day at **http://prisonsecrets.com/2011/02/13/first-day-in-prison-part-1/**.

Find information about each federal correctional facility at **www.bop.gov/locations/index.jsp**.

Read about employment opportunities for correctional officers at **www.bls.gov/oco/ocos156.htm**.

The National Institute of Corrections has information on the jail, prison, and community corrections system of each state at **http://nicic.gov/StateStats/**.

Learn about education in prison at **www.ceanational.org/index2.htm**.

Prison Life

"Prison. . . destroys you on the inside long before its effects are evident on the outside . . . It is a den of indifference and spiritual emptiness. It is a place where you learn to hate."

—Diane Metzger, *Author and Prisoner at Baylor Women's Correctional Institution*

1 Describe the characteristics of prisoners in state and federal prison.

2 Explain the elements of prison life that define the incarceration experience, and apply deprivation or importation theory to each of these elements.

3 Identify the benefits and challenges of having inmates work while incarcerated.

4 Clarify the key ways prisoners use the sub rosa economy for profit.

5 Compare and contrast security threat groups and play families in terms of their structure, purpose, and management.

6 Summarize the various forms of individual-level inmate violence, including assault and sexual assault.

7 Identify how collective violence begins and why it is sustained as a part of prison life.

8

Source: © Mikael Karlsson/Alamy

ARE PRISON RIOTS A COLLECTIVE CALL FOR HELP?

INTRO

At the California Institution for Men in Chino, a riot suddenly broke out in a dayroom at 7:45 PM on August 8, 2009, where inmates grouped together by race/ethnicity. Fighting continued in six different housing units at other parts of the prison where only two officers were staffed for every 100 inmates. The prisoners destroyed sinks, bed frames, mattresses, and windows in order to quickly avail themselves with weapons such as pipes, broken glass, and ceramic shards for protection. Despite receiving information two days ahead of time that led to efforts to restrict prisoner movement, there were too many inmates for the capacity and the riot lasted for 11 hours before authorities could regain control. The riot left over 200 people injured and two housing units burned to the ground. There were no fatalities, but over 1,100 homeless prisoners were transferred to other units around the state.

While it appeared that the triggering event of the riot was racial tensions, experts contend that the predisposing factors were a severely overcrowded state prison system, inmate idleness, massive treatment program cuts, and dangerously understaffed facilities. At that time, California had nearly 155,000 prisoners in facilities designed to hold fewer than 85,000 prisoners. Back in June 2007, a federal three-judge panel ordered that California reduce the inmate population by nearly 43,000 prisoners. At around that same time, the U.S. economy went into a recession that has affected state budgets across the country.

As a result of California's continued prison budget crisis, it came as no surprise when on August 28, 2010, a different riot was started by 200 inmates in a Folsom prison yard. Correctional officers quelled the riot after 30 minutes by shooting into the yard with loaded guns. There were no fatalities, but seven inmates were hospitalized with injuries, of which five had gunshot wounds.

Sources: (James 2009; McNary 2010; and CNN Wire Staff 2010)

> **DISCUSS** What should the state of California do to restore order and safety to its prisons in the face of such severe budget cuts?

Diane Metzger's quote at the beginning of the chapter sets the stage for understanding several important themes of today's prisons. First, prison is a long-term sentence that permanently changes a person. The adjustments many individuals make in order to endure a prison sentence too often result in greater social challenges, anger, and individuals who are released with the same problems (drug abuse, parenting, job skills, etc.) that they had before they were arrested. One explanation for the negative impact prison has on many inmates is the social structure and environment of the prison itself. But first we examine who is in prison.

▶ Who is in Prison?

Individuals in prison originate from all kinds of family backgrounds, nationalities, occupations, and socioeconomic backgrounds. However, prisoners also share some similarities. First, most prisoners must overcome some sort of challenge to rebalance their lives in some way. They have either become excessively focused on a single behavior—such as drug addiction, money, or power—or they lack a fundamental skill or ability that has affected their lives in a significant way—such as their inability to control their emotions, lack of education, or employment in which they can make a livable wage. Many times, people who end up in prison are in both groups—they have lived a life of excess and of deficits.

When we consider demographics, most prisoners are young men between the ages of 18 and 35. The average age of prisoners is actually 35, but averages factor in both the younger crowd and the older group between 35 and 75 years of age. The number of women in the prison population has always been **disproportionately** less than their percent in the general population. For example, if women prisoners were proportional to the percent they represent in the general population, we would expect female prisoners to comprise about 51 percent of the prison population. However, women accounted for only 7 percent of all prisoners nationwide, which makes women *disproportionately underrepresented* in prison.

most prisoners have either become excessively focused on a single behavior or they lack a fundamental skill or ability that has affected their lives in a significant way

 7% women accounted for only 7 percent of all prisoners nationwide

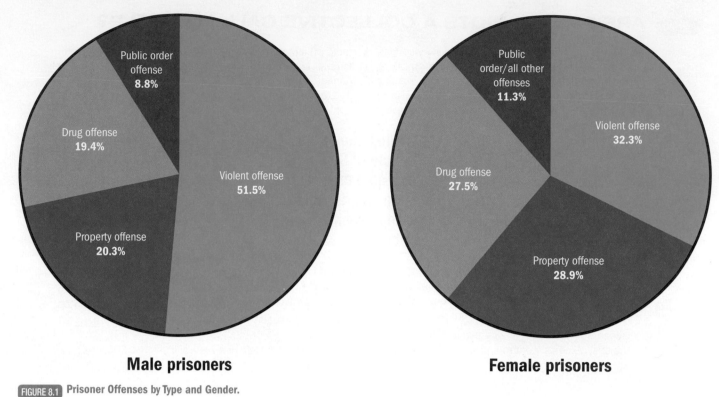

Male prisoners

Female prisoners

FIGURE 8.1 **Prisoner Offenses by Type and Gender.**
Source: Sabol, W. J., West, H. C., & Cooper, M. (2009). *Prisoners in 2008*. NCJ 228417. Washington, DC: U.S. Department of Justice, Appendix Table 16, p. 37.

Most prisoners tend to come from impoverished backgrounds riddled with childhood abuse, from parents who neglected them, and from underfunded school districts. Related to socioeconomic status is race/ethnicity, in which a disproportionate number of African-American and Hispanic individuals are in prison. For females, the national average was 27.6 percent African-American, 48 percent Caucasian, and 16.4 percent Hispanic. For men, 39.2 percent were African-American, 33.3 percent were Caucasian, and 20.6 percent were Hispanic (Sabol, West, & Cooper 2009).

One out of every four federal prisoners was *not* a U.S. citizen

Federal Prisoners

Individuals who have committed a serious federal offense are under authority of the **Bureau of Prisons (BOP)**. Federal prisoners comprise 9 percent of all prisoners held in the United States. As of 2011, there were 210,380 federal offenders; 93 percent were in a prison and 7 percent in a community-based or other short-term residential facility (Federal Bureau of Prisons 2011). The BOP inmate population is changing in composition as well as in number. While drug offenders account for half of all federal offenses, more than one out of every four federal prisoners was *not* a U.S. citizen. BOP prisoners who were non-U.S. citizens had citizenship in Mexico, Columbia, Dominican Republic, or

Offense Type	State Offenses	Federal Offenses
VIOLENT	• Murder/manslaughter • Robbery • Rape/sexual assault • Assault	• Kidnapping • Bank robbery • Explosives • Weapons offenses
PROPERTY	• Larceny/motor vehicle theft • Bribery • Fraud/forgery	• Extortion • Bribery • Fraud
DRUG	• Possession • Selling	• Trafficking • Organized distribution
OTHER	• Driving while intoxicated	• Immigration-related

FIGURE 8.2 **Examples of Common Felony Offenses.**
Sources: (Federal Bureau of Prisons 2011; Sabol, West, & Cooper 2009)

ICE officers apprehend 1.5 million aliens every year. Most aliens are temporarily detained and deported without being charged, while a small number serve time for convictions that happened within U.S. borders—ranging from violent crimes (32 percent) and drug offenses (30 percent) to property and public order crimes (U.S. Immigration and Customs Enforcement 2011). In your opinion, should government resources be increased to build ICE facilities to house convicted non-U.S. citizens for offenses committed within our borders, or is it more effective to just immediately deport? Should we even be worried about non-U.S. citizens who are law abiding? Why or why not?

Source: J. Emilio Flores/La Opinion/Newscom

Cuba (Federal BOP 2011). Some non-U.S. citizens were convicted of felony crimes for which they must serve time before being deported. Others were detained longer in one of 63 Immigration and Customs Enforcement (ICE) facilities, to investigate suspected roles in human trafficking, illegal drug distribution, and identity fraud. Some offenders are convicted for immigration offenses such as arriving without proper documents or overstaying a visa. Immigration offenses comprised 11 percent of all federal offenses.

▶ *Learning Prison Norms*

Every society has a set of norms and values that are considered "mainstream," defined by those wielding the most power and influence. Individuals who operate inside mainstream norms are rewarded and those who do not are considered "deviant" and ostracized. To first-timers, prison is a new experience that takes some time to adjust; it is a learning process of mainstream prison culture. Clemmer (1966) used the term **prisonization** to explain the process by which prisoners were socialized into prison life or the **inmate subculture** with its own norms, values, and beliefs. While prison society shares many aspects of dominant culture, prisoners have developed their own informal rules, language, economic system, and groups that exhibit a strong influence on life in prison (Santos 2004). The degree that prisoners adopt prison values as their own largely depends on the length of their sentence and the custody level of the prison to which they're assigned (Terry 2003). Short-term prisoners doing two years or fewer are typically housed in lower-custody facilities and within that span can resist the pressures of the prison environment and not become a "regular" or a convict. Individuals with longer sentences in maximum custody find it difficult to remain connected to the world outside for that long, and succumb to their situation to make their own life easier (Santos 2004).

The Big House era and the traditional convict code was replaced by a new code of conduct that provided predatory inmates the opportunity to exploit vulnerable fellow inmates

Deprivations of the Big House

During the **Big House** era when prisons were located in remote areas, routines were highly disciplined and prisoners lacked access to media sources. Prisons were **total institutions** and convicts and building tenders were in charge at the top of the social and political hierarchy. Building tenders controlled the housing units and were rewarded through informal accommodations and staff favoritism. The focus of prison was on the **deprivation model**.

Once the courts mandated the end of the building tender system (where building tenders were replaced with new generation correctional officers) and the rise of the rehabilitative ideal, this created a very different culture. Many senior guards retreated to positions where they could continue to avoid contact with prisoners (like it was when the building tenders were in charge), some out of resentment and others out of fear. The prison environment was open for a new group of prisoners —prison gangs—to take over. Unlike the elite convicts and building tenders who had the same goals of controlling the masses, prison gangs were in competition with each other for scarce resources and prisons became less safe. The Big House era and the traditional convict code was replaced by a new code of conduct that provided predatory inmates the opportunity to exploit vulnerable fellow inmates (Johnson 1993; Winfree, Newbold, & Tubb 2002). The focus of mainstream prison culture turned more toward the **importation model**, or the code of the streets.

LEARNING OUTCOMES 2 Explain the elements of prison life that define the incarceration experience, and apply deprivation or importation theory to each of these elements.

GLOSSARY

prisonization The process by which the prisoners learn the norms of life in prison.

inmate subculture A society with its own norms and values defined by inmates with the most power and influence.

Big House A maximum-security penitentiary with a convict subculture, lasting between the early 1800s until about 1980.

total institution A regimented facility that is physically separate from the larger society and meets the survival needs of its occupants.

deprivation model Assumes that prison culture developed out of the pains of imprisonment through adaptations that prisoners make to circumvent these losses.

importation model Assumes that prison life is an extension of street life of marginalized people from impoverished communities who dominate the prison.

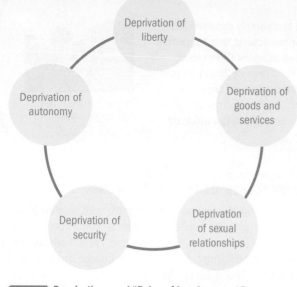

FIGURE 8.3 **Deprivations and "Pains of Imprisonment."**
Source: Adapted from (Sykes 1958)

Inmate Code

The **inmate code** is an informal, unwritten set of ideal norms that directs an inmate's behavior. But unlike formal prison rules, the inmate code is learned by word of mouth, and if not followed, inmates enforce the norms via bullying, harassment, or violence. These principles have remained fairly constant over the last 60 years (Sykes & Messinger 1960; Winfree, Newbold, & Tubb 2002). The inmate code is similar across many prisons in the world.

Code of Conduct for Women

Women prisoners seem to have a slightly different inmate code than men. Violence is not glorified to obtain respect nor is there necessarily a need to join gangs for protection. Women also seemed more tolerant of mixed-race groupings than men (Alarid 1996). Pollock (2002) observed that women were less likely than men to "Do their own time" as the subcultural norms in women's prisons did not prohibit or discourage individuals getting involved in another woman's problems. Women were more likely than men to "spread rumors and gossip about one another's activities as a form of social control or merely as a social pastime" (Pollock 2002, 131). Interaction with correctional officers is not prohibited for female inmates—it is more casual and social. There is even some indication that female prisoners look to staff, as well as to each other, for support. As a result, staff may be more likely to bend the rules. As one woman explained, a main part of the code is

"Don't snitch," but she quickly added, "It is good to tell for certain things, like if someone gets jumped or somebody got stabbed" (Owen 1998, 178).

Prison Argot

Prison argot or **"prison-proper"** is the language, slang, and physical gestures used to communicate meaning in prison. According to Encinas (2001), argot is influenced by the region of the country or the dominant race/ethnic group incarcerated in that area. For example, prisons in the Southwest that are influenced by Latino prisoners use slightly different slang than prisons dominated by African-American prisoners. Argot terms describe the inmate world as one that is hardened, lacks tolerance, and is filled with racist and sexist terminology. K.C. Carceral, a federal prisoner, provides more detail:

> Prison-proper perpetuates prejudice and stereotyping based on skin color. For example, African-American prisoners call whites Square Johns, crackers, pecker-woods, white boyees, and honkies. After twenty years behind bars, many black prisoners still look at me with rejection and suspicion. Everything comes down to the fact

inmate code A system of unwritten rules that directs inmate behavior.

prison argot or **"prison-proper"** The language, slang, and physical gestures used to communicate meaning in prison.

players Prisoners who embrace mainstream prison culture that values manipulating and intimidating others.

squares Inmates who oppose mainstream prison culture by being well-behaved and who take advantage of every self-improvement program they can to keep themselves busy. Also known as *bootlickers*.

snitch Inmates who are targeted by predatory inmates because they have passed along information to staff that has gotten another inmate in trouble. Also known as *player haters*.

punk Inmates who are targeted by predatory inmates because they are perceived as physically or mentally weak and afraid to fight back.

fish First-time inmate that is vulnerable because he or she has not yet been prisonized.

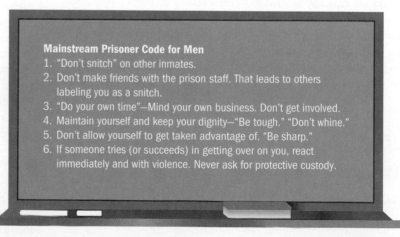

Mainstream Prisoner Code for Men
1. "Don't snitch" on other inmates.
2. Don't make friends with the prison staff. That leads to others labeling you as a snitch.
3. "Do your own time"—Mind your own business. Don't get involved.
4. Maintain yourself and keep your dignity—"Be tough." "Don't whine."
5. Don't allow yourself to get taken advantage of. "Be sharp."
6. If someone tries (or succeeds) in getting over on you, react immediately and with violence. Never ask for protective custody.

FIGURE 8.4 **Mainstream Prisoner Code for Men.**
Sources: (Sykes & Messinger 1960; Winfree, Newbold, & Tubb 2002)

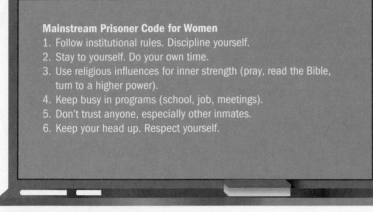

Mainstream Prisoner Code for Women

1. Follow institutional rules. Discipline yourself.
2. Stay to yourself. Do your own time.
3. Use religious influences for inner strength (pray, read the Bible, turn to a higher power).
4. Keep busy in programs (school, job, meetings).
5. Don't trust anyone, especially other inmates.
6. Keep your head up. Respect yourself.

FIGURE 8.5 **Mainstream Prisoner Code for Women.**
Source: WOMEN OFFENDERS' PERCEPTION OF CONFINEMENT: Behavior Code, Acceptance, Hustling, and Group Relations in Jail and Prison by Leanne F. Alarid (1996). An unpublished Doctoral Dissertation. Huntsville, TX, Sam Houston State University.

Inmates who choose not to assimilate to convict norms do harder time as outcasts, but because they've been "living on the outside in their head," they will likely remain free after release

that I am white. Of course, I see the same prejudicial attitude when white prisoners look at black prisoners. Both groups justify their hatred because of ignorance and intolerance of diversity…. There are [also] many terms that are derogatory toward women. It helps create and support an uncaring place where feminine qualities are seen as a target for predatory behavior. (2004, 28)

Carceral's observations support how race/ethnic identification and separatism become a primary way that defines the prison experience, particularly for men (Alarid 2000). While some prisoners enter the institution with racist attitudes, Carceral's view suggests that most prisoners simply give in to the norms that staying with one's own race is the only way to avoid trouble, and do not go against the norms because of the bullying and potential violent consequences: "The prison identity is grounded in hatred, learned racism, and a willingness to resort to violence when necessary" (Carceral 2004, 127).

A study of prison argot provides a window into understanding what qualities are valued and what is despised. For example, individuals who are prison gang leaders, organized crime figures, or traffickers are given the most respect by other inmates. Prison gang members are second because they are part of the networked power structure. The vast majority of individual prisoners fall into one of two groups: they are either **players** or **squares** as every prisoner chooses whether to embrace the mainstream norms or oppose prison culture (Terry 2003). At the bottom of the hierarchy are inmates who have committed sex-related crimes against children or who are perceived as **snitches** or **punks** (Carceral 2004).

It seems that the individuals who undergo the most radical transformations in prison come in as **fish**, make the key connections with the

players, and decide to fully assimilate themselves into the prison world. Inmates who choose not to assimilate to convict norms do harder time as outcasts, but because they've been "living on the outside in their head," they will likely remain free after release (Terry 2003, 74). An explanation of the classic outcasts are protective custody inmates who are "… generally the nonviolent intelligent ones, have to live with limited privileges, whereas the regular inmates, who are generally the violent ones and losers, have all the privileges permitted" (Harkleroad 2000, 164).

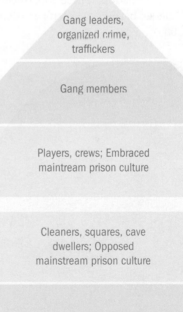

Gang leaders, organized crime, traffickers

Gang members

Players, crews; Embraced mainstream prison culture

Cleaners, squares, cave dwellers; Opposed mainstream prison culture

Punks

Snitches, Player haters, Sex offenders

FIGURE 8.6 **Prisoner Hierarchy.**

Think About It...

A prison's physical structure restricts a person's freedom of movement and ability to control what he or she eats, where he or she lives or works, and even the ability to control the room temperature. To most prisoners, not having independence or control greatly affects their sense of dignity, emotional well-being, and over time, their decision-making ability. On the one hand, some call this situation "punishment" while others believe it severely prevents inmates from learning the tools they need to keep a job and control their behavior after they leave prison. What can be done to teach prisoners what they need to learn to be successful in mainstream America while being incarcerated as punishment?

Source: trekandshoot/Dreamstime.com

► Prisoner Job Assignments

American culture is occupation-dominated in which a job organizes routines, behavior, and even one's identity. In prison culture, administrators initially used inmates for cheap labor to decrease incarceration costs and to make a profit through the leasing system and through manufacturing prison-made goods. Later, working became an important source of informal social control and keeping inmates occupied. However, the main challenge today is there are more prisoners than work available to keep each occupied for eight hours; therefore, the work is spread around so that most inmates actually work two to three hours per day.

Most inmates are assigned to menial **institutional maintenance** jobs that help to operate and maintain the prison in areas such as food preparation, laundry, cleaning all surfaces and floors, and lawn care. Specialty maintenance jobs exist, in which **trustys** can be promoted, that offer more freedom of movement or access to information. These jobs include hall janitors, porters, stock clerks, barbers, warden's assistants, and library clerks (Alarid 2005).

A second category of prison jobs exists primarily in southern regions of the United States, where there is open land for agriculture—growing crops and raising cattle and pigs. This work is traditionally for inmates with disciplinary problems. **Agricultural** work is hard and hot—as it is done using shovels and aggies—and the inmates work in rows under the watchful eye of armed officers on horses (Alarid 2005). Some states offer good time, but do not pay prisoners for institutional maintenance or agricultural jobs, while others offer wages such as $0.10 per hour.

LEARNING OUTCOMES 3 Identify the benefits and challenges of having inmates work while incarcerated.

GLOSSARY

institutional maintenance Unskilled jobs that inmates are assigned in order to assist with daily prison operations (food preparation, laundry, cleaning).

trustys Minimum-security-level inmates who earn the status through not causing behavioral problems.

agriculture Outdoor field work jobs involving prisoners' growing crops and raising livestock; prevalent in southern states.

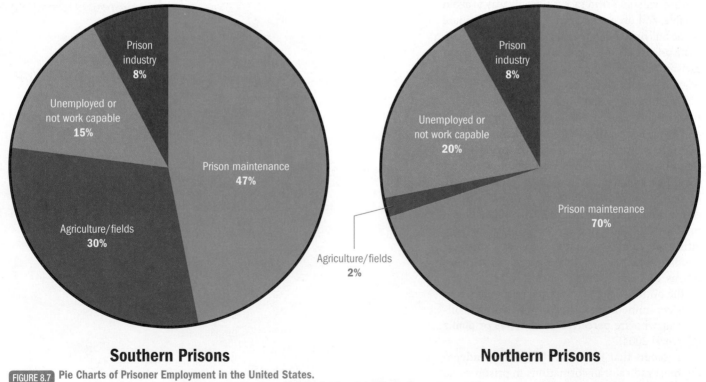

Southern Prisons — Prison maintenance 47%, Agriculture/fields 30%, Unemployed or not work capable 15%, Prison industry 8%

Northern Prisons — Prison maintenance 70%, Unemployed or not work capable 20%, Prison industry 8%, Agriculture/fields 2%

FIGURE 8.7 Pie Charts of Prisoner Employment in the United States.
Source: Derived from data in "Turning a Profit of Just Passing the Time? A Gender Comparison of Prisoner Jobs and Workplace Deviance in the SubRosa Economy" by L. F. Alarid, (2005) Deviant Behavior, 6, 621–624. Taylor & Francis Ltd.

Timeline of Prison Labor Laws

1929	**1935**	**1940**	**1979**
Hawes-Cooper Act	**Ashurst-Sumners Act**	**Ashurst-Sumners Amendment**	**Prison Industries Enhancement (PIE) Act**
Prison-made goods were subjected to control of the receiving state's laws.	It became a federal offense to transport prison-made goods into states that had barred them under Hawes-Cooper.	This allowed state *agricultural* prison products to be sold in other states.	This increased opportunities for public–private cooperation.
One state can prohibit another state from selling its prison-made goods there.		Twenty-two states mandated that state agencies purchase certain products made at state prisons.	It restricted the number of jurisdictions and industries.

Prison industry jobs are highly competitive and are sought after by inmates because they provide the most realistic work environment of six to eight-hour days and the best pay. There are few slots available for these jobs only because they are highly regulated by the government. The prison industry is typically a manufacturing plant or factory that produces prison-made goods for either **open markets** or **sheltered markets**. The greatest concern is that prisoner labor might again unfairly compete with free-world labor, so restrictions were placed on the prison industry that operates under a **free enterprise** system.

UNICOR was established by Congress in 1934 to provide prison-made goods for all federal agencies. UNICOR is not only self-sustaining, but it makes significant profits every year. For example, during 2010, UNICOR employed about 9 percent of work-eligible inmates in 94 factories across the country. The prisoners are paid between $0.23 and $1.15 per hour to make such things as clothing, office furniture, electronics, fleet management and vehicular components, and industrial products (UNICOR 2010).

Another open market system is the heavily restricted PIE prison industry programs that operate with private business in up to 50 jurisdictions around the United States. The PIE program allows preselected inmates to work in a realistic environment, get paid for their efforts at wages that are equal for similar work elsewhere, and allow them to learn a trade. The inmates must be at minimum-custody level, hold at least a GED or a high school diploma, and have not received a disciplinary report for six months. The government also requires that the PIE program,

- Must not displace private-sector workers.
- Inmates apply voluntarily and are selected based on predefined standards.
- Inmate wages must be similar to those paid to private-sector employees.
- Between 5 and 20 percent of inmate wages goes to pay court fines, victim restitution, or child support.

The PIE program is enjoying considerable success and compliance with requirements (National Correctional Industries Association 2011).

prison industry A skilled job within the prison that provides inmates training while incarcerated (manufacturing, construction, auto repair, welding, etc.).

open market Prison-made products are sold, either by private companies or by the state, to prospective buyers.

sheltered market Restricts the sale of prison-made products only to other state and local government markets. Also known as the *government or state use models*.

free enterprise A private sector entrepreneurial model of doing business.

System	Market	Control	Product Examples
Government use or state use	Sheltered	Government 100%	Traffic signs, license plates, furniture, dairy
Joint-venture	Sheltered	Government 50% (wage scales, hiring) Private firm 50% (product design, marketing, distribution)	Joint Venture Program (California) Corcraft (New York)
Corporate	Open	Private more control than government	PRIDE (Florida) UNICOR (Federal BOP)
Free enterprise	Open	Private sector 100%	PIE products Prison Blues® (Oregon)

FIGURE 8.8 **Contemporary Prison Industry Systems.**
Source: Adapted from (Dwyer and McNally 1993)

Prisoner Labor Benefits	Challenges of Prisoner Labor
• Maintains day-to-day facility operations	• Prisoners can use their jobs to profit by moving contraband and commissary.
• Cost-effective goods can be made.	• Private companies feel that it is unfair to compete with prison-made goods.
• Government profits	• Congress passed legislation restricting prison-made products and made it difficult for prisons to be too profitable.
• Victim restitution, child support, and court-ordered fines can be garnished from wages.	• Many inmates do not get paid at all for their labor or payment is not enough to garnish wages.
• Reduces idleness during incarceration	• Idleness still exists when there are more prisoners than jobs—unemployment rate of 10–30%.
• Choice jobs that inmates earn reduce institutional misconduct.	• Behavioral problems with the lower-ranked jobs (hoe squad, field work)
• Private businesses receive tax incentives, avoid payment of employee benefits such as retirement, vacation, and sick leave; and they have a reliable workforce.	• Prison spends much effort with job placement, promotions, demotions, and getting work crews to work on time; work schedule revolves around prison security; occasional work stoppages occur.
• Inmates learn employable skills.	• May Interfere or compete with the free labor market.

FIGURE 8.9 Benefits and Challenges of Prisoner Labor.

EVIDENCE-BASED PRACTICE—DOES IT WORK?

Prisoner Job Training

Until recently, job training program results were either anecdotal or based on less rigorous methodological studies. Past evaluations of prisoners that received job training were already a different group than a comparison group that did not seek out training, because the trained group already had more motivation while incarcerated. Eight job training programs that used *random group assignment* were analyzed to look at whether the program reduced rearrest after release. Job training programs for ex-offenders had *no significant effect* on the likelihood that the treatment subjects would be rearrested compared to the group who did not receive such services.

Source: (Visher, Winterfield, & Coggeshall 2005)

▶ Sub Rosa Economy

Every jail and prison has a bartering system of reciprocity based on negotiation and exchange of goods and services between prisoners without the use of cash. This illicit, underground economy is forbidden, and is known as the **sub rosa economy**. Prisoners secure items of value through favors and trades. Most of the items are state supplies and are considered more of a nuisance for prison officials than a real security threat. Thus, officers may disregard or overlook minor acts that do not interfere with institutional security. Some groups provide **commissary** or loan items to friends on disciplinary status (Alarid 1997). Other individuals are well-known in the prison for their entrepreneurial spirit. For example, **merchants** control scarce resources by running a prison store out of their cell. **Jailhouse lawyers** use their legal knowledge and skills to conduct legal research, and write writs and grievances. Many inmates perfect a skill such as artwork, making cards, and writing poems and sell, trade, or barter that skill for goods (such as snacks, stamps, etc.) or services (ironing a uniform, cleaning a cell, cooking a late-night meal). Alarid (2005) found that about 27 percent of men and women inmates admitted to using their assigned prison job to yield a personal profit, while prison industry workers were the least likely to participate in the sub rosa economy. Skimming and pilfering food, laundry bleach, and office supplies were group efforts carried out in maintenance jobs. Other inmates admitted to using their freedom of movement in their jobs to pass contraband, food, and

Every jail and prison has a bartering system of reciprocity based on negotiation and exchange of goods and services between prisoners without the use of cash.

information (Santos 2004). Terry (2003, 64) provides an account of how he used his job as a receiving clerk for profit:

> This position gave me access to information about who would be arriving in the institution the day before they arrived. One of the things I was expected to do [by inmates] … and was taught to me by the man I replaced, including making three lists of these soon-to-be-new prisoners… of their names, race, county of origin, and crime. Once completed, I gave a copy to a black, brown, and white prisoner…. In return, I was rewarded with something tangible, such as cigarettes or a small amount of marijuana, and social status. This process served the purpose of screening incoming prisoners… for determining who could stay, or who had to go.

27% of men and women inmates admitted to using their assigned prison job to yield a personal profit in the sub rosa economy.

A more serious form of behavior that is of concern to prison officials is smuggling in **contraband** that prove to be lucrative such as weapons, drugs, cell phones, cigarettes, or cash. The extent of contraband in each prison depended on the level of staff enforcement rather than the custody level. Lankenau (2001) found that minimum-security facilities had the most organized cigarette black markets compared to medium- or maximum-security prisons because minimum-security inmates had more contact with visitors, more movement, and more access to work release, where they were unsupervised on the outside.

LEARNING OUTCOMES 4 — Clarify the key ways prisoners use the sub rosa economy for profit.

GLOSSARY

sub rosa economy Underground economy based on negotiation and exchange of goods and services between prisoners without the use of cash.

commissary Snacks, hygiene items, and other items available for purchase at the prison store.

merchants Inmates who control scarce resources by running a prison store.

jailhouse lawyers Inmates who use their legal knowledge and skills to write writs and grievances.

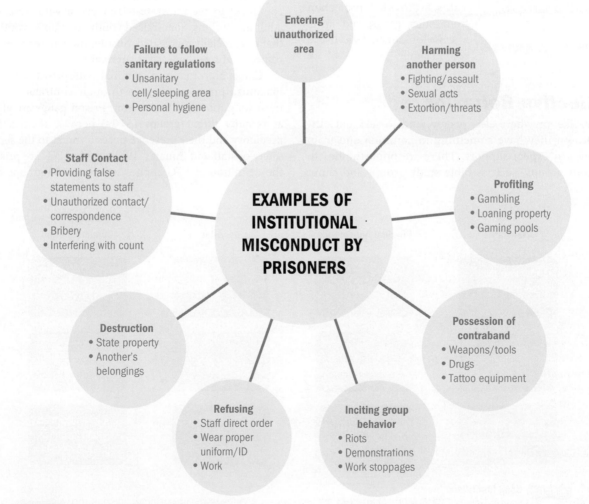

EXAMPLES OF INSTITUTIONAL MISCONDUCT BY PRISONERS

Entering unauthorized area

Harming another person
• Fighting/assault
• Sexual acts
• Extortion/threats

Profiting
• Gambling
• Loaning property
• Gaming pools

Possession of contraband
• Weapons/tools
• Drugs
• Tattoo equipment

Inciting group behavior
• Riots
• Demonstrations
• Work stoppages

Refusing
• Staff direct order
• Wear proper uniform/ID
• Work

Destruction
• State property
• Another's belongings

Staff Contact
• Providing false statements to staff
• Unauthorized contact/correspondence
• Bribery
• Interfering with count

Failure to follow sanitary regulations
• Unsanitary cell/sleeping area
• Personal hygiene

FIGURE 8.10 Examples of Prisoner Misconduct.

Gangs control the institution's drug transactions, gambling, loans, prostitution, and debt-collection rackets. In addition, they increase an inmate's status, provide protection from other gangs, and instill a sense of camaraderie like a second family.

contraband Forbidden items that compromise institutional safety and security.

crews Small cliques of prisoners that spend time together, but there is no initiation or formal alliances. Some crews can be networked and predatory, but they are more loosely associated and are not an institutional security threat.

Movement of contraband typically involves **crews**, but a large amount of the most lucrative part of the illegal economy is claimed by prison gangs (Santos 2004). Gangs control the institution's drug transactions, gambling, loans, prostitution, and debt-collection rackets. In addition, they increase an inmate's status, provide protection from other gangs, and instill a sense of camaraderie like a second family.

▶ *Collective Behavior*

In prisons, like anywhere else, people tend to seek out others with whom they have something in common and from whom they can expect support. There are opportunities to join religious groups, such as bible study groups and choir.

There are athletic leagues that have organized teams that play basketball, volleyball, or flag football. There are chess clubs and groups such as Alcoholics Anonymous that address addiction. These groups are allowed by the prison because they aid in the prisoner's self-development, and they keep prisoners busy.

Another reason to be part of a crew is for self-protection. Ross and Richards (2002, 133) observed that in some prisons "you absolutely need to affiliate with a group that will protect you. The loners, the people without social skills or friends, are vulnerable to being physically attacked or preyed upon." We begin first by discussing men's prison gangs, and then we discuss groups in women's institutions.

Prison Gangs and Security Threat Groups

Growth of prison gangs throughout the 1960s and 1970s were closely tied to racial conflicts between African-American and Caucasian prisoners and instability caused by the ending of the building tender system. With the dismantling of the convict subculture, Latino prisoners saw potential early on for using gangs to control the drug economy in prison and, at the same time, protect them from being victimized by outsiders (Irwin 1980). As the numbers of Latino gang members increased and became a perceived threat, black and white prisoners responded by creating their own groups. In the 1980s and 1990s, gangs continued to recruit **state-raised youth** who were waived to adult institutions. State-raised youth grew up in youth facilities that were racially segregated, hostile, and where violence earned respect and stealing was for survival.

Gangs are organized criminal enterprises that attempt to maximize power and profit through contraband and drug-trafficking movement in prison. Prison gangs are also known as **security threat groups (STGs)** because their activities are predatory and their presence poses a threat to the security and safety of staff and inmates. While most STGs are prison gangs, the definition of *STG* applies to over 1,000 groups consisting

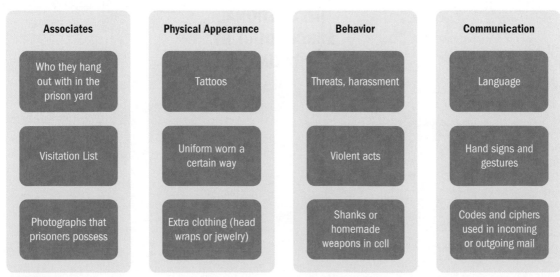

FIGURE 8.11 **Gang Identifiers.**
Source: From THE PROBLEM OF GANGS AND SECURITY THREAT GROUPS (STGs) IN AMERICAN PRISONS TODAY: Recent Research Findings from the 2004 Prison Gang Survey ed. by George W. Knox, Ph.D. Copyright © 2005. Reprinted by permission of National Gang Crime Research Center.

TABLE 8.1 | Examples Of Security Threat Groups.

Group Formation	Latino Groups	Caucasian Groups	African-American Groups
1950s	Latin Kings	Ku Klux Klan (1800s)	Vice Lords
	Mexican Mafia (CA La Eme)	Hell's Angels MC (1948)	
		Pagans MC	
1960s	Nuestra Familia	Aryan Brotherhood	Black P Stones
	Texas Syndicate	Diablos MC	CRIPs/Folk Nation
	Florencia 13	Sons of Silence MC	Bloods/People Nation
	Surenos	Warlocks MC	Black Guerilla Family
	Maniac Latin Disciples	Vagos MC	Black Panther Party
	Bandidos MC	Brother Speed MC	
	Mongols MC		
1970s	Neta	Nazi Low Riders	DC Blacks
	Nortenos	Simon City Royals	
1980s	Mexikanemi (TX)	Skinheads	El Rukns
	Barrio Azteca	Peckerwoods	Gangster Disciples
	Raza Unida	Aryan Circle	Nation of Islam
	Hermanos de Pistoleros Latinos	Public Enemy Number One	Five Percenters
	Border Brothers	Dirty White Boys	
1990s	Mara Salvatrucha 13	White Knights	United Blood Nation
	Tri-City Bombers	Dead Man, Inc.	Fruits of Islam
	Texas Chicano Brotherhood	United Aryan Brotherhood	
	Tango Blast/Four Horsemen	White Aryan Resistance	
2000s		Asatru	
		Christian Identity	
		World Church of the Creator	

MC = Motorcycle club

Source: Gang Identification Task Force. Retrieved from http://gangtaskforce.blogspot.com/.

LEARNING OUTCOMES 5 Compare and contrast security threat groups and play families in terms of their structure, purpose, and management.

GLOSSARY

state-raised youth Inmates who grew up in youth prisons and who tend to be more violent than the average prisoner.

of motorcycle clubs, militias, mafia families, Asian gangs, and occult groups—all of which require constant monitoring (Winterdyk & Ruddell 2010).

Active membership varies widely by each state, with some states having significant STG problems (California, Texas, New York, Florida, Illinois, Wisconsin) than others. Prevalence of STGs average between 19 and 26 percent who were gang members before imprisonment (Winterdyk & Ruddell 2010), and an additional 12 percent of male inmates were recruited into a gang during imprisonment (Knox 2005). Official data is supported by self-reported pressures by 20 percent of males and 16 percent of Caucasian female inmates to join a gang in an urban county jail (Alarid 2000a).

In total, that translates into an estimated 500,000 STG members currently in jail and prison throughout the United States. However, the number varies because some members are more active than others, making it more difficult for prison authorities to confirm memberships. In the post-9/11 era, concern remains that prisons are possible breeding grounds for future terrorists, particularly by religious extremist groups during chapel services. For example, the leader of the Black P. Stones was convicted of conspiring with Libya in a terrorist plot to shoot down American planes (Knox 2005).

35% Prevalence of STGs average between 19 and 26 percent who were gang members before imprisonment and an additional 12 percent of male inmates were recruited into a gang during imprisonment

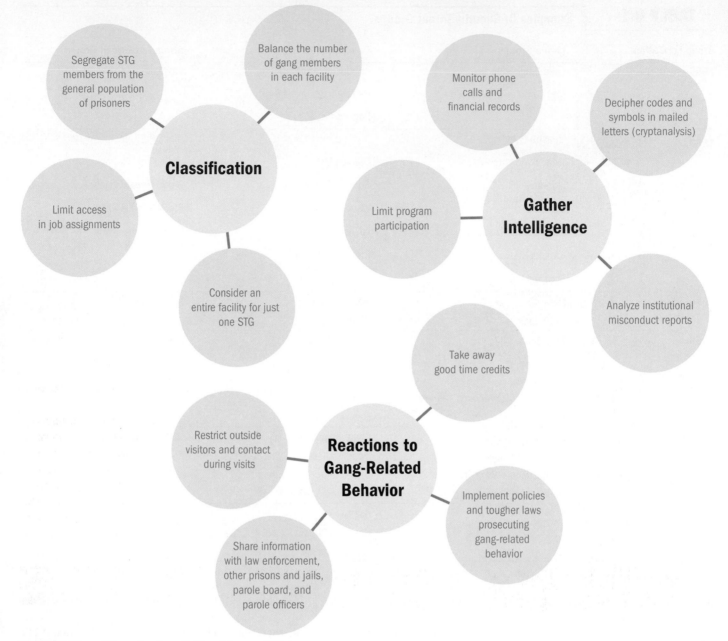

FIGURE 8.12 Ways of Managing Security Threat Groups (STGs).
Sources: (Knox 2005; Winterdyk & Ruddell 2010)

The circles in the figure contain the following text:

Classification
- Segregate STG members from the general population of prisoners
- Balance the number of gang members in each facility
- Limit access in job assignments
- Consider an entire facility for just one STG

Gather Intelligence
- Monitor phone calls and financial records
- Decipher codes and symbols in mailed letters (cryptanalysis)
- Limit program participation
- Analyze institutional misconduct reports

Reactions to Gang-Related Behavior
- Take away good time credits
- Restrict outside visitors and contact during visits
- Implement policies and tougher laws prosecuting gang-related behavior
- Share information with law enforcement, other prisons and jails, parole board, and parole officers

Gang intelligence officers (GIs) collect information on suspected gang members using the list of gang identifiers, along with information from correctional officers and other inmate informants (Knox 2005). Once active STG members are identified, prison officials place restrictions on them, such as removal from the general prison population, reclassification to a higher custody level, and placement in administrative segregation for the remainder of their prison term (Winterdyk & Ruddell 2010). A small number of prisons have programs that encourage members to permanently renounce their gang membership and "debrief," which means to share confidential information. However, less than 10 percent of validated gang members renounce their membership because of the consequences of assaults or death (Knox 2005). Despite efforts to control STGs, prison gangs maintain

Despite efforts to control STGs, prison gangs maintain a stronghold in maximum and supermax prisons throughout the United States.

Although their numbers are growing, women tend to recruit less actively and are less likely to make group membership a security threat issue.

a stronghold in maximum and supermax prisons throughout the United States. Unfortunately, drugs are brought in primarily by visitors and the occasional corrupt prison employee or naïve volunteer. That situation makes it even more difficult for prison administrators to control the introduction of drugs into the prison and to negatively impact the growth of prison gangs (Winterdyk & Ruddell 2010).

Groups in Women's Prisons

Although their numbers are growing, women tend to recruit less actively and are less likely to make group membership a security threat issue. Less than 4 percent of female inmates are recruited into a gang during imprisonment, and 6.3 percent of female prisoners were gang members before imprisonment (Knox 2005). Female gang members seem to be less active while incarcerated, as the environment inside the institution does not support gang behavior (Owen 1998; Petersen 2000). Instead, female groups were organized based on make-believe families, friendships, and couples that crossed racial lines. Small, close-knit make-believe families were encouraged because being well-connected was still important to being part of "the drama" or "the mix." "Their advocacy is emotional and personal; their allegiance is to a few rather than to many" (Pollock 2002, 138).

Instead, female groups were organized based on make-believe families, friendships, and couples that crossed racial lines.

10% Less than 4 percent of female inmates are recruited into a gang during imprisonment, and 6.3 percent of female prisoners were gang members before imprisonment

Close friendships were the most prevalent type of relationship found in women's prisons. Most women had between one and ten close friends that they considered to be trustworthy, with an average of two close friends. Friendships allowed women to share problems and commissary, but were not used very often for hustling goods and services or for protection (Alarid 1996). Only 12 percent of adult women reported being loners. These women were not necessarily social outcasts or unable to form social bonds. Rather, loners chose a different path, after deciding that "commissary and sex games" were not the way to do time (Alarid 1996).

One of the most widely documented aspects of the social structure of women's prisons is a fabricated kinship network that has been called *pseudofamilies*, *make-believe families*, or *prison families*. The most common term is **play families**, which refers to relationships among women prisoners that borrow the structure, terminology, and function of families in larger society. About 4 in 10 women joined play families in prison, while only 12 percent reported doing so in jail. Play families shared commissary, persuaded members to be compliant with prison rules, and protected each other from predatory inmates (Alarid 1996). Women chose either a masculine or feminine role. However, most play families existed as mentoring relationships, where the play mother is the family's center (Alarid 1996). The most common roles are mother–daughter and sister–sister. Mothers, especially, may have several daughters for whom they listen to problems and offer advice. The relationships created in the play family likely do not represent the women's real-life experiences. Instead, the play mother may be a better mother to her inmate daughters than her real-life mother was to her while growing up, or better than the inmate was to her own children before imprisonment. Generally, women's prisons had less incidents of serious misconduct than men's facilities.

Factors That Accurately Predict More Misconduct	Factors That Do Not Accurately Predict More Misconduct

• Current age
  – Younger inmates more than older
• Gender
  – Males involved more than females
• History of violence
  – Recent history predicted continuation
• Mental illness
• Lack of program participation
• Gang membership
	• Drug and alcohol use
	• History of escape
	• Sentence length
	• Severity of offense
	• Time left to serve

FIGURE 8.13 **Predicting Misconduct while Incarcerated.**
Source: From EVIDENCE-BASED PRACTICE: Principles for Enhancing Correctional Results in Prisons by Ralph C. Serin (2005). Washington, DC: National Institute of Corrections.

▶ Prison Violence

Potential for violence exists in all institutions, but violence is clearly concentrated in higher-security units and within certain groups because the subculture of violence is stronger. An environment that encourages violence to create a reputation, bully or harass as a show of power, impose fear when necessary to avoid being victimized, and settle problems without staff are all circumstances that sustain violent behavior (Carceral 2004). Prison officials have a duty under the Eighth Amendment to keep prisoners safe from violence by other prisoners, but staff is not liable for assaults unless the prisoner can prove that staff exhibited **deliberate indifference**.

The most common acts of violence involving two people are inmate–inmate threats, assaults, and sexual assault. Threats are the most common, but are

An environment that encourages violence to create a reputation, bully or harass as a show of power, impose fear when necessary to avoid being victimized, and settle problems without staff are all circumstances that sustain violent behavior

undocumented in official statistics. Cases of assault and sexual assault/rape are underreported out of fear of being labeled a snitch (Santos 2004). Documented cases are therefore the worst ones that involve medical attention. Some known facts about assault in prison are as follows:

- Incidents of assault in women's prisons were less likely to involve deadly weapons and less related to race/ethnic tension. Jealousy, sexual pressuring, and unreciprocated attention were the most frequently cited reasons that led to assault.

- For men, *intraracial* assaults by inmates of the same race were more common than interracial inmate assaults (Trulson & Marquart 2002).

- For men, STG members committed acts of violence at two to three times the rate of inmates who were not STG members in units of the same security level.

- Of all documented assaults in men's prisons, two-thirds were inmate–inmate assault and one-third were inmates who assaulted a staff member. In six states (Kansas, Mississippi, Missouri, Ohio, South Carolina, and Wisconsin), inmate assaults against staff exceeded the number of inmate–inmate assaults. However, assaults against staff were less likely to

require medical attention and more often to be referred for prosecution (Camp, Camp, & May 2003).

Sexual Assault and Rape

Sexual behavior between inmates, and especially between inmates and staff members, has always been prohibited—this includes sexual assault (intentional touching) or nonconsensual sexual acts. In the past, a climate of acceptance that rape and sexual harassment was part of the punishment dominated prisons across the United States. "Turning out" a vulnerable inmate by force was a way for another prisoner to enhance his or her own status among peers, whether it was blatantly through rape, or through more subtle strategies like loaning new prisoners more than they could ever afford to pay back and then demanding payment through sex (Santos 2004). Sexual harassment, derogatory or profane comments, or acts of staff sexual misconduct (indecent exposure, voyeurism, or requested sexual acts) had few, if any negative consequences. Prison conditions have greatly improved since the 1970s, but anecdotal evidence suggested that sexual assault was still entrenched in prison culture because it was overlooked by correctional officers and encouraged by the prisoner subculture.

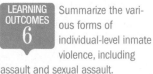

LEARNING OUTCOMES 6 Summarize the various forms of individual-level inmate violence, including assault and sexual assault.

GLOSSARY

deliberate indifference When officers know about a situation and don't take action to prevent it.

Reducing sexual victimization of prison inmates became a priority with the 2003 passage of the Prison Rape Elimination Act (PREA). PREA sought for the first time to measure the incidence of prison rape in federal, state, and local institutions, and to provide guidelines to protect prisoners from rape. The provisions of the act included staff training on the new law, a zero-tolerance policy of sexual misconduct and rape incidents, victim access to counseling and protective custody housing, and establishing a national commission to develop more permanent standards (PREA 2003).

Five years after PREA's passage, the nationwide rate of inmates who, when surveyed, reported sexual victimization at least once within a prior 12-month period was still 4.4 percent in prisons and 3 percent in jails. This equated to 88,500 incidents every year. At some units around the country, rates ranged from less than 1 percent to a high of nearly 20 percent (Beck, Harrison, & Guerino 2010). Facilities with higher rates of sexual abuse had a higher number of violent offenders, high racial conflict, dormitory housing, places without video surveillance, and they were understaffed compared to the number of offenders (English & Heil 2005). About 90 percent of these incidents that inmates anonymously reported to researchers were *not* reported to prison officials, in part because few incidents could be substantiated (proven that they occurred) due to lack of evidence.

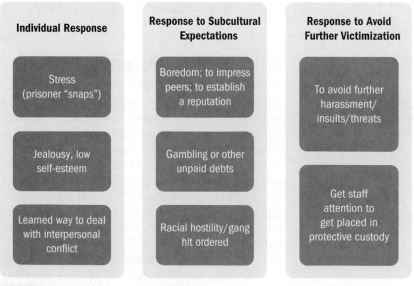

Individual Response	Response to Subcultural Expectations	Response to Avoid Further Victimization
Stress (prisoner "snaps")	Boredom; to impress peers; to establish a reputation	To avoid further harassment/ insults/threats
Jealousy, low self-esteem	Gambling or other unpaid debts	Get staff attention to get placed in protective custody
Learned way to deal with interpersonal conflict	Racial hostility/gang hit ordered	

 **FIGURE 8.14** Causes of Individual-Level Violence.

4.4% Five years after PREA's passage, the nationwide rate of inmates who reported sexual victimization at least once within a prior 12-month period was still 4.4 percent in prisons and 3 percent in jails.

Most incidents of sexual abuse of inmates were committed by staff members rather than by other inmates. In both men's and women's units, staff member sexual abusers were more likely to be of the opposite sex relative to the inmate victim (Beck, Harrison, & Guerino 2010). The unequal power relationship that exists between correctional staff and confined prisoners was particularly important to address due to these findings. All sexual acts involving staff are considered to be forms of coerced sexual misconduct and may result in termination and/or additional criminal charges.

Inmate *perpetrators* of sexual assault tend to have spent time in juvenile facilities, have committed a violent crime as an adult, be gang affiliated, be more likely to be involved in all types of misconduct, and be under age 30. Targeted inmate *victims* tended to be young, first-time, nonviolent, Caucasian, and from a middle-class background. Individual characteristics that increased victimization even more (whether they were actual or perceived by others) were those who were developmentally disabled or mentally ill, unaffiliated with a group, known to be gay or bisexual, perceived to be a snitch, possessed certain physical traits (effeminate traits if a man and masculine traits if a woman), and those who were convicted of a crime against a minor (English & Heil 2005; English, Heil, & Dumond 2010). Victims who reported being sexually abused were targeted between three to five times during that year.

Most sexually coerced incidents by other inmates involved sexual harassment or forced sexual assault. Sexual coercion led to incidents of sexual assault when other prisoners perceived their advances were being ignored. Once a woman was targeted for physical and/or sexual violence, it was difficult to escape the situation. If rape occurred, it involved a group of women (Alarid 2000b).

To reduce incidences of prison sexual assault and violence

- Separate predatory inmates from targeted inmates
- Provide prisoner and staff training on sexual assault
- Encourage staff to be part of the solution (rather than the problem)
- Provide counseling intervention for sexual assault victims
- Encourage consistent rule enforcement by staff
- Aggressively investigate and prosecute rapes
- Provide protective custody for inmates targeted for sexual assault
- Use video cameras to prevent sex abuse
- Allow housing changes and facility transfers for victims
- Implement criminal sanctions for any inmates or staffers engaging in abuse

FIGURE 8.15 **Reducing Incidents of Prison Sexual Assault and Violence.**
Source: Based on Hensley, et al., 2002; Austin, et al., 2006; Zweig, et al., 2007.

Most incidents of sexual abuse of inmates were committed by staff members rather than by other inmates. In both men's and women's units, staff member sexual abusers were more likely to be of the opposite sex relative to the inmate victim

The national standards for reducing prison rape were published by the attorney general for public comment in early 2011 before being finalized later that year. The national standards require each state to have a special unit to investigate and prosecute sexual assault and rape committed during incarceration. States are also required to educate staff members about sexual assault and separate likely abusers from potential victims. The national standards are immediately binding to federal facilities, and states have one year to comply, or risk losing 5 percent of their federal funding.

Collective Violence

Most acts of collective violence are for the purpose of prisoners vehemently communicating some form of change. Prisoners have engaged in group hunger strikes, work stoppages, and **voluntary lockdowns**. Acts of collective violence in prison can be differentiated into disturbances and riots. **Disturbances** are quite common—occurring once or twice per week in maximum security and once every few months in minimum security correctional facilities throughout the United States. Most disturbances involve fighting/assault because of racial tension, gang rivalries, or retaliation. Other incidents were disruptive, meaning they involved noise and property damage, including banging on cell doors, flooding cells (by stopping up toilets), setting fire to property, throwing feces/urine at officers, and cell extraction problems (Corrections Compendium 2002b). Most disturbances occur in large areas where many inmates congregate, such as the prison yard, the chow hall, the dormitories, and the dayroom. Most disturbances can cause injury to inmates and property damage, but they usually end within minutes. Most importantly, the prison remains in control at all times. Disturbances in female prisons occur less often than with men and are most often group strikes, fires, and fights.

Prison Riots

More attention has been paid to **prison riots** because they involve a large number of inmates who plan to forcibly take control of the prison. Once the control of the prison changes hands from officers to prisoners, a disturbance officially becomes a riot. Rioting stems from prisoners viewing violence as their best response to adverse conditions or way to achieve change of **predisposing factors** that, over an extended period of time, provide the riot's foundation. Predisposing

GLOSSARY

voluntary lockdown When prisoners refuse to leave their cells.

disturbance An altercation involving three or more inmates, resulting in official action, but where staff control of the facility is maintained.

prison riot A situation involving a large number of inmates making a forcible attempt to take control of a sizable area of the prison for a substantial amount of time.

predisposing factors Underlying conditions that occur over an extended period of time and provide the foundation for a riot.

triggering event One or several specific events that sparked the riot.

conditions could be administrative breakdown, severe staff shortages, perceived oppressive conditions, continuous staff confrontation, or ongoing racial tension. Predisposing factors are more likely to occur in higher-custody-level prisons (such as in Chino and Folsom prisons in California) than in medium- or minimum-level facilities.

The **triggering event** is what actually starts the riot, *but is not the cause*. The triggering event in the Chino riot in 2009 was racial tension in the dayroom, but the riot occurred because of oppressive conditions due to overcrowding and idleness. Once a riot has begun, some inmates will seek safety and remove themselves from the rioters. Others will rejoice in their newfound freedom and partake in binges of drinking, drug use, and property damage (Wicker 1994). There may also be violence among inmates as old grudges are settled or snitches are harmed or even killed.

The vast majority of riots today are contained in a small area of the prison and never make it to a full-scale organized plan because they are extinguished by prison officials within a few hours. Riots between the 1950s and 1970s, however, lasted longer and involved organized negotiation by a few inmate leaders that challenged abuses of power by corrections officers. For example, the Attica, New York, riot in 1971 was a complete prison takeover; it lasted five days and involved negotiations between inmate leaders and prison authorities to improve prison conditions and inmate treatment. In the eager attempt to reclaim the prison, law enforcement officers killed 39 inmates and 10 correctional officers, and wounded more than 80 others. Three inmates were intentionally killed at the hands of other inmates, and one officer died two days later of head wounds inflicted when the inmates took his keys (Wicker 1994).

The Santa Fe riot provides an interesting contrast to the Attica riot. On February 2, 1980, inmates at the New Mexico State Penitentiary began what would be a 36-hour riot. Before it was over, 33 inmates were dead and over 100 others were beaten and sexually assaulted by fellow prisoners. There were some similarities in the predisposing conditions (Colvin 1997), but the biggest differences were the absence of organization and the brutal violence against each other. Property damage amounted to over

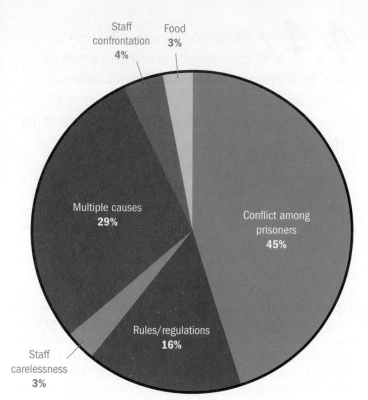

*Note: Some of the causes were triggering events, while others were predisposing factors

FIGURE 8.16 **Causes* of Prison Riots and Disturbances.**
Source: From A HISTORY OF CORRECTIONAL VIOLENCE: An Examination of Riots and Correctional Disturbances by Reid H. Montgomery & Jordan A. Crews. Copyright © 1998. Reprinted by permission of American Correctional Association, Alexandria, VA.

$100 million, and a new prison had to be built to replace the one that was destroyed.

Montgomery and Crews (1998) examined 255 U.S. prison riots between 1900 and 1995, and found that 7 out of 10 riots did not involve hostages, most riots involved a small area of the prison that was taken over (as opposed to the whole prison), the inmates conceded within a one- to five-hour span after the riot began, and the reasons for the riot varied widely—likely because some of what was reported were triggering events while others were predisposing factors. Although riots still happen from time to time, more is known about how to respond and most importantly, how to prevent riots from occurring in the first place.

- Consistent and fair rule enforcement by staff
- Adequate ratios of both treatment and security staff per inmate
- Quality food
- Vigilance for abrupt changes in prisoner or staff behavior (inmates requesting transfers, staff who call in sick)
- "No hostage" policy—administrators will not negotiate if hostages are taken
- Riot plan and continuous training
- Open lines of communication among management, staff, and inmates (decreases rumors)
- Good classification system

FIGURE 8.17 **Preventing Prison Riots.**

Decreasing Violence through the Inmate Subculture

Resolve to Stop the Violence Project (RSVP) began in a San Francisco jail to decrease violence in prisoners with a history of street violence or institutional misconduct. RSVP is unique from most programs in that it changes the institutional subculture of violence within one dorm through peer mentoring, direct and consistent staff supervision, and race/ethnic composition that reflects the composition of program participants. RSVP is known as a peer mentoring program because it uses more senior-level clients as change agents for newer participants and also focuses on changing the *institutional culture* that permeates the problem.

The second main component in RSVP is its restorative justice concepts to bring about victim empathy, repair the harm done to others, and to repair harm done to themselves. Part of behavioral change in RSVP mandates that the offender apologize to people he or she has hurt or victimized. Exposure to the program is for 12 hours per day for six days per week. The length of stay depended largely on their sentence, but it averaged 165 days (most ranged from two months to six months).

RSVP has support from community groups including the District Attorney's Office, the Probation Department, domestic violence shelters, and other victim advocate groups. The community groups developed concrete ways that violent offenders convicted of domestic violence, robbery, assault, rape, and terrorist threats

can take responsibility for their actions and restore the harm they caused to their victims, their own families, and to the larger community.

The first way is that as inmates progress through the program, each inmate is expected to take on a greater leadership role with newcomers. The senior status inmates confront newcomers about their violent behavior in a controlled group setting and help them to recognize how their early gender socialization, such as suppressing their feelings and expressing a tough macho image, has contributed to their anger problems.

The second phase is victim impact in which victims of violent crime describe in vivid detail how that crime has devastated their lives. This phase also allows the inmates to begin to reflect on how they have been victimized and witnessed violence in their own lives. The third phase involves artistic expression through a one-act play that each inmate writes that represents a traumatic incident that led him or her to become a violent person. The play is performed by inmates, and could have alternate endings. The final step is the continued participation in group sessions for one year after returning to the community. Since the program began, violent incidents in the rest of the jail have decreased because the predatory inmates are transferred to the program dorm. As program duration increases from 8 weeks to 16 weeks, rates of recidivism significantly decrease when the RSVP group was compared to a group not exposed to RSVP. Over 4,000 offenders have participated, with 87 percent who have *not* been rearrested for another violent offense.

The RSVP provides hope for change in the following questions:

1. What characteristics do peer mentoring programs (such as therapeutic communities for drug addicts and the RSVP program for violent offenders featured here) share in common?

2. Are there any challenges with peer mentoring programs that you can think of?

3. What other programs could be modeled after the RSVP program to change other undesirable behaviors in the prisoner subculture?

Sources: (Lee & Gilligan 2005; WABC-TV/DT 2008)

Source: © Mikael Karlsson/Alamy

Describe the characteristics of prisoners in state and federal prison.

LEARNING OUTCOMES 1

Prisoners are primarily young men who lacked skills and education. Women accounted for a disproportionately small group of offenders compared to men, but are still growing at a greater rate. Non-U.S. citizens and aliens, detained in special ICE units now comprise one out of four federal prisoners.

1. What differences are there between state and federal prisoners?

2. Why do prisoners tend to come from impoverished communities, and why do they lack education?

3. What can be done in other parts of the criminal justice system about this situation?

disproportionate When the group under study has a substantially greater or lesser percentage than exists in the larger population.

Bureau of Prisons Where federal prisoners go when they have violated an incarcerable federal offense.

Explain the elements of prison life that define the incarceration experience, and apply deprivation or importation theory to each of these elements.

LEARNING OUTCOMES 2

The norms and values of the inmate subculture are the result of a combination of losses inherent in prison conditions and importation of street norms and behaviors that represent the code of the streets. The elements of prison life that define the incarceration experience include socialization, the inmate code, language, group membership, working a job, disciplinary reports, and involvement in the sub rosa economic system.

1. How would a new prisoner best learn the ropes of prison life without getting victimized in the process?

2. Are there ways that staff members can influence or change the inmate subculture? If so, how? If not, why not?

3. Which theory (deprivation or importation) best explains the sub rosa economy?

4. Which theory (deprivation or importation) best explains women's play families and why?

prisonization The process by which the prisoners learn the norms of life in prison.

inmate subculture A society with its own norms and values defined by inmates with the most power and influence.

Big House A maximum-security penitentiary with a convict subculture, lasting between the early 1800s until about 1980.

total institution A regimented facility that is physically separate from the larger society and meets the survival needs of its occupants.

deprivation model Assumes that prison culture developed out of the pains of imprisonment through adaptations that prisoners make to circumvent these losses.

importation model Assumes that prison life is an extension of street life of marginalized people from impoverished communities who dominate the prison.

inmate code A system of unwritten rules that directs inmate behavior.

prison argot or "prison-proper" The language, slang, and physical gestures used to communicate meaning in prison.

players Prisoners who embrace mainstream prison culture that values manipulating and intimidating others.

squares Inmates who oppose mainstream prison culture by being well-behaved and who take advantage of every self-improvement program they can to keep themselves busy. Also known as *bootlickers*.

snitch Inmates who are targeted by predatory inmates because they have passed along information to staff that has gotten another inmate in trouble. Also known as *player haters*.

punk Inmates who are targeted by predatory inmates because they are perceived as physically or mentally weak and afraid to fight back.

fish First-time inmate that is vulnerable because he or she has not yet been prisonized.

Identify the benefits and challenges of having inmates work while incarcerated.

Most prisoners are assigned to work a part-time maintenance job, and have the opportunity to attend school or other programs. Less than 10 percent of prisoners are chosen to work full-time jobs in the prison industry, which more closely mirrors working life in outside society. Prison-made goods are mainly sold in sheltered markets, but some private businesses partner with prisons to sell goods on the open market.

1. While prisoner labor should not compete with free-world labor, with all the private businesses relocating to other countries, isn't the relocation (India, China, etc.) a greater threat than simply allowing U.S. prisoners that same opportunity?

2. What would happen if our government increased the number of jurisdictions that could have a private factory inside a prison from 50 across the whole United States to 500?

3. How can the unemployment rate inside prisons be reduced?

4. Would you support paying all inmates a wage for their work, and then deducting that money for rent, utilities, and paying restitution? Debate the pros and cons of this policy.

institutional maintenance Unskilled jobs that inmates are assigned in order to assist with daily prison operations (food preparation, laundry, cleaning).

trustys Minimum-security-level inmates who earn the status through not causing behavioral problems.

agriculture Outdoor field work jobs involving prisoners' growing crops and raising livestock; prevalent in southern states.

prison industry A skilled job within the prison that provides inmates training while incarcerated (manufacturing, construction, auto repair, welding, etc.).

open market Prison-made products are sold, either by private companies or by the state, to prospective buyers.

sheltered market/government/state use model Restricts the sale of prison-made products only to other state and local government markets. Also known as the *government or state use models*.

free enterprise A private sector entrepreneurial model of doing business.

Clarify the key ways prisoners use the sub rosa economy for profit.

The sub rosa economy is used illicitly by prisoners for personal profit and to obtain goods and services in an environment that lacks access to resources. Smuggling and movement of contraband is controlled by prison gangs.

1. If it is known that stealing and other workplace deviance exists in prisoner jobs, then why have prisoners work at all?

2. How can common illicit behaviors—such as loaning, gambling, extortion, running commissary stores, etc.—be minimized?

3. Would cracking down on the sub rosa economy affect correctional officers' rapport too much with inmates?

4. How much illicit behavior is tolerated simply because officers are so outnumbered by inmates?

sub rosa economy Underground economy based on negotiation and exchange of goods and services between prisoners without the use of cash.

commissary Snacks, hygiene items, and other items available for purchase at the prison store.

merchants Inmates who control scarce resources by running a prison store.

jailhouse lawyers Inmates who use their legal knowledge and skills to write writs and grievances.

contraband Forbidden items that compromise institutional safety and security.

crews Small cliques of prisoners that spend time together, but there is no initiation, or formal alliances. Some crews can be networked and predatory, but they are more loosely associated and are not an institutional security threat.

Compare and contrast security threat groups and play families in terms of their structure, purpose, and management.

The social structure of men's prisons is built on crews and gangs—many of which are racially and ethnically segregated. *Security threat groups* are widespread in men's prisons and have a formalized structure and constitution with rigid rules. In some states, active STG leaders and members are segregated in an attempt to decrease prison violence. The social structure of women's prisons is less influenced by violence, gangs, and race/ethnicity. Play families reflect an informal structure built on bonding, social control, and economic assistance; they do not pose an institutional threat, so fewer attempts are made to control them.

1. Given what you know about the prisoner subculture and the limited freedoms, how can racial hostility in jails and prisons be realistically reduced?

2. Can prison gangs be abolished in prisons, or are they just too powerful?

3. Which strategies do you think are most effective in managing security threat groups?

4. Are play families problematic in women's prisons? If so, how?

state-raised youth Inmates who grew up in youth prisons and who tend to be more violent than the average prisoner.

security threat group An organized group whose activities are predatory and criminal and whose presence in a correctional institution/agency poses a real and imminent threat to the security and safety of staff and inmates.

play families Relationships among women prisoners that mimic the structure, terminology, and function of families in general society.

Summarize the various forms of individual-level inmate violence, including assault and sexual assault.

Individual-level violence for men is most often caused by personality clashes, racial tensions, unpaid debts, sexual assault, and retaliation. Violence for women is caused most often by jealously, unreciprocated love, and sexual coercion/harassment. The PREA act was passed to further reduce inmates from getting sexually assaulted and harassed.

1. What forms of individual-level violence do you see as most problematic and why?

2. Discuss how the following three policies for *staff* would or would not reduce prisoner sexual assault in prisons on their own merit:

   a. Provide staff training on sexual assault

   b. Mandate staff intervention for sexual assault victims

   c. Encourage staff to consistently enforce the rules for predatory inmates

3. Discuss how the following three policies for *prisoners* would or would not reduce sexual assault in prisons on their own merit:

   a. Provide prisoner training on sexual assault

   b. Provide condoms to inmates

   c. Increase conjugal visitation

deliberate indifference When officers know about a situation and don't take action to prevent it.

Special Correctional Populations

"If they are terminal or incapacitated and not at risk to commit a crime… [prison] is not the place for them. We need to be concentrating on people who are dangerous to the community and need to be locked up."

—Dr. Louis Shicker, Medical Director, Illinois Department of Corrections

1 Summarize various treatment programs within a prison.

2 Summarize the issues regarding sex offenders.

3 Describe the alternatives that pregnant mothers have once they give birth to their babies while incarcerated.

4 Summarize the issues regarding offenders with infectious diseases.

5 Outline the issues of aging and terminally ill prisoners in terms of their medical care, housing, and release options.

9

Identify how collective violence begins and why it is sustained as a part of prison life.

Most acts of collective violence are classified as disturbances involving small groups of prisoners or security threat groups. Disturbances are different from riots in that they do not involve any intent to take over a prison. Riots have the intent of prisoners taking over the control of a prison.

1. Can disturbances lead to riots, or are they completely different events?

2. How can prison riots be decreased or prevented?

voluntary lockdown When prisoners refuse to leave their cells.

disturbance An altercation involving three or more inmates resulting in official action, but where staff control of the facility is maintained.

prison riot A situation involving a large number of inmates making a forcible attempt to take control of a sizable area of the prison for a substantial amount of time.

predisposing factors Underlying conditions that occur over an extended period of time and provide the foundation for a riot.

triggering event One or several specific events that sparked the riot.

MyCJLab

Go to the Chapter 8 section in *MyCJLab* to test your understanding of this chapter, access customized study content, engage in interactive simulations, complete critical thinking and research assignments, and view related online videos.

Additional Links

First-Time in Prison: Learning the Ropes can be viewed here: **www.youtube.com/watch?v=PAS4uSDJe9k&feature=relmfu**.

Lockdown: Maximum Security (as a National Geographic program in 5 separate parts) Part 1 can be found at **www.youtube.com/watch?v=RiQZpRbEPfM&feature=related**.

Visit the National Correctional Industries Association and click on the "News" section to see all the prisoner-made goods **www.nationalcia.org/**.

The MS-13 Gang from El Salvador is featured in this documentary: **www.youtube.com/watch?v=PrZx2YdZFOk**.

The Nuestra Familia Prison Gang is featured in the following video: **www.youtube.com/watch?v=vRMqOumehWk&feature=related**.

View the 29 minute video about violence reduction in correctional facilities, entitled Visionaries with Sam Waterston: Resolve to Stop the Violence at **www.youtube.com/watch?v=HDAelT3K5w4**.

Visit the Federal Bureau of Prisons website to view the different prisons and programs: **www.bop.gov**.

For the latest news about supermax prisons, visit **www.supermaxed.com**.

INTRO IS KEEPING BILL HEIRENS BEHIND BARS WORTH $73,000?

Bill Heirens was 17 years old when he was sentenced to Stateville prison for three life terms, with release opportunity once rehabilitated. He confessed to stabbing two women to death during two different house burglaries. He was also linked to kidnapping, strangling, and dismembering six-year-old Suzanne Degnan in a heavily publicized media case—all back in 1946. Although he confessed, the police investigation process and evidence remains questionable as to whether Heirens actually killed Suzanne Degnan. While incarcerated, he completed 250 college credits and was the first Illinois prisoner to earn a bachelor of arts degree. He became a role model for others to complete their GED, yet, he is continuously denied parole and clemency petitions.

Now at age 82, Heirens lives in the geriatric ward of Dixon Correctional Center. Journalist Jessica Pupovac received special permission to visit Dixon and interview Heirens, who is now Illinois' longest serving prisoner. Pupovac (2011) described Heirens' condition as

> ... [he] can't get out of bed or bathe himself, and his cataract-plagued eyes have left him unable to read. He has severe diabetes and gets shots of insulin twice a day, along with a cocktail of other medications. Nurses constantly change bandages on his legs, where diabetic sores weep fluids. They say he is beginning to show signs of dementia. Last year, he collapsed while inching his way down the hall, grasping the handrail, and was sent by ambulance to UIC medical center, where he stayed for four days. Though he is clearly too frail to injure

DISCUSS Do you think Heirens should be paroled to a nursing home? Why or why not?

anyone, the state will pay $73,000 this year to keep Heirens behind bars, feed him, and treat his ever-expanding list of ailments.

A sister of one of Heiren's victims believes the cost, even now, is worth it to protect the public and as an example to others. A large part of the cost is that each time a prisoner needs to see a specialist, the prisoner must be transported to an outside hospital. Prison policy requires that a correctional officer accompany the prisoner and remain at his or her bedside the entire time. In comparison, if Heirens were in an elderly nursing home on the streets, the estimated cost is $57,000.

William Heirens is seen standing outside the Dixon Correctional Facility in Illinois. Heirens now uses a wheel chair to get around, having served nearly 65 years in prison after killing three people in 1946.
Credit: AP Photo/Peter Thompson
Source: AP WideWorld Photos

▶ Treatment Programs in Prison

We discussed earlier in several previous chapters that evidence-based correctional practices require an initial risk/needs assessment at intake. All offenders are rescored at least once per year, or earlier if a major situation occurs such as a disciplinary infraction, change in physical or mental health, or need to transfer to a different unit for treatment. Reassessments allow for the opportunity to address any new treatment needs that surface.

In-prison treatment programs based on cognitive behavioral interventions can reduce future recidivism between 20 and 30 percent (Landenberger & Lipsey 2005). These

interventions assume that thought patterns and feelings determine behavior and that identifying and changing thinking errors will ultimately change behavior. The key in the treatment process is for the offender to admit how **thinking errors** resulted in failure to accept responsibility, dysfunctional habits, addictions, and criminal behaviors.

Psychologists who work with offenders describe them as emotionally and cognitively immature. Exposure to thinking errors is a starting point for change, but true change comes from the individual's genuine willingness to become a better person.

Some treatment programs address offender needs that require specialized treatment, attention, and/or medical care. These specialized treatment

LEARNING OUTCOMES 1 Summarize various treatment programs within a prison.

GLOSSARY

thinking errors Ways that people use to avoid taking responsibility for their own behavior, or ways to make themselves look good by making others look bad.

20% In-prison treatment programs based on cognitive behavioral interventions can reduce future recidivism between 20 and 30 percent

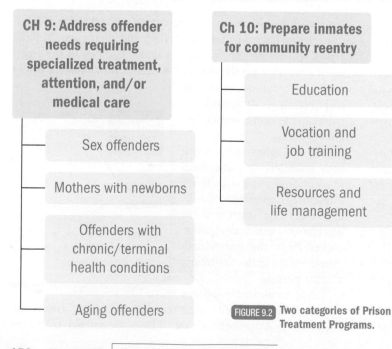

Victim Stance
- Portrays self as the victim

Minimizing Injury to Others
- Feels justified in taking what he or she wants, and does not see self as injuring others (despite leaving an evident path of destruction and injury)

Blaming
- Blaming others to avoid responsibility; putting others down to build self up

Pride
- Overly high evaluation of oneself and performance

Entitlement
- Views people as pawns or property to move around

Anger
- Uses intimidation or threats as a way of controlling others; helps avoid other unpleasant feelings such as fear, sadness, or shame

FIGURE 9.1 **Examples of Thinking Errors.**
Source: Samenow, S. E. (1984). *Inside the criminal mind.* New York: Times Books.

programs can include offenders with mental illness, which was fully covered in Chapter 6, so it will not be covered here. Other treatment programs prepare inmates for reentry; that is the subject of the next chapter. In this chapter, we address sex offenders, pregnant and parenting inmates, offenders with HIV/AIDS, and aging and terminally ill prisoners.

CH 9: Address offender needs requiring specialized treatment, attention, and/or medical care
- Sex offenders
- Mothers with newborns
- Offenders with chronic/terminal health conditions
- Aging offenders

Ch 10: Prepare inmates for community reentry
- Education
- Vocation and job training
- Resources and life management

FIGURE 9.2 **Two categories of Prison Treatment Programs.**

▶ *Treatment that Addresses Sex Offending*

One of the principles of evidence-based practices (EBP) is that treatment interventions should target higher risk offenders and behaviors most closely associated with criminal activity. Sex offenders meet both of these criteria. Furthermore, mandatory polygraph testing as part of the treatment makes this type of treatment unique from all other types. In this section, the antisocial attitudes, thinking errors, and treatment of different types of sex offenders are discussed.

Sex offenses are inappropriate sexual acts against children or sexual acts against a victim's will. The three main types of sexual offenders are child molesters, incest offenders, and rapists (Harris 2004). Victims of sex offenses can be children or adults—in both cases, victims more often already know their perpetrator than a stranger whom they've never previously met. Roughly one-third of all sex offenses are reported to the police, based on comparing arrests and convictions with self-reported information gathered from polygraphs of known sex offenders. Sex offenses are more often reported when the perpetrator is a stranger than when the perpetrator and the victim know each other.

Sex offenders are a very heterogeneous group, each having different motivations, thinking patterns, targeted victims, and personality styles. Treatment approaches must reflect these differences. Sex offender treatment programs use multiple regimens that include cognitive-behavioral therapy to address thinking errors and minimization, victim empathy, polygraph to avoid denial and aid in divulging previous sex offenses, and **aversive conditioning**. Medications such as **antiandrogens** or **selective serotonin reuptake inhibitors** may be used along with therapy (Harris 2004).

Child molesters require resolution for their own victimization, as well as intense behavioral modification to change their focus from children to adults. Rapists need help with managing their anger, chemical dependency, and choosing nonviolent responses. Finally, how staff relate to sex offenders is extremely important to achieving lasting behavioral

LEARNING OUTCOMES 2 — Summarize the issues regarding sex offenders.

GLOSSARY

sex offenses Inappropriate sexual contact with family members/acquaintances, child molestation, sexual assault or rape of adults.

aversive conditioning The use of negative stimuli (painful thoughts, putrid smells, etc.) to reduce or eliminate sexual arousal.

antiandrogens Hormones that lower the male sex drive by decreasing testosterone levels. Examples include cyproterone acetate or medroxyprogesterone acetate.

selective serotonin reuptake inhibitors Medications that increase serotonin levels in the brain to decrease libido and cause erectile dysfunction.

Principles of Becoming Socially Competent

I will recognize my own patterns of thinking, feeling, and perceiving.

I will differentiate my healthy thoughts, feelings, and perceptions from my dysfunctional ones.

Through repetitive modeling, role playing, and rehearsal, I will learn how to change the dysfunctional thought processes by stopping them when they occur.

I will stop and consider the consequences before acting.

I resolve to consider various alternatives of responding and how my behavior may impact someone else.

Source: Reprinted from "Probation and Cognitive Skills" by F. R. Chavaria (1997) Federal Probation, 61 (2), 57–60. Washington, DC: Judiciary Branch of the United States Government.

change. Understanding criminal thinking errors, requiring polygraphs, drug testing, and disapproving of the behavior—not the person—is important to reducing recidivism for this group of offenders. Perhaps Robert Johnson (2002, 12) summarized it best when he said "Yet whatever criminals do—and criminals do some terrible things—they remain human beings,

Victims of sex offenses more often already know their perpetrator than a stranger whom they've never previously met.

Child Molesters	Incest Offenders	Rapists
Low self-esteem, socially awkward as children, not married	Socially competent and most resembles other law-abiding citizens	Have experienced violence and/or sexual abuse in the past
Were likely sexually victimized as a child and did not resolve or cope	Married/cohabitating and has children or step-children	Share similar characteristics to other non-sexual violent offenders
Earlier age of onset (molesting starts as an adolescent)	60% are adults and 40% are adolescents when offending first occurs	Later age of onset
Highest use of deviant or child pornography	Most secretive and most difficult to identify; victim least likely to report	Most likely (compared to incest and CM) to abuse substances

FIGURE 9.3 **"They're Not All the Same": Typical Profiles of Three Types of Sex Offenders.**
Source: (Harris 2004)

Think About It...

Polygraphs for Treatment? Most sex offender treatment programs require participants to undergo polygraphs to acknowledge all prior sex offenses and do not guarantee immunity against prosecution for such confessions. Prisoners who refuse to cooperate are removed from the program and reclassified to a maximum-security unit with reduced privileges. A Kansas prisoner challenged the polygraphs, saying that they violated his Fifth Amendment privilege against self-incrimination. The U.S. Supreme Court ruled in favor of the prison system's confessionary requirement, citing that accepting responsibility is the first step in the rehabilitation process and that the program was developed for treatment, not for law-enforcement or investigatory purposes (*Warden* v. *Lile* 2002). Based on the court's ruling, could polygraphs be used with other types of offenders, such as with domestic violence offenders who attend battering treatment, or in substance abuse treatment programs?

Source: pefostudio5/Shutterstock

Prisons, then, pose difficult tests of our values because the conditions of our prisons are a measure of our capacity to recognize and respect the humanity of offenders, people we fear and hate.

however miserable or flawed. ... Prisons, then, pose difficult tests of our values because the conditions of our prisons are a measure of our capacity to recognize and respect the humanity of offenders, people we fear and hate."

▶ Pregnant and Parenting Women

All people who are incarcerated—particularly parents with young children miss important milestones in their children's lives or in the lives of other family members—births, baby's first steps, first days of school, birthdays, proms, graduations, weddings, and even funerals. Incarceration is particularly difficult for single-parent caretakers who become dismayed and overcome by feelings of failure and guilt at not being there for their children.

Prisoners are encouraged to remain in contact with family or friends by writing letters/sending cards, or calling collect on the phone, but prisoners on disciplinary status may not make phone calls or receive personal visits. There was a difference by gender of the rate that prisoners made effort to contact family on

TABLE 9.1 | Percent of State Prisoners Who Had Contact with Their Children

	Fathers	Mothers
Telephone		
At least once a week	25.4	38.3
At least once a month	16.6	15.3
Less than once a month	15.5	13.8
Never	42.5	32.6
Mail		
At least once a week	26.6	45.2
At least once a month	23.3	20.6
Less than once a month	18.6	13.2
Never	31.6	21.0
Personal Visits		
At least once a week	7.2	9.1
At least once a month	13.8	14.7
Less than once a month	22.2	22.1
Never	56.8	54.1

Source: (Mumola 2000)

Describe the alternatives that pregnant mothers have once they give birth to their babies while incarcerated.

the outside. Mothers were generally more likely to write more letters and use the telephone than fathers. Having contact with outside family members can be a double-edged sword. While it gives some prisoners something to hold on to, others find it more bearable to do time if they cut off all family ties while incarcerated (Crawley & Sparks 2006). Perhaps the most revealing was the large number of prisoners who never received a personal visit from their children (and may have wanted it that way). For prisoners who look forward to visits, visits are stressful on family because of the long distance, the cost, the lack of transportation, and the painful reminder of seeing their family locked up. For example, for one person to take a bus round-trip to a prison located over 250 miles away, and to be there for the predefined visiting hours, the visitor needs to leave around 5:00 AM, with $150–$200 for transportation, food, and any gifts. Visits are stressful on inmates, from the anticipation leading up to the visit, to the depression that immediately follows (Christian 2005). Some prisons are now experimenting with "virtual visits" (similar to Skype) that allow children to see their parents on a computer screen from home while communicating with them on the telephone.

Being Pregnant while Incarcerated

A related problem with lack of contact with parents and their outside family is the infants born to incarcerated mothers. Between 6 and 10 percent of women enter prison pregnant, but

6% Between 6 and 10 percent of women enter prison pregnant, but this is a conservative estimate since only half of all state prisons screen for pregnancy at intake

this is a conservative estimate since only half of all state prisons screen for pregnancy at intake. Pregnant inmates are definitely in need of special care, so they are transferred to a facility that is located near a hospital, where they can receive prenatal diets. Once she is in labor, she is transported to a regular hospital off facility grounds to have her baby. A correctional officer remains with her the entire time, and in some states, she may be chained to the bed, even during labor. Shackling prison inmates during labor is a safety hazard to the women and their fetuses, and the American Civil Liberties Union (ACLU) is attempting to encourage states to pass policies that ban this practice (National Women's Law Center 2010). The new mother may only get from a few minutes to a few hours to hold her baby, depending on its health when it arrives. The mother is transported back to the jail or prison the same day after giving birth to minimize the security costs.

Once the baby is ready to leave the hospital, prisons expect a temporary guardian or relative to pick up the newborn within 24 hours. If family members are unavailable or unwilling to accept the temporary custody and care of an infant born in jail or prison, the infant becomes a ward of the state (Sharp 2003). Many incarcerated women fear losing parental rights

When Mom goes to prison, who takes care of the children?

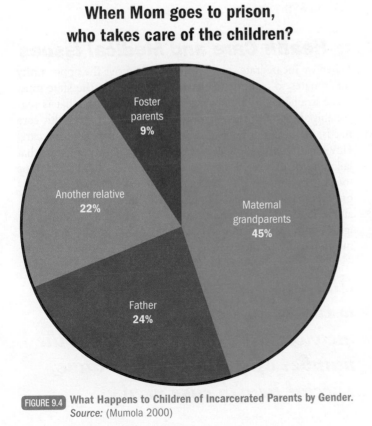

Foster parents 9%

Another relative 22%

Father 24%

Maternal grandparents 45%

When Dad goes to prison, who takes care of the children?

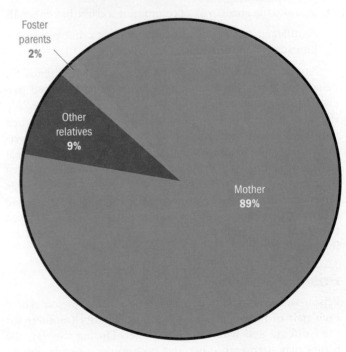

Foster parents 2%

Other relatives 9%

Mother 89%

FIGURE 9.4 **What Happens to Children of Incarcerated Parents by Gender.** *Source:* (Mumola 2000)

The United States is one of the few developed countries that routinely separates children from their mothers upon incarceration.

and therefore encourage family members to take care of their children. Unfortunately, the fear of parental termination may result in a family placement that is unsafe and abusive for children (Sharp 2003). Foster parents can be a short-term option, but in some states, there is a limit on the length of time a child can be in foster care before permanently terminating the rights of the biological parents.

The United States is one of the few developed countries that routinely separates children from their mothers upon incarceration based on two assumptions:

1. That incarceration is supposed to punish offenders by limiting freedoms and taking away what is cherished, and that includes family.

2. A convicted mother or father must be a bad parent.

Research shows that a young infant who is unable to bond with his or her mother or father during the first two years of life suffers lifelong attachment difficulties—a situation that routinely occurs when the infant and mother are permanently separated within a few hours of birth. Compared with children who do not have an incarcerated parent, children between 5 and 17 who have at least one parent behind bars experience the following:

- Higher levels of anxiety and depression

- Poorer academic performance

- Significantly greater risk of committing a crime before age 18

- Significantly greater chance of continuing crime patterns into adulthood (Carlson & Cervera 1992)

Another reason for separating parents and children is the belief that a convicted mother or father must be a bad parent. While this may be true in cases of child abuse or neglect, the vast majority of children are better off being with their biological parents if possible. Some extended family members may not be able to afford adequate care. There is also the fear that some children will experience physical or sexual abuse that their mother (or father) experienced when they were younger. One out of ten children who were raised by grandparents had a history of violence (Sharp 2003). But are young children better off living with their mothers when their mothers are incarcerated?

Prison Nurseries

Prison nurseries are separate facilities inside prison where each pair of infants and mothers must qualify (mothers for their offense and babies for their age). During the day, the babies play with each other and each mom is responsible to

Thirty-five percent of imprisoned women had a family member incarcerated at the same time.

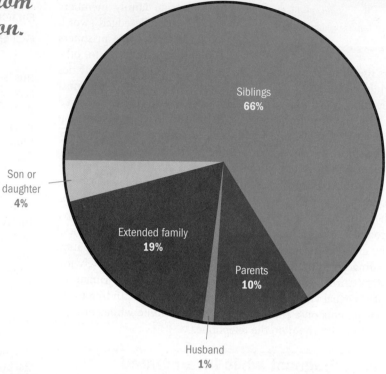

FIGURE 9.5 Incarceration is Intergenerational and Interfamilial.
Source: (Moses 1995)

watch her child. At night, the infant sleeps in a crib in the mother's cell. A case study of a prison nursery is described at the end of the chapter.

▶ Health Care and Medical Issues

When we incarcerate someone, we also remove the opportunity for inmates to care for themselves. As a result, the state must make available to inmates a level of medical care that is reasonably designed to meet routine and emergency health care needs, including physical ills, dental care, and psychiatric care. However, the prevailing principle of less eligibility suggests that jail and prison conditions must be more severe than conditions for law-abiding people. Regarding medical care, jails and prisons are not only obligated to provide medical care for incarcerated offenders, but staff can also be held legally accountable for ignoring medical conditions based on a standard of "deliberate indifference" (*Estelle* v. *Gamble* 1976). Inmates do not have the

The number one issue that is linked to rising costs of incarceration is the growth in the number of prisoners who have special health care needs.

TABLE 9.2 | Benefits and Concerns about Prison Nurseries

Benefits of Prison Nurseries	Concerns about Prison Nurseries
Biological parent retains custody	Potential liability concerns within the facility
Child establishes a bond with his or her mother	Extra money is unavailable to take care of dependent children
Mother learns parental responsibility, positive reinforcement, and how to respond to negative behavior appropriately (consistent and assertive, but not aggressive)	The welfare of a child is the main responsibility of child protective services—it is an additional responsibility that is beyond the scope of prisons
Allows inmates to serve as positive role models for their children and each other	Questionable whether children in prison nurseries benefit significantly more than children who live with extended family or in foster care while parents are incarcerated
Reduces recidivism chances of mother and child	No scientific evidence that prison nurseries lower recidivism compared to women with dependent children who do not get to take advantage of the prison nursery

right to better medical care than free-world citizens, and the courts restrict the recourse that inmates have for inadequate medical care (Vaughn & Carroll 1998).

When offenders enter correctional facilities, most need immediate testing and medical attention because they have neglected their health while living on the streets and they have engaged in lifestyles that may put them at risk, such as intravenous drug use and unprotected sex (Rhodes, Johnston, McMullen, & Hozik 2000). The number one issue that is linked to rising costs of incarceration is the growth in the number of prisoners who have special health care needs. Jails and prisons provide all the basic health care services that an average clinic does, including examinations, diagnostic testing, and treatment. As prisoners serve longer sentences, they may contract communicable diseases, terminal illnesses, and an increasing number of them have aged and now require special care. More specific treatments and procedures requiring surgery may necessitate a supervised trip to a hospital outside the walls.

Nearly 40 state prisons and 39 percent of jails deduct between $2.00 and $8.00 for each infirmary visit as a co-payment to curb rising health care costs (American

LEARNING OUTCOMES 4 — Summarize the issues regarding offenders with infectious diseases.

Correctional Association 2004; Kerle 2004). If an inmate requests a visit and has no money, he or she cannot be denied medical treatment.

Prisoners with HIV/AIDS

Individuals who engage in criminal activity are also more likely to engage in behaviors that place them at risk for HIV and other communicable diseases, such as intravenous drug use. Thus, it is no surprise that there is a disproportionate number of HIV positive persons in correctional facilities—1.5 percent of male and 1.9 percent of female state prisoners—compared with 0.17 percent of U.S. residents outside of prison who are living with HIV or AIDS (Center for Disease Control 2003; Maruschak 2009). The number has steadily declined since the mid-1990s due primarily to prevention efforts and improvements in care

1.5% there is a disproportionate number of HIV positive persons in correctional facilities— 1.5 percent of male and 1.9 percent of female state prisoners—compared with 0.17 percent of U.S. residents outside of prison who are living with HIV or AIDS

TABLE 9.3 | Arguments For and Against Charging Inmates Medical Co-Payments

For	Against
Inmates should share responsibility for their own health	The inmate's family is the one who pays because they deposit money
Reduces frivolous requests to pass the time	Inmates may forgo preventive medical care because they don't want to pay
Reduces money spent on high-calorie junk food	Collecting and tracking these fees adds administrative cost

Source: (Nolan 2003; Sanborn 2003)

TABLE 9.4   Number and Percent of HIV-Positive Prisoners, 1995–2008

Year	Estimated Number of HIV-Positive Inmates	Percent HIV/AIDS in Prisoner Population
Male Inmates		
1995	21,144	2.3%
2000	21,894	2.1
2003	20,060	1.8
2008	20,075	1.5
Female Inmates		
1995	2,230	4.0%
2000	2,472	3.4
2003	2,131	2.7
2008	1,912	1.9

Sources: (Maruschak and Beavers 2009; Maruschak 2005 and 2004)

for HIV/AIDS with the protease inhibitors and antiretroviral therapies. Still, 1 out of every 12 deaths in state prisons is due to complications from an AIDS-related illness.

HIV-infected inmates live among the general population so they have equal opportunities and will not be treated differently or discriminated against. Only Alabama and South Carolina continue to keep known HIV-positive prisoners separate from the general prisoner population. This is despite objections by the ACLU and possible legal consequences by the Justice Department if the states do not desegregate (American Civil Liberties Union 2010). Once HIV-infected inmates contract AIDS (about one out of four HIV positive prisoners), they are segregated from the general prison population for their own safety—only when separate housing is required to be away from airborne diseases prevalent among the general population.

Lessening the spread of HIV/AIDS may be effective with a number of policies, including education, testing, notifying partners, and issuing protection supplies.

- Many facilities provide education programs on how HIV is transmitted and how it progresses to AIDS.

- Testing inmates for HIV occurred at admission in 23 states, at release in 6 states, and more frequently upon request in all states. Additional testing is conducted on inmate request, by a court order, by clinical judgment, or for anyone who is involved in an incident that might have increased his or her exposure risk (Maruschak 2009).

- Correctional officers are issued disposable gloves for pat searches and cell searches; some have one-way face shields for first aid on someone with breathing difficulties (Alarid 2009).

- Inmates are issued bleach for cleaning living areas.

Treatment of Other Communicable Diseases

Besides HIV/AIDS, inmates are tested for other communicable diseases at intake and treated if necessary, including tuberculosis (TB), hepatitis B, hepatitis C, syphilis, and gonorrhea. Like with HIV/AIDS, many of these communicable diseases exist at greater rates in correctional facilities due to their link with intravenous drug use and unprotected sex. One reason that TB is five times higher inside jail is that it spreads in places of confinement where crowded conditions and poor ventilation provide ideal conditions, and inmates move around the facility as well as transfer to other facilities. Thus, inmates with active TB must be quarantined in an airtight isolated room until the

(Think About It...

Should Condoms Be Issued to Inmates? Sexual activity is prohibited within institutions, so providing condoms places prison officials in a predicament of approving conduct that violates prison rules. Advocates of condom distribution argue that sexual behavior is a fact of life, and prisons have an obligation to protect lives. Critics argue that condoms can also be used to pass contraband (swallowing balloons of drugs) or to fill with bodily fluids or excrement to throw at others. Should condoms be provided to all inmates, only to certain inmates at highest risk of HIV, or not at all? Defend your position.

Source: Alexandr Shevchenko/ Shutterstock

TABLE 9.5 | **How Much Does It Cost?**

Estimated Annual Costs per Person for Inmates with Three Different Health Situations

Cost	General Population (Average Health)	Inmates with HIV	Inmates with AIDS
Housing/Security	$24,000	$38,500	$38,500
Clinic Visits	$1,750	$1,752	$1,752
Case Management	$500	$1,200	$1,200
HIV/TB Prev Education	-----	$440	$440
Medications	$500	$22,800	$46,440
Lab Tests	$200	$420	$420
Hazardous Waste Disposal	-----	$1,200	$1,200
Special Diets	-----	$2,160	$2,500
Hospital Stays	-----	$1,400	$3,750
Security for Hospital	-----	$4,750	$5,250
Outpatient Tests	$200	$2,800	$3,850
TOTAL COST:	$27,150	$80,400	$106,000

Sources: (Bozzette et al. 2001; Ekwueme et al. 2003; Gebo et al. 2010; Zaller, Thurmond, & Rich, 2007)

TB is no longer contagious. While correctional facilities play an important role in the reduction of TB, recovering fully from TB takes from six to nine months, which is longer than most jail sentences—inmates with active TB are released from confinement before they complete the cycle. While releasees are provided with enough medication to finish the cycle, they are no longer being supervised. For some people, the partially treated TB is still contagious and over time, can become resistant to antibiotics (Parvez, Lobato, & Greifinger 2010).

Hepatitis C is a virus that affects the liver and is spread primarily through injected drug use, unsafe sexual practices, and unsterile tattooing (Hellard, Aitken, & Hocking 2007). A disproportionately higher number of the 5 million people with hepatitis C are arrested and incarcerated, making the rate of Hepatitis C in confinement between 8 and 20 times higher than what exists in the general population. Between 23 percent and up to one-third of all prisoners tested positive for hepatitis C (Beck & Maruschak 2004; Macalino et al. 2004). Most states tested only targeted inmates for hepatitis B and C based on high-risk behaviors, inmate request, or on a doctor's request. While there is a vaccine for hepatitis B, there is no vaccine to protect against hepatitis C. However, chronic hepatitis C can be treated with antiviral medications at a cost of $7,000 to $20,000 per person for one cycle, with a success rate of 30 to 40 percent (Allen et al. 2003; Beck & Maruschak 2004).

▶ Aging Prisoners

Graying of U.S. prisons began in the mid-1980s as longer prison sentences for recidivists and reductions in the use of parole began expanding the number of inmates that remained. The National Institute of Corrections and most state prisons define an **elderly prisoner** as being age 50 and over. Although this is considered "middle age" outside the prison walls, the stress of the prison experience, coupled with prisoners who led a fast life of drug use, poor health, and lack of preventive care prior to incarceration seems to age a person faster than their chronological age. Prisoners over the age of 50 are the fastest growing segment within the general prisoner population (Reimer 2008). Older inmates now make-up about 13 percent of the prisoner population, which is more than double that of the previous decade. Unless changes are made, current protocol will continue to increase the number of elderly in prison in the coming decade.

According to Reimer (2008), various categories of aging prisoners include the following:

1. First-time felons over age 50 with no prior prison experience
2. Lifers who grew old due to serving a long sentence
3. Recidivists who cycle in and out as adults

LEARNING OUTCOMES 5 Outline the issues of aging and terminally ill prisoners in terms of their medical care, housing, and release options.

GLOSSARY

elderly prisoner A prisoner who is age 50 and over.

geriatric prisons Separate facilities specifically designed for elderly inmates where they have no contact with the younger general population.

compassionate release Available on a case-by-case basis for inmates who are permanently incapacitated, have less than one year to live, and for those who no longer pose an imminent danger to the community. Also known as medical parole.

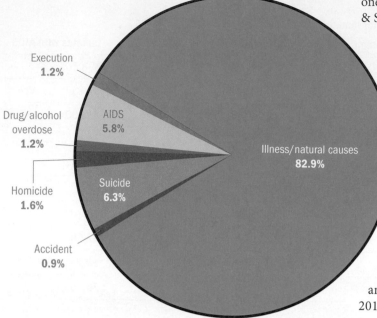

FIGURE 9.6 **Causes of Prisoner Death (%), 2001–2007.**
Source: Adapted from Bureau of Justice Statistics. (2010). Percent of state prisoner deaths, by cause of death, 2001–2007. Retrieved from http://bjs.ojp.usdoj.gov/content/dcrp/tables/dcst07spt2.pdf.

Graying of U.S. prisons began in the mid-1980s as longer prison sentences for recidivists and reductions in the use of parole began expanding the number of inmates that remained.

Eighty male prisoners between the ages of 65 and 84 were interviewed about coping with their prison experience (Crawley & Sparks 2006). Most were either first-timers or were at the other end of the spectrum as lifers. The older first-time felons reported being anxious and depressed by how prison disrupted their former lives, particularly the ones who had family and spouses on the outside. Lifers, or men who had spent many years in prison, had not been on the streets in so long that they lost touch with the outside world and doubted their own decision-making capabilities. At this stage of life, many prisoners reported thinking about getting medical help in the middle of the night if needed and dying in prison. The prisoners who were most enthusiastic about release were the

13% Older inmates now make-up about 13 percent of the prisoner population, which is more than double that of the previous decade

ones who had family waiting for them on the outside (Crawley & Sparks 2006).

Studies have consistently shown that the vast majority of people age out of crime, which means that if and when they are released, the likelihood of continuing criminal behavior decreases as people get older. This is supported through data provided by the Illinois Department of Corrections. Older inmates are less likely to commit new offenses within three years after being released—3.6 percent recidivism for those 70–79 years old compared to 30 percent for prisoners under age 50 (Pupovac 2011).

The number one concern of managing older prisoners is not violence or recidivism, but maintaining health. The special health needs of older prisoners cost about three times more than a younger inmate of average health. For example, the Illinois Department of Corrections spends about a third of its annual budget ($428 million) on aging prisoners (Pupovac 2011). The situation in Illinois represents the situation all over the United States.

A decline in visual abilities and a loss of hearing may make the older offender more vulnerable to harm by the very structure of the prison, and it can cause depression, post-traumatic stress disorder, and result in social isolation. Studies report that many older male prisoners exhibit signs of trauma, stress, and mental illness, and thus feel unsafe and vulnerable to attack by younger inmates (Haugebrook, Zgoba, Maschi, Morgen, & Brown 2010). The physical condition and structure of many prisons are also cause for concern about physical safety. Prisons were, after all, designed for young, active inmates and had stairs in tiered cell blocks and long distances to walk from one place to the next.

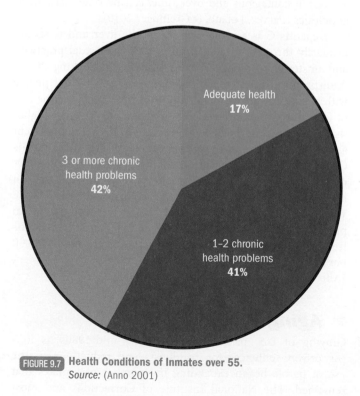

FIGURE 9.7 **Health Conditions of Inmates over 55.**
Source: (Anno 2001)

TABLE 9.6 — Should Terminally Ill Prisoners Be Released on Parole?

Arguments in Favor	Arguments Against
Cost savings realized with the same levels of care still offered in a community-based hospice	Prisons are alleviating responsibility to care for the prisoner's full medical needs
Opens space for an able-bodied person who poses a threat to public safety	If the prisoner wasn't terminally ill, he or she would still be in prison; releasing for an illness is the wrong reason
The inmate is still on parole supervision	May go against victim's wishes
Chance of committing a new crime is extremely low	There is still a chance that a prisoner could feel well enough to commit a crime again
The prisoner's family could more easily visit and prepare for death	Prisoner may live longer than predicted

3x The special health needs of older prisoners cost about three times more than a younger inmate of average health.

Geriatric prisons are separate facilities specifically designed for aging inmates with three or more chronic conditions, physical limitations, and/or inmates of any age who are terminally ill. In about half of all states, chronically ill prisoners are housed with or near elderly prisoners because both groups have similar medical and dietary needs. These facilities are more like infirmaries, hospice care, or chronic care facilities that offer safety from predatory inmates. Geriatric prisons offer unique programming or services geared specifically toward this population of prisoners, who will not likely be employed (or employable) once they return to society. Thus, involvement in GED or occupational training is not offered. Instead, inmates in these facilities tend to care for each other instead of placing each other in jeopardy. Oxygen generators and wheelchairs are kept on hand, and medication time becomes as important as count time. Aging trustys complete the facility operation work, such as changing sheets, bedpans, laundry, cooking, and cleaning.

In light of high medical costs, the issue of early release of terminally ill prisoners from prison has received new attention. Many states have **compassionate release** or medical parole available on a case-by-case basis for inmates who are permanently incapacitated, have less than one year to live, and for those who no longer pose an imminent danger to the community (American Correctional Association 2003). Release must be made in most cases by the governor or a parole board, after a team of physicians makes a recommendation on the prisoner's medical condition. Currently, about 100 prisoners are released every year in this way (Reimer 2008).

Prison Hospice

Hospices based inside prison are available for terminally ill prisoners whose sentences do not qualify them for medical parole or their application was denied. Prison hospices began in the late 1980s and the National Prison Hospice Association formed in 1991 to address the large increase of AIDS-related deaths (Wright & Bronstein 2007). Prison hospices operate similar to community-based hospice services in that the inmates are provided with medication to manage pain; they are cared for by a team of nurses, social workers, dieticians, pharmacists, and clergy; and the environment resembles a secure hospital rather than a prison atmosphere. Some of the more unique volunteers are other able-bodied prisoners who are there to emotionally console dying prisoners when they have no family left or family members are unable or unwilling to visit. The correctional officers have respect for the care and companionship that they see as necessary to allow every person, no matter how they behaved on the streets, to die with dignity (Reimer 2008; Wright & Bronstein 2007).

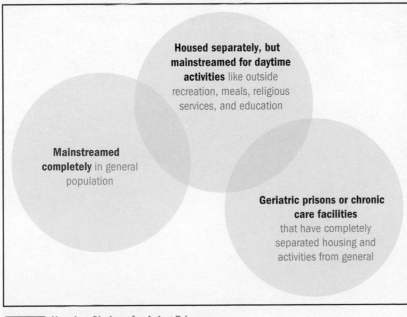

Housed separately, but mainstreamed for daytime activities like outside recreation, meals, religious services, and education

Mainstreamed completely in general population

Geriatric prisons or chronic care facilities that have completely separated housing and activities from general

FIGURE 9.8 Housing Choices for Aging Prisoners.

Should Infants and Toddlers of Incarcerated Moms Be Raised in Prison?

New York's Bedford Hills opened the first prison nursery over 100 years ago and remains the oldest operating prison nursery in the United States. Up to 29 mothers are selected if they have been convicted of a nonviolent offense and have no history of child abuse or neglect. Mothers can live and raise their child for up to 18 months, or until the child reaches two years old—whichever occurs first. In an effort to emulate conditions in the real world, mothers return to work at the prison (or outside, if they are eligible for work release) six weeks after their babies are born (National Women's Law Center 2010). Other inmates at the prison, who are specially trained and participate in parenting classes, may serve as caregivers. The program is thus inmate-centered, in that women prisoners teach each other about parenting. When they are not at work, mothers assume full responsibility for their children (Kauffman 2006). The parenting experience of most women is quite different than what they've ever experienced on the streets, because it is the first time they've been a parent while clean and sober.

From the early 1900s to the 1950s most women's prisons had nurseries for the needs of babies born inside the facility. Except for Bedford Hills, all other nurseries closed their doors by the 1970s due to litigation worries and concern for the effect it had on children. The mother/child bond during the first two years of an infant's life was important enough to convince several states to reinstitute prison nurseries programs once again (Byrne 2006). New York expanded its nursery program across the street at Taconic Correctional Facility. While 13 state department of corrections claim to allow mothers access to a prison nursery, three allow stays up to one month, and six states allow infants and moms to live together in prison for up to eighteen months (National Women's Law Center 2010). Most prison nurseries limit the age of children to two or younger.

Nurseries in women's prison raise two interesting issues:

1. What are the potential benefits for infants up to age two being raised by their mothers? What are the potential problems?

2. What are the potential benefits to mothers to raise a child while doing time? What are the potential problems?

Source: © Mikael Karlsson/Alamy

Summarize various treatment programs within a prison.

Some treatment programs address offender needs that require specialized treatment, such as for sex offenders. Others pay attention to health and medical care of pregnant inmates, infants born to incarcerated mothers, prisoners with HIV or other communicable diseases, and elderly inmates.

Other treatment programs prepare inmates for community reentry by teaching new skill sets.

1. What other types of special needs inmates are there?

2. What other types of thinking errors are typical with criminal offenders?

thinking errors Ways that people use to avoid taking responsibility for their own behavior, or ways to make themselves look good by making others look bad.

Summarize the issues regarding sex offenders.

Sex offenders are a heterogeneous group with different motivations, thinking patterns, targeted victims, and personality styles. The three main types are rapists, child molesters, and incest offenders.

Sex offender treatment programs use multiple regimens that include cognitive-behavioral therapy to address thinking errors and minimization, victim empathy, polygraphs, and aversive conditioning. For child molesters and incest offenders, medication to decrease libido is imperative. Long-term treatment and medication regimens of sex offenders can significantly reduce rearrest rates after release.

1. What kind of staff qualifications (educational background, practical experience, type of person, personal characteristics, etc.) might be most effective for in-prison sex offender treatment?

2. Research the term "chemical castration." What is your view on "chemical castration" as a treatment regimen for sex offenders?

3. Should rapists and child molesters/incest offenders be housed together within the prison? Why or why not?

sex offenses Inappropriate sexual contact with family members/acquaintances, child molestation, sexual assault or rape of adults.

aversive conditioning The use of negative stimuli (painful thoughts, putrid smells, etc.) to reduce or eliminate sexual arousal.

antiandrogens Hormones that lower the male sex drive by decreasing testosterone levels. Examples include cyproterone acetate or medroxyprogesterone acetate.

selective serotonin reuptake inhibitors Medications that increase serotonin levels in the brain to decrease libido and cause erectile dysfunction.

Describe the alternatives that pregnant mothers have once they give birth to their babies while incarcerated.

Most incarcerated parents will resume custody of their children when released, so contact with outside family members is encouraged.

Pregnant women who have their babies while incarcerated must find outside family members who are available and willing to accept temporary custody, or else the children go to foster care or become wards of the state.

A small number of states provide prison nurseries where qualified mothers can care for their newborns while incarcerated.

1. Given what you know about why family members do not visit, what ideas do you have for how prisons can increase visitation?

2. Do you agree that a pregnant prisoner should be shackled while being transported to the hospital? Should she be shackled while in labor? If so, why? If not, how are you going to assure that she doesn't escape?

3. Discuss the pros and cons of raising children in correctional institutions. How would you expand or limit such programs?

Summarize the issues regarding offenders with infectious diseases.

The number of prisoners with HIV has steadily declined; however, it remains disproportionately higher per 100,000 people compared to outside society. While about half of all states test for HIV at admission, most will test upon request of the prisoner or a doctor. Inmates with HIV are housed in the general population until they become too weak with AIDS.

Other communicable diseases that are problematic inside correctional facilities are tuberculosis (TB), hepatitis B, hepatitis C, syphilis, and gonorrhea.

TB has become a serious problem in places of confinement where crowded conditions and poor ventilation provide ideal conditions for the spread of an infectious disease.

1. Discuss the issue of patient confidentiality of medical records versus the right of staff to know of prisoner medical conditions. Under what conditions would the right to know be acceptable?

2. How would a jail or prison control an outbreak of tuberculosis in the facility if 15 people tested positive who all had casual contact with a carrier in general population? How can prisoners be effectively quarantined to avoid infecting the whole facility?

Outline the issues of aging and terminally ill prisoners in terms of their medical care, housing, and release options.

As prisoners serve longer sentences, they also age in prison. Prisoners over the age of 50 are the fastest growing segment in the prisoner population.

Geriatric prisons are separate facilities for elderly inmates where they have no contact with the younger general population.

Terminally ill prisoners either experience prison-based hospice programs or are released through medical parole supervision.

1. What do you think about the policy of releasing terminally ill prisoners to the community?

2. What could be done to ensure that these prisoners do not pose a safety risk to the community if released?

3. Write a medical parole policy that allows or limits the following: medical condition of offender, age of offender, type of offense committed, who decides release (individual or committee composed of whom), does the victim have a vote/ opinion, what care will the offender get from the state, what care will the offender (or offender's family) have to pay for, and what are the conditions of the parole?

elderly prisoner A prisoner who is age 50 and over.

geriatric prisons Separate facilities specifically designed for elderly inmates where they have no contact with the younger general population.

compassionate release Available on a case-by-case basis for inmates who are permanently incapacitated, have less than one year to live, and for those who no longer pose an imminent danger to the community. Also known as medical parole.

Additional Links

View the four-minute video about being pregnant in jail and a prison nursery in Nebraska. **http://videos.howstuffworks.com/discovery-health/38897-im-pregnant-and-in-prison-nursery-conditions-video.htm**.

View the nine-minute video, narrated by Mary Byrne, about her research with prison nurseries: **www.youtube.com/watch?v=2GUfn1Sjic0**.

For publications on correctional health care standards, go to the National Commission on Correctional Health Care at **www.ncchc.org/pubs/index.html**.

View the 27-minute video about health care and aging in prison entitled "Life in Prison: A Project Envision documentary": **www.youtube.com/watch?v=alcK_QBE7h8**.

View the 22-minute video about release and hospice solutions for aging and terminally ill prisoners at **www.youtube.com/watch?v=Xvqj8hgxRfg&feature=relmfu**.

View the 23-minute video about the mentally ill from prison **www.youtube.com/watch?v=bPUsdxMBEOQ&feature=related**.

View the eight-minute video about California's struggle with reducing its prison population and cutting treatment services, including health care: **www.pbs.org/newshour/extra/video/blog/2009/08/broke_california_struggles_to.html**.

Reentry Programs and Institutional Release

"Correctional officials [and the public] need to have a stake in the success of prisoners returning to the community, not a vested interest in their returning to prison."

—Justice Anthony M. Kennedy, U.S. Supreme Court Justice (1936–)

1 Describe the reentry process and the challenges that prisoners face when they are released from prison.

2 Understand the role of education and vocational programs as they contribute to reducing recidivism.

3 Explain the key ways in which community programs play a role in the reentry process.

4 Summarize the history of parole, along with the various forms of unconditional versus conditional release.

10

Source: © Andrew Aitchison/Alamy

FORMER GOVERNOR IS NOW EX-CON

Former Louisiana governor Edwin Edwards was released from federal prison in 2011 after having served over eight years of a ten-year sentence for 17 counts on activities that included fraud, money laundering, extortion, and racketeering. Edwards, who turned 84 in August 2011, was a well-known political figure over a span of nearly three decades, including four terms as governor. Over the years, he was allegedly involved in gambling, bribery, corruption, and

> **DISCUSS** What type of adjustment and/ or reentry issues does former governor Edwards potentially face?

accepting illegal campaign contributions, but was acquitted of these charges in the 1980s. Federal charges resulted in a conviction in the late 1990s. As a part of Edward's mandatory supervised release conditions, he lived with his daughter under home confinement and reported to a federal halfway house three times a week for six months. During this time, Edwards was required to work and to avoid media contact as a part of his reentry into society.

In the broadest sense, about 95 percent of all prisoners incarcerated right now will eventually return to the community. Every year, 12 million people leave county jail and an additional 753,000 people are released from prison (Ingley 2004). While short-term jail releasees leave in the middle of the night with their own street clothes and no extra money, there is greater concern about the release of state and federal prisoners who have arguably served more time away. Long-term prisoners must go through a period of readjustment in transition from the rigidity of institutional life to living with choices in larger society. **Reentry** is a process of release preparation that

95% about 95 percent of all prisoners incarcerated right now will eventually return to the community

begins within the institution and continues in the community. Reentry begins by asking the question, "What is needed to effectively prepare an offender to lead a law-abiding life in the community?"

▶ Challenges in the Reentry Process

A reentry process model was developed by the National Institute of Corrections to help state correctional departments develop their own transition programs from prison to the community. A prison case manager develops a "transitional accountability plan" that serves as an assessment of what each offender needs to accomplish prior to the release date and in the community. Offenders are transferred to a "transitional housing unit" (similar to prerelease centers) when they are close to release to ensure they have met some of the plan goals and to move them toward concrete strategies for obtaining employment and housing before or upon release (Missouri Department of Corrections 2004). To be

Reentry therefore focuses on a wide variety of positive relationships and community program resources that offenders need to assist them in stabilizing their lives so that they may eventually become fully independent.

successful, state corrections departments must form partnerships with social services, mental health, economic development, health and senior services, and courts administrators. At least nine jurisdictions have implemented the model: District of Columbia, Georgia, Indiana, Michigan, Missouri, New York, North Dakota, Oregon, and Rhode Island.

Some state correctional institutions are working more closely with community agencies in the areas of identification, clothing, housing, and employment needs. Some would say that the government has an obligation to make the reentry process less shocking from the "time warp" where prisoners are living with monotonous and restricted rules to the immediate need to "catch up" on living a free life that prisoners may feel they missed while away. Others would say that more attention needs to be paid to helping new releasees, such as tax incentives to encourage businesses to hire former offenders.

Just what issues do prisoners themselves face when transitioning from prison to the community? The challenges overlap and multiply when various facets of their lives are mismanaged, neglected, or mistreated. This includes mental health, physical health, physical abuse, deficits in education, underemployment, lack of social support, and dysfunctional prior relationships. Drug use may be a response to dealing with problems.

Professionals who work with ex-offenders report that the desire to remain free is seldom enough by itself to keep someone straight (Snider 1999). Reentry therefore focuses

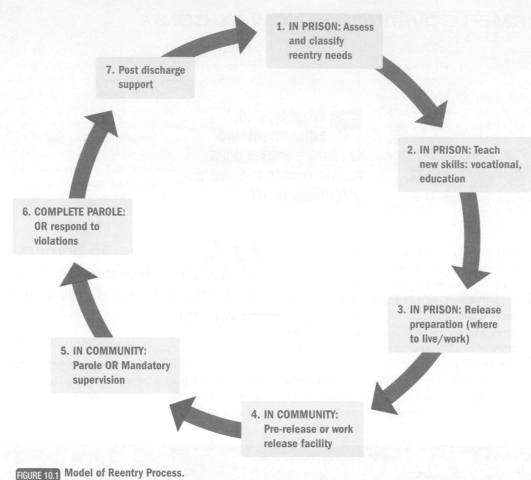

FIGURE 10.1 **Model of Reentry Process.**
Source: National Institute of Corrections Model of Transition from prison to the community. Retrieved from www.in.gov/idoc/2520.htm.

on a wide variety of positive *relationships* and *community program* resources that offenders need to assist them in stabilizing their lives so that they may eventually become fully independent. To meet this goal, the **Second Chance Act** was signed into law in April 2008 to allow for three years of federal funding for a variety of reentry initiatives that include housing assistance, employment, mentoring, and substance abuse treatment.

In February of each year, the Office of Management and Budget releases the President's Budget for the following fiscal year. The President's Budget is reviewed between March and June in both the House and the Senate Appropriations Subcommittee on Commerce, Justice, Science and Related Agencies. In June 2011, the Second Chance Reauthorization Act was introduced to the Senate for continued funding of prisoner reentry programs.

We know that if prisoners are not given transitional resources or if an appointment is not made prior to entering the community, many will not continue their medical care, mental health care, or their medication due mainly to a lack of income or a lack of available community resources. With the confidentiality of medical records, many community-based agencies are not coordinated with shared databases or medical records to directly accept former prisoners from the institution. If applicable, indigent releasees must be reenrolled for federal and/or state medical and mental health benefits following their release, since they are not eligible for federal benefits such as Medicaid, social security, or disability income while incarcerated. There may be a lengthy gap of time between release and the time when insurance benefits begin (Hammett, Roberts, & Kennedy 2001). Because of these gaps, offenders begin release preparation when they are within three to twelve

LEARNING OUTCOMES 1 Describe the reentry process and the challenges that prisoners face when they are released from prison.

GLOSSARY

reentry The process of release preparation that begins within the institution and continues with community supervision.

Second Chance Act Federal legislation that authorizes reentry grants to state and local agencies and nonprofit organizations to provide employment assistance, substance abuse treatment, housing, and mentoring to reduce recidivism for ex-offenders returning to communities from correctional facilities.

ESTABLISHING STRUCTURE AND STABILITY IN A MYRIAD OF CHOICES

- Finding affordable and stable housing
- Securing employment that pays a sufficient income
- Securing basic supplies (bus pass, identification, eyeglasses, clothes) with little or no money
- Making sound decisions on a daily basis
- Reliable public transportation

CHOOSING SUPPORTIVE RELATIONSHIPS

- Creating new connections that reinforces non-criminal attitudes and behaviors
- Regaining legal and physical custody of children
- Negotiating stigmatization from the community, suspicion from police, and the constant need to prove self as worthy and changed
- Making decisions about continuing prior intimate relationships, which may have been exploitative, or sexually or physically abusive

CONNECTING TO SOCIAL SERVICES AND COMMUNITY AGENCIES

- Sobriety and recovery from alcohol or drug addiction
- Parole obligations
- Reinstatement of Medicaid benefits and/or Supplemental Security Income
- Insight into problems and self understanding of behavior

FIGURE 10.2 Challenges Offenders Face with Reentry.
Sources: (Brown 2004; Dodge & Pogrebin 2001; O'Brien 2002; Travis & Petersilia 2001)

months of release in state facilities and within 24 months of release in federal institutions. While there is no uniform curriculum, reentry programs share a common set of elements.

Reentry programs have done some innovative things for releasees. For example, a reentry program in Delaware invited representatives from the Department of Labor to discuss how to initiate the job search and a representative from the Department of Motor Vehicles to speak about how to get back a suspended license or how to apply for identification. Delaware's program also integrates peer teaching (offenders helping one another) and invites family members to be part of the process (Finn 1998). Another example is Oregon's prison-based program called Turning Point. Life skills are combined with drug education, anger management, and relationship development; it is offered to both men and women over a period of nine to twelve months. Additional aftercare is for six months following release (Morash, Bynum, & Koons 1998).

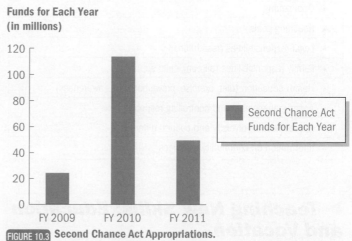

Funds for Each Year (in millions)

FIGURE 10.3 Second Chance Act Appropriations.
Sources: http://reentrypolicy.org/government_affairs/second_chance_act

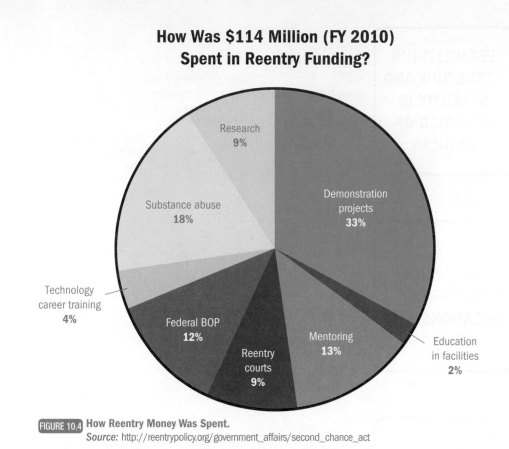

How Was $114 Million (FY 2010) Spent in Reentry Funding?

- Research 9%
- Substance abuse 18%
- Technology career training 4%
- Federal BOP 12%
- Reentry courts 9%
- Demonstration projects 33%
- Mentoring 13%
- Education in facilities 2%

FIGURE 10.4 How Reentry Money Was Spent.
Source: http://reentrypolicy.org/government_affairs/second_chance_act

Elements of Most Reentry Programs

- Job search
- Mock job interviews
- Securing identification and vocational/educational certificates
- Credit, finance, and banking (balancing a checkbook, opening a savings account)
- Motor vehicle registration
- Consumer skills
- Goal setting
- Reaching goals
- Legal responsibilities (restitution)
- Family responsibilities (alimony, child support)
- Health education (diet, exercise, prevention, AIDS awareness)
- Anger management and controlling response
- Appreciation of diversity and cultural differences
- Information on community resources

► *Teaching New Skills: Education and Vocation*

Many students reading this book have learned how to set educational goals and reach them incrementally through taking classes part time or full time. Getting a degree is not instantaneous, as it takes time, effort, and sacrifice. Most former prisoners "remain largely uneducated, unskilled, and usually without solid family support systems—and now they have the added burden of a prison record and the distrust and fear that it inevitably elicits" (Petersilia 2002, 154). Think about what it would be like to live in poverty without setting or reaching goals and yet not having the skills or motivation to improve your life the "slow" way. Instead, individuals with learning or speech disabilities (many of them undiagnosed) drop out of school. Other reasons for dropping out of school include behavioral problems, family or personal problems, socioeconomic difficulties, entered the work force early, or joined the military (Harlow 2003).

About 4 in 10 of all adult inmates in jails and prisons had not completed high school nor received the equivalent general equivalency diploma (GED). The lack of education makes it very difficult to find a well-paying job, and explains why other sources of income are needed to make ends meet.

Evidence-based correctional practices stress the importance of increasing levels of educational achievement. At intake, inmates are given a **test for adult basic education (TABE)** to determine at what level the prisoner is functioning academically. Illiterate individuals are best taught through Corrective Reading, a beginning adult

LEARNING OUTCOMES 2 Understand the role of education and vocational programs as they contribute to reducing recidivism.

GLOSSARY

test for adult basic education (TABE) Test given to inmates to determine the prisoner's level of academic ability.

TABLE 10.1 Education Levels of State Prisoners.

	Percent of State Prison Inmates	
	Male	Female
Educational Attainment		
8th grade or less	14.3%	13.6%
Some high school	25.3	28.2
GED	28.9	22.3
High school diploma	20.4	21.6
Postsecondary/some college	8.8	11.2
College graduate	2.3	3.1

Source: Harlow, C. W. (2003). *Bureau of Justice statistics special report: Education and correctional populations.* Washington, DC: U.S. Department of Justice.

Evidence-based correctional practices stress the importance of increasing levels of educational achievement.

40% 4 in 10 of all adult inmates in jails and prisons had not completed high school nor received the equivalent general equivalency diploma (GED)

reader program (Coulter & Brookens 2003). Federal offenders who are not proficient in the English language are required to achieve at least an eighth-grade proficiency level (U.S. General Accounting Office 2001). State prisoners are generally less educated at admission than federal prisoners, but only a small number of states established a mandatory literacy level, varying between the fifth and the twelfth grade (McCollum 1994).

The National Adult Literacy Survey measures literacy based on performance across a variety of tasks encountered in daily life (for example, writing letters, filling out forms, understanding information from agencies and companies, and doing basic arithmetic). A randomly selected national sample of prisoners was compared with a randomly selected national sample of adults not in prison. Haigler, Harlow, O'Connor, and Campbell (1994)

TABLE 10.2 Pre-arrest Income Sources of Prisoners by Gender.

	State Prisoners		Federal Prisoners	
	Male	Female	Male	Female
Source of Income in Month before Current Arrest[a]				
Wages or salary	68.3%	43.6%	68.4%	57.1%
Government benefits[b]	13.3	41.8	7.1	33.3
Family/friends	17.8	26.1	12.7	22.2
Child support OR alimony	0.1	6.5	0.2	6.3
Illegal sources	27.1	28.1	31.1	23.7
Other[c]	3.4	18.4	6.1	4.1

[a]May add to more than 100 percent because prisoners may have had multiple sources of income.
[b]Includes welfare, Social Security, supplemental Social Security income, and compensation payments such as unemployment insurance, workman's compensation, and veteran's compensation
[c]Includes pensions, educational assistance, investments, and other unspecified types of income
Source: Mumola, C. J. (2000). *Bureau of Justice statistics special report: Incarcerated parents and their children.* Washington, DC: U.S. Department of Justice, Office of Justice Programs.

TABLE 10.3 | Meaning of TABE Scores.

TABE Score	Definition	Solution
1–6	Considered to be illiterate	Adult Literacy
6–8	Functions between sixth and eighth grade	Adult Basic Education
8.5–11	Functions between eighth and eleventh grade	Eligible for GED classes
12	Functions at a twelfth grade education level	Eligible to take GED test

found that prisoners are more likely than nonprisoners to have difficulty integrating or synthesizing information and are also more likely to have difficulty in performing quantitative tasks and setting up problems to solve. Being behind academically seems to start early. Juveniles who got into trouble with the law had significantly more problems in all areas of math, reading, and written and oral language skills than did juveniles who had never been in trouble. Even among juvenile delinquents, recidivists were academically behind first-time offenders (Foley 2001).

GED and Secondary Education

The Federal BOP requires inmates without a diploma to earn a GED before release to earn the maximum amount of good-time credits (U.S. General Accounting Office 2001). Inmates who scored over an 8.5 on the TABE are placed in a GED program. About 25 percent of all state inmates reported taking basic education, high school–level courses,

Juveniles who got into trouble with the law had significantly more problems in all areas of math, reading, and written and oral language skills than did juveniles who had never been in trouble.

25% About 25 percent of all state inmates reported taking basic education, high school–level courses, and earning their GED while serving time

and earning their GED while serving time (Harlow 2003). Many GED programs are self-paced so that students do not become bored or frustrated, as may happen in a traditionally structured classroom.

College Programs

The 1960s G.I. bill provided tuition assistance to veterans of World War II and did not limit these benefits if the vets ever became incarcerated. In the 1960s, federal grants provided assistance for tuition to low-income individuals, including inmates. These benefits provided the impetus for college programs in prison. Although prisoners received less than 1 percent of the Pell grants offered annually by the government, the principle of this practice became so controversial with the public that these benefits were discontinued in 1994. College-level classes became virtually extinct as a result of the provision that denied all prisoners access to federal Pell grants. Enrolling in college classes has been made possible again through online courses and correspondence programs, although prisoners are responsible for paying their own tuition and fees.

One federally funded distance learning program called Correctional Learning Network provides general education

TABLE 10.4 | Educational and Vocational Programs Offered in Correctional Facilities.

Program	State Prisons	Federal Prisons	Private Prisons	Local Jails
Adult Literacy	80.4%	97.4%	61.6%	24.7%
GED/Secondary education	83.6%	98.7%	70.7%	54.8%
Special education	39.6%	59.7%	21.9%	10.8%
Vocational training	55.7%	93.5%	44.2%	6.5%

Note: Percentages will not add to 100 percent because facilities may have more than one educational program.

Sources: Bureau of Justice Statistics. (2000). *Census of state and federal adult correctional facilities*. Washington, DC: U.S. Department of Justice: Office of Justice Programs; Bureau of Justice Statistics. (1999). *Census of jails*. Washington, DC: U.S. Department of Justice: Office of Justice Programs; Harlow, C. W. (2003). *Bureau of Justice statistics special report: Education and correctional populations*. Washington, DC: U.S. Department of Justice.

classes that lead to an associate's degree. Most prisoners who attend college classes while incarcerated are a select group and unrepresentative of most prisoners in the larger population. That said, most studies comparing recidivism of prisoners who enroll in college classes to general population prisoners suffer from self-selection bias, in that college-level prisoners already have characteristics that are different from the rest.

Vocational Programs

Vocational training efforts have a long history in prisons. Beginning in the mid-1800s, inmates received vocational training in a multitude of fields such as welding, auto mechanics, or masonry, but it was primarily for the benefit of the institution. In the 1970s, the focus shifted to vocational training for reentry. At that same time, prison administrators were criticized for not providing enough variety of opportunities for women to learn vocational skills that would assist them in obtaining good jobs. Court

rulings have recognized the right to equivalent programming, but opportunities "... should be based on the interests and needs of the female inmates rather than short-sighted efforts to duplicate the programs offered at male institutions" (*Glover* v. *Johnson* 1979 [478 F.Supp. 1075, E.D. Mich.], 1087). Women inmates are offered training in the types of jobs they want, and prison administrators are merely giving women what they want (Lahm 2000).

Another view of this issue suggests that women do not seek fields that pay better because they are not educated on the choices they have beyond the stereotypical low-paying service and sales jobs. They seek out the familiar jobs they have been successful at in the past, or they seek an area similar to a fellow inmate they know. Many prison administrators, on the other hand, feel that male-dominated vocational skills are of little interest to women. This is an excuse, critics say, for not spending the money to open up more opportunities for women: "The majority of the jobs these women are being trained for are among the most underpaid and unstable jobs in society.

EVIDENCE-BASED PRACTICES—DOES IT WORK?

Education as a Buffer Against Recidivism

There are a number of in-prison programs provided to prisoners: education, vocation, and work programs. So which one is most effective? Wilson, Gallagher, and MacKenzie (2000) compared education, vocational, and work programs by examining recidivism rates of 33 different studies. They found that involvement in postsecondary education programs in prison resulted in greater reductions in recidivism after release than did involvement in-prison vocational and work programs. This same conclusion was found by Brewster and Sharp (2002) who found that completion of a GED lowered

recidivism, but completion of a vocational program actually increased the likelihood of rearrest.

So, it seems that education does work to lower recidivism and produce higher earnings (Steurer & Smith 2003). But there are so many levels of education—so what are we talking about here? While college education counteracts the negative stigma of a criminal record and produced the most positive results of all education programs (Batiuk et al. 2005), postsecondary education, in particular, received the best post-prison results for the majority compared to lesser adult basic education/literacy programs which are only classified as "promising" (Chappell 2004).

TABLE 10.5 | Vocational Program Examples by Gender.

Women	Men
Cosmetology, sewing, custodial/maintenance, food service, horticulture, clerical, data entry/processing, service dog trainer	Auto repair, business, barber, drafting, data entry/processing, building/construction, computer repair, carpentry, culinary/baking, drafting, food service, furniture/upholstery, computer graphics, horticulture, machining, painting, printing, welding, masonry, office/clerical, raising livestock, service dog trainer

"A woman leaving prison with minimal skills, earning minimum wage, will not be able to support herself or her family, and thus may turn to the government for aid or recidivate and find herself back in prison" (Lahm 2000, 45).

A woman leaving prison with minimal skills, earning minimum wage, will not be able to support herself or her family, and thus may turn to the government for aid or recidivate and find herself back in prison" (Lahm 2000, 45). Until women begin to demand more valuable job skills, women's prisons will not provide the same opportunities for women that prisons provide men.

▶ Community Corrections in Reentry

Community corrections programs were discussed in detail in Chapter 5. Many of these programs are vitally important for persons being released from prisons or jails. The community-based programs that are most often used in the reentry process include residential community corrections facilities (halfway houses and prerelease centers), outpatient substance abuse relapse prevention aftercare programs, day reporting centers, electronic monitoring/global positioning devices, and reparation boards. Instead of repeating material here (refer back to Chapter 5 for descriptions of each program if needed), we will discuss a few ways that these programs are applied to reentry.

Prerelease Facilities

First, when a prisoner is getting ready for release, he or she is typically transferred to a minimum-custody facility either within the department of corrections (still considered prison-based) or to a facility in the community (prerelease center). A **prerelease center** is a minimum-security step down facility that either houses prisoners who have not yet been granted parole, or houses prisoners who have met the parole board and been promised a future parole date if they can successfully complete 6–12 months in a community-based facility.

Prerelease facilities that are prison-based or community-based grant furloughs. A **furlough** is an authorized temporary overnight leave of absence from 24–72 hours. Acceptable reasons for a furlough include seeking postrelease employment or housing, attending funerals, or simply establishing community contacts and maintaining family ties. About 5 percent of all prerelease prisoners received at least one furlough while at a minimum-security facility. Of the ones approved for a furlough, most inmates visited family to get gradually reacquainted, and about 17 percent of both federal and state inmates attended a funeral. Some furloughs that are granted while the inmate is still in prison must receive special permission and sometimes the prisoner's family must agree to pay for officer security to accompany the releasee during the leave period.

Community Reparation Boards

Restorative justice (introduced in Chapter 5) plays an important role in the reentry process. Involvement of community members and treatment providers in offender reentry is known as **community reparation boards** and is particularly valuable for offenders. Herman and Wasserman (2001, 429) suggest that in addition to the community, crime victims can assist with reentry by "providing decision makers with important and relevant information; offering experience and expertise; encouraging offender accountability; and furthering the goals of victim empowerment, safety, restitution, and reintegration." Community reparation boards are useful in assisting the offender with finding a job, and in turn, influence employer's perceptions of former offenders. Some reparation boards have an offender sign a contract that incrementally moves the offender toward self-sufficiency and independent living. Areas that participated in a federal initiative known as Reentry Partnership Initiative (RPI) used reparation boards in the reentry process in places such as Baltimore, Maryland; Spokane, Washington; Lowell, Massachusetts; Las Vegas, Nevada; Columbia, South Carolina; Kansas City, Missouri; Lake City,

LEARNING OUTCOMES 3 Explain the key ways in which community programs play a role in the reentry process.

GLOSSARY

prerelease center A minimum-security prison-based or community-based facility that either houses prisoners who have not yet been granted parole, or houses prisoners who have met the parole board and been promised a future parole date.

furlough An authorized temporary overnight leave of absence from 24 to 72 hours.

community reparation board Group that facilitates involvement of community members in an offender's reentry to society.

Source: © Bob Daemmrich/The Image Works

Community reparation boards are useful in assisting the offender with finding a job, and in turn, influence employer's perceptions of former offenders.

Florida; and Burlington, Vermont (Byrne, Taxman, & Young 2002). Now that we've discussed reentry issues and reentry programs, we move to getting released from jail and prison.

▶ Release from Prison

There are four ways to leave prison: two of which involve no supervision and two involve continued supervision in the community. **Unconditional release** refers to returning prisoners to the streets without postrelease supervision. Two reasons for unconditional release are sentence expiration and commutation. An expired sentence means that the maximum time on the prison sentence has been served. While an attempt is made to transition prisoners down to lower security levels one to two years prior to release, prisoners with disciplinary infractions or protective custody levels may be released directly from maximum security.

Commutation of sentence involves a discretionary reduction of the sentence length by a designated individual in the executive branch. State prisoners can be commuted by a governor or a parole board, while federal prisoners are commuted by the president of the United States. A sentence might be commuted if it is found to be excessive or if the governor or board simply believes commutation would be in the society's best interest. Prisoners must file an application for commutation, typically after they have served a minimum amount of time. All commutations are considered, but most go to prisoners on death row who get their sentences reduced to life without parole, nonetheless the conviction remains on record. It is rare for prisoners to be released from prison due to a commuted sentence.

Conditional release involves postrelease supervision in the community. The governing authority that releases the prisoner is the parole board in **discretionary parole** and the law in mandatory supervision. Discretionary parole is the most common release method used in northeastern states and comprises just over half of all releases in southern states. **Supervised mandatory release**

includes all inmates who—by law—are automatically released to the community when they have completed their maximum prison sentence less any good-time credit they have received. Mandatory parole entries are persons whose releases from prison were not decided by a parole board. This includes those entering because of determinate sentencing statutes, good-time provisions, or emergency releases. But because the full sentence is not really completed, the inmate's release is conditional and requires supervision. Supervised mandatory release is the most common release mechanism in the United States today, particularly in the western and midwestern regions. We first examine the history of discretionary parole in the United States, which began on the other side of the globe, near Australia.

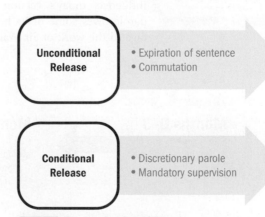

Unconditional Release
• Expiration of sentence
• Commutation

Conditional Release
• Discretionary parole
• Mandatory supervision

FIGURE 10.5 Ways to Get Out of Prison.

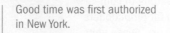
1800s	**1817**	**1854**	**1944**
British prisoners who were banished to Australia were able to work off a certain portion of their sentence before being set free.	Good time was first authorized in New York.	Sir Walter Crofton implemented the ticket-of-leave in Ireland.	All states in U.S. used indeterminate sentencing and parole.
	1836–1840	**1876**	
	Captain Alexander Maconochie implemented the Marks system at Norfolk Island.	Zebulon Brockway implemented the Irish system at Elmira, New York.	

Maconochie, Captain Alexander Governor of Norfolk Island from 1836–1840, one of the toughest penal colonies for English prisoners.

mark system Developed by Maconochie, this system rewarded positive behavior and work ethics.

Irish system Mid-nineteenth-century prison philosophy that asserted punishment's most direct purpose should be to reform the criminal.

Brockway, Zebulon Credited with implementing the Irish system in the United States at the Elmira Reformatory in Elmira, New York, in the late 1870s.

parole board Group of citizens, typically appointed by the state governor, who meet periodically to review the files of those prisoners eligible for parole.

parole agreement/order Document that the parolee signs at first meeting with parole officer where he or she agrees to abide by certain conditions while on parole.

History of Parole

Norfolk Island was one of the toughest penal colonies for English prisoners. Norfolk Island had a reputation for housing the most unruly and violent prisoners and for using a management style that included severe beatings and physical labor (Morris 2002). When he arrived, **Captain Alexander Maconochie** significantly changed the way that prisoners were managed. He abolished corporal punishment and chain gangs, and rewarded positive behavior and work ethics through a daily **mark system**. Prisoners who participated in work and education programs were credited with marks, while marks were removed for disciplinary violations. When prisoners accumulated enough "marks," they were released early from the island (Morris 2002).

In addition to Maconochie's influence, today's version of parole owes some of its heritage to the work of Sir Walter Crofton and the application of indeterminate sentencing. Sir Walter Crofton, appointed as director of the Irish Prison System, was especially intrigued with this concept of conditional release. Borrowing some ideas from Maconochie, Crofton developed a system of increasing privileges that was known as the **Irish system**.

While under a ticket-of-leave, releasees were not under supervision per se, but were expected to keep police informed of their whereabouts. The ticket-of-leave is parole's predecessor, but at that time, prisoners on leave were not being formally supervised, nor were there any revocation procedures for failing to notify law enforcement.

In the United States, prison officials realized the necessity of having ways to encourage good behavior by prisoners. With the first complaints of crowding, officials saw a need for procedures that would help control the size of the prison population by releasing some prisoners early to make room for new arrivals. The answer could be found in the Irish system's reliance on indeterminate sentencing and the ticket-of-leave. When the new institution opened at Elmira, New York, penologist **Zebulon Brockway** implemented Maconochie's mark system and Crofton's graduated release leading to a supervised ticket-of-leave. Inmates released from Elmira were supervised at first by volunteer citizens. After its successful use at Elmira, the indeterminate sentence and parole became the dominant philosophy.

The Parole Decision

Granting parole requires first that a prisoner meet the minimum eligibility criteria and second that a majority of board members agree that the prisoner is ready. Prisoners are given a date on which they are first eligible for early

Months 0–3
Solitary confinement on reduced rations and not allowed to work

Months 4–9
Solitary confinement with full rations and allowed to work

Months 10–Release
Transferred to general population, worked with other inmates, and earned one mark per day until enough were earned for obtain a **ticket-of-leave**.

FIGURE 10.6 The Irish System.

Uses of Parole
1. Assist released inmates to lead a more law-abiding life under restrictions
2. Encourage inmate conformity to prison rules
3. Backdoor population reduction strategy
4. Reduce judicial sentencing disparity

Granting parole requires first that a prisoner meet the minimum eligibility criteria and second that a majority of board members agree that the prisoner is ready.

release on parole according to their sentence minus good time earned during the sentence. For example, consider an offender with a six to ten year sentence (in which six is the minimum amount of time and ten is the maximum) in a state where good time is given at a rate of one day of good time for each day served. Assuming that good time is earned every day, that inmate would be eligible for parole after serving three years in prison, because the six year minimum sentence has been met after only three years. But the emphasis is still on the words *eligible* and *can be considered*. Parole, after all, is a privilege and not a right.

The next step in the process is to determine which of the eligible prisoners will receive a parole release. The **parole board**, appointed by the state governor, meets to review the files of those prisoners eligible for parole. In some cases, the board interviews the prisoner and reviews the file, and in other cases, the board reviews the file only. If the board members agree that a person should be released on parole, they set a specific parole date. The prisoner knows that, barring any infractions or problems with the parole plan, he or she can expect to be released on that date. If the board members do not believe the time for release is quite right, parole is deferred or delayed for 12–24 months.

The common goal, regardless of specific criteria used, is to predict the offender's future conduct. Parole boards routinely use scoring instruments to help them assess risk. Male prisoners under age 25, convicted of a property offense, with severe untreated drug addiction, and with several prior convictions represent a higher risk of recidivism than women, older prisoners, offenders with less serious drug abuse histories, and those who were employed prior to arrest.

Decrease of Discretionary Parole and Rise of Mandatory Supervision

During the 1970s, parole was attacked on the grounds that parole boards had too much discretion on a prisoner's release date, which meant persons convicted of similar crimes could end up serving very different amounts of time in prison. A second criticism centered on a perceived lack of effectiveness in treating offenders given an early release. By the 1990s, many states revised their sentencing laws and began using determinate sentencing for violent crimes. This change to determinate sentencing also necessitated replacing discretionary parole

with supervised mandatory release. With supervised mandatory release, prisoners are automatically released to the community when they have completed their maximum prison sentence less any good-time credit they have received. But because the full sentence is not really completed, the inmate's release is conditional and requires community supervision. Mandatory release takes the decision making away from a parole board and gives it to legislators who revise sentencing laws.

The rate of supervised mandatory releases has grown significantly, and there are now more mandatory releases than discretionary. Supervised mandatory release is used in the states where parole boards have been abolished. Mandatory release is also used in the federal system and for violent crimes in about 21 states. A small number of states reinstated discretionary release because the prisons became too crowded under mandatory release.

Field Parole Officers and Supervision

Once the eligible offender is granted a release date on mandatory or discretionary supervision, a field officer must verify the release plan to ensure that the living arrangements are acceptable. Being that most parolees cannot afford their own place upon release, they must rely on staying with someone else. A field officer verifies that the family members agree to house the parolee and agree to parole officer visits. If housing plans are still not solidified, a halfway house facility is an available option. Once the release plan has been accepted, the

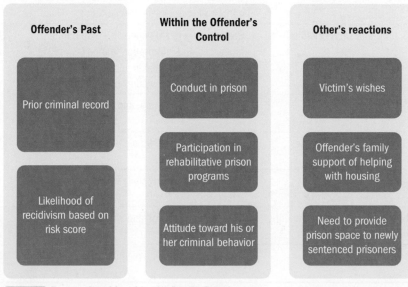

FIGURE 10.7 Factors Considered by the Parole Board.

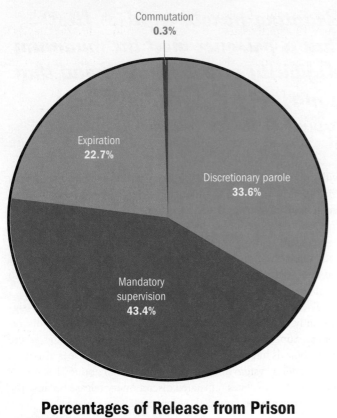

Commutation
0.3%

Expiration
22.7%

Discretionary parole
33.6%

Mandatory
supervision
43.4%

Percentages of Release from Prison

FIGURE 10.8 **Prison Release Methods.**
Source: Sabol, W. J., West, H. C., & Cooper, M. (2009). *Prisoners in 2008*. NCJ 228417. Washington, D.C.: U.S. Department of Justice.

offender is released from prison and is ordered to report to his or her parole officer within 24–48 hours. At that first visit, the offender signs a **parole agreement** or **parole order**. The term *agreement* is used when parole is discretionary, while an *order* more often suggests parole is mandatory and the parolee is aware of (though may not necessarily agree with) the rules. Parole conditions are nearly identical to those for probationers, so they will not be repeated.

Just as there is similarity between conditions of probation and parole, there is similarity among the duties assigned to manage each type of case no matter if they are on discretionary or mandatory parole. The two positions are enough alike that in the federal system and in many states, supervision officers have combined caseloads of probation and parole clients. Parole field officers are responsible for ensuring through supervision and assistance that the reentry plan is continued and their parolees do not pose a threat to public safety. In states with reentry initiatives, the parole officer focuses on reworking the transitional accountability plan to ensure a continuity of services the offender needs.

Contemporary models of parole supervision include neighborhood-based supervision by zip code; partnerships with law enforcement; and attempting to change the offenders' lives through personal, family, and neighborhood interventions. At the core, these models move toward matching offender needs with community resources, strengthening victim services for victims who have an offender in the community, offender

TABLE 10.6 | A Comparison of Traditional and Contemporary Parole.

Characteristic	Traditional Parole	Contemporary Parole
Program Development	Programs should be provided through the Department of Corrections prior to being paroled.	POs have input into the development of programs and are familiar with program resources in their communities.
Offender Treatment Plans	One size fits all and conducted for the sake of paperwork, but largely disregarded	Specific to each offender's criminogenic needs, realistic goals, and the foundation of case management
PO Work with Crime Victims	Case managers are generally isolated from processes and information related to working with victims, and they are not entirely comfortable responding to victims or their concerns.	Case managers are trained and knowledgeable about victim issues, comfortable with issues related to confidentiality, and have tools to respond effectively to victims.
PO Training	Procedures, paperwork, and rules	Evidence-based practices, cognitive-behavioral interventions, motivational interviewing
PO Help with Employment	Unemployed offenders are encouraged to look for work.	With community workforce staff, the PO assists the offender in job search and placement.
Evaluations of POs	Based on number of contacts PO makes with offender by risk level	Based on offender's successful implementation of case plans and whether PO contacts help with treatment goals
Style of PO Case Management	Reactive to problems and violations	Proactive and addresses offenders' crime-producing needs to prevent new crimes or violations
Parole Supervisors	Office-bound, working regular business hours	Develops partnerships with local social service agencies; supervises officers directly in the community

Source: Burke, P. B. (2004). *Parole violations revisited* [NIC #019833]. Washington, DC: National Institute of Corrections, p. 39.

accountability and positive community contributions, and decreasing the number of prisoners who return to prison.

The length of time a person is on parole varies considerably, but the average time is one to two years. Looking at differences among states, we can find some examples in which time on parole cannot exceed six months or the offender's maximum sentence date, whichever comes first; in other states, the parolees are discharged no later than one year after their release. States with mandatory parole typically specify time on parole as varying—for example, one to five years—depending on the crime. For instance, the state legislature might determine that conviction of a class 3 felony will require two years on parole after completing whatever prison sentence the judge imposes. Like probationers, parolees try to complete supervision successfully through discharge rather than an unsuccessful revocation.

Parole officer responses, like the model pictured in Figure 10.9, differentiate among low, medium, and high levels of parolee behavior. Behaviors defined as "low" are considered less consequential than "high" behaviors (Burke 2004). The far left-hand column of this model shows how officers can reward positive behavior as well as sanction negative parolee behavior (shown in the far right-hand column). For example, a parolee who is on electronic monitoring and who is violation-free for 90 days might be eligible for regular parole supervision without the electronic surveillance. However, if that same parolee had a drug test that showed he or she used multiple illegal substances (a medium-risk behavior), the parolee would be required to enroll in an in-house drug program. Most states have solid parole policies that sanction negative behavior but seem to neglect rewarding positive behavior.

LEVELS

Suggested Response	POSITIVE BEHAVIOR		NEGATIVE BEHAVIOR	Suggested Response
• Verbal recognition • Letter of recognition • Certificate of completion • 6-month compliance certificate	• 90 days clean • 90 days employed • 6 months stable residence • Completed first school semester or 30 days regular GED attendance • Outpatient program completion • 30 days electronic monitoring (EM) violation-free • 2 months perfect attendance at cognitive skills course	LOW	• Positive drug test(s) • Program nonattendance • Failure to report • EM violations (minor) • Assessment not attended • Failure to support dependents • Unemployed (short period) • Special condition violation • Fee arrearage $60 or less • Technical violation—other	• Specific issue hearing • Outpatient program • Self-help program • PO letter of reprimand • PO verbal reprimand • Increased screening • Increased reporting • Verbal warning
• 1-year compliance certificate • Mr./Ms. Clean Award • Letter of recognition • EM early termination • Certificate of completion • Reduced reporting • Chief recognition • Decrease supervision level	• 12 months stability (employment and residence, few to no violations) • 6 months clean • 2 months perfect attendance at cognnitive skills class • Completed 1 year of school or 6 months of regular GED attendance • 90 days EM violation-free • Outpatient program completion • Cognitive skills course completion	MEDIUM	• Misdemeanor arrest • Multiple positive drug tests • Multiple program nonattendance • EM violations (serious) • Unemployed (lengthy) • Assessment not attended (multiple) • Sex offender violations (minor) • Fee arrearage $100 or less	• Administrative hearing • In-house program • Restart program • EM extension • Outpatient program • Specific issue hearing • Increased screening • Increased reporting • Verbal reprimand—chief • Restorative/community service work • Increase supervision level
• Commutation request • Donated gift certificate (GED/school graduation) • Cognitive skills graduation • Lifestyle Commitment Award • Second Mr./Ms. Clean Award • Reduced reporting	• 24 months stability • Completed school or GED • 12 months clean • Volunteer work, church affiliation • Prosocial activities	HIGH	• Felony arrest • Violent misdemeanor arrest or DUI • Positive drug tests (critical) • Program nonattendance (critical) • Sex offender violation (serious) • EM violations (critical) • Possession of a weapon • Absconding • Failure to attend administrative hearing • Unemployed (critical) • Fee arrearage over $100	• Request revocation • Short-term incarceration (local detention) • Electronic monitoring • In-house program • Administrative hearing • Outpatient program • EM extension • Whitworth Detention Center

FIGURE 10.9 **Behavior Response Guide for Parole Officers.**
Source: Burke, P. B. (2004). *Parole violations revisited* [NIC #019833]. Washington, DC: National Institute of Corrections, and Silver Spring, MD: Center for Effective Public Policy, p. 35.

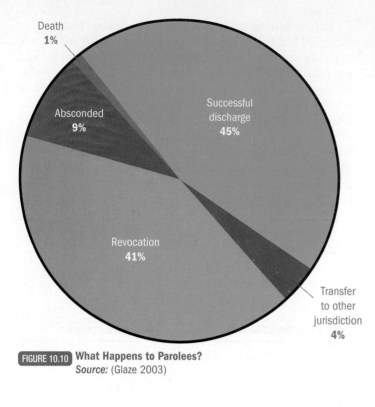

Death
1%

Absconded
9%

Successful
discharge
45%

Revocation
41%

Transfer
to other
jurisdiction
4%

FIGURE 10.10 **What Happens to Parolees?**
Source: (Glaze 2003)

Revoking Parole

Upon becoming aware of the possible commission of a new crime or technical violations, a parole officer may wish to revoke parole, but the final decision is up to the parole board. If formal revocation is sought, there must be a preliminary hearing and a formal revocation hearing following arrest. The parolee is not entitled to many of the rights at a criminal trial, such as an attorney, a jury of peers, or privilege against self-incrimination. However, parole revocation represents a loss of liberty, so some due process rights are permitted. They are as follows:

1. Written notice of alleged parole violations

2. Disclosure of evidence against parolee

3. Opportunity to be heard in person and to present witnesses and evidence

4. Right to confront and cross-examine adverse witnesses (unless the hearing officer finds good cause not to allow such confrontation)

5. A neutral and detached hearing body

6. A written statement by the fact-finder as to the evidence relied upon and reason(s) for revoking parole (*Morrissey* v. *Brewer,* (1972) 408 U.S., 471)

A revocation for technical violations may not always result in removal from the community. In some jurisdictions like Colorado, intermediate sanctions like day reporting centers or residential community facilities are the preferred cost-effective alternative to jail or prison. If jail is inevitable, some states still limit the amount of time that can be served for a revocation. For example, Kentucky allows parole officers discretion to incarcerate a technical violator for up to 30 days per every 365 day period on parole (VERA Institute of Justice 2010). Due to the economic deficits that most states have recently faced, many have explored reducing overall costs to the correctional system by way of increasing parole rates, increasing probation as an alternative to prison, and decreasing prison as an option for parole or probation revocation. This has unfortunately meant larger caseloads for parole officers (primarily due to a state hiring freeze) and thus a reduced ability to supervise them. The future of larger community caseloads and less parole and probation officers remains to be seen.

Faith-Based Reentry

Correctional facilities rely on volunteers to provide a wide range of spiritual opportunities such as worship services, bible study, clergy visits, and publications for many denominations. Prison Fellowship Ministries (PFM), founded by ex-felon Charles Colson, provides Christian-based opportunities for prisoners and their families (Paynter 2004). In 1997, PFM started the first Christian prison community called InnerChange Freedom Initiative (IFI) under the belief that criminal behavior, drug use, alcoholism, homosexuality, and dishonesty are sinful behaviors that can be cured by being saved by Jesus. Inmate volunteers are transferred to the specific prison IFI unit. All IFI treatment staff members and inmates are of the Christian denomination. The program has four phases:

- *Phase One, Transformation* (18 months): This involves intense Bible study and weekly testing on the concepts for more than ten hours per day (Paynter 2004). This phase includes admitting sins, taking responsibility, and seeking repentance.

- *Phase Two, Reentry Preparation* (6 months): This involves off-site prison work programs and involvement in reentry classes while still incarcerated. Reading the Bible, attending church service, and strengthening one's relationship with God are expected throughout all phases.

- *Phase Three, Community Facility* (6 months): Inmates develop a relationship with a PFM mentor who aids them in finding a more permanent job and housing.

An empirical study of the Texas IFI program compared 177 participants (75 graduates and 102 who quit or were paroled before completing) to 1,700 inmates who met the initial IFI selection criteria but did not participate. Johnson and Larson (2003) tracked recidivism rates of both groups for two years beyond their prison release dates and found no significant difference between IFI participants (36 percent rearrested and 24.3 percent reincarcerated) and nonparticipants (35 percent rearrested and 20 percent reincarcerated). Although a separate comparison of the 75 IFI program graduates showed lower rearrest (17.3 percent) and reincarceration rates (8 percent), it is difficult to say whether the lower recidivism is because of the program or because there are qualities about program completers that differ from program dropouts and nonparticipants.

IFI programs currently operate in five states with over 1,000 total participants. While state funds can pay only for costs that are not faith-based, PFM pays all faith-based costs after the U.S. District Court ordered PFM to repay the state of Iowa $1.53 million in faith-based costs that violated the separation of church and state (*Americans United* v. *Prison Fellowship Ministry* 2006).

The InnerChange Freedom Initiative raises some interesting issues:

1. Given that an inmate of another religious denomination cannot practice at IFI, is this a violation of First Amendment rights? Why or why not? What accommodations can be made?

2. How would you classify IFI as a reentry program? Does it work? Is it promising?

3. In tough budget times, IFI may be an attractive option for states facing possible prison closures. Would you advocate in favor of or against expansion of IFI to other treatment programs like those for sex offenders? Why?

Source: © Andrew Aitchison/Alamy

LEARNING OUTCOMES 1

Describe the reentry process and the challenges that prisoners face when they are released from prison.

Reentry programs are directed at offenders who are within three to twelve months of release and assist with securing identification, housing, finding a job, remaining sober, and making healthy decisions.

1. Should the Second Chance Act be reauthorized by Congress? Why or why not?

2. What else can we do to help former offenders who are released from prison? Make a list of as many ideas as you can think of that might help.

reentry The process of release preparation that begins within the institution and continues with community supervision.

Second Chance Act Federal legislation that authorizes reentry grants to state and local agencies and nonprofit organizations to provide employment assistance, substance abuse treatment, housing, and mentoring to reduce recidivism for ex-offenders returning to communities from correctional facilities.

LEARNING OUTCOMES 2

Understand the role of education and vocational programs as they contribute to reducing recidivism.

Educational programs in prison include literacy and basic education, obtaining a GED, and some college programs. Recidivism was lower as a result of involvement in educational programs while incarcerated. While literacy and GED programs are abundant, few college opportunities exist for prisoners.

Vocational programs are available for inmates who have at least a GED, but fewer choices exist for women than for men. Studies that have tracked inmates to see if vocational programs increased success found vocational programs to be less successful than traditional education programs.

1. Should prisoners receive financial aid or scholarships to attend college classes while incarcerated. Why or why not?

2. In order to qualify for vocational training programs, discuss the pros and cons of requiring inmates to have a GED or diploma as a prerequisite.

test for adult basic education (TABE) Test given to inmates to determine the prisoner's level of academic ability.

LEARNING OUTCOMES 3

Explain the key ways in which community programs play a role in the reentry process.

1. Should prerelease centers be expanded in the community? Argue for or against your choice.

2. How does the principle of forgiveness relate to restorative justice and the reentry process?

3. Would you be willing to volunteer on a community reparation board? Why or why not?

prerelease center A minimum-security prison-based or community-based facility that either houses prisoners who have not yet been granted parole, or houses prisoners who have met the parole board and been promised a future parole date.

furlough An authorized temporary overnight leave of absence from 24 to 72 hours.

community reparation board Group that facilitates involvement of community members in an offender's reentry to society.

LEARNING OUTCOMES 4

Summarize the history of parole, along with the various forms of unconditional versus conditional release.

1. As a citizen, which form of supervised release do you think is more effective for recent releasees—discretionary parole or mandatory release? Why?

2. If you were a prisoner, would you prefer to get out early on parole supervision, or would you prefer to do all your time behind bars and get out on unconditional release? What factors weigh on this decision?

3. How does the early marks system resemble the contemporary model of responding positively and negatively to parolee behavior?

unconditional release The return of prisoners to the larger community without supervision.

commutation of sentence When a leader in the executive branch of government reduces an offender's punishment.

discretionary parole Conditional early release from imprisonment at the discretion of a state paroling authority and continued supervision in the community.

supervised mandatory release When an inmate is automatically released by law to the community when he or she has completed his or her maximum prison sentence less any good-time credit the inmate has received.

Maconochie, Captain Alexander Governor of Norfolk Island from 1836–1840, one of the toughest penal colonies for English prisoners.

mark system Developed by Maconochie, this system rewarded positive behavior and work ethics.

Irish system Mid-nineteenth-century prison philosophy that asserted punishment's most direct purpose should be to reform the criminal.

Brockway, Zebulon Credited with implementing the Irish system in the United States at the Elmira Reformatory in Elmira, New York, in the late 1870s.

parole board Group of citizens, typically appointed by the state governor, who meet periodically to review the files of those prisoners eligible for parole.

parole agreement/order Document that the parolee signs at first meeting with parole officer where he or she agrees to abide by certain conditions while on parole.

MyCJLab

Go to the Chapter 10 section in *MyCJLab* to test your understanding of this chapter, access customized study content, engage in interactive simulations, complete critical thinking and research assignments, and view related online videos.

Additional Links

View a five-minute interview with a former prisoner about what challenges he faced when first released: **www.youtube.com/watch?v=wnmoVyYO7nU**.

The Michigan Reentry Prisoner Initiative can be found at these two websites: **www.youtube.com/watch?v=Q_Qy2ybXaF4&feature=related** and **www.michigan.gov/corrections/0,1607,7-119-1435---,00.html**.

How women offenders view reentry programs can be accessed at **www.youtube.com/watch?v=dbuav6irGJE&feature=related**.

Visit the Urban Institute to review various policy research projects related to prisoner reentry: **www.urban.org**.

Visit Texas's prison entrepreneurship reentry program for how prisoners are taught to start their own businesses: **www.prisonentrepreneurship.org**.

Court Services and Offender Supervision Agency is the federal parole and probation entity exclusively for Washington, DC: **www.csosa.gov**.

Visit the Vera Family Justice Program and listen to the podcast entitled "Introducing Family Justice" from December 2, 2009, about how it assists in the reentry process: **www.vera.org/centers/family-justice-program**.

Visit the National Conference on State Legislatures Fall Forum, held in December 2010. Speakers discuss initiatives to disrupt the recidivism cycle following an offender's release from prison: **www.ncsl.org/default.aspx?tabid=21839**.

Complete the "Parole Decision Maker" to provide you with a glimpse of the factors the parole board considers: **www.insideprison.com/parole_decision_making.asp**.

Legal Issues in Corrections

"A prisoner is not wholly stripped of constitutional protections when he is imprisoned for crime. There is no iron curtain drawn between the Constitution and the prisons of this country."

—*Justice Byron White*, Wolff *v.* McDonnell *(1974)*

1 Outline the development and sources of prisoners' rights.

2 Describe types of inmate lawsuits using access to courts and issues of religion as examples.

3 Describe how inmate litigation is limited.

4 Summarize the issues associated with the loss of civil rights.

5 Explain procedures by which civil rights can be restored.

11

Oklahoma City bombing conspirator, Terry Nichols, is serving a life sentence at the Federal Administrative Maximum prison in Colorado for conspiracy and involuntary manslaughter in the 1995 bombing of the Alfred P. Murrah Federal Building. In 2009, Nichols filed a lawsuit claiming his constitutional rights were being violated because the prison food did not meet his medical and religious needs. He claimed to need a fiber-rich diet of whole grain foods, bran products, and unpeeled and uncooked fruits and vegetables. Nichols argued that not only does he have a medical condition requiring such a diet, but his Christian belief is that God created our food to be consumed in their whole unrefined state. In 2010, a federal judge ruled his claims to be invalid, saying that Nichols did not prove his diet constituted cruel and unusual punishment nor did he offer proof that it violated his Christian beliefs (Doucette 2010).

Lyralisa Stevens is one of more than 300 inmates in the California state prison system diagnosed with gender identity disorder. This psychiatric condition is treated with hormone replacement therapy and, in some case, sex

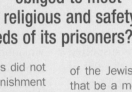

DISCUSS Are prisons obliged to meet the religious and safety needs of its prisoners?

reassignment surgery. Stevens was born male but lives as a female. She is serving 50 years to life for killing a woman in a dispute over clothes. In a 2011 lawsuit, Stevens asked the court to require California to pay for a sex-change operation. She claims that that removal of her penis and testicles and transfer to a women's prison are the best way to protect her from rape and abuse by male inmates (Dolan 2011). Her fears seem well-founded since at least one study has found that transgender prisoners are 13 times more likely to suffer sexual assault than other inmates (Jenness 2009).

Both of these cases present issues related to prisoners' rights. Nichols's argument may seem silly, but what if he was of the Jewish faith and asking for kosher meals? Would that be a more legitimate request? Whether you consider the Stevens case to be frivolous or not, there certainly are issues of safety to be considered. Would it be irresponsible for prison officials to put a 17-year-old juvenile who was convicted and sentenced as an adult in a cell with a convicted child molester? Does the state have some responsibility for the safety of prisoners?

Two positions can be taken regarding rights of convicted and imprisoned persons:

- The **rights-are-retained** position argues that prisoners keep all the rights of an ordinary citizen, except those that are expressly or by necessity taken away from them by law.

- The **rights-are-lost** position says prisoners are wholly without rights except those expressly conferred by law or necessity.

Importantly, but confusingly, neither position accurately identifies the approach held by the courts. The

rights-are-retained view comes directly from a federal appeals court decision in 1944 (*Coffin* v. *Reichard*), but federal courts have issued many other decisions that suggest prisoners may only have rights that are compatible with the goals of prison administration. In the absence of a clear and consistent approach, it is not surprising that the public, prison officials, and even judges have difficulty understanding or describing the rights of prisoners. However, before discussing how the courts have responded to this "rights-retained" or "rights-lost" dilemma, we consider from where the presumed rights come.

▶ *Sources of Prisoners' Rights*

Proponents of having inmates retain some rights during incarceration point at state and federal constitutions and state and federal laws to support their claim. State constitutions and laws are too numerous to cover here, so we concentrate on federal-level sources. First we will look at articles of the U.S. Constitution and two of the constitution's amendments to understand how they serve as the basis for many inmate claims. Then we consider the Civil Rights Act (U.S. Code, Title 42 Section 1983) as an example of a federal statute that is increasingly being used to support inmate claims of discrimination.

The U.S. Constitution

When introducing the concept of individual rights under the U.S. Constitution, Ferdico states how much easier enforcing criminal laws would be if suspected criminals were presumed guilty; could be detained for long periods of time without a hearing; had no privilege against self-incrimination; and could

have their bodies, vehicles, and homes searched at will (2005, 4). But because the United States was founded as a direct response to what early colonists saw as British abuses in these kinds of areas, there has always been a strong commitment to protecting individual rights from government abuse. With the ratification in 1788 of the U.S. Constitution, and with the addition in 1791 of the Bill of Rights, America's commitment to individual rights was guaranteed. As a result, persons suspected of crime are, among other things, presumed innocent, cannot be detained long

LEARNING OUTCOMES 1 Outline the development and sources of prisoners' rights.

GLOSSARY

rights-are-retained Argues that prisoners keep all the rights of an ordinary citizen, except those that are expressly or by necessity taken away from them by law.

rights-are-lost Argues that prisoners are wholly without rights except those expressly conferred by law or necessity.

Important Prisoners' Rights Court Cases

1871	1970	1972	1974
Ruffin v. Commonwealth A Virginia Supreme Court ruling that prisoners are a "slave of the state" and have forfeited all personal rights except those the state chooses to give him.	**Holt v. Sarver** Federal district court ruling that something is cruel and unusual if it amounts to torture, is grossly excessive in proportion to the offense, is inherently unfair, unnecessarily degrading, or is shocking or disgusting to people of reasonable sensitivity.	**Cruz v. Beto** Prisoners with "nontraditional" beliefs, Buddhism in this case, cannot be denied an opportunity to practice their religion.	**Wolff v. McDonnell** In contrast to *Ruffin v. Commonwealth*, the Wolff decision said "a prisoner is not wholly stripped of constitutional protections when he is imprisoned for crime."

Source: © Arnold Gold/ New Haven Register/ The Image Works

without a hearing, are not forced to incriminate themselves, and have protection against unreasonable searches and seizures.

In addition to concern about the rights of persons suspected and accused of crimes, the U.S. Constitution and the Bill of Rights also cover the rights of persons convicted of a crime. For example, Section 9 of Article 1 provides the privilege of the **writ of** *habeas corpus* (for our purposes, such a writ directs the person—the warden, for example—detaining the prisoner to show the legality of the detention). On the other hand, Section 10 of Article 1, through its prohibition against **ex post facto law**, prevents imposing a greater punishment for a crime than was in effect when the crime was committed. The Eighth Amendment's prohibition against cruel and unusual punishments is the obvious example of concern for convicted persons,

but so is the Fourteenth Amendment's due process requirement. *Habeas corpus* action and complaints of *ex post facto* law violations are still brought by offenders today. But this overview concentrates on issues related to the Eighth and Fourteenth Amendments.

The Eighth Amendment to the U.S. Constitution prohibits cruel and unusual punishments. Even persons claiming that offenders forfeit all their rights after conviction are likely to make an exception to the constitutional protection against cruel and unusual punishment. The problem is determining to what this prohibition refers. Is it cruel and unusual to serve an inmate only one meal per day? To tie an inmate to a hitching post for hours in the hot sun? To prohibit any out-of-cell exercise for an inmate? To punish an inmate by banning him from

TABLE 11.1 | What Constitutes Cruel and Unusual Punishment?

The term *cruel and unusual punishment* cannot be specifically defined because it is flexible and broadens as society pays more regard to human decency and dignity. In general, however, cruel and unusual punishment is that which "amounts to torture, when it is grossly excessive in proportion to the offense for which it is imposed, or that is inherently unfair, or that is unnecessarily degrading, or that is shocking or disgusting to people of reasonable sensitivity" (*Holt* v. *Sarver* 1970, 309 F. Supp. at 362). Recent court decisions reflect the difficulty inherent in dealing with such issues:

Does Violate the Eighth Amendment

- The U.S. Supreme Court found that handcuffing an Alabama prisoner to a "hitching post" for two hours (the first time) and seven hours (a second time) in the hot sun without bathroom or water breaks, and taunting him by pouring water out in front of him, violated the Eighth Amendment (*Hope* v. *Pelzer* 2002).

- A U.S. Court of Appeals found Michigan's policy of terminating all inmate visits (except from attorneys and clergy) as a way to punish inmates with two or more violations of the department's substance abuse policy to be an Eighth Amendment violation. The court described the ban on visits as cruel and unusual because it, in part, destroyed the social, emotional, and physical bonds of parent and child (*Bazzetta* v. *McGinnis* 2002).

- In *Knop* v. *Johnson* (1987), a federal district court ruled that Michigan had failed to provide inmates with winter coats, hats, and gloves and thereby subjected them to cruel and unusual punishment. Boots, however, were not required as long as the state provided adequate winter socks and kept the walkways and outdoor exercise areas free from snow.

Does Not Violate the Eighth Amendment

- A Kentucky jail did not violate a prisoner's Eighth Amendment rights by serving him only one meal a day for 15 consecutive days because the one meal was sufficient to maintain normal health for the 15 days involved (*Cunningham* v. *Jones* 1982).

- When an Arkansas prison refused to allow out-of-cell exercise for the first 15 days of a prisoner's time in punitive isolation, a federal court said the policy may be severe, and even harsh, but it was neither cruel nor barbaric (*Leonard* v. *Norris* 1986).

- An Illinois inmate complained that the prison failed to provide him with toilet paper for five days, or with soap, toothpaste, or a toothbrush for ten days. The federal court (*Harris* v. *Fleming* 1988) found that because the inmate suffered merely some unpleasantness, the temporary neglect was not intentional and did not reach unconstitutional proportions.

DISCUSS *Can you determine from these cases just what criteria the courts are using to conclude if something constitutes cruel and unusual punishment? If more cases were cited, do you think it would be possible to identify a clear standard? Why or why not?*

1987

Turner v. Safley Considered by some to be the most important USSC case on prison law because it sets the legal standard for judging whether prison regulations infringe on prisoners' rights. It says that prison regulations are valid as long as they are reasonably related to legitimate penological interests.

2002

Porter v. Nussle The Prison Litigation Reform Act's requirement that inmates must exhaust all administrative grievance procedures before a lawsuit can be filed applies not only to general prison conditions, but also to individual incidents such as accusations of excessive force.

Source: Patrick Tehan/MCT/Newscom

2005

Wilkinson v. Austin Although the extreme deprivation and punishment found in supermax prisons warrant protections for prisoners' due process rights, the procedures used in Ohio to transfer inmates to the supermax facility provided sufficient protection to comply with the Fourteenth Amendment.

writ of *habeas corpus* Judicial mandate to a prison official ordering that an inmate be brought to the court in order to determine the legality of the prisoner's detention.

ex post facto law A law imposing a greater punishment for a crime than was allowed when the crime was committed.

incorporation Legal theory arguing that all provisions of the Bill of Rights are made applicable to the states through the due process clause.

having visits with family members? Does a prison violate an inmate's Eighth Amendment rights when it fails to provide adequate winter clothing or does not supply the inmate with toilet paper, soap, toothpaste, or toothbrush? These questions represent some of the complaints brought by prisoners who believe they are being subjected to cruel and unusual punishment.

The Fourteenth Amendment has significant importance to the concept of individual rights. Prior to the passage of the Fourteenth Amendment, the Bill of Rights served primarily to define the relationship between citizens and the federal government. Each state had its own state constitution, and many of those identified rights held by citizens against injustices by their state government. But the U.S. Constitution's first ten amendments referred only to the protections citizens had against the federal government. This meant that a person might have certain rights when interacting with the federal government but not have those rights when associating with the state government.

> *Prior to the passage of the Fourteenth Amendment, the Bill of Rights served primarily to define the relationship between citizens and the federal government.*

Such a situation was not considered inappropriate under a federal republic in which states shared sovereignty with the federal government, nor was it necessarily confusing because many of the state constitutions were modeled after the federal constitution. There were, however, some rights guaranteed in the Bill of Rights that were being denied by some states.

After the Civil War, the Thirteenth Amendment was passed (1865) to correct the obvious violation of individual rights where states continued to allow slavery and involuntary servitude. Because other infringements on individual rights continued in some states, the Fourteenth Amendment was ratified in 1868. Its importance to individual rights is best understood through the theory of **incorporation**, which argues that all provisions of the Bill of Rights are made applicable to the states (that is, they are incorporated) by the amendment's due process clause. So, when the amendment says that "no State shall deprive any

PROCEDURES TO FOLLOW WHEN DISCIPLINING PRISONERS

In a 1974 decision, the U.S. Supreme Court identified the basic procedural requirements that prison officials must follow when taking disciplinary action that could result in a prisoner receiving punitive segregation or a loss of good time (*Wolff v. McDonnell*).

- The prisoner must be given written notification of the charges at least 24 hours in advance of the hearing so that he or she might prepare a defense.
- There must be a written statement by the fact-finders as to the evidence relied on and the reasons for the disciplinary action.
- Inmates facing disciplinary proceedings should be allowed to call witnesses and present documentary evidence in their defense as long as it does not unduly jeopardize institutional safety or correctional goals.
- There is no constitutional requirement that prison disciplinary hearings allow for cross-examination procedures, nor does the inmate have a right to either retained or appointed counsel in the proceedings. In some cases (for example, the inmate is illiterate or the case is particularly complex), a staff member or another inmate may act as substitute counsel.
- The inmate's hearing should be conducted by an impartial official or panel.

2006

Beard v. Banks Denying dangerous inmates access to newspapers, magazines, and photographs does not violate the First Amendment when the prison policy meets the *Turner* v. *Safley* standard.

2011

Brown v. Plata Finding that conditions in California's overcrowded prisons are so bad that they amount to cruel and unusual punishment, the U.S. Supreme Court ordered the state to dramatically reduce its overcrowded conditions through early release of prisoners, new prison construction, transfer to other states, or to county jails. California has two years (with a possibility of extensions) to comply with the order.

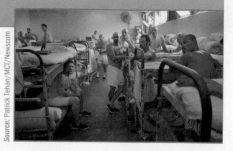

Source: Patrick Tehan/MCT/Newscom

person of life, liberty, or property, without due process of law," it is requiring each state to abide by the Bill of Rights.

The Fourteenth Amendment also prohibits any state from denying "any person within its jurisdiction the equal protection of the law." Therefore, because of the Fourteenth Amendment, individual states must abide by the Bill of Rights and must obey federal court rulings about whether the state

1. followed due process of law when depriving a person of life, liberty, or property (the **due process clause**).

2. provided equal protection of the law to all people within its jurisdiction (the **equal protection clause**).

Offenders have often used the Fourteenth Amendment's due process and equal protection clauses when claiming their rights have been violated.

Examples of prisoner due process violation claims are those linked to whether a hearing is required before prison officials can discipline or transfer inmates. Everyone probably agrees that it would be a denial of due process to keep suspects in jail for weeks or months without having them appear before a judge to hear the charges against them and be told of their right to counsel. But

what about inmates suspected of misbehavior while in prison? In its 1974 *Wolff* v. *McDonnell* decision, the U.S. Supreme Court distinguished between due process requirements for a defendant at trial and those required for an inmate at a disciplinary hearing. The Court held that because "prison disciplinary proceedings are not part of a criminal prosecution, the full panoply of rights due a defendant in such proceedings does not apply" (418 U.S. at 556). However, although prison officials are not bound to the same procedures as found in criminal court, the prison disciplinary hearings must abide by some level of due process and the Court identified specific steps that must be followed, such

due process clause That section of the Fourteenth Amendment requiring all states to abide by the Bill of Rights when depriving a person of life, liberty, or property.

equal protection clause That section of the Fourteenth Amendment prohibiting any state from denying equal protection of the law to persons within its jurisdiction.

Section 1983 claim A claim brought under the authority of U.S. Code Title 42, Section 1983 that civil rights have been violated.

TABLE 11.2	Fourteenth Amendment Equal Protection Claims.
Racial/Ethnic discrimination	State statutes requiring segregation of races in prisons and jails violates the Fourteenth Amendment (*Lee* v. *Washington* 1968 and *Holt* v. *Sarver* 1970), as does the subjection of African-American or Hispanic prisoners to disparate and unequal treatment (*Ramos* v. *Lamm* 1979). Importantly, the *Lee* v. *Washington* decision did say that prison officials acting in good faith, and in particular circumstances, can take racial tensions into account to maintain security, discipline, and good order. But when racial tensions are used to justify actions such as segregation, those considerations should be made after a danger to security, discipline, and good order has become apparent and not before (*Wilson* v. *Kelley* 1968).
Gender discrimination	In what is probably the most well-known case on women's prison issues, a United States district court was asked to rule on programs and facilities provided by the state of Michigan for its women prisoners compared to those for its men prisoners. Women prisoners in Michigan claimed they were not receiving access to vocational courses equal to those for male prisoners, and the numbers seemed to support the women's position. Men had access to twenty-two vocational courses while women had access to only three. In addition, the courses available to the men led to marketable skills but those for women did not. One of the prison teachers testified that the "women were taught at a junior-high level because the attitude of those in charge was 'keep it simple, these are only women'" (Muraskin 1993, 218). The court (*Glover* v. *Johnson* 1979) held that women inmates must be provided with treatment facilities that are substantially equal but not necessarily identical to those provided the men. As a result of the *Glover* ruling, Michigan had to provide to its women prisoners postsecondary education, counseling, vocational programs, and a legal education program.

Although federal and state courts have not consistently followed either a rights-are-retained or rights-are-lost position, it is possible to identify historical periods according to the courts' willingness to be involved in prison administration issues. These periods move from an initial time of noninvolvement (called the hands-off doctrine) to a time of active intrusion (the hands-on doctrine) and most recently to a deference doctrine wherein court rulings should respect the assessment of prison officials.

1. The Hands-Off Doctrine. Federal and state courts, before the early 1960s, held the view that prisoners had only those rights specifically granted by statute or by policy. Prison conditions were free from outside scrutiny, and prison administrators governed without any outside interference. State and federal courts were reluctant to intervene in prison administration unless there appeared to be a clear violation of the Eighth Amendment's protection against cruel and unusual punishment. The hands-off doctrine espoused by the courts was justified on several grounds including the argument that correctional administration was a technical matter that was best left to experts in corrections rather than to the courts, which are not equipped to make appropriate evaluations regarding the running of prisons.

2. The Hands-On Doctrine. After nearly 170 years of keeping the courts out of the prison management business, the hands-off doctrine began eroding. By the mid-1960s, federal district courts were seriously considering prisoners' claims. An important reason for the courts' new interest in prisoners was simply a reflection of the times, which also saw increased interest in areas such as civil rights, student rights, public welfare, and general institutional reform. Several of the earliest cases heard by the courts involved racial and religious discrimination brought by Black Muslims in prison. With the new hands-on doctrine, courts (especially the lower federal courts) began supporting prisoners' claims to rights in areas such as privacy, communication, safety, and due process.

3. The Deference Doctrine. Since 1980, the U.S. Supreme Court and lower federal courts have based decisions regarding the constitutionality of prison restrictions with deference to the assessment of prison officials. In *Bell* v. *Wolfish*, for example, Justice Rehnquist expressed a belief that courts had become too involved in the minutiae of prison operations. Rehnquist, writing for the majority, explained that court involvement in prison management must be limited to whether a particular prison requirement violates the Constitution. An example of the new deference to the discretion of prison authorities is *Turner* v. *Safley* (1987), which found that prison requirements that impinge on inmates' constitutional rights are valid if they are reasonably related to legitimate penological interests.

as advance written notice of the alleged infraction and a written statement of the findings. States are welcome to provide more procedural protections than required by *Wolff* and many jurisdictions do so—for example, by allowing cross-examination.

The Fourteenth Amendment's equal protection clause is also frequently used in inmate claims. Although this clause does not require the government to treat everyone alike in all circumstances, it does forbid unjustified or malicious discrimination or classification. Because prison officials can often articulate a rational basis for their actions, it is difficult for inmates to win an equal protection claim in a prison case. For example, the courts have not found equal protection violations when prisoners have been denied things such as temporary release programs (for example, work release), even though other prisoners with equally—or even more—deplorable records were involved in the programs.

Furthermore, having different visiting privileges for those on death row and those in the general population does not violate the equal protection clause (*Jamieson* v. *Robinson* 1981), nor does a pay differential between two different prisons (*Beatham* v. *Manson* 1973). Courts have, however, been sympathetic to equal protection clause claims in racial and gender-based discrimination.

The Civil Rights Act

Civil rights are those personal, natural rights that protect people against arbitrary or discriminatory treatment. Clearly the Constitution, including its Bill of Rights and other amendments, provides the first source of civil rights in the United States. However, there are civil rights not specifically mentioned in the Constitution but that are recognized by the courts, including

Think About It...

Rev. Martin Luther King, Jr.'s famed "I Have a Dream" speech galvanized the nation's civil rights movements and led to the passage of the 1964 Civil Rights Act—one of several important civil rights acts passed at the federal level. As a result of these acts, citizens (including prisoners) have rights and privileges such as freedom from discrimination. The primary vehicle for prisoner civil rights claims is Section 1983 of the Civil Rights Act of 1871, which was designed to guarantee the rights of newly freed slaves and to allow people direct access to the federal courts. The provision has been used successfully in class-action suits challenging institutional conditions. Why do you think it is important that citizens (including inmates in state prisons) have direct access to federal courts (rather than having to progress through state courts) when they are claiming violation of their civil rights?

> *Because Christian inmates were allowed to read the Bible and Jewish inmates could have Hebrew literature, the prison officials found it difficult to explain why Muslim prisoners could not have the Qur'an or receive Arabic documents.*

such rights as to live and work where we wish; to marry and to have children; and to participate in the political, social, and cultural processes of society (Ferdico 2005). Because the Constitution does not enumerate all civil rights, Americans can turn to other sources in which their rights are identified. For the purposes of discussing prisoners' rights, some of the most important relate to the Civil Rights Act, which is found in the U.S. Code as Title 42, Section 1983. For brevity, this is usually referred to as "Section 1983" and prisoner claims are typically called **Section 1983 claims**.

Early recognition that prisoners could sue for civil rights violations involved cases of religious freedom brought by Black Muslims. In 1962 Black Muslim leader Thomas X. Cooper filed suit in Illinois against Stateville Prison warden Frank Pate. Cooper claimed that his confinement in segregation was retribution for his religious beliefs. The basis for his claim was Section 1983 of the Civil Rights Act. Cooper was being denied access to the Qur'an, to Muslim literature such as the newspaper *Muhammad Speaks*, and to Muslim clergy. At a 1965 trial, ordered by the U.S. Supreme Court (*Cooper v. Pate* 1964), prison officials had to justify their refusal to recognize the Muslims as a religious group. Because Christian inmates were allowed to read the Bible and Jewish inmates could have Hebrew literature, the prison officials found it difficult to explain why Muslim prisoners could not have the Qur'an or receive Arabic documents (Jacobs 1977). In the end, Cooper won on some points (Muslims had to have access to the Qur'an, to communicate and visit with Muslim ministers, and to attend Muslim religious services). On other points, the court sided with prison officials (contemporary Muslim literature and Arabic textbooks did not have to be allowed).

Although the religious points were important in opening First Amendment rights to prisoner claims, *Cooper v. Pate* is important because the suit was based on a civil rights act. From the rather narrow issue of religious freedom, prisoners used Section 1983 to bring claims of civil rights violations in cases involving inadequate medical care, brutality by prison staff, and inmate-on-inmate assaults.

▶ A Sampling of Prisoner Rights Issues

Because of the many issues that could be addressed in this section, we review only a few. We cover those in only a cursory manner to provide a basic overview of the types of issues confronting prisoners and prison authorities. Specifically, this section considers inmate access to the courts and the issue of religion.

Access to the Courts

Possibly the most basic right for prisoners is access to the courts. Without it, any other rights would be moot because prisoners would be unable to bring their claims to the court's attention. This issue actually has two components:

1. Procedures by which inmates get their claims before the court

2. Having the necessary legal knowledge to make their access effective

The "getting a claim to court" issue was resolved in 1941 when a Michigan State Prison inmate challenged the prison policy of requiring prisoners to first submit all types of legal documents to prison authorities. The prison officials would then forward to the appropriate court those documents they considered to be properly written. The U.S. Supreme Court held (*ex parte Hull*) that prison authorities cannot restrict an inmate's right to apply to a federal court for a writ of *habeas corpus*.

But having direct access to courts via a writ of *habeas corpus* is only one step in the process of accessing the courts. Prisoners who are not familiar with the law may need assistance to ensure their right to access is meaningful. Similarly, prisoners who are familiar with the law can only have meaningful access if items such as law books and other legal materials are made available for their use.

In *Bounds* v. *Smith* (1977), the Court addressed the question of what constitutes meaningful access and ruled that prisons must provide adequate law libraries (for example, holding such references as state statutes, court reports, legal dictionaries, and law textbooks) or adequate legal assistance from persons trained in the law (for example, lawyers, paralegal assistants, and/or law student interns). In *Lewis* v. *Casey* (1996), the Court provided further explanation saying that *Bounds* did not create a freestanding right to a law library or even to legal assistance. Instead, *Bounds* simply established the right of prisoners to access the courts. So, for a violation of *Bounds* to occur, prisoners must show that the provided prison library or legal assistance program is hindering their efforts to pursue a legal claim.

Issues of Religion

Of the two religion clauses found in the First Amendment (the establishment clause and the free exercise clause), the issue of free exercise presents greater problems in a prison environment. The free exercise clause itself has been taken to have two aspects: the freedom to believe and the freedom to act. In *Cantwell* v. *Connecticut* (1940), the Court decided that "the first is absolute but, in the nature of things, the second cannot be. Conduct remains subject to [governmental] regulation for the protection of society" (310 U.S. at 303). With this decision,

> *Possibly the most basic right for prisoners is access to the courts.*

Congress shall make no law respecting an establishment of religion, or prohibiting the free exercise thereof....

First Amendment to the U.S. Constitution

the Court understands that the First Amendment gives all people the absolute right to whatever religious beliefs they wish but not necessarily to every action they may want to carry out. The most frequent reason for limiting an inmate's religious freedom has been the duty of prison officials to maintain security within an institution. A clear example of this is found in aspects of the Black Muslims' fight for recognition and rights in prisons and jails.

Smith (1993) highlights court decisions beginning in the 1960s that allowed restrictions on the freedom of the Nation of Islam (Black Muslims) to practice their religion. Prison officials readily acknowledge that Black Muslims were not afforded the same opportunity to practice their religion as were followers of more traditional faiths. But, the officials argued, the Black Muslims presented security problems that other religions did not present, and, as a result, the officials felt restrictions were proper. For example, the California Supreme Court (*In re Ferguson* 1961) said prison authorities were allowed to prohibit Black Muslims from worshiping and from studying church literature because the Muslims' philosophy and assertive behavior threatened the correctional institution (Smith 1993).

With the *Cooper* v. *Pate* decision (discussed earlier under the Civil Rights Act), Black Muslims began having some success in gaining privileges similar to those granted to the more traditional religions. And in a federal district court decision (*Northern* v. *Nelson* 1970), the court held that the prison library was obliged to make copies of the Qur'an available and that prisoners must be allowed to receive *Muhammad Speaks* unless it could be clearly demonstrated that a particular issue would substantially disrupt prison discipline.

The requirement that prison officials must prove that an inmate's religious freedom threatens prison security and must be restricted continues in more recent court decisions. In *O'Lone* v. *Estate of Shabazz* (1987), the court heard arguments on a New Jersey prison policy that prevented Muslim inmates from attending weekly congregational service (*Jumu'ah*). The Muslim prisoners argued that the service was central to the observation of the Muslim faith and that their participation was a necessary component to their freedom of religion. Muslim inmates with work assignments outside the prison's main buildings were unable to return for the Friday afternoon service. Seeking alternatives that would allow them to attend the services without missing any work hours, the inmates asked to be placed on inside work detail or be given substitute weekend tasks. The prison rejected these proposals as unacceptable given scarce prison personnel and potential security problems. The court, although agreeing that *Jumu'ah* was of central importance to the Islamic faith, said the prison policy did not violate the inmates' constitutional rights because the policy was reasonably related to **legitimate penological interests**—that is, rather than being arbitrary or developed without any appreciation of the importance of the services to Muslims, the policy was established out of concern for prison order and security.

The Turner v. Safley Standards

Reference to legitimate penological interests in the *O'Lone* v. *Estate of Shabazz* is of particular importance in understanding contemporary court decisions on prisoners' rights. In its 1987 *Turner* v. *Safley* decision (made one week before *O'Lone* v. *Estate of Shabazz*), the U.S. Supreme Court laid out four factors to be considered when deciding if a prison regulation that interferes with a prisoner's constitutional rights is a valid policy:

1. Does the regulation have a valid, rational connection to a legitimate governmental interest?

the First Amendment gives all people the absolute right to whatever religious beliefs they wish but not necessarily to every action they may want to carry out

Think About It...

Since its passage by Congress in 2000, the Religious Land Use and Institutionalized Persons Act (RLUIPA) has been the basis for many prison lawsuits related to prisoners' religious rights. The RLUIPA requires states to allow prisoners to practice their religious beliefs unless those officials can show that restricting religious practices is both necessary for an important and legitimate goal (security, for example) and that it is the least restrictive way they can achieve that goal. More states are now allowing sweat lodges, which are an important aspect of Native American spirituality. What type of religious practices do you think are probably allowed in most prisons? What do you suppose are some that could be legitimately disallowed?

Source: James Estrinn/Redux Pictures

Because prison officials are obliged to maintain security and discipline within the institution, prison officials may have to occasionally restrict what would otherwise be a constitutionally protected right of prisoners.

2. Do inmates have available alternate means to exercise the asserted right?

3. How would accommodation of the right affect correctional officers, inmates, and prison resources?

4. Are there ready alternatives to the regulation?

The importance of *Turner* is noted by del Carmen, Ritter, and Witt (2005), who point out that the ruling provides a single test (that is, is the restriction reasonably related to legitimate penological interests?) for responding to prisoner complaints and gives prison officials more power and authority in prison administration. Because prison officials are obliged to maintain security and discipline within the institution (making those things legitimate penological interests), prison officials may have to occasionally restrict what would otherwise be a constitutionally protected right of prisoners. As a result, when prison authorities can show that such restrictions are necessary for security and disciplinary reasons, the courts will typically approve the prison policy under the *Turner* v. *Safley* standards.

Using those standards, courts have restricted publications coming into a prison when the warden determines them to be detrimental to the security, good order, or discipline of the institution (*Thornburgh* v. *Abbott* 1989; *Beard* v. *Banks* 2006); restricted treating a prisoner with antipsychotic drugs against his or her will and without a judicial hearing (*Washington* v. *Harper* 1990); and placed restrictions on prison visitations (*Overton* v. *Bazetta*, 2003) and other aspects of life in prison.

▶ Limiting Inmate Litigation

By the mid-1990s, prison and jail inmates were bringing annually to federal court more than 40,000 new lawsuits challenging the conditions of their confinement. The cases were noteworthy for their sheer number and for being the federal court case type with the lowest plaintiff win rate. These statistics highlight two qualities long associated with prisoner lawsuits: their volume and the low rate of plaintiffs' success (Ostrom, Hanson, & Cheesman II 2003; Schlanger 2003).

Many of the lawsuits were filed at taxpayer expense because the prisoners claimed they lacked funds to pay filing fees (that is, they took *in forma pauperis* status). The nature of many of the lawsuits, their growing number, the increasing burden they placed on federal courts, and the expense to taxpayers having to support the judicial system's handling of the

Three PLRA provisions affecting prisoner litigation may be summarized as follows:

1. *Frequent filer provision:* To discourage prisoners from filing meritless lawsuits *in forma pauperis*, inmates must pay the full $150 fee (and costs, where applicable) when filing a complaint, or they must make an initial down payment followed by periodic installment payments. A truly indigent prisoner can still file his or her claim or appeal without paying the fee, but he or she may accumulate a substantial bill over time.

2. *Three-strikes provision:* To keep prisoners from filing meritless claims, indigent prisoners are prohibited from filing new lawsuits when they have previously filed three or more actions that were dismissed as frivolous or malicious. That provision is waived if there is an immediate threat of physical harm.

3. *Exhausted remedies provision:* Inmates must exhaust all available administrative remedies through the inmate grievance systems at their place of confinement before filing a complaint.

cases resulted in strong public opinion for reform.

Congress's response to the public outcry was the **Prison Litigation Reform Act (PLRA)**. The act attempted to limit the ability of prisoners to complain about conditions of their confinement or alleging violation of their constitutional rights. That goal was to be achieved by discouraging *in forma pauperis* lawsuits (frequent filer provision), reducing meritless claims (three-strikes provision), and requiring inmates to first use the prison's grievance procedures (exhausted remedies provision).

LEARNING OUTCOMES 3 Describe how inmate litigation is limited.

GLOSSARY

Prison Litigation Reform Act (PLRA) Intended to reduce the volume of prisoner litigation and to improve the merit of filed claims, including limiting nongovernmental organizations to legally challenge prison conditions and automatically terminates court orders after two years regardless of compliance.

With these provisions, the PLRA was intended to reduce the volume of prisoner litigation and to improve the merit of those claims that are filed. Research indicates it has been successful at both, with most studies concluding that the PLRA has produced a statistically significant decrease in both the volume and trend of Section 1983 lawsuits since its passage. Similarly, research on the "more meritorious" question suggests the PLRA has weeded out the more frivolous cases (Cheesman II, Ostrom, & Hanson 2004; Ostrom et al. 2003; Schlanger 2003).

▶ Civil Disabilities and Other Postconviction Sanctions

Walter Mosley's fictional character, Socrates Fortlow, is an ex-con trying to readjust to life on the streets. His sentiment expressed in the following quote is shared by many released inmates who find that many opportunities remain blocked. In many jurisdictions, persons convicted of a felony lose some of their civil rights, meaning that they are not legally full citizens even after finishing their sentence. That status hinders full

1. cannot be evaluated as to their effectiveness, impact, or even how they are implemented.
2. typically take effect outside of the traditional sentencing framework. That is, rather than being part of a sentence, they are collateral consequences of a sentence.
3. are often created without public debate and typically remain unknown to the public.

"Just 'cause they let you outta prison that don't mean you're free."

—*Socrates Fortlow (in Walter Mosley's Walkin' the Dog)*

reintegration and contributes to recidivism. The sanctions imposed on convicted felons after serving time are discussed in this section. These sanctions are defined as "civil" rather than criminal in nature and as "disabilities" rather than punishments.

Under early English common law, a convicted offender might, in addition to his sentence, lose all his civil rights and have to forfeit his property. As a result of this **civil death** sanction, offenders forfeited all rights and privileges of citizenship, including things such as the right to enter into a contract (even marriage) or the right to sue. They were, in other words, civilly dead. Today, criminal offenders are more likely to suffer **civil disabilities**—that is, partial rather than absolute loss of civil rights—and, in this sense, are more civilly disabled than civilly dead. States and the federal government impose these civil disabilities in ways that can affect offenders both during incarceration and after release. The disabilities that continue to affect the offender after release from prison are the concern of this section.

Invisible Punishments

We typically think of punishments as being rather obvious—certainly to the person being punished, but also to others in society. The person who has been fined, required to report to a probation officer, or placed in jail or prison certainly considers his or her punishment to be quite obvious. The punishments are also made visible to anyone else who is interested enough to find out what punishments were imposed in a particular case.

TABLE 11.3	**Examples of Invisible Punishments.**
Welfare benefits	The welfare reform package passed by Congress in 1996 included a lifetime ban on receiving welfare and food stamp benefits for anyone convicted of any federal or state felony drug offense (for example, involving the use or sale of drugs). Congressional proponents of the ban argued that the government should neither feel nor have an obligation to support drug offenders—especially when the welfare benefits could be used to support drug habits.
	The bans on welfare benefits have had an especially harsh impact on women of color convicted on drug offenses. Critics of the ban argue that loss of welfare benefits makes it difficult for women to become self-sufficient, provide for their children, and be active participants in their community. Low-income women and their children are hindered in their ability to move out of poverty and as a result can increase child welfare caseloads.
Public housing	Federal laws passed in the late 1990s allow public housing agencies to deny housing to anyone who had engaged in drug-related or violent criminal activity, or other criminal activity that would adversely affect the health, safety, and enjoyment of the premises of others. A tenant and/or a tenant's visitor who possesses or uses drugs on the premises is a basis for eviction from public housing. Persons convicted of drug offenses who can show they have been rehabilitated can reapply for housing after a three-year waiting period.
Student loans	People convicted of drug offenses while enrolled in school and while receiving federal financial assistance become ineligible for federal student loans, grants, and work assistance unless they complete a treatment program. The length of ban depends on the conviction and evidence of rehabilitation.

DISCUSS *Which of these bans do you support? Why or why not? What punishment philosophy do you feel these bans are trying to accomplish? Do you think the ban is successful in helping to achieve that penal goal?*

Depending on the state, a person with a felony conviction could be prohibited from getting (or could have revoked or suspended) a license or permit to engage in certain occupations. Examples of occupations that may require a license or permit—again, depending on the state, include the following:

- Acupuncturists
- Bar tenders and managers
- Barber/Beautician
- Construction contractors
- Hearing aid dealers

- Horse and dog racetrack employees
- Insurance sales people
- Interior designers
- Labor union officers
- Nurses

- Private detectives
- Real estate appraisers or brokers
- Security guards
- Social workers

When a state places restrictions on entering or continuing in certain occupations as the result of a felony conviction, the restriction could be permanent or time-restricted (for example, the prohibition is lifted five or ten years after the felony conviction).

DISCUSS *What do you suppose are some reasons for preventing convicted felons from employment in these areas? What other types of occupations do you suspect may be prohibited for convicted felons in some states? How would you distinguish those occupations from which a convicted felon should be forever banned from those occupations that they could engage in after a certain number of years?*

---

invisible punishments have accompanying or secondary consequences beyond the actual sentence that was imposed.

LEARNING OUTCOMES 4 Summarize the issues associated with the loss of civil rights.

GLOSSARY

civil death Convicted offenders forfeit all rights and privileges of citizenship, including things such as the right to enter into a contract or the right to sue.

civil disabilities Convicted offenders suffer a partial, rather than an absolute, loss of civil rights because of a criminal conviction.

invisible punishments Sanctions operating mostly beyond public view, yet having very serious, adverse consequences for the individuals affected.

They could see it or hear about it through various media or might even look it up in court records. But oftentimes there are other punishments accompanying those visible ones that surprise even the offender. Did the convicted burglar realize that even after completing his sentence he will not be able to vote? Did the convicted drug distributor know that she may not be able to receive welfare or nutrition assistance as a result of that conviction? Possibly even more surprised may be the teenage daughter of that convicted drug distributor upon hearing that her mother may not be allowed to live in public housing—leaving the daughter to wonder where she and her family will live.

Those examples of disenfranchisement (loss of the right to vote), being prohibited from receiving welfare, and not being able to live in public housing are examples of sanctions that Travis has termed **invisible punishments** (2002) because they operate mostly beyond public view, yet have very serious, adverse consequences for the individuals affected.

Invisible punishments are especially important because they add **collateral consequences** to the sentence. This means the invisible punishments have accompanying or secondary consequences beyond the actual sentence that was imposed. Those collateral effects tend to increase the negative consequences of a criminal conviction and they can be described as falling into three categories (Periman 2007):

1. Impaired access to, or enjoyment of, the ordinary rights and benefits associated with citizenship or residence (for example, not being allowed to vote, losing your driver's license, or having restriction placed on where you can live)

2. Impaired economic opportunity, primarily through reduction of the range of available employment (for example, not being allowed to get a beautician's license or sell insurance)

3. Increased severity of sanctions in any subsequent criminal proceeding brought against the offender (for example, in some states a prior felony conviction can trigger forfeiture of a car or boat that is used in a subsequent crime involving alcohol)

Two specific types of invisible punishments with far-reaching collateral consequences are sex offender registration and notification laws and the disenfranchisement of felons. We will take a closer look at each of these.

Sex Offender Registration, Notification, and Residence Restriction Laws

A particularly controversial topic related to restrictions placed on the ordinary rights of residency is linked to a specific type of crime—sex offenses. Collateral consequences of a sex offense conviction include **sex offender registration laws** and **public notification laws**. The former requires persons convicted of sex offenses to register in a community, even after they have completed their sentence for that conviction. The notification laws are an additional provision that requires the public be notified of the name and location of certain sex offenders in the community.

Do Notification Laws Encourage Residents to Modify Their Behavior?

Research on how community notification laws affect community members has consistently found that although the laws increase reported fear among residents, they have strong public support and are seen as providing an important public service. However, the research also shows that most residents do not access the available community notification information (Bandy 2011). In addition, the findings are mixed as to whether notification prompts protective behavior. This point is important because an assumption of notification laws is that by providing people with knowledge about a person who poses a potential threat to their safety, they will change their behavior to lessen that risk.

Bandy (2011) studied that assumption with research in Minneapolis. Her results were consistent with other studies that found no statistically significant relationship between receiving notification about a high-risk sex offender and the adoption of self-protective behaviors.

However, Bandy also found that parents who received information about a high-risk offender did adopt more protective behaviors to protect their children against victimization than did parents who had not received notification. So, although community members strongly support notification laws and report feeling safer as a result of knowing where sex offenders live, they engage in few protective behaviors as a result of the notification—except being slightly more likely to take protective action on behalf of their children (Levenson 2011).

DISCUSS *Since most child sexual abuse victims know their perpetrator, and since most offenders are not subject to notification laws, what do you think is gained by notification? What are some examples of protective behaviors that parents may adopt? Will those behaviors realistically protect their children from the people most likely to victimize them?*

14 By July 2011, only fourteen states had been identified by the Justice Department as having substantially implemented SORNA

Under the federal Sex Offender Registration and Notification Act (SORNA), all U.S. jurisdictions are required to pass registration and notification laws that conform to federal minimum standards or risk a penalty in receiving federal grants. SORNA's goal is to strengthen the nationwide network of sex offender registration and notification programs by (Office of Justice Programs 2011b)

- Extending the jurisdictions in which registration is required beyond the 50 states, the District of Columbia, and the principal U.S. territories, to also include federally recognized Indian tribes

- Incorporating a more comprehensive group of sex offenders and sex offenses for which registration is required

- Requiring registered sex offenders to register and keep their registration current in each jurisdiction in which they reside, work, or go to school

- Requiring sex offenders to provide more extensive registration information

- Requiring sex offenders to make periodic in-person appearances to verify and update their registration information

- Expanding the amount of information available to the public regarding registered sex offenders

- Making changes in the required minimum duration of registration for sex offenders

Although all states and the District of Columbia had registration and notification laws before SORNA's passage in 2006, those laws were not necessarily consistent with SORNA's minimum requirements. A 2008 national survey found inconsistencies between the federal mandates and state practices and that there are many barriers preventing states from implementing SORNA (Harris & Lobanov-Rostovsky 2010). By July 2011, only fourteen states had been identified by the Justice Department as having substantially implemented SORNA (Office of Justice Programs 2011a).

Delaware, as a recognized SORNA conformer, provides a good example of a state's sex offender registration and notification law (see the synopsis at City of Newark 2011). Both adults and juveniles convicted of certain sex-related offenses are categorized according their risk assessment with Tier III being high risk, Tier II being moderate risk, and Tier I being low risk. Persons convicted of a defined sex offense must register with the Delaware State Bureau of Identification within seven days of their conviction, change of address, or

Think About It...

Public notification of law breakers is designed to shame offenders and deter against future offending, as demonstrated by judges that order convicted sex offenders to display a sign in their front yard as part of the punishment. Is it sufficient to let people call their local law enforcement agency or check on a website to determine if there are registered sex offenders in their neighborhood, or would it be better to require signs to be posted? What are some of the implications of either approach?

the general assumption is that all sex offenders victimize children and, most likely, children who are strangers to them ... both of those ideas are inaccurate.

upon establishing residency in Delaware. Failure to register is a felony. The community notification aspect of Delaware's law can include any method devised specifically to notify such public facilities as schools, day care, libraries, and members of the public who are likely to encounter a sex offender. Those methods include notification via mail, electronic mail, telephone, newspapers, or door-to-door appearances.

As in many states, Delaware restricts the public's ability to access information about registered sex offenders according to the perceived risk presented by the offender to the public. For both Tier II and Tier III sex offenders, local law enforcement must make searchable records (for example, the person's name, address, physical description, and conviction information) available to the public. For Tier II offenders, local law enforcement may also use community notification efforts, but for Tier III offenders community notification must be provided—including door-to-door notification in the neighborhood where the offender resides, works, or attends school.

In addition to the registration and notification laws, sex offenders are also subject to **residence restriction laws** that may require them to live in certain areas or restrict them from living in other areas. Tewksbury (2011) points out that limits on where registered sex offenders may live have been widely shown to impose negative consequences on both offenders and their families. For example, registered sex offenders end up being concentrated in either very dense, socially disorganized communities or in rural communities lacking employment, treatment, and transportation options. Despite those negative consequences, residential restrictions are increasingly common across the nation.

Presumably, if residence restriction laws contributed to public safety, the negative consequences on the offenders would not be of much concern. However, existing research suggests residential restrictions are likely to contribute very little to public safety. This is probably because of the faulty assumptions upon which residence restriction laws are based. For example, the general assumption is that all sex offenders victimize children and, most likely, children who are strangers to them. Tewksbury (2011) points out that both of those ideas are inaccurate. In addition, residence restrictions assume that if offenders live farther away from schools, day cares, and so on, they are unable or unlikely to access those facilities. That, of course, ignores the point that motivated offenders can use public transportation. When the proof of negative consequences to offenders and their families are set against the unproven assumptions that residence restrictions increase public safety, an increasing number of scholars and policy makers question the need for the residence restriction laws.

Civil Disenfranchisement

Another controversial loss that affects essentially all felons is **civil disenfranchisement**, or the loss of the right to vote. A person's eligibility to vote is regulated at the state level—even for national elections. The U.S. Constitution prohibits any state from denying the right to vote based on grounds of race, sex, or age (citizens age 18 and older may vote), but beyond those basic qualifications, eligibility is regulated by each state. Of concern in this section is the ban that some states have imposed on persons convicted of a crime. This is no small group, with some 5.3 million Americans denied the right to vote because of laws disenfranchising people with criminal convictions (Porter 2010). In most cases those refer to felony convictions—and that is the general reference here—but it is important to note that ten states and the District of Columbia also restrict some people with a misdemeanor conviction from voting (those states are listed at ProCon.org 2010, April 8).

A state-by-state breakdown of the provisions (see Table 11.4) shows that only two states (Maine and Vermont) do not disenfranchise convicted felons. Of the 12 most restrictive states, some will restore this right automatically for some offenders or have provisions allowing some offenders to apply for re-enfranchisement.

Supporters of disenfranchisement offer several reasons for restricting a convicted felon from voting. Uggen, Behrens, and Manza (2005) discuss the primary ones as falling into the categories of retribution, deterrence, incapacitation, and rehabilitation. Felon disenfranchisement is retributive to the extent that it provides a sense of just deserts. But, as Uggen et al. note, a blanket disenfranchisement of all people convicted of felonies calls into question the proportionality of the punishment—especially when that disenfranchisement is permanent.

5.3M some 5.3 million Americans are denied the right to vote because of laws disenfranchising people with criminal convictions

> "At a minimum, proponents of any restrictive policy in a modern democracy must explain how the proposed exclusion would strengthen our democracy and protect the public good. Advocates of disenfranchisement fail that test."
>
> Alec C. Ewald,
> Assistant Professor of Political Science
> at the University of Vermont

> "Individuals who have shown that they are unwilling to follow the law cannot claim the right to make laws for the rest of us ... We have certain minimum standards of trustworthiness before we let people participate in the serious business of self-government, and people who commit serious crimes don't meet those standards."
>
> Roger Clegg, JD,
> President and General Counsel
> at the Center for Equal Opportunity

FIGURE 11.1 **The Right to Vote Should Automatically Be Restored upon Release from Prison.**
Quote sources: http://felonvoting.procon.org/view.answers.php?questionID=001319 (ProCon.org 2009, January 23)

DISCUSS *What is your position on automatic restoration of voting rights to felons? If you agree that persons who have been convicted of a felony should have their voting rights restored, do you also agree that prisoners should be allowed to vote while in prison? Explain your responses.*

An argument for any deterrent effect in disenfranchisement relies on a belief that if people attach great significance to the right to vote they will not commit another crime after having lost the right to vote while under a criminal sentence (specific deterrence) or will refrain from committing a crime for fear of losing that right (general deterrence). This point is supported by comments from George Steinbrenner, former owner of the New York Yankees baseball team. As a result of his conviction for making an illegal campaign contribution to Richard Nixon's 1972 reelection campaign, Steinbrenner lost his right to vote. Although his voting rights were restored by a pardon from President Reagan, Steinbrenner was still commenting some 30 years later about the pain caused him by the disenfranchisement (Manza & Uggen 2006, 5). However, for most people losing the right to vote would likely not be the determining factor in whether they commit a crime.

It is difficult to justify felon disenfranchisement on the basis of incapacitation, since removing the right to vote cannot

33% only 33 percent of the respondents thought people in prison should be allowed to vote, but 80 percent supported the right to vote for persons convicted of a crime who have served their entire sentence

prevent people from committing other crimes unrelated to voting. Even for the few convicted of such crimes as electoral fraud, the ability of felon disenfranchisement to prevent repeat offending is questionable. In short, disenfranchisement prevents political participation, but not criminal activity.

The idea that disenfranchisement might be rehabilitative seems counterintuitive. Presumably, disenfranchisement could be rehabilitative if reenfranchisement was a reward for good behavior; but restoration of voting rights is rarely conditioned on good behavior. Instead, it is triggered automatically when a sentence is completed or a waiting period has passed. More likely, restricting voting rights hinders rehabilitative efforts. As Manza and his colleagues suggest, it is more plausible that participation in this fundamental act of citizenship may foster respect for laws and the institutions that make and enforce them (2006). That point is not farfetched, since at least one study has shown that among people with an arrest history about 27 percent of nonvoters were rearrested compared to 12 percent of voters in the sample (Manza & Uggen 2006, 312). Possibly there is at least a correlation between voting and recidivism among people who have had some official contact with the criminal justice system.

Other justifications for disenfranchisement have been offered, such as the idea that allowing criminals to vote dilutes the votes of law-abiding citizens and the suggestion that voting criminals might band together to oust government officials who are tough on crime. But those arguments are less mainstream than the others. Public opinion actually seems to favor restoring voting rights—at least for some. A Harris Interactive Poll found that only 33 percent of the respondents thought people in prison should be allowed to vote, but 80 percent supported the right to vote for persons convicted of a crime who have served their entire sentence and are now living in the community (ProCon.org 2009, April 13).

An argument against disenfranchisement that is considered to be especially persuasive by those favoring voting rights is that the policy is racially discriminatory. Although felon disenfranchisement laws are race neutral on their face, their origins are tainted. After ratification of the Fifteenth Amendment (giving blacks the right to vote), many states specifically considered whether to retain the disenfranchisement of felons. Several southern state legislatures kept the felon restriction as one of several tools to lessen the ability of blacks to exercise their new right (Fellner & Mauer 1998). A study of historical changes to state felon disenfranchisement laws concluded that states with greater non-white prison populations have been more likely to ban convicted felons from voting than states with proportionally fewer non-whites in the criminal justice system (Behrens, Uggen, & Manza 2003, 596). Supporters of disenfranchisement respond to these charges with arguments that the uneven representation of black Americans among the disenfranchised felons is a result of their disproportionate representation among persons committing felonies and not a result of racial discrimination in the laws themselves.

TABLE 11.4 | State Felon Voting Laws *(Current as of April 08, 2010).*

The legal ability of people with felony convictions to vote varies from state to state. Some states allow felons to vote from prison while other states permanently ban felons from voting even after being released from prison, parole, and probation, and having paid all their fines. This table shows the restrictions found in each state and the District of Columbia.

People with felony convictions are barred from voting in these states if they are	Incarcerated, on parole, or on probation[i]	Incarcerated, on parole, or on probation[ii]	Incarcerated or on parole[iii]	Incarcerated[iv]
	12 states	**18 states**	**5 states**	**13 states & DC**
1. Alabama	✔			
2. Alaska		✔		
3. Arizona	✔			
4. Arkansas		✔		
5. California			✔	
6. Colorado			✔	
7. Connecticut			✔	
8. District of Columbia				✔
9. Delaware	✔			
10. Florida	✔			
11. Georgia		✔		
12. Hawaii				✔
13. Idaho		✔		
14. Illinois				✔
15. Indiana				✔
16. Iowa		✔		
17. Kansas		✔		
18. Kentucky	✔			
19. Louisiana		✔		
20. Maine		NO RESTRICTIONS		
21. Maryland		✔		
22. Massachusetts				✔
23. Michigan				✔
24. Minnesota		✔		
25. Mississippi	✔			
26. Missouri		✔		

People with felony convictions are barred from voting in these states if they are	Incarcerated, on parole, or on probation[i]	Incarcerated, on parole, or on probation[ii]	Incarcerated or on parole[iii]	Incarcerated[iv]
	12 states	18 states	5 states	13 states & DC
27. Montana				✔
28. Nebraska	✔			
29. Nevada	✔			
30. New Hampshire				✔
31. New Jersey		✔		
32. New Mexico		✔		
33. New York			✔	
34. North Carolina		✔		
35. North Dakota				✔
36. Ohio				✔
37. Oklahoma		✔		
38. Oregon				✔
39. Pennsylvania				✔
40. Rhode Island				✔
41. South Carolina		✔		
42. South Dakota			✔	
43. Tennessee	✔			
44. Texas		✔		
45. Utah				✔
46. Vermont	NO RESTRICTIONS			
47. Virginia	✔			
48. Washington	✔			
49. West Virginia		✔		
50. Wisconsin		✔		
51. Wyoming	✔			

Source: Reprinted with permission of ProCon.org. "State Felon Voting Laws" chart available at http://www.felonvoting.procon.org.

[i] The states in this column are considered the most restrictive. In some of these states the right to vote is lost permanently. Some felons may vote depending on the crime committed, date of the offense, and other variables. For details see http://felonvoting.procon.org/view.resource.php?resourceID=000286.

[ii] Although similar to the column at the left, these states are considered less restrictive because people with felony convictions may vote upon completion of all supervised release.

[iii] People with felony convictions may vote upon completion of parole.

[iv] People with felony convictions may vote upon release from prison.

LEARNING
OUTCOMES
5

Explain procedures
by which civil rights
can be restored.

GLOSSARY

certificate of rehabilitation
Generic term for an official recognition that a criminal offender has shown reliability and good character over time and deserves to regain lost civil rights.

▶ Restoring Civil Rights Following a Conviction

Every U.S. jurisdiction has some legal mechanism for mitigating or avoiding the collateral consequences of a felony conviction, but the ways in which that can be accomplished vary considerably across the country. Love (2006) provides the best attempt at such a source with her survey of the legal mechanisms available in each state for avoiding or mitigating collateral penalties and disabilities accompanying a criminal conviction. In some jurisdictions for some offenses, restoration of rights is automatic after sentence completion or some specific time period following sentence completion. For example, the right to vote is routinely restored in most states upon completing the court-imposed sentence (Love 2005). When restoration is not automatic, it is most often the result of a pardon, an expungement or sealing of records, or limits on having a criminal conviction being a criterion for restricting employment or licensing.

Although pardon, expungement, and laws prohibiting employment discrimination based on a criminal conviction are more well-known, Love (2006, October 1) identifies other interesting mechanisms that are used in some states. For example, six states (California, Connecticut, Illinois, Nevada, New Jersey, and New York) offer administrative **certificates of rehabilitation** (a generic term for an official recognition that a criminal offender has shown reliability and good character over time and deserves to regain lost civil rights) that may restore some or all legal rights and privileges. New York's version is especially unique. Two types of certificates are offered in New York: a certificate of relief from disabilities (CRD) and a certificate of good conduct (CGC). They differ primarily in their eligibility requirements with the CRD available to misdemeanants and first-time felons and the CGC available to repeat offenders. Both certificates have a similar legal effect in that they create a presumption of rehabilitation that must be considered by employers and licensing boards.

Despite their availability, few offenders take advantage of—or may even be aware of—these remedies to the collateral consequences of a criminal conviction. When noting the very complex and unclear procedures facing offenders who wish to put their criminal past behind them, Love comments that, "As a practical matter, in most jurisdictions people convicted of a crime have no hope of ever being able to fully discharge their debt to society" (2005).

WAYS CIVIL RIGHTS MIGHT BE RESTORED WHEN NOT DONE AUTOMATICALLY

1. Executive pardon power. In many U.S. jurisdictions, an executive pardon by the state's governor or an appointed board is the only way civil disabilities can be mitigated. However, although it remains the most common relief mechanism across the country, the pardon is used less and less frequently. Love (2005) notes that in at least a dozen states where a governor's pardon is the only way to mitigate collateral disabilities, the governor has not granted pardons with any regularity. That reluctance may result from perceived political troubles that could result from granting a pardon (or too many pardons). For example, Love found only 13 states where more than a handful of pardons have been granted each year since 1995.

2. Judicial expungement, sealing, or setting aside of adult felony convictions. Love (2005, 2006, October 1) found several states (Arizona, Kansas, Massachusetts, Nevada, New Hampshire, Oregon, Utah, and Washington) where this procedure is available through the courts but it seems widely used in those jurisdictions. In some of these states the option is available only to first offenders or to

misdemeanants. Serious or violent offenders are almost always ineligible for this method. When a conviction has been expunged or sealed, the person is frequently able to deny their conviction when, for example, completing employment forms. However, the conviction normally remains available for law enforcement purposes. Versions of expungement or sealing are also available in Michigan, New Jersey, Ohio, and Rhode Island (Love 2006, October 1).

3. Laws limiting consideration of conviction in employment and licensing. Thirty-three states have laws that attempt to limit consideration of conviction when a person is applying for employment and/or licensing. These "nondiscrimination" laws might, for example, allow disqualification because of a criminal conviction only if the criminal offense is directly or substantially related to the employment or license sought. Love (2005) points out that many states have no mechanism for enforcement of the provision, so it is difficult to determine how effective the laws are in discouraging employers from hiring or firing based on knowledge of a conviction.

Proof of Rehabilitation

In 2010, reporter Dawn Turner Trice brought Darrell Langdon's story to *Chicago Tribune* readers (2010, July 29, 2010, September 26). It is a compelling story of a man who made a mistake two decades earlier and worked hard to pay his debt to society and to become a productive, law-abiding citizen. His success in doing so was even formally acknowledged by a court-granted Certificate of Good Conduct that attests to a person's rehabilitation.

Langdon had been convicted of possessing a half gram of cocaine in 1985 and he was sentenced to serve six months on probation and pay a $100 fine. At the time of his conviction he worked for the Chicago Public Schools (a job he was allowed to keep after his conviction) until 1995 when he was laid off during a major restructuring. He worked as a mortgage broker and also as a building engineer until 2008 when he applied for another job with Chicago Public Schools (CPS). His application was denied because the Illinois School Code prohibits persons with records such as Langdon from working in public schools. Langdon told Trice that he had been sober since 1988, reared two sons as a single parent, and has a very good work history since the conviction.

1. A CPS spokesperson said "This individual sounds like he did everything he should be doing to rehabilitate himself into professional and private community. We're glad to see that, but the delicate balance is that we need to ensure we're hiring people who won't put our children in jeopardy" (quoted in Trice 2010, July 29). What things could CPS or any other workplace use to determine whether someone is rehabilitated and safe to have work around children?

2. In 2010, under a newly revised law, Langdon applied for a Certificate of Good Conduct that lifts statutory barriers to employment for persons with lower-grade felony convictions. That certificate allowed CPS to hire Langdon and, after an initial denial, they did so under new rules established in response to Langdon's case. Pardon and expungement of adult criminal records is becoming increasingly rare. *Do you think certificates of rehabilitation will be the main process by which civil rights are restored in the future? What do you see as some problems and benefits of this procedure?*

Source: trekandshoot/Shutterstock.com

LEARNING OUTCOMES 1

Outline the development and sources of prisoners' rights.

Rather than taking an extreme position of constitutional rights being either totally lost or all retained upon entering prison, the courts have tried to determine what rights can be compatible with the goals of prison administration. When making that determination, courts turn to a variety of sources including state constitutions and laws passed by federal and state legislators; but prisoners' rights are primarily found in the U.S. Constitution, including the Bill of Rights, and the Civil Rights Act.

1. Identify and explain at least three important prisoners' rights cases.

2. How would you describe to a layperson what is meant by the phrase "cruel and unusual punishment"?

3. Explain the Fourteenth Amendment's due process clause and its equal protection clause. Give examples of how both have been used in prisoners' rights cases.

4. What are civil rights and how do they relate to prisoner claims?

rights-are-retained Argues that prisoners keep all the rights of an ordinary citizen, except those that are expressly or by necessity taken away from them by law.

rights-are-lost Argues that prisoners are wholly without rights except those expressly conferred by law or necessity.

writ of *habeas corpus* Judicial mandate to a prison official ordering that an inmate be brought to the court in order to determine the legality of the prisoner's detention.

***ex post facto* law** A law imposing a greater punishment for a crime than was allowed when the crime was committed.

incorporation Legal theory arguing that all provisions of the Bill of Rights are made applicable to the states through the due process clause.

due process clause That section of the Fourteenth Amendment requiring all states to abide by the Bill of Rights when depriving a person of life, liberty, or property.

equal protection clause That section of the Fourteenth Amendment prohibiting any state from denying equal protection of the law to persons within its jurisdiction.

Section 1983 claim A claim brought under the authority of U.S. Code Title 42, Section 1983 that civil rights have been violated.

LEARNING OUTCOMES 2

Describe types of inmate lawsuits using access to courts and issues of religion as examples.

Prisoners have claimed violations of many types of constitutional rights linked to such things as conditions of their confinement, lack of attention to medical needs, violation of privacy rights, and others. Of the types of lawsuits filed, ones related to prisoner access to courts is particularly important because without that access prisoners would not be able to have a hearing on any of their other claims. Another important type of inmate lawsuit is when prisoners claim violation of the ability to practice their religion. Courts have responded differently over the years to these and the other inmate claims as they moved from an early "hands-off" position that essentially let prison officials make decisions without interference from the courts to a period when the courts were very much involved in deciding how prisons should operate to a current position wherein the courts are more likely to defer to the reasonable assessment of prison officials as to what rights may require violation.

1. Why is access to courts such an important right for prisoners?

2. Summarize what steps the courts require prison officials to take so that prisoners have access to courts.

3. List and explain the three eras of judicial involvement in prison administration.

4. Distinguish the freedom to believe and the freedom to practice as they relate to freedom of religion. Which one can prison officials restrict? Why that one and not the other?

5. Explain the meaning and importance of the phrase "legitimate penological interests."

legitimate penological interests Standard used by courts to determine whether a prison policy was developed in an arbitrary manner or out of concern for prison order and security.

Describe how inmate litigation is limited.

In an attempt to limit what was becoming a very large number of inmate lawsuits, Congress passed the Prison Litigation Reform Act (PLRA) in 1995. That Act was intended to reduce the volume of prisoner litigation and improve the merit of those claims that are filed. Indications are that the Act has succeeded at both.

1. What do you think would be examples of frivolous lawsuits that prisoners might file? Why would prisoners file such lawsuits knowing that they will likely be tossed out by the courts?

2. Explain the frequent-filer provision of the PLRA. Do you think this presents desirable and appropriate restrictions? Why or why not?

3. Explain the three-strikes provision of the PLRA. Do you think this presents desirable and appropriate restrictions? Why or why not?

4. Explain the exhausted remedies provision of the PLRA. Do you think this presents desirable and appropriate restrictions? Why or why not?

Prison Litigation Reform Act (PLRA) Intended to reduce the volume of prisoner litigation and to improve the merit of filed claims, including limiting nongovernmental organizations to legally challenge prison conditions and automatically terminates court orders after two years regardless of compliance.

Summarize the issues associated with the loss of civil rights.

A criminal conviction (usually a felony, but sometimes a misdemeanor) can result in the loss of certain rights that are typically associated with full citizenship. Depending on the jurisdiction, these lost civil rights might include the ability to vote, serve on a jury, receive welfare benefits, or engage in certain occupations. Because these sanctions are less obvious than the actual sentence an offender receives they have been called invisible punishments and are important because of the collateral consequences they add to the sentence. Examples of those invisible punishments and their collateral consequences are sex offender registration and notification laws and the disenfranchisement of felons.

1. Explain what is meant by the text book quote "Just 'cause they let you outta prison that don't mean you're free."

2. Distinguish between civil death and civil disabilities.

3. What is meant by the concept of invisible punishments?

4. Should defendants be told of collateral consequences associated with a felony conviction—much like suspects are informed of their rights when Miranda warnings are read? Why or why not?

5. Distinguish between sex offender registration laws and public notification laws.

6. What are some reasons offered in support of restricting convicted felons from voting? Which, if any, do you find persuasive?

7. On what basis do some people claim that felon disenfranchisement laws were and are racially discriminatory?

civil death Convicted offenders forfeit all rights and privileges of citizenship, including things such as the right to enter into a contract or the right to sue.

civil disabilities Convicted offenders suffer a partial, rather than an absolute, loss of civil rights because of a criminal conviction.

invisible punishments Sanctions operating mostly beyond public view, yet having very serious, adverse consequences for the individuals affected.

collateral consequences Secondary consequences beyond the actual sentence that was imposed.

sex offender registration laws Requires persons convicted of sex offenses to register in a community, even after they have completed their sentence for that conviction.

public notification laws Requires the public be notified of the name and location of certain sex offenders in the community.

residence restriction laws Require sex offenders to live in certain areas or restrict them from living in other areas.

civil disenfranchisement The loss of the right to vote due, for example, to a felony conviction.

Explain procedures by which civil rights can be restored.

Although every U.S. jurisdiction has a legal mechanism by which at least some civil rights can be restored after a felony conviction (including automatic restoration), those methods vary across the country. The most popular means are through an executive pardon, an expungement or sealing of records, or placing limits on the extent to which criminal records can be used when making employment or licensing decisions. In addition to those common methods, an increasingly popular technique is to issue some version of a certificate of rehabilitation.

1. Explain how a pardon affects civil rights.

2. Although expunging or sealing of juvenile records is rather commonplace, doing the same with adult records is less common. Why? Do you think the practice should be more widely available for adults who have successfully completed their sentence? Why or why not?

3. Nondiscrimination laws are designed to discourage employers from using an applicant's criminal conviction as the sole criterion for denying employment. Do you think such laws are effective at doing that? Why or why not?

4. Explain the idea behind a certificate of rehabilitation and whether you think it can be an effective way to lessen the negative effect of collateral consequences.

certificate of rehabilitation Generic term for an official recognition that a criminal offender has shown reliability and good character over time and deserves to regain lost civil rights.

MyCJLab

Go to the Chapter 11 section in *MyCJLab* to test your understanding of this chapter, access customized study content, engage in interactive simulations, complete critical thinking and research assignments, and view related online videos.

Additional Links

Visit the ACLU Prisoners' Rights page at **www.aclu.org/prisoners-rights** for news and cases.

Read about the award winning film *Writ Writer* at **www.writwritermovie.com/index.html** for an interesting portrayal of a self-taught jailhouse lawyer who challenged the constitutionality of prison conditions in Texas in the 1960s.

Read about the civil disabilities imposed in your state by visiting the Legal Action Center's roadblocks to reentry page: **www.lac.org/roadblocks-to-reentry/main.php?view=law.**

Get more information about felon disenfranchisement at **www.sentencingproject.org/template/page.cfm?id=133**.

Capital Punishment

"If we are to abolish the death penalty, I should like to see the first step taken by my friends the murderers."

—Alphonse Karr (for the retentionists)

"The death penalty is an excessive and unnecessary punishment that violates the Eighth Amendment."

—Justice Thurgood Marshall (for the abolitionists)

1 Outline the history of capital punishment in the United States.

2 Explain the legal provisions for capital punishment in the United States.

3 Summarize the characteristics of current death-row prisoners.

4 Summarize the arguments for and against the use of the death penalty.

Source: © Presselect/Alamy

LETTING THE MURDER VICTIM'S FAMILY SPEAK

On February 18, 2011, the Lakeland (FL) Ledger read "Jurors Cry as Victim's Son Testifies in Leon Davis Murder Trial." The story went on to explain how several jurors dabbed at tears as 11-year-old Damon Lugo told them how lonely and sad his family is now that his mother is gone. "We were a happy family of four," Damon said. "Now we are a family of three, lonely and sad" (Schottelkotte 2011). Just a few days earlier, the same jury had found Leon Davis, Jr., guilty of murdering Yvonne Bustamante, Damon's mom. The jury was now in the penalty phase and was hearing testimony from both victim and offender family members.

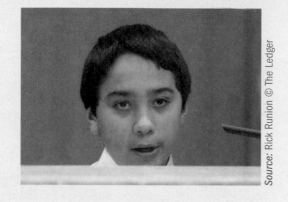

Source: Rick Runion © The Ledger

The opportunity to speak during the penalty phase of a capital trial is provided as way for jurors to hear thoughts and feelings that would not have been allowed during the trial.

The U.S. Supreme Court (*Payne* v. *Tennessee*, 1991) recognized that victims have rights in criminal cases—including the right to explain how a crime has affected their life. In murder cases, the victim's family is allowed to tell about the victim and about the harm caused by the offender. A concern expressed by some is that allowing these victim impact statements in capital cases could arouse the emotions of jurors and bias them in favor of imposing death. A study by Paternoster and Deise (2011) suggests that this concern might be valid. According to their research, when victim impact evidence was used, the research subjects were more likely to have favorable perceptions of the victim and the victim's family and unfavorable perceptions of the offender. Those positive feelings toward the victim and the victim's family were related to a heightened risk of them imposing the death penalty.

DISCUSS If victim impact statements do bias jurors toward imposing death, should they still be allowed? Why?

The topics of capital punishment and the use of the death penalty give rise to some of the most emotional, yet academically interesting, debates of any criminal justice issue. The breadth and depth of issues are too many to tackle here, so we begin with a brief review of the history of capital punishment. Then we consider some of the related legal issues before moving to the characteristics of persons on death row. We conclude with arguments for and against the death penalty.

▶ *Capital Punishment Yesterday and Today*

The history of the death penalty in the United States is best understood by viewing it as two historical periods: the early period prior to 1972 and the modern period from 1972 forward. The distinguishing event was the 1972 United States Supreme Court decision in *Furman* v. *Georgia* that (as we see later) began the modern era of capital punishment. We cover these periods in a brief history of capital punishment.

A Short History of Capital Punishment in the United States

When British settlers came to the new world, they brought with them the practice of capital punishment. It had been a well-established punishment in England and during the sixteenth-century reign of Henry VIII (1509–1547), an estimated 72,000 men and women were executed for a variety of offenses. By the 1700s, more than 200 crimes were punishable by death in Britain, including stealing and cutting down a growing tree. Even into the 1800s there were more than 100 crimes punishable by death (Death Penalty Information Center 2010f; Kronenwetter 1993).

With that heritage, it is not surprising that the American colonies came to rely on capital punishment as well. The first recorded execution in the colonies was in 1608 in the Jamestown Colony of Virginia when Captain George Kendall was executed for being a spy for Spain. The death penalty could also be applied in Virginia during the early 1600s for such minor offenses as stealing grapes, killing chickens, and trading with Indians. In the mid-1600s, the New York Colony punished by death such crimes as striking one's mother or father (Death Penalty Information Center 2010f).

LEARNING OUTCOMES 1 Outline the history of capital punishment in the United States.

By the start of the American Revolution, the death penalty was used in all 13 colonies, with Rhode Island being the only

The history of the death penalty in the United States is best understood by viewing it as two historical periods: the early period prior to 1972 and the modern period from 1972 forward.

First- and second-degree murder are differentiated, with the death penalty increasingly reserved for first-degree.

+

Executions are moved from public locations to jails or prisons in order to avoid disorder caused by the public spectacle.

+

Rather than automatically imposing a death sentence for first-degree murder, it was made an option—typically decided by a jury.

→ Death penalty changes in the nineteenth century

FIGURE 12.1 Factors Influencing Changes in the Death Penalty during the Nineteenth Century.

colony that did not have at least ten crimes punishable by death (ProCon.org 2011). The colonies had fairly similar death statutes that covered arson, piracy, treason, murder, sodomy, burglary, robbery, rape, horse stealing, slave rebellion, and often counterfeiting. Hanging was the usual sentence. But it did not take long before changes began occurring in the death penalty's application.

As explained in Chapter 3, continued reliance on corporal and capital punishment as the primary sanctions for criminal behavior began falling out of favor by the middle to late 1800s. The Pennsylvania Quakers worked to have long-term imprisonment accepted as a humanitarian alternative to the existing punishments and various death penalty abolitionist societies began appearing across the country. Other key changes during the nineteenth century included

DISCUSS *What international and national events may help explain why support for the death penalty was at its lowest level from the late 1950s to the early 1970s (see Figure 12.3)? What might explain its popularity from the late 1980s to the mid-1990s?*

making a distinction between first- and second-degree murder, a discontinuance of public executions, and a movement from mandatory to discretionary capital punishment statutes (Bohm 2003; del Carmen, Vollum, Cheeseman, Frantzen, & San Miguel 2005).

During the first half of the twentieth century, there were increased calls for the death penalty's abolition. However, after a period in the early 1900s, when several states abolished then reinstated capital punishment, there was resurgence in its use from the 1920s to the 1940s. In the 1930s there were more executions in America than there have been in any other decade—averaging 167 executions per year (Bohm 2003). By the 1950s, public sentiment in America—and in many of the allied nations that had fought in World War II—had turned away from the death penalty and the number of executions in the United States dropped dramatically. A Gallup poll in 1966 showed support for the death penalty at only 42 percent—still the lowest level of support found in any Gallup poll since 1937 (see Figure 12.3).

Between 1608 (America's first execution) and 1972, there were more than 14,000 executions in colonial America and the United States. Forty-nine percent of those executed were black, 41 percent were white, and the remainder fell into the other category (Death Penalty Information Center 2010d). In the period from 1930 to 1976, most of those executed were African-Americans (54 percent) and men (99 percent). Executions were typically for murder (86 percent, with blacks accounting for 49 percent of these executions), and 12 percent were for rape in which blacks accounted for 90 percent of the executions (Office of Justice Programs 1978).

African-Americans constituted between 10 and 12 percent of the total U.S. population during the twentieth century. Their 54 percent representation among persons executed in the mid-twentieth century was very lopsided. This disproportionate representation of African-Americans among those executed was one of the factors leading the United States Supreme Court to declare the death penalty unconstitutional in 1972, and that decision marked the end of capital punishment's early period in America.

Capital Punishment in the Modern Era

Specifics of the U.S. Supreme Court decision that marked the beginning of the death penalty's modern era in the United States are covered below in the section on "Capital Punishment and the Law." Suffice it to say that in 1972 the death penalty was placed in a limbo status as states tried to create death penalty statutes that the U.S. Supreme Court would find to be constitutional. Here, as we cover capital punishment's history, we concentrate on how the death penalty has been implemented during this modern era from 1972 to the present.

34 states plus the federal government and the U.S. military have death penalty statutes

1890

At Auburn Prison in New York, William Kemmler becomes the first person executed by electrocution after killing his lover with an ax.

Source: © Reuters/CORBIS

1924

Nevada becomes the first jurisdiction in the world to legally execute a person with cyanide gas.

1936

The last public execution in the United States is a hanging in Owensboro, Kentucky.

1977

Gary Gilmore's execution by a firing squad in Utah marks the return of the death penalty's use after a ten year pause.

Source: © Mark Jenkinson/CORBIS

1982

Virgina executes Velma Barfield by lethal injection, and she becomes the first woman to be executed since the death penalty was reinstated in 1976.

At the start of the second decade of the twenty-first century, 34 states plus the federal government and the U.S. military have death penalty statutes. All of those jurisdictions (except the U.S. military, which had its last execution in 1961) have held at least one execution since 1976. Statistics from the Death Penalty Information Center (2011) show that through October 21, 2011, more than 1,200 executions took place in the United States since 1976. Texas, Virginia, and Oklahoma (in order) accounted for 54 percent of those executions. Of the persons executed during that period, 56 percent were white, 35 percent were black, 7 percent were Hispanic, and 2 percent were of

Today, all 34 states with the death penalty and the U.S. government use lethal injection as their primary method of execution.

another race/ethnicity. More than 80 percent of the executions have occurred in the South and less than one percent have taken place in the Northeast (see Figure 12.4).

Source: © Helder Almeida/Fotolia

Hanging

- This is the primary execution method in the United States until the 1890s.
- If the inmate has strong neck muscles, if he or she is very light, if the "drop" is too short, or if the noose has been wrongly positioned, the fracture-dislocation is not rapid and death results from slow asphyxiation.
- It is currently an option in New Hampshire and Washington, but lethal injection is the primary method in both states.

Source: © Helder Almeida/Fotolia

Electrocution

- This was first used in 1888 by New York as a more humane method of execution than hanging.
- It was presumed to be a relatively painless way to die because death would be virtually immediate, but others suggested that the body fluids must heat close to the boiling point of water in order to generate the steam or wisps of smoke that were often seen after an electrocution.
- It is currently an option in nine states, but lethal injection is the primary method in each.

Source: © Ilene MacDonald/Alamy

Gas Chamber

- This was introduced in Nevada in 1924 as a more humane way of execution.
- It is currently an option in four states, but lethal injection is the primary method in each.
- Crystals of sodium cyanide are released into the pail beneath a chair where the condemned prisoner is strapped. A chemical reaction occurs that releases hydrogen cyanide gas. The prisoner is instructed to breathe deeply to speed up the process, but most prisoners try to hold their breath and some struggle.
- Some have suggested that the gas chamber tortures the spectators more than the condemned because it is an unpleasant thing to watch.

FIGURE 12.2 **Popular Twentieth-Century Execution Methods.**
Source: (Death Penalty Information Center 2010; Wikberg 1992)

1993	1996	1999	2001	2009	2010
Maryland prisoner Kirk Bloodworth becomes the first death row inmate to be exonerated with DNA evidence.	The hanging of convicted double-murderer Bill Bailey in Delaware is America's last execution by hanging.	After twice refusing offers of lethal injection, Walter LaGrand is executed in an Arizona gas chamber and becomes America's last prisoner to be executed by the gas chamber.	Oklahoma City bomber Timothy McVeigh becomes first federal prisoner to be executed in 38 years.	Ohio becomes the first state to execute a death-row inmate with a one-drug intravenous lethal injection rather than the three-drug cocktail used in most states.	Utah death-row inmate Ronnie Lee Gardner chooses the firing squad over a lethal injection and becomes the last person in America to be executed by firing squad.

Source: Splash News/Splash News/Newscom

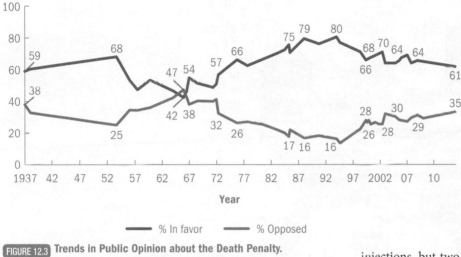

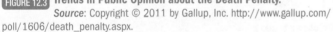

FIGURE 12.3 **Trends in Public Opinion about the Death Penalty.**
Source: Copyright © 2011 by Gallup, Inc. http://www.gallup.com/poll/1606/death_penalty.aspx.

The primary features of capital punishment's modern era concern legal challenges to the death penalty (as reviewed in the "Capital Punishment and the Courts" section), but a particularly interesting aspect of the period was a change in the method of execution. This most recent version of execution is actually a return to one of the oldest—administering a lethal drug. More than 2,300 years ago, Socrates was executed by drinking a cup of hemlock, and in 1982 Charlie Brooks, Jr., received lethal injections of sodium thiopental (an anesthetic), pancuronium bromide (a muscle relaxant designed to paralyze), and potassium chloride (to stop the heart and cause death). He died, as planned, from the overdose of sodium thiopental, and

in this way dying was presumed to be "no more traumatic than falling asleep" ("A new executioner: The needle" 1981).

The execution of Brooks made Texas the first state—and the first jurisdiction in the world—to use lethal injection as a method of execution. Texas officials lauded the new technique as less painful, less offensive, and more palatable. Since 1982, lethal injection has become the technique of choice in most of the states with death penalty statutes.

Today, all 34 states with the death penalty and the U.S. government use lethal injection as their primary method of execution. Almost all the states use the same three-drug combination for lethal injections, but two states (Ohio and Washington) use only the anesthetic (sodium thiopental) for executions.

▶ Capital Punishment and the Law

The Eighth Amendment to the United States Constitution states that cruel and unusual punishments will not be inflicted. Unfortunately, for those preferring simple directions, the Constitution defines neither *cruel* nor *unusual*. But most constitutional scholars believe the Founding Fathers intended to allow for the death penalty. Not only was capital punishment authorized in all 13 colonies, but there also are specific provisions in the Constitution that suggest the taking of life is possible (for example, the Fifth Amendment's

Think About It...

In response to concerns about the potential for improper administration of the three drugs, Ohio executed a death-row inmate in 2009 using a one-drug intravenous lethal injection. That method—essentially a large dose of anesthetic similar to how animals are euthanized—was never before used on a human. The new method is said to be painless and an improvement over the three-drug cocktail used in most states. Do you think the use of one-drug rather than three-drugs will quiet the controversy regarding lethal injection?

Source: Paul Harris pacificcoastnews/Paul Harris pacificcoastnews/Newscom

1775

The death penalty is used in all 13 U.S. colonies at the outbreak of the American Revolution

Crimes typically covered were arson, treason, murder, burglary, robbery, rape, horse-stealing, and slave rebellion. Hanging was the usual method.

1910

Weems v. United States
In ruling that a penalty was too harsh considering the nature of the offense, the USSC establishes precedents on cruel and unusual punishment.

Source: © Natalia Bratslavsky/Fotolia

1947

Louisiana ex rel. Francis v. Resweber USSC finds that a second execution attempt following a technical malfunction does not constitute cruel and unusual punishment.

1968

Witherspoon v. Illinois USSC forbids the dismissal of jurors based on personal opposition to capital punishment.

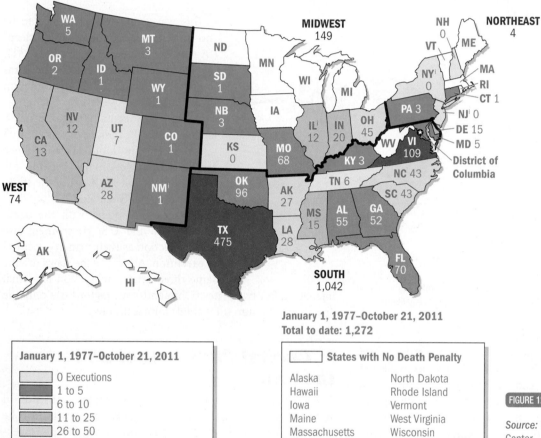

January 1, 1977–October 21, 2011
Total to date: 1,272

January 1, 1977–October 21, 2011

	0 Executions
	1 to 5
	6 to 10
	11 to 25
	26 to 50
	51 to 100
	Over 100

ᴵExecutions occurred between 1977 and the state's abolition.

☐ **States with No Death Penalty**

Alaska	North Dakota
Hawaii	Rhode Island
Iowa	Vermont
Maine	West Virginia
Massachusetts	Wisconsin
Michigan	District of Colombia
Minnesota	

FIGURE 12.4 **Executions by State, January 1, 1977–October 21, 2011.**

Source: Data from Death Penalty Information Center. (October 21, 2011). Number of Executions by State and Region Since 1976. Retrieved October 21, 2011, from www.deathpenaltyinfo.org/number-executions-state-and-region-1976.

When the three-drug protocol is properly administered, the first drug ensures that the prisoner does not experience any pain associated with the paralysis and cardiac arrest caused by the second and third drugs.

The three-drug protocol is problematic because the initial anesthetic may not take hold, and the other two drugs can cause excruciating pain. One of those drugs, a paralytic, would render the prisoner unable to express his or her discomfort.

FIGURE 12.5 The Lethal Injection Controversy.

provision that no person shall be deprived of life without due process). But the ambiguous nature of the terms *cruel* and *unusual* and the Supreme Court's finding that the Eighth Amendment "must draw its meaning from the evolving standards of decency that mark the progress of a maturing society" (*Trop* v. *Dulles* 1958, 356 U.S. at 101), have kept the topic of capital punishment at the forefront among social and legal issues. This section looks first at legal issues related to whom the death penalty applies, and then it considers key court cases that have shaped how the death penalty is implemented.

1972	1976	1977	1986

Furman v. Georgia USSC determines that the death penalty does not violate the Constitution but that the arbitrary and capricious manner of its application in many states does.

Gregg v. Georgia Georgia's new death penalty statute is deemed constitutional, and the stage is set for capital punishment to be reinstated in other states.

Source: ROGER L. WOLLENBERG/ UPI/Newscom

Coker v. Georgia USSC rules that use of the death penalty in rape cases is unconstitutional for rape of an adult woman when the victim is not killed.

Ford v. Wainwright USSC rules that executing the mentally insane is cruel and unusual and therefore unconstitutional.

Entering Death Row

To the surprise of some people (who, for example, think *all* murderers should be subject to execution), the death penalty is reserved for only the most heinous crimes. Bohm (2003) notes that the U.S. Supreme Court has ruled that the death penalty should be limited to aggravated or capital murder. In fact, all executions since 1976 have been for murder with aggravating circumstances.

Although there have been no executions since 1976 for crimes other than murder with aggravating circumstances, there are state and federal statutes that provide for the death penalty in cases other than those involving the death of the victim. State statutes for nonmurder capital crimes include the following (Death Penalty Information Center, 2010a):

- Treason (Arkansas, California, Colorado, Georgia, Louisiana, Mississippi, Missouri, Washington)
- Aggravated kidnapping (Colorado, Idaho, Missouri, Montana)
- Drug trafficking (Florida, Missouri)
- Aircraft hijacking (Georgia, Missouri)
- Placing a bomb near a bus terminal (Missouri)
- Aggravated assault by incarcerated, persistent felons, or murderers (Montana)

Despite those statutes, the likelihood that the Supreme Court will allow someone to be executed for a crime not involving murder is very remote. The Court has already ruled in *Coker* v. *Georgia* (1977), *Eberheart* v. *Georgia* (1977), and *Kennedy* v. *Louisiana* (2008) that the death penalty was disproportionate, and therefore unacceptable, to the crime of rape of an adult woman who was not killed (*Coker*), the crime of kidnapping when the victim was not killed (*Eberheart*), and the rape of a child that did not result in the victim's death (*Kennedy*).

there have been no executions since 1976 for crimes other than murder with aggravating circumstances

Capital Punishment and the Courts

In the 1960s, there was a decline in use of the death penalty and an unofficial moratorium meant no executions occurred in the United States from 1968 to 1977. The moratorium resulted from increasing legal challenges to the death penalty in the 1960s. During this moratorium, the states with death penalty statutes were unsure about the Supreme Court's view of the constitutionality of the laws, so they refrained from any executions. Their concern was well founded, because the Court's 1972 *Furman* v. *Georgia* decision held that the death penalty—as it was then being used—amounted to cruel and unusual punishment.

The Furman Decision

What is referred to as the **Furman decision** actually involved three cases, each with a black defendant, that the U.S. Supreme Court heard together: *Furman* v. *Georgia*, *Jackson* v. *Georgia*, and *Branch* v. *Texas*. *Furman* v. *Georgia*, however, is the cited case when reviewing the Court's decision.

Furman, a 26-year-old black man with a sixth-grade education, tried to enter a private home at night. The homeowner surprised Furman while he was in the act of burglary. While trying to escape, Furman shot and killed the homeowner with one pistol shot fired through a closed kitchen door from the outside. At his trial, Furman said he accidentally tripped over a wire while backing away, causing the gun to fire.

In Furman v. Georgia (1972) the U.S. Supreme Court determined that the death penalty was cruel and unusual because it was imposed in an arbitrary and capricious manner.

Prior to his trial, Furman was committed to the Georgia Central State Hospital for a psychiatric exam on his plea of insanity. Initially, the superintendent reported that the diagnostic staff had concluded that Furman's diagnosis was of mild to moderate mental deficiency, with psychotic episodes associated with convulsive disorder. The physicians agreed

Thompson v. Oklahoma People aged 15 or younger when they committed a crime may not be sentenced to death.

Atkins v. Virginia USSC prohibits execution of the mentally retarded but leaves to the states the determination of what constitutes mental retardation.
Ring v. Arizona USSC rules that jurors, rather than a judge or panel of judges, must determine whether a convicted murderer should receive the death penalty.

Source: HO/UPI/Newscom

Roper v. Simmons People aged 17 or younger when they committed a crime may not be sentenced to death. Christopher Simmons was 17 when he kidnapped and killed Shirley Cook.

Kennedy v. Louisiana The death penalty cannot be imposed on those convicted of raping a child when the crime did not result in the child's death.

---

that Furman was not presently psychotic but said he was incapable of cooperating with his counsel in preparing his defense. Furthermore, the staff believed that he needed further psychiatric hospitalization and treatment. However, at a later time, the superintendent reported that, although the staff diagnosis was the same, he concluded that while Furman was not currently psychotic, he knew right from wrong and was able to cooperate with his counsel in preparing his defense. All the jury knew about Furman was that he was black, 26 years old, and worked at an upholstery shop. After deliberating about 90 minutes, the jury returned a verdict of guilt and a sentence of death.

In *Furman* v. *Georgia* (1972) the U.S. Supreme Court determined that the death penalty was cruel and unusual. Two of the justices said it is cruel and unusual in all cases, but the majority said it was cruel and unusual because it was imposed in an arbitrary and capricious manner. Justice Douglas, taking the arbitrary and capricious position, said it was not possible to determine from the facts of the three cases that the defendants were sentenced to death because they were black. However, he expressed concern that the laws left the decision of death or imprisonment to "the uncontrolled discretion of judges or juries" and in doing so, "people live or die, dependent on the whim of one man or of 12" (*Furman* v. *Georgia*).

In the Furman case, three of the five justices in the majority took the position that the death penalty was cruel and unusual because it was applied arbitrarily. The other two justices in the majority believed the death penalty was cruel and unusual in itself. Had the majority held the second position, the death penalty would essentially have been abandoned throughout the United States. But the "arbitrary" position left the door open for laws that would allow for nonarbitrary use of the death penalty. Said differently, in the *Furman* decision, the Court's ruling was not against capital punishment itself; it was against the way it was being imposed. Under that reasoning, states assumed, death penalty statutes that removed the arbitrary nature of executions would be constitutional.

The Gregg Decision

Because each Court justice wrote a separate opinion in *Furman*, it was not immediately clear just what kind of death penalty law would be acceptable to the Court. Two major types of laws were tried by different states: mandatory and guided discretion. The mandatory laws tried to completely eliminate discretion in capital sentencing by requiring the death penalty upon conviction of specific crimes. Those types were held unconstitutional in a series of 1976 rulings (see *Roberts* v. *Louisiana* and *Woodson* v. *North Carolina*).

The **guided discretion** statutes require juries to administer capital punishment after considering both aggravating and mitigating circumstances. The Court upheld these statutes in several other 1976 rulings (*Gregg* v. *Georgia*, *Jurek* v. *Texas*, and *Proffitt* v. *Florida*), but the **Gregg decision** is typically cited as initiating the guided discretion era. The Georgia, Texas, and Florida statutes each require a **bifurcated trial**, with the first stage being the traditional trial to determine guilt. When guilt is established, the second stage takes place to decide the sentence—death or life imprisonment. It is during the second stage that guided discretion occurs; this is when the sentencing authority hears about aggravating and mitigating factors that will affect the sentencing decision.

Further refinements to the death penalty laws have included decisions such as *Coker* v. *Georgia* (the death penalty was not warranted for the crime of rape of an adult woman wherein the victim is not killed), *Eberheart* v. *Georgia* (the death penalty is not warranted for the crime of kidnapping wherein the victim was not killed), and *Kennedy* v. *Louisiana* (the death penalty is not warranted for the rape of a child when the victim did not die) decisions. In addition, the Court has ruled that it is unconstitutional to execute persons who are mentally insane (*Ford* v. *Wainwright*), mentally retarded (*Atkins* v. *Virginia*), or were younger than age 18 when they committed their crime (*Roper* v. *Simmons*).

LEARNING OUTCOMES 2 Explain the legal provisions for capital punishment in the United States.

GLOSSARY

Furman decision In *Furman* v. *Georgia* the U.S. Supreme Court determined that the death penalty was cruel and unusual because it was imposed in an arbitrary and capricious manner.

guided discretion A requirement that juries, after determining guilt in the first stage of a death penalty trial, consider both aggravating and mitigating circumstances during the sentencing stage of the trial.

Gregg decision Death penalty statutes that provide for bifurcated trials and that direct juries to use guided discretion in deciding the sentence are allowed under the Constitution.

bifurcated trial A requirement that death penalty cases have two stages, with the first stage being the traditional trial to determine guilt and a second stage to decide the sentence—death or life imprisonment.

▶ Characteristics of Death-Row Prisoners

Based on the review of legal issues related to capital punishment, we know some of the characteristics of persons who are on death row in America. Basically, they are offenders who have been convicted of first-degree murder with aggravating circumstances, who are neither mentally ill nor mentally retarded, and who were at least age 18 when committing their crime. There are other interesting characteristics beyond those, however.

Summarize the characteristics of current death-row prisoners.

Most (53 percent) of the prisoners on death row in the United States are in the South and the fewest (7 percent) are in the Northeast. California, with more than 600, has the greatest number of prisoners on death row, and New Hampshire and Wyoming have the fewest with one each. Just over half of all death-row prisoners are in the states of California, Texas, Florida, and Pennsylvania (Snell 2010). As shown in Table 12.1, most of prisoners on death row in 2009 were white non-Hispanic males who had never been married.

1/2 Just over half of all death-row prisoners are in the states of California, Texas, Florida, and Pennsylvania

Among death-row inmates for whom criminal history information was available, 66 percent had prior felony convictions, including 9 percent with at least one previous homicide conviction (Snell 2010). Most of the people on death row were not involved in the criminal justice system at the time of the capital offense. However, those who were "in the system" were more likely to be on parole (15 percent) than probation (11 percent).

Most death-row prisoners actually leave death row without being executed—through appellate court action or clemency

TABLE 12.1 — Demographic Characteristics of Prisoners under Sentence of Death, 2009

Characteristic	Yearend	Admissions	Removals
Total inmates	3,173	112	149
Sex			
Male	98.1%	98.2%	100%
Female	1.9	1.8	0
Race[a]			
White	56.1%	58.0%	53.7%
Black	41.5	37.5	45.6
All other races[b]	2.4	4.5	0.7
Hispanic Origin			
Hispanic	13.5%	19.4%	12.4%
Non-Hispanic	86.5	80.6	87.6
Number unknown	396	19	12
Age			
20–24	1.2%	11.6%	0%
25–29	5.5	14.3	4.7
30–34	12.3	18.8	7.4
35–39	16.8	19.6	16.1
40–44	17.0	5.4	12.1
45–49	17.9	16.1	19.5
50–54	13.3	5.4	19.5
55–59	7.8	4.5	5.4
60–64	5.6	3.6	10.7
65 or older	2.6	0.9	4.7
Mean age	44	38	47
Median age	44	36	47
Education			
8th grade or less	13.5%	8.1%	10.5%
9th–11th grade	36.0	38.4	49.2
High school graduate/GED	41.5	47.7	29.0
Any college	9.0	5.8	11.3
Median	12th	12th	11th
Number unknown[c]	532	26	25
Marital Status			
Married	21.9%	17.0%	25.0%
Divorced/separated	20.5	33.0	21.3
Widowed	2.8	1.1	4.4
Never married	54.7	48.9	49.3
Number unknown	376	18	13

Note: Calculations are based on those cases for which data were reported. Detail may not add to total due to rounding.

[a] Includes persons of Hispanic/Latino origin.

[b] At yearend 2009, inmates in "all other races" consisted of 26 American Indians, 36 Asians, and 14 self-identified Hispanics. During 2009, one Asian and four self-identified Hispanic inmates were admitted, and one Native American was removed.

[c] Due to a large number of cases with missing data on the education variable, users are advised to use caution when interpreting the distribution on this variable.

Source: T. L. Snell. (2010). Capital punishment, 2009 (statistical tables). Retrieved April 22, 2011, from http://bjs.ojp.usdoj.gov/content/pub/pdf/cp09st.pdf.

56% From 1976 to the present, most of the executions were of whites (56 percent) rather than blacks, but were still primarily men (all but 12), and have involved a murder charge.

Most death-row prisoners actually leave death row without being executed—through appellate court action or clemency—but many have their death sentence carried out. Statistics from the Death Penalty Information Center (2011) show that through the end of 2010, 1,245 executions had taken place in the United States since 1976. Texas, Virginia, and Oklahoma (in order) accounted for 54 percent of those executions. Of the persons executed during that period, 56 percent were white, 35 percent were black, 7 percent were Hispanic, and 2 percent were of another race.

Executions in the modern era (that is, post-*Furman*) were to have been imposed in a more equitable manner. Executions between 1930 and 1976 were usually of African-Americans (54 percent), men (99 percent), and took place in the South (60 percent). Most of the executions were for murder (86 percent, with African-Americans accounting for 49 percent of these executions), and 12 percent were for rape in which African-Americans accounted for 90 percent of the executions (Department of Justice 1978). From 1976 to the present, most of the executions were of whites (56 percent) rather than blacks, but were still primarily men (all but 12), and have involved a murder charge.

▶ Arguments For and Against Capital Punishment

One would be hard pressed to find another criminal justice topic that occasions such passion as the death penalty. The topic has been debated on the basis of such topics as morality, deterrence, retribution, irrevocable mistake, cost comparison of death versus life imprisonment, discrimination by race and social class, and the quality of defense counsel available to capital crime defendants. A sampling of those topics is provided here.

Deterrence

The idea that people will be deterred from committing murder out of fear that they will be executed seems inherently logical. In fact, a belief that the death penalty provides a general deterrent is one of the oldest reasons for its use. Public executions were held to deliberately dissuade those who might be thinking about committing murder or some other capital crime of the time. But murder and other crimes continued, and the public executions themselves were often a stimulus to criminal behavior.

Even when the death penalty is carried out in a private setting, reason seems to suggest that it should deter persons from doing

YES
The death penalty deters.

"People fear nothing more than death. Therefore, nothing will deter a criminal more than the fear of death."

Ernest van den Haag
late Professor of Jurisprudence at Fordham University

NO
The death penalty does not deter.

"There is no credible evidence that the death penalty deters crime more effectively than long terms of imprisonment."

American Civil Liberties Union

FIGURE 12.6 **Does the Death Penalty Deter?**

something for which they could be executed. That belief goes back to the logic of the classical school, in which people such as Beccaria and Bentham (see Chapter 2) argued that under conditions of certainty, severity, and swiftness, punishment can effectively keep the rational person from committing a crime. Issues of certainty, severity, and swiftness are admittedly important, but an overriding matter is the assumption of rationality. **Abolitionists** (those favoring the abolition of the death penalty) argue, for example, that murder is seldom a rational act. Quite the contrary; it typically occurs in the heat of the moment and frequently involves alcohol or drugs in the victim, offender, or both. This lethal mix does not create a setting for rational decision making. If a punishment only deters when the potential offender can rationally weigh the pros and cons of a proposed act, the death penalty will not deter the majority of murders, because they are emotional, not rational, acts.

Retentionists (those who favor keeping the death penalty) respond to the rationality argument by suggesting that the death penalty's deterrent effect is achieved through the socialization process. Throughout his or her life, the individual comes to internalize the association of act and penalty. Good behavior becomes something that occurs naturally rather than something that results from constant weighing of pros and cons throughout the day. Goldberg (1991) uses an analogy of angry husbands to make the point. Most husbands, he argues, slam doors, shout, or sulk when they are angry. Some husbands, when angry, murder their wives: "The question is not what deterred the person who did murder (nothing did), but what deterred the person who didn't" (Goldberg 1991, 114). The slamming, shouting, sulking husband has presumably instilled

Think About It...

In the third Bush–Gore debate leading up to the 2000 presidential election, George W. Bush answered the following to the question: "Do both of you believe that the death penalty actually deters crime?" Bush said, "I do, that's the only reason to be for it. I don't think you should support the death penalty to seek revenge. . . . I think the reason to support the death penalty is because it saves other people's lives" (cited at ProCon.org 2009). Do you agree with President Bush? Why or why not?

a psychological resistance to murder—not because he makes a rational decision in the heat of the moment, but because he has internalized the link between killing and the death penalty.

Interesting though the philosophical debate on deterrence might be, much of the discussion about deterrence and the death penalty has relied on statistics. Use of statistical analysis is especially popular among abolitionists because the evidence has consistently supported the position that the death penalty does not serve as a general deterrent to murder—with some exceptions noted next. Kronenwetter (1993) notes that as early as 1919, statistical studies showed that there was no measurable relation between the homicide rate and the existence or absence of the death penalty. Since then, researchers have repeatedly failed to find a general-deterrent effect in executions (see Table 12.2). The studies are consistent in finding that factors other than execution are responsible for the variation and trends in murder rates.

There are, however, some studies that claim to have found a deterrent effect. Sociologist Ted Goertzel (2004) explains that these studies primarily use econometric modeling wherein complex mathematical models are constructed on the assumption that the models mirror what happens in the real world. Some of these econometric models show that capital punishment deters homicide, but others do not (Fagan 2005; Goertzel 2004). One of the first such studies was conducted with data from the mid-twentieth-century United States. Isaac Ehrlich (1975) concluded that eight murders were prevented by each execution. His findings were roundly criticized, and attempts at replication failed to confirm a deterrent effect (Paternoster 1991). The greatest damage to Ehrlich's study came from a board of experts commissioned by the National Academy of Sciences to review his findings. They determined that it offered no useful evidence for a deterrent effect of capital punishment (Kronenwetter 1993).

There has been a resurgence of interest in econometric modeling to test deterrence and capital punishment. Columbia Law School professor Jeffrey Fagan reviewed more than a dozen studies published since 1995 claiming the death penalty can prevent anywhere from three to thirty-two murders (Fagan 2005 and 2006). Some of the studies claim that pardons, commutations, and exonerations cause murders to increase; others claim murders of passion can be deterred; and some even claim that executions can reduce robberies and even some nonviolent crimes.

TABLE 12.2 — Deterrence Research and Capital Punishment

Found Deterrent Effect?	Authors (Year)*	Findings
NO	Bailey & Peterson (1994) Peterson & Bailey (1991)	Using a monthly time-series analysis, the authors found no evidence of a deterrent effect on police killings (Bailey & Peterson 1994) nor any consistent relationship between the number of executions and the rate of felony murder (Peterson & Bailey 1991).
NO	Peterson & Bailey (1998)	After thoroughly reviewing the empirical literature on a deterrent effect of capital punishment, the authors conclude that factors other than execution are responsible for the variation and trends in murder rates.
NO	Sorensen, Wrinkle, Brewer, & Marquart (1999)	Suggesting that if the death penalty can have any general deterrent effect at all, it would have one in Texas (the most active death penalty state), researchers found that "the number of executions did not appear to influence either the rate of murder in general or the rate of felony murder in particular" (pp. 489–490).
NO	Donohue & Wolfers (2005) Donohue & Wolfers (2006)	Following a thorough assessment of the statistical evidence that claims to support a deterrent effect for capital punishment, the authors conclude that the view the death penalty deters is the product of belief, not evidence.
YES	Ehrlich (1975)	This highly controversial study, using econometric methods, concludes the death penalty reduces homicide in the United States.
YES	Land, Teske, & Zheng (2009)	Based on a time-series analysis and independent-validation tests, the authors found evidence in Texas of modest, short-term reductions in homicides in the first and fourth months following an execution.
YES	Dezhbakhsh & Rubin (2010)	In disagreeing with Donohue and Wolfers (2005), these authors claim deterrence findings based on econometric methods are, in fact, robust.

*See references section for complete citation.

"When one considers all the evidence the empirical support for the proposition that the death penalty deters is __at best__ weak and inconclusive" (Donohue & Wolfers 2006, 2).

These "econometric illusions"—as Goertzel (2004) calls them—have serious methodological problems that include the following:

- **Ignoring large amounts of missing data** in important states such as Florida

- **Failing to show that murderers** are, *first of all*, aware of executions in their own state (much less in faraway states) *and* that they rationally decide to forego homicide as a result

- **Failing to consider the deterrent effect of life-without-parole sentences**, which have the same incapacitative effect as do execution

- **Applying econometric modeling to a problem with very limited data** (there are few executions each year) when the methodology is most successful where there is a large flow of data for testing (Fagan 2005 and 2006; Goertzel 2004)

The statistical evidence so far is on the abolitionists' side. Reviews of deterrence studies (Bohm 2003; Donohue & Wolfers 2006; Fagan 2005 and 2006; Goertzel 2004; Radelet & Borg 2000) consistently support Paternoster's summary that "after years of research with different methodologies and statistical approaches, the empirical evidence seems to clearly suggest that capital punishment is not a superior general deterrent" (1991, 241). Or, as Donohue and Wolfers put it, "When one considers all the evidence the empirical support for the proposition that the death penalty deters is *at best* weak and inconclusive" (Donohue & Wolfers 2006, 2). Importantly, however, even with statistics on their side, abolitionists have trouble responding to the retentionists' point that only the times when the death penalty has not deterred can be counted because only then is there something to count. There is no way of knowing when it did deter because there is nothing to count when the murder does not happen.

Fairness

Several issues are raised when discussing the fairness of the death penalty. Many of those issues are based on statistics that show the death penalty applying most often to men, disproportionately to African-Americans and Hispanics, and invariably to poor defendants. Women, Caucasians, and rich people also commit capital crimes, but they have not been executed quite as regularly.

Regarding fairness and gender, it is clear that the death penalty has been applied to both men and women throughout history and across cultures. However, women have not been executed in the United States as often as their number on death row suggests they could be. Women account for about 2 percent of all death sentences imposed in the United States. But rather than comprising 2 percent of the persons executed, women make up about 1 percent of the total.

In 2004, the American Civil Liberties Union (King & Bellin 2004) released findings from the first-ever national survey of women on death row. Key findings from the survey are shown in Table 12.3.

The report concludes with recommendations to ensure that women receive fair and adequate defense counsel when charged with a capital offense (for example, train defense counsel to litigate issues of abuse in death penalty cases) and to improve conditions for women on death row (for example, integrate women on death row into regular prison units).

TABLE 12.3 | Women on Death Row

Findings	Recommendations
• Women on death row often had ineffective counsel or were subjected to official misconduct by prosecutors during their trials.	• To ensure that every woman receives fair and adequate defense, programs should be established to educate lawyers about abuse and domestic violence so they can adequately represent their clients.
• Half of the women on death row acted with at least one other person, but in most of those cases the codefendant received a sentence other than death—even in cases where they appeared to be equally culpable.	• Defense attorneys should be provided with adequate access to expert witnesses and mitigation specialists to help them identify mental illness and mental retardation issues that could be raised at trial and/or sentencing.
• Nearly two-thirds of the women on death row were convicted of killing family members or people they knew. Although no one has calculated the number of men on death row for killing the same categories of people, we know from the general prison population that women who are in prison are more likely than men to have killed family members or intimates.	• Many women on death row were convicted of crimes that were directly or indirectly related to abuse they received as children or as adults. Counseling programs to address child abuse and domestic violence must be provided to these women.
• Most women on death row, probably because of their small numbers, live in almost complete isolation, rarely leaving their cells. Such conditions may lead to psychosis or can exacerbate existing mental illness.	• In states with very low numbers of women sentenced to death, the states should integrate those women into a regular prison unit.

Findings and recommendations are from the first-ever national survey of women on death row (King & Bellin 2004).

Source: Derived from THE FORGOTTEN POPULATION: A Look at Death Row in the United States through the Experiences of Women by R. King & J. Bellin (December 2004). Published by American Civil Liberties Union. http://www.aclu.org/files/FilesPDFs/womenondeathrow.pdf.

DISCUSS *In what ways might the findings in Table 12.3 also apply to men on death row. Could any of the recommendations also be appropriate for men on death row?*

A second important topic related to fairness and the death penalty concerns social class. Supreme Court Justice William Douglas commented (*Furman* v. *Georgia*) that "one searches our chronicles in vain for the execution of any member of the affluent strata of this society" (408 U.S. 251–252).

The characteristics of persons on death row seem to reflect those of the poor and lower class in society as a whole. Although most of the criminal justice system's clients are poor, death-row inmates are among the poorest. Unfortunate and unfair as it is, persons from the lower socioeconomic classes elicit little sympathy from justice system officials, jurors, or the general public. We know that punishments for other crimes, such as marijuana possession, have eased as more and more of the middle class indulge in the behavior. Those offenders do draw sympathy from officials, jurors, and the community, with a result being a lessening of penalties associated with the behavior. One wonders how long the death penalty would have lasted if most of those executed had reflected typical middle-class characteristics.

Proponents of the death penalty argue that inequities in the application of the death penalty should draw criticism of its application, not of its use. As van den Haag argues, "If guilty whites or wealthy people escape the gallows and guilty poor people do not, the poor or black do not become less guilty nor do they deserve less punishment because others did not get the punishment they deserve" (1991, 158).

Because a good, experienced lawyer will improve the defendant's chances at each stage in the legal process, "the better the lawyer, the better the defendant's chances of escaping execution" (Kronenwetter 1993, 36). Unfortunately, almost all defendants in capital cases cannot afford their own attorney, so they are provided a public defender or court-appointed attorney.

YES

The death penalty is unfair because it is applied mostly to the lower socioeconomic class.

The death penalty is imposed mostly on society's poor and lower class because they cannot afford good lawyers. As Supreme Court Justice Ruth Bader Ginsburg put it: "People who are well represented at trial do not get the death penalty" (CBS News, 2001).

NO

If the death penalty is applied mostly to the lower socioeconomic class that makes its application bad, not its use.

"If guilty whites or wealthy people escape the gallows and guilty poor people do not, the poor or black do not become less guilty nor do they deserve less punishment because others did not get the punishment they deserve" (van den Haag).

FIGURE 12.7 Is the Death Penalty Unfair Because of its Discrimination by Social Class?

"the better the lawyer, the better the defendant's chances of escaping execution"
(Kronenwetter 1993, 36)

Certainly there are good, well-trained, and imminently qualified public defenders and court-appointed attorneys handling death penalty cases around the country, but there are also public defenders and court-appointed attorneys who are overworked, underpaid, or who lack the trial experience required for death penalty cases. In a study of death penalty cases in Texas, researchers found that capital defendants with court-appointed lawyers were more than twice as likely to receive a death sentence as were those able to hire their own attorneys (Kronenwetter 1993).

Important as issues of gender and social class are, one of the most discussed areas of fairness and the death penalty deals with race and ethnicity. Concern about the disproportionate minority group representation in the criminal justice system has been present for years—and especially so in how the death penalty is applied. Traditionally, the bias has been recognized as relating to the offender's race and ethnicity; more recently, attention has turned to the victim's race and ethnicity. We look first at the offender's characteristics.

In a report on race and the death penalty, Amnesty International USA (1999, April 30) concluded that there is no evidence that current legal safeguards have eliminated racial bias in the application of the death penalty. The report notes the potential for racial bias is linked to prosecutorial discretion because it is unreasonable to think individual prosecutors are not influenced by the racial divisions affecting American society. To support the existence of prosecutorial bias, the report notes that only 2 percent of the nation's district attorneys are non-white and cites studies showing that prosecutors in some jurisdictions seem to selectively apply the death penalty on the basis of race (see also Pokorak 1998). However, as an editorial in the *New York Post* notes, because the death penalty can only be sought when aggravating circumstances are present, it is possible that such circumstances appear disproportionately by race ("Amnesty International is dead wrong" 1999). If that is true—and at least one study suggests it may be (see Rothman & Powers 1994)—prosecutors may bring death penalty charges against black defendants more often because of the circumstances of their alleged crime rather than because of their race. The issue, like so many linked to the death penalty, is complex.

The racial/ethnic distribution on death row is as follows (NAACP Legal Defense Fund 2010):

- 44 percent white non-Hispanic
- 42 percent black non-Hispanic
- 12 percent Hispanic
- 1 percent Native American
- 1 percent Asian

Of persons executed since 1976 (NAACP Legal Defense Fund 2010),

- 56 percent white non-Hispanic
- 35 percent black non-Hispanic
- 7 percent Hispanic
- 1 percent Native American
- 1 percent Asian

Because the percentage of minorities being executed is less than it was before 1976, and because the number of minorities executed is now close to their percentage on death row, there seems to have been some improvement in the death penalty's application. Importantly, however, minorities still make up a much higher percentage of the death-row population than they do of the population as a whole. That disproportionate representation of minorities on death row has been used in court to argue that the death penalty is unconstitutional; but an even more persuasive argument has been how the victim's race might influence who receives the death penalty.

Disparity in the imposition of the death penalty has often looked at the offender's demographic factors, but more recent studies have added an interest in victim demographics. Since 1976, African-Americans (47 percent of homicide victims) and whites (51 percent) were the victims of homicide in almost equal

YES

The race of the defendant, and especially the victim, influences who gets the death penalty.

"A systematic racial bias in the application of the death penalty exists at both the state and federal level."
American Civil Liberties Union

NO

Since 1976 the death penalty has not been applied in a racially biased manner.

"The fact that blacks and Hispanics are charged with capital crimes out of proportion to their numbers in the general population may simply mean that blacks and Hispanics commit capital crimes out of proportion to their numbers."

Roger Clegg
General Counsel at the Center for Equal Opportunity

FIGURE 12.8 **Does Race Affect the Application of the Death Penalty?**

numbers (Fox & Zawitz 2011). Since African-Americans comprise 13 percent of the U.S. population their percentage among homicide victims is very disproportionate, but it is still instructive to note the similarity in homicide victim race. That is because despite blacks comprising nearly half of the murder victims, 78 percent of the people executed since 1977 were convicted of murdering white victims (NAACP Legal Defense Fund 2010). Does the victim's race influence whether an offender receives the death penalty? If so, that would clearly be an extralegal factor and one that should play no role in prosecuting, adjudication, or sentencing decisions.

One of the first studies noting the predictive value of victim race in death sentences was conducted by Baldus, Pulaski, and Woodworth (1983) and was used by the U.S. Supreme Court case of *McCleskey* v. *Kemp* (1987). McCleskey, a black man who had been convicted of murdering a white police officer, used the Baldus study (as it has come to be called) in his claim that he was being discriminated against on the basis of his race and that of his victim. The Baldus study found a large racial disparity in the way Georgia juries had imposed the death penalty between 1973 and 1978. For example, Baldus and his colleagues found that offenders charged with killing a white person were 4.3 times more likely to be sentenced to death in Georgia than those charged with killing a black person.

The Court rejected McCleskey's claims, deciding that a statistical study suggesting that racial considerations entered into capital sentencing in Georgia does not establish purposeful discrimination—which the Court said a successful Fourteenth Amendment claim must show. In addition, the justices noted that although the Baldus study found a correlation between race factors and sentencing, it did not prove that race entered into the sentencing decision. For a defendant to be successful in an appeal, "exceptionally clear proof" must be provided that the decision makers had acted with discriminatory intent (*McCleskey* v. *Kemp* 481 U.S. at 297).

Studies continue to find racial disparity when applying the death penalty. Paternoster and Brame, for example found (2003) and reaffirmed (2008) that the death penalty is more likely to be imposed in Maryland when the victim is white and in cases with black defendants and white victims. But the

78% despite blacks comprising nearly half of the murder victims, 78 percent of the people executed since 1977 were convicted of murdering white victims

courts continue to find such studies lacking in "exceptionally clear proof." In 2001, a U.S. Court of Appeals agreed that the racial imbalance in Ohio's capital sentencing system was "extremely troubling" (*Coleman* v. *Mitchell*, 6th Cir.), but it is no more so than was deemed permissible by *McCleskey*. Such decisions led Baldus, Woodworth, and Grosso (2008) to comment that for all practical purposes, the McCleskey decision precludes the bringing of race claims in federal courts when the evidence of discrimination is a statewide statistical study (p. 145). So, despite what the research might show, the courts have not yet found the statistical analysis compelling enough to find racial disparities in capital sentencing unconstitutional.

Retribution

Another popular capital punishment debate topic is that of *lex talionis*—the "eye for an eye, tooth for a tooth" position. In many ways this is the most difficult to debate because technically it provides no basis for debate. Newman (1985) says retributivists, the prime supporters of this view, are often asked the trap question, "Why must a wrongful act be punished?" Any reply made by the retributivist will be utilitarian, and of all the punishment philosophies, retribution is the only one that is nonutilitarian. If the retributivist tries to answer a question such as "Why should the death penalty be used?" the response will inevitably lean toward things such as deterrence, public safety, or reinforcing the moral order. But each of these answers has a utilitarian aspect, and the retributivist does not require, or even want, such a link.

Newman (1985) suggests the only nonutilitarian response available to retributivists is "Because the act was wrong." But that response merely restates the assertion—that is, retribution claims that a wrongful act must be repaid by punishment, so saying that the reason for punishment is to repay the wrongful act is merely redundant, unless the statement "A wrongful act must be punished" is a statement of fact rather than simply an assertion. And, Newman suggests, that is exactly what the statement is. He argues that saying "A wrongful act must be punished" verges on being a social law. The resulting problem is finding another position to take in order to have a debate. If retributivists say that punishment—the death penalty, for example—is inherently right, even required, the only "other side" one could take is to claim the statement is not a fact, let alone a social law. This becomes more of a philosophical discussion than a utilitarian debate. That is not a bad thing; it just means that the "discussers" must not get hung up on topics such as what punishment achieves. In other words, even if there was clear and convincing evidence that the death penalty is not needed to achieve specific deterrence, does not provide general deterrence, and is applied in a biased manner, the retributivist

MUST A RETRIBUTIVIST BE PRO-DEATH PENALTY?

Achieving a strict principle of *lex talionis* is very difficult and, as a result, some self-described retributivists are actually against the death penalty. Paternoster (1991) offers three limitations to *lex talionis* that turn some retributivists into abolitionists.

1. Rigid adherence to the *lex talionis* principle of equality would mean that the death penalty is appropriate only for murder. Crimes of rape, kidnapping, and armed robbery would not be punished by execution, but all murderers would be. Under contemporary legal requirements (that is, only murders with aggravating circumstances are eligible for the death penalty) the principle of equity is tempered with a dose of mercy.

2. Strict following of *lex talionis* would result in ridiculous and uncivilized punishments since society cannot always treat criminals exactly as they treated their victims. We do not rape the rapists, set fire to the arsonists, or steal from thieves. Nor can we administer several executions to the serial murderer.

3. The principle of equity cannot be met in instances of brutal murder since a strict *lex talionis* would require that brutal murderers be treated brutally by tormenting those who tortured, dismembering those who cut up their victims, and so on. Such behavior by the state would require imitation of the very acts the public so intensely despises.

would still favor capital punishment because it is the "right" thing to do.

Because strict adherence to the principle of *lex talionis* would seemingly require that all murderers be executed—not just those who committed murder with aggravating circumstances—and that executions be conducted in very uncivilized ways, some retributivists argue for **proportional retributivism**. Rather than requiring an exactly similar punishment for a criminal, "proportional retributivism requires only that the worst crime in any society be punished with the worst penalty" (Paternoster 1991, 258). In abandoning the requirement of *lex talionis*, this version of retribution would require that a murderer receive the most severe penalty that society currently would morally tolerate. That punishment must be severe enough so as not to trivialize the victim's injury. Consider, for example, a prison sentence for rapists. Ten years in prison is not equivalent injury for one who has raped another, but it is a severe enough penalty that it does not do an injustice to the victim. Similarly, life imprisonment without the possibility for parole does not duplicate the harm to the murder victim, but it is not a penalty that is out of proportion to murder.

Innocence

Between 1973 and the end of 2010, 138 people in twenty-six states had been released from death row with evidence of their innocence (Death Penalty Information Center 2010e). In seventeen of those cases, DNA was a substantial factor in establishing innocence. For the other cases, defendants either had their original conviction overturned and were acquitted at a retrial (or all charges were dismissed) or were given an absolute pardon by the governor based on new evidence of innocence. Sharp criticizes the criteria the Death Penalty Information Center (DPIC) uses to determine the number of innocent people released from death row as often blurring a distinction between actual innocence and legal innocence (Sharp 2004). Instead, after reviewing several studies that closely analyzed the DPIC list of innocents, Sharp allowed that 17 might be a credible number for actual innocents released from death row between 1973 and 2004. Whether the number is greater than 100 or

138 Between 1973 and the end of 2010, 138 people in twenty-six states had been released from death row with evidence of their innocence

fewer than 20, the possibility of executing an innocent person is reason enough for many people to be against using death sentences. Others, however, suggest that the horror of a rare mistake is outweighed by the benefits of execution when it is appropriate.

Although cases of innocent people being released from death row have convinced some death penalty proponents to become opponents, others simply point to these close calls as examples of the system working—they were caught in time, the argument goes. Reliance on the justice system to catch its own errors before tragedy occurs may be misplaced, however. In many of the exonerations, it was not a diligent justice system that identified the condemned man's innocence but rather an independent nonprofit organization established to assist prisoners (including those on death row) who could be proven innocent through DNA testing. **The Innocence Project** (www.innocenceproject.org/) has been instrumental in 17 DNA exonerations of persons who had served time on death row and is actively involved in reforming the criminal justice system to prevent future injustices.

Regardless of whether the exoneration of an innocent death-row inmate resulted from a diligent justice process or a diligent nonprofit organization, the point for some capital punishment proponents is that the execution did not occur. So, they suggest, there is no reason to believe an innocent person has ever actually been executed (Sharp 2004). Abolitionists agree it is difficult to prove an innocent person has been executed since courts do not generally entertain claims of innocence when the defendant is dead. Further, the need to work on cases of people living on death row who may be innocent takes precedence over cases of people already executed. The Death Penalty Information Center identifies nine people executed since 1976 as possibly having been innocent (2010c), but it is especially interesting to note that the public seems to believe

YES

There can be no margin of error when taking a person's life.

"It is a central pillar of our criminal justice system that it is better that many guilty people go free than one innocent should suffer... Let us pause to be certain we do not kill a single innocent person. This is really not too much to ask for a civilized society."

Russ Feingold
U.S. Senator from Wisconsin

NO

The benefits of execution outweigh the horror of a rare mistake.

"The inevitability of a mistake should not serve as grounds to eliminate the death penalty any more than the risk of having a fatal wreck should make automobiles illegal."

Steven Stewart
Clark County Indiana Prosecuting Attorney

FIGURE 12.9 **Should the Death Penalty Be Banned Because an Innocent Person Could Be Executed?**

that innocent people have been executed. Gallup poll data find that 59 percent of Americans believe that an innocent person has been executed in the last five years, but the same poll found that 64 percent of the public favor capital punishment (2010).

Questions of whether the death penalty deters, is applied in a fair manner, provides retribution for society, or may present an irrevocable mistake, are ones with which we continue to struggle. In the end, one's position regarding the death penalty must be arrived at through personal decisions based on variables ranging from morality to assessment of statistical research.

In the end, one's position regarding the death penalty must be arrived at through personal decisions based on variables ranging from morality to assessment of statistical research.

Should You Be Able to Watch an Execution on Television or Your Smartphone?

On August 14, 1936, the last public execution was held in the United States. Rainey Bethea was hanged in Owensboro, Kentucky, for the rape and murder of a 70-year-old woman. Some 20,000 people came to witness the event, which also involved the country's first hanging conducted by a woman (National Public Radio 2001). The carnival atmosphere—as some reporters called it—is believed by some to have encouraged the eventual banning of public executions in America. But the suitability of public executions in contemporary society still pops up on occasion, as some argue that it could increase the death penalty's deterrent effect and others say it would only serve to desensitize people to violence.

In 1991, a public television station sought permission to videotape and televise a California execution. The request was denied, in part, out of respect for the privacy of prison personnel who participate in the execution process and their concern that harm could come to themselves or their families in retaliation from those opposed to the execution. Proponents of televised executions argue that private nighttime executions leave the public uninformed about the facts surrounding capital punishment—with a result being the degrading of America's democracy by restricting public access to information and suppressing public debate.

More recently, Timothy McVeigh said he had no objection to the broadcast of his 2001 execution for the 1995 Oklahoma City bombing that killed 168 people. In the end, McVeigh's execution had a restricted broadcast to more than 200 survivors and family members who watched on a closed-circuit television feed in Oklahoma City.

1. A presumed benefit of public executions is to maximize the deterrent effect of capital punishment. When it is obvious to everyone that the death penalty will be used—and, humiliatingly, with thousands of others watching—it will discourage others from committing a capital offense. *Is the potential for general deterrence sufficient to reintroduce public executions?*

2. An argument against public executions is that it could desensitize people to violence. *Do you agree or disagree with that argument? What other reasons can you think of for why executions should not be public?*

3. In agreeing to a closed-circuit television broadcast of his execution, McVeigh wondered why it should not be truly public via public broadcast. *Would you have watched a televised execution of Timothy McVeigh? Why or why not?*

Source: © Presselect/Alamy

Outline the history of capital punishment in the United States.

Following the British lead, American colonists relied on capital punishment as a primary punishment for criminal offenders. However, in the 1800s capital punishment began falling out of favor and by the 1940s it was used less frequently. In 1972, the death penalty was declared unconstitutional as it was then used and there was a moratorium on American executions until 1976 when new death penalty statutes were approved by the U.S. Supreme Court. Today, the death penalty is authorized in 34 states plus the federal government and the U.S. military. All those jurisdictions use lethal injection as their primary method of execution.

1. Both corporal and capital punishment were once the norm in America. Corporal punishment (for example, whipping, branding, and the stocks) is no longer practiced but capital punishment is. Why?

2. What event distinguishes the early and modern eras of capital punishment in the United States?

3. What were the popular methods of execution during the early era of capital punishment in the United States?

4. How have public opinions about the death penalty varied over the last century?

5. In which area of the country are the states less likely to have death penalty statutes? Why?

Explain the legal provisions for capital punishment in the United States.

Although the Eighth Amendment prohibits cruel and unusual punishment, neither term is defined in the Constitution and the U.S. Supreme Court has determined that terms must be considered in the context of evolving community standards. This means legal challenges to the death penalty are constantly heard by the courts. Some of those challenges focus on to whom the death penalty can apply and others center on the procedures to be used when applying it. As a result, today the death penalty may be used in cases of first-degree murder with aggravating circumstances (the "who" question) following procedures that provide for both a trial phase and a penalty phase (the "how" question).

1. What crimes other than aggravated murder are included in the death penalty statues of some states? Do you agree or disagree that those crimes should receive the death penalty?

2. Is it important that an execution method be humane? Why or why not?

3. On what basis did the U.S. Supreme Court (*Furman* v. *Georgia*) determine that the death penalty was being imposed in an unconstitutional manner?

4. Other than the *Furman* and *Gregg* decisions, what three or four U.S. Supreme Court cases do you believe have had the greatest impact on the death penalty? Why?

Furman decision In *Furman* v. *Georgia* the U.S. Supreme Court determined that the death penalty was cruel and unusual because it was imposed in an arbitrary and capricious manner.

guided discretion A requirement that juries, after determining guilt in the first stage of a death penalty trial, consider both aggravating and mitigating circumstances during the sentencing stage of the trial.

Gregg decision Death penalty statutes that provide for bifurcated trials and that direct juries to use guided discretion in deciding the sentence are allowed under the Constitution.

bifurcated trial A requirement that death penalty cases have two stages, with the first stage being the traditional trial to determine guilt and a second stage to decide the sentence—death or life imprisonment.

Summarize the characteristics of current death-row prisoners.

Since the U.S. Supreme Court has ruled that the death penalty cannot be given to persons who are mentally ill, mentally retarded, or were under age 18 at the time of their crime, none of the death-row prisoners should have those characteristics. Demographic descriptions tell us that those on death row are mostly white males who have never been married. They were likely to have had prior felony convictions but were not involved in the criminal justice system (for example, were not of probation or parole) at the time of the capital offense. Although most death-row prisoners leave death row through appellate court action or clemency, those that are executed were probably white males in a Texas, Virginia, or Oklahoma prison.

1. Describe prisoners on death row in terms of age. What does that characteristic tell you about persons convicted of capital murder?

2. Describe prisoners on death row in terms of their education. What does that characteristic tell you about persons convicted of capital murder?

3. Despite U.S. Supreme Court rulings, there are defense claims that mentally ill and mentally retarded persons are on death row. Do you think that is true? If so, how is possible?

4. What does it mean to say that most death-row prisoners leave death row through appellate court action or clemency?

LEARNING OUTCOMES 4

Summarize the arguments for and against the use of the death penalty.

Arguments for and against the death penalty are many and complex. One popular argument is centered on the question of general deterrence. That is, are others discouraged from committing murder because they could be executed? Other common debate topics concern whether execution is an appropriate way to exact retribution; whether having the death penalty is worth the risk of executing an innocent person; and whether the death penalty is handed out in a fair manner or if gender, class, and race/ethnicity issues are influencing decisions about who will be executed. As with other significant issues related to social control, we are left with our own personal punishment philosophy to influence our position on this important topic.

1. Of the four general debate topics (deterrence, fairness, retribution, irrevocable mistake), which is of most importance in forming your personal opinion about the death penalty? Why?

2. The death penalty is available only for murder with aggravating circumstances. Most murders are not of that type. Can the death penalty deter "typical" murders even though it is only used for aggravated murders?

3. Raise some capital punishment debate topics that were not covered in this chapter (for example, cost) and present an argument favoring or opposing the death penalty based on that topic.

abolitionists Those favoring the abolition of the death penalty.

retentionists Those who favor keeping the death penalty.

proportional retributivism Requires that the worst crime in any society be punished with the worst penalty.

The Innocence Project An organization instrumental in securing DNA exonerations of persons who had served time on death row.

MyCJLab

Go to the Chapter 12 section in *MyCJLab* to test your understanding of this chapter, access customized study content, engage in interactive simulations, complete critical thinking and research assignments, and view related online videos.

Additional Links

Some of the most current and comprehensive information about the death penalty is available from the Death Penalty Information Center at **www.deathpenaltyinfo.org/**.

The National Center for State Courts **www.ncsc.org/Topics/Criminal/Capital-Punishment-The-Death-Penalty/Resource-Guide.aspx** provides a helpful Resource Guide on capital punishment.

The Criminal Justice Legal Foundation provides summaries of research supporting a deterrent effect of capital punishment **www.cjlf.org/deathpenalty/DPDeterrence.htm**.

To review information related to both sides of the death penalty debate, visit Pro-Death Penalty. com at **http://prodeathpenalty.com/** and Amnesty International at **www.amnesty.org/en/death-penalty**.

Amnesty International promotes abolitions of the death penalty and provides a world view on the topic at **http://web.amnesty.org/pages/deathpenalty-index-eng**.

Listen to podcasts on such death penalty topics as race, representation, innocence, and victims at **www.deathpenaltyinfo.org/dpic-podcasts**.

Juvenile Corrections

"We make criminals out of children who are not criminals by treating them as if they were criminals."

—Frederick Wines
Secretary of the Illinois Board of Charities and a noted penal reformer

1 Outline the development of the juvenile justice system.

2 Explain the age limits and types of offenses handled in the juvenile justice system.

3 Describe the juvenile court process and the characteristics of juvenile offenders.

4 Explain how juvenile offenders may be transferred to adult court.

5 Describe community-based treatment programs for juvenile offenders.

6 Describe juvenile residential facilities and the treatment programs available in them.

7 Summarize issues confronting juvenile corrections.

13

INTRO FROM JAIL TO YALE

You may know Charles Dutton from his television or movie roles (for example, *Roc* or *Gothika*). What you may not know is that this respected and award winning actor and director was sent to a juvenile reform school at age 13. When he was 17 he was convicted of manslaughter and sentenced to five years' imprisonment in the Maryland State Prison. He was released on parole, but after only a few months he returned to prison for possession of a handgun. During that return, he hit a correctional officer when a riot broke out and an additional eight years were added to his sentence.

Dutton's life began taking a more positive direction when he read a play while he was doing time in solitary confinement for refusing to clean toilets. The play sparked his interest in acting and he began participating in a prison drama program. While still in prison he received his GED and then an associate's degree in theater. After his release from prison, he earned a bachelor's degree in theater from Towson State University then went

to Yale University's School of Drama for graduate work.

In 2009, Dutton and several other former juvenile offenders who went on to become productive and valued members of society (for example, former U.S. senator Alan Simpson [R-WY] and acclaimed writer, activist, and poet D. Luis Rodriguez) filed a brief before the U.S. Supreme Court arguing against sentences to life imprisonment without possibility of parole for juvenile offenders. Dutton and the others believe

Source: /ZUMA Press/Newscom

that when a juvenile commits a crime—even a serious one— the justice system should not assume there is no possibility of rehabilitation (Equal Justice Initiative, n.d.).

> **DISCUSS** Should authorities estimate a juvenile's chances for rehabilitation based on the crime he or she commits?

Juveniles (youths younger than age 18) account for about 26 percent of all persons arrested for property offenses (burglary, larceny-theft, motor vehicle theft, and arson) and about 16 percent of all arrests for violent crimes (murder, forcible rape, robbery, and aggravated assault). After remaining fairly constant in the 1980–1994 period, juvenile property crime arrests began to fall and by 2006 they were at their lowest level since the 1970s. Although there has been a slight increase in recent years, the property crime index arrest rate is lower than it was in the early 1990s. A similar trend is found with juvenile arrests for violent crimes. After substantial increases between 1980 and 1994, juvenile arrests for violent crime index offenses have fallen to levels that are lower than any year in the 1990s (Puzzanchera 2009).

Despite the very welcome decline since the 1990s in juvenile arrests for both property and violent offense, there is a clear link between age and criminal behavior. In fact, the link is so fundamental that it is called the **age-crime curve**. This refers to the tendency for offending to rise during adolescence, peak around age 18, and then drop thereafter. The age factor is so closely tied to offending behavior that some cynics

have facetiously suggested the most effective crime policy would be to incarcerate everyone in the country on their thirteenth birthday and not release them until they reach age 30. Statistically, such action should dramatically reduce the nation's crime rates. Presumably, there are less dramatic proposals to consider—and we do so in this chapter. We begin with a brief overview of the decision to respond differently to juvenile offenders than we do to adult offenders.

some cynics have facetiously suggested the most effective crime policy would be to incarcerate everyone in the country on their thirteenth birthday and not release them until they reach age 30.

▶ *Development and Operation of the Juvenile Justice System*

A separate system of juvenile justice did not appear in the United States until 1899, when the first juvenile court was established in Cook County (Chicago), Illinois. Other communities had made informal movements to respond differently to juvenile offenders before Cook County's formal action, but the Cook County juvenile court clearly became the model around the country. The court was established to provide for both the care and control of juveniles.

The court's "care" function was based on the concept of **parens patriae**, which is the idea that the court is the

The court was established to provide for both the care and control of juveniles.

LEARNING
OUTCOMES
1
Outline the development of the juvenile justice system.

GLOSSARY

age-crime curve Refers to the tendency for offending to rise during adolescence, peak around age 18, and then drop thereafter.

parens patriae The idea that the court is the ultimate parent of all minors and therefore has final responsibility for its younger citizens.

ultimate parent of all minors, and therefore has final responsibility for its younger citizens. This philosophy came from the English system wherein children who were not receiving proper parental care could be brought before the Chancery Court. That court was concerned with protecting property rights of juveniles and the child's general welfare. It was with this philosophy in mind that the Illinois legislators gave the juvenile court concern for, and authority over, a child's welfare. In this manner, children deemed in need of supervision—those who are dependent, neglected, or abused—are taken to the juvenile court, which has incorporated the old English Chancery Court care functions.

The need to control misbehaving young people was a second function of the new juvenile court. Prior to the court's establishment, there was no age distinction (in Chicago or anywhere else in the country) as to how younger and older defendants were treated—everyone accused of a crime was handled in the regular criminal justice system. As far as the criminal courts were concerned, a ten-year-old was simply a small, misbehaving adult. But that began changing in the late-nineteenth century as widespread interest in bringing about child-welfare

reforms took hold across the country. The result was a desire to control misbehaving young people with more compassion than was present in the criminal justice system. As Frederick Wines said before the Illinois Conference of Charities,

> We make criminals out of children who are not criminals by treating them as if they were criminals. What we should have, in our system of criminal jurisprudence, is an entirely separate system of courts for children, in large cities, who commit offenses which would be criminal by adults. We ought to have a "children's court" in Chicago, and we ought to have a "children's judge," who should attend to no other business. (Quoted in Platt 1969, 132)

As a result, when America's version of a separate justice system for juvenile offenders began in 1899, the guiding philosophy of the new juvenile courts was clearly protective and rehabilitative. The dual functions of care and control are still part of today's juvenile justice system, but the control function is not so clearly protective and rehabilitative. Instead, there has been some movement back toward a view that at least some juvenile offenders are best handled as adult offenders. But before looking at those situations, it is necessary to understand better just who comes under the juvenile justice system's jurisdiction and what happens to them once they are there.

▶ Processing Juvenile Offenders

The ways in which juvenile offenders are processed through the juvenile justice system are different enough from the ways adults are processed in the criminal court system that it is not possible to elaborate in detail here (the case flowchart in Figure 13.1

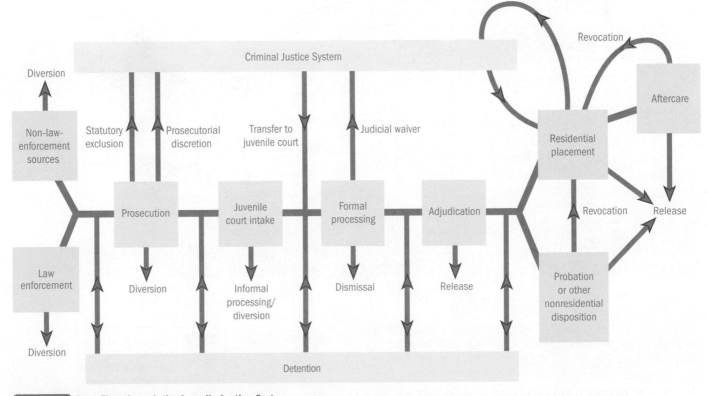

FIGURE 13.1 Case Flow through the Juvenile Justice System.
Source: www.ojjdp.gov/ojstatbb/structure_process/case.html

LEARNING OUTCOMES 2

Explain the age limits and types of offenses handled in the juvenile justice system.

GLOSSARY

status offense Misbehavior that is considered wrong only because society does not consider the juvenile old enough for such activity.

delinquency offense Act that would be criminal had it been done by an adult.

provides an overview of the stages involved). However, it is necessary to give brief attention to the process so we can understand to whom this system applies and the reasons for which juvenile offenders can be processed.

Age Limits: Who are the Juveniles?

Determining who will be processed in the juvenile justice system rather than the adult criminal justice system is not as easily accomplished as one might suppose. Figure 13.2 shows the oldest age at which a state's juvenile court can have jurisdiction over the juvenile. But even the map is a bit deceiving since many states have higher ages of juvenile court jurisdiction in such matters as abuse or neglect. For example, a young person identified by the juvenile court as having been neglected by his or her parents could be under the court's jurisdiction through age 20. In addition, many states exclude married or otherwise emancipated juveniles from juvenile court jurisdiction.

Juvenile Offense Categories: Reasons for Coming to Juvenile Court

Because of the *parens patriae* doctrine, the initial philosophy of the juvenile court was to assume that all the court personnel were interested in the welfare of the child and constantly had the child's best interests in mind. The result was a juvenile court system with jurisdiction over three perceived problem areas:

1. Situations wherein the child or juvenile has been neglected, abused, exploited, or in some other way mistreated

2. Certain offenses committed by juveniles that are deemed inappropriate or undesirable for persons under a certain age

3. Offenses committed by juveniles that would be a crime if committed by an adult

It is those last two items that occupy most of the juvenile court's time, because they deal with the juvenile's actual misbehavior. Misbehavior that is considered wrong only because society does not consider the juvenile old enough for certain kinds of activities is called a **status offense**; these include violating administrative rules (such as staying out past a city's curfew, skipping school, and purchasing and using alcohol and tobacco) or being "out of control" (for example, running away from home, not obeying parents, sexual promiscuity). Before 1974, many states responded to status offenders in the same way they responded to delinquents. It was assumed

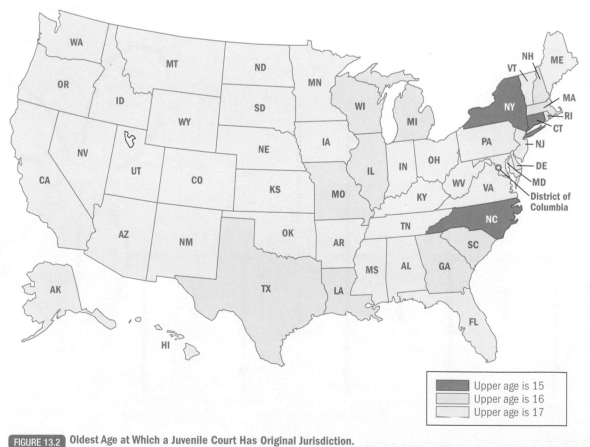

FIGURE 13.2 **Oldest Age at Which a Juvenile Court Has Original Jurisdiction.**
Source: Prepared with information from Snyder, H. N. & Sickmund, M. (2006). Juvenile offenders and victims: 2006 National Report (NCJ 212906). Washington, DC: Office of Juvenile Justice and Delinquency Prevention, 103.

that a runaway or truant would quite likely become involved in delinquent activities if some formal action was not taken. Consequently, juveniles were placed on probation or put in a correctional institution for nothing more than running away from home or being unmanageable. Today it is more typical for status offenders to be handled separately under some nondelinquent categories such as PINS (persons in need of supervision), JINS (juveniles in need of supervision), CHINS (children in need of supervision), and MRAI (minors requiring authoritative intervention). These supervision categories allow the state to become involved in the child's life but do not confer the stigma of delinquency proceedings or the effects of such formal action as incarceration.

Status offenses present a dilemma for society. On the one hand, it is argued that young people who are truant, have run away from home, are using alcohol, or are generally beyond their parents' control are in great danger of committing crimes. Property crimes might support the runaway, vandalism may give the truant something to do, or violent acts could be a way for the ungovernable to express their continued frustration. A desire to prevent those more serious violations by "doing something" when the acts are merely at the status offense level has been the motivation for most of the status offense laws. But critics of those laws argue that "doing something" may actually push the offender further toward delinquency.

The third type of misbehavior that can bring a young person before the juvenile court is the one people are most familiar with—**delinquency offenses**, or committing an act that would be criminal had it been done by an adult. Such acts include both petty and serious offenses ranging from shoplifting to murder. Since this type of behavior is the one to which the juvenile corrections system responds we use it to discuss the juvenile court's operation.

▶ Juvenile Offenders in Juvenile Court

Youths come to juvenile court officials' attention mostly as the result of police contact but also through social service agencies, schools, parents, probation officers, and victims. Upon getting a referral, an intake officer, prosecutor, or judge decides whether to handle the case informally or formally. The informal

Most delinquency cases are handled formally through a petition

response involves a nonjudicial disposition that is referred to as a **nonpetitioned case** (see Figure 13.3). Dispositions available at this point include probation (more accurately, **informal probation**), some other sanction, or having the case dismissed. Nearly every state has authorized informal probation, and the practice is commonly used across the country. Typically juveniles are placed on informal probation only when they have admitted to the charges against them, and they and their parents have voluntarily agreed to submit to the conditions of the informal probation. In the absence of such admission and agreement, the case will be dismissed or formally processed. Critics of the practice argue that it allows the imposition of substantial constraints on the youth's liberty without providing adequate due process safeguards.

Most delinquency cases are handled formally through a petition (see Figure 13.3). This involves the filing of a petition that requests an adjudicatory hearing. During this hearing, the juvenile court judge or referee determines whether the youth will be adjudicated (found) delinquent. That decision is made after evidence and witnesses are presented by a prosecuting attorney (in some cases and jurisdictions this is done by a probation officer), and after the juvenile or his attorney presents evidence and cross-examines witnesses. The juvenile may admit to the charges at the hearing, but when an admission is not forthcoming, the judge or referee must dismiss the case or must find beyond a reasonable doubt that the juvenile is delinquent.

When a finding of delinquency is made, a disposition (or sentencing) proceeding follows. Sometimes the disposition stage occurs immediately after the adjudication stage—especially if a predisposition investigation has already been prepared to expedite matters—but it might also be delayed until a social history is completed. Figure 13.3 shows that most of the

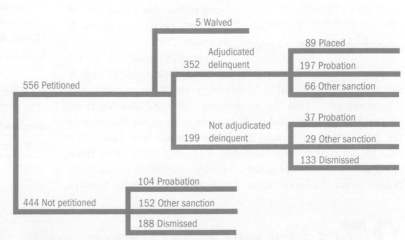

FIGURE 13.3 Case Flow for a Typical 1,000 Delinquency Cases in 2007.
Source: Knoll, C., & Sickmund, M. (2010). Delinquency cases in juvenile court, 2007. (NCJ 230168). Retrieved from www.ncjrs.gov/pdffiles1/ojjdp/230168.pdf.

Key Events in the Juvenile Justice System

1899	**1966**	**1967**	**1970**	**1974**
First Juvenile Court established in Cook County, Illinois. By 1925 most states have juvenile courts or probation services.	**Kent v. United States** USSC rules that courts must provide the "essentials of due process" in transferring juveniles to the adult system.	**In re Gault** USSC determines that, in hearings that could result in commitment to an institution, juveniles have four basic constitutional rights.	**In re Winship** USSC requires the state to prove its case beyond a reasonable doubt in delinquency matters. Prior to this ruling the civil nature of juvenile court proceedings meant that the burden of proof was only a preponderance of evidence (that is, evidence more convincing than the evidence offered in opposition).	Congress amends the 1968 Juvenile Crime and Delinquency Prevention Act to require that states keep their juvenile justice systems segregated from the adult systems and banned detention for status offenders.

LEARNING OUTCOMES 3 Describe the juvenile court process and the characteristics of juvenile offenders.

GLOSSARY

nonpetitioned case The informal response to a juvenile court case.

informal probation Upon the voluntary agreement of child and parents, the juvenile agrees to submit to certain probation conditions without being formally charged or adjudicated as delinquent.

preponderance of evidence Burden of proof that requires evidence supporting a charge to have greater weight or be more convincing than the evidence offered in opposition to it.

beyond a reasonable doubt Burden of proof that requires evidence supporting a claim to offer fully satisfying and entirely convincing evidence establishing the accused's guilt.

adjudicated cases resulted in either probation or placement in a residential facility.

Characteristics of Juvenile Offenders

Most delinquency cases handled by the juvenile courts involve property offenses as the most serious charge (36 percent), followed by public order offenses (28 percent), person offenses (25 percent), and drug offenses (11 percent). Public order offenses include such activities as obstruction of justice, disorderly conduct, and liquor law violations. The rankings vary by gender (for females the most serious charge is person offenses, followed by public order, property, and drug offenses), by race (see Table 13.1), and by age—with the juveniles younger than age 14 at the time of their referral being responsible for 24 percent of the person offenses (Knoll & Sickmund 2010).

Females make up about 27 percent of the delinquency caseload nationwide (Knoll & Sickmund 2010). That is a relatively small proportion, but it is noteworthy that the proportion increased steadily from 19 percent in 1985. Not only has there been an increase in the proportion of female caseloads overall, but Table 13.2 also shows that female caseloads increased more than male caseloads for each four general offense categories. Particularly notable were the large increase in person offenses for females

TABLE 13.1 | Race Profile of Delinquency Cases, 2007

Most Serious Offense	Total	White	Black	American Indian	Asian
Total delinquency	100%	64%	33%	1%	1%
Person	100	56	41	1	1
Property	100	66	30	2	2
Drugs	100	72	25	1	1
Public order	100	63	34	1	1

Note: Detail may not add to totals because of rounding.
Source: Knoll, C., & Sickmund, M. (2010). Delinquency cases in juvenile court, 2007. (NCJ 230168). Retrieved from www.ncjrs.gov/pdffiles1/ojjdp/230168.pdf.

DISCUSS *What explanations can you offer for why white offenders have drugs as their highest offense category and why black offenders have person offenses as their highest category? What about the respective lowest categories?*

and the increase in property offense cases for females, whereas males saw a decrease during the same period.

Most juveniles processed through the juvenile court are white, but black youths are disproportionately represented. Although accounting for 16 percent of the U.S. juvenile population, young African-Americans were 33 percent of all delinquency cases (Knoll & Sickmund 2010). This overrepresentation is especially high for crimes against persons, but less so for drug offenses.

TABLE 13.2 | Percent Change, 1985–2007

Most Serious Offense	Female	Male
Total delinquency	101%	30%
Person	233	95
Property	22	-24
Drugs	163	144
Public order	210	122

Source: Knoll, C., & Sickmund, M. (2010). Delinquency cases in juvenile court, 2007. (NCJ 230168). Retrieved from www.ncjrs.gov/pdffiles1/ojjdp/230168.pdf.

27% Females make up about 27 percent of the delinquency caseload nationwide

| **Thompson v. Oklahoma** USSC decides that society's "evolving standards of decency" now prohibit the execution of juveniles who committed their crime when under the age of 16. | **United Nations Convention on the Rights of the Child** reflects international consensus against execution and life imprisonment of juvenile offenders in its statement that "neither capital punishment nor life imprisonment without possibility of release shall be imposed for offenses committed by persons below 18 years of age." The United States does not ratify the convention. | **Roper v. Simmons** USSC abolishes the death penalty for defendants who were under age 18 when they committed their crime. The decision is controversial in part because the majority of the Justices cited overwhelming international consensus against the juvenile death penalty and the dissenting Justices did not agree that U.S. law should be influenced by international opinion. | **Graham v. Florida** USSC ruled that juvenile offenders may not be sentenced to life in prison without parole for nonhomicide cases. |

Most juveniles processed through the juvenile court are white, but black youths are disproportionately represented.

Due Process and Juveniles

The juvenile court was established without adversarial proceedings wherein a prosecutor tries to prove the defendant's guilt and the defense works to assure that the defendant has all the required legal protection. The absence of adversarial proceedings meant that due process protections for the juvenile were not really needed. After all, because the prosecution, defense, and judge were all looking out for the juvenile's rights and interests, why clog things up with procedural trappings? As a result, the juvenile court developed into a rather informal proceeding with a goal of treating rather than punishing the misbehaving juvenile.

Concern about the lack of procedural protection for juveniles did not attract much public or judicial attention until the 1960s. The U.S. Supreme Court had taken the position that the juvenile court's rehabilitative rather than penal philosophy made it an exception to the procedural guidelines of the Constitution. As Justice Blackmun said, "If the formalities of the criminal adjudicative process are to be superimposed upon the juvenile court system, there is little need for its separate existence" (*McKeiver* v. *Pennsylvania*, 403 U.S. at 551). But by the mid-1960s, it was becoming evident that in the name of treatment, juveniles were subjected to essentially the same punishments as were adult defendants.

In 1966, the U.S. Supreme Court heard the case of Gerald Gault, a 15-year-old who was taken into custody by Arizona authorities on the charge of making a lewd phone call (he was accused of asking a female neighbor, "Do you have big bombers?"). Gerald was eventually committed by the juvenile court to the State Industrial School until he reached age 21. Had Gerald been an adult making similar phone calls, Arizona law provided for a maximum penalty of a $50 fine or two months imprisonment. Gault's parents challenged the legality of his confinement and the case eventually reached the U.S. Supreme Court. In a 1967 (*In re Gault*), the Court reversed the Arizona court action

and identified minimum due process requirements for juvenile courts to follow in cases where institutional commitment was possible. Specifically, juveniles were given the following:

1. The right to fair notice of the charges to allow sufficient time to prepare a defense
2. The right to representation by counsel
3. The right to face their accusers and cross-examine the witnesses
4. The privilege against self-incrimination

The *Gault* decision was also important for what it did not say. For example, after *Gault*, rights still unavailable to juveniles included the right to trial by jury, to release on bail, and to protection against double jeopardy. In addition, because *Gault* pertained only to juveniles whose delinquent actions may result in institutionalization, jurisdictions have differed in the extent to which they have carried out the decision. In some states, the protections provided by *Gault*, such as the right to counsel, pertain only to delinquent charges. In other jurisdictions the protections have been expanded to apply to status offenders and in neglect and dependency proceedings.

In 1970, a second Supreme Court decision dealing with juveniles brought changes in juvenile court proceedings. *In re Winship* dealt with the burden of proof in delinquency hearings. The civil nature of the juvenile court proceedings meant that only a **preponderance of evidence**—that is, evidence having greater weight or being more convincing than the evidence offered in opposition to it—was required to establish a child's delinquency. In the *Winship* decision, the Court held that the standard of proof used in criminal court was applicable to juveniles in delinquency hearings. As a result, adjudication of delinquency required proof **beyond a reasonable doubt**—that is, fully satisfying and entirely convincing evidence establishing the accused's guilt. See the timeline for other Supreme Court decisions affecting juveniles.

Had Gerald been an adult making similar phone calls, Arizona law provided for a maximum penalty of a $50 fine or two months imprisonment.

► *Juvenile Offenders in Adult Court*

Even as the first juvenile courts were being established there was concern that some of the more serious offenses by juveniles should be handled in criminal court. A rise in juvenile violence in the 1980s and 1990s brought the issue to a head, and virtually every state allowed juveniles to be tried as adults in criminal court under certain circumstances. This transfer can occur in one of three ways:

1. Judicial waiver: Juvenile court judge waives jurisdiction in the matter
2. Direct file: Prosecutor decides to try the juvenile as an adult
3. Statutory exclusion: Criminal courts have original jurisdiction for certain crimes committed by juveniles

It is possible that any particular state will have all three or just one or two of the strategies in place (see Table 13.3). It is important to note that about half the states also have provisions for transferring cases from criminal court to juvenile court under certain circumstances (called reverse waiver), but we are interested here in those cases that end up in criminal court.

The Three Models

Transfer by **judicial waiver** is possible in all states except Massachusetts, Montana, Nebraska, New Mexico, and New York (Griffin 2011). Under this mechanism, a juvenile court judge can waive jurisdiction over a case and transfer it to criminal court. Prosecutors usually are the ones requesting such action, although in some states juveniles or their parents can request the transfer. Statutes typically limit judicial waiver by age, offense, or offense history and might also require the judge to consider the juvenile's amenability to treatment. In addition, waiver provisions are entirely discretionary in some states, whereas in others it is either presumed or mandatory that the

TABLE 13.3	Juvenile Transfer Laws by State								
	Judicial Waiver								
	Discretionary	Presumptive	Mandatory	Direct File	Statutory Exclusion	Reverse Waiver	Once/ Always	Juvenile Blended	Criminal Blended
Total States	45	15	15	15	29	24	34	14	18
Alabama	X				X		X		
Alaska	X	X			X			X	
Arizona	X			X	X	X	X		
Arkansas	X			X		X		X	X
California	X	X		X	X	X	X		X
Colorado	X	X		X		X		X	X
Connecticut			X			X		X	
Delaware	X		X		X	X	X		
District of Columbia	X	X		X			X		
Florida	X			X	X		X		X
Georgia	X		X	X	X	X			
Hawaii	X						X		
Idaho	X				X		X		X
Illinois	X	X	X		X		X	X	X
Indiana	X		X		X		X		
Iowa	X				X	X	X		X
Kansas	X	X					X	X	
Kentucky	X		X			X			X
Louisiana	X		X	X	X				

| | Judicial Waiver | | | | | | | | |
	Discretionary	Presumptive	Mandatory	Direct File	Statutory Exclusion	Reverse Waiver	Once/ Always	Juvenile Blended	Criminal Blended
Maine	X	X					X		
Maryland	X				X	X	X		
Massachusetts					X			X	X
Michigan	X			X			X	X	X
Minnesota	X	X			X		X	X	
Mississippi	X				X	X	X		
Missouri	X						X		X
Montana			X	X	X		X		
Nebraska					X	X			X
Nevada	X	X			X	X	X		
New Hampshire	X	X					X		
New Jersey	X	X	X						
New Mexico					X			X	X
New York					X	X			
North Carolina	X		X				X		
North Dakota	X	X	X				X		
Ohio	X		X				X	X	
Oklahoma	X			X	X	X	X		X
Oregon	X				X	X	X		
Pennsylvania	X	X			X	X	X		
Rhode Island	X	X	X				X	X	
South Carolina	X		X		X				
South Dakota	X				X	X	X		
Tennessee	X					X	X		
Texas	X						X	X	
Utah	X	X			X		X		
Vermont	X			X	X	X			X
Virginia	X		X	X	X	X	X		X
Washington	X				X		X		
West Virginia	X		X						X
Wisconsin	X				X	X	X		X
Wyoming	X			X		X			

Source: From Griffin, Patrick, 2011. "National Overviews." STATE JUVENILE JUSTICE PROFILES. Pittsburgh, PA: National Center for Juvenile Justice. Online. Available: http://www.ncjj.org/stateprofiles/. Reprinted by permission of National Center for Juvenile Justice.

LEARNING OUTCOMES 4 Explain how juvenile offenders may be transferred to adult court.

GLOSSARY

judicial waiver Juvenile court judge waives jurisdiction over a case and transfers it to criminal court.

direct file Prosecutor decides to try a juvenile as an adult.

statutory exclusion Criminal courts have original jurisdiction for certain crimes committed by juveniles.

juvenile blended sentence Juvenile court judge can impose both juvenile and adult sanctions on certain categories of serious juvenile offenders.

criminal blended sentences In cases where a juvenile is tried as an adult, the criminal court judge can impose juvenile sentences that would ordinarily be available only to juvenile court.

judge waive the case. Snyder and Sickmund (2006) report that less than 1 percent of all formally handled delinquency cases are waived nationally. Most of the cases waived involve offenses against a person or property offenses. Most of the waived cases involve black males who were 16 years or older at the time of the referral to juvenile court.

In some states, statutes give prosecutors the authority to file certain juvenile cases in either juvenile or criminal court. This **direct file** procedure—also called *prosecutorial discretion* or *concurrent jurisdiction*— is usually limited by age and offense criteria. For example, in Virginia prosecutors can direct file against a child at least age 14 who is charged with murder or such crimes as malicious wounding of a police officer or carjacking. In Florida, prosecutors have discretion to file in criminal court those cases in which juveniles age 16 or older are charged with any felony offense or any misdemeanors if committed by a juvenile with two prior adjudications, one for a felony. Interestingly, if a Florida prosecutor declines the option to direct file in cases where it is possible to do so, he or she may be formally obliged to move for a transfer in juvenile court, or at least to provide the court with written reasons for failing to do so (Griffin 2011).

State legislatures effectively transfer young offenders to criminal court by **statutorily excluding** them from juvenile court jurisdiction. Essentially, legislators in these states have predetermined which court is appropriate and have taken the decision out of both prosecutors' and judges' hands. Although this may not technically be a transfer, the large and increasing number of juveniles affected by these statutes makes it an important strategy for getting cases to criminal court. In 29 states, minors accused of certain offenses cannot have their case heard by the juvenile court. In some states those offenses are only the most serious kind—for example, in New Mexico only first-degree murder by a child at least 15 years old is excluded. But in other states the range of excluded offenses is quite broad. For example, in Mississippi all felonies committed by 17-year-olds are excluded as are any capital crimes (including attempts) by persons at least age 13 (Griffin 2011).

DISCUSS *What other pro/con arguments can you come up with? For ideas, see http://debatepedia.idebate.org/en/index.php/ Debate:_In_some_cases_juveniles_should_be_tried_as_adults.*

CONS

The legal consequences of criminal court felony convictions are too harsh.

Brain studies show adolescent capacity for judgment is not fully developed.

Juveniles are more likely to be rehabilitated in the juvenile system.

Being convicted as an adult carries more social stigma and has longer-term negative consequences than does a juvenile court conviction.

PROS

Juvenile court sanctions are weak retribution for the serious criminal behavior of some juveniles.

Juveniles recieve more due process rights in adult courts.

Juries in adult courts may be more sympathetic to minors.

Juvenile crime and young offenders have changed since the juvenile justice system was first established and that system is no longer appropriate for for today's youth.

FIGURE 13.4 Pros and Cons of Transferring Juveniles to Adult Court.

Blended Sentencing

Comparing sentences of transferred juveniles is complicated by some states using creative alternatives that essentially mix juvenile and adult sentences. These blended sentences allow the court to impose either juvenile or adult sanctions, or a combination of these sanctions. In this manner, the blended sentence resembles transfer laws in that they define juveniles who may be treated as though they were adults (Snyder & Sickmund 2006). Importantly, in all states where juveniles in juvenile court are at risk of receiving adult sanctions, those juveniles are entitled to the basic procedural rights afforded to criminal defendants (for example, the right to a jury trial).

When used in juvenile court, these **juvenile blended sentences** allow the juvenile court judge to impose both juvenile and adult sanctions on certain categories of serious juvenile offenders. In most of the 15 states using juvenile blended sentencing, any adult sanction imposed is suspended and functions as a kind of guarantee of good behavior. If the juvenile cooperates, he or she will remain in the juvenile system; if not, he or she may be sent to the adult system (Griffin 2011).

When juveniles are tried and convicted as adults, 17 states authorize their criminal courts to impose, under some circumstances, juvenile sentences that would ordinarily be available only to juvenile court. In this way, juveniles who have left the juvenile system for criminal prosecution may be returned to it for sanctioning purposes (Griffin 2011). These **criminal blended sentences** may be a combination of juvenile and criminal sanctions.

Think About It...

In *McKeiver* v. *Pennsylvania*, the Court found no constitutional requirement to a trial by jury in juvenile court. But the justices went on to say that individual states should be free to experiment and may install a jury system or use an advisory jury to assist the judge. Some states have responded with advisory juries composed of other juveniles. These teen courts (also called *youth courts* or *peer courts*) began taking shape in the 1970s and remain popular today (Butts & Buck 2002). The National Association of Youth Courts (www.youthcourt.net/) identifies more than 1,000 active programs as of early 2011. Youth court advocates believe the programs increase young people's respect for the law and for authority figures, and reduce recidivism. Have you or a friend had any experience with a youth or teen court? What impression did you or your friend have about such courts? What advantages or disadvantages do you see with youth or teen courts?

If the resulting sentence involves incarceration, there are three common ways it can be implemented:

- Straight adult incarceration: Juveniles are sentenced and imprisoned as adults with little differentiation in programming between juveniles and adults.

- Graduated incarceration: Juveniles are sentenced as adults but imprisoned in juvenile or separate adult correctional facilities until they reach a certain age. At that age, they may be released or transferred to adult facilities to serve the remainder of their sentence.

- Segregated incarceration: Juveniles are sentenced as adults but housed in separate facilities for younger adult offenders (usually 18- to 25-year-olds), and occasionally with specialized programming (Torbet 1997).

Trends in Judicial Waiver

Transfer laws generally (including judicial waiver, direct file, and statutory exclusion) expanded dramatically during the 1980s and 1990s. Statistics are most easily kept on the waiver procedures and the use of waivers over time reflects variation in justice policy. For example, from 1989 through 1992, drug offenses were more likely to be waived to adult court than any other offense category. Between 1993 and 2007, person offense cases were more likely to be judicially waived than cases involving other offenses (Adams & Addie 2010).

waivers are being used less often today than in the past

In addition to changes in the type of offense most likely to receive judicial waiver, it is important to note that waivers are being used less often today than in the past. In 1994, more than 13,000 cases were waived nationally, but in 2007 the number had dropped to 8,500—a level similar to what it was in the mid-1980s (Adams & Addie 2010). The vast majority of waived cases involve white males age 16 or older.

▶ Community-Based Responses to Juvenile Offenders

Several community-based programs for juvenile offenders exist for all offense types. As you will recall from Figure 13.3, most of the formally processed (petitioned) cases result in probation; but even quite a few of those that are informally processed (nonpetitoned) will also result in probation (called *informal probation* in these cases). Especially in the formally processed probation dispositions, there will also be accompanying requirements such as drug counseling, weekend confinement, or community service. The structure of juvenile probation and the work of juvenile probation officers are very similar to adult probation, so they do not need elaboration here. However, brief mention of some successful programs is useful.

Think About It...

As the Justice Police Institute points out (Petteruti, Velazquez, & Walsh 2009), youths placed in custodial facilities have a higher recidivism rate than youths who have received community-based sanctions. In addition, imprisoning youths can have severe detrimental effects on those young people and their long-term economic productivity. One reason is that imprisonment disrupts the process that normally allows many youths to "age-out" of crime. What other reasons can you offer for the detrimental effects of placing young offenders in custodial facilities? Does the goal of retribution override those detrimental effects?

Community-based programs are appropriate for youths placed on either informal or formal probation, but also for those returning to the community after residential placement. Greenwood (2008) explains that the most successful programs are those emphasizing family interactions—possibly because they include the providing of skills to the adults who supervise and train the child. Two particularly effective programs for juveniles on probation are Functional Family Therapy and Multisystemic Therapy.

Functional Family Therapy (FFT) targets youths aged 11–18 who are facing problems with delinquency, substance abuse, or violence. It is designed as a short-term intervention program with an average of 12 sessions over a three- to four-month period. The program can be offered in both clinic and home settings, but has also been successfully used in schools, probation offices, and mental health facilities. The focus, which is on altering interactions between family members, seeks to improve family functioning by increasing family problem-solving skills, enhancing emotional connections, and strengthening parents' ability to provide appropriate structure, guidance, and limits for their children (Center for the Study and Prevention of Violence 2007; Functional Family Therapy 2010; Greenwood 2008). The program has been found to be effective for a wide range of problem youths and with different types of therapists.

Multisystemic Therapy (MST) is also a family-based program but it has a community-based aspect as well. MST views the individual as part of a complex network that includes family, peers, school, and neighborhood. Parents learn to deal effectively with their youth's behavior

LEARNING OUTCOMES 5 — Describe community-based treatment programs for juvenile offenders.

GLOSSARY

Functional Family Therapy An effective short-term intervention program targeting youths aged 11–18 who are facing problems with delinquency, substance abuse, or violence.

Multisystemic Therapy An effective family-based program for serious juvenile offenders that views the individual as part of a complex network that includes family, peers, school, and neighborhood.

the most successful programs are those emphasizing family interactions

problems by recognizing barriers to effective parenting and learning to address problems through collaboration with a social support network that might include other family members, teachers, or other adults supervising the youths. Intervention may be necessary in any one or a combination of the network units, so MST could be provided in the home, school, or other community locations. Master-level counselors provide 50 hours of face-to-face contact and continuous crisis intervention over four months. As with FFT, MST has been proven an effective program for serious juvenile offenders (Center for the Study and Prevention of Violence 2007; Greenwood 2008).

There are, of course, community-based programs that focus on the individual offender rather than on the family. However, these have been found to be much less successful than the family- and community-based programs. Other programs such as intensive supervision probation, probation with extra services, and deterrence approaches such as Scared Straight have not been found effective (Greenwood 2008).

▶ Residential-Based Responses to Juvenile Offenders

Juvenile offenders whose disposition involves out of home placement are typically sent to a residential institution such as a group home, camp, or correctional facility. After reviewing the characteristics of those facilities and the juveniles in them, we consider some of the successful programs that can be used in an institutional setting.

Characteristics of Custody Facilities and the Youths in Them

According to the most recent census of juvenile residential facilities (Livsey, Sickmund, & Sladky 2009), about 2,800 facilities nationwide hold nearly 95,000 juvenile offenders. Most of

Think About It...

The traditional absence of procedural restrictions on the juvenile court is the result of three factors:

1. The juvenile court is not a criminal court; it is a statutory court (that is, it was created in state statutes by the legislatures) with powers provided for and limited by state law.
2. Because it is not a criminal court, no determination of guilt is involved. Instead, a misbehaving juvenile is adjudicated (pronounced) delinquent.
3. The juvenile court's goal is to treat rather than punish; therefore, procedural safeguards relevant and necessary for criminal court are neither relevant nor necessary for juvenile court.

Are these good enough reasons to not provide juveniles with basic due process rights that are given to adults in criminal court? If not, what due process rights should juveniles have in juvenile court?

69% most juvenile offenders (69 percent) are held in large public facilities

Females are more likely to be in custody as the result of a status offense or an assault without a weapon.

the facilities are small and privately operated (58 percent), but most juvenile offenders (69 percent) are held in large public facilities. About one-third of youths in custody live in coed facilities, but fewer than 10 percent of the facilities have coed living units (Sedlak & McPherson 2010).

LEARNING OUTCOMES 6 Describe juvenile residential facilities and the treatment programs available in them.

GLOSSARY

Missouri Model A model for juvenile institutions that emphasizes rehabilitation in small groups, constant therapeutic interventions, and minimal force.

Youths in custody are much more likely to have not been enrolled in school compared with their peers in the general population (21 percent versus 5 percent) and about half of youths in custody are functioning below grade level for their age. Because the link between education and delinquency is well established, an obvious need for juveniles held in residential facilities is an ability to continue their education. Most facilities evaluate the juveniles in terms of their educational needs and the majority of juveniles attend school while in the facility. Both middle-school and high-school educational services are available in most facilities and many provide special education services and GED preparation. Fewer provide vocational or technical education (Livsey et al. 2009).

The majority of juveniles in custody facilities are being held for delinquency offenses—more often for offenses against

persons (43 percent) than for offenses against property (26 percent)—and for drug offenses (10 percent), status offenses (10 percent), and public order offenses (3 percent). The remaining 7 percent are in custody for technical violations of probation or parole or some other reason (Sedlak & Bruce 2010).

Although most of the youths in custodial facilities are male (85 percent) there are interesting differences between male and female offenders in terms of their offense patterns. As shown in Figure 13.5, greater percentages of males than females have murder, rape, kidnapping, robbery, drug offenses, and public order offenses as their most serious current offense. Females are more likely to be in custody as the result of a status offense or an assault without a weapon. The high proportion of female simple assault offenses is probably not so much a result of females being more violent as it is a result of mandatory domestic violence arrest laws—juvenile females are being arrested for altercations with family members whereas in the past such cases were handled informally or documented as status offenses (Sedlak & Bruce 2010).

Institutional Programs

Treatment programs for youths in residential facilities have been evaluated over several years and some consistent patterns have emerged (Greenwood 2008). Generally speaking,

1. Programs that support mental health issues are more successful than those focusing on punishment—so treatment programs administered by mental health professionals are more effective than similar programs administered by regular correctional staff.

2. Programs focusing on specific skills (for example, behavior management, interpersonal skills training, family counseling, group counseling, individual counseling) have all demonstrated positive effects in institutional settings.

 DISCUSS *Significantly more juvenile females are in custodial facilities for "assault without a weapon" offenses than are juvenile males. Why? For which other offense categories do you find the male/ female differences interesting?*

FIGURE 13.5 **Males and Females in Custody by Their Most Serious Current Offense.** *Source:* www.ncjrs.gov/pdffiles1/ojjdp/227730.pdf

(Bar chart titled "Most Serious Current Offense" with vertical axis "Percentage of Sex Group" ranging 0 to 30. Categories: Murder, rape, kidnapping; Robbery*; Assault with weapon*; Assault, no weapon*; Property; Drug, public order*; Status*; Technical violation/other. Legend: Male, Female.)*

Can Juveniles Receive Successful Treatment in an Institution?

The Mendota Juvenile Treatment Center (MJTC) is a secured correctional facility located in Madison, Wisconsin. MJTC provides specialized treatment and programs for delinquent youths whose behaviors present a serious problem to themselves or to others. The MJTC program has been evaluated in one quasi-experimental and two preexperimental studies and is included in the National Registry of Evidence-based Programs and Practices (http://nrepp.samhsa.gov/). The program provides school services and group therapy focused on anger management, improved social skills and problem solving, and issues of substance abuse and sexual offenses. Youths in the program typically have several individual counseling sessions each

week with a psychologist, psychiatrist, or social worker. Program goals are to help youths accept responsibility for their behavior, learn social skills, resolve mental health issues, and build positive relationships with families (Substance Abuse and Mental Health Services Administration 2010; Wisconsin Department of Corrections 2011).

Research findings show that the program had the greatest benefit on serious violent offenders with those youth in the treatment group being more than six times less likely to engage in felony violence than a comparison group. Youth who received treatment in the MJTC program were also less likely than a comparison group to be involved in community violence within two years of release (Substance Abuse and Mental Health Services Administration 2010).

3. Cognitive-behavioral therapy, with its goal of changing the thinking process, has been found to work well with institutionalized youths.

4. Aggression replacement training, such as "anger control," which teaches participants what triggers their anger and how to control their reactions, has also been shown to work well with institutionalized youths.

Although effective institutional treatment programs are clearly needed, one state has undertaken a bigger change than mere program implementation. When facilities for juvenile offenders were first considered, not much thought was given to whether they should physically resemble those for adult offenders—it was just assumed they would. They were often given nicer-sounding names (reformatories, training schools, and so on), but they were essentially large congregate-care facilities that, at best, were built on a campus-style design rather than a cellblock or dormitory plan.

For many years, Missouri saw no reason to rely on anything other than the traditional congregate-care training school institution. In the 1970s, the Missouri Division of Youth Services (DYS) began questioning having youths mostly kept under the watchful gaze of correctional officers in a setting that was not especially conducive to the DYS stated mission of rehabilitation. Instead, the DYS began experimenting with smaller correctional programs by securing small sites across the state—abandoned school buildings, large residential homes, a convent—and outfitted them to house delinquent teens. As it invested in these community-based alternatives to incarceration, Missouri changed the philosophy and operation of its long-term secure confinement facilities to provide counseling and education in a more homelike setting. The largest of these new facilities housed only 36 juveniles (Mendel 2003).

Today, this emphasis on rehabilitation in small groups, constant therapeutic interventions and minimal force is known as the **Missouri Model** and is influencing the direction taken by other states such as Florida, Illinois, and Louisiana (Moore 2009). The Missouri facilities are positioned in

five regions (allowing confined youths to be within driving distance of homes and family), and each facility is staffed mostly with college-educated youth specialists (selected more for their interest in nurturing than guarding) who receive extensive training. Most importantly, the approach seems to be working. Missouri has one of the lowest recidivism rates in the country with 75 percent of youths released after 24 months remaining law-abiding and 67 percent remaining law-abiding after 36 months (Missouri Department of Social Services 2009).

▶ Issues Confronting Juvenile Corrections

The juvenile justice system as a whole is seen by many people as in urgent need of reform (for example, Arya 2011). Issues covered earlier in this chapter such as due process rights for juveniles, transferring juveniles to adult court, and applying adult sanctions to juvenile offenders are concerns that occasion much discussion among practitioners, policy makers, and the general public. There are other problems as well, including accusations of abuse and neglect in juvenile institutions, the significantly greater number of American youths in secure confinement compared with the youths of other countries, and the negative consequences of imprisonment on a young person's long-term economic productivity. Each of those deserve closer attention, but in this section we concentrate on the equally compelling issues of overrepresentation by minorities in the juvenile justice system and the problems of dealing with girls in a system designed for boys.

LEARNING OUTCOMES 7 Summarize issues confronting juvenile corrections.

GLOSSARY

Disproportionate Minority Contact Refers to the overrepresentation of minorities in virtually all aspects of the juvenile justice system.

Disproportionate Minority Contact

Data from 1910 indicate that the early juvenile facilities were used more frequently for white than for black juvenile offenders. Of white youths sentenced to correctional facilities, 69 percent went to reformatories for delinquents, whereas 31 percent were sent to traditional prisons, jails, and workhouses. The reverse was true for black youths—29 percent were committed to juvenile facilities and 71 percent to prisons, jails, and workhouses (Cahalan 1986). The discrepancy was eased as more states built facilities for juveniles and as racial segregation in public institutions was halted.

Throughout most of the twentieth century, white youths (not including Hispanics) made up the greatest percentage of the population in public and private custody facilities for juveniles, although minority youths were still confined at disproportionate levels. Today, minority youths ages 10–17 account for about one-fifth of the U.S. juvenile population but comprise more than half the juvenile arrests for violent crimes, more than one-third of the delinquency cases, and more than half of youths in residential placement facilities (Knoll & Sickmund 2010; Puzzanchera 2009; Sedlak & Bruce 2010). Non-Hispanic black juveniles make up about 16 percent of the nationwide juvenile population but account for 32 percent of juveniles in

1/5 Today, minority youths ages 10–17 account for about one-fifth of the U.S. juvenile population but comprise more than half the juvenile arrests for violent crimes, more than one-third of the delinquency cases, and more than half of youths in residential placement facilities

residential placement (Sedlak & Bruce 2010). Hispanic youths (of any race) comprise about 16 percent of the juvenile population but make up 24 percent of juveniles in residential placement (Hsia, Bridges, & McHale 2004; Sedlak & Bruce 2010; Snyder & Sickmund 2006).

The issue of disproportionate minority representation in virtually all aspects of the juvenile justice system is referred to as **Disproportionate Minority Contact** (DMC). For present purposes, we concentrate specifically on the disproportionate representation of minority youths in residential placement facilities. Four general factors have been suggested as contributing to minority overrepresentation (Devine, Coolbaugh, & Jenkins 1998; Hsia et al. 2004):

1. Activities occurring in the juvenile justice system itself
2. Socioeconomic conditions
3. Educational system inadequacies
4. Family dynamics

The impact and interaction of each area is complex. Family factors such as single-parent homes, economic stress, and limited time for supervision are controversial but apparent factors. Also, the absence of school programs to adequately serve minority juveniles—or the failure of minority youths to fully participate in the educational system—can encourage involvement in delinquent behavior. And poor socioeconomic conditions likely play a role by limiting job opportunities, providing low incomes, and restricting social support services.

Finally, the juvenile justice system itself contributes to DMC through activities that occur well in advance of the actual confinement. For example, racial stereotyping and cultural insensitivity (both intentional and

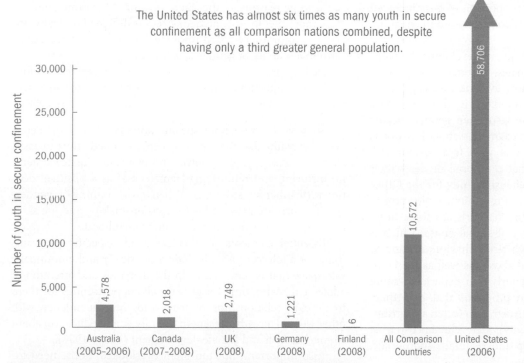

U.S. Youth in Secure Confinement Compared with Youth from other Countries.
Source: From p. 1 in FINDING DIRECTION: Expanding Criminal Justice Options by Considering Policies of Other Nations by Justice Policy Institute, April 2011. Reprinted by permission of Justice Policy Institute. http://www.justicepolicy.org/uploads/justicepolicy/documents/juvenile_justice.pdf.

DISCUSS *What reasons can you suggest for why the United States has so many of its youths in secure confinement compared with other countries? Can it simply be explained as a result of the United States having a greater population of young people than might the comparison countries? The Justice Police Institute (2011) suggests that U.S. policy tends to first find fault in the youth for committing the crime, whereas other countries tend to ask why the crime was committed and what services should be provided to encourage more positive life outcomes. Do you agree that this could be a reasonable explanation?*

unintentional) seem to affect processing decisions in many juvenile justice systems. A procedure known as *selection bias* occurs when actions or histories of minority youth are scrutinized more carefully than are the actions or histories of nonminority juveniles. For example, some studies show that police officers are more likely to stop and question a group of minority youths but only glance at a similar group of nonminority youths. According to other research, prosecutors have been found to look at a minority youth's prior system involvement as a stronger indication of a tendency toward continued crime than the same record predicts for a nonminority youth (Devine et al. 1998). When selection bias is combined with influences from the educational system, the family, and prevailing socioeconomic conditions, DMC is one of several negative consequences.

Girls in a System Designed for Boys

Girls entering the juvenile justice system are typically placed in programs that were created for delinquent boys (Bloom, Owen, Piper Deschenes, & Rosenbaum 2002). We know very little about the appropriateness of those programs for girls. Bloom and her colleagues explain that the "what works" literature has focused primarily on boys and men, leaving us to wonder about the applicability of the programs to girls and women. Program evaluations typically describe the proportion of girls included in the sample, but differences in outcome based on gender are not examined.

As we better understand the different developmental pathways followed by females and males, the need for gender-specific programming becomes more evident. Just as girls and boys develop physically and emotionally in different ways, their pathways to delinquency are also often gender-specific (Belknap & Holsinger 1998). For example, scholarly work is making it increasingly apparent that girls face specific risk factors because of their gender that can derail or delay their healthy development. In a comprehensive study for the Office of Juvenile Justice and Delinquency Prevention, senior project manager Sheila Peters (1998) notes that girls are three times as likely as boys to have experienced sexual abuse, which is often an underlying factor in high-risk behaviors leading to delinquency. The impact of sexual abuse (as well as the emotional and/or physical abuse that girls also experience more frequently) means that girls need programs that help them address their feelings of anger and frustration (often a contributor to involvement in criminal activity); their reluctance to trust others; and how they can develop and maintain appropriate, healthy boundaries in relationships.

Peters (1998) lists some of the things that girls need for healthy development (for example, physical safety, validation from caring adults, positive female role models) and some of the challenges they face (violence, substance abuse, family dysfunction, sexism,

academic failure) that may put them at greater risk for delinquency. Specific risks (other than sexual and/or physical abuse) of special concern to girls include the following:

- **Substance abuse:** Psychosocial development can be interrupted by substance abuse, as suggested in the anecdote that it is not unusual for a 16-year-old girl to check into a residential drug treatment program with both her needle and syringe and a well-worn stuffed animal hidden in her backpack.

- **Teen pregnancy:** Female juvenile delinquents engage in sexual activity at an earlier age than nonoffenders, which puts them at higher risk of unwanted pregnancy. Teen mothers (most of whom drop out of high school, earn less than half the poverty-level income, and live in poor housing in poor neighborhoods) are more likely to raise a child who goes to prison than are mothers who delay having children until their early twenties.

- **Poor academic performance:** The most significant risk factor relating to early onset of delinquency. A disproportionate number of female juvenile offenders have learning disabilities and may have developed a negative attitude about learning.

- **Societal factors:** Girls and boys don't get into trouble for the same reasons, in the same ways, or at the same rate. Because the juvenile justice system is designed to deal with boys, community-based resources for girls are scarce. Add to that scarcity of gender-specific resources a perceived need to "protect" girls and we may have an explanation for the disproportionate number of girls who are committed to residential facilities, often for status offenses (Peters 1998).

So, what might gender-specific programs look like? Peters (1998) explains that they involve a concentrated effort to assist all girls (not only those involved in the juvenile justice system) in nurturing and reinforcing "femaleness" as a positive identity with inherent strengths. When programming is gender-specific, girls are provided with decision-making and life skills that assist in their development into womanhood.

Essential elements of effective gender-specific programming for adolescent girls include a physically and emotionally safe space that is removed from the demands and attention of adolescent males, time for girls to talk, opportunities for them to develop relationships of trust and interdependence with other women already present in their lives, and education about women's health and female development (Peters 1998).

Also important, but too often overlooked, is the need for specialized training for staff members who are working with adolescent girls. Because working with girls and young women presents unique challenges, staff training is especially important in terms of relationship and communication skills, gender differences in delinquency, substance abuse education, and appropriate placement (Bloom et al. 2002; Daniel 1999).

Rather than continuing to squeeze girls into a justice system designed for boys, or to simply separate delinquents according to gender, it is necessary to have gender-specific programs for girls that provide a comprehensive approach to female delinquency rooted in the experience of girls (Peters 1998). There is movement in that direction, but a long journey remains.

Girls entering the juvenile justice system are typically placed in programs that were created for delinquent boys

Should Juveniles Receive a Life Sentence?

When Terrance Graham was 16 years old he was convicted of armed burglary and attempted armed robbery. Under a plea agreement, the Florida trial court sentenced Graham to probation, but six months later he violated that probation by committing an additional crime, a home-invasion robbery. The trial court revoked his probation and sentenced him to life imprisonment for the original armed burglary charge. Because Florida has abolished its parole system, the life sentence was essentially one without possibility of parole. Graham argued that the life sentence without possibility of parole constituted cruel and unusual punishment (Denniston 2009; The Oyez Project 2011). The case reached the U.S. Supreme Court in 2009 and the question before the Court was whether the Eighth Amendment is violated when a life sentence is imposed on a juvenile convicted of a nonhomicide crime. In 2010 (*Graham v. Florida*) the Court decided that such a sentence does indeed violate the Eighth Amendment's prohibition against cruel and unusual punishment.

If life imprisonment without parole is unconstitutional for juveniles convicted of nonhomicide crimes, might it also be unconstitutional for juveniles convicted on homicide crimes? Cases asking that question began making their way to the Supreme Court in 2011 when attorneys with the Equal Justice Initiative asked the U.S. Supreme Court to address whether it is constitutional to impose life imprisonment without parole sentences on juveniles convicted of homicide (Equal Justice Initiative 2011). In one case, Kuntrell Jackson was convicted of murder after his older cousin and friend shot a video store clerk during a robbery attempt. He received a mandatory sentence to die in prison. In another case, Evan Miller, who suffered physical and emotional abuse so severe that he tried to kill himself when he was just seven years old, was convicted of capital murder and received a mandatory life sentence without any consideration of his age or the abuse and neglect he suffered throughout his short life.

1. In its 2005 *Roper* v. *Simmons* decision, the U.S. Supreme Court ruled that it is unconstitutional to execute persons who were under age 18 when they committed their crime. In a Missouri case that resulted in mandatory life imprisonment for a 15-year-old boy convicted of killing a police officer, State Supreme Court Judge Michael Wolff wrote, "Juveniles should not be sentenced to die in prison any more than they should be sent to prison to be executed" (*Missouri* v. *Andrews*, No. SC91006; 2010). *Do you agree or disagree with Judge Wolff? Why?*

2. Some of the factors considered by the justices when ruling in favor of defendant Graham, were the belief that teenagers are different from older criminals because they are less mature, more impulsive, more susceptible to peer pressure, and more likely to be rehabilitated. *Which, if any, of those reasons do you believe are especially compelling in the argument that juvenile offenders should not be given sentences of life imprisonment without parole?*

LEARNING OUTCOMES 1

Outline the development of the juvenile justice system.

The country's first juvenile court was established in 1899 in Cook County, Illinois. The court's philosophy was based on the English concept of *parens patriae*, which meant the court was considered to be the ultimate parent of all minors. In that role, the juvenile court came to have both a care function and a control function over children and adolescents.

1. What is meant by the *age-crime curve* concept?

2. Do you accept the legitimacy of the concept of *parens patriae*? Why or why not?

3. What is meant by the statement that the juvenile court has both a care and a control function?

age-crime curve Refers to the tendency for offending to rise during adolescence, peak around age 18, and then drop thereafter.

parens patriae The idea that the court is the ultimate parent of all minors and therefore has final responsibility for its younger citizens.

LEARNING OUTCOMES 2

Explain the age limits and types of offenses handled in the juvenile justice system.

The states vary in terms of the age for which its juvenile court has jurisdiction over juveniles, but the most typical oldest age is 17—that is, adult court starts on the defendant's eighteenth birthday. Although the juvenile court will hear cases in which the juvenile is more a victim than an offender (for example, cases of neglect or abuse) the court's control function requires it to also hear cases involving certain behavior by juveniles. The types of behavior that can result in a juvenile court appearance include some actions that are perfectly acceptable when done by an adult (for example, purchasing and using alcohol) and other offenses that would be criminal had they been done by an adult.

1. What is the youngest "age limit" for juvenile court jurisdiction in the United States?

2. Many states exclude married juveniles from juvenile court jurisdiction even if they are at an appropriate age for juvenile court? Do you agree or disagree with that exclusion? Why?

3. What term is used for cases brought to the juvenile court that involve behavior that is wrong only because the juvenile is not considered old enough for those kinds of activities?

4. What is the corresponding criminal justice term for these juvenile justice system terms: *delinquent child, adjudication, disposition?*

status offense Misbehavior that is considered wrong only because society does not consider the juvenile old enough for such activity.

delinquency offense Act that would be criminal had it been done by an adult.

Describe the juvenile court process and the characteristics of juvenile offenders.

Cases come to the juvenile court primarily through referral by the police. The case can be handled either informally or formally. Formal processing means there will be a hearing at the juvenile court and a decision is made as to whether the youth will be found delinquent. When a finding of delinquency is made, the court decides what sanctions will be imposed. Most delinquency cases involve property offenses by white male youths, but the proportion of females has increased steadily over the last few decades.

1. Do you think placing a juvenile on informal probation is a fair or unfair practice? Why?

2. What are the most frequently imposed sanctions in adjudicated delinquency cases?

3. How does involvement in the four categories of delinquency cases (property, person, drugs, public order) vary according to gender, race, and age?

4. What explanations can you offer for why female property offenses cases increased during a period when male property offenses cases decreased?

5. What are the four basic due process rights given to juveniles under the *In re Gault* decision?

6. Distinguish "preponderance of evidence" and "beyond a reasonable doubt" as burden of proof requirements.

nonpetitioned case The informal response to a juvenile court case.

informal probation Upon the voluntary agreement of child and parents, the juvenile agrees to submit to certain probation conditions without being formally charged or adjudicated as delinquent.

preponderance of evidence Burden of proof that requires evidence supporting a charge to have greater weight or be more convincing than the evidence offered in opposition to it.

beyond a reasonable doubt Burden of proof that requires evidence supporting a claim to offer fully satisfying and entirely convincing evidence establishing the accused's guilt.

Explain how juvenile offenders may be transferred to adult court.

Responding to a rise in juvenile violence in the 1980s and 1990s, states increasingly allowed juveniles to be transferred to adult court under certain circumstances. That transfer occurs in one of three ways, with judicial waiver being the one most commonly found across the country. Judicial waiver is most often used today for cases involving person offenses, but it is important to note that judicial waiver is used less often today than it has been in the past. When juveniles who have been transferred to adult court are sentenced, it is possible that they may receive a mix of both juvenile and adult sanctions.

1. What are the three ways under which a juvenile can be transferred to adult court?

2. Which transfer model is found in all but four states?

3. Distinguish juvenile blended sentences from criminal blended sentences.

4. What are the three common ways of implementing a sentence of incarceration when a juvenile is convicted in adult court?

5. What are some of the pros and cons of transferring juveniles to adult court?

judicial waiver Juvenile court judge waives jurisdiction over a case and transfers it to criminal court.

direct file Prosecutor decides to try a juvenile as an adult.

statutory exclusion Criminal courts have original jurisdiction for certain crimes committed by juveniles.

juvenile blended sentence Juvenile court judge can impose both juvenile and adult sanctions on certain categories of serious juvenile offenders.

criminal blended sentences In cases where a juvenile is tried as an adult, the criminal court judge can impose juvenile sentences that would ordinarily be available only to juvenile court.

LEARNING OUTCOMES 5

Describe community-based treatment programs for juvenile offenders.

The most frequently used community sanction for adjudicated juvenile offenders is probation. As part of their probation, juveniles may also be required to participate in such programs as drug counseling or community service. The most successful community-based programs are those emphasizing family interactions. Two good examples of such programs are Functional Family Therapy and Multisystemic Therapy.

1. Although juvenile and adult probation have more similarities than differences, what do you think are some problems confronting juvenile probation officers that adult probation officers do not have?

2. Why are programs emphasizing family interactions especially successful for juvenile offenders?

3. Describe Functional Family Therapy.

4. Describe Multisystemic Therapy.

Functional Family Therapy An effective short-term intervention program targeting youths aged 11–18 who are facing problems with delinquency, substance abuse, or violence.

Multisystemic Therapy An effective family-based program for serious juvenile offenders that views the individual as part of a complex network that includes family, peers, school, and neighborhood.

LEARNING OUTCOMES 6

Describe juvenile residential facilities and the treatment programs available in them.

Juveniles who are placed outside the home are generally sent to a group home, camp, or correctional facility. Most of these residential facilities are small and private, but the large public facilities are where most juvenile offenders are held. Youths in these facilities are less likely than their peers to have been enrolled in school and many of them are functioning below grade level. Most facilities respond to this situation by providing educational services in the facility. Offense patterns of youths in custodial facilities show gender differences wherein females are more likely to be in custody as the result of a status offense or simple assault.

1. Since learning to interact with the opposite sex is important for all juveniles, should more juvenile residential facilities be coed? Why or why not?

2. Is a custodial facility appropriate for a juvenile whose most serious offense is a public order offense? Why or why not?

3. What are some general characteristics of successful treatment programs in residential facilities?

4. Describe the Missouri Model.

Missouri Model A model for juvenile institutions that emphasizes rehabilitation in small groups, constant therapeutic interventions, and minimal force.

LEARNING OUTCOMES 7 Summarize issues confronting juvenile corrections.

The juvenile justice system as a whole is confronted with questions about the need for due process rights when processing juveniles, the appropriateness of transferring juveniles to adult court, and the desirability of applying adult sanctions to juvenile offenders. Particular concerns for the corrections component of the juvenile justice system include the high number of American youth in confinement compared with the youth of other countries and the type of treatment they receive in those custodial facilities. Two issues of particular note are the disproportionately high representation of minorities in all aspects of the juvenile system, but especially in residential facilities, and the consequences of applying a system designed for boys to an increasing number of girls.

1. Describe some of the issues confronting the juvenile justice system as a whole and identify one that you consider to be especially problematic. Why did you choose that one?

2. Should we care that the United States has more youths in custody than do other countries? Why or why not?

3. What are some of the negative consequences that imprisonment can have on a young person's long-term economic productivity?

4. Explain what is meant by Disproportionate Minority Contact. Do you think this is a legitimate concern for America's juvenile justice system? Why or why not?

5. Are you convinced that there should be gender-specific programs in the juvenile justice system? Why or why not?

Disproportionate Minority Contact Refers to the overrepresentation of minorities in virtually all aspects of the juvenile justice system.

MyCJLab

Go to the Chapter 13 section in *MyCJLab* to test your understanding of this chapter, access customized study content, engage in interactive simulations, complete critical thinking and research assignments, and view related online videos.

Additional Links

The National Center for Juvenile Justice provides an online resource that profiles each state's juvenile justice system (see **www.ncjj.org/stateprofiles/**), including its transfer procedures.

Read and watch a video about Functional Family Therapy at **www.colorado.edu/cspv/blueprints/modelprograms/FFT.html**.

Find a Youth or Teen Court in your area at **www.youthcourt.net/?page_id=3**.

Visit the Justice Policy Institute page at **www.justicepolicy.org/research/2322** and download the Juvenile Justice fact sheet for more comparison of America's juvenile justice system with that of other countries.

Revisiting Evidence-Based Practices and What Works

"When you put all of this together—the very high cost [of prison] and the relatively low returns, along with the emerging field of evidence-based practices—it is increasingly persuasive to state policymakers and at the federal level as well that we *can* do something about this."

—Adam Gelb, Director of the Public Safety Performance Project, Pew Center on the States

1 Summarize the main evidence-based practices in corrections in terms of what works.

2 Describe how correctional budgets impact policy related to sustaining institutional and community-based correctional programs.

3 Discuss how rationality can be returned to correctional policy.

4 Explain the future of corrections as it relates to performance-based outcomes.

14

IS A NATIONAL CRIMINAL JUSTICE COMMISSION NECESSARY TO MAKE SYSTEM-WIDE CHANGES?

In 2011, Virginia State Senator Jim Webb introduced Senate Bill 306 into the 112th U.S. Congress to create a bipartisan 14-member president's commission to examine the criminal justice system as a whole, what works, what does not work, and make specific policy recommendations for the future (U.S. Senate Bill 306 2011). Known as the "National Criminal Justice Commission Act of 2011," this bill would authorize the commission to be appointed by the president and members of the house and senate within 45 days of its passage. Over an 18-month period, the commission would examine issues such as the over-incarceration of nonviolent and drug offenders, prison violence reduction, reentry programs, treatment of the mentally ill in the system, transnational crime, prison gangs, and drug cartels. The first (and last) time a comprehensive study of the criminal justice system was commissioned by Congress was in 1965 when Congress authorized the President's Commission on Law Enforcement and the Administration

of Justice. This commission released its final report as a publicly available book entitled "The Challenge of Crime in a Free Society" and it was the impetus for dramatic changes in the criminal justice system for the next two decades. These changes included minimizing pretrial detention for defendants prior to conviction, installing call management and arrest records systems tied to 911 in every police department, installing mainframe computers in every courthouse to process cases, and increasing alternatives to incarceration. The most recent bill was initially introduced by Senator Webb back in 2009 as Senate Bill 714. Webb's bill received wide bipartisan support, was backed by the Senate Judiciary Committee, and was passed by the House of Representatives, but it was blocked for unknown reasons in the U.S. Senate.

DISCUSS Look up Senate Bill 306. What are the arguments in favor of and arguments against this bill? What changes would you suggest making, if any?

Sources: http://webb.senate.gov/newsroom/pressreleases/ 02-08-2011-02.cfm; http://webb.senate.gov/issuesandlegislation/ criminaljusticeandlawenforcement/Criminal_Justice_Banner.cfm

---

▶ What Works in Corrections

This text presents an evidence-based approach to how correctional practices and research in institution and community-based systems can be improved. We began by introducing the principles of evidence-based practices (EBP), most of which were the mechanics of how supervision and treatment in corrections is to be applied by practitioners to offenders to get the most dramatic reductions in recidivism. These principles of effective intervention included establishing rapport and positive reinforcement for offenders (Chapter 5), accurately measuring risk and needs (Chapter 7), targeting criminogenic needs (such as the violence reduction program in Chapter 8), using cognitive-behavioral methods (Chapter 9), the importance of reentry (Chapter 10), and graduated sanctions for youths and adults who may backslide while on community supervision (Chapter 10 and 13). EBP included important methodological and evaluation considerations, which were introduced in Chapter 1 and shown throughout the text, to allow individuals to determine whether a research study is of high enough quality to have confidence in the results. In this chapter, the salient points of some correctional interventions will be revisited, along with examining the cost of these interventions, and how more informed decisions can be made in correctional policy. We begin first by discussing the goals of punishment.

are more about the idea of carrying out the punishment than about the results. Changing offender attitudes and behaviors through treatment is one of the main goals of the correctional system that is tied to EBP. However, not all treatment programs are equally effective. The most effective type of treatment for offenders is the cognitive-behavioral approach, in that it assumes that behavioral change

LEARNING OUTCOMES 1 Summarize the main evidence-based practices in corrections in terms of what works.

Cognitive-Behavioral Treatment

In Chapter 2, we learned that there are many different philosophies about why we punish. Some of the goals, such as deterrence, are difficult to measure and others, such as retribution,

TABLE 14.1	What Do We Expect from the Corrections System?
Enforcement	Court orders, parole board orders
Community Protection	No further harm while on supervision (no new criminal behaviors or escapes)
Restoration	Victim and/or community reparations (community service and restitution completion)
Deterrence	Former offender does not return to criminal behavior
Rehabilitation	Reformed offender creates a new life with changed thinking and behaviors
Retribution	Victims and others have a feeling that the offender has received his or her just deserts

can only come about through the understanding that there are errors in the way offenders think about certain issues, such as the thought that violence is the way to resolve disagreements with another individual (Lipsey & Cullen 2007).

Cognitive-behavioral treatment can take place in prison, in residential community programs, or as outpatient community programs. Prison-based EBP treatment programs have been found to benefit prisoners by changing their behavior and reducing misconduct while they are still incarcerated (French & Gendreau 2006). These same prison programs that reduced institutional misconduct were also associated with larger reductions in recidivism after release. In fact, researchers estimate that for every $1 spent on treatment, approximately $7 was saved in reduced recidivism costs and fewer hospital episodes (Harrison & Martin 2003).

Therapeutic communities (TCs) use cognitive behavioral treatment methods for drug addicts. TC graduates had lower rearrest rates, less drug relapse, and greater employment rates, particularly if they received aftercare following the residential phase. After three years, recidivism rates for the TC/aftercare group were between 25 and 31 percent, while for the TC participants only, recidivism varied between 45 and 79 percent (Welsh & Zajac 2004). After five years, *postrelease treatment* became the key variable in delaying a return to crime and increasing employment retention after release (Prendergast, Hall, Wexler, Melnick, & Cao 2004).

Cognitive-behavioral treatment for offenders while on community supervision is also important for change. The type and duration of treatment is more important to recidivism reduction than the probation supervision itself (intensive,

1:7 For every $1 spent on treatment, approximately $7 was saved in reduced recidivism costs and fewer hospital episodes.

regular, or electronic monitoring). More specifically, treatment that incorporates anger management and interpersonal problem solving had larger reductions in later recidivism than those that contained victim impact and behavioral modification (Lipsey, Landenberger, & Wilson 2007). The duration of treatment contact hours should be a minimum of 300 hours for high-risk offenders (who have the highest priority to get treated), 200 hours for medium risk, and 100 hours for low-risk offenders (who have the lowest priority of getting treated) for the maximum benefits (Bourgon & Armstrong 2006; Latessa 2004). Finally, long-lasting change is a *process*, so we should prepare for opportunities for intervention, such as offering technical violators treatment rather than jail (MacKenzie et al. 1999).

The type and duration of treatment is more important to recidivism reduction than the probation supervision itself (intensive, regular, or electronic monitoring).

EVIDENCE-BASED PRACTICE—DOES IT WORK?

Correctional Intervention Effectiveness

What Works	What Does Not Work
Prison for violent and predatory offenders who endanger the public/victims	Prison for nonviolent and drug offenders
Drug courts and mental health courts	Jail diversion for mentally ill offenders
Risk and needs assessments based on dynamic and static factors	Long-term administrative segregation
Vocational training, job preparation, and provided work opportunities	Expecting ex-offender to find employment on his or her own
Probation or parole supervision with treatment	Long-term community supervision (more than five years)
Residential community facilities or day reporting centers	Discipline-oriented boot camps
Teen courts, diversion for low-risk juveniles	Scared Straight
Reentry programs from prison	Expiration release from prison
Motivational interviewing and positive reinforcements to induce change	Negative punishments and threats
Multisystemic or Functional Family Therapy	Drug Abuse Resistance Education (DARE) or therapies based on fear or moral appeal
Intensive, residential programs for at-risk youths	Short-term nonresidential placements for at-risk youths

Source: Findings from many studies are available at www.campbellcollaboration.org.

Community Supervision

Probation supervision with treatment is effective in reducing the likelihood that offenders will engage in nonviolent crime and alcohol/drug use while on supervision, particularly for women (MacKenzie et al. 1999).

> Even when the differences between male and female probationers are taken into account, females perform better on probation with respect to technical violations and new arrests. This may be the case because females may have different motivations for completing their probation sentence successfully, such as keeping or regaining custody of children, the emotional support provided by interactions with probation officers, or access to treatment that otherwise would not be available to them. (Olson, Lurigio, and Seng 2000, 77)

Since women pose less of a risk of violence than men (in general), EBP suggest minimizing the interventions with the low-risk offenders. The higher risk offenders should be receiving longer treatment doses and more structured supervision. Residential facilities in the community, such as halfway houses and prerelease centers can fill this role, since they cater to clients with greater needs than regular probation or parolees. These needs are typically related to mental health, drug/alcohol abuse, and are criminogenic, in that they relate to their criminal history. RCCF offenders committed about the same number of new crimes as traditional probationers who resided at their own home. This is good news for RCCFs—showing that they work—because RCCF offenders posed no greater risk to the public despite their more complicated needs and assumed likelihood of greater failure (Lowenkamp & Latessa 2004).

Jail and Prison

Prison and more intensive correctional interventions are reserved for those individuals who pose the highest risk to public safety, while community-based options are more effective for lower risk offenders. Unlike community-based corrections and treatment programs, jails and prisons have fewer options for evidence-based

TABLE 14.2 — Outcome on Community Supervision

	Successful	Not successful
AGE	Over age 30	Under age 30
SKILLS	Stable employment and educational skills	Deficient employment and educational skills
HOUSING	Stable housing	Mobile or transient housing
FAMILY SUPPORT	Lived with their spouses or children	No support system
TREATMENT	Completed substance abuse and/or sex offender treatment programs	Did not complete treatment programs

Sources: (Makarios, Steiner, & Travis 2010; Roy 2004)

To learn more about specific programs that work, begin your search through the Bureau of Justice Assistance Center for Program Evaluation and Performance Measurement or use the interactive links provided at the end of the chapter.

practices that work to reduce long-term recidivism so we must be extremely selective. Most correctional facilities focus on creating a safe and secure prison environment that minimizes escapes, violence, and sexual assault. As we learned in Chapter 7, risk assessments are important to manage and reduce violence among prisoners within the institutional setting. Another important element to safe prisons that are free of contraband is to value correctional staff through decent pay, benefits, and to reward them with extra bonuses for reduced violence and keeping contraband out. This will minimize the perceived need to ignore illegal activities in prison or being part of the problem. As discussed in Chapter 11, the staff members must observe prisoners' legal rights, and treat prisoners fairly and consistently. If we are truly interested in safe environments that are not mere schools of crime, we must be willing to pay for better trained and higher caliber staff; that is part of the solution. Finally, offenders learning new skills while incarcerated, such as increasing education levels and employment skills, is important to help with reentry. To learn more about specific programs that work, begin your search through the Bureau of Justice Assistance Center for Program Evaluation and Performance Measurement or use the interactive links provided at the end of the chapter.

▶ Cost of Correctional Interventions

Now that we have a clearer idea of what correctional interventions work and what does not work, a prudent step is to factor in the idea of getting the biggest crime reduction benefit for the cost to administer the program. We begin with figuring the cost of incarceration, which are rough estimates. The cost of incarceration varies widely according to the cost of living in the area and also according to the security level of the prison

LEARNING OUTCOMES 2 — Describe how correctional budgets impact policy related to sustaining institutional and community-based correctional programs.

66% Nearly two-thirds of a corrections budget pays for staff members' salaries, wages, and benefits.

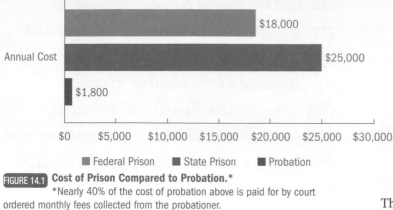

Annual Cost

$18,000
$25,000
$1,800

$0 $5,000 $10,000 $15,000 $20,000 $25,000 $30,000

■ Federal Prison   ■ State Prison   ■ Probation

FIGURE 14.1 **Cost of Prison Compared to Probation.***

*Nearly 40% of the cost of probation above is paid for by court ordered monthly fees collected from the probationer.

(cost is lower for minimum security and nearly doubles for maximum security).

Nearly two-thirds of a corrections budget pays for staff members' salaries, wages, and benefits. The most costly expense for prisoners is health care, and that is only expected to increase. Nearly one-fifth of all other operating expenses are for everything else, including food, transportation, programming and treatment, utilities, supplies, and other expenses (Stephan 2004).

Facility Construction

Facility construction and remodeling is a capital expenditure and is a small part (only 4 percent) of overall correctional budgets in most states. Some states borrowed money through lease revenue bonds to finance new prisons. For example, by the time the debt is paid, Florida taxpayers will pay over $1 billion in principal and interest on debt for bonds issued to build new

The most costly expense for prisoners is health care.

prisons as of 2010 (Collins Center for Public Policy/ Florida Tax Watch 2011). Estimated costs of building one maximum-security prison cell is over $110,000. Being that most prisons built today house between 1,500 and 2,000 inmates, the cost of building a single prison ranges between $140 and $200 million. Once a facility is built, about $12 million is needed each year to keep it operational.

The entire criminal justice system (police, courts, and corrections combined) comprised about 7 percent of all state and local government spending, which was about the same amount spent on health care and hospitals (Kyckelhahn 2010). With a less stable economy, decline in tax-based revenues, and increases in health care costs, the amount spent on criminal justice is predicted to decrease. States must either raise taxes or reduce spending through program cuts and hiring freezes for state institutions such as police, schools, universities, social services, probation, and prisons. For example, a decline in state funding for higher education has caused college tuition increases (National Association of State Budget Officers 2011). The disjuncture between state spending on prisons

$100k The estimated cost of building one maximum security prison cell is over $110,000.

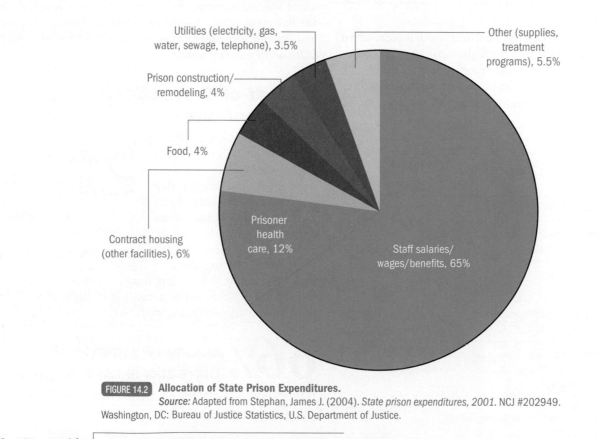

Utilities (electricity, gas, water, sewage, telephone), 3.5%

Prison construction/ remodeling, 4%

Food, 4%

Contract housing (other facilities), 6%

Prisoner health care, 12%

Other (supplies, treatment programs), 5.5%

Staff salaries/ wages/benefits, 65%

FIGURE 14.2 **Allocation of State Prison Expenditures.**
Source: Adapted from Stephan, James J. (2004). *State prison expenditures, 2001.* NCJ #202949. Washington, DC: Bureau of Justice Statistics, U.S. Department of Justice.

TABLE 14.3 | Program Costs and Estimated Benefits of Correctonal Interventions

Program	Benefits (value of reduced crime)	Initial Investment Program Costs (2007 dollars)	Benefits Divided by Cost (return on investment for every dollar invested)
Prison-Based			
Education	$18,621	$ 985	$18.90
Prison Industry	$14,387	$ 427	$33.69
Therapeutic Community	$14,357	$ 1,642	$ 8.74
Sex Offender	$16,945	$12,881	$ 1.31
Violent Mentally Ill	$46,452	$27,617	$ 1.68
Community-Based			
Drug Treatment	$12,443	$ 588	$21.16
Drug Courts	$12,988	$ 4,474	$ 2.90
Work Release	$ 2,904	$ 615	$ 4.72
Intensive Supervision Probation with No Treatment	$ 0	$ 3,869	$ 0
Electronic Monitoring	$ 0	$ 926	$ 0

Source: (Adapted from Drake, Aos, and Miller 2009, Table 1 p. 184–185)

The entire criminal justice system (police, courts, and corrections combined) comprised about 7 percent of all state and local government spending, which was about the same amount spent on health care and hospitals

and higher education is even more pronounced in California, Florida, Maryland, and New York. As we learn more about reducing costs, retaining what works, and cutting what does not work, it is time to explore returning rationality to correctional policy and sentencing.

▶ Returning Rationality to Corrections Policy

Corrections policy has become overrun by politics, union control, and emotionally based reactions to terrible tragedies, along with not enough administrative accountability and transparency. Academic scholars and not-for-profit groups such as the Sentencing Project are deeply committed to rational crime control policy, which focuses on appropriate responses to harm suffered by the victim or by communities. Tonry

(2004) suggested that crime policy making be altogether delegated away from politics and to a specialized administrative agency. This idea is in line with his other suggestion to make prosecutors and judgeships into career civil servant tracts and to get away from the election and political appointment process. Mauer (1999, 16–17) outlined concrete ways that crime control policy can become more rational. These ways include the following:

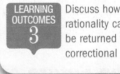

LEARNING OUTCOMES 3 — Discuss how rationality can be returned to correctional policy.

- Require sunset provisions for mandatory sentencing policies so these laws must be reviewed if they are to be continued.
- Transfer more resources away from institutional corrections and toward community-based options.
- Develop more restorative justice and conflict mediation solutions.
- Incorporate front-end crime prevention programs which are less costly than reacting to control crime after it has occurred.
- Present corrections policy as either a public safety or as a public health issue. Policies should no longer be seen as a choice between victim rights versus rights of the convicted offender, as concerned parties are ultimately in favor of increasing safety for both victims and offenders.
- All local entities to use solutions specific to their problems. Crime solutions that are "one size fits all" may not work everywhere.

▶ *The Future of Corrections*

We predict that the future of corrections looks very promising, as changes are made toward evidence-based practices and programs that work to reduce recidivism. No longer will programs be funded solely on the number of persons incarcerated or on the caseload sizes on probation. We predict that funding will instead be allocated for programs that can meet certain **performance-based measures** such as recidivism reduction, decreasing revocations back to jail, increasing employment rates for offenders on supervision, increasing the amount of restitution collected, and the amount of community supervision completed. This only works with accurate data, if community service officers are dedicated to helping offenders succeed instead of playing the **"gotcha" game**, and if parole boards and judges agree to a progressive sanction model over automatic jail or prison revocations. Ultimately, with less offenders going back to institutions, the state saves a significant amount of money.

Local jurisdictions that have saved the state money by reducing their prison populations (such as in Michigan, Ohio, and Oregon) have been approved to use the savings on crime prevention programs in their own communities. The practice of redistributing money is known as "Justice Reinvestment" (Tucker & Cadora 2003) or as "Reclaim" in Ohio. Essentially, if prison populations dropped over time, the money saved from funds that were initially budgeted by a state to incarcerate offenders could be redirected to job training, or to support schools, libraries, public housing, and other forms of community restoration in high-crime neighborhoods. Another use of federal funds was to encourage states to apply for grant money to use on interventions that simultaneously reduced prison populations and increased public safety in the neighborhoods where most prisoners return (Clear 2011). Examples of Justice Reinvestment projects include diverting people from the prison system, increasing drug treatment beds, closing prisons, and reducing parole and probation technical violation rates. Every intervention must use data to show measurable declines in the prison population and how the intervention affects neighborhood public safety.

Many state and local correctional systems are hampered with outdated data systems and simply do not collect the type of data necessary to make sound policy decisions. To help this situation, a shared performance-based measures database allows administrators to use the same database platform to collect, store, and analyze data for their institution. This database also allows one institution to compare performance against other similar institutions around the country using standardized measures that compute rates by factoring in the raw number by a standard denominator. The performance-based measures database contains seven main areas of available data primarily for jails and prisons: public safety, institutional safety, mental health, substance abuse, justice, education, and physical health.

Corrections managers in juvenile and adult corrections will need to become more accountable and transparent through information collected as well as through professional associations like the American Corrections Association or the **Association of State Correctional Administrators** (ASCA). As we venture into the future, we may be looking at an entire paradigm change from one that focused on an offender's deficits and shortcomings to one built on positive incentives, strengths, aspirations, and talents that have the potential of becoming exceptional and changed behavior. Focusing on positive behavior along with reinvesting in vulnerable communities, incarceration rates will be reduced without compromising public safety.

LEARNING OUTCOMES 4 Explain the future of corrections as it relates to performance-based outcomes.

GLOSSARY

performance-based measures system A Web-based database that allows users to analyze their own institutional environment and compare to other states using standardized measures.

"gotcha" game A style of offender supervision where the officer is less interested in helping the offender succeed, and is more interested in tracking failures and acting on rule violations; as a result, the officer has a high turnover of cases.

Association of State Correctional Administrators A national organization for state department of corrections directors that seeks to educate top administrators on broad correctional issues and influence correctional policy.

TABLE 14.4 | **Performance Standards for Corrections**

Public Safety

Facility escapes (medium custody and above)

Walkaways

Institutional Safety

Staffing ratios per shift (number of inmates for every officer)

Riots and disturbances

Prisoner homicides

Prisoner suicides

Contraband recovered

Inmate-on-inmate assaults and victims

Uses of force by staff

Staff injuries resulting from inmate assault

Inmate-on-inmate sexual assaults

Staff sexual misconduct

Treatment Provided

Type and frequency of treatment programs provided

Positive drug tests

Psychiatric beds

Treatment staff (type, number of hours providing services)

Offender Recidivism

Commitment type (technical violation or new crime)

New offense type

Number of crime-free days (release date to new offense date)

Source: Adapted from Wright, K., Brisbee, J., and Hardyman, P. (2003) *Defining and measuring performance*. Washington, DC: U.S. Department of Justice, Table 7 pp. 58–60.

Arizona's Getting Ready Program: Does a "Parallel Universe" Work?

Corrections Director Dora Schriro observed that a person defined as a "model inmate" learned how to obey orders and avoided disciplinary reports, but the offenders were not taught how to make good decisions when they were on their own that would keep them from returning to prison. As a result, Schriro developed a "Parallel Universe" for inmates in Arizona and Missouri that incorporates incentives for positive behavior.

First, a case treatment plan is developed for every inmate. All inmates are expected to work and/or be completing their GED before release. Prison jobs are ranked by entry level or skilled. Skilled jobs can be acquired only by inmates that have received their GED and have been disciplinary free. There is a three-tiered incentive system based on earning it through behavior—what inmates defined they would like to receive if they work toward these incentives. An example of an incentive is a contact visit with family where the family can bring homemade food. Other incentives are special commissary purchases (as long as inmates have their own money on the books) and dinner and a movie.

Performance-based data in Arizona were compared one year before the program started and then compared with outcome data four years later in 2007. The evaluation found that there was a decrease in negative behavior in prison, which included less major rule violations, assaults, sexual assaults, grievances, and drug use. Recidivism (defined by returning to prison) declined 2.75 percent from 30 percent to 27.25 percent after one year following release.

The "Parallel Universe" concept in Arizona raises several interesting questions:

1. Do you consider the "Parallel Universe" an example of a Justice Reinvestment program (in that it can reduce prison populations and increase public safety)? Why or why not?

2. Should inmates be paid comparable wages for all prison jobs, and charged bills such as rent and utilities, just like outside of prison? Argue for or against this concept.

Source: © Mikael Karlsson/Alamy

LEARNING OUTCOMES 1

Summarize the main evidence-based practices in corrections in terms of what works.

The principles of effective intervention include establishing rapport, positive reinforcement for offenders, accurately measuring risk and needs, targeting criminogenic needs, using cognitive-behavioral methods, reentry, and graduated sanctions. Prison is only for those individuals who pose the highest risk to public safety, while community-based options are more effective for lower-risk offenders.

1. Are offenders getting enough correctional intervention to adequately change their path?

2. EBP in corrections seems to focus entirely on offenders and seems to ignore victims in this process. How can EBP be explained or sold to victims or victims' rights groups so that they will support EBP?

LEARNING OUTCOMES 2

Describe how correctional budgets impact policy related to sustaining institutional and community-based correctional programs.

In this age of uncertain budgets and economic shortfalls, estimating the costs and benefits of reduced crime from these programs is as important to implementing what works as it is to deciding which programs should be funded.

1. How can correctional staff members' salaries and benefits, which comprise the largest portion of correctional costs, be reduced, yet still be able to pay staff what they're worth?

2. How can correctional budgets be decreased without compromising institutional safety and public safety?

LEARNING OUTCOMES 3

Discuss how rationality can be returned to correctional policy.

Move away from the political arena and into professionalizing key decision-making positions. Examine the broader effects of our decisions on the justice system and on communities outside the system. Reinvest dollars saved on incarceration into social service programs in low-income communities.

1. What negative consequences might there be by minimizing political influences?

2. If we are unable to separate from political influences, what limits must be set and/or standards be met for legislators and those in elected positions to minimize the irrational decisions of the past?

LEARNING OUTCOMES 4

Explain the future of corrections as it relates to performance-based outcomes.

Future correctional budgets will fund programs that work, and will base funding on whether the system can achieve outcomes such as recidivism reduction and accounting for victim restitution and community service completion. This will necessitate transparency and access to centralized data.

1. What kinds of things need to happen in order for this new correctional paradigm to be transformed and embraced?

2. What kind of balance should there be between institutional transparency and privacy?

performance-based measures system A Web-based database that allows users to analyze their own institutional environment and compare to other states using standardized measures.

"gotcha" game A style of offender supervision where the officer is less interested in helping the offender succeed, and is more interested in tracking failures and acting on rule violations; as a result, the officer has a high turnover of cases.

Association of State Correctional Administrators A national organization for state department of corrections directors that seeks to educate top administrators on broad correctional issues and influence correctional policy.

MyCJLab

Go to the Chapter 14 section in *MyCJLab* to test your understanding of this chapter, access customized study content, engage in interactive simulations, complete critical thinking and research assignments, and view related online videos.

Additional Links

View the 60-minute Justice Reinvestment Initiative panel session, sponsored by BJA, in January 2010: **www.youtube.com/watch?v=QNU7tJOsgPM.**

View Dr. Edward Latessa's summary of how community corrections can be strengthened using evidence-based practices at **www.youtube.com/watch?v=MYY6jQ2LAuc&feature=relmfu**.

Begin your search for EBPs that work through the Bureau of Justice Assistance Program Evaluation and Performance Measurement resources page: **www.ojp.usdoj.gov/BJA/evaluation/evidence-based.htm**.

Continue your search for more EBPs that work in criminal justice, juvenile justice, and victimology through the Office of Justice Program-sponsored website: **www.crimesolutions.gov/**.

Visit the Campbell Collaboration website to look up the latest meta-analytic research on what works in the criminal justice system: **www.campbellcollaboration.org**.

Look up evidence-based substance abuse and/or mental health programs that work through the U.S. Dept. of Health and Human Services Substance Abuse and Mental Health Services Administration interactive database: **http://nrepp.samhsa.gov**.

Visit the Center for the Study and Prevention of Violence to search for EBP that work for juveniles: **www.colorado.edu/cspv/blueprints/**.

Glossary

1779 Penitentiary Act Passed by the English Parliament, this act relied on John Howard's ideas to make significant reforms to the prison system.

abolitionists Those favoring the abolition of the death penalty.

age-crime curve Refers to the tendency for offending to rise during adolescence, peak around age 18, and then drop thereafter.

aggravating circumstances An event or condition that makes an offense more serious than it might otherwise be.

agriculture Outdoor field work jobs involving prisoners' growing crops and raising livestock; prevalent in southern states.

antiandrogens Hormones that lower the male sex drive by decreasing testosterone levels. Examples include cyproterone acetate or medroxyprogesterone acetate.

Association of State Correctional Administrators A national organization for state department of corrections directors that seeks to educate top administrators on broad correctional issues and influence correctional policy.

Auburn system Prison system established with the Auburn Prison in New York, which used a modified version of the Pennsylvania system wherein prisoners were kept separate from each other at night but allowed to work and eat together, in silence, during the day.

aversive conditioning The use of negative stimuli (painful thoughts, putrid smells, etc.) to reduce or eliminate sexual arousal.

bail bond A written agreement by the defendant to pay cash or relinquish property to the court if the defendant fails to attend required court appearances.

beyond a reasonable doubt Burden of proof that requires evidence supporting a claim to offer fully satisfying and entirely convincing evidence establishing the accused's guilt.

bifurcated trial A requirement that death penalty cases have two stages, with the first stage being the traditional trial to determine guilt and a second stage to decide the sentence—death or life imprisonment.

Big House A maximum-security penitentiary with a convict subculture, lasting between the early 1800s until about 1980.

booked When a suspect is identified and fingerprinted in jail after being arrested for an alleged crime.

Brockway, Zebulon Credited with implementing the Irish system in the United States at the Elmira Reformatory in Elmira, New York, in the late 1870s.

Bureau of Prisons Where federal prisoners go when they have violated an incarcerable federal offense.

caseload The number of individuals that one probation officer can effectively supervise based on predefined risks and needs posed.

certificate of rehabilitation Generic term for an official recognition that a criminal offender has shown reliability and good character over time and deserves to regain lost civil rights.

citation A police-issued ticket ordering a citizen to pay a fine for a minor law violation.

citizen circles An Ohio restorative justice program at the prisoner reentry stage that encourages community collaboration with offenders during their supervision in the community.

civil death Convicted offenders forfeit all rights and privileges of citizenship, including things such as the right to enter into a contract or the right to sue.

civil disabilities Convicted offenders suffer a partial, rather than an absolute, loss of civil rights because of a criminal conviction.

civil disenfranchisement The loss of the right to vote due, for example, to a felony conviction.

classification The process and procedures by which prison officials determine the risk posed by each offender and the offender's individual treatment needs.

co-occurring disorders A client with a mental disorder and a substance abuse problem.

Code of Hammurabi The first known body of law, established by King Hammurabi about 4,000 years ago, lays out the basis of criminal law.

cognitive behavioral approaches Changing thinking patterns and habits that lead to criminal behavior, such as self-control, anger management, social perspective taking, moral reasoning, problem solving, and attitudinal change.

collateral consequences Secondary consequences beyond the actual sentence that was imposed.

commissary Snacks, hygiene items, and other items available for purchase at the prison store.

community corrections Court-ordered supervision and treatment while the offender remains at liberty in the community.

community reparation board Group that facilitates involvement of community members in an offender's reentry to society.

community service Court-ordered special condition that mandates that offenders complete unpaid work for non-profit organizations.

commutation of sentence When a leader in the executive branch of government reduces an offender's punishment.

compassionate release Available on a case-by-case basis for inmates who are permanently incapacitated, have less than one year to live, and for those who no longer pose an imminent danger to the community. Also known as medical parole.

concentration approach Prisoners are grouped together in special prisons or special units within a prison, and their activities and movements are severely restricted and highly monitored.

concurrent sentencing Allows an offender convicted of multiple offenses to serve those offenses at the same time.

conditional release The return of prisoners to the larger community with a brief period of supervision with rules such as curfew, treatment completion, and maintaining employment. Can be used either pretrial or postconviction.

congregate and silent Key words distinguishing the Auburn system, which required prisoners to remain silent, even while working and eating together.

continuum of sanctions One or more sentencing options within the community or an institution that can be combined with one another to achieve a range of sentencing goals.

contraband Forbidden items that compromise institutional safety and security.

correctional officer The person responsible for maintaining order within the institution and enforcing prison rules and regulations.

corrections The network of government and private agencies responsible for the pre- and postconviction custody, supervision, and treatment of persons accused or convicted of crimes.

crews Small cliques of prisoners that spend time together, but there is no initiation or formal alliances. Some crews can be networked and predatory, but they are more loosely associated and are not an institutional security threat.

crime control policy A course of action to respond to criminal behavior in the best interest of the public.

criminal blended sentences In cases where a juvenile is tried as an adult, the criminal court judge can impose juvenile sentences that would ordinarily be available only to juvenile court.

criminogenic Factors that cause or tend to cause criminal behavior.

cultivation theory Repeated viewing and cumulative exposure to violence in the media eventually creates a sense of insecurity and irrational fear of violent victimization and about people in the world in general.

day reporting center A nonresidential community corrections sanction that blends high levels of control with the delivery of specific services needed by offenders.

decentralization A principle popular in the South during the first half of the nineteenth century wherein the administration of justice was left to local authorities instead of being centralized at the state level.

deliberate indifference When officers know about a situation and don't take action to prevent it.

delinquency offense Act that would be criminal had it been done by an adult.

department of corrections The state agency responsible for managing and operating the state's adult prison system.

deprivation model Assumes that prison culture developed out of the pains of imprisonment through adaptations that prisoners make to circumvent these losses.

design capacity The number of inmates that facility planners or architects intended for the facility.

determinate sentencing A system wherein the convicted offender receives a sentence to a specific time period rather than a time range.

deterrence Discouraging future criminal acts by both the offender and others in the population.

detoxification A process of sudden withdrawal from all drugs and alcohol so that treatment can begin.

differential response Term applied to society's response to women offenders when emphasis was on having separate and different-style prisons, different programs, and different sentencing practices for women offenders.

direct file Prosecutor decides to try a juvenile as an adult.

direct supervision Inmate supervision method wherein custodial staff are placed—for their entire shift—in the inmates' living area.

discretionary parole Conditional early release from imprisonment at the discretion of a state paroling authority and continued supervision in the community.

dismissed When a case is dropped for lack of evidence and does not proceed any further.

dispersion approach Prison administrators spread troublemakers to prisons throughout the system or in various units of the prison.

disproportionate When the group under study has a substantially greater or lesser percentage than exists in the larger population.

Disproportionate Minority Contact Refers to the over-representation of minorities in virtually all aspects of the juvenile justice system.

disturbance An altercation involving three or more inmates resulting in official action, but where staff control of the facility is maintained.

diversion A form of community supervision for individuals who have not been formally sentenced, but who agree to complete stipulations such as treatment or community service in exchange for having their charges dropped.

due process clause That section of the Fourteenth Amendment requiring all states to abide by the Bill of Rights when depriving a person of life, liberty, or property.

dynamic factors Individual characteristics that can be changed, such as antisocial attitudes, values and beliefs, poor self-control, criminal peers, and criminal thinking patterns.

earned good time Good-time credits resulting from good behavior or through participation in work or education programs.

economic mobility The likelihood that individuals can rise and maintain a higher socioeconomic status than they were born into, through employment and earnings.

elderly prisoner A prisoner who is age 50 and over.

electronic monitoring When a probationer or parolee is monitored in the community by wearing an electronic device that tracks his or her location.

equal protection clause That section of the Fourteenth Amendment prohibiting any state from denying equal protection of the law to persons within its jurisdiction.

evidence-based practices Correctional interventions for which there is consistent and solid scientific evidence showing that they work to meet the intended outcomes, such as recidivism reduction.

evidence-based sentencing Involves the use of scientific research to improve the quality of judicial decision making when determining sentences and sentencing conditions.

ex post facto **law** A law imposing a greater punishment for a crime than was allowed when the crime was committed.

external classification A stage in the classification process wherein a prisoner's custody level is determined and, based on that custody level, in which the prison inmate begins serving the sentence.

fines A fixed financial penalty imposed by the judge, with the amount determined by the severity of the offense.

fish First-time inmate that is vulnerable because he or she has not yet been prisonized.

free enterprise A private sector entrepreneurial model of doing business.

Functional Family Therapy An effective short-term intervention program targeting youths aged 11–18 who are facing problems with delinquency, substance abuse, or violence.

furlough An authorized temporary overnight leave of absence from 24 to 72 hours.

Furman decision In *Furman* v. *Georgia* the U.S. Supreme Court determined that the death penalty was cruel and unusual because it was imposed in an arbitrary and capricious manner.

general deterrence Seeks to prevent crime by using punishment to discourage people from committing a crime in the first place.

general incapacitation Imprisonment is acceptable and desirable on an extensive scale for a wide range of offenders as a means of crime prevention.

geriatric prisons Separate facilities specifically designed for elderly inmates where they have no contact with the younger general population.

good time Reduction of days from a sentence as a result of statutory provisions, the offender's good behavior, or extra work done by the offender.

"gotcha" game A style of offender supervision where the officer is less interested in helping the offender succeed, and is more interested in tracking failures and acting on rule violations; as a result, the officer has a high turnover of cases.

Gregg decision Death penalty statutes that provide for bifurcated trials and that direct juries to use guided discretion in deciding the sentence are allowed under the Constitution.

guided discretion A requirement that juries, after determining guilt in the first stage of a death penalty trial, consider both aggravating and mitigating circumstances during the sentencing stage of the trial.

home detention Requires offenders to remain at home at all times, except for such purposes as employment, school, treatment, medical emergencies, or approved shopping trips.

hospice facilities Late-sixteenth and early-seventeenth century institutions that promoted the idea of isolating offenders from each other.

houses of correction Sixteenth-century institutions for offenders that emphasized the importance of hard work at disagreeable tasks.

importation model Assumes that prison life is an extension of street life of marginalized people from impoverished communities who dominate the prison.

incapacitation Restricting an offender's freedom of movement through isolation from the general population.

incarceration rate The proportion of people in jail and prison per 100,000 residents in a given area.

incorporation Legal theory arguing that all provisions of the Bill of Rights are made applicable to the states through the due process clause.

indeterminate sentencing A system wherein the convicted offender receives a sentence that covers a time range rather than a fixed period.

Indian Country Land within an Indian reservation or land that is technically owned by the federal government but held in trust for a tribe or tribal member.

indirect supervision Inmate supervision method wherein custodial staff observe and interact with inmates remotely by watching through windows and listening via microphones.

informal probation Upon the voluntary agreement of child and parents, the juvenile agrees to submit to certain probation conditions without being formally charged or adjudicated as delinquent.

inmate code A system of unwritten rules that directs inmate behavior.

inmate subculture A society with its own norms and values defined by inmates with the most power and influence.

institutional corrections Incarceration of offenders in a jail or prison, apart from the community.

institutional maintenance Unskilled jobs that inmates are assigned in order to assist with daily prison operations (food preparation, laundry, cleaning).

integrated jail–prison systems A state government, rather than the more typical local government agency, is responsible for the administration and operation of jails located throughout the state.

intermittent supervision Inmate supervision method wherein custodial staff members are able to observe or interact with inmates only on an irregular or sporadic basis.

internal classification Establishes the prisoner's housing, program, and work assignments within the prison.

invisible punishments Sanctions operating mostly beyond public view, yet having very serious, adverse consequences for the individuals affected.

Irish system Mid-nineteenth-century prison philosophy that asserted punishment's most direct purpose should be to reform the criminal.

iron law of imprisonment The realization that almost all prisoners will return to free society.

jailhouse lawyers Inmates who use their legal knowledge and skills to write writs and grievances.

jails Confinement facilities usually operated by city or county governments and typically managed by that government's law enforcement agency.

judicial waiver Juvenile court judge waives jurisdiction over a case and transfers it to criminal court.

jurisdiction A predefined geographic area.

Justice Reinvestment Initiative A data-driven approach to encourage states to reduce correctional spending and reinvest savings in strategies designed to prevent crime. States and localities collect and analyze data on factors related to prison population growth and costs, implement changes to increase efficiencies, and measure both the fiscal and public safety impacts of those changes.

juvenile blended sentence Juvenile court judge can impose both juvenile and adult sanctions on certain categories of serious juvenile offenders.

lease system Prison officials lease a prisoner to a private contractor to do labor for a specified sum and for a fixed time.

legal violation When a probationer commits a new criminal act and the original probation sentence can be revoked.

legitimate penological interests Standard used by courts to determine whether a prison policy was developed in an arbitrary manner or out of concern for prison order and security.

levels system A behavior modification program that increases a client's community freedom with good behavior.

lex talionis The law of retaliation.

linear facilities Jails and prisons designed with single- or multiple-occupancy cells aligned along corridors that, in turn, are often stacked in tiers.

Maconochie, Captain Alexander Governor of Norfolk Island from 1836–1840, one of the toughest penal colonies for English prisoners.

mandatory sentencing Requires a prison sentence for some crimes and some offenders.

mark system Developed by Maconochie, this system rewarded positive behavior and work ethics.

mass media Broadcast and print forms of expression for consumer news, education, and entertainment, such as television, movies, internet, DVDs, video games, radio, books, newspapers, and magazines.

maximum-security facility Designed for the fullest possible supervision, control, and surveillance of general population inmates. Also known as *close-security prisons*.

medical model An orienting philosophy that views criminals not so much "bad" as "sick" and in need of treatment.

medium-security facility Institutions where inmates receive more supervision than at minimum-security prisons, but still have considerable freedom to move around to work assignments and programming activities.

mega jails The country's largest jails holding over 1,000 people.

mental health disorder A broad category used to identify convicted offenders who are considered to have mental health problems as a result of self-reported clinical diagnosis or treatment by a mental health professional.

mental health screening An examination performed on each newly admitted inmate that usually includes a review of the medical screening, behavior observations, an inquiry into any mental health history, and an assessment of suicide potential.

merchants Inmates who control scarce resources by running a prison store.

meritorious good time Good-time credits given to inmates who perform exceptional acts or services such as firefighting or working in emergency conditions.

minimum-security facility Institutions where inmates have considerable personal freedom and more relaxed supervision.

Missouri Model A model for juvenile institutions that emphasizes rehabilitation in small groups, constant therapeutic interventions, and minimal force.

mitigating circumstances An event or condition that makes an offense less serious than it might otherwise be.

Mosaic Law The Hebrew legal system, which started when God gave Moses two stone tablets containing the Ten Commandments.

motivational interviewing A style of personal interaction between the officer and client that involves rapport, trust, and persuasion to help bring about positive behavior change.

Multisystemic Therapy An effective family-based program for serious juvenile offenders that views the individual as part of a complex network that includes family, peers, school, and neighborhood.

net widening When offenders receive a level of correctional control or punishment that is greater than what they really require, resulting in bringing more people into the system.

new generation jails Facilities using a specific architectural design and inmate supervision model in order to reduce violent and destructive behavior by the inmates.

nonpetitioned case The informal response to a juvenile court case.

norm of reciprocity The view of punishment as a natural response, or reciprocation, to a wrongful act.

objective classification system Classification procedures that have a factual, impartial, and observable base rather than the intuitive footing of subjective systems.

open market Prison-made products are sold, either by private companies or by the state, to prospective buyers.

outpatient treatment Drug treatment programs for participants who live and work independently in the community.

parens patriae The idea that the court is the ultimate parent of all minors and therefore has final responsibility for its younger citizens.

parole agreement/order Document that the parolee signs at first meeting with parole officer where he or she agrees to abide by certain conditions while on parole.

parole board Group of citizens, typically appointed by the state governor, who meet periodically to review the files of those prisoners eligible for parole.

Pennsylvania Quakers Members of the Society of Friends who, in 1787, argued that solitude and hard labor were humanitarian alternatives to the existing punishments.

Pennsylvania system Prison system established with the Eastern State Penitentiary in 1892 in Philadelphia that assumed offenders would more quickly repent and reform if they could reflect on their crimes all day in silence and separated from others.

performance-based measures system A Web-based database that allows users to analyze their own institutional environment and compare to other states using standardized measures.

play families Relationships among women prisoners that mimic the structure, terminology, and function of families in general society.

players Prisoners who embrace mainstream prison culture that values manipulating and intimidating others.

police Law enforcement officials who are sworn to uphold the law, keep social order, and preserve public safety.

predisposing factors Underlying conditions that occur over an extended period of time and provide the foundation for a riot.

preponderance of evidence Burden of proof that requires evidence supporting a charge to have greater weight or be more convincing than the evidence offered in opposition to it.

prerelease center A minimum-security prison-based or community-based facility that either houses prisoners who have not yet been granted parole, or houses prisoners who have met the parole board and been promised a future parole date.

presentence investigation report A report developed from information derived through a presentence investigation that is provided to the judge to assist in sentencing decisions.

presentence investigation An inquiry interview and data-collection method used by a probation officer to summarize information about a convicted offender.

presumptive sentencing guidelines Required, rather than suggested, guidelines for a judge to use when deciding a sentence.

pretrial jail time Time spent in jail, either pretrial or after conviction, that could be counted toward a convicted offender's sentence.

pretrial supervision The community supervision of a defendant who has not yet been convicted but is waiting for his or her next court hearing date.

prison argot or "prison-proper" The language, slang, and physical gestures used to communicate meaning in prison.

prison hulks Eighteenth-century British merchant and naval ships converted into floating prisons.

prison industry A skilled job within the prison that provides inmates training while incarcerated (manufacturing, construction, auto repair, welding, etc.).

Prison Litigation Reform Act (PLRA) Intended to reduce the volume of prisoner litigation and to improve the merit of filed claims, including limiting nongovernmental organizations to legally challenge prison conditions and automatically terminates court orders after two years regardless of compliance.

prison riot A situation involving a large number of inmates making a forcible attempt to take control of a sizable area of the prison for a substantial amount of time.

prison risk assessment A determination of the risk an offender poses to escape or to be a management problem for prison officials.

prisonization The process by which the prisoners learn the norms of life in prison.

private prison A correctional facility operated by a non-governmental organization that is under contract with federal or state authorities to provide security, housing, and programs to adult offenders.

probation The court-ordered community supervision of an offender by an officer who enforces conditions for a specified length of time.

problem-solving courts An alternative court process for people who get arrested and have a history of alcohol or drug abuse, or a mental illness.

progressivism Reform movement that began in the 1890s and resulted in widespread, significant political and social reforms in many social institutions, including prisons.

proportional retributivism Requires that the worst crime in any society be punished with the worst penalty.

public notification laws Requires the public be notified of the name and location of certain sex offenders in the community.

public risk assessment A determination of the risk posed by an offender to the general public.

punk Inmates who are targeted by predatory inmates because they are perceived as physically or mentally weak and afraid to fight back.

rated capacity The maximum number of beds or inmates allocated by a rating official to institutions in the states.

reclassification A stage in the classification process wherein an inmate's custody level, treatment program, or work assignment is reevaluated to be sure they are still appropriate.

reentry The process of release preparation that begins within the institution and continues with community supervision.

reformatory A system of prison discipline that incorporates a more humanitarian approach to confinement and has an interest in preparing inmates for their eventual return to the community.

rehabilitation Providing the offender with skills, attitudes, and norms that enable him or her to be law-abiding.

release on recognizance Pretrial release based only on the defendant's promise to appear for trial (not backed with money or property).

reparative probation program A Vermont restorative justice program at the postconviction stage that combines a suspended probation sentence with elements of community reparation boards.

residence restriction laws Require sex offenders to live in certain areas or restrict them from living in other areas.

residential community correction facility (RCCF) A modern term for *halfway house*; community-based correctional center in which the offender lives under supervision and must obtain permission to leave for work and leisure.

responsivity The process in which prisoners are assigned to treatment programs designed to address their particular set of dynamic criminogenic needs.

restitution A court-ordered cash payment that an offender makes to the victim to offset some of the losses incurred from the crime.

restoration Restoring the victim, community, and offender through accountability, respect for the law and the legal process, and attention to victim needs.

restorative justice The process, also called community justice, wherein victim, offender, and community representatives determine a fair or just way to restore the balance that the crime had upset.

retentionists Those who favor keeping the death penalty.

retribution Just and adequate punishment.

rights-are-lost Argues that prisoners are wholly without rights except those expressly conferred by law or necessity.

rights-are-retained Argues that prisoners keep all the rights of an ordinary citizen, except those that are expressly or by necessity taken away from them by law.

Second Chance Act Federal legislation that authorizes reentry grants to state and local agencies and nonprofit organizations to provide employment assistance, substance abuse treatment, housing, and mentoring to reduce recidivism for ex-offenders returning to communities from correctional facilities.

Section 1983 claim A claim brought under the authority of U.S. Code Title 42, Section 1983 that civil rights have been violated.

security threat group An organized group whose activities are predatory and criminal and whose presence in a correctional institution/agency poses a real and imminent threat to the security and safety of staff and inmates.

selective incapacitation Imprisonment is reserved for those very few offenders who must truly be locked away for society's protection.

selective serotonin reuptake inhibitors Medications that increase serotonin levels in the brain to decrease libido and cause erectile dysfunction.

sentencing disparity A type of injustice wherein sentencing policy has the unintended effect of targeting a population group—often minority—and resulting in members of that group being disproportionately represented among persons in the correctional system.

sentencing guidelines Impose a predefined sentence length based on crime severity and prior criminal history, with the opportunity for the judge to depart from the guidelines when circumstances warrant.

sentencing When a court imposes a penalty on a person convicted of a crime.

separate and silent Key words distinguishing the Pennsylvania system, which sought to keep prisoners separate from each other and required them to remain silent.

serious mental illness A narrow category used to identify convicted offenders suffering from such conditions as bipolar disorder, schizophrenia spectrum disorder, or major depression.

sex offender registration laws Requires persons convicted of sex offenses to register in a community, even after they have completed their sentence for that conviction.

sex offenses Inappropriate sexual contact with family members/acquaintances, child molestation, sexual assault or rape of adults.

sheltered market/government/state use model Restricts the sale of prison-made products only to other state and local government markets. Also known as the *government or state use models*.

short-term inpatient residential programs Drug treatment programs of three to six months in length for less severe drug abusers.

snitch Inmates who are targeted by predatory inmates because they have passed along information to staff that has gotten another inmate in trouble. Also known as *player haters*.

social learning Changing old behavior through modeling new skills and desirable behavior.

special conditions Requirements in addition to the standard conditions, such as paying fines or undergoing electronic monitoring.

specific deterrence Seeks to prevent crime by using punishment to discourage that person from committing additional crimes.

squares Inmates who oppose mainstream prison culture by being well-behaved and who take advantage of every self-improvement program they can to keep themselves busy. Also known as *bootlickers*.

standard conditions Commitments every probationer agrees to abide by in return for remaining at liberty in the community.

state-raised youth Inmates who grew up in youth prisons and who tend to be more violent than the average prisoner.

static factors Individual characteristics that are constant or happened in the past and cannot be changed, such as a person's gender, age at first arrest, or number of prior arrests.

status offense Misbehavior that is considered wrong only because society does not consider the juvenile old enough for such activity.

statutory exclusion Criminal courts have original jurisdiction for certain crimes committed by juveniles.

statutory good time Reduction of days from a sentence usually given automatically as a prison management tool to relieve overcrowding.

statutory penalties Sentences linked via legislation to specific crimes, or to specific classes of felonies or misdemeanors, with a minimum and maximum time period.

sub rosa economy Underground economy based on negotiation and exchange of goods and services between prisoners without the use of cash.

substance abuse When the use of one or more chemical substances disrupts normal living patterns.

supermax prison Prisons at the highest security level, with prisoners isolated from the general population and from each other. Also known as *control units* or *secured housing units*.

supervised mandatory release When an inmate is automatically released by law to the community when he or she has completed his or her maximum prison sentence less any good-time credit the inmate has received.

technical violation When a probationer repeatedly fails to abide by conditions of probation, and the probation sentence can be revoked.

technological incapacitation Using technologies such as critical organ surgery, chemical treatment, and electronic monitoring to restrict an offender's freedom of movement.

test for adult basic education (TABE) Test given to inmates to determine the prisoner's level of academic ability.

The Innocence Project An organization instrumental in securing DNA exonerations of persons who had served time on death row.

therapeutic communities Long-term peer-led programs for chronic addicts using group confrontational methods.

thinking errors Ways that people use to avoid taking responsibility for their own behavior, or ways to make themselves look good by making others look bad.

three strikes and you're out Laws that authorize, or mandate in some cases, longer periods of incarceration after a certain number of prior convictions ("strikes").

total institution A regimented facility that is physically separate from the larger society and meets the survival needs of its occupants.

transportation The removal of criminals to a remote location where they could be used as laborers.

triggering event One or several specific events that sparked the riot.

trustys Minimum-security-level inmates who earn the status through not causing behavioral problems.

truth-in-sentencing When the length of time served in a sentence is close to the time imposed by the courts.

Twelve Tables The earliest form of written Roman law, which provided the basis for private rights of Roman citizens.

unconditional release The return of prisoners to the larger community without supervision.

unsecured bond When a defendant is released without having to make any payment but is liable for the full bail amount if required court appearances are missed.

victim compensation A general fund by which state governments disperse money to qualifying victims of violent crimes for payment of bills and lost wages.

victim impact classes Restorative justice program, typically offered in prison, wherein prisoners hear violent crime survivors share their experiences with the hope of effecting positive change in the offender.

victim–offender mediation An application of restorative justice principles at the sentencing stage by having mediation sessions involving both offender and victim take the place of traditional sentencing by a judge.

voluntary lockdown When prisoners refuse to leave their cells.

voluntary sentencing guidelines Suggested, rather than required, guidelines that stipulate a time range for a judge to use when deciding a sentence.

Walnut Street Jail Opened in Philadelphia in 1776 to house petty offenders, debtors, and serious offenders and operated only as a jail until 1792 when a penitentiary addition was completed.

writ of *habeas corpus* Judicial mandate to a prison official ordering that an inmate be brought to the court in order to determine the legality of the prisoner's detention.

wrongful convictions A type of injustice wherein a person is convicted and punished for a crime he or she did not commit.

References

Chapter 1, An Evidence-Based Approach to Corrections

Applegate, B. K. and Davis, R. K. (2006). Public views on sentencing juvenile murderers. *Youth Violence and Juvenile Justice,* 4(1): 55–74.

Applegate, B. K., Davis, R. K., & Cullen, F.T. (2009). Reconsidering child saving. *Crime & Delinquency,* 55(1): 51–77.

Cassidy, R. T. (2010). Collateral consequences of criminal convictions: Our law is a tragedy. Retrieved from http://onlawyering.com/2010/06/collateral-consequences-of-criminal-convictions-our-law-is-a-tragedy/.

Crime and Justice Institute. (2004). *Implementing evidence-based practice in community corrections: The principles of effective intervention.* Longmont, CO: National Institute of Corrections.

Cullen, F., Fisher, B., & Applegate, B. (2000). Public opinion about punishment and corrections. *Crime and Justice* 27: 1–79.

Dowler, K., Fleming, T., & Muzzatti, S. L. (2006). Constructing crime: Media, crime, and popular culture. *Canadian Journal of Criminology and Criminal Justice,* 48(6): 837–850.

Glaze, L. E. & Bonczar, T. P. (2010). *Probation and parole in the United States, 2009.* NCJ 231674. Washington, DC: U.S. Department of Justice.

Gorham, B. W. (2006). News media's relationship with stereotyping: The linguistic intergroup bias in response to crime news. *Journal of Communication,* 56(2): 289–308.

Harcourt, B. E. (2010). Risk as a proxy for race. (September 16). Criminology and Public Policy, Forthcoming; University of Chicago Law & Economics Olin Working Paper No. 535; University of Chicago Public Law Working Paper No. 323. Available at SSRN: http://ssrn.com/abstract=1677654.

Lowenkamp, C. T. & Whetzel, J. (2009). The development of an actuarial risk assessment for U.S. pretrial services. *Federal Probation,* 73(2): 33–36.

Mauer, M. (1999). The crisis of the young African-American male and the criminal justice system. Washington, DC, *The Sentencing Project.*

McKenzie, W., Stemen, D., and Coursen, D. (2009). Prosecution and racial justice: Using data to advance fairness in criminal prosecution. New York, NY Vera Institute of Justice. Retrieved online from www.vera.org/centers/prosecution-and-racial-justice.

Pew Charitable Trusts. (2010). *Collateral costs: Incarceration's effect on economic mobility.* Washington, DC: The Pew Charitable Trusts.

Sherman, L. W., Gottfredson, D., MacKenzie, D., Eck, J., Reuter, P., & Bushway, S. (1997). *Preventing crime: What works, what doesn't, what's promising.* Washington, DC: National Institute of Justice.

Tonry, M. (2004). *Thinking about crime: Sense and sensibility in American penal culture.* New York, Oxford University Press.

Walker, S., Spohn, C., & Delone, M. (2012). *The color of justice: Race, ethnicity, and crime in America,* 5th edition. Cengage.

Unnever, J.D. & Cullen, F.T. (2010). The social sources of Americans' punitiveness: A test of three competing models. *Criminology,* 48(1), 99–129.

Vera Institute of Justice (2010). *The continuing fiscal crisis in corrections: Setting a new course.* New York, NY: Vera Institute of Justice.

Yanich, D. (2004). Crime creep: Urban and suburban crime in local TV news. *Journal of Urban Affairs,* 26: 535–563.

Zgoba, K. M. (2004). Spin doctors and moral crusaders: The moral panic behind child safety legislation. *Criminal Justice Studies,* 17(4), 385–404.

Chapter 2, Why Do We Punish?

Alabama Sentencing Commission. (2000). Statute creating the Alabama Sentencing Commission. Retrieved from http://sentencingcommission.alacourt.gov/statute.html.

Council of Europe. (2009). Report to the Czech Government on the visit to the Czech Republic carried out by the European Committee for the Prevention of Torture and Inhuman or Degrading Treatment or Punishment (CPT). Retrieved from www.cpt.coe.int/documents/cze/2009-08-inf-eng.htm.

Dolan, J. (2010). Charles Manson had a cellphone? *Los Angeles Times,* (December 2). Retrieved from Article collections website: http://articles.latimes.com/2010/dec/02/local/la-me-prison-cellphones-20101203.

Easton, A. (2009). Poland chemical castration is law. (November 27). Retrieved from BBC News website: http://news.bbc.co.uk/2/hi/europe/8383698.stm.

Ellis, R. D., & Ellis, C. S. (1989). *Theories of criminal justice: A critical reappraisal.* Wolfeboro, N.H.: Longwood Academic.

Fagan, J., & Meares, T. L. (2008). Punishment, deterrence and social control: The paradox of punishment in minority communities. *Ohio State Journal of Criminal Law,* 6, 173–229.

Gannon, T. A., & Cortoni, F. (Eds.). (2010). *Female sexual offenders: Theory, assessment, and treatment.* Oxford, UK: Wiley-Blackwell.

Hudak, S. (2010). Creative sentences a growing trend, but legal experts question effectiveness. *Standard-Examiner,* (October 28). Retrieved from www.standard.net/.

Humphrey, J. A., Burford, G., & Huey, M. P. (2007). Reparative versus standard probation: Community justice outcomes. Retrieved from Vermont Department of Corrections Agency of Human Services Published Reports website: www.doc. state.vt.us/about/reports/.

Hyun-jung, B. (2010). Child rapists to get chemical castration. *The Korea Herald,* (June 30). Retrieved from www.koreaherald.com/national/Detail. jsp?newsMLId=20100630000789.

Judicial Council of California. (2010). California rules of court. Retrieved from www.courtinfo.ca.gov/rules/index. cfm?title=four&linkid=rule4_410.

Katz, J. (1988). *Seductions of crime: Moral and sensual attractions in doing evil.* New York: Basic Books.

Kurki, L. (1999). Incorporating restorative and community justice Into American sentencing and corrections. (NCJ 175723). Retrieved from National Criminal Justice Reference Service website: www.ncjrs.gov/pdffiles1/ nij/175723.pdf.

Maletzky, B. M., Tolan, A., & McFarland, B. (2006). The Oregon depo-Provera Program: A Five-Year Follow-Up. *Sex Abuse, 18,* 303–316. doi: 10.1177/107906320601800308.

Meyer, W. J., III, & Cole, C. M. (1997). Physical and chemical castration of sex offenders: A review. *Journal of Offender Rehabilitation, 25*(3–4), 1–18.

Millhollon, M. (2008). Jindal signs chemical castration bill. Retrieved from The Advocate website: www.2theadvocate. com/news/21656994.html.

Newman, G. R. (1985). *The punishment response* (2nd ed.). Albany, N.Y.: Harrow and Heston.

Norman-Eady, S. (2006). Castration of sex offenders. Retrieved from State of Connecticut website: www.cga. ct.gov/2006/rpt/2006-R-0183.htm.

Office for Victims of Crime. (2010). The case for evidence-based programming. Retrieved from Victim impact: Listen and learn website: www.ovcttac.gov/victimimpact/ evidence_based.cfm.

Redding, R. E. (2009). Evidence-based sentencing: The science of sentencing policy and practice. *Chapman Journal of Criminal Justice, 1*(1), 1–19. Retrieved from SSRN website: http://ssrn.com/paper=1424008.

Reynolds, E. (2010, December 11). Should criminals be sentenced to read? Retrieved from www.newyorker.com/ online/blogs/books/.

Rhine, E., Matthews, J. R., Sampson, L. A., & Daley, R. H. (2003). Citizen's circles: Community collaboration in reentry. *Corrections Today, 65*(5), 52–64.

Severson, K., & Brown, R. (2011). Outlawed, cellphones are thriving in prisons. *New York Times,* (January 2). Retrieved from www.nytimes.com/2011/01/03/us/ 03prisoners.html.

State of Colorado. (2010). Colorado revised statutes (18-1-102.5). Retrieved from www.state.co.us/gov_dir/leg_dir/ olls/colorado_revised_statutes.htm.

State of Ohio. (2007). Citizen circles. Retrieved from Ohio Department of Rehabilitation and Correction website: www. drc.ohio.gov/web/Citizen/citizencircle.htm.

State of Texas. (2009). Chapter 1. General provisions; Sec. 1.02. Objectives of code. Retrieved from penal code website: www.statutes.legis.state.tx.us/.

State of Vermont. (2002). 28 V.S.A. § 2a. Restorative justice. *Vermont Statutes Annotated.* Retrieved from www.leg.state. vt.us/statutesMain.cfm.

T.I. says new prison sentence is his final lesson. (2010). *USA Today,* (October 19). Retrieved from www.usatoday.com/.

Travis, J. (2005). Prisoner reentry: The iron law of imprisonment. In R. Muraskin (Ed.), *Key correctional issues* (pp. 64–71). Upper Saddle River, NJ: Pearson Prentice Hall.

Umbreit, M. S., Vos, B., Coates, R. B., & Brown, K. A. (2003). *Facing violence: The path of restorative justice and dialogue.* Monsey, NY: Criminal Justice Press.

Urban Institute. (2006). Understanding the challenges of prisoner reentry: Research findings from the Urban Institute's prisoner reentry portfolio. Retrieved from www. urban.org/UploadedPDF/411289_reentry_portfolio.pdf.

Vermont Department of Corrections. (2010). Facts and figures 2010. Retrieved from Agency of Human Services Published Reports website: www.doc.vermont.gov/ about/reports.

Walker, N. (1991). *Why punish?* Oxford England: Oxford University Press.

Weihofen, H. (1971). Punishment and treatment: Rehabilitation. In S. E. Grupp (Ed.), *Theories of punishment* (pp. 255–263). Bloomington, IN: Indiana University Press.

Wong, C. M. (2001). Chemical castration: Oregon's innovative approach to sex offender rehabilitation, or unconstitutional punishment? *Oregon Law Review, 80*(1), 267–301. Retrieved from https://scholarsbank.uoregon.edu/ xmlui/handle/1794/4593.

Zimring, F. E., & Hawkins, G. (1995). *Incapacitation: Penal confinement and the restraint of crime.* New York: Oxford University Press.

Chapter 3, Correctional Practices from Ancient to Contemporary Times

Abadinsky, H. (1994). *Probation and parole: Theory and practice.* Englewood Cliffs, NJ: Prentice Hall.

Barnes, H. E., & Teeters, N. K. (1943). *New horizons in criminology: The American crime problem.* New York: Prentice Hall.

Barnes, H. E., & Teeters, N. K. (1959). *New horizons in criminology* (3rd ed.). Englewood Cliffs, NJ: Prentice-Hall.

Cahalan, M. W. (1986). *Historical corrections statistics in the United States, 1850–1984*. Washington, DC: Department of Justice.

Chesney-Lind, M. & Pollock, J. M. (1995). Women's prisons: Equality with a vengeance. In A. V. Merlo & J. M. Pollock (Eds.), *Women, law, and social control* (pp. 155–175). Boston: Allyn and Bacon.

Christianson, S. (1998). *With liberty for some: 500 years of imprisonment in America*. Boston, MA: Northeastern University Press.

Cohen, A. (2007). My morning at Supermax. *CBS News* (September 12). Retrieved from www.cbsnews.com/8301-500803_162-3253653-500803.html.

Colvin, M. (1997). *Penitentiaries, reformatories, and chain gangs: Social theory and the history of punishment in nineteenth-century America*. New York: St. Martin's Press.

Dobash, R. P., Dobash, R. E., & Gutteridge, S. (1986). *The imprisonment of women*. New York: Basil Blackwell.

Drug Policy Alliance. (2006). Proposition 36: Improving lives, delivering results. (March). Retrieved from www.drugpolicy.org/docUploads/Prop36March2006.pdf.

Eriksson, T. (1976). *The reformers: An historical survey of pioneer experiments in the treatment of criminals* (C. Djurklou, Trans.). New York: Elsevier.

Freedman, E. B. (1974). Their sisters' keepers: An historical perspective on female correctional institutions in the United States: 1870–1900. *Feminist Studies, 2*(1), 77–95.

Hindus, M. S. (1980). *Prison and plantation: Crime, justice, and authority in Massachusetts and South Carolina, 1767–1878*. Chapel Hill, NC: University of North Carolina Press.

Hirsch, A. J. (1992). *The rise of the penitentiary: Prisons and punishments in early America*. New Haven, CT: Yale University Press.

Johnston, N. (1973). *The human cage: A brief history of prison architecture*. Philadelphia: American Foundation Inc.

Kurshan, N. (1992). Women and imprisonment in the U.S.—History and current reality. In W. Churchill & J. J. Vander Wall (Eds.), *Cages of steel: The politics of imprisonment in the United States* (pp. 331–358). Washington, DC: Maisonneuve Press.

Lodine-Chaffey, J. (2010). From Newgate to the new world: A study of London's transported female convicts, 1718–1775. *The Early America Review, 9*(2). Retrieved from www.earlyamerica.com/review/2010_winter_spring/female-convicts.html.

McKelvey, B. (1977). *American prisons: A history of good intentions*. Montclair, NJ: Patterson Smith.

Old Bailey Proceedings Online. January 1760, trial of Joseph Tedar (t17600116-17). Retrieved from www.oldbaileyonline.org.

Peter D. Hart Research Associates. (2002). Changing public attitudes toward the criminal justice system. (February). Retrieved from U.S. Programs Criminal Justice website: www.soros.org/initiatives/usprograms/focus/justice/articles_publications/publications/hartpoll_20020201.

Pew Center on the States. (2010). National research of public attitudes on crime and punishment. (September). Retrieved from the Pew Center on the States website: www.pewcenteronthestates.org/initiatives_detail.aspx?initiativeID=60775.

Pew Charitable Trusts. (2010). Prison count 2010: State population declines for the first time in 38 years. (April 1). Retrieved from Sentencing and corrections website: www.pewtrusts.org/our_work_report_detail.aspx?id=57797.

PortCities London. (n.d.). Prison hulks on the River Thames. Retrieved from Crime and punishment website: www.portcities.org.uk/london/server/show/ConNarrative.56/Prison-hulks-on-the-River-Thames.html.

Rafter, N. H. (1990). *Partial justice: Women, prisons, and social control* (2nd ed.). New Brunswick, NJ: Transaction Publishers.

Rafter, N. H. (1993). Equality of difference? *Female offenders: Meeting needs of a neglected population* (pp. 7–11). Laurel, MD: American Correctional Association.

Rappold, R. S. (2006). Bomber expresses no remorse for victims. *The Gazette* (December 10). Retrieved from www.gazette.com/articles/rudolph-11114-wrote-supermax.html.

Reichel, P. L. (1997). Transportation. In F. Schmalleger & G. M. Armstrong (Eds.), *Crime and the justice system in America: An encyclopedia* (pp. 235–237). Westport, CT: Greenwood Press.

Roth, M. P. (2011). *Crime and punishment: A history of the criminal justice system* (2nd ed.). Belmont, CA: Wadsworth Cengage.

Schuster, H. (2007). Producer's notebook: My trip to Supermax. *CBS News*, (October 14). Retrieved from 60 Minutes website: www.cbsnews.com/stories/2007/10/13/60minutes/main3364113.shtml?tag=contentMain;contentBody.

Smith, M. L. (1997). Progressives. In F. Schmalleger (Ed.), *Crime and the justice system in America: An encyclopedia* (p. 198). Westport, CT: Greenwood Press.

Spierenburg, P. (1995). The body and the state: Early modern Europe. In N. Morris & D. J. Rothman (Eds.), *The Oxford history of the prison* (pp. 49–77). New York: Oxford University Press.

Sullivan, L. E. (1990). *The prison reform movement: Forlorn hope*. Boston: Twayne Publishers.

UCLA issues new report on Prop. 36. (2008). *e! Science News* (October 15). Retrieved from Psychology & sociology website: http://esciencenews.com/articles/2008/10/15/ucla.issues.new.report.prop.36.

Vaver, A. (2009). Transported convicts in the New World (6): Adjusting to America. *Convict Transportation* (June 10). Retrieved from Early American Crime website: www.earlyamericancrime.com/convict-transportation/in-the-new-world/adjusting-to-america.

West, H. C. (2010). Prison inmates at midyear 2009—Statistical Table. (NCJ 230113). Retrieved from Bureau of Justice Statistics website: http://bjs.ojp.usdoj.gov/index.cfm?ty=pbdetail&iid=2273.

Chapter 4, Sentencing

Aos, S., Miller, M., & Drake, E. (2006). Evidence-based public policy options to reduce future prison construction, criminal justice costs, and crime rates. Retrieved from Washington State Institute for Public Policy website: www.wsipp.wa.gov/pub.asp?docid=06-10-1201.

Bazelon, E. (2010). Arguing three strikes. *New York Times,* (May 21). Retrieved from www.nytimes.com.

Bierman, J., & Dorenbaum, J. (2010). 'Three strikes' law is a human travesty. *The Sacremento Bee,* (December 17). Retrieved from Opinion - Viewpoints website: www.sacbee.com.

Bluestein, G. (2010). Wesley Snipes tax evasion case: Snipes hoping for new trial. *The Christian Science Monitor,* (June 25). Retrieved from www.csmonitor.com.

Carlton, J. (2011). Texan declared innocent after 30 years in prison. *The Statesman,* (January 4). Retrieved from www.statesman.com/.

Casey, P. M. (2010). Reducing recidivism with evidence-based sentencing. Retrieved from National Center for State Courts Digital Archive website: http://contentdm.ncsconline.org/cdm4/item_viewer.php?CISOROOT=/criminal&CISOPTR=187&REC=1.

Crime and Justice Institute. (2004). Implementing evidence-based practice in community corrections: The principles of effective intervention. Retrieved from National Institute of Corrections Library website: http://nicic.gov/Library/019342.

Davey, M. (2010, September 18). Missouri tells judges cost of sentences, *New York Times*. Retrieved from www.nytimes.com.

Dittmann, M. (2004). Accuracy and the accused (article sidebar: Recommendations for police lineups). *Monitor on Psychology, 35*(7). Retrieved from www.apa.org/monitor/julaug04/lineups.aspx.

Garrett, B. L. (2010). The substance of false confessions. *Stanford Law Review, 62*(4), 1051–1119.

Hodgson, G. (2010). Wesley Snipes suggests race a factor in his sentencing. (December 8). Retrieved from Monsters and Critics - People website: www.monstersandcritics.com/.

Itzkoff, D. (2010). Wesley Snipes surrenders to begin sentence on tax convictions. Retrieved from http://artsbeat.blogs.nytimes.com/.

Milkman, H., & Wanberg, K. (2007). Cognitive-behavioral treatment: A review and discussion for correctional professionals. Retrieved from National Institute of Corrections Library website: http://nicic.gov/Library/021657.

National Center for State Courts. (2009). Evidence-based sentencing to improve public safety & reduce recidivism: A model curriculum for judges. Retrieved from National Center for State Courts Digital Archive website: http://contentdm.ncsconline.org/cdm4/item_viewer.php?CISOROOT=/criminal&CISOPTR=185&REC=3.

Northwestern University School of Law. (2010). Victims of erroneous eyewitness I.D. Retrieved from Center on Wrongful Convictions website: www.law.northwestern.edu/wrongfulconvictions/issues/causesandremedies/erroneouseyewitness/Index.html.

Phillips, R. (2008). Snipes gets the max—3 years—in tax case. (April 24). Retrieved from CNN Justice website: http://articles.cnn.com/.

Redding, R. E. (2009). Evidence-based sentencing: The science of sentencing policy and practice. *Chapman Journal of Criminal Justice, 1*(1), 1–19. Retrieved from SSRN website: http://ssrn.com/paper=1424008.

TMZ Staff. (2011). Wesley Snipes—Downward-facing inmate. (January 1). Retrieved from www.tmz.com.

Warren, R. K. (2007). Evidence-based practice to reduce recidivism: Implications for state judiciaries. Retrieved from National Institute of Corrections website: http://nicic.gov/Downloads/PDF/Library/023358.pdf.

Warren, R. K. (2009). Arming the courts with research: 10 evidence-based sentencing initiatives to control crime and reduce costs. *Public Safety Policy Brief,* (8). Retrieved from the Pew Center on the States website: www.pewcenteronthestates.org/report_detail.aspx?id=51750.

Wodahl, E. J., Ogle, R., Kadleck, C., & Gerow, K. (2009). Offender Perceptions of Graduated Sanctions. *Crime & Delinquency*. doi: 10.1177/0011128709333725.

Chapter 5, Community Supervision

Bearden v. *Georgia,* 461 U.S. 660 (1983).

Bureau of Prisons. (2010). Active community corrections/residential reentry center contract listing, July 2010. Retrieved from www.bop.gov/locations/cc/RRcontracts_0710.pdf.

Davis, R. C., Smith, B., & Hillenbrand, S. (1991). Increasing offender compliance with restitution orders. *Judicature, 74*(5), 245–248.

Dickman, M. (2009). Should Crime Pay? A critical assessment of the mandatory victim's restitution act of 1996. *California Law Review, 97*(6), 1687–1718.

Dunn, S. (1999). Offenders bypass service with donations. *Greeley Tribune*: A1, A10.

Ekstrand, L. E. & Burton, D.R. (2001). *Prisoner releases: Trends and information on reintegration programs*. Publication GAO-01-483. Washington, DC: U.S. General Accounting Office.

French, M. T., Popovici, I., & Tapsell, L. (2008). The economic costs of substance abuse treatment: Updated estimates and cost bands for program assessment and reimbursement. *Journal of Substance Abuse Treatment,* 35(4), 462–469.

Glaze, Lauren E. & Bonczar, Thomas P. (2010). *Probation and parole in the United States, 2009.* NCJ 231674. Washington, DC: U.S. Department of Justice.

Goldfarb, R. L., & Singer, L.R. (1973). *After conviction.* New York, Simon & Schuster.

Gowen, D. (2001). Remote location monitoring—A supervision strategy to enhance risk control. *Federal Probation,* 65(2), 38–41.

Greek, C. E. (2002). The cutting edge: Tracking probationers in space and time: The convergence of GIS and GPS systems. *Federal Probation,* 66(1), 51–53.

Greenfield S. F., Brooks, A. J., Gordon, S.M., Green, C. A., Kropp, F., McHugh, R. K., Lincoln, M., Hien, D., & Miele, G. M. (2007). Substance abuse treatment entry, retention, and outcome in women: A review of the literature. *Drug and Alcohol Dependence,* 86(1), 1–21.

Grella, C. E. (1999). Women in residential drug treatment: Differences by program type and pregnancy. *Journal of Health Care for the Poor and Underserved,* 10(2), 216–229.

Hepburn, J. R. & Griffin, M. L. (2004). An analysis of risk factors contributing to the recidivism of sex offenders on probation. Report submitted to the National Institute of Justice (January). Washington, DC: U.S. Department of Justice.

Kim, D., Joo, H., & McCarty, W. P. (2008). Risk assessment and classification of day reporting center clients: An actuarial approach. *Criminal Justice and Behavior,* 35(6), 795–812.

Morris, N. & Tonry, M. (1990). *Between prison and probation: Intermediate punishments in a rational sentencing system.* New York: Oxford University Press.

Office for the Victims of Crime (2010). OVC Fact Sheet: What is the Office for Victims of Crime? (April). Retrieved from www.ovc.gov/publications/factshts/what_is_OVC2010/fs_000321.html.

Rozek, D. (2011). Probation in murder of man whose dog urinated on lawn. *The Herald News,* updated January 11. http://heraldnews.suntimes.com/3067498-418/clements-funches-judge-prison-dog.html.

Ruback, R. B., Schaffer, J. N., & Logue, M. A. (2004). The imposition and the effects of restitution in four Pennsylvania counties: Effects of size of county and specialized collection units. *Crime and Delinquency,* 50(2), 168–188.

Sarteschi, C. M. (2009). *Assessing the effectiveness of mental health courts: A meta-analysis of clinical and recidivism outcomes.* An unpublished doctoral dissertation, University of Pittsburgh. Retrieved online from http://challenger.library.pitt.edu/ETD/available/etd-08272009-143525/unrestricted/CMSarteschiAug2009Dissertation.pdf.

Stalans, L. J., Yarnold, P. R. Seng, M., Olson, D. E., & Repp, M. (2004). Identifying three types of violent offenders and predicting violent recidivism while on probation: A classification tree analysis. *Law and Human Behavior,* 28(3), 253–271.

Thompson, M., Osher, F., & Tomasini-Joshi, D. (2008). *Improving responses to people with mental illnesses: The essential elements of a mental health court.* New York: The Council of State Governments Justice Center.

Tsenin, K. (2000). One judicial perspective on the sex trade. *Research on women and girls in the justice system: Plenary papers of the 1999 conference on criminal justice research and evaluation—Enhancing policy.* Washington, DC, National Institute of Justice.

van Kalmthout, A. M. & Tak, P. (1988). *Sanctions-systems in the member-states of the Council of Europe, Part I.* Norwell, MA, Kluwer Law and Taxation Publishers.

Vanstone, M. (2004). *Supervising offenders in the community: A history of probation theory and practice.* Burlington, VT: Ashgate.

van Wormer, K. (2010). *Working with female offenders: A gender-sensitive approach.* New Jersey: John Wiley and Sons.

Welsh, W. N. & Zajac, G. (2004). A census of prison-based drug treatment programs: Implications for programming, policy, and evaluation. *Crime and Delinquency,* 50(1), 108–133.

Chapter 6, Jails and Pretrial Release

Applegate, B., & Paoline, E. (2007). Jail officers' perceptions of the work environment in traditional versus new generation facilities. [Article]. *American Journal of Criminal Justice,* 31(2), 64–80. doi: 10.1007/s12103-007-9005-z

Beck, A. R. (2006). Deciding on a new jail design. Retrieved from Justice Concepts Inc. website: www.justiceconcepts.com/design.htm.

Belcher, J. (1988). Are jails replacing the mental health system for the homeless mentally ill? *Community Mental Health Journal,* 24, 185–195.

Bowker, G. M. (2002). Jail resource issues: What every funding authority needs to know. Washington, DC: National Institute of Corrections.

Case, B., Steadman, H. J., Dupuis, S. A., & Morris, L. S. (2009). Who succeeds in jail diversion programs for persons with mental illness? A multi-site study. *Behavioral Sciences & the Law,* 27(5), 661–674. doi: 10.1002/bsl.883

Cohen, T. H., & Kyckelhahn, T. (2010). Felony defendants in large urban counties, 2006. (NCJ 228944). Retrieved from Bureau of Justice Statistics website: http://bjs.ojp.usdoj.gov/index.cfm?ty=pbdetail&iid=2193.

Cohen, T. H., & Reaves, B. A. (2006). Felony defendants in large urban counties, 2002. (NCJ 210818). Retrieved from Bureau of Justice Statistics Publications & Products website: http://bjs.ojp.usdoj.gov/index.cfm?ty=pbse&sid=27.

Cohen, T. H., & Reaves, B. A. (2007). Pretrial release of felony defendants in state courts. (NCJ 214994). Retrieved from Bureau of Justice Statistics website: http://bjs.ojp.usdoj.gov/index.cfm?ty=pbdetail&iid=834.

Council of State Governments. (2002). Criminal justice / mental health consensus project report. Retrieved from http://consensusproject.org/downloads/Entire_report.pdf.

Council of State Governments. (n.d.). Frequently asked questions about new study of serious mental illness in jails. Retrieved from Justice Center Publications website: http://consensusproject.org/jc_publication.

Ditton, P. M. (1999). Mental health and treatment of inmates and probationers. (NCJ 174463). Retrieved from Bureau of Justice Statistics website: http://bjs.ojp.usdoj.gov/index.cfm?ty=pbdetail&iid=787.

Fletcher, M. L. M. (2009). Addressing the epidemic of domestic violence in Indian Country by restoring tribal sovereignty. Retrieved from American Constitution Society for Law and Policy website: www.acslaw.org/sites/default/files/Fletcher%20Issue%20Brief.pdf.

Gilliard, D. K. (1999). Prison and jail inmates at midyear 1998. (NCJ 173414). Retrieved from http://bjs.ojp.usdoj.gov/content/pub/pdf/pjim98.pdf.

Grissom, B. (2011). As mental health cuts mount, psychiatric cases fill jails. *New York Times*, (February 24). Retrieved from www.nytimes.com.

Hagar, G. M., Ludwig, T. E., & McGovern, K. (2008). Program evaluation for a jail-based mental health treatment program. *Journal of Correctional Health Care, 14*(3), 222–231. doi: 10.1177/1078345808318257

Harrison, P. M., & Beck, A. J. (2006). Prison and jail inmates at midyear 2005. Retrieved from http://bjs.ojp.usdoj.gov/content/pub/pdf/pjim05.pdf.

James, D. J., & Glaze, L. E. (2006). Mental health problems of prison and jail inmates. (NCJ 213600). Retrieved from Bureau of Justice Statistics website: http://bjs.ojp.usdoj.gov/index.cfm?ty=pbdetail&iid=789.

Minton, T. D. (2010). Jail inmates at midyear 2009–Statistical Tables. (NCJ 230122). Retrieved from Bureau of Justice Statistics website: http://bjs.ojp.usdoj.gov/index.cfm?ty=pbdetail&iid=2200.

Minton, T. D. (2011). Jails in Indian country, 2009. (NCJ 232223). Retrieved from Bureau of Justice Statistics website: http://bjs.ojp.usdoj.gov/index.cfm?ty=pbdetail&iid=2223.

National Institute of Corrections. (2006). Direct supervision jails: 2006 sourcebook. (Accession Number: 021968). Retrieved from NIC Corrections Library website: http://nicic.gov/Library/021968.

Phillips, M. T. (2008). Bail, detention, & felony case outcomes. *CJA Research Brief*, (No. 18). Retrieved from New York City Criminal Justice Agency website: www.cjareports.org/reports/brief18.pdf.

Sabol, W. J., & Minton, T. D. (2008). Jail inmates at midyear 2007. (NCJ 221945). Retrieved from Bureau of Justice Statistics website: http://bjs.ojp.usdoj.gov/index.cfm?ty=pbdetail&iid=1005.

Senese, J. D. (1997). Evaluating jail reform: A comparative analysis of podular/direct and linear jail inmate infractions. *Journal of Criminal Justice, 25*(1), 61–73. doi: 10.1016/s0047-2352(96)00052-9

Steadman, H. J., Osher, F. C., Robbins, P. C., Case, B., & Samuels, S. (2009). Prevalence of serious mental illness among jail inmates. *Psychiatric Services, 60*(6), 761–765. doi: 10.1176/appi.ps.60.6.761

Stevenson, B., & Legg, S. (2010). Pretrial services agencies: The first responders in the reentry process. *Corrections Today, 72* (April), 104–107.

Summerill, J. (2005, February). The state of Indian jails in America. *Corrections Today, 67*, 64–67.

Tartaro, C., & Levy, M. (2010). The impact of jail environment on inmate suicide. *American Jails, 24*(1), 48.

Torrey, E. F., Kennard, A. D., Eslinger, D., Lamb, R., & Pavle, J. (2010). More mentally ill persons are in jails and prisons than hospitals: A survey of the states. Retrieved from Treatment Advocacy Center Reports and Presentations website: www.treatmentadvocacycenter.org/storage/documents/finaljailsvhospitalsstudy.pdf.

U.S. Department of the Interior. (2004). "Neither safe nor secure" An assessment of Indian detention facilities. (Report No. 2004-I-0056). Retrieved from Office of Inspector General website: www.doioig.gov/images/stories/reports/pdf/IndianCountryDetentionFinal%20Report.pdf.

VanNostrand, M. (2007). Legal and evidence based practices: Application of legal principles, laws, and research to the field of pretrial services. Retrieved from EBP Box Set Paper website: www.cjinstitute.org/boxset.

Veysey, B. M., De Cou, K., & Prescott, L. (1998). Effective management of female jail detainees with histories of physical and sexual abuse. *American Jails* (May/June), 50–54.

VanNostrand, M. (2007). Legal and evidence based practices: Application of legal principles, laws, and research to the field of pretrial services. Retrieved from EBP Box Set Paper website: www.cjinstitute.org/boxset.

Wener, R. (2005). The invention of direct supervision. *Corrections Compendium, 30*(2), 4–7, 32–34.

Wener, R. (2006). Effectiveness of the direct supervision system of correctional design and management. *Criminal Justice and Behavior, 33*(3), 392–410. doi: 10.1177/0093854806286202

West, H. C., Sabol, W. J., & Greenman, S. J. (2010). Prisoners in 2009. (NCJ 231675). Retrieved from Bureau of Justice Statistics website: http://bjs.ojp.usdoj.gov/index.cfm?ty=pbdetail&iid=2232.

Zupan, L. L. (1991). *Jails: Reform and the new generation philosophy*. Cincinnati, OH: Anderson.

Chapter 7, Managing Prisons and Prisoners

Adams, K., & Ferrandino, J. (2008). Managing mentally ill inmates in prisons. *Criminal Justice and Behavior, 35*(8), 913–927. doi: 10.1177/0093854808318624

ADMIN. (2011). First day in prison (part 1). Retrieved from Prison Secrets website: http://prisonsecrets.com/2011/02/13/first-day-in-prison-part-1/.

American Correctional Association. (2007). Correctional officers—Hiring requirements and wages: Survey summary. *Corrections Compendium, 32*(3), 12–13.

American Correctional Association. (2008a). Correctional officer education and training: Survey summary. *Corrections Compendium, 33*(4), 11.

American Correctional Association. (2008b). Inmate mental health care: Survey summary. *Corrections Compendium, 33*(5), 12–13.

Austin, J. (2003). Findings in prison classification and risk assessment. Retrieved from National Institute of Corrections Library website: http://nicic.gov/Library/018888.

Austin, J., & Coventry, G. (2003). A second look at the private prison debate. *The Criminologist, 28*(5), 1, 3–9.

Blakely, C. R., & Bumphus, V. W. (2004). Private and public sector prisons—A comparison of select characteristics. *Federal Probation, 68*(1), 27–31.

Bureau of Labor Statistics. (2011). Occupational employment and wages news release. (May 17). Retrieved from www.bls.gov/news.release/ocwage.htm.

Bureau of Prisons. (2009). State of the Bureau 2009. Retrieved from Publications from the Bureau of Prisons website: www.bop.gov/locations/index.jsp.

Bureau of Prisons. (2011). Federal prison facilities. Retrieved from Federal Bureau of Prisons website: www.bop.gov/locations/index.jsp.

Bureau of Prisons. (2011, April 23). Quick facts about the Bureau of Prisons. Retrieved from www.bop.gov/news/quick.jsp.

Bureau of Prisons. (n.d.). A brief history of Alcatraz. Retrieved from Federal Bureau of Prisons website: www.bop.gov/about/history/alcatraz.jsp.

Camp, C. G. (Ed.). (2003). *The 2002 Corrections Yearbook: Adult Corrections*. Middletown, CT: Criminal Justice Institute.

Corrections Corporation of America. (2008). About CCA. Retrieved May 26, 2011, from www.cca.com/about/.

Dammer, H. R. (1996). Religion in prisons. In M. D. McShane & F. Williams III (Eds.), *Encyclopedia of American prisons* (pp. 399–402). New York: Garland.

Gaes, G. G. (2008). The impact of prison education programs on post-release outcomes. (February 18). Retrieved from CEA Correctional Education Research website: www.ceanational.org/docs/Gaes.pdf.

Gazis-Sax, J. (1998). Alcatraz: Frequently asked questions. Retrieved from www.notfrisco2.com/alcatraz/faq/faq3.html.

Hauser, B. (2008). The changing of the guard. *New York Times*, (September 28). Retrieved from www.nytimes.com.

Kahler, H. L. (1999). Prison recreation. In P. M. Carlson & J. S. Garrett (Eds.), *Prison and jail administration: Practice and theory* (pp. 94–99). Gaithersburg, MD: Aspen Publishers.

Lawrence, R., & Mahan, S. (1998). Women correctional officers in men's prisons: Acceptance and perceived job performance. *Women & Criminal Justice, 9*(3), 63–86.

Logan, C. H. (1990). *Private prisons: Cons and pros*. New York: Oxford University Press.

Lundahl, B., Kunz, C., Brownell, C., Harris, N., & Van Vleet, R. (2007). Prison privatization: A meta-analysis of cost effectiveness and quality of confinement indicators. Retrieved from http://ucjc.law.utah.edu/wp-content/uploads/86.pdf.

McKelvey, B. (1977). *American prisons: A history of good intentions*. Montclair, NJ: Patterson Smith.

Newton, C., Rough, G., & Hensley, J. J. (2010). Arizona inmate escape puts spotlight on state private prisons. *The Arizona Republic*, (August 22). Retrieved from www.azcentral.com/.

Oppel, R. A., Jr. (2011). Private prisons found to offer little in savings. *New York Times*, (May 18). Retrieved from New York Times website: www.nytimes.com/2011/05/19/us/19prisons.html.

Seidel, J. (2009). Female inmate described rapes in lawsuit against state. *Detroit Free Press*, (January 7). Retrieved from www.freep.com.

Seiter, R. P. (2002). *Correctional administration: Integrating theory and practice*. Upper Saddle River, NJ: Prentice Hall.

Stephan, J. J. (2008). Census of state and federal correctional facilities, 2005. (NCJ 222182). Retrieved from Bureau of Justice Statistics website: http://bjs.ojp.usdoj.gov/index.cfm?ty=pbdetail&iid=530.

United Nations Office on Drugs and Crime. (2008). *Handbook for prison managers and policymakers on women and imprisonment*. New York, NY: United Nations.

Vose, B., Lowenkamp, C. T., Smith, P., & Cullen, F. T. (2009). Gender and the predictive validity of the LSI-R. *Journal of Contemporary Criminal Justice, 25*(4), 459–471. doi: 10.1177/1043986209344797

West, H. C. (2010). Prison inmates at midyear 2009—Statistical Table. (NCJ 230113). Retrieved from Bureau of Justice Statistics website: http://bjs.ojp.usdoj.gov/index.cfm?ty=pbdetail&iid=2273.

West, H. C., Sabol, W. J., & Greenman, S. J. (2010). Prisoners in 2009. (NCJ 231675). Retrieved from Bureau of Justice Statistics website: http://bjs.ojp.usdoj.gov/index.cfm?ty=pbdetail&iid=2232.

Zupan, L. L. (1992). The progress of women correctional officers in all-male prisons. In I. Moyer (Ed.), *The changing role of women in the criminal justice system* (pp. 323–343). Prospect Heights, IL: Waveland.

Chapter 8, Prison Life

Alarid, Leanne F. (1996). *Women offender's perception of confinement: Behavior code acceptance, hustling, and group relations in jail and prison.* An Unpublished Doctoral Dissertation. Huntsville Texas, Sam Houston State University.

Alarid, Leanne F. (1997). Female inmate subcultures. *Correctional contexts: Contemporary and classical readings.* J. W. Marquart, & J. R. Sorensen. Los Angeles, Roxbury.

Alarid, Leanne F. (2000a). Along racial and gender lines: Jail subcultures in the midst of racial disproportionality. *Corrections Management Quarterly* 4(1), 8–19.

Alarid, Leanne F. (2000b). Sexual assault and coercion among incarcerated women prisoners: Excerpts from prison letters. *The Prison Journal* 80(4): 391–406.

Alarid, Leanne F. (2005). Turning a profit or just passing the time? A gender comparison of prisoner jobs and workplace deviance in the sub rosa economy. *Deviant Behavior, 6,* 621–641.

Beck, A. J., Harrison, P. M., & Guerino, P. (2010). *Sexual victimization in prisons and jails reported by inmates, 2008–2009.* Washington, DC: U.S. Department of Justice.

Camp, C. G., Camp, G., & May, B. (2003). *The 2002 Corrections Yearbook.* Middletown, CT, Criminal Justice Institute, Inc.

Carceral, K. C. (2004). *Behind a convict's eyes: Doing time in a modern prison.* Bernard, T. J., Leanne F. Alarid, Bruce Bikle, & Alene Bikle, Eds. Belmont, CA, Wadsworth.

Clemmer, D. (1966). *The prison community.* New York: Holt.

CNN Wire staff (2010). Guards open fire during major riot at California's prison. August 28, 2010. Retrieved from http://articles.cnn.com/2010-08-28/justice/california.prison.riot_1_prison-yard-prison-staff-members-inmates?_s=PM:CRIME.

Colvin, M. (1997). *Penitentiaries, reformatories, and chain gangs: Social theory and the history of punishment in nineteenth-century America.* New York: St. Martin's Press.

Corrections Compendium. (2002a). Prison violence—Table 1: 2000 numbers and Table 2: 2001 numbers. *Corrections Compendium 27*(5), 6–10.

Corrections Compendium. (2002b). Prison violence—Table 3: Disturbances. *Corrections Compendium 27*(5): 11–14.

Dwyer, D. C. and McNally, R. B. (1993). Public policy prison industries, and business: An equitable balance for the 1990s. *Federal Probation, 57*(2), 30–36.

Encinas, Gilbert L. (2001). *Prison argot: A sociolinguistic and lexicographic study.* University Press of America.

English, K. & Heil, P. (2005). Prison rape: What we know today. *Corrections Compendium 30*(5), 1–5, 42–44.

English, K., Heil, P., & Dumond, R. (2010). *Sexual assault in jail and juvenile facilities: Promising practices for prevention and response.* Denver, CO: Colorado Division of Criminal Justice. Retrieved from http://dcj.state.co.us/ors/pdf/PREA/FINAL%20PREA%20REPORT%20June%2028%202010.pdf.

Federal Bureau of Prisons. (2011). Quick Facts about the Bureau of Prisons. Retrieved from www.bop.gov/news/quick.jsp.

Harkleroad, J. (2000). Prison is a Place. In R. Johnson and H. Toch (Eds.), *Crime and punishment: Inside views* (pp. 163–164). Los Angeles, CA: Roxbury.

Irwin, J. (1980). *Prisons in turmoil.* Boston, MA, Little, Brown, & Company.

James, R. (2009). A brief history of prison riots. *Time,* Aug 11, 2009. Retrieved from www.time.com/time/nation/article/0,8599,1915665,00.html.

Johnson, R. H. (1993). *Hard time: Understanding and reforming the prison* (3rd edition). Belmont, CA: Wadsworth.

Jones, T. R. & Pratt, T. C. (2008). The prevalence of sexual violence in prison: The state of the knowledge base and implications for evidence-based correctional policy making. *International Journal of Offender Therapy and Comparative Criminology, 52*(3), 280–295.

Knox, G. W. (2005). *The problem of gangs and security threat groups (STGs) in American prisons today: Recent research findings from the 2004 prison gang survey.* Retrieved from www.ngcrc.com.

Lankenau, S. E. (2001). Smoke 'em if you got 'em: Cigarette black markets in U.S. prisons and jails. *The Prison Journal 81*(2), 142–161.

Lee, B. & Gilligan, J. (2005). The resolve to stop violence project: Transforming an in-house culture of violence through a jail-based programme. *Journal of Public Health, 27*(2), 149–155.

McNary, S. (2010). After the prison Chino riot. KPCC, Southern California Public Radio. Retrieved from www.scpr.org/specials/prison/.

Metzger, D. H. (2000). Life in a microwave. In R. Johnson and H. Toch (Eds), *Crime and punishment: Inside views* (pp. 138–139). Los Angeles, CA: Roxbury.

Montgomery, R. H. & Crews, G. A. (1998). *A history of correctional violence: An examination of riots and correctional disturbances*. Lanham, MD: American Correctional Association.

National Correctional Industries Association. (2011). Prison Industry Enhancement (PIE) Certification Program. Retrieved from www.nationalcia.org/wp-content/uploads/2008/10/pie-overview-final2.pdf.

Owen, B. (1998). *In the mix: Struggle and survival in a women's prison*. Albany, NY: State University of New York.

Petersen, R. D. (2000). Gang subcultures and prison gangs of female youth. *Free Inquiry in Creative Sociology 28*(2), 27–42.

Pollock, J. M. (2002). *Women, prison & crime* (2nd ed.). Belmont, CA: Thomson/Wadsworth.

The Prison Rape Elimination Act. (2003). 108th Congress, 2003, 117 Stat. 972.

Ross, J. I. & Richards, S. C. (2002). *Behind bars: Surviving prison*. Indianapolis, IN, Alpha Books.

Sabol, W. J., West, H. C., & Cooper, M. (2009). *Prisoners in 2008*. NCJ 228417. Washington, DC: U.S. Department of Justice.

Santos, M. G. (2004). *About prison*. Belmont, CA: Wadsworth/Thomson.

Serin, R. C. (2005). *Evidence-based practice: Principles for enhancing correctional results in prisons*. Longmont, CO: National Institute of Corrections.

Struckman-Johnson, C., Struckman-Johnson, D., Rucker, L., Bumby, K., & Donaldson, S. (1996). Sexual coercion reported by men and women in prisons. *The Journal of Sex Research 33*(1), 37–76.

Sykes, G. M. (1958). *The society of captives*. Princeton, Princeton University Press.

Sykes, G. M. & Messinger, S. (1960). The inmate social system. In *Theoretical Studies in Social Organization of the Prison* (pp. 5–19). New York: Social Science Research Council.

Terry, C. M. (2003). *The fellas: Overcoming prison and addiction*. Belmont, CA: Wadsworth.

Trulson, C. R., & Marquart, J. W. (2002). Racial desegregation and violence in the Texas prisons system. *Criminal Justice Review 27*(2), 233–255.

UNICOR. (2011). *2010 Annual Financial Management Report*. Retrieved from www.unicor.gov/information/publications/pdfs/corporate/FY2010.Q4.FPI-final.pdf.

U.S. Immigration and Customs Enforcement. (2011). *Fact Sheet of the Detention and Removal Operations: Alternatives to Detention*. Retrieved from www.ice.gov.

Visher, C. A., Winterfield, L., & Coggeshall, M. B. (2005). Ex-offender employment programs and recidivism: A meta-analysis. *Journal of Experimental Criminology, 1*(3), 295–316.

WABC-TV/DT. (2008). RSVP program helps inmates with anger. (June 10, 2008). Eyewitness News, WABC, New York. Retrieved from http://abclocal.go.com/wabc/story?section=news/local&id=6197063.

Wicker, T. (1994). *A time to die: The Attica prison revolt*. University of Nebraska Press.

Winfree, L. T., Newbold, G., & Tubb, S. H. (2002). Prisoner perspective on inmate culture in New Mexico and New Zealand: A descriptive case study. *The Prison Journal, 82*(2), 213–233.

Winterdyk, J. & Ruddell, R. (2010). Managing prison gangs: Results from a survey of U.S. prison systems. *Journal of Criminal Justice, 38*(4), 730–736.

Chapter 9, Special Correctional Populations

Alarid, L. F. (2009). Risk factors for potential occupational exposure to HIV: A study of correctional officers. *Journal of Criminal Justice 37*(2), 114–122.

Allen, S. A., Rich, J. D., Schwartzapfel, B., & Friedmann, P. D. (2003). Hepatitis C Among Offenders—Correctional Challenge and Public Health Opportunity. *Federal Probation 67*(2), 22–26.

American Civil Liberties Union. (2010). ACLU and Human Rights Watch report calls on South Carolina and Alabama to stop segregating prisoners with HIV. April 14, 2010. Retrieved from www.aclu.org/hiv-aids-prisoners-rights/aclu-and-human-rights-watch-report-calls-south-carolina-and-alabama-stop-s.

American Correctional Association. (2004). Inmate health care: Table 7: Co-pay plans and release medications. *Corrections Compendium 29*(6), 28–29.

American Correctional Association. (2003). Inmate health care Part 2—Table 1: Specialized services. *Corrections Compendium 28*(11): 11–14.

Anno, B. J. (2001). *Special needs prisoners*. Washington, DC: National Institute of Justice.

Beck, A. J. & Maruschak, L. M. (2004). Hepatitis testing and treatment in state prisons. *Bureau of Justice Statistics Special Report*. Washington, DC, U.S. Department of Justice, Office of Justice Programs.

Bozzette, S. A., Joyce, G., McCaffrey, D. F., Leibowitz, A. A., Morton, S. C., Berry, S. H., Rastegar, A., Timberlake, D., Shapiro, M. F., & Goldman, D. F. (2001). Expenditures for the care of HIV-Infected patients in the era of highly active antiretroviral therapy. *New England Journal of Medicine, 344*(11), 817–820.

Bureau of Justice Statistics. (2010). Percent of state prisoner deaths, by cause of death, 2001–2007. Retrieved from http://bjs.ojp.usdoj.gov/content/dcrp/tables/dcst07spt2.pdf.

Byrne, M. W. (2006). *Responsive parenting support during the prison nursery and reentry years: Highlights from a study in progress: Maternal and child outcomes of a prison nursery program* (Nov. 6 power point presentation,). Retrieved from http://archives.drugabuse.gov/meetings/children_at_risk/pdf/Byrne.pdf.

Carlson, B. & Cervera, N. (1992). *Inmates and their wives: Incarceration and family life*. Westport, CT, Greenwood.

Center for Disease Control. (2003). Estimated rates of adults and adolescents per 100,000 living with HIV or AIDS in the United States. Retrieved from www.cdc.gov/hiv/surveillance/resources/reports/2003report/pdf/map1-2.pdf.

Chavaria, F. R. (2006). Probation and cognitive skills. In Kenneth C. Haas and Geoffrey P. Alpert (Eds.), *The dilemmas of corrections*, 5th edition (pp. 453–460). Long Grove, IL: Waveland.

Christian, J. (2005). Riding the bus: Barriers to prison visitation and family management strategies. *Journal of Contemporary Criminal Justice* 21: 31–48.

Crawley, E. & Sparks, R. (2006). Is there life after imprisonment? How elderly men talk about imprisonment and release. *Criminology & Criminal Justice, 6*(1), 63–82.

Ekwueme, D. U., Pinkerton, S. D., Holtgrave, D. R., & Branson, B. M. (2003). Cost comparison of three HIV counseling and testing technologies. *American Journal of Preventive Medicine, 25*, 112–121.

Gebo, K. A., Fleishman, J. A., Conviser, R., Hellinger, J., Hellinger, F. J., Josephs, J. S., Keiser, P., Gaist, P., & Moore, R. D. (2010). Contemporary costs of HIV healthcare in the HAART era. *AIDS, 24*(17), 2705–2715.

Grinstead, O., Eldridge, G., MacGowan, R., Morrow, K. M., Seal, D. W., Sosman, J. M., & Zack, B. (2008). An HIV, STD, and hepatitis prevention program for young men leaving prison: Project START. *Journal of Correctional Health Care, 14*, 183–196.

Hanson, R. K., & Bussiere, M. T. (1998). Predicting relapse: A meta-analysis of sexual offender recidivism. *Journal of Consulting and Clinical Psychology* 66(2), 348–362.

Harris, D. A. (2004). *A typological approach to exploring pathways for rapists, child molesters, and incest offenders.* An unpublished master's thesis. College Park: University of Maryland.

Haugebrook, S., Zgoba, K. M., Maschi, T., Morgen, K., & Brown, D. (2010). Trauma, stress, health and mental health among ethnically diverse older adult prisoners. *Journal of Correctional Health Care, 16*, 220–229.

Hellard, M. E., Aitken, C. K., & Hocking, J. S. (2007). Tattooing in prisons- Not such a pretty picture. *American Journal of Infection Control, 35*(7), 477–480.

Johnson, R. (2002). *Hard time: Understanding and reforming the prison.* Belmont, CA: Wadsworth.

Kauffman, K. (2006). Prison nurseries: New beginnings and second chances. In R. Immarigeon (Ed.), *Women and girls in the criminal justice system: Policy issues and practice strategies* (pp. 1–7 in Chap 20). Kingston, NJ: Civic Research Institute, Inc.

Kerle, K. (2004). Inmates as victims of crime. *American Jails.* 18: 35–37.

Landenberger, N. A. & Lipsey, M. W. (2005). The positive effects of cognitive-behavioral programs for offenders: A meta-analysis of factors associated with effective treatment. *Journal of Experimental Criminology, 1*(4), 451–476.

Lowden, K., Hetz, N., Harrison, L., Patrick, D., English, K., & Pasini-Hill, D. (2003). *Evaluation of Colorado's prison therapeutic community for sex offenders.* Denver, CO, Colorado Division of Criminal Justice, Office of Research and Statistics.

Macalino, G. E., Viahov, D., Stanford-Colby, S., Patel, S., Sabin, K., Salas, C., and Rich, J. D. (2004). Prevalence and incidence of HIV, hepatitis B virus, and hepatitis C virus infections among males in Rhode Island prisons. *American Journal of Public Health, 94*(7), 1218–1223.

Marushchak, L. M. (2005). *HIV in prisons, 2003.* Washington, DC: U.S. Department of Justice, Office of Justice Programs.

Marushchak, L. M. (2004). *HIV in prisons, 2001.* Washington, DC: U.S. Department of Justice, Office of Justice Programs.

Marushchak, L. M. & Beavers, R. (2009). *HIV in prisons, 2007–08.* Washington, DC: U.S. Department of Justice, Office of Justice Programs.

Moses, M. C. (1995). Keeping incarcerated mothers and their daughters together: Girl Scouts beyond bars. *National Institute of Justice Program Focus.* Washington, DC, U.S. Department of Justice, Office of Justice Programs.

Mumola, C. J. (2000). *Bureau of Justice Statistics Special Report: Incarcerated Parents and Their Children.* Washington, DC: U.S. Department of Justice, Office of Justice Programs.

National Women's Law Center. (2010). Mothers behind bars: A state-by-state report card and analysis of federal policies on conditions of confinement for pregnant and parenting women and the effect on their children. Retrieved from www.nwlc.org/sites/default/files/pdfs/mothersbehindbars2010.pdf.

Nolan, P. (2003). Inmate user fees: Fiscal fix or mirage. *Corrections Today* 65(5): 23.

Paris, J. E. (2010). Three cases of correctional litigation: Learning from the root causes. *Journal of Correctional Health Care, 16*, 39–47.

Parvez, F. M., Lobato, M. N., & Greifinger, R. B. (2010). Tuberculosis control: Lessons for outbreak preparedness in a correctional facility. *Journal of Correctional Health Care, 16*, 239–242.

Pupovac, J. (2011). Guarding grandpa. *Chicago Reader,* January 5, 2011. Retrieved from www.chicagoreader.com/chicago/illinois-prisons-budget-elderly-old-inmates/Content?oid=3013140.

Reimer, G. (2008). The graying of the U.S. prisoner population. *Journal of Correctional Health Care, 14*, 202–208.

Rhodes, W., Johnston, P., McMullen, Q., & Hozik, L. (2000). *Unintended consequences of sentencing policy: The creation of long-term healthcare obligations.* Cambridge, MA, Washington, DC, ABT Associates, Inc., National Institute of Justice.

Samenow, S. E. (1984). *Inside the criminal mind.* New York: Times Books.

Sanborn, M. M. (2003). The pay-to-stay debate: Inmates must take financial responsibility. *Corrections Today* 65(5): 22.

Sharp, S. F. (2003). Mothers in prison: Issues in parent–child contact. In S. F. Sharp (Ed.), *The incarcerated woman: Rehabilitative programming in women's prisons* (pp. 151–165). Upper Saddle River, NJ, Prentice Hall.

Sylla, M., Harawa, N., & Reznick, O. G. (2010). The first condom machine in a US jail: The challenge of harm reduction in a law and order environment. *American Journal of Public Health, 100*(6), 982–985.

Vaughn, M. S. & Carroll, L. (1998). Separate and unequal: Prison versus free-world medical care. *Justice Quarterly* 15(1), 3–40.

Wright, K. N. & Bronstein, L. (2007). An organizational analysis of prison hospice. *The Prison Journal, 87*(4), 391–407.

Zaller, N., Thurmond, P., & Rich, J. D. (2007). Limited spending: An analysis of correctional expenditures on antiretrovirals for HIV-Infected prisoners. *Public Health Reports 122*(1), 49–54.

Chapter 10, Reentry Programs and Institutional Release

American Bar Association Justice Kennedy Commission. (2004). Report to the house of delegates: Recommendations on prison conditions and prisoner reentry. Washington, DC, American Bar Association.

American Correctional Association. (2004). Reentry/reintegration. *Corrections Compendium* 29(2): 8–9.

Americans United v. *Prison Fellowship Ministry.* (2006). 432 F. Supp. 2d. 862.

Batiuk, M. E., Lahm, K. F., McKeever, M., Wilcox, N. & Wilcox, P. (2005). Disentangling the effects of correctional education. *Criminal Justice, 5*(1), 55–74.

Brewster, D. R., & Sharp, S. F. (2002). Educational programs and recidivism in Oklahoma: Another look. *The Prison Journal, 82*(3), 314–334. doi: 10.1177/0032885502082000302

Brown, J. D. (2004). Managing the transition to community: A Canadian parole officer perspective on the needs of newly released federal offenders. *Western Criminology Review* 5(2): 97–107.

Bureau of Justice Statistics. (2000). *Census of state and federal adult correctional facilities*. Washington, DC: U.S. Department of Justice: Office of Justice Programs.

Bureau of Justice Statistics. (1999). *Census of jails*. Washington, DC: U.S. Department of Justice: Office of Justice Programs.

Burke, P. B. (2004). *Parole violations revisited* [NIC #019833]. Washington, DC: National Institute of Corrections, and Silver Spring, MD: Center for Effective Public Policy.

Byrne, J. M., Taxman, F. S., & Young, D. (2002). *Emerging roles and responsibilities in the reentry partnership initiative: New ways of doing business*. Washington, DC: National Institute of Justice. Retrieved from www.ncjrs.gov/pdffiles1/nij/grants/196441.pdf.

Chappell, C. A. (2004). Post-secondary correctional education and recidivism: A meta-analysis of research conducted 1990–1999. *The Journal of Correctional Education, 55*(2), 148–162.

Coulter, G. & Brookens, E. (2003). Corrective reading: A systemwide program to improve basic reading performance for adult basic education students. *Corrections Compendium* 28(10): 1–4, 28–30.

Dodge, M. & Pogrebin, M. R. (2001). Collateral costs of imprisonment for women: Complications of reintegration. *The Prison Journal* 81(1): 42–54.

Finn, P. (1998). Program focus: The Delaware department of corrections life skills program. Washington, DC: National Institute of Justice.

Foley, R. M. (2001). Academic characteristics of incarcerated youth and correctional education programs: A literature review. *Journal of Emotional and Behavioral Disorders* 9(4): 248–259.

Glaze, L. E. (2003). *Probation and parole in the United States, 2002*. Washington, DC: Bureau of Justice Statistics, U.S. Department of Justice.

Glover v. *Johnson*. (1979). 478 F. Supp. 1075, E.D. Mich., 1087.

Haigler, K. O., Harlow, C., O'Connor, P., & Campbell, A. (1994). *Executive summary of literacy behind prison walls: Profiles of the prison population from the National Adult Literacy Survey*. Retrieved from http://nces.ed.gov/pubsearch/pubsinfo.asp?pubid=94102.

Hammett, T., Roberts, C., & Kennedy, S. (2001). Health-related issues in prisoner reentry. *Crime and Delinquency* 47(3): 390–409.

Harlow, C. W. (2003). *Education and correctional populations*. Washington, DC: U.S. Department of Justice, Bureau of Justice Statistics.

Herman, S., & Wasserman, C. (2001). A role for victims in offender reentry. *Crime and Delinquency* 47(3): 428–445.

Ingley, S. J. (2004). Reentry or preentry? *American Jails*. 18: 7.

Johnson, B. R., & Larson, D. B. (2003). The InnerChange Freedom initiative: A preliminary evaluation of faith-based prison programs. Center for Research on Religion and Urban Civil Society, University of Pennsylvania.

Kennedy, A. M. (2004). Commission of the American Bar Association.

Lahm, K. F. (2000). Equal or equitable: An exploration of educational and vocational program availability for male and female offenders. *Federal Probation* 64(2): 39–46.

McCollum, S. G. (1994). Prison college programs. *The Prison Journal* 73(1): 51–61.

Meyer, S. J., Fredericks, L., Borden, C. M., and Richardson, P. L. (2010). Implementing postsecondary academic programs in state prisons: Challenges and opportunities. *Journal of Correctional Education, 61*(2), 148–183.

Missouri Department of Corrections. (2004). Department hosts inaugural TPCI symposium. *The Horizon* 18(4): 1, 10–11.

Morash, M., Bynum, T. S., & Koonz, B. A. (1998). Women offenders: Programming needs and promising approaches. *National Institute of Justice Research In Brief.* Washington, DC: U.S. Department of Justice, Office of Justice Programs, National Institute of Justice.

Morrissey v. *Brewer.* (1972) 408 U.S., 471.

Morris, Norval. (2002). *Maconochie's gentlemen: The story of Norfolk Island and the roots of modern prison reform.* New York, Oxford University Press.

Mumola, C. J. (2000). *Bureau of Justice statistics special report: Incarcerated parents and their children.* Washington, DC: U.S. Department of Justice, Office of Justice Programs.

National Institute of Corrections Model of Transition from Prison to the Community. (n.d.). Retrieved from www.in.gov/idoc/2520.htm.

O'Brien, P. (2002). *Reducing barriers to employment for women ex-offenders: Mapping the road to reintegration.* Chicago, IL: Safer Foundation.

Paynter, B. (2004). Jesus is in the big house. *The Pitch.* Kansas City, MO: 13–21.

Petersilia, J. (2002). *Reforming probation and parole in the 21st century.* Lanham, MD, American Correctional Association.

Sabol, W. J., West, H. C., & Cooper, M. (2009). *Prisoners in 2008.* NCJ 228417. Washington, DC: U.S. Department of Justice.

Scram, K. (2011, January 13). Former governor to spend three days a week at halfway house. WGMB Fox 44 News, Baton Rouge, LA. Retrieved from www.fox44.com/news/halfway-house-critical-to-edwards-success-after-prison.

Second Chance Act of 2007, Pub. L. No. 110-199, 122 Stat. 657 (2008).

Snider, E. (1999). The road to freedom. Retrieved from www.exoffender.org.

Steurer, S. J., & Smith, L. G. (2003). *Education reduces crime: Three-state recidivism study.* Lanham, MD. Correctional Education Association.

Travis, J. & Petersilia, J. (2001). Reentry reconsidered: A new look at an old question. *Crime and Delinquency* 47(3): 291–313.

United States General Accounting Office. (2001). *Prisoner releases: Reintegration of offenders into communities.* Washington, DC: U.S. General Accounting Office.

VERA Institute of Justice (2010). *The continuing fiscal crisis in corrections: Setting a new course.* (October). New York, NY. Retrieved from www.vera.org/download?file=3072/The-continuing-fiscal-crisis-in-corrections-10-2010-updated.pdf.

Wilson, D. B., Gallagher, C. A., & MacKenzie, D. L. (2000). A meta-analysis of corrections-based education, vocation, and work programs for adult offenders. *Journal of Research in Crime and Delinquency* 37(4): 347–368.

Chapter 11, Legal Issues in Corrections

Bandy, R. (2011). Measuring the impact of sex offender notification on community adoption of protective behaviors. *Criminology & Public Policy, 10*(2), 237–263. doi: 10.1111/j.1745-9133.2011.00705.x

Behrens, A., Uggen, C., & Manza, J. (2003). Ballot manipulation and the "Menace of Negro Domination": Racial threat and felon disenfranchisement in the United States, 1850–2002. *American Journal of Sociology, 109*(3), 559–605.

Cheesman II, F. L., Ostrom, B. J., & Hanson, R. A. (2004). A tale of two laws revisited: Investigating the impact of the Prisoner Litigation Reform Act and the Antiterrorism and Effective Death Penalty. Retrieved from National Center for State Courts website: www.ncsconline.org/d_research/descriptions.html.

City of Newark. (2011). Synopsis of Delaware's sex offender law. Retrieved from www.cityofnewarkde.us/index.aspx?NID=388.

del Carmen, R. V., Ritter, S. E., & Witt, B. A. (2005). *Briefs of leading cases in corrections* (4th ed.). Newark, NJ: Lexis Nexis Anderson Publishing.

Dolan, J. (2011). Lawsuit asks state to pay for inmate's sex-change operation. *Los Angeles Times*, (April 20). Retrieved from Article Collections website: http://articles.latimes.com/.

Doucette, B. (2010). Nichols' lawsuit over prison food dismissed by federal judge. (August 13). Retrieved from The Oklahoman's NewsOK website: www.newsok.com/.

Fellner, J., & Mauer, M. (1998). Losing the vote: The impact of felony disenfranchisement laws in the United States. (October). Retrieved from The Sentencing Project Publications website: www.sentencingproject.org/template/page.cfm?id=131.

Ferdico, J. N. (2005). *Criminal procedure for the criminal justice professional* (9th ed.). Belmont, CA: Thompson/Wadsworth.

Harris, A. J., & Lobanov-Rostovsky, C. (2010). Implementing the Adam Walsh Act's Sex Offender Registration and Notification Provisions: A survey of the states. *Criminal Justice Policy Review, 21*(2), 202–222. doi: 10.1177/0887403409346118

Jenness, V. (2009). Transgender inmates in California's prisons: An empirical study of a vulnerable population. Retrieved from University of California - Irvine Center for Evidence-Based Corrections website: http://ucicorrections.seweb.uci.edu/pubs#powerpoint.

Levenson, J. S. (2011). Sex offender policies in an era of zero tolerance. *Criminology & Public Policy, 10*(2), 229–233. doi: 10.1111/j.1745-9133.2011.00704.x

Love, M. C. (2005). *Relief from the collateral consequences of a criminal conviction: A state-by-state resource guide* (Executive summary). Retrieved from The Sentencing Project website: www.sentencingproject.org/detail/publication.cfm?publication_id=115.

Love, M. C. (2006). *Relief from the collateral consequences of a criminal conviction: A state-by-state resource guide*. Buffalo, NY: William S. Hein.

Love, M. C. (2006, October 1). Certificates of rehabilitation and other forms of relief from the collateral consequences of conviction: A survey of state laws. Retrieved from Margaret Colgate Love's Selected Publications and Reference Materials website: www.pardonlaw.com/articlesandpublications.html.

Manza, J., & Uggen, C. (2006). *Locked out: Felon disenfranchisement and American democracy*. New York, NY: Oxford University Press.

Muraskin, R. (1993). Disparate treatment in correctional facilities. In R. Muraskin & T. Alleman (Eds.), *It's a crime: Women and justice* (pp. 211–225). Englewood Cliffs, NJ: Prentice Hall.

Office of Justice Programs. (2011a). Justice department finds 24 jurisdictions have substantially implemented SORNA requirements. (July 28). Retrieved from SMART Press Releases website: www.ojp.usdoj.gov/newsroom/pressreleases/2011/SMART_PR-072811.htm.

Office of Justice Programs. (2011b). SORNA. Retrieved from Office of Sex Offender Sentencing, Monitoring, Apprehending, Registering, and Trafficking website: www.ojp.usdoj.gov/smart/sorna.htm.

Ostrom, B. J., Hanson, R. A., & Cheesman II, F. L. (2003). Congress, courts and corrections: An empirical perspective on the Prison Litigation Reform Act. *Notre Dame Law Review, 78*(5), 1525–1560.

Periman, D. (2007). The hidden impact of a criminal conviction: A brief overview of collateral consequences in Alaska. *Alaska Justice Forum, 24*(3). Retrieved from http://justice.uaa.alaska.edu/forum/24/3fall2007/a_collateral.html.

Porter, N. D. (2010). Expanding the vote: State felony disenfranchisement reform, 1997–2010. Retrieved from Sentencing Project Publications website: www.sentencingproject.org/template/page.cfm?id=131.

ProCon.org. (2009, April 13). Opinion polls/surveys. Retrieved from Felon Voting website: http://felonvoting.procon.org/view.resource.php?resourceID=000666.

ProCon.org. (2009, January 23). Should felons be allowed to vote? Retrieved from Core Question website: http://felonvoting.procon.org/view.answers.php?questionID=001319.

ProCon.org. (2010, April 8). State felon voting laws. Retrieved from Felon Voting website: http://felonvoting.procon.org/view.resource.php?resourceID=000286.

Schlanger, M. (2003). Inmate litigation. *Harvard Law Review, 116*(6), 1555–1706.

Tewksbury, R. (2011). Policy implications of sex offender residence restrictions laws. *Criminology & Public Policy, 10*(2), 345–348. doi: 10.1111/j.1745-9133.2011.00712.x

Travis, J. (2002). Invisible punishment: An instrument of social exclusion. Retrieved from Urban Institute Publications website: www.urban.org/url.cfm?ID=1000557.

Trice, D. T. (2010, July 29). CPS: Good conduct certificate not good enough. *Chicago Tribune*. Retrieved from Chicago Tribune Article Collections website: http://articles.chicagotribune.com/.

Trice, D. T. (2010, September 26). CPS reverses itself, gives job candidate a 2nd chance. *Chicago Tribune*. Retrieved from Chicago Tribune Article Collections website: http://articles.chicagotribune.com/.

Uggen, C., Behrens, A., & Manza, J. (2005). Criminal disenfranchisement. *Annual Review of Law and Social Science, 1*(1), 307–322. doi: 10.1146/annurev.lawsocsci.1.041604.115840

Chapter 12, Capital Punishment

Amnesty International is dead wrong. (1999). *New York Post* (May 22). Retrieved from Archive website: www.nypost.com/nypostarchives.

Bailey, W. C., & Peterson, R. D. (1994). Murder, capital punishment, and deterrence: A review of the evidence and an examination of police killings. *Journal of Social Issues, 50*(2), 53–74. doi: 10.1111/j.1540-4560.1994.tb02410.x

Baldus, D. C., Woodworth, G., & Grosso, C. M. (2008). Race and proportionality since *McCleskey* v. *Kemp* (1987): Different actors with mixed strategies of denial and avoidance. *Columbia Human Rights Law Review, 39*, 143–177.

Bohm, R. M. (2003). *Deathquest II: An introduction to the theory and practice of capital punishment in the United States* (2nd ed.). Cincinnati, OH: Anderson Publishing.

CBS News. (2001). Justice backs death penalty freeze (April 10). Retrieved from Capital punishment website: www.cbsnews.com/stories/2001/04/10/deathpenalty/main284850.shtml.

Death Penalty Information Center. (2010a). Death penalty for offenses other than murder. Retrieved from Death Penalty Information Center website: www.deathpenaltyinfo.org/death-penalty-offenses-other-murder.

Death Penalty Information Center. (2010b). Description of execution methods. Retrieved from Death Penalty Information Center website: www.deathpenaltyinfo.org/descriptions-execution-methods#hanging.

Death Penalty Information Center. (2010c). Executed but possibly innocent. Retrieved from Death Penalty Information Center website: www.deathpenaltyinfo.org/executed-possibly-innocent#cam.

Death Penalty Information Center. (2010d). Executions in the U.S. 1608–2002: The Espy File. Retrieved from Death Penalty Information Center website: www.deathpenaltyinfo.org/executions-us-1608-2002-espy-file.

Death Penalty Information Center. (2010e). Innocence and the death penalty. Retrieved from Death Penalty Information Center website: www.deathpenaltyinfo.org/innocence-and-death-penalty.

Death Penalty Information Center. (2010f). Part 1: Introduction to the death penalty. Retrieved from History of the Death Penalty website: www.deathpenaltyinfo.org/history-death-penalty.

Death Penalty Information Center. (2011). Facts about the death penalty. (April 1). Retrieved from Death Penalty Information Center website: www.deathpenaltyinfo.org/documents/FactSheet.pdf.

del Carmen, R. V., Vollum, S., Cheeseman, K., Frantzen, D., & San Miguel, C. (2005). *The death penalty: Constitutional issues, commentaries, and case briefs*. Cincinnati, OH: Anderson Publishing.

Department of Justice. (1978). *Capital punishment 1977*. (NCJ 49657). Washington, DC: Bureau of Justice Statistics.

Dezhbakhsh, H., & Rubin, P. H. (2010). From the 'econometrics of capital punishment' to the 'capital punishment' of econometrics: On the use and abuse of sensitivity analysis. *Applied Economics*. doi: 10.1080/00036841003670804

Donohue, J. J., & Wolfers, J. (2006). The death penalty: No evidence for deterrence. *The Economists' Voice, 3*(5). doi: 10.2202/1553-3832.1170

Donohue, J. J., & Wolfers, J. (2005). Uses and abuses of empirical evidence in the death penalty debate. *Stanford Law Review, 58*(3), 791–845. Retrieved from www.stanfordlawreview.org/content/article/uses-and-abuses-empirical-evidence-death-penalty-debate

Ehrlich, I. (1975). The deterrent effect of capital punishment: A question of life and death. *American Economic Review, 65*(3), 397–417.

Fagan, J. (2005). Deterrence and the death penalty: A critical review of new evidence. (January 21). Retrieved from Death Penalty Information Center website: www.deathpenaltyinfo.org/FaganTestimony.pdf.

Fagan, J. (2006). Death and deterrence redux: Science, law, and causal reasoning. *Ohio State Journal of Criminal Law, 4*, 255–320.

Fox, J. A., & Zawitz, M. W. (2011). Homicide trends in the U.S. (April 13). Retrieved from Trends by race website: http://bjs.ojp.usdoj.gov/content/homicide/race.cfm#.

Gallup. (2010). Death penalty. (October 7-10). Retrieved from www.gallup.com/poll/1606/death-penalty.aspx.

Goertzel, T. (2004). Capital punishment and homicide: Sociological realities and econometric illusions. *Skeptical Enquirer*. Retrieved from www.deathpenaltyinfo.org/article.php?scid=12&did=1176.

Goldberg, S. (1991). The death penalty deters murder. In C. Wekesser (Ed.), *The death penalty: Opposing viewpoints* (pp. 113–118). San Diego, CA: Greenhaven Press.

King, R., & Bellin, J. (2004). The forgotten population: A look at death row in the United States through the experiences of women. Retrieved from American Civil Liberties Union website: www.aclu.org/files/FilesPDFs/womenondeathrow.pdf.

Kronenwetter, M. (1993). *Capital punishment: A reference handbook*. Santa Barbara, CA: ABC-CLIO.

Land, K. C., Teske, R. H. C., & Zheng, H. U. I. (2009). The short-term effects of executions on homicides: Deterrence, displacement, or both? *Criminology, 47*(4), 1009–1043. doi: 10.1111/j.1745-9125.2009.00168.x

NAACP Legal Defense Fund. (2010). Death row U.S.A.—Winter 2010. (January 1). Retrieved from http://naacpldf.org/files/publications/DRUSA_Winter_2010.pdf.

National Public Radio. (2001). The last public execution in America. (May 1). Retrieved from Morning Edition website: www.npr.org/programs/morning/features/2001/apr/010430.execution.html.

A new executioner: The needle. (1981, 14 September). *Time*, 80.

Newman, G. R. (1985). *The punishment response* (2nd ed.). Albany, N.Y.: Harrow and Heston.

Office of Justice Programs. (1978). Capital punishment, 1977. (NCJ 49657). Retrieved from Bureau of Justice Statistics website: http://bjs.ojp.usdoj.gov/index.cfm?ty=pbdetail&iid=1249.

Paternoster, R. (1991). *Capital punishment in America*. New York: Lexington Books.

Peterson, R. D., & Bailey, W. C. (1991). Felony murder and capital punishment: An examination of the deterrence question. *Criminology, 29*, 367–395.

Peterson, R. D., & Bailey, W. C. (1998). Is capital punishment an effective deterrent for murder? An examination of the social science research. In J. R. Acker, R. M. Bohm, & C. S. Lanier (Eds.), *America's experiment with capital punishment: Reflections on the past, present, and future of the ultimate sanction* (pp. 157–182). Durham, NC: Carolina Academic Press.

Paternoster, R., & Brame, R. (2003). An empirical analysis of Maryland's death sentencing system with respect to the influence of race and legal jurisdiction. College Park: University of Maryland.

Paternoster, R., & Brame, R. (2008). Reassessing race disparities in Maryland capital cases. *Criminology, 46*(4), 971–1008. doi: 10.1111/j.1745-9125.2008.00132.x

Paternoster, R., & Deise, J. (2011). A heavy thumb on the scale: The effect of victim impact evidence on capital decision making. *Criminology, 49*(1), 129–161. doi: 10.1111/j.1745-9125.2010.00220.x

Pokorak, J. J. (1998). Probing the capital prosecutor's perspective: Race of the discretionary actors. *Cornell Law Review, 83*(6), 1811–1820.

ProCon.org. (2009). Does the death penalty deter crime? (January 13). Retrieved from Deterrence & Retribution website: http://deathpenalty.procon.org/view.answers.php?questionID=000983.

ProCon.org. (2011). Historical timeline. Retrieved from Death Penalty website: http://deathpenalty.procon.org/view.resource.php?resourceID=003096.

Radelet, M. L., & Borg, M. J. (2000). The changing nature of death penalty debates. *Annual Review of Sociology, 26*, 43–61.

Rothman, S., & Powers, S. (1994). Execution by quota? *The Public Interest, 116*(Summer), 3–17.

Ruddell, R., & Urbina, M. G. (2004). Minority threat and punishment: A cross-national analysis. *Justice Quarterly, 21*(4), 903–931.

Schottelkotte, S. (2011). Jurors cry as victim's son testifies in Leon Davis murder trial (February 18). Retrieved from www.theledger.com/article/20110218/NEWS/102185010&tc=ix.

Shaked-Schroer, N., Costanzo, M., & Marcus-Newhall, A. (2008). Reducing racial bias in the penalty phase of capital trials. *Behavioral Sciences & the Law, 26*(5), 603–617. doi: 10.1002/bsl.829

Sharp, D. (2004). Innocence issues—The death penalty. Retrieved from Pro-Death Penalty.com Innocence website: www.prodeathpenalty.com/Innocence.htm.

Snell, T. L. (2010). Capital punishment, 2009—Statistical tables. (NCJ 231676). Retrieved from Bureau of Justice Statistics website: http://bjs.ojp.usdoj.gov/index.cfm?ty=pbdetail&iid=2215.

Sorensen, J., Wrinkle, R., Brewer, V., & Marquart, J. W. (1999). Capital punishment and deterrence: Examining the effect of executions on murder in Texas. *Crime & Delinquency, 45*(4), 481–493.

van den Haag, E. (1991). Guilt overrides the importance of death penalty discrimination. In C. Wekesser (Ed.), *The death penalty: Opposing viewpoints* (pp. 156–159). San Diego, CA: Greenhaven Press.

Wikberg, R. (1992). The horror show. In W. Rideau & R. Wikberg (Eds.), *Life sentences: Rage and survival behind bars* (pp. 284–303). New York: Times Books.

Chapter 13, Juvenile Corrections

Adams, B., & Addie, S. (2010). Delinquency cases waived to criminal court, 2007. (NCJ 230167). Retrieved from NCJRS website: www.ncjrs.gov/app/Search/Abstracts.aspx?id=252199.

Arya, N. (2011). Juvenile Justice (Chapter 8). The Smart on Crime Coalition (Ed.) *Smart on crime: Recommendations for the Aministration and Congress*. Retrieved from www.besmartoncrime.org/pdf/Complete.pdf.

Belknap, J., & Holsinger, K. (1998). An overview of delinquent girls: How theory and practice have failed and the need for innovative changes. In R. T. Zaplin (Ed.), *Female offenders: Critical perspectives and effective interventions* (pp. 31–64). Gaithersburg, MD: Aspen Publishers.

Bloom, B., Owen, B., Piper Deschenes, E., & Rosenbaum, J. (2002). Improving juvenile justice for females: A statewide assessment in California. *Crime & Delinquency, 48(4)*, 526–552.

Cahalan, M. W. (1986). *Historical corrections statistics in the United States, 1850–1984*. Washington, DC: Department of Justice.

Center for the Study and Prevention of Violence. (2007). Functional Family Therapy. Retrieved from Model Programs website: www.colorado.edu/cspv/blueprints/modelprograms.html.

Daniel, M. D. (1999). The female intervention team. *Juvenile Justice, 6(1)*, 14–21. Retrieved from www.ncjrs.org/pdffiles1/ojjdp/178254.pdf.

Denniston, L. (2009). Inquiring into the juvenile mind. Retrieved from SCOTUSblog website: www.scotusblog.com/?p=12559.

Devine, P., Coolbaugh, K., & Jenkins, S. (1998). Disproportionate minority confinement: Lessons learned from five states. *Juvenile Justice Bulletin*, (NCJ 173420). Retrieved from www.ncjrs.gov/html/ojjdp/173420/contents.html.

Equal Justice Initiative. (n.d.). Success stories: Kids change. *Sullivan and Graham media resource kit*. Retrieved from http://eji.org/eji/childrenprison/deathinprison/sullivan.graham/resourcekit.

Equal Justice Initiative. (2011). Death in prison for 13- and 14-year-olds. Retrieved from EJI Children in Adult Prison website: www.eji.org/eji/childrenprison/deathinprison.

Functional Family Therapy. (2010). The clinical model. Retrieved from About FFT website: www.fftinc.com/about_model.html.

Greenwood, P. W. (2008). Prevention and intervention programs for juvenile offenders. *Juvenile Justice, 18*. Retrieved from www.princeton.edu/futureofchildren/publications/journals/journal_details/index.xml?journalid=31.

Griffin, P. (2011). Which states try juveniles as adults and use blended sentencing? *State Juvenile Justice Profiles*. Retrieved from National Overviews website: http://70.89.227.250:8080/stateprofiles/overviews/transfer_state_overview.asp (no longer active).

Hsia, H. M., Bridges, G. S., & McHale, R. (2004). Disproportionate minority confinement: 2002 update. (NCJ 201240). Retrieved from Office of Justice Programs website: www.ojjdp.gov/publications/PubAbstract.asp?pubi=201240.

Justice Policy Institute. (2011). Factsheet: Juvenile justice. *Finding Direction: Expanding Criminal Justice Options by Considering Policies of Other Nations*. Retrieved from www.justicepolicy.org/research/2322.

Knoll, C., & Sickmund, M. (2010). Delinquency cases in juvenile court, 2007. (NCJ 230168). Retrieved from www.ncjrs.gov/pdffiles1/ojjdp/230168.pdf.

Livsey, S., Sickmund, M., & Sladky, A. (2009). Juvenile residential facility census, 2004: Selected findings. *National Report Series Bulletin* (NCJ 222721). Retrieved from NCJRS website: www.ncjrs.gov/App/publications/Abstract.aspx?id=244623.

Mendel, D. (2003). Small is beautiful: The Missouri Division of Youth Services. (NCJ 202528). Retrieved from NCJRS website: www.ncjrs.gov/App/publications/Abstract.aspx?id=202528.

Missouri Department of Social Services. (2009). Missouri Division of Youth Services Annual Report, 2009. Retrieved from Research and Evaluation website: www.dss.mo.gov/re/dysar.htm.

Moore, S. (2009). Missouri system treats juvenile offenders with lighter hand. *New York Times* (March 27). Retrieved from www.nytimes.com.

Peters, S. R. (1998). Guiding principles for promising female programming: An inventory of best practices. Retrieved from www.ojjdp.ncjrs.org/pubs/principles/contents.html.

Petteruti, A., Velazquez, T., & Walsh, N. (2009). The costs of confinement: Why good juvenile justice policies make good fiscal sense. Retrieved from www.justicepolicy.org/research/78.

Platt, A. M. (1969). *The child savers*. Chicago: University of Chicago Press.

Puzzanchera, C. (2009). Juvenile arrests 2008. (NCJ 228479). Retrieved from Office of Justice Programs website: www.ojjdp.gov/publications/PubAbstract.asp?pubi=250498.

Sedlak, A. J., & Bruce, C. (2010). Youth's characteristics and backgrounds: Findings from the survey of youth in residential placement. *Juvenile Justice Bulletin* (NCJ 227730). Retrieved from Office of Justice Programs website: www.ojjdp.gov/publications/PubAbstract.asp?pubi=249737.

Sedlak, A. J., & McPherson, K. S. (2010). Conditions of confinement: Findings from the survey of youth in residential placement. *Juvenile Justice Bulletin* (NCJ 227729). Retrieved from NCJRS website: www.ncjrs.gov/app/publications/Abstract.aspx?id=249736.

Snyder, H. N., & Sickmund, M. (2006). Juvenile offenders and victims: 2006 national report. Retrieved from Office of Juvenile Justice and Delinquency Prevention website: www.ojjdp.gov/ojstatbb/nr2006/index.html.

Substance Abuse and Mental Health Services Administration. (2010). Mendota juvenile treatment center program. Retrieved from SAMHSA's National Registry of Evidence-based Programs and Practices website: http://nrepp.samhsa.gov/ViewIntervention.aspx?id=38.

The Oyez Project. (2011). *Graham v. Florida*, 560 U.S. ____ (2010). Retrieved from www.oyez.org/cases/2000-2009/2009/2009_08_7412.

Torbet, P. (1997). State responses to serious and violent juvenile offenders. *Corrections Today* (June), 121–123.

Wisconsin Department of Corrections. (2011). Mendota juvenile treatment center. Retrieved from Juvenile Corrections website: www.wi-doc.com/MJTC.htm.

Chapter 14, Revisiting Evidence-Based Practices and What Works

Bourgon, G. & Armstrong, B. (2006). Transferring the principles of effective treatment into a real world setting. *Criminal Justice, 32*(1), 3–25.

Center on Juvenile and Criminal Justice. (2002). From classrooms to cell blocks: A national perspective. San Francisco, CA: Center on Juvenile and Criminal Justice.

Clear, T. R. (2011). A private-sector, incentive-based model for Justice Reinvestment. *Criminology & Public Policy, 10*(3), 585–608.

Collins Center/Florida Tax Watch. (2011). A billion dollars and growing: Why prison bonding is tougher on Florida taxpayers than on crime. Collins Center for Public Policy, Florida. Retrieved from www.collinscenter.org/resource/resmgr/prison_bonding/prisonbondingreport.pdf.

Drake, E. K., Aos, S., & Miller, M. G. (2009). Evidence-based public policy options to reduce crime and criminal justice costs: Implications in Washington state. *Victims and Offenders, 4,* 170–196.

French, S. A. and Gendreau, P. (2006). Reducing prison misconducts: What works! *Criminal Justice and Behavior, 33*(2), 185–218.

Harrison, L. D., & Martin, S. S. (2003). *Residential substance abuse treatment for state prisoners: Implementation lessons learned.* Washington, DC: Bureau of Justice Assistance.

Kyckelhahn, T. (2010). *Justice expenditure and employment extracts, 2007.* Washington, DC: Bureau of Justice Statistics.

Latessa, E. J. (2004). The challenge of change: Correctional programs and evidence-based practices. *Criminology and Public Policy, 3*(4), 547–560.

Lipsey, M. W. & Cullen, F. T. (2007). The effectiveness of correctional rehabilitation: A review of systematic reviews. *Annual review of law and social science, 3,* 297–320.

Lipsey, M. W., Landenberger, & Wilson, S. J. (2007). *Effects of cognitive-behavioral programs for criminal offenders.* The Campbell Collaboration. Retrieved from www.campbellcollaboration.org.

Lowenkamp, C. T. & Latessa, E. J. (2004). Residential community corrections and the risk principle: Lessons learned in Ohio. *Ohio Corrections Research Compendium,* Volume II, Columbus, OH: Ohio Department of Rehabilitation and Correction. Retrieved from www.uc.edu/ccjr/Articles/Risk_Principle_Lessons_Learned.pdf.

MacKenzie, D. L., Browning, K., Skroban, S. B. & Smith, D. A. (1999). The impact of probation on the criminal activities of offenders. *Journal of Research in Crime and Delinquency 36*(4): 423–453.

Makarios, M., Steiner, B., and Travis, L. F. (2010). Examining the Predictors of Recidivism of men and women released from prison in Ohio. *Criminal Justice and Behavior, 37*(12), 1377–1391.

Mauer, Marc (1999). Why are tough on crime policies so popular? *Stanford Law and Policy Review* 11(1): 9–21.

National Association of State Budget Officers. (2004). *The Fiscal Survey of States.* Washington, DC, National Governor's Association and National Association of State Budget Officers.

Olson, D. E., Lurigio, A. J., & Seng, M. (2000). A comparison of female and male probationers: Characteristics and case outcomes. *Women and Criminal Justice* 11(4): 65–49.

Prendergrast, M. L., Hall, E. A., Wexler, H. K., Melnick, G. & Cao, Y. (2004). Amity prison-based therapeutic community: 5-year outcomes. *The Prison Journal 84*(1): 36–60.

Roy, S. (2004). Factors related to successful recidivism in a day reporting center. *Criminal Justice Studies* 17(1): 3–17.

Schriro, D. (2009). Getting Ready: How Arizona has created a parallel universe for inmates. *NIJ Journal, 263*, 2–9. Retrieved from www.ncjrs.gov/pdffiles1/nij/226870.pdf.

Stephan, J. J. (2004). *State prison expenditures, 2001* (NCJ 202949). Washington, DC: Bureau of Justice Statistics.

Tonry, M. (2004). *Thinking about crime: Sense and sensibility in American penal culture.* New York, Oxford University Press.

Tonry, M., & Petersilia, J. (1999). *Prisons research at the beginning of the 21st century.* Washington, DC: National Institute of Justice. Retrieved from www.ncjrs.org/pdffiles1/nij/184478.pdf.

Tucker, S. B., & Cadora, E. (2003). Ideas for an open society: Justice Reinvestment. *Open Society Institute 3*(3): 1–8. Retrieved from www.soros.org/resources/articles_publications/publications/ideas_20040106/ideas_reinvestment.pdf.

U.S. Senate Bill 306. (2011). National Criminal Justice Commission Act of 2011. Retrieved from www.scribd.com/doc/48650143/S306-2011-CrimJ-Commission-Act.

Welsh, W. N., & Zajac, G. (2004). A census of prison-based drug treatment programs: Implications for programming, policy, and evaluation. *Crime and Delinquency 50*(1): 108–133.

Wright, K., Brisbee, J., and Hardyman, P. (2003). *Defining and measuring performance.* Washington, DC: U.S. Department of Justice.

Name Index

Subject Index